Newsroom Management

Newsroom Management

A Guide to Theory and Practice

Robert H. Giles

Media Management Books, Inc.
P.O. Box 1326
Detroit, MI 48231
1991

The research for this book was generously supported in connection with the fiftieth anniversary of the Gannett Foundation, 1985.

© 1991 by Robert H. Giles

Library of Congress Catalog Number:
87-71124

Fifth Printing

ISBN 0-9621094-0-1

Previously published by R.J. Berg & Co.

All rights reserved. No part of this publication may be reproduced, stored in a retrieval system, or transmitted, in any form or by any means, electronic, mechanical, photocopying, recording, or otherwise, without the prior written persmission of the copyright owner.

Printed in the United States of America

For Nancy, Dave, Megan, and Rob, whose love and support were a source of continuing inspiration.

Contents

	Preface ix
	Acknowledgments xvii
1	Management Theories and Human Behavior 1
2	Newsroom Work Groups 15
3	Motivating Journalists............................. 41
4	Communication in the Newsroom.................... 79
5	Newsroom Supervisors............................ 113
6	Newsroom Management Roles 137
7	Leadership and Power............................ 179
8	Styles of Management............................ 213
9	Understanding Individual Potential................ 245
10	Rating Performance 275
11	Pay, MBO, and Other Rewards 335
12	Managing Change in the Newsroom................ 369
13	Managing Conflict in the Newsroom 401
14	Stress and Survival............................... 441
15	Hiring, Training, and Promoting 501
16	Managing Upwards 559
17	The Changing Face of the Newsroom............... 585
	Case Studies 623
	Review Questions 649
	Glossary 665
	Appendix.. 677
	Bibliography 703
	Index... 727

Preface

The idea for this book took seed many years ago in the newsroom of the *Akron Beacon Journal*, where the late Ben Maidenburg was the presiding editor. An awesome figure in the eyes of a young and impressionable reporter, Ben stood well over six feet tall and weighed two hundred pounds. His impatience with the seeming stupidities of his staff could boil into action quickly, and we all dreaded the moment when a mistake or a misjudgment would capture Ben's attention and ignite his temper. At those times, he would stride across the newsroom, a copy of the offending story clutched in one hand and an unlit cigar in the other, his eyes dark and angry. You could *feel* him coming, a towering giant. The power of his voice guaranteed that the message would not be missed. On those occasions, the work of the newspaper stopped while everyone watched.

One of Ben's rituals was to call the city editor into his office late in the afternoon to discuss the day's transgressions. The meeting was by invitation; Ben would peer over the glass divider of his office and shout the city editor's name. One day, after years of watching Ben grind down other city editors, it was my turn. Ben would sit me next to his desk and grill me about how a story or staff situation had been handled. The discussion would wind its way around to what I now remember as the moment-of-wisdom-about-being-an-editor. "Bob," he would say, crossing one long leg over the other and staring at his cigar, "you've got to learn to be a son of a bitch."

Maidenburg had a powerful influence on me. He was a mentor in the best sense of the word: He shared his knowledge and his experiences, and he challenged me to find my own answers. They weren't often the answers he would have chosen, and this became a source of continuing conflict. The central question Ben forced me to answer was this: How can I do what he wants me to do and still be myself? Unwittingly, I think, he reinforced my basic instinct that there are other ways to run a newsroom than by being a son of a bitch.

Over the years and under different editors, I continued to run up against the same paradox: We put out pretty good newspapers, but we don't give much thought to managing people. I began to wonder about other factors that were common to newsroom life: high levels of stress in an environment that encourages creativity and individuality, where the best thrived but mediocrity was tolerated; few editors who knew or cared about "human behavior"—their mission was to get the story, whatever the cost.

The cost, in fact, has been great. Insensitive management has driven thousands of talented, bright, hard-working journalists from daily newspaper jobs. They turned to new careers in television or public relations or government or free-lance writing. Publishers and senior editors were slow to recognize the features of newsroom life that were creating the talent drain: high stress, low pay, lack of opportunity for growth, uncaring management. The turnover didn't matter, they said, because there was plenty of talent waiting to be hired.

For most newspaper editors, their first supervisory assignment came when they were promoted from reporter to assistant city editor. Typically, that advancement came without training and without preparation, even though they were taking on responsibilities that would require them to spend more than half of their time working with people. Many senior editors remember the grim and uncertain experiences of learning to be a "boss" as being among the darkest of their newspaper lives.

The newspaper editor's job has changed dramatically in the past twenty years. In addition to the traditional editing role, there are new and difficult demands on the editor:

- The need to be effective in running a staff that is ambitious, well educated, and sophisticated in its expectation of sensitive management.
- The need to be supportive of women and minorities in their quest for equality and opportunity.
- The need to help staffers motivate themselves and to see human potential with the same vision and creativity used in recognizing a good story.
- The need to build a climate of trust based on a willingness to listen and to invite ideas from others.
- The need to let staffers know where they stand through regular evaluations that are objective and job-related.
- The need to help staffers chart career paths and receive the training and development that will prepare them for larger responsibilities.
- The need to be sensitive to readers who question the integrity of the news report.
- The need to understand the high technology that is now the foundation of writing, editing, graphics, photography, and newspaper production.
- The need to develop and execute changes in news content and news focus based on marketing and readership research.
- The need to participate in the responsibility for the profit and marketing strategies of the newspaper company.

Clearly, there is a distinction between the news skills demanded of an editor—critical judgment, a strong sense of events, and the capacity to act quickly under pressure—and those qualities required to manage the professional careers of able, creative, self-motivated men and women. Editors are willing to help manage the careers of their staffers, but they are finding this to be a complex and demanding responsibility for which they are not adequately prepared.

Editors are discovering, too, that in an information era, competition is resulting from the explosion of media companies. Journalism graduates have a growing range of opportunities for media careers. Newspapers are losing top journalism school graduates to media competitors as well as to graduate programs such as law and business. The new media opportunities appear to be exciting to many young people, particularly when compared to the stereotype that newspapers pay and manage poorly. In the years ahead, it is clear that newspapers can compete for the most able journalists only if there is a broad commitment by editors and publishers to place a higher premium on good managers and good management practices.

The newspaper editor no longer is able to be independent from the economics of the newspaper business. Newspapers are a major industrial employer. The press in the United States has become one of the largest and one of the most profitable of the nation's economic giants. Three fundamental changes that have taken place in less than a quarter of a century explain the ascendent position of newspapers:

First is the decline of competition and the rise of monopoly ownership of newspapers. The local daily newspaper is a monopoly in all but about thirty cities, giving the owners the unchallenged opportunity to set advertising rates and circulation prices.

Second is the growth of newspaper companies whose stock is traded publicly. This has changed the ownership pattern in which newspapers were almost entirely owned by individuals or families. In 1986, shares were being publicly traded in fifteen companies that accounted for nearly 30 percent of total daily circulation in the United States. Stock prices and the opinions of market analysts and shareholders are influencing corporate newspaper managers to adopt strategies that put a greater importance on the bottom line.

Third is the reduction in newspaper production jobs as a result of new technology. Composing-room staffs are a fraction of their size in the 1960s. In another decade, converting the image of a news page on a pagination screen directly into a press plate will be commonplace, eliminating the composing room altogether. The introduction of the computer in newspaper production and the disappearance of Linotype operators, stereotypers, makeup personnel, and others has helped the bottom line, but the potential for future payroll cuts is limited. The computer is making other areas of the newspaper faster and more efficient, but no less labor-intensive. Newsroom editing systems have not lessened the need for reporters and editors. The work of the advertising department and the circulation department—two major employment centers—will continue to depend on people who sell and service customers. Computers will assist them but not replace them.

These three factors are playing an increasingly large role in the lives of editors and underscoring the need for editors to be smart and sophisticated managers who have a role in the profit planning and marketing strategies of their newspapers. It has not been easy for editors to accept these broader responsibilities. Few of them feel at ease with the numbers in an operating budget or with the challenge to understand the behavior of people at work. My own experiences in developing a performance-appraisal system and in studying how stress affects the lives of editors suggest that there are many editors who are willing to be good managers but who lack the information that tells them how. In their answers to questions about stress, editors revealed their frustration at not knowing how to handle the pressure of the job or how to deal emotionally with challenges to their control of the newsroom. Their wide interest in the performance appraisals used at the Rochester newspapers suggests that employee evaluations—perhaps the centerpiece of good newsroom management—is just now being looked at seriously.

There is a widely recognized need for enriching the instruction of newspaper management in the journalism-school curriculum. Journalism magazines and trade journals report an increase in the teaching of management, although deans and professors of journalism emphasize the difficulty of attempting to teach management without an appropriate text.

The world of journalism into which students will step is destined to become ever more professional. In preparing students to begin a career, journalism education has to satisfy three requirements:

First are the special skills of journalism: teaching students to report, write, and edit with clarity and precision.

Second is the knowledge that is beyond professional skill: the social, economic, historical, political, scientific, and behavioral issues of our time.

Third is what lies beneath professional journalistic skill: the institutional context in which the journalistic skills are practiced.

There is a continuing debate over the degree to which journalism schools should be captives of their professions. This preoccupation is understandable, since a major role of journalism education is to teach the tasks of newspaper work. But a vigorous journalism education program also should address the larger problems and convey to students the meaning of what they will find in the newsroom that is beyond their own special orbit of reporting or copy editing. Journalism graduates should have a conscious sense of the institutions to which they are applying for work and which they expect to support their skills. The management of newsrooms, newspapers, and other media institutions is one of the modes of a professional education for which journalism schools must construct an educational sequence that will serve the needs of contemporary newsrooms.

This book grew out of my own conviction that there is a connection between good management and good newspapers—a link that will become more and more important. Newspaper executives in the coming years will be tested by their ability to manage ideas. The vision to transform ideas into effective newspaper operating strategies will determine, in a large sense, whether newspapers continue to grow and thrive into the twenty-first century. This has implications for management at each step along the way: for management education, for management training and development, and for management selection, as well as for the individual responsibilities of publishers, editors, and other newspaper executives.

Newsroom Management: A Guide to Theory and Practice, is based on many of the behavioral-science theories about management that have been developed in American business and industry. The theories and the research that supports them are presented to help students understand some of the fundamental ideas about the behavior of people at work. Not all of these theories have application to newspaper work, of course, but where it seemed appropriate, they have been translated into newsroom situations with emphasis on strategies and guidance for students, both in the classroom and in the newsroom. *Newsroom Management* seeks to be both theoretical and practical, and is intended to be useful as a textbook for students and a reference for publishers, editors, and other practitioners.

Acknowledgments

Since I began the research for this book in early 1983, many friends and colleagues have provided information, ideas, criticism, and help that made the finished product more readable and useful than it otherwise might have been.

Gene Dorsey and Jerry Sass of the Gannett Foundation generously invested grant money in the belief that a newsroom management book was needed.

Editors, reporters, publishers, corporate executives, teachers, and scholars willingly shared their time and their thoughts. Some sat for extensive interviews. Some read portions of the book and made important suggestions that improved the writing and the thoroughness of the material. Others shared their own research on newspaper problems. Each made a contribution for which I am deeply grateful. The list is long and incomplete, but it certainly would include J. D. Alexander of the *San Diego Union*, R. W. Apple, Jr. of the *New York Times*, Ed Baron of Gannett, Edward Bassett of Northwestern University, James Batten of Knight-Ridder Newspapers, Larry Beaupre of the *Rochester Times-Union* and later the Westchester Rockland Newspapers, Eric Best of the *San Francisco Examiner*, George Blake of the *Cincinnati Enquirer*, Marge Bratcher of the Poynter Institute for Media Studies, Del Brinkman of the University of Kansas, Judee and Michael Burgoon of the University of Arizona, Bill Burleigh of Scripps-Howard Newspapers, Bob Clark of Harte-Hanks Newspapers, Roy Peter Clark of the Poynter Institute for

Media Studies, Neale Copple of the University of Nebraska, Ellis Cose of the Institute for Journalism Education, Phil Currie of Gannett, Everette Dennis of the Gannett Center for Media Studies, Colleen Dishon of the *Chicago Tribune,* Al Fitzpatrick of Knight-Ridder Newspapers, Larry Fuller of the *Sioux Falls Argus Leader,* the late Richard Gray of Indiana University, Loren Ghiglione of the *News* of Southbridge, Massachusetts, Bob Haiman of the Poynter Institute for Media Studies, David Hall of the *Denver Post,* Jay Harris of the *Philadelphia Daily News,* Byron Harless of Knight-Ridder Newspapers, Ralph Holsinger of Indiana University, John B. Jaske of Gannett, Madelyn Jennings of Gannett, Max Jennings of the *Mesa Tribune,* Larry Jinks of Knight-Ridder Newspapers, Ivan Jones of Knight-Ridder Newspapers, Dorothy Jurney, a newspaper researcher of Philadelphia, Michael Kautsch of the University of Kansas, Dolly King of the *Charlotte Observer,* Ralph Langer of the *Dallas Morning News,* Kurt Luedtke, formerly of the *Detroit Free Press,* John McMillan of the *Salem Statesman-Journal,* John Quinn of Gannett, Paul Pohlman of the University of Chicago, Robert Ritter of the *San Bernadino Sun,* Denise Rousseau of Northwestern University, Susanne Shaw of the University of Kansas, Jay Silverberg of the *Rockford Register Star,* Ardyth Sohn of the University of Colorado, Bill Thomas of the *Oakland Press,* Vince Spezzano of Gannett Rochester Newspapers, Chris Waddle of the *Anniston Star,* Jim Wells of the Knight-Ridder Institute of Training, G. Cleveland Wilhoit of Indiana University, Jean Gaddy Wilson of the University of Missouri, and Nancy Woodhull of *USA TODAY.*

Of critical importance was the contribution of two friends whose skills and perceptions helped clarify early drafts: Christine Landauer, my former assistant and later director of personnel for the Gannett Rochester Newspapers, whose thoughtful ideas and wise counsel kept me pointed in the right direction, and Debbie Gump of Knight-Ridder News Service, whose skillful editing was invaluable. Esther Wiger, my executive secretary, worked long hours in library searches turning up countless texts and research journals. Marcia Hart, my administrative assistant at the *Detroit News,* helped in the final editing by tracking down several bibliographical citations.

Acknowledgments

John Curley, president and chief executive officer of the Gannett Company, Inc., shared his file of notes and articles for a newspaper management book he once planned to write. Rich Egan of the *Times-Union* gave me an understanding of personal computers and shared a full menu of shortcuts for manipulating a manuscript. Christine Wells, library director at *USA TODAY*, traced elusive source material through the paper's swift and efficient electronic library. Kevin Miles Smith, staff artist at the *Times-Union*, easily captured the sense of many of the management theories in his illustrations for the book. Peter Ford, library manager for the *Times-Union* and *Democrat and Chronicle*, faithfully tracked obscure facts and footnote citations. Jim Mahler, wireroom supervisor for the *Times-Union* and the *Democrat and Chronicle*, and B. Lee McQuinn, newsroom typist, invested long hours transcribing taped interviews.

My ability to complete the manuscript and tend to my other responsibilities at the Rochester Newspapers was enhanced by the continuing counsel, support, and patience of Pat Rissberger, my administrative assistant, Christy Bradford and J. Ford Huffman, my managing editors, and two publishers, Vince Spezzano and George Dastyck.

Two special contributors were Ray Berg and Ginny Berg of Indianapolis. Ray, the publisher and a fervent believer in the value of a newsroom management book, was a continuing source of encouragement and guidance. Ginny, the editor, made enormous contributions to the quality of the text through her perceptive suggestions, her gift for precision, and her sense for rhythm in text.

An author could not ask for a more supportive environment in which to labor over a text than the one provided by Nancy Giles and our three children, David, Megan, and Rob. They share fully in whatever success this project achieves.

My predispositions about newspaper management are the product of experiences that can be traced to the early 1960s. Many hundreds of friends and associates at the *Akron Beacon Journal*, the *Times-Union*, the *Democrat and Chronicle*, the University of Kansas, and in two eminently valuable professional organizations, the Associated Press Managing Editors Association and the American Society of Newspaper Editors, provided the experiences that shaped my thinking and my values. They know who they are and they know that I remembered them as I wrote this book.

1

Management Theories and Human Behavior

How often have we heard a manager say, "People are our greatest asset"? That truism has particular meaning for newspapers. The only real difference between one newspaper and another is the performance of the people on their staffs. Electronic editing systems, marketing strategies, modern presses, and reliable delivery trucks are important, but they don't make the critical difference in performance. Only people can do that.

Yet, of all the resources available to newspaper publishers and editors, human *potential* is the least utilized. Newspaper executives may speak of people as assets, but in their management roles, these same executives all too often translate humans into problems, procedures, and costs.

Those in charge of the business side of newspapers look at the news staff as "overhead." Newsroom productivity cannot be measured in traditional ways—there are no customers to serve, no new accounts to generate, no profit goals to meet. So, to those involved with the newspaper's finances, the news staff is an operating expense rather than an investment or an asset that makes an essential contribution to the quality, and therefore the success, of the newspaper.

The management structure of newspapers is similar to that of other business organizations, and many of the general management theories apply. In a newspaper company, power is centralized at the top. Information and authority flow downward. The work is specialized. But within this common framework, the news operation is quite different from the newspaper's business office or circulation department or advertising department.

Working in the newsroom is a highly social process, involving much discussion, challenge, give-and-take, and many questions in the sometimes fractious, sometimes agonizing process of deciding how to play the day's news. Contact between boss and worker is routine, a natural part of an environment in which aggressive, independent-minded individuals honor both teamwork and disagreement. Their ability to work together effectively depends as much on their *human skills*—that is, their interactions with others—as on their *technical skills*. In the newsroom, the editor-manager's challenge of instilling responsibility and the desire for achievement in the news staff is different than in other departments; not more difficult necessarily, just different.

Yet, "the people managing the newsroom," says Paul Pohlman, codirector of management-development seminars at the University of Chicago and a frequent lecturer on newspaper management, "are professional journalists—reporters and writers who have spent the better part of their careers developing and using their journalistic skills. They are experts in their fields—skilled in developing story ideas, news judgment, and editing—but they have spent little or no time developing managerial skills or looking at issues of organizational structure and development, hiring practices, and similar concerns."[1]

Management involves working with and through individuals and groups of individuals to achieve the goals of the newspaper. The roles of management include planning, organizing, staffing, directing, and controlling, and each of these roles utilizes human, financial, and material resources. Regardless of their title, position, or level, every member of the newsroom management team performs these five management functions. In addition, the broad definition of management includes the specific tasks of supervising, managing, and leading. While each of these tasks is different from the others, they are interrelated and present in the management styles of effective editors.

This chapter and those that follow set the stage for the journey toward understanding and developing the management skills that many editors who rise from the ranks of reporter or copy editor are lacking. These chapters introduce basic theories of behavioral science, and ideas concerning the essence of management and human behavior. As such, they will be the foundation for the principles of managing in the newsroom.

MANAGEMENT THEORIES

Classical Management Theories

Over the years, an array of ideas, concepts, principles, theories, and methods has given us a broad understanding of what management is and how we should approach it as a field of study.

The early theories had little to do with people. These theories arose from advances in technology, and their applications focused on the vast amounts of raw materials and labor required to manufacture products effectively and cheaply.

The first ideas about management were known as *classical management theories*. They took root during the Industrial Revolution in England following the invention of steam-powered machinery. Pioneers in classical management offered advice on making production more efficient. Their thinking reckoned with management as both an art and a science.

One of the first voices in the classical school was that of Charles Babbage (1792–1871), a British mathematician. In 1832, he published a book, *On the Economy of Machinery and Manufacturers*, which explained his observation that the most important principle of management was "the division of labor amongst the persons who perform the work."[2]

Frederick Winslow Taylor (1856–1915), an American engineer, was called the Father of Scientific Management. Drawing from his work as an executive, consultant, production specialist, and efficiency expert, he wrote about the applications of scientific methods to factory problems. Taylor was a pioneer in time-and-motion studies, which sought ways to reduce worker fatigue and improve efficiency and output. He advocated a system of pay based on each individual worker's output, a concept that came to be known as piecework. A modern-day application of Taylor's principles is found in job specialization on factory assembly lines.[3]

Henry L. Gantt (1861–1919), a disciple of Taylor, encouraged a movement away from authoritarian management. He introduced a program of wages which paid a fixed amount for below-standard work, a bonus if standards were met, and an additional amount when standards were exceeded.[4] Gantt also developed the Gantt Chart, which describes a desired end product and outlines each step needed to produce it, creating a planning tool known by modern engineers and architects as a critical path.

Henri Fayol (1841–1925), a French industrialist, is recognized as the leader in elevating the role of administration in classical management theory. He believed that the ability to manage was not a personal talent, but a skill that could be taught. He developed a guide for managers based on fourteen principles (see fig. 1.1). These principles were drawn from his own experience, and they still provide modern managers with sound guidelines for organizing and administering companies. Fayol also identified the five basic management functions: planning, organizing, staffing, commanding (directing), and controlling.[5]

Fig. 1.1

CLOSE-UP

Henri Fayol's principles for management, although decades old, provide a solid foundation for today's editors who seek constructive direction for administering their staffs and their newsrooms. Fayol's fourteen principles are:

1. *Division of work.* Specialization allows workers and managers to acquire ability, sureness, and accuracy that will increase output. More and better work will be produced with the same effort.

2. *Authority and responsibility.* The right to give orders and the power to exact obedience are the essence of authority. Its roots are in the person and the position. Responsibility is a natural consequence of and essential counterpart of authority.

3. *Discipline.* Discipline is composed of obedience, application, energy, behavior, and outward marks of respect between employers and employees. It is essential to any business. Without it, no enterprise can prosper.

4. *Unity of command.* For any action whatsoever, an employee should receive orders from one superior only. One person, one boss. More than one boss creates a perpetual source of conflicts.

5. *Unity of direction.* One head and one plan should lead a group of activities having the same objective. It is the condition essential to unity of action, coordination of action, and focusing of strength.

6. *Subordination of individual interest to general interest.* The interest of one person or group in a business should not prevail over that of the organization as a whole. Ignorance, ambition, selfishness, laziness, weakness, and all human passions tend to undermine the general interest and promote individual interest. A perpetual struggle has to be waged against such tendencies.

7. *Remuneration of personnel.* The price paid for services rendered should be fair and satisfactory to both employees and employer. A level of pay depends on an employee's value to the organization and on factors independent of an employee's worth, such as cost of living, availability of personnel, and general business conditions. Wages should encourage keenness by rewarding well-directed effort.

8. *Balanced centralization.* Everything that serves to reduce the importance of an individual subordinate's role is centralization. Everything that increases the subordinate's importance is decentralization. All situations call for a balance between the two positions.

9. *Chain of command.* The chain formed by managers from the highest to the lowest is called a chain of command. Managers are the links in the chain. They should communicate to and through the links. Links may be skipped or circumvented only when superiors approve and a real need to do so exists.

10. *Order.* This principle is simple advocacy of a place for everyone, and everyone in his or her place; a place for everything, and everything in its place. The objective of order is to avoid loss and waste.

Fig. 1.1, continued

11. *Equity.* Kindliness and justice should be practiced by people in authority to extract the best that their subordinates have to give.

12. *Stability of tenure of personnel.* Reducing the turnover of personnel will result in more efficiency and fewer expenses. If turnover is repeated indefinitely, the work will never be properly done. Generally, the managerial personnel of prosperous concerns is stable; that of unsuccessful ones is unstable.

13. *Initiative.* People should be allowed the freedom to propose and to execute ideas at all levels of an enterprise. A manager who is able to permit the exercise of initiative on the part of subordinates is far superior to one who is unable to do so.

14. *Esprit de corps.* In unity there is strength. Managers have the duty to promote harmony and to discourage and avoid those things that disturb harmony.

Source: Henri Fayol, *General and Industrial Management,* 6th ed. (London: Sir Isaac Pitman & Sons, 1959), 20–41.

Chester Barnard (1886–1961), while at the American Telephone Company, emphasized leadership as the most important task of any manager. He wrote that the basic function of a manager is to provide the basis for cooperative effort, and defined organization as a system of goal-oriented cooperative activities. Barnard's success as an executive proved his own theories about management and leadership. He believed that after managers set goals and assembled resources, they should concentrate on leading so as to gain acceptance for their authority.[6]

Behavioral Management Theories

Veering from the path of classical management theory, the behavioral management theorists focused their studies on employees as individuals, as parts of work groups, as persons with needs to be met by the company. They forced managers to look at work from another point of view, to value employees as assets to be worked with and developed.

Robert Owen (1771–1858), a Scottish factory owner, was one of the first authors to argue that people are as important as machines. In an 1813 address to the "Superintendents of Manufactories," Owen said that the quality and quantity of workers' output were influenced by conditions on and off the job. He demonstrated in his own textile mills that it made good economic sense to devote as much attention to "vital machines" (people) as to "inanimate machines."[7]

In the 1920s, Mary Parker Follett (1868–1933) emerged as one of the first management thinkers to suggest that the principles of psychology be applied to business. Although not a manager, she wrote so convincingly that she was recognized as a major contributor to modern thinking about problems in personal and group relationships. Follett advocated the application of social science teachings to industrial settings. She said that effective leaders could motivate others and could coordinate plans, actions, and relationships. She believed that individuals could reach their full potential only through groups.[8]

Australian Elton Mayo (1880–1949), a faculty member at Harvard University's School of Business Administration, initiated the *human relations movement*, the study of people working together. In the late 1920s, Mayo began a series of experiments at the Hawthorne, Illinois, plant of the Western Electric Company. His research introduced the idea that people worked for something in addition to money, that it was important to be part of a group and to feel important in the eyes of the company.[9]

Another major contributor to the study of behavioral science was Douglas McGregor (1906–1964), an industrial psychologist and consultant. In 1960, in a book titled *The Human Side of Enterprise*, he presented the classic "Theory X–Theory Y." Theory X assumes that most people don't like to work. They prefer to be directed, are not interested in assuming responsibility, want safety above all, and are motivated by money, fringe benefits, and the threat of punishment. Theory Y holds that people are not lazy and unreliable, that they can be self-directed and creative at work if properly motivated. McGregor concluded that, under Theory Y, an essential task of management was to unleash this individual potential.[10] (For further discussion of Theory X–Theory Y, see Chapter 3.)

Behavioral Science in the Newsroom

To many of us, the word *science* brings to mind the physical part of our world, the subjects that we studied in chemistry or physics or biology classes in school. Human behavior also is a science, and we can expand our understanding of how humans behave on the job by studying management through a scientific approach known as *behavioral science.*

Using behavioral-science principles to understand organizational behavior is a field of study that draws on older disciplines such as psychology, sociology, business administration, and industrial relations. Editors can use behavioral-science principles to improve the individual work of journalists and the collective effort of the news staff. For example, a reporter's behavior is influenced by his or her personal characteristics as well as by the newsroom environment. Motivation is only one of many aspects of behavior the editor can examine using scientific principles. When we speak of motivating reporters, we are talking about creating a link between the reporter's characteristics and the characteristics of the newsroom that will result in desired behavior. Such relationships are complex, involving the individual reporter's capabilities, goals, needs, expectations, attitudes, and perceptions.[11] If we can define how reporters are motivated, then we can look at ways in which the editor can strengthen communication to improve the reporter's motivation.

A primary objective of the editor is to exert a degree of control over the behavior of the news staff. The editor can achieve control by understanding the dynamics of human behavior and by using that knowledge to predict how patterns of behavior in the newsroom will be influenced by his or her own actions and by the actions of others on the staff.

As a matter of science, it is easier to measure a liquid in the chemistry lab than it is to understand how to motivate a human being. The complexity of human behavior is such that the editor who is trying to help motivate a staffer must employ a good deal of guesswork. The editor is not sure whether a single factor or a combination of factors might produce an improvement in the staffer's performance.

Some of the theories of behavioral science are backed by sufficient research to give us confidence that they work. Other theories are still subject to controversy. Like all scientific knowledge, they represent partial truth.[12]

Without theories of human behavior to use as a guide, however, the editor would face each staff problem as if it were the first such encounter. Unable to draw on his or her own experience in solving earlier problems, the editor simply would improvise. Behavioral science gives us the advantage of knowing what might cause a problem and what might help correct it. It helps editors bring a consistency and a sense of control to their style of management.

The five general principles of behavioral science, as summarized here, can be the basis for a philosophy of supervision and management in the newsroom:

1. All people are different. No two journalists have the same values, attitudes, feelings, goals, or abilities. This is one of the factors that makes an editor's job difficult.

2. There is no one best way. Some management strategies may work consistently, but there are always exceptions—a fact that is reinforced by differences in people.

3. Personalities cannot be changed. One of the editor's biggest challenges is dealing with a variety of personalities. It is not uncommon in a business that attracts people with strong egos to find that personality clashes can affect performance. These situations are always difficult for the editor, but behavior can be changed; personalities cannot.

4. Perfection with people is impossible. The editor will not be able to solve all of the staff's "people problems," nor should the attempt be made. Disappointed will be the editor who expects staff members to behave perfectly.

5. Natural motivations are more powerful than artificial ones. Natural motivations are those that are inherent, such as the capacity for hard work or the drive to achieve. Editors will find it easier to help motivate people by accepting them for

what they are and by working with their natural strengths, talents, and characteristics than by trying to make people into something they aren't.[13]

DEVELOPING MANAGERIAL SKILLS

Today, the gospel of good management recognizes the value of successful managers possessing human skills. John D. Rockefeller, who founded the Standard Oil Company, said, "I will pay more for the ability to deal with people than any other ability under the sun." Rockefeller's ideas are echoed in a report by the American Management Association in which two hundred managers participating in a 1960s survey agreed that the most important single skill of an executive is his or her ability to get along with people.[14]

The importance of human skills in the selection of top executives was emphasized in the results of a 1982 study at the Center for Creative Leadership, a nonprofit research and educational institution in Greensboro, North Carolina. In the study, twenty-one executives—successful people who had been expected to go even higher in the organization but had failed—were compared with twenty executives who had made it to the top. The two groups were found to be "astonishingly" alike.

Each executive in both groups possessed remarkable strengths and was flawed by one or more significant weaknesses. The flaw that led to failure more often than any other was insensitivity to people. Other qualities that sealed the fate of these individuals included arrogance, betrayal of trust, and immoderate ambition. Out of ten categories of failure, only two—specific performance problems and an inability to think strategically—were linked to technical skills. All of the others were problems of working with people. The authors of the study concluded that the ability—or inability—to consider other people's perspectives was the most striking difference between those who succeeded and those who did not.[15]

The technical skills of a newspaper editor are acquired over many years. These skills begin, for many, with journalism-school courses that teach reporting and copy editing, and they are sharpened as the student moves to a job as reporter or copy editor on a newspaper. In time, the reporter or copy editor demonstrates behavior that attracts the attention of the senior editors: highly skilled reporting and writing or copy editing; good ideas; strong news sense; high motivation; great commitment to newspaper work; productive. In the nature of the news business, individuals with these qualities get "promoted to the desk." Whatever the specific job titles, they are now supervisors with the responsibility to manage others and produce results.

During all of the years when the reporter or copy editor was moving toward the moment he or she would become "a boss," the experience was bound up in developing technical skills. To be sure, there was always human interaction going on—whether with a teacher or a city editor, a high level of communication helped in the development of technical skills. But for the young journalist, either as a student or a professional, there was no emphasis placed on the human side of the job. There was no training in what it was like to be an editor, no discussion of what young editors should know to have an impact on the behavior of people.

Technical skills are critical to the success of an editor. But a gifted writer or talented copy editor moving into a supervisory position may not know how to get results from individuals whose diverse personalities and independent views bring forth a natural skepticism of their bosses. The ability to evaluate a news event is not easily translated into the judgment and discretion required to manage a staff of reporters or copy editors.

What kind of expertise do editors need to be effective managers of people?

First, in order to get things done through other people, editors need to understand why people behave the way they do. The literature of management focuses on patterns of past behavior and motivation. Editors need to combine the lessons and theories of general management with their specific knowledge of behavior in the newsroom.

Second, the ability to predict patterns of behavior will help the editor manage people effectively. It is essential to understand why staffers did what they did yesterday. Even more important is being able to anticipate how they are going to behave today, tomorrow, next week, and next month under similar as well as changing conditions.[16]

Finally, the effective editor needs to use this understanding of behavior to direct and control the staff and bring change to the newspaper. Control plays a prominent role in management, utilizing the editor's understanding of past events in the newsroom and expectations—that is, his or her ability to use past experience to anticipate future behavior. Control does not mean manipulation; rather, it draws on analysis and critical judgment to help the editor absorb all factors necessary to make an effective decision and to direct the staff in its implementation.

CHAPTER SUMMARY

The first ideas about management were known as classical management theories, which took root during the Industrial Revolution in England. Pioneers in classical management offered advice on how to make production more efficient.

Behavioral management theories focused on employees as individuals and as assets to be worked with and developed. Beginning in the early nineteenth century, authors and researchers in the field of management established the idea that workers were as important as machines, that people worked most effectively in groups, that being made to feel an important part of the company was more important to workers than working conditions, and that people can be self-directed and creative at work if properly motivated.

Behavioral-science principles can help build an understanding of how humans behave on the job. This knowledge can be used to improve the work of individual journalists and the collective effort of the news staff—a skill that can serve as a major building block in the development of an effective editor-manager.

Five general behavioral-science principles are the basis for effective supervision: (1) all people are different, (2) there is no one best way, (3) personalities cannot be changed, (4) perfection with people is impossible, and (5) natural motivations are more powerful than artificial ones.

Journalists acquire technical skills throughout their newspaper work, beginning in journalism school. On the job, some journalists are promoted and assume the responsibility for supervising others. At that point, the new supervisors tend to be proficient in writing or editing, but they may have little knowledge of the human skills that will be crucial to their success as editors.

There are three keys to being an effective editor-manager: First is to understand why people behave as they do. Second is the ability to predict how people might behave in the future. Third is to use this knowledge to control the news staff, give it direction, and introduce change.

NOTES

1. Virginia Tadie, "Management: Editors Changing Their Tune," *presstime*, February 1984, 10.
2. Warren R. Plunkett and Raymond F. Attner, *Introduction to Management* (Boston: Kent, 1983), 17.
3. Ibid., 17–19.
4. Ibid., 18–19.
5. Ibid., 20.
6. Ibid., 19.
7. Ibid., 22–23.
8. Ibid., 23.
9. Paul Hersey and Kenneth Blanchard, *Management of Organizational Behavior*, 4th ed. (Englewood Cliffs, N.J.: Prentice-Hall, 1982), 46.
10. Ibid., 48–49.
11. Douglas McGregor, *The Professional Manager* (New York: McGraw-Hill, 1967), 6.
12. Ibid., 5.
13. Jerry L. Gray, *Supervision* (Boston: Kent, 1984), 15.
14. Hersey and Blanchard, *Management of Organizational Behavior*, 6.
15. Morgan W. McCall, Jr., and Michael M. Lombardo, "What Makes a Top Executive?" *Psychology Today*, February 1983, 26–31.
16. Hersey and Blanchard, *Management of Organizational Behavior*, 9.

2

Newsroom Work Groups

Newsroom management requires an understanding of individual behavior and group behavior, each of which influences the other. Groups are a fact of newsroom life, either as part of the formal newsroom structure or in the informal clusters of staffers known as peer groups. Power, status, influence, conflict, cohesiveness, discord—all are products of the group dynamic. The nature of groups and how groups affect the operation of the newsroom are topics of high interest to editors.

WHY PEOPLE WORK

A logical first step in learning about managing newspaper journalists is to develop an understanding of why people work. Is work merely an impersonal exchange of labor for money? Is it only money that workers want, so they can meet their needs for food, shelter, and material goods? Or are there other dimensions to work that are ultimately more satisfying?

In the early days of American industry, management believed that the chief characteristic of workers was their economic self-interest. As a result, management searched for ways to use that self-interest to increase productivity. Better pay and working conditions, it was thought, would produce more work.

For many years, efficiency experts tried a mix of working methods, working hours, and working conditions as a stimulus to greater production. They experimented with piecework, using a system advocated by Frederick Winslow Taylor, a self-taught American engineer. Taylor proposed a system of paying workers based on individual output: The more work done, the more money earned. However, none of these efforts provided what management was seeking: a reliable formula to motivate workers to do more work.

In 1924, efficiency experts at the Western Electric Company's Hawthorne, Illinois, plant organized a study of the effects of lighting on productivity. Two groups of employees were selected for the experiment. The test group worked under a variety of lighting conditions; the control group worked under the normal illumination at the plant. It was anticipated that as the light was increased for the test group, their output would increase—and that's what happened. The efficiency team thought there would be no change in the output of the control group because it continued to work under regular lighting conditions, but the control group produced more work, too.

Baffled by the results, the efficiency experts at Hawthorne decided in 1927 to expand their study. They consulted with Elton Mayo of Harvard University's School of Business Administration, and the resulting research offered the first insight into why people work—findings that caused management to reassess its views that workers were motivated largely by money.[1]

Mayo and his team began their work at the Western Electric plant with a group of five women. For eighteen months, Mayo's researchers enhanced the working conditions of this group, adding such innovations as scheduled rest periods, company-provided lunches, and shorter work weeks. Then, without warning, they took away all the improvements, returning the working conditions to the way they had been at the beginning of the experiment. The researchers thought this would have a tremendous negative psychological impact on the workers and would reduce production. Instead, productivity jumped to a new high.

As Mayo began to unravel the puzzle, he found that the stimuli for greater productivity were not related to working conditions, but to the human aspects of the job. The experimenters had lavished great attention on the group of workers, who responded by feeling that they were an important part of the company. The traditional attitude that coworkers were isolated individuals who just happened to work together in the same room gave way to the sense that they were part of a congenial, cohesive work group. They began to experience feelings of affiliation, competence, and achievement—needs that had long been unsatisfied by their work alone. As a result, the group members worked harder and more effectively.

On the other hand, Mayo's discoveries suggested that when the group believed its own goals were in opposition to those of management, productivity fell. This was particularly true in situations where workers were closely supervised and had no significant control over their jobs or environment. It was from these discoveries that Mayo began to identify the value of informal work groups and to recognize that the needs for satisfactory association with others at work had a direct relationship to productivity.

Mayo's Harvard team continued its inquiry from 1927 to 1932, expanding its interviews until about twenty thousand employees from all departments of the company had been included. The researchers wanted to know what the workers thought about their jobs, their working conditions, their supervisors, and their company. Workers were asked what bothered them and whether those feelings might influence their productivity.

Mayo's interviews had an immediate, therapeutic effect on the Hawthorne work force. The workers had an opportunity to express their feelings, and as a result, wholesale changes in their attitudes took place. Because many of their suggestions were being implemented, the workers began to feel they were important to management, both as individuals and as a group.

More significantly, the Hawthorne research signaled the need for management to study and understand the relationships among people and the influences that resulted in the development of informal groups within the work force. In these studies, as well as in others that followed, the most significant factor affecting productivity was found to be interpersonal relationships that developed on the job, not just pay and working conditions.

A colleague of Mayo's wrote, "A change in morale had also been observed. No longer were the girls isolated individuals, working together only in the sense of an actual physical proximity. They had become participating members of a working group with all the psychological and social implications peculiar to such a group."[2]

Mayo saw the development of informal work groups as an indictment of the traditional view of workers as insensitive machines concerned only with money. He said workers' lack of satisfaction led to tension, anxiety, frustration, and feelings of helplessness—reactions to conditions in which workers thought of themselves as unimportant and unattached.

According to Mayo, too many managers assumed that society consisted of a mass of individuals whose only concern was self-preservation or self-interest. These managers believed that people were motivated by physiological and safety needs, wanting to make as much money as they could for as little work as possible. It was Mayo's view that, as a result, management organized work around the idea that workers, on the whole, were a contemptible lot.[3]

DEFINING WORK GROUPS

A standard definition of a *work group* is any set of two or more people who are working toward a common objective and are in physical proximity to each other.[4] Other factors that affect the group process, or how members of groups interact, are the size of the group, how much time the group spends together, and how stable the membership is.

There are two kinds of work groups: formal and informal. In a newsroom, the city desk is a *formal work group*. Organized by the newspaper's management, it is one of the building blocks of the newsroom. Authority to run the city desk is assigned to the city editor. The rules and procedures for operating the city desk are established by management.

Informal work groups, or peer groups, as identified in Elton Mayo's research, are defined by the group members and are not bound by official lines of authority. It is easy to recognize factors that can bring journalists together in informal groups. The copy desk is a good example of a formal work group whose members

Kinds of Work Groups

FORMAL WORK GROUP

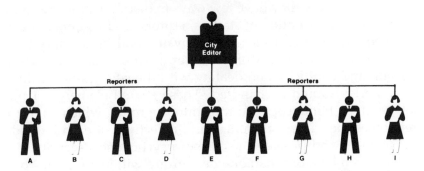

INFORMAL WORK GROUP

Fig. 2.1.

The formal work group, one of the building blocks of the newsroom, is organized by management. The informal work group is defined by group members.

share many common interests and relate to each other as a peer group as well. Copy editors sit close together, often around one large desk or group of desks. Their common tasks include editing stories and writing headlines on deadline. Because copy editors may think they have few ways to distinguish themselves or to draw the attention of staffers, editors, and readers to their work, qualities such as seniority, loyalty, and punctuality take on added importance. Moreover, copy editors may encounter tension and conflict when dealing with the city desk regarding how stories should be handled. These shared elements of the job tend to bond copy editors into a group, which in turn reinforces the values, attitudes, and objectives of each individual member and provides a sense of psychological security.

There can be more than one peer group within a formal work group—for example, the senior reporters, or those who are regarded as the best writers on the staff, can form a peer group. And, reporters who cover government and other public agencies have common interests that draw them together, as do reporters who are assigned to cover suburban or regional communities. In each case, individual and collective self-interests are involved. Perception plays an important role in the creation of informal newsroom groups: If the individuals see themselves as a group, then a group exists.

Classical management theorists have searched unsuccessfully for ways to identify the right size for the various types of informal work groups, finally concluding that there simply is no right number for most group activities.[5]

In 1956, Harvard University researchers Robert F. Bales and Edgar F. Borgatta published a series of studies on how the size of groups influenced the way individuals in the group interacted. They did this by observing work groups and recording who said what to whom. In smaller groups of two to four, Bales and Borgatta found greater tension, agreement, and opinion seeking. In groups of five to seven, there was greater release of tension and more sharing of suggestions and information. Each member of the group is under pressure to maintain an adequate relationship with other group members. As the size of the group increases, each member has more relationships to maintain and less time to do so.[6]

Figure 2.2 lists other differences in group interaction that were observed in the Bales-Borgatta studies.

Fig. 2.2

Small Groups	**Large Groups**
Fewer relationships to maintain and more time to do so.	More relationships to maintain and less time to do so.
Less pressure to give suggestions and more time to seek opinions.	More pressure to give suggestions and less time to seek opinions.
Harmony is crucial and people have more time to develop thoughts and opinions.	Individuals need to be more direct because of increased competition for attention.
Statements evaluating one's position are less inhibited.	Statements evaluating one's position are relatively more inhibited.
Getting agreement is relatively less difficult.	Getting agreement is relatively more difficult.
Participation of all members of the group will be relatively high.	Relatively more group members will participate minimally.
Persons who might be tense about greater involvement in the group will have fewer opportunities for anonymity.	Persons who might be prone to show tension if forced into greater involvement will have more opportunities for anonymity.

Source: Robert F. Bales and Edgar F. Borgatta, "Size of Group as a Factor in the Interaction Profile," in *Small Groups: Studies in Social Interaction*, rev. ed., edited by A. Paul Hare, Edgar F. Borgatta, and Robert F. Bales (New York: Knopf, 1966), 490–500.

In a later study by Lyman W. Porter of the University of California and Edward E. Lawler of Yale, people working in smaller work units reported higher levels of satisfaction than those in larger units.[7] Among blue-collar workers, smaller work units are characterized by lower absenteeism, lower turnover, fewer labor disputes, and greater satisfaction. Porter and Lyman argue that the evidence suggests small work units are desirable because individuals typically receive greater attention and are made to feel that they are an important part of the group—findings that support Elton Mayo's early conclusions.

Applying these results to the city staff of a newspaper would suggest that as the staff increases in size, it is more difficult to maintain high cohesion and good communication, due in part to a greater tendency toward specialization. The result may be higher job dissatisfaction. A simplistic conclusion would be that a reporter on a small city desk is likely to be more satisfied with his or her work than a reporter on a large city desk. But as we will see in Chapter 3, other factors play a powerful role in influencing the satisfaction of newspaper journalists.

Fig. 2.3

CLOSE-UP

It is important to establish early in our discussion of informal work groups whether there is a difference in how groups organize at large and small newspapers. Chris Waddle, who has been a managing editor of the *Kansas City Times* (circulation 300,000) and the *Anniston* (Alabama) *Star* (circulation 33,000), talks about the differences.

"The concept of peer groups is universal. On large papers, peer groups tend to be a little more antagonistic. In bigger organizations, you need more desperately to find other people to identify with. The group gives a kind of positive reinforcement. In good management, we hope that the positive reinforcement comes from the editors. On larger papers, the time between visits from editors is longer and the peer group can provide the reinforcement the reporter needs. Sometimes, of course, peer groups run away with the initiative and the reporters end up getting more feedback from the group than from management.

"Because of the complexity of getting the paper out in large newsrooms, editors have a stronger management orientation. They become a kind of professional class of managers. The reporters may find that they have more things in common with the peer group than they have with the managers.

"On smaller papers, I see a lot less time between visits from editors. The environment is smaller; the access is easier. The pace may not be easier, but because you are in closer quarters and see each other regularly, an editor is more likely to make a decision with the reporter present.

"On small newspapers, there is less chance to hire editors from the outside and a greater tendency to promote from the inside so that, quite often, the person who is city editor was a reporter last year and still has the respect of colleagues.

"On our metro desk [*Anniston Star*], we have fourteen reporters and they are organized in three groups based on their assignments. There are cross-relationships, of course, because it is such a small group overall. They tend to party together. But when I see them going out to lunch, it is the city people going together and those who cover the other counties going together."

Source: Chris Waddle, interview with author, November 1984.

PEER GROUPS

How Peer Groups Are Formed

Peer groups grow and develop over time in several stages. Bruce W. Tuckman of the Naval Medical Research Institute in Bethesda, Maryland, created a model of group development based on observations of patients in therapy. Tuckman's model consists of four stages: (1) forming, (2) intragroup conflict, (3) cohesion, and (4) role distinction.[8] Although the full sequence of these four stages may not always be present, Tuckman's ideas provide a framework for looking at how peer groups develop or, more particularly in the case of a newsroom, how a newcomer to the staff adapts to an existing peer group.

In the first weeks or months on staff, the new reporter is testing his or her behavior in an effort to form relationships with others on the staff. The reporter is trying to determine what behavior is acceptable and what is not. In this process, the new staffer is heavily dependent on others to provide clues to successful behavior. This is the *forming* stage.

Once the reporter is accepted by the group, he or she searches for a niche and for a way to contribute to the group. A number of personal factors, including talent, motives, ambition, and personality, will influence the degree to which the new staffer will have an effect on the group. This is the *intragroup-conflict* stage. This stage is always present, even if the newcomer is satisfied with a place at the bottom of the group hierarchy and wants only the companionship the group offers.

Over time, the third stage, *cohesion*, occurs. The new reporter is fully accepted by the group and develops a commitment to whatever unity of purpose binds the group.

In the final stage, *role distinction*, the reporter understands that his or her role on the staff is different from his or her role in a peer group. He or she discovers that it is the strength of performance, and not the influence of the peer group, that will determine the reporter's future on the paper. With this understanding, the reporter is able to strike a realistic balance between the effect of performance and the effect of the group on new opportunities at the paper.

Fig. 2.4

CLOSE-UP

In most newsrooms, peer groups have been in existence for years. Over time they take on different qualities and different roles because of staff turnover, changing leadership, or management practices.

How would groups emerge at a new newspaper? What would happen if a staff of strangers were being assembled to create a newspaper? Some understanding of this process can be seen in the experience at *USA TODAY*.

In the summer of 1982, the first members of a news staff of 340 began work in Gannett's Arlington, Virginia, newsroom. More than half of the staffers had worked on other Gannett papers, some in top newsroom management positions. Others were new to Gannett.

In the beginning, each of the four news departments was small. The reporters and editors in each department gathered for lunch or drinks after work. Getting the paper ready for its September 1982 launch consumed most of the staff's waking hours. It was an exciting and demanding time. The initial groups were largely social outlets.

As more and more staffers came on board, groups began to form along traditional lines. Sports reporters recognized their common self-interests, as did midlevel editors and specialists on the "Money" desk.

Sometimes the force of geography influenced the formation of groups. Because parts of the newsroom were still under construction, reporters from different editorial sections worked temporarily in the same areas. Two reporters from the "Money" section and five reporters from the "Life" section worked together in a small area away from the rest of the staff. They developed a bond even though there was little common ground in the subjects they covered.

A major influence on the early friendships that developed was the life-style outside of *USA TODAY*. Staffers who were on loan from other Gannett papers lived in apartments made available by the company. They were away from their families and were drawn to each other for companionship and such activities as dinner and weekend trips.

The second group was composed largely of people who had been hired from other newspapers. They had made their bargain with Gannett. They felt secure in their jobs. Many of them had rented apartments, had brought their families to the Washington area, and went home at night.

The "loaners" had been uprooted. While they were eager for the opportunity, they didn't always believe they had a good picture of their future at *USA TODAY*. They weren't as confident as many of those who had been hired. The loaners were drawn to each other out of a need for security and survival, the need to be with people who were in the same situation, and the need for information that might give them clues about their prospects of staying with the paper.

Heavy travel and the coming and going of loaners disrupted the stability of the initial peer groups. The editors tried to encourage a cohesive spirit. They held cocktail parties where staffers could mix with each other. As the staff's life-style directions began to settle down, professional attitudes influenced the adjustment of peer groups.

One group believed in the idea of *USA TODAY*, was dedicated to making it work, and was especially sensitive to the professional barbs about the newspaper. Another group wanted to be part of *USA TODAY* out of curiosity. This group was doing its part toward the paper's progress, but was prepared to move on when and if it became necessary. A smaller third group was sympathetic to outside criticism

Fig. 2.4, continued

of *USA TODAY* and was trying to save the paper from itself—it wanted *USA TODAY* to be a more traditional newspaper rather than a new and different kind of paper. Many members of this group moved on at the end of the year.

News instincts also contributed to another combination of peer relationships, especially among members of the editing team. *USA TODAY*'s initial dual personality of newspaper and newsmagazine generated two peer groups around the news conference table: The first included those strongly identified with daily newspapering, who clung together, pushing the new newspaper toward a harder news image and unconventional ways to report conventional news. The second group included those linked to news features and magazines, who frequently joined forces to mold the newspaper into the big-picture, one-shot feature approach, looking to unconventional news in conventional ways.

Source: John C. Quinn, editor, *USA TODAY*, correspondence with author, January 1985; J. Ford Huffman, managing editor, *Times-Union*, Rochester, N.Y., Nancy Woodhull, managing editor/enterprise, *USA TODAY*, and Vince Spezzano, publisher, *Times-Union* and *Democrat and Chronicle*, Rochester, N.Y., interviews with author, January 1985.

Why Peer Groups Are Formed

Security, friendship, recognition, support, and the need for information are the most common reasons journalists form or join peer groups. Let's look at each of these in detail.

Security. "Strength in numbers" is an attraction for many workers, including journalists. The group protects the individual from outsiders and offers a feeling of belonging. Groups provide a degree of certainty and predictability in interpersonal relationships.[9]

A peer group can provide security in the newsroom in many ways. The sense of belonging is important because the nature of newspaper work encourages a high level of personal interaction. In such an environment, the individual reporter works closely with his or her editor. The reporter finds that being part of a peer group is an essential way to play off his or her relationship with editors. The editor is a leader of a formal work group and represents authority to the reporter. The reporter's association with a group of peers involves no authority figure and gives the reporter the freedom to express opinions and complaints with impunity. Thus, the need for social satisfaction from the group complements the need for job satisfaction through individual achievement.

Friendship. In addition to the professional benefits that come from belonging to a peer group, many journalists build strong personal ties to other members of the group. Friendships grow quite naturally because people in the newsroom spend many hours together each week. The first link in the bond is the common interest in their work. When reporters have lunch together or go out after work, the makeup of the group often is influenced by the informal organization within the reporting staff. For example, the government reporters or the feature writers or the younger staffers may be drawn together by common interests and common problems, a collective self-interest.

As these relationships grow into friendships, the activities that result may have little bearing on the individuals' work. Friendships and leisure interests can create subgroups that cut across traditional peer-group lines. Sports enthusiasts, music lovers, gourmet cooks, and movie aficionados will naturally seek each other out, and these friendships can have a unifying influence on the newsroom.

Recognition. While reporters, photographers, and artists get more public recognition from their work than editors and copy editors, all of the individuals on the news staff need to have their personal accomplishments noticed by their coworkers. The city editor may neglect to applaud the county government reporter's story, but if the city hall reporter and the politics writer come by to say "Good job," that's important.

Attention may be drawn to a member of the peer group in other ways. For example, a reporter who is a good storyteller or the originator of outrageous pranks will attract attention. And the peer group that remembers to celebrate a member's birthday is helping satisfy that person's need for recognition.

Fig. 2.5

CLOSE-UP

Peer groups can influence decisions and the results of those decisions in the newsroom in a number of ways. Because of the input reporters have in the story process, for example, they can affect editors' content decisions.

This influence begins when reporters initiate story ideas that reflect their own personal or professional interests. Reporters who have an ideological commitment to social causes are a prime example—or the intensive news hawks: investigative reporters, government reporters, the journalists who want to ferret out the "crooks" at the courthouse.

The interests of these reporters help form the decisions about which stories to cover, how to cover the stories, and how to write the stories. Group members often exchange story ideas before they try them out on the editors.

A curious editor could get a sense of how this influence works by clipping every local story and tracing how it got in the paper. Was it an assignment from the editors? If so, who was the highest ranking editor having something to do with the story being assigned? Was the story idea volunteered by a reporter to the desk? If so, how is the reporter linked to the content of the story? Is it from the reporter's beat? Does the story idea reflect a personal interest of the reporter seeking the assignment or another reporter in the peer group? Did the idea come from outside the office? Did it come over the phone? Was it a tip from a source or a reader? Did a public relations person give it to a particular reporter?

By tracking the origin of each story, the editor would begin to understand how individual reporters or reporter groups can influence the content of the newspaper.

Support. A reporter who is having difficulty on the job ideally would turn to his or her editor for support. The editor may be empathetic and offer some good tips on "how you can improve." But the reporter also knows that revealing such problems to the editor could cause the editor to react in a way that could endanger the reporter's reputation. No matter how sensitively the editor deals with the situation, the reporter's need for additional support from his or her peers remains.

Tension typically exists between the editor and a reporter who is not performing well. While the reporter may feel critical of the editor's actions or judgment, he or she knows it is not appropriate to voice those feelings to the editor. Instead, the reporter turns to colleagues in his or her peer group, seeking their counsel, a sympathetic ear, a bit of sage advice, or a comforting word.

Information. People on the news staff always want to know more about the operations of the newspaper than what is offered by management's channels of communication (see Chapter 4). The network of individuals in a peer group gives the group's members access to information they otherwise might not get. Information that comes through informal channels is unofficial, but it is often accurate. The grapevine is a common source of news about plans, changes, and promotions that have not been formally announced. Sometimes editors will "leak" information into the grapevine. Or, if staffers suspect something, they will circulate a story, filling in any gaps with their own information, in hopes of smoking out the truth in the process. Underground channels of information, especially where peer groups are effective, are part of the reality of the newsroom.

Group Norms

Each peer group creates its own standards of behavior, or *group norms*, which suggest clues for what is right and what is wrong. Norms are also the ideals or goals that bond individuals together, but they apply only to behavior—not to private thoughts or feelings. Norms provide a frame of reference, and they can be both powerful and pervasive.

Although norms are an important influence on individual behavior, they are not consciously mandated by the group. In most situations, the establishment of norms for newsroom peer groups is not a formal process; rather, it is the social process through which individuals interact that determines the norms for the group.

Individual behavior typically is regulated through the enforcement of norms by group members—for example, sharing news tips is a common activity among reporters. If a member of the group violates that norm by refusing to pass along information, others in the group might "discipline" the staffer by withholding news tips from him or her. Or, a reporter who accepts confidences from other staffers and then passes them on to an editor would be disregarding the norms of the group.

The officers of a newsroom union would expect staff members in the bargaining unit to conform to the norms of the union. Staffers may be required to engage in activities such as picketing or other confrontive behavior that is designed to reinforce the union's bargaining position with the newspaper's management.

Norms generally develop gradually and are limited to behaviors that are viewed as most important by group members; however, group members can choose to shortcut this gradual process by declaring that "from now on," this norm will exist.

Not all norms apply to everyone. High-status members of the group have more freedom to deviate from the letter of the norm than do others.[10] In an informal and more closely knit peer group, such as one involving the best writers on the staff, the norms may be more subtle and, therefore, more difficult for the editors to identify. If those norms involve the preparation of news stories, they are important to the editors; if the norms have to do with who eats lunch with whom, they are little more than a curiosity to the editors. Since members of a work group are expected to behave according to that group's norms, editors need to understand the norms that influence the collective behavior of the group.

In his book, *Behind the Front Page*, Chris Argyris identifies three kinds of reporter peer groups: (1) Traditional Reporter, (2) Reporter-Researcher, and (3) Reporter-Activist, each of which has different norms:[11]

1. The norms of Traditional Reporters are that reporting is a craft of "common sense," that they strive to present the news as objectively as possible, and that the satisfactions come from applying their craft under pressure.

2. The norms of Reporter-Researchers emphasize scholarship and the need to use their analytical and conceptual skills. They believe they are at the edge of influencing events.

3. The norms of Reporter-Activists focus on using journalism to change or shake up the world. "Their need to dig beneath everything is much stronger," says Argyris, "and their paranoia is exceeded only by their deep disappointment that the men they had revered in public life are human to a fault."

Fig. 2.6

CLOSE-UP

One newsroom peer group whose norms tend to be somewhat different involves the assistant desk editors. On newspapers where there are two or more assistant city editors, for example, the desk is normally organized so that a great deal of cooperation and coordination is required among the assistant editors. They have to acknowledge that they are on equal footing and that management has given each the same basic authority and responsibility.

Yet in that equality, there has to be give-and-take; there has to be a group dynamic that allows the best ideas and solutions to prevail. The process is heavily influenced by talent—not just the talent of being a good journalist, but the talent of getting along. If the assistants are equally talented, democratic acceptance of others' ideas is more likely. If levels of talent vary, the more talented editors are not as likely to accept the ideas of those they consider less talented.

Editors often wonder why staffers comply with a group's norms when those norms seem to work against what the editor considers to be the best interests of the newspaper. For example, it is puzzling to editors why staffers would be willing to sign a petition for a newsroom union contending that the company pays low wages. What concerns editors is that many of these staffers may be well paid and may know that the petition represents exaggerated or untruthful statements that can be damaging to the public image of the newspaper. Indeed, many who sign such a statement have little commitment to the union, but they sign to support the principle of unity. Studies show that personality is a major factor in such instances—for example, staffers who show high levels of intelligence, tolerance, and ego-strength are less likely to conform to the norms of a group. Those who submit easily to authority are more inclined to conform to group norms.

Conformity also can be influenced by ambiguity. If a new management policy or an order from the editor is confusing or ambiguous, the tendency to conform to group norms is greater; that is, staffers will continue to do what they did before the new order. In this situation, conformity provides a sense of protection and security in new and perhaps threatening circumstances. Moreover, conformity is higher if there is unanimity among group members. In the case of a new directive from management, conformity will be stronger if the group has been successful in ignoring or blunting the effect of previous policy changes.[12]

The editor can have an impact on group norms, but it is often limited. If the city editor is popular with the reporting staff, the norm may be that a reporter does not go to the managing editor to complain about how the city editor handled a story. If the popular city editor retires and management hires a replacement from another newspaper, the various peer groups in the newsroom will rethink their norms.

Fig. 2.7

CLOSE-UP

"Peer pressure" is a familiar expression. We've heard it at school and around the office. It means that the group attempts to influence the individual to conform. A classic study of conformity was conducted in the 1950s by psychologist Solomon Asch at Swarthmore College.

Asch brought the subject of the experiment into a room and introduced him to several people, all of whom knew each other and were confederates of the experimenter.

Each person in the room was asked to match the length of a given line (X) with one of three unequal lines, as shown on the following page:

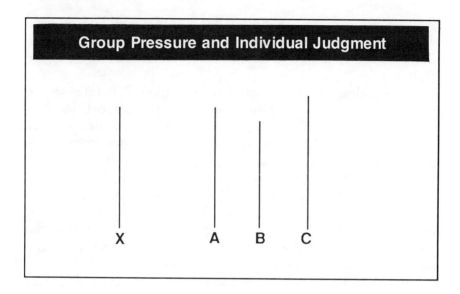

The accomplices in the experiment spoke first. As instructed, they identified line C as the line closest in length to line X, even though line A was clearly the correct answer.

In more than one-third of the trials in this experiment, the naïve subjects denied the evidence of their own senses that line A was correct and confirmed the wrong answer of the group.

Asch concluded that, when confronted by a unanimous answer to a question by others in the group, a large percentage of individuals choose to go along with the group rather than express a conflicting opinion that they are certain is correct.

Source: Solomon Asch, "Studies of Independence and Conformity: A Minority of One Against a Unanimous Majority," *Psychological Monographs* 70 (1956), 7.

Peer-Group Leaders

Informal leaders in the newsroom tend to exemplify the norms and values of their peer groups. Differences in status occur in peer groups in the same way they do in formal groups. Certain individuals become leaders for a variety of reasons: charisma, intelligence, technical skills, age, seniority. In formal groups, leaders are appointed by management; in informal groups, they are chosen casually by the members of the group. But the qualities required for success in either type of group are quite similar.

While leaders of peer groups can be influential, because of the particular cohesiveness of the newsroom, their importance usually does not rival that of the key first-line supervisors, such as the city editor or the sports editor, who supervise nonmanagement employees. If the peer group's goals conflict with those of the editors, however, the situation can be difficult. The informal leader has added influence and can cause problems for the editors when such a group has unity of purpose. And in management's eyes, there will be an incongruity between the professional skills of the leader and his or her role in leading the challenge to a management policy or decision.

Editors who are sensitive to the presence of informal leaders can learn to use the natural influence of those individuals. The network of staffers in the peer group has an "agenda," things that frustrate or concern them. The items on the agenda come through the grapevine or are based on the perceptions of individuals in the group. They may have "heard" that the publisher has cut back the newsroom travel budget or they may think that the baseball writer is getting a "bad deal" from the sports editor. The editor can tune in to that agenda through the informal leaders.

For the top editors, observing the activities of peer groups and picking up signals from the leadership may produce a sign that management's appointed leader, say the city editor, is not functioning properly. If there is weak direction from the top, staff members will seek direction themselves. The existence of tightly bonded, active peer groups may be a response to newsroom leadership that is inconsistent or ambiguous.

The editor can analyze newsroom groups by understanding that they are affected by personal factors and by conditions under which groups can be formed. Figure 2.9 illustrates how these forces come together. Personal factors include attitude, ability, individual motives, personality, and background. The conditions include the type of group, reasons for membership in the group, and the state of group development. The personal and conditional elements influence the structure of the group:

its size, its norms, its role and status relationships, and its cohesiveness. The result is a group process that is shaped by communication, conflict, decision making, power and politics, and leadership. Finally, the outcome is expressed in the attitudes and behavior of the members of the group.

Peer-Group Influence in the Newsroom

The shape and character of peer groups change from desk to desk and from newspaper to newspaper, but however organized, these groups can wield considerable influence in the newsroom. The effectiveness of peer groups suggests that the organizational chart doesn't tell all. Personal and social relationships arise spontaneously as staff members respond to the need for one another's company and the benefits that result.

Understanding peer groups is particularly important to first-line supervisors such as the city editor or features editor. Although editors must manage individual reporters and copy

---

Fig. 2.8

CLOSE-UP

The editors of a midwestern newspaper hired a new city editor from another paper. Although the new city editor had full authority to run the staff, the reporter group quickly recognized that the true leader on the city desk was one of the assistant city editors, an editor who had been in that position when the new city editor took over. Whenever possible, reporters dealt with the assistant. They wanted to avoid the city editor, whom they found intimidating and inconsistent in his directions to the staff. The frustration the reporters felt because of the ambiguous signals from the city editor pulled them into a close working relationship with the assistant city editor.

The senior editors worked hard to help the city editor become effective. However, after eighteen months, they acknowledged their mistake and moved him to another job in the newsroom. The assistant was promoted to city editor. The day the changes were announced, the leader of the reporter group asked the executive editor, "What took you so long? We knew months ago that he wouldn't make it."

---

editors, these staffers invariably belong to one or more peer groups that can influence their individual behavior.

Peer groups can affect the formal operation of the newsroom in a variety of ways, both negatively and positively:

Problems

Peer groups can resist change by putting roadblocks in the path of an editor's attempt to alter the operating practices or the focus of the newspaper. By resisting an editor's efforts, members of the group believe they are protecting their beliefs and values.

If the peer group and the editor both command loyalty, conflict can result for the staffer who tries to serve both masters. What comes into conflict most often are the staffer's need for social satisfaction and the editor's need for productivity.

The peer-group grapevine can circulate rumors that may upset the stability or the concentration of the staff. The strength and cohesiveness of the peer group create pressure for individuals to conform to group norms. Obviously, peer pressure can create problems for the editor if the goals of the group are at cross-purposes with the goals of the newspaper. This is sometimes the case when a newsroom union may pressure individuals to behave in ways that may not be in the best interests of the paper.[13]

Benefits

If a peer group blends well with the formal newsroom operation, it helps the staff function more effectively—for example, the city editor can share plans for a new beat structure with the staff, knowing that the staff will volunteer a thoughtful reaction which may help refine the plan.

Individual editors can draw support from peer groups. Reporters who pass along news to the city desk or who immediately call an editor's attention to an error in a headline or a story are helping build a cooperative environment based on trust.

A peer group can bring stability to a newsroom by giving individual staffers a feeling of being wanted, by helping them maintain a positive feeling about the newspaper, and by giving

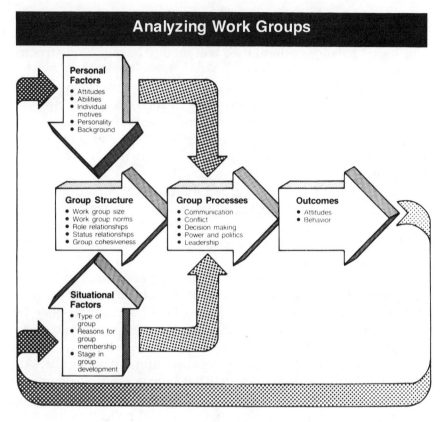

Fig. 2.9.

The organization of groups is affected by personal factors as well as by conditions under which groups can be formed. This illustration demonstrates how these forces come together and influence the group process.

Source: Adapted from Terence R. Mitchell, *People in Organizations* (New York: McGraw-Hill, 1978).

---

them a place to vent frustrations. All of these things contribute to reducing staff turnover.

The same channels of communication that spread rumors can be used by the editors to circulate useful information about the work of the newspaper.

Effective peer groups also can encourage better management in the newsroom. If editors recognize that peer groups serve as a check-and-balance system, they will tend to be more sensitive in making changes.[14]

Research into the social forces in the newsroom suggests that while it is easy for peer groups to be formed, their real effect is restrained by the common goals and ideals that editors and reporters share.[15] The staff and the newsroom managers share the vision that their newspaper is more than just a business enterprise.

Also, many editors are regarded with respect and admiration. Their professional credentials are impressive. They may serve as mentors, or they may support reporters with news sources or push them for promotions or rearrange the staff schedule to get someone an extra day off.

Younger staffers particularly have keen ambitions for status achievements. They want to move ahead quickly. They want to be considered for the best assignments. Challenging policy or editors, either individually or through the peer group, is seen as a serious bar to advancement.

There are few conflicts that may cause informal peer groups to interfere with newsroom policy. That is true even in organized newsrooms because unions, such as the Newspaper Guild, have not attempted to influence a paper's internal policies or journalistic standards. The Guild's interest is the economic welfare of its members and the traditional political interests of organized labor.

Strategies for Working with Peer Groups

In working with peer groups and their leaders, editors should keep the following points in mind:

- Try to align the peer groups' goals with the editors' goals.
- Work toward building relationships with peer-group leaders that will provide open communication. Trust and the willingness to share confidences are at the heart of such relationships.

- Rely on peer-group leaders to help dispel rumors and to disseminate facts to group members.

- Avoid actions that will threaten the existence of peer groups or embarrass their leaders.

- Do not give the groups or their leaders any reason to doubt the editors' credibility.

CHAPTER SUMMARY

Research by Elton Mayo in the 1920s produced findings that began to change management's view that people work only to make money. Mayo's studies showed the importance of interpersonal relationships on the job and the need for belonging to groups.

Work groups are important building blocks in the newsroom. There are two kinds of groups: (1) formal groups, such as the city desk, where management assigns the roles, writes the rules, and selects the leaders; and (2) informal groups, or peer groups, in which individuals come together out of common interests.

Peer groups grow and develop in four stages: (1) forming, (2) intragroup conflict, (3) cohesion, and (4) role distinction.

Journalists are drawn to peer groups for a variety of reasons, including security, friendship, recognition, support, and the need for information. Peer groups create their own standards of behavior, called group norms. Members of a group are expected to conform to group norms, which are used to control the behavior of the group's members. Peer-group leaders tend to exemplify the norms and values of their peer groups.

Peer-group power in newsrooms is somewhat restrained since staffers and editors typically hold common objectives and ideals. They often share a vision of what they want the newspaper to be.

Editors find it useful to have a trusting relationship with peer-group leaders, who may be willing to share information about their groups' concerns and frustrations.

NOTES

1. For detailed descriptions of Elton Mayo's research, see Fritz J. Roethlisberger and William J. Dickson, *Management and the Worker*, 15th ed. (Cambridge: Harvard University Press, 1970). Also, Elton Mayo, *The Human Problems of an Industrial Civilization* (New York: Macmillan, 1935).
2. Roethlisberger and Dickson, *Management and the Worker*, 86.
3. This account of Elton Mayo's research at the Hawthorne Plant of Western Electric was taken from Paul Hersey and Kenneth Blanchard, *Management of Organizational Behavior*, 4th ed. (Englewood Cliffs, N.J.: Prentice-Hall, 1982), 45–47.
4. Jerry L. Gray, *Supervision* (Boston: Kent, 1984), 203.
5. Richard M. Steers, *Introduction to Organizational Behavior*, 2d ed. (Glenview, Ill.: Scott, Foresman, 1984), 225–26.
6. Robert F. Bales and Edgar F. Borgatta, "Size of Group as a Factor in the Interaction Profile," in *Small Groups: Studies in Social Interaction*, rev. ed., ed. A. Paul Hare, Edgar F. Borgatta, and Robert F. Bales (New York: Knopf, 1966), 490–500.
7. Lyman W. Porter and Edward E. Lawler III, "Properties of Organization Structure in Relation to Job Attitudes and Job Behavior," *Psychological Bulletin* 64 (1965): 34–40.
8. Bruce W. Tuckman, "Developmental Sequence in Small Groups," *Psychological Bulletin* 64 (1965): 384–99.
9. Gray, *Supervision*, 203.
10. J. Richard Hackman, *Group Influences on Individuals in Organizations* (Springfield, Va.: National Technical Information Service, 1976), 95–98.
11. Chris Argyris, *Behind the Front Page* (San Francisco: Jossey-Bass, 1974), 47–53.
12. Steers, *Introduction to Organizational Behavior*, 230.
13. David R. Hampton, Charles E. Summer, and Ross A. Webber, *Organizational Behavior and the Practice of Management*, 3d ed. (Glenview, Ill.: Scott, Foresman, 1978), 195–96.
14. Keith Davis, *Human Behavior at Work: Organizational Behavior*, 6th ed. (New York: McGraw-Hill, 1981), 328–30.
15. Warren Breed, "Social Control in the Newsroom: A Functional Analysis," *Social Forces*, May 1955, 330–31.

3

Motivating Journalists

For the newspaper editor, a thorough understanding of the basic motivational process is essential. *Motivation*—a word that derives from the Latin *movere*, which means to move—deals with an individual's needs, with personal differences, and with the ways in which workers respond to different rewards. Editors can enhance their managerial skills by knowing what causes good or bad performance on the job.

The motivational process has four components: (1) the need, (2) the goal, (3) the behavior or action toward the goal, and (4) the feedback. Motivation is the impetus that causes an individual to pursue a goal.

After Elton Mayo's Hawthorne studies opened a new phase in the management of American business and industry (see Chapter 2), researchers began to examine the nature of people and their performances at work. This research into human nature has given us an abundance of ideas and theories about motivation. While some of the theories failed the tests of scientific examination, others remain, and the challenge for editors in learning about motivation is deciding which of these theories may work for journalists.

MORALE AND MOTIVATION

Among the initial conclusions drawn from the Hawthorne studies was that as employee morale improved, productivity increased as well. The women at the Hawthorne plant had high morale because management made them feel important; as a result, they produced more at work.

The idea that happy workers are productive workers first became popular in the 1940s. To boost employee morale, management implemented innovative techniques such as participative management, loose supervision, better communication, and employee counseling.[1]

In the late 1950s and early 1960s, new research began to expose weaknesses in the morale-productivity theory. Evidence showed that it was not difficult to find unproductive workers with high morale as well as unhappy workers who were strong performers.

The focus of management research thus shifted to job satisfaction, emphasizing employees' feelings and attitudes about their jobs. Researchers concluded that motivation and performance were linked to the degree of satisfaction and challenge workers experienced in their jobs. Studies showed that increased motivation would occur if jobs could be redesigned to give workers more responsibility, greater opportunity for growth, and increased feelings of achievement. These ideas were embodied in a concept known as job enrichment.[2]

Fig. 3.1

CLOSE-UP

While morale is no longer a valid theory of motivation, worker morale nonetheless remains a consideration for managers. A study of Peace Corps volunteers in the 1960s revealed a pattern of morale that has application to many human experiences.

During the early years of the Peace Corps, volunteers dropped out of the program at an alarming rate. Puzzled Peace Corps officials wanted to know what had changed for the young men and women who, just months earlier, had embarked for foreign countries highly motivated and full of the belief that they could make a difference.

The Peace Corps asked a group of psychiatrists, led by Walter Menninger of the Menninger Foundation in Topeka, Kansas, to investigate the problem.

Menninger's interviews revealed a pattern of behavior that he characterized as the *morale curve*. The Peace Corps volunteers reached their new country in high spirits. Within a few weeks, they encountered the frustrations of adjusting and trying to bring change to an unfamiliar culture. The reality of their situations didn't match their idealistic dreams. Within six months, morale and motivation dropped dramatically and some of the volunteers quit.

In developing his concept of the morale curve, Menninger identified four points or crises which appeared typical to those individuals interviewed:

1. The first point, the *crisis of arrival*, is a time of emotional high. The volunteers were eager for the adventure. Their training and education had prepared them for this moment. For many, there also was a sublayer of apprehension and the private question, Did I make the right decision?

2. After about six months, attitudes changed. Morale and motivation declined. The volunteers had discovered the realities of Peace Corps life. Menninger calls this second point on the morale curve the *crisis of engagement*. Morale is characterized by depression, a realization of losses—both real and fancied—limited outlets, and frustration. It is difficult to express anger because the old support systems are at home and the new ones haven't matured to the point where anger is acceptable. This period marked the time when some of the volunteers gave up.

3. For those who stayed, however, the strength of mind, ego, and body helped them move to the *crisis of acceptance*, the third of the four points on the morale curve. These volunteers decided to get involved. Their work began to take on a pattern. They felt comfortable with their surroundings and their associates. The depression lifted, freeing their energies for more constructive work. The crisis of acceptance can go on for months or years. For the Peace Corps volunteers, it lasted until their overseas tour was completed.

4. As they prepared to return home, the volunteers entered the fourth point on the morale curve, the *crisis of reentry*. They faced this period with mixed reactions: They were eager to go home but sorry to leave. The idea of giving up the Peace Corps experience was felt as a loss and the future offered uncertainty. The experience, says Menninger, is the psychological equivalent of depression.

Fig. 3.1, continued

We experience the morale curve throughout life. Apply its four points to your first year in school or your first job on a newspaper. You can't avoid it, but by understanding the rhythm of mood swings that it characterizes, you can recognize what is happening to you.

Source: Layne Longfellow, "The Morale Curve," presented at a seminar for business executives at the Menninger Foundation, Topeka, Kansas, July 1977.

When focusing on job enrichment, researchers did not discard the importance of morale, but they saw it as unrelated to job performance. Poor morale could inhibit job satisfaction, but the key to performance was how challenging the job was for the workers. In other words, good *human-relations* practices would not result in high productivity if the job were not basically satisfying.

The flaw in the job-enrichment approach was the assumption that everyone wanted a more challenging job. Investigations of

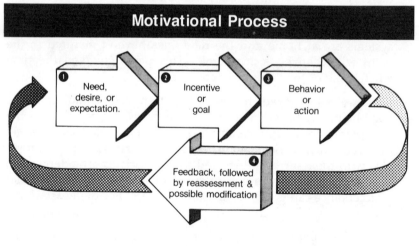

Fig. 3.2.

This model shows the four essential steps in the basic motivational process: the need, the goal, the behavior, and the feedback.

Source: Adapted from Richard M. Steers, *Introduction to Organizational Behavior*, 2d ed. (Glenview, Ill.: Scott, Foresman, 1984).

the late 1960s and early 1970s revealed many workers who were highly satisfied in dead-end jobs. Companies discovered that some workers did not want more responsibility. In addition, implementing the job-enrichment concept, especially for supervisors, often meant a major redesign of workflow and responsibilities, steps that top management was hesitant to take.[3]

More recent research concentrates on a concept that seems particularly valid for journalists: individual differences. This suggests that no single theory of motivation will always work because people have different experiences, needs, and goals. The contemporary approach is to tailor a motivation strategy to the individual differences of workers. Managers view employees as potential *human resources,* and it is management's responsibility to tap these resources in such a way that both the workers' and the organization's needs and goals are served.

MASLOW'S HIERARCHY OF NEEDS

Our exploration of motivation theories begins with Abraham Maslow (1908–1970), a clinical psychologist who played a major role in changing our view of human nature and human possibilities. His published works form a bold and original psychological theory. He began the early developmental work on his *hierarchy of needs* in the 1940s among children with mental or emotional problems.[4] His idea was that human needs can be arranged in an order or hierarchy:

1. At the first level of the hierarchy are the basic physiological needs: food, clothing, and shelter.

2. At the second level, the needs center on a safe and secure physical and emotional environment—both at home and at work. Programs such as tenure agreements, seniority clauses in union contracts, and pension and health-insurance programs reflect the need for safety and security on the job.

3. The third rung in Maslow's hierarchy involves the need to belong and to relate to others. The social elements—love, friendship, companionship—are paramount at this level.

Satisfaction at work is influenced by interaction with other workers and by securing a place in the group.

4. The fourth level focuses on the desire to have a good self-image. At this stage, satisfaction comes from recognition, esteem, attention, and the acknowledgment or appreciation of one's abilities by others. People for whom this need is satisfied have a feeling of confidence and a sense of true worth. Lack of satisfaction leads to feelings of helplessness, weakness, or inferiority. At work, a strong self-image is promoted by successful performance, by important titles in the organization, and through recognition by peers and superiors.

5. The fifth and highest level in Maslow's hierarchy is what he calls self-actualization. It expresses the desire to reach one's full potential. On the job, satisfaction at this level comes from the work itself.

Maslow described the first three levels of needs—physiological, safety, and belonging—as deficiency needs. He said that once the basic deficiency needs were adequately fulfilled, the growth needs—esteem and self-actualization—emerged.

People move up and down the hierarchy by a process of deprivation and gratification. When a particular need is deprived or unfulfilled, it will dominate the individual's attention. Once satisfied, this need recedes and the next higher need comes to the fore. A need level must be satisfied only to a relative degree before behavior is motivated by the next higher level. The level of relative satisfaction changes over time as individuals mature and encounter new experiences. A job that is satisfying today may become boring in a year. The intellectual growth that takes place will cause us to see the job as less demanding over time.

Maslow saw this process as a dynamic cycle that is reflected in the basic state of one's life; that is, if we have enough to eat and drink, a place to live, and family and friends, the focus of our needs is on matters of self-worth and self-fulfillment. We can

Fig. 3.3.

Abraham Maslow developed an early theory of motivation based on the idea that human needs can be arranged in an order or hierarchy. This illustration identifies the needs in each of the five levels of Maslow's hierarchy.

understand this by thinking of the daily cycles in our lives when, for example, the momentary need for a meal or a cup of coffee or shelter from the rain takes temporary priority over activities related to the growth process.

For Maslow, the self-actualizing person is not a normal person with something added, but a normal person with nothing taken away. In his study of historical figures such as Thomas Jefferson, Albert Einstein, Eleanor Roosevelt, Albert Schweitzer, and Jane Addams, Maslow concluded that one of the most striking characteristics of self-actualizing people is that they are strongly focused on problems outside of themselves. They generally have a mission in life; they delight in bringing about justice, stopping cruelty and exploitation, fighting lies and untruth. They have a clear perception of reality along with a keen sense of the false and the phony. They are spontaneous and creative, sometimes displaying what might be called a mature childlikeness, a "second naïveté." They are autonomous, not bound tightly to the customs and assumptions of their particular culture. The makeup of their character is highly democratic so that their friendships tend to cut across the boundaries of class, education, politics, or ethnic background. At the same time, they are marked by a certain detachment and a need for privacy; they generally limit themselves to a small circle of friends.[5]

Maslow's theory spawned new research into motivation. One study found that managers in higher echelons of organizations generally are more able to satisfy their growth needs than lower-level managers. The top managers have more challenging, autonomous jobs where it is possible to pursue growth needs seriously. Lower-level managers tend to have more routine jobs, which are less likely to satisfy their growth needs.[6] Is this a valid comparison to draw between the job of executive editor and the job of city editor?

Fig. 3.4

CLOSE-UP

How can Maslow's hierarchy of needs be applied to journalists? What kinds of psychological needs are important to them? How have these needs changed over the years? Two major studies—one by sociologists at the University of Illinois, the other by members of the journalism faculty at Indiana University—can offer some insight into these questions.

In a 1971 sociological portrait of American journalists and their work, John W. C. Johnstone, Edward J. Slawski, and William W. Bowman of the University of Illinois reported that public service—the chance to help people—was the most important aspect of newspaper journalism. From their interviews with 3,194 staff members at daily newspapers, the researchers suggested that autonomy on the job was second most important and freedom from supervision third. Next came job security, followed by pay and fringe benefits.

A more recent major survey conducted in 1982–83 by David H. Weaver, Richard G. Gray, and G. Cleveland Wilhoit of Indiana University covered the same topics in interviews with 1,001 newspaper journalists. As the Illinois study found, public service still ranked first as the most important aspect of newspaper work. Interestingly, job security was second, while autonomy and freedom from supervision fell to fourth and seventh.

Why would job security become the second most important job characteristic among newspaper journalists? The evidence is only circumstantial, but the Indiana interviews were conducted some ten years later than those at Illinois, at a time when hiring freezes and other belt-tightening measures were common in U.S. newsrooms and when the industry was reeling from the closing of several major newspapers. Between 1981 and 1983, the *Cleveland Press, Philadelphia Bulletin, Minneapolis Star, Buffalo Courier-Express,* and *Washington Star* went out of business. Other newspapers were in trouble, including the *New York Daily News* and *St. Louis Globe Democrat,* which made well-publicized retrenchment and restructuring efforts in order to survive.

In addition, evening newspapers in many communities were being combined with morning counterparts or were being changed to a morning publication cycle. Thousands of journalists lost their jobs when their newspapers failed. Many thousand others felt the pinch brought on by the recession of 1981. Still others were threatened by the prospect that their newspapers would go under or that their working life-styles would be altered sharply by having to learn to work to the beat of a different publishing cycle.

In this shaky environment, the need to feel secure in their jobs may have taken precedence, as Maslow has suggested, over some of the higher needs of newspaper journalists.

Sources: John W. C. Johnstone, Edward J. Slawski, and William W. Bowman, *The News People* (Urbana, Ill.: University of Illinois Press, 1976), 109–111, 229; David H. Weaver, Richard G. Gray, and G. Cleveland Wilhoit, "Portrait of the U.S. Journalist," (Indiana University School of Journalism, October 1984).

McGREGOR'S THEORY X AND THEORY Y

Maslow's work paved the way for the development of Theory X and Theory Y, a now-classic set of ideas about motivation first proposed in 1960 by Douglas McGregor of the Massachusetts Institute of Technology.[7] His thesis was that management makes certain assumptions about human nature.

One group of assumptions was defined as "Theory X." Managers who accept Theory X believe that workers are, by nature, lazy, irresponsible, immature, and unreliable. They dislike work, and close supervision and control are necessary to force productivity. McGregor thought this was an inaccurate view of human behavior and an ineffective style of management. Drawing on Maslow's hierarchy of needs, McGregor argued that Theory X was a questionable method for motivating individual workers whose physiological and safety needs are reasonably satisfied and whose social, esteem, and self-actualization needs are emerging and becoming predominant.[8]

McGregor developed "Theory Y" as an alternate theory of behavior to reflect a more accurate understanding of human nature and motivation. This theory assumes that people like work, that they are able to direct their own efforts, and that they can be creative at work if properly motivated.

We should not conclude that Theory X is "bad" and Theory Y is "good." For example, an editor's natural management style may correspond with Theory Y: He or she is supportive, encouraging, and avoids close supervision. However, such a Theory-Y style and its assumptions about human nature may not work with some staffers. A short-term Theory-X approach of authoritarian and tightly controlled supervision may be necessary to help alter a staffer's poor work behavior so that a Theory-Y approach can then be effective.

HERZBERG'S TWO-FACTOR THEORY

One of the most interesting series of motivation studies was conducted in the early 1960s by psychologist Frederick Herzberg and his associates at Western Reserve University in Cleveland.[9] Their two-factor theory came from data collected in extensive interviews of two hundred engineers and accountants from eleven industries in the Pittsburgh area. These workers were asked what kinds of things on the job made them happy or satisfied and what kinds of things made them unhappy or dissatisfied.

In his analysis of the interviews, Herzberg saw two different and independent categories of human needs that affect behavior in separate ways. The things that tended to make people

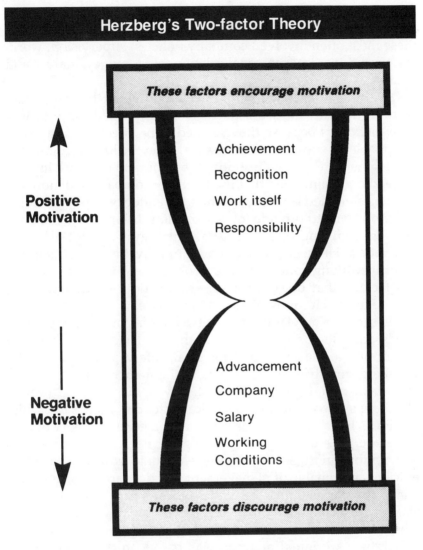

Fig. 3.5.

Frederick Herzberg identified two categories of human needs. Those things that tended to make people unhappy with their jobs resulted in negative motivation. Those things that made people feel good about their jobs could lead to positive motivation.

unhappy with their jobs were found in the working environment. Identified by Herzberg as *hygiene* or *maintenance factors*, these most often involved company policies, supervision, working conditions, interpersonal relationships, money, status, and security.

The things that made people feel good about their jobs had more to do with the work itself. Herzberg called these factors *needs motivators* because they seemed to be effective in motivating people to superior performance. They include recognition, achievement, responsibility, advancement, and the work itself.[10]

Herzberg maintained that the failure of companies to motivate workers stemmed from management's tendency to rely on working conditions to provide job satisfaction. In this way, companies were reducing dissatisfaction, but they were not affecting motivation. Herzberg concluded that motivation is not likely to occur if working conditions are poor. If working conditions are satisfactory, that does not assure motivation; it only creates a climate in which motivation can take place.

We can see a relationship between Maslow's hierarchy of needs and Herzberg's two-factor theory. Herzberg's hygienes correspond to Maslow's physiological, safety, and social needs. Herzberg's motivators are similar to the higher-order needs for self-worth and fulfillment on Maslow's hierarchy. However, Herzberg's theory relates specifically to the workplace while Maslow's hierarchy of needs represents a general theory of life.

Herzberg's studies have meaning for newspaper publishers and editors in this way: If the electronic editing system is efficient and reliable, if management practices are consistent and fair, if the pay is equitable, if the newsroom is comfortable, if staffers are a congenial group and feel reasonably secure in their jobs, then a climate exists in which the staff can be motivated.

Herzberg's original analysis was based on data taken from scientific and professional people, but subsequent investigation suggests that his theory does not work in all cases. In the newsroom, for example, there may be staffers who are genuinely motivated by interpersonal relationships (a hygiene factor) that they develop with coworkers on the paper and among their sources. Who can doubt that the reporters who labor for years on the national political beats are motivated by their association with the powerful and the influential?

Fig. 3.6

CLOSE-UP

In 1972 and 1973, Harold Shaver, an assistant professor of journalism at Kansas State University, surveyed journalism graduates from seven universities to test whether they developed satisfaction and dissatisfaction with jobs in the way Herzberg predicted. The 404 participants had been in the news-editorial or advertising sequences in journalism school and were members of the classes of 1960 and 1970. More than 70 percent of the respondents were from the class of 1970.

Shaver's questionnaire listed twenty-four specific satisfiers and dissatisfiers drawn from the general factors identified by Herzberg's hygiene-motivation theory. While the responses indicated that journalism graduates develop satisfaction and dissatisfaction with jobs in the way Herzberg predicts, one exception was worth noting.

High on the list of satisfiers or motivators was "interpersonal relations with peers." Herzberg considered this a hygiene factor, but its ranking as the fifth most important satisfier underscores the importance of personal interaction in the newsroom. It also suggests why peer groups are such a natural element in newsroom dynamics.

"Possibility of growth" was the most important single satisfier and the second ranked dissatisfier. The opportunity to acquire new professional skills and stature is clearly significant, both for those who succeed and those whose ambitions are frustrated.

Poorly handled company policy and administration was the dissatisfier mentioned most often. Salary ranked third.

Overall, Shaver found, job satisfaction was generally positive.

Source: Harold C. Shaver, "Job Satisfaction among Journalism Graduates," *Journalism Quarterly* 55 (Spring 1978): 54–61.

McCLELLAND'S ACHIEVEMENT MOTIVATION THEORY

Also in the early 1960s, a third theory of motivation was developed by psychologist David McClelland and his colleagues at Harvard. McClelland's fascination with achievement was the impetus behind his research and his classic book, *The Achieving Society*, which considered the question: Why are some societies able to produce great historical figures, writers, scientists, and entrepreneurs when others just barely manage to survive?[11]

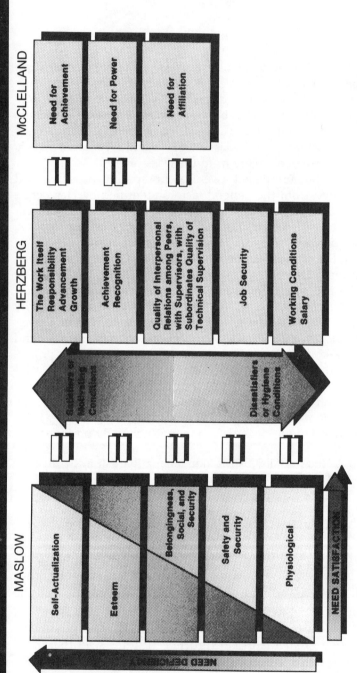

Fig. 3.7.

Similarities can be seen in comparing David McClelland's achievement, affiliation, and power needs to the upper levels of the Maslow and Herzberg theories.

Source: Adapted from James L. Gibson, John M. Ivancevich, and James H. Donnelly, Jr., *Organizations: Behavior, Structure, Processes,* 3d ed. (Dallas: Business Publications, 1979).

McClelland's research led him to propose that the need for achievement is a distinct human motive, one that can be distinguished from other needs. More important, the achievement motive can be isolated and assessed in any group.[12] Unlike the Maslow and Herzberg theories, McClelland's theory has considerable scientific support and is of practical value to managers.

McClelland identified three needs—achievement, affiliation, and power—as the primary motivators of human behavior. These needs are present in varying degrees in all individuals, and they are not expressed in a sequence of one following another as Maslow had suggested.

Fig. 3.8

CLOSE-UP

David McClelland illustrated some of the human achievement characteristics by describing a laboratory experiment. Participants were asked to throw rings over a peg from any distance they chose. Many people tended to throw at random—now close, now far away. Individuals with a high need for achievement seemed to measure carefully where they were most likely to get a sense of mastery—not too close to make the task ridiculously easy or too far away to make it impossible. They set moderately difficult but achievable goals. In biology, this is known as the *overload principle*. It is exemplified through the principles of weight lifting where, for example, strength cannot be increased if the weights are too light or so heavy that the lifter risks injury. Strength can be increased by lifting weights that are difficult but realistic enough to stretch the muscles.

Source: Paul Hersey and Kenneth H. Blanchard, *Management of Organizational Behavior*, 4th ed. (Englewood Cliffs, N.J.: Prentice-Hall, 1982), 38.

Achievement. This is the need to excel or reach challenging goals. McClelland explains that high achievers demonstrate the following characteristics:

- They focus on personal improvement, on doing things better by themselves. They want to excel, to do the task better than it has been done before. Success in meeting the challenge is a greater motivator than the rewards associated with it. Money is valuable primarily as a measure of better performance.

- They prefer to work alone and to take personal responsibility for the work rather than leave the outcome to others. High achievers are often seen as loners who have difficulty delegating work.

- They set moderate but challenging goals for themselves. They want to excel, so they avoid easy goals; but they are not risk takers, so they won't set the goals too high. They prefer a moderate degree of chance because they are confident that their efforts and abilities can influence the outcome.

- They like to maintain control over the means to achieve their goals. They want to be sure that the probability for success is high because if they fail to make the goal, for whatever reason, there is no satisfaction of achievement.

- They want short-term feedback on their performance so that they can tell how well they are doing. Rapid feedback helps high achievers measure their progress toward the goal. And they want feedback related to the work they are doing as opposed to how helpful or how cooperative they are.[13]

McClelland says that achievement-motivated people spend a lot of time thinking about how to do things better. As a result, they are more successful as students or as employees than those of equal intelligence who have weaker achievement needs.

The pure high achievers may be found in only 5 percent of the work force. They tend to be drawn to entrepreneurial work, such as self-employment or commission sales, where they can satisfy their need for achievement.[14]

We can see why a high achiever might not be satisfied as a reporter for a daily newspaper where the tasks are defined by the editor, where the means of performing tasks or achieving goals are restrained by tradition, where the cooperation of copy editors and editors is necessary, and where the pay is on an hourly or salary basis. Journalists who are true high achievers tend to become the top news executives, specialists in reporting fields, free-lance writers, photographers, or artists.

Staffers with a high achievement drive demand a lot of attention from editors. The challenge for the editor is to fit their needs for feedback and independence into the framework of an efficient news operation.

Affiliation. The second of McClelland's needs involves the desire for friendship, close cooperation, and interpersonal relationships. This need is identified with people who gain great satisfaction from deep and long-lasting personal relationships. They value friendships. They want to be liked. They are concerned with other people's feelings about them.

Staffers with strong affiliation needs are likely to be involved with informal work groups in the newsroom. They also require attention from editors; they want to know that editors share their concern for interpersonal matters, such as a congenial working environment or a caring management style. Editors can influence these staffers' improvement on the job by suggesting how continued poor performance will affect the editors' regard for their value to the newspaper. If editors can match the talents and skills of these employees with jobs that will permit them to interact with others, it is likely that they will be highly motivated.

If asked to make a choice, individuals with a strong affiliation need would give priority to a working relationship that offers companionship with other staffers. A high achiever, on the other hand, would choose a working relationship with key staffers who could help the achiever reach his or her goals.

Power. The third motivator identified by McClelland focuses on the need to control or have influence over others. Managers have a high need for power, and this is important because a major task of managers is to influence the behavior of others. Some employees are motivated by a desire for personal power. They want to dominate.

Staffers with the need for power often assume leadership roles in newsroom organizations such as informal peer groups or the bargaining unit of a union. Editors can make use of strong performers with power needs by providing them with an arena, such as a special-projects task force or a planning committee, where their special skills or knowledge can be influential. Power seekers who are marginal performers can be motivated if the editor demonstrates how their poor performance is weakening their power base, such as their influence over other staffers.

As managers, personal-power types want their subordinates to be responsible to them rather than the organization. Those driven by the need for institutional power feel personally responsible for the success of the organization. They are willing to sacrifice their own self-interests for the welfare of the company. They tend to be mature individuals with a strong sense of justice.[15]

Another twist to the power needs of journalists is control over one's work. For example, the city government reporter who knows more about city hall than the editors can pretty much set his or her own agenda: what meetings to cover, what officials to interview, what stories to write. For the reporter, this represents control—a form of power that is often highly satisfying.

Fig. 3.9

CLOSE-UP

During my interviews with journalists in preparing to write this book, I asked what they thought motivated them or other successful newspaper people they know. Following are some of their observations:

"I think young reporters are motivated by the idealism, by the excitement, by the glamour and the extensive ideals of social responsibility and social blessings which they believe fall on the shoulders of people who write for newspapers. My experience is that they bring more enthusiasm and idealism to their work than people in many, many other professions. They are still imbued with a notion that their work can make a difference, that they can change the world, that they can make it a better place, and that they can afflict some of the comfortable. They believe they can find personal fulfillment in ways that are difficult to find in many other businesses or professions."

Robert J. Haiman
President and Managing Director
Poynter Institute
St. Petersburg, Florida

"I am idealistic about work. For a Catholic, I have a Protestant work ethic. I love to do the job well, whatever it is. I have a very good idealistic belief in journalism. I really believe that we accomplish good by sharing knowledge. I believe that we are a good force in society. I have a great allegiance to what would be considered the traditional wisdom of journalism. A basic motivation for young reporters is a sense of accomplishment and that they are learning and improving. They want to be involved in big stories and to do well because that seems to move them ahead in the field, whether it moves them up to a higher job or a bigger paper or whether it is simply the stature and respect that they command."

Larry Beaupre
Executive Editor
Westchester-Rockland Newspapers
Harrison, New York

"Curiosity. I would stick with that, but I would reach for some others. When I was in college, I realized I had made a lot of decisions about reporting that had to do with the fun of learning things and being in a place where I can pick up the phone and legitimately ask anybody in the world a question. Now I love that. I derive tremendous satisfaction from that because, in a way, the opportunity that the profession affords you is the opportunity to create a universe out of your own curiosity. If you want to, you can go anywhere, see anything, ask anything, learn anything you want to. If you want to get highfalutin' about it, this is a way to get paid for intellectual existentialism."

Eric Best
Assistant City Editor
San Francisco Examiner
San Francisco, California

"Seeing a story on page one is probably a motivator for a lot of people. Money is a motivator. If you are paid well, you are probably going to be happier than if you are not. But there has got to be more than money to make the job satisfying. I think that good leadership,

Fig. 3.9, continued
for example, can be a motivator. If I have a boss who is a very hard worker and who sometimes amazes me at how much he does, then I can do some of those things that are bothering me. In that sense, motivation comes from leadership by example. I am motivated by trust and honesty and sincerity and sharing information."

> Phil Currie
> Vice-president/News
> Gannett Company, Inc.
> Arlington, Virginia

Sources: Robert J. Haiman, interview with author, 19 January 1984; Larry Beaupre, interview with author, 7 January 1984; Eric Best, interview with author, 7 February 1984; Phil Currie, interview with author, 11 January 1984.

CONTEMPORARY MOTIVATION THEORIES

The theories of Maslow, McGregor, Herzberg, and McClelland are valuable because they identify the needs that trigger motivated behavior. Their work inspired continuing research into motivation. Contemporary investigations have advanced ideas that suggest why employees display different types of motivated behavior. Among the contemporary theories, three are worth examining.

Expectancy Theory

The literature of motivation was enlarged in the early 1960s by the work of Victor H. Vroom, a professor of psychology at Carnegie Institute of Technology in Pittsburgh, whose contribution was the first theory that attempted to incorporate individual differences.[16] His expectancy theory suggests that an individual's choice of behaviors is influenced by the expectation of a desirable outcome.

Vroom's model has three variables:

1. Valence defines the value of the goal to the individual—how attractive is the reward? The reward has greater value if it represents an unsatisfied need of the individual. If employ-

Motivating Journalists

ees do not value the rewards offered by the company, they are not likely to be motivated to perform well.

2. Instrumentality deals with the probability that if an employee works harder, this behavior will actually lead to the desired outcome or reward. The employee's ability to control the behavior that would produce the expected outcome is important.

3. Expectation involves an employee's evaluation of how much effort or energy is necessary to be successful in achieving the goal.

To illustrate Vroom's concepts, let us look at a newsroom where the pay is low in comparison to salaries at other local newspapers. Money as a reward does not have a high value in

Expectancy Theory of Motivation

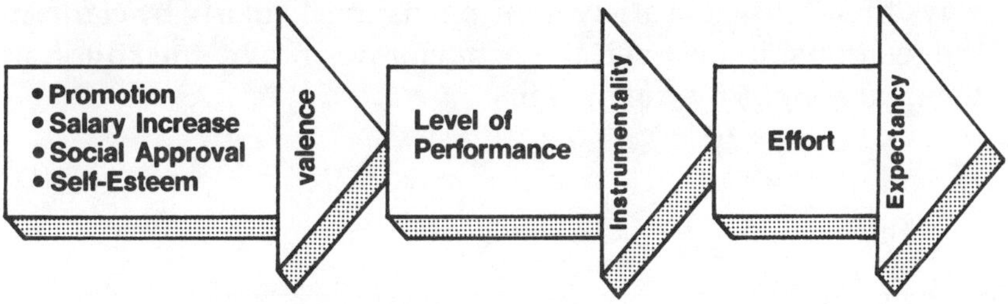

- Promotion
- Salary Increase
- Social Approval
- Self-Esteem

valence → Level of Performance → Instrumentality → Effort → Expectancy

Fig. 3.10.

Victor H. Vroom's expectancy theory suggests that an individual's choice of behaviors is influenced by the expectation of a desirable result. In this model, *valence* is the value of the goal, *instrumentality* deals with the probability that certain behavior will lead to the reward, and *expectation* represents the individual's sense of how much effort is necessary to be successful.

Source: Adapted from James L. Gibson, John M. Ivancevich, and James H. Donnelly, Jr., *Organizations: Behavior, Structure, Processes*, 3d ed. (Dallas: Business Publications, 1979).

this newsroom. The staff is not highly motivated. The publisher is aware of the problem and introduces a merit-pay plan that is designed to increase the earnings of the strongest performers. Money suddenly takes on greater value as a reward. That's valence.

Individual staffers now begin to calculate the probability that by improving the coverage on their beats or by writing better headlines, they can qualify for merit pay. That's instrumentality.

Having concluded that money has value as a reward and that the probability is good that better work will lead to additional pay, the staffers assess how much extra effort is necessary to claim the reward. That's expectation.

In the expectancy theory, the role of the editor in the motivation process is clear. The editor must know the goals of the individuals on the staff—that is, what do reporters aspire to? What short-term career objectives do copy editors have? Unless these questions are answered, the editor cannot be an effective motivator.

Once employees' goals are understood, the editor can suggest ways their jobs can satisfy their needs, particularly by clarifying the relationship between the behavior desired by the editor and the goal sought by the staffer.

Equity Theory

The equity theory is the most popular social comparison concept that focuses on individuals' feelings or perceptions of how fairly they are being treated as compared to others.[17]

Formulated by J. Stacy Adams in 1965, the equity theory rests on two basic assumptions about human behavior. The first assumption is that individuals evaluate their social relationships much as they would evaluate an economic transaction in the marketplace. Relationships are seen as an exchange. Individuals make investments in relationships and, in return, they expect certain outcomes. Second, individuals compare their own situations with the situations of others to determine whether an exchange was fair. You compare the price of a new car with what

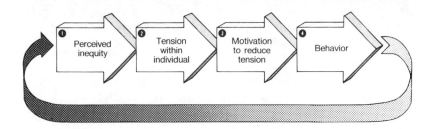

Fig. 3.11.

The equity theory rests on two assumptions: that individuals evaluate social relationships and that they compare their own situation with others. As this model shows, an inequity causes tension, which leads to motivation, which leads to behavior that seeks to reduce the tension.

Source: Adapted from Richard M. Steers, *Introduction to Organizational Behavior*, 2d ed. (Glenview, Ill.: Scott, Foresman, 1984).

---

your neighbor paid. You appraise the apparent value of your personal or professional relationships against those of your colleagues.[18]

The equity theory has clear meaning for the workplace. Behavior is influenced by the rewards workers receive or are going to receive, underscoring the basic human desire to be treated fairly.

The individual's perception is a crucial element in determining whether a state of equity or inequity exists. An individual can have a distorted view of things, believing that he or she is getting a low reward for a high effort. The inequity will not exist, however, if coworkers are satisfied with a similar exchange.

Adams found that when an inequity exists, the following consequences are likely to occur: Individuals who believe they are being treated unfairly will experience tension. The tension will be proportionate to the magnitude of the inequity and will motivate individuals to attempt to reduce the inequity. The strength of the drive to reduce the inequity will be proportionate to the perceived inequity.[19]

For editors faced with the problem of recognizing a perceived inequity, here are six possible scenarios drawn from Adams's research:

1. A staffer may alter the input. Employee input may be increased or decreased, depending on whether the inequity is advantageous or disadvantageous. For example, an underpaid reporter might reduce the level of effort or increase absenteeism; a reporter who is overpaid might work harder.

2. A staffer might alter the outcome. Outcome would be increased if the reporter responded to a pay increase and an enhancement in working conditions by improving his or her effort.

3. A staffer may distort input or outcome. The reporter who feels underpaid may downplay or diminish the status of the job with remarks such as, "I really don't work all that hard on this beat." This artificial distortion balances the ratio of effort to reward and helps the reporter feel more content.

4. A staffer may distort the work of others. In the face of an injustice, the reporter may conclude that another staffer who gets a greater reward also works harder. Or, the reporter may attempt to diminish the value of another's work, saying, for example, that the other staffer's page-one stories always require heavy reworking on the copy desk.

5. A staffer may choose another point of comparison. The reporter may discard one comparison and select another where the balance between effort and reward is more in line with his or her own. For example, the reporter may shift comparisons of pay or beat significance from the stars on the staff to those on the next lower level.

6. A staffer may go to another paper. The desire to quit or find another job is born of the desire to find a better balance between effort and reward.

These are techniques individuals use to cope with situations they believe are unfair. Their motivations and efforts are aimed at returning to a state of equity and reduced tension. They continually try to understand their environment and to act on it in a way that satisfies their more pressing needs, desires, and expectations.[20]

Goal-setting Theory

In 1968, psychologist Edwin A. Locke of the American Institutes for Research put forward a theory suggesting that supervisors can influence the motivation of their subordinates. Locke determined that motivation has two basic elements: values, and intentions or goals.[21] Individuals attach values to their tasks; for example, in the newsroom, a strong work ethic can produce a goal of accomplishing more, which can cause employees to work longer hours. Thus, the value (work ethic) influences the goal (get more done), which influences behavior (work longer hours).[22]

The basic premise of goal setting—that a supervisor can help employees achieve their work goals—contradicts Herzberg's

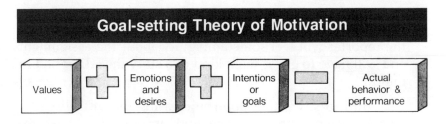

Fig. 3.12.

The premise of goal setting is that motivation has two basic elements: *values* and *goals*. This model shows how values influence desires, which influence goals, which result in actual behavior.

Source: Adapted from Richard M. Steers, *Introduction to Organizational Behavior*, 2d ed. (Glenview, Ill.: Scott, Foresman, 1984).

idea that supervision can only cause dissatisfaction and that achievement in the job itself can only cause satisfaction. Yet, in reality, the actions of the boss are often seen as major contributors to whether one has a good day or a bad day at the office. Locke sees supervisors who can be described as "pleasant," "considerate," or "friendly" as possessing important traits in common with workers. By helping subordinates attain high production, solve problems, and perform competent work, a supervisor can help workers reach such goals as higher earnings and promotions.

Locke identified two aspects of motivation that are interrelated: satisfaction with job and supervisor, and work performance. Satisfaction reflects the degree to which workers believe the job fulfills or allows the fulfillment of their job values. It follows, Locke concluded, that a supervisor can influence satisfaction by either helping or hindering workers in pursuit of their goals.[23]

Further studies of Locke's thesis developed six characteristics that enhance the translation of goals into performance:[24]

1. Specific goal. A goal that is clearly defined will result in higher performance levels than a goal that is described in general terms. If, after asking a reporter to interview the mayor, the city editor helps shape the questions to be asked, the reporter will have a clear understanding of the assignment. If the city editor simply says, "Go talk to the mayor," the reporter will feel some ambiguity about the assignment and will have to guess what kind of a story the editor had in mind.

2. Goal difficulty. Up to a point, increasing the difficulty of a goal heightens the challenge and encourages a stronger effort. This is particularly true for the high achievers identified by McClelland. However, if difficult goals are not routinely reinforced, they may lose their motivating potential. Moreover, if an employee has failed to achieve earlier goals, the motivating effect of setting difficult goals in the future may be minimized.

    A police reporter may be told by the city editor that before he or she can be considered for the courthouse beat, an improvement in story organization is necessary. The reporter accepts that as a goal and begins to work on it. But during the next six months, the city editor doesn't mention story organization again to the reporter. Without reinforcement from the editor, the reporter loses interest in the goal and slips back into bad habits. Consequently, when the courthouse beat goes to someone else, the reporter becomes wary of new goals the city editor might set in connection with a different assignment.

3. Participation. An employee's participation in goal setting has long been thought of as desirable, not only for achievement but also for employee satisfaction. It is easy to understand that a reporter would prefer to have the city editor help define a goal rather than say to the reporter, "You've got to organize your stories better and here is how you are going to do it."

4. Feedback. Receiving feedback is an important influence on the effectiveness of goal setting for employees. It serves to keep staffers on target and encourages them to push for a greater effort. It is clear that a reporter can correct a story-organization problem more effectively if the city editor routinely offers suggestions and observations.

5. Peer competition. In a newsroom, where strong egos reside, peer competition is part of the life-style. Editors recognize that performance can be enhanced by competition. Reporters generally work independently of each other and are responsible for their own stories. In this environment, competition can be highly effective. However, there can be only one winner if an assistant city editor slot is coming open, and if the staff believes that performance will determine who gets the new opportunity, the peer competition can be quite lively.

6. Acceptance. What ties these goal-setting characteristics together is the acceptance of goals by individual workers. If the goal of becoming assistant city editor fits the personal aspirations of individual reporters, each of them will be strongly motivated to perform. Or, if a reporter disagrees with the

city editor that a story-organization problem exists, the possibility is slim that the reporter will be motivated to change.[25]

BEHAVIOR MODIFICATION

The ideas of noted behavioral scientist B. F. Skinner are thought of more as techniques for motivating employees than a theory of work motivation.[26] Managers who employ Skinner's behavior-modification principles understand that employees can be conditioned to behave according to the standards of the company. People behave in ways that help them avoid punishment and achieve pleasant results.

Three of Skinner's ideas form the foundation for behavior modification:

1. The first of Skinner's ideas about behavior modification suggests that individuals are basically passive. They react to events rather than initiating behavior that influences events. This is in contrast to some other theories of motivation, which state that people make conscious decisions about their behavior and take an active role in shaping their environment.[27]
2. Skinner's second point was that only behavior that could be observed and measured could be modified. Needs, attitudes, and goals—those nonobservable elements of most motivation theories—could not be factored into a behavior-modification plan.
3. Finally, Skinner contended that reinforcement was essential to create permanent change through behavior modification. Individuals can learn different behaviors if they are positively reinforced.

To use behavior modification in the newsroom, the editor must be able to define those behaviors associated with good performance. A pertinent example, which will be discussed in Chapter 10, is a performance-review program based on behavioral standards that can be observed and measured. A regular performance review can help editors pinpoint trouble spots. Editors can translate performance weaknesses as well as career ambitions into goals for each staffer. The positive reinforcement occurs when the editor praises the staffer for demonstrating the desired behavior.

Studies show that most behavior-modification programs fail because managers neglect to specify detailed goals for altering behavior.

Fig. 3.13

CLOSE-UP

In a 1985 survey of 1,335 daily newspaper journalists for the Associated Press Managing Editors, respondents were asked how important several possible career motivations were to them. The two motivators cited by three-quarters of the respondents as "very important" were: "The work is important and gives you a feeling of accomplishment" and "The work is satisfying and makes good use of your skills and talents." Nearly half of the journalists cited "public service—the chance to help people" as "very important."

Other motivations were singled out as "very important" by fewer of the journalists interviewed. These included "job security" (39 percent); "chances for advancement" (38 percent); "pay" (33 percent); "autonomy" (31 percent); "fringe benefits" (28 percent); "the newspaper is one of the best in the country" (21 percent); and "freedom from supervision" (16 percent).

Source: Robert Ritter, Michael Waller, and Kris McGrath, *Journalists and Readers: Bridging the Credibility Gap* (Associated Press Managing Editors, 1985).

IS MONEY A MOTIVATOR?

Money can mean whatever people want it to mean. Its value as a motivator is entangled with all other human needs, and its importance to individuals is difficult to determine. According to Maslow and Herzberg, money is not the only thing, but it is the first thing.

Editors looking for clues to explain the value of money to

themselves and to the journalists on their news staffs will be interested in the results of three studies:

1. The first study focused on workers in a midwestern factory in the late 1940s who had been asked to produce on an incentive plan. The more work they did, the more money they would earn. William F. Whyte of Cornell University found that for 90 percent of these employees, the work group was more important than the incentive for higher pay.[28] In the situations Whyte studied, the work group had decided to resist management's desire for greater production. By ignoring the incentive plan, Whyte concluded, workers were giving a higher value to the work group—that is, opinions of fellow workers, comfort and enjoyment on the job, and long-range security—than to the opportunity to make more money.

2. Two psychologists at the University of Minnesota, Robert L. Opsahl and Marvin D. Dunnette, evaluated several research studies in which money was found to have a number of meanings for workers. They discovered that money is a goal and an incentive; money is a source of satisfaction; money is a source of material goods; money is a standard of comparison of one's worth to the company; and money is a reinforcer when it is tied to a certain level of performance.[29]

3. In his book, *Pay and Organizational Effectiveness,* psychologist Edward E. Lawler of Yale University proposed that if the following conditions are present, money can act as a motivator: Trust level between managers and subordinates is high. Individual performance can actually be measured. Pay rewards are higher for strong performers than for average or weak performers. Workers perceive few negative consequences of good performance.[30]

Based on this research, one can see that merit pay has the potential to be a stronger motivator for journalists than a pay program in which every staffer gets an equal increase. Feedback and effective performance reviews also are essential to a climate in which money can contribute to improved performance.

Fig. 3.14

CLOSE-UP

Psychologist Neil P. Lewis says that while many editors think they have serious motivation problems with newsroom employees, what they really have is management problems.

"Most reporters are just plain not very well managed. They don't know what their mission is. They're not sure what their goals are. They have no real plan to get there from here, and they never get any meaningful feedback on how they are doing.

"It's no wonder so many reporters wander off in strange directions, try hard to do their own thing, and eventually become disillusioned with the whole business and leave.

"It is clear the only way to 'motivate' newsroom people is to manage them better. For some, the concepts of management and authority seem contrary to many of the egalitarian and humanistic notions so many of us hold dear. However, it is not that people really resent being managed, directed, or told what to do. What they resent is being managed poorly, unfairly, insufficiently, or, for that matter, not at all.

"In managing, it is helpful to assume that (1) people have a variety of conscious goals that are typically very complex and often in competition with each other; the achievement of one goal may be incompatible with the achievement of another; (2) much of human behavior is consciously goal-directed and purposive; and (3) people have strong emotional reactions to the outcomes they obtain as a result of their behavior."

Source: Neil P. Lewis, "How to Motivate People," *The Bulletin of the American Society of Newspaper Editors* (March 1981), 16–18.

SOLVING THE MOTIVATION RIDDLE

Most of the motivation experiments discussed in this chapter involved factory workers, engineers, or accountants. To date, little research exists among newspaper journalists to suggest how these theories and techniques might apply in the newsroom. However, we can see that there are links between motivation research and the kind of work done by newspaper journalists. Noted management consultant Peter F. Drucker suggests that the greatest opportunities for effective motivation that will increase productivity are to be found in knowledge work, and especially in management.[31]

Drucker sees *knowledge workers*—managers, researchers, planners, designers, and innovators—as the most productive resource. The variety of tasks performed by newspaper journalists—from reporter to editor—suggests that there are significant responsibilities for research, planning, design, and innovation at every level.

Drucker argues that managing and motivating knowledge workers are far more demanding than managing and motivating manual workers. For one thing, the weapon of fear is not effective. Fear of economic suffering and fear of job security do not work as newsroom management strategies except in those cases where performance is clearly unacceptable.

The focus of motivation, particularly for knowledge workers, has to be in terms of achievement. Each staffer, whatever the individual differences and needs, has to recognize that there is a clear path of opportunity for those who perform well. Editors can keep the path clear through a management process that rewards outstanding performance.

Fig. 3.15

CLOSE-UP

At newspaper management seminars, discussions about motivation invariably invite the question, How do you motivate the old-timer on the staff, the fellow who has been sitting on the rim for fifteen years? He's fifty-eight years old, drinks a bit too much, isn't very friendly, and is only marginally competent. His zest for work has waned. He's not bad enough to fire, but he doesn't contribute much either.

The first point to remember is that the editors of the newspaper share the responsibility for the situation. They tolerated the staffer's poor performance for years without giving him the essential choice of doing better or leaving. As a result, he has been conditioned to believe that mediocre performance is acceptable.

In the time-honored tradition of respect for elders, a young editor may shy away from criticizing the old-timer's work, evaluating performance, and counseling. Instead, the editor may simply tolerate the situation, putting him "out to pasture" and giving him assignments that are routine, innocuous, and unchallenging.

A turnaround is not always possible, but here are some steps to be tried:

- Pay attention to the staffer. Make him believe that he is a valued employee, important to the success of the newspaper. Be alert to opportunities to reinforce a positive self-image.
- Tell him specifically what he has to do to improve the quality of his work. Let him know the consequences if his work continues to be marginal. This can include termination.
- Help him set short-term goals for improvement.
- Reinforce his progress with praise.
- Schedule frequent meetings to review his work. Go over both the strong and weak points in performance. Reinforce the need to continue working on the goals. Be firm in insisting that improvement is necessary.
- Assign him tasks that will draw on his strengths, such as experience and knowledge of the community. Treat him as an authority. Emphasize that his lifetime of experience and learning has value. His recall of places, streets, and people can be valuable. Ask him to give a workshop for new staffers on the history of the community. Give him a special project to edit.
- If his drinking is a problem at work, obtain the help of a professional.
- Be patient. You are asking him to change a long-standing pattern of behavior. But insist that he work toward his goals.
- Record performance failures in writing. If there is no progress, warn him that continued poor work can result in termination.
- Maintain a balance in your mind between the needs of the individual and the rest of the staff. After a reasonable time, you may conclude that his poor performance may be forcing others to carry an unfair share of the work load. Then it may be appropriate to terminate him by offering a package of early retirement and other incentives—an arrangement commonly called a "buy out."

Many of the motivation approaches seek to increase productivity. But, in the newsroom, productivity is a vague concept. It is impossible to define or measure productivity for most newspaper jobs. Is increased productivity more stories? Or longer stories? Or fewer errors? We can count the number of stories or the number of bylines, but that is not a true measure of a reporter's productivity.

If productivity is difficult to define, achievement is more so. For each staffer, but especially for editors, there may be a different answer to the question, What is particularly satisfying about my job? The answer will contain unequal parts of other questions: Am I making a contribution? Am I performing up to my standards? Am I serving my values? Is the job fulfilling?

For the newsroom-motivation equation, there is yet another ingredient. The research of Daniel Yankelovich, a highly respected analyst of social trends and public attitudes, suggests that a key element of the cultural revolution of the 1960s and 1970s was a shift in the definition of a fulfilling life. Yankelovich says the new dimensions of the American life-style created a mismatch between the goals of Americans seeking self-fulfillment and the means they use to achieve those goals. The boundaries of self-fulfillment moved beyond earning a good wage. People were drawn to adventures outside work that enlarged their lives: leisure, participation, pleasure, vitality, stimulation, autonomy, creativity. The joy of living took on a new aspect, and as it did, workers—including journalists—decided that the meaning of life was not limited to an exhausting commitment to one's job or to one's duty.

So, we have before us a bewildering array of ideas and theories about motivation. How can they be useful to an editor who is stumped by the behavior pattern of a reporter? Reexamining the major motivation theories and drawing from each the essentials to help editors pondering the riddle of motivation would produce the following checklist:

- Basic needs have to be satisfied before motivation can be effective. This includes pay, management practices, working conditions, and intergroup relationships. (Maslow and Herzberg)
- Satisfaction on the job is most likely to come from feelings of self-worth and the work itself. (Maslow and Herzberg)

- People like to work, are able to direct their own efforts, and, under proper guidance, can be creative. (McGregor's "Theory Y")
- The need for achievement is paramount among journalists. They seek challenge and they strive to excel. The need for friendships and the desire to control their own work also are important. (McClelland)
- High achievers require motivation strategies that are different from those for workers with high affiliation or high power needs. (McClelland)
- Individual differences are important. The editor should attempt to relate the newspaper's goals to the individual's goals. (Vroom's "Expectancy Theory")
- A staffer's choice of behaviors is influenced by the expectation of a desirable outcome. Individual values, the probability that harder work will produce the expected reward, and the amount of effort required for success are variables that influence behavior. (Vroom)
- Staffers compare their situations with those of others. They want to be treated fairly. If they believe there is equity, they are more easily motivated. (Adams's "Equity Theory")
- Values, such as the work ethic, can influence individual goals, which in turn influence behavior. (Locke's "Goal Setting")
- Staffers should participate in setting goals. Goals should be specific and challenging. The editor should provide feedback and reinforcement. Journalists respond well to peer competition. (Locke)
- Staffers can learn to change their behavior. Only behavior that can be observed and measured can be modified. Positive reinforcement is critical to learning new behaviors. (Skinner)
- Money has many different meanings for journalists. Money can be effective as a motivator if trust exists between management and staff, if individual performance is evaluated

fairly, and if outstanding work is rewarded differently from average or poor work. (Lawler)

CHAPTER SUMMARY

Motivation deals with an individual's needs, with personal differences, and with the ways in which workers respond to different rewards. The many theories about morale and motivation can guide newspaper editors in deciding on the most effective strategy to encourage better performance by individual journalists.

Maslow's hierarchy of needs is an early theory that relates motivation to unsatisfied needs. His hierarchy prescribes the order in which physiological, security, social, ego, and self-fulfillment needs motivate behavior.

McGregor's Theory X assumes workers to be lazy, disliking work, and requiring close supervision and control to force productivity. His Theory Y assumes that people like to work, are able to direct their own efforts, and, under proper guidance, can be creative.

Herzberg's two-factor theory distinguishes between needs that cannot motivate but can cause dissatisfaction if left unmet, called hygiene factors, and elements that can bring job satisfaction, called motivation factors.

McClelland's research on achievement motivation poses three needs as major motivators: (1) achievement, (2) affiliation, and (3) power. These needs are not dependent on each other. McClelland's studies suggest that high achievers need to be managed differently than employees with high affiliation needs.

Contemporary motivation theories—the expectancy theory, the equity theory, and the goal-setting theory—attempt to show that human behavior is planned and that workers often make conscious decisions about their behavior.

B. F. Skinner's ideas about behavior modification challenge the assumptions of the contemporary theories. Skinner argues that people are passive and do not initiate changes in behavior. He says they can be taught to change their behavior, provided that the required behavior can be observed and measured and that they receive positive reinforcement.

Money has a variety of values to individuals, including value as a motivator under circumstances that include trust, feedback, and special rewards for outstanding performance.

To be effective motivators, editors should consider the individual needs, goals, and talents of their staff members in designing a motivation plan that will benefit both employee and company.

NOTES

1. Jerry L. Gray, *Supervision* (Boston: Kent, 1984), 126–27.
2. Frederick Herzberg, Bernard Mausner, and Barbara Snyderman, *The Motivation to Work* (New York: John Wiley & Sons, 1959), 132–34.
3. Gray, *Supervision*, 127–28.
4. Abraham H. Maslow, *Motivation and Personality* (New York: Harper & Row, 1954), 35–57.
5. George Leonard, "Abraham Maslow and the New Self," *Esquire*, December 1983, 332.
6. Lyman W. Porter, "A Study of Perceived Need Satisfaction in Bottom and Middle Management Jobs," *Journal of Applied Psychology* 45 (1961): 1–10.
7. Douglas McGregor, *The Human Side of Enterprise* (New York: McGraw-Hill, 1960), 33–57.
8. Paul Hersey and Kenneth Blanchard, *Management of Organizational Behavior*, 4th ed. (Englewood Cliffs, N.J.: Prentice-Hall, 1982), 48.
9. Frederick Herzberg, "One More Time: How Do You Motivate Employees?" *Harvard Business Review* 46 (January–February 1968): 53–62.
10. Hersey and Blanchard, *Management of Organizational Behavior*, 57–58.
11. David C. McClelland, *The Achieving Society* (Princeton: Van Nostrand, 1961).
12. Hersey and Blanchard, *Management of Organizational Behavior*, 38.
13. David C. McClelland and David Burnham, "Power Is the Great Motivator," *Harvard Business Review*, March–April 1976, 100–110.
14. Gray, *Supervision*, 156.
15. Richard M. Steers, *Introduction to Organizational Behavior*, 2d ed. (Glenview, Ill.: Scott, Foresman, 1984), 150–51.
16. Victor H. Vroom, *Work and Motivation* (New York: John Wiley & Sons, 1964), 14–28.
17. J. Stacy Adams, "Toward an Understanding of Equity," *Journal of Abnormal and Social Psychology*, November 1963, 422–36.
18. Steers, *Introduction to Organizational Behavior*, 165.
19. Adams, "Toward an Understanding of Equity," 422–36.

20. Steers, *Introduction to Organizational Behavior*, 167–68.
21. Edwin A. Locke, "Toward a Theory of Task Performance and Incentives," *Organizational Behavior and Human Performance* 3 (1968): 157–89.
22. Steers, *Introduction to Organizational Behavior*, 170–71.
23. Edwin A. Locke, "The Supervisor as 'Motivator': His Influence on Employee Performance and Satisfaction," in *Motivation and Work Behavior*, 2d ed. (New York: McGraw-Hill, 1979), 376.
24. Richard M. Steers and Lyman W. Porter, "The Role of Task-Goal Attributes in Employee Performance," *Psychological Bulletin* 81 (1974): 434–51.
25. B. F. Skinner, *Beyond Freedom and Dignity* (New York: Alfred A. Knopf, 1971), 87–100.
26. Steers, *Introduction to Organizational Behavior*, 201–2.
27. William F. Whyte, ed., *Money and Motivation* (New York: Harper & Row, 1955), 210–17.
28. Robert L. Opsahl and Marvin D. Dunnette, "The Role of Financial Compensation in Industrial Motivation," *Psychological Bulletin* 66 (1966): 94–96.
29. Edward E. Lawler, *Pay and Organizational Effectiveness* (New York: McGraw-Hill, 1971), 132, 159–60.
30. Peter F. Drucker, *Management* (New York: Harper & Row, 1974), 176–77.
31. Daniel Yankelovich, *New Rules: Searching for Self-fulfillment in a World Turned Upside Down* (New York: Random House, 1981), 4–15.

4

Communication in the Newsroom

Communication is the vital link that influences both individual motivation and group behavior in the newsroom. Timely, precise, accurate, complete information affects the quality of decisions that editors must make and the quality of work the staff produces. However, in every newsroom, in every one-on-one relationship, there are natural barriers to communication. The editor's understanding of effective skills and strategies for overcoming communication barriers is an essential part of his or her management responsibility.

HOW WE COMMUNICATE

An editor, frustrated over an instruction that was misunderstood, snaps, "We may be in the communications business, but we sure don't know how to communicate!" The editor's lament acknowledges that while communication may be at the heart of newsroom performance, it also may be the most common source of problems in the newsroom. The techniques for developing good communication skills are widely known, but rarely practiced. We tend to take communication for granted. We assume we are communicating with people without checking to see if this is so. We also assume that others have the same information we do, so we become careless about keeping them up-to-date.

Communication is sharing information with others in terms of their own experiences. An editor discussing a story assignment with a reporter uses reporters' lingo: "Go see the city budget director and get three grafs of insert material to support the mayor's contention that taxes are going up." When talking to the production director about a press run, the editor communicates in terms of straight and collect runs, balloon formers, and other jargon of the pressroom. In addressing the issue of credibility, editors write columns explaining the workings of the newspaper, but often find that their efforts founder because readers are not able to relate to newspaper work in terms of their own experiences.

Perception—the awareness and understanding of our surroundings—is one of the keys to communication; that is, we can perceive only what we are capable of perceiving. In today's world, with the explosion of new forms of communication and devices to transmit information, human perception does not always keep pace. We can see computers and touch them, but if we cannot understand how they enhance the flow of information, then computers, for us, cannot become communication. Modern music is beyond the range of perception for some. We hear it; we see it performed on television. But if we cannot accept it, music does not, for us, become communication.

Communication is more complicated than simply sending messages. Many things can happen between the time a message is sent and the time it is received. In the newsroom, the extent to which employees accurately receive job instructions from supervisors may be influenced by their opinions of their editors. If a staffer perceives the editor as an incompetent manager, chances are that whatever the boss says will not be regarded seriously. On the other hand, if the boss is seen as influential and powerful, everything he or she says may be interpreted as important.[1]

Communication also appeals to motivation—if the editor's explanation of a story assignment fits with the aspirations, values, and purposes of the reporter, the communication can be a strong motivator. For example, a reporter who believes the newspaper has been slow to investigate reports of payoffs in the police department will be highly motivated and attentive in taking an assignment from the city editor to do the story. If the proposed assignment goes against the reporter's sentiments, there will be little communication and the reporter may misunderstand or miss completely the nuances of the assignment.

Individual editors have different styles of communicating with their subordinate editors and the staff. Some are compulsive memo writers. Others are talkers who convey information more effectively in conversation. Still others rely on meetings to get the message out. Each of these methods of communication is appropriate. If the message is complicated or if it represents a change in policy, a memo to the staff may be necessary. If speed is a factor, a conversation may be effective. If feedback is important, such as in the planning of a special reporting project or examining the daily news budgets, a meeting may be appropriate.

The interpersonal-communication process is also influenced by the organizational structure. The decentralized nature of the newsroom invites a high degree of participation between editors and staffers. This means that messages relating to reporting and editing assignments do not have to travel through many layers of the hierarchy. The city editor or assistant city editor, for example, talks directly to a reporter about a story. The result is that opportunities for message distortion are reduced if effective communication skills are used. However, if a message from the publisher is transmitted orally through several levels of editors, distortion—and thus, misunderstanding—is probable.

As journalists, we communicate not only with coworkers about the process of producing the newspaper, but we also communicate in the paper through the written word. Writing a news story begins with self-communication. If a reporter is working with information that exceeds his or her capacity for perception, the story will reflect this. The ritual of preparing to write a lead is really a struggle to communicate with ourselves before we can communicate with our readers.

Peter F. Drucker notes that "communication is expectation. We perceive, as a rule, what we expect to perceive. We see largely what we expect to see, and we hear largely what we expect to hear. What is truly important is that the unexpected is usually not received at all. It is not seen or heard, but ignored or misunderstood. The human mind attempts to fit impressions and stimuli into a frame of expectations. It resists vigorously any attempts to make it 'change its mind,' that is, to perceive what it does not expect to perceive or not to perceive what it expects to perceive. Before we can communicate, we must anticipate what the recipient expects to see and hear. Only then can we know whether communication can utilize his or her expectations."[2]

For years, the wire services have provided newspapers with one-paragraph tidbits known as fillers. They contain seemingly irrelevant details, such as the number of pigs in Iowa, and are used to fill out news columns. Editors are amazed to learn of the high readership and high retention rate of these items. Many readers can recall them more easily than almost anything else in the paper. Drucker explains that the fillers make no demands. Because of their irrelevancy, they are perceived as requiring nothing of readers; consequently, they are remembered.[3] News stories, on the other hand, are about life in our world today. Messages carried in many of those news stories make readers angry, sad, or fearful. The stories provide information readers may not like, and the details are not as easily remembered.

The validity and reliability of information increases when human emotions, including values, expectations, and perceptions, can be set aside, paving the way for effective communication.

Communication as it works in the newsroom has two dimensions: communication between individuals, and organizational communication that flows up or down through the various levels of authority. Let's take a close look at each dimension.

Fig. 4.1

CLOSE-UP

When written with taste and care, the memorandum can be an excellent communication tool. For the editor, the memo should not be an outlet for anger or a way to cut up staffers without having to look at them. The memo should teach, offer praise, seek information, provide extended commentary on news situations or staff performance, and send "zingers" when they are warranted.

The most gifted memo writer in my memory was the late John Dougherty, who served as managing editor of the *Times-Union* and later the *Democrat and Chronicle* in Rochester. Dougherty disliked meetings and used memos as a way of getting the floor. They became his "bloody pulpit" from which he pursued the professional qualities he wanted in his newspapers.

Following is a Dougherty sampler:

"In all the hours we spend defending, apologizing for, and explaining our newspapers to everyone from ethnic groups to bowling league proprietors, one lesson comes through for all of us: A lousy, overstated headline cannot really be defended."

"If I may offer a sad comment, perhaps one reason our BRIEFS are so well read is that our longer stories are so poorly written. At least sometimes. And there is nothing here that a pencil couldn't correct. Sharpen them!"

"Being easy ain't the way. Being so soft that goldbricks impose on you and that you never criticize mistakes will help neither the product nor the morale. In fact, it can backfire, for good people will resent the fact that others get away with murder while they, operating on their own initiative or 'protestant ethic' or whatever, are putting out every day."

"Affidavit, dammit!"

"That nice, shiny book next to the pillar in the newsroom is a dictionary. It doesn't seem to be showing the wear it should. Today I saw the word 'siaciatric' in copy. It's 'psychiatric'."

"There are two M's in accommodate. There are two M's in accommodate. There are two M's in accommodate. There are two M's etc., etc., etc., etc."

"I want the editor who wrote this headline and the editor who passed it to twist slowly in the wind while long bamboo splinters are inserted under their fingernails."

"Shun not the obits. Every morning I read them first, and if the average age of the obits is less than mine, I get up and go to work. The wire services sometimes just run a paragraph; you can get more from them, from our library, from the clips. Use a picture, but use one showing the person at his famous activity—Oswald Jacoby playing bridge, Roger Bannister running, John Glenn going into space. An exception to this rule: Xaviera Hollander, the Happy Hooker."

INTERPERSONAL COMMUNICATION

Communication in the newsroom takes place in a variety of ways: meetings, memos, conversations in the hallway, one-on-

one discussions at the city desk, telephone calls, bulletin-board postings, talking shop over lunch or after work—all are part of the communications mix in the newsroom. Research shows that managers spend about 80 percent of their time in oral communication with others, more often listening than talking. Managers prefer oral communication because it is an "action" medium and because it provides current information and immediate feedback.[4]

Interpersonal communication, in whatever manner, serves four basic purposes:[5] (1) to influence others; (2) to express feelings and emotions; (3) to provide, receive, or exchange information; and (4) to reinforce the formal structure of the organization, such as using formal channels of communication.

Within this framework, the editor's role as a communicator takes several forms:[6]

Translator. In a highly social environment such as the newsroom, the status or rank of the communicators can affect the flow of information, even dictating who speaks to whom and how one responds. For example, a reporter may choose different words and assume a more formal attitude when talking to the city editor than when talking to another reporter. Although communication in the newsroom is quick and casual as a rule, barriers imposed by rank can interfere with the accuracy and the understanding of the message.

As a translator, the editor must cut through any status barriers to make sure that he or she has a clear understanding of the information. The city editor may be asked to convey a complaint from a reporter to the managing editor. Before carrying the problem to the managing editor's office, the city editor must understand the details, the technical points that may be involved, and the nuances that such messages often carry.

The editor also translates messages from the publisher or other top executives. If the message is a sharp rebuke, the editor may filter the anger and recast the information so that it focuses on the problem. The offending staffer should know that the complaint originated in the publisher's office, but should be spared the news that it was accompanied by an unduly loud and harsh tirade against the individual.

Informer. The staff depends heavily on the editor for information. Staffers resent being kept in the dark because it is a signal that the editor does not consider the staff important or lacks confidence in the staff's ability to deal with the information effectively. For the editor, deciding what to share and what to withhold becomes a delicate balancing act. Negative or discouraging information is more likely to be held back in the interest of staff morale. If the editor doesn't share what staffers want to know, they will turn to an unofficial network for information. Information obtained from the grapevine is less reliable, but it becomes accepted unless the editor sets the record straight. Sometimes the editor reacts too late to correct a patchwork version of events created by the staff, and the incomplete account is regarded as the truth.

Buffer. Information from top management often is of little interest or little use to the staff. As a buffer, the editor is able to stop the flow of information that would waste the staff's time. The editor also filters information from the newsroom, telling the publisher only what he or she needs to know. In this way, the editor is a gatekeeper, sorting out information that is potentially useful.

Secretaries, too, serve as important gatekeepers. They are buffers for their bosses in screening mail, telephone calls, and access by the staff.

Liaison. In this role, the editor serves as a go-between, linking various desks in the newsroom or other departments in the organization with the newsroom. As the news-department representative to the publisher's circle of department heads, the editor helps build bridges between the news side and the other operations at the paper. On many occasions, it is necessary for the editor to be a spokesperson for the newsroom, interpreting for readers or for other officers of the newspaper company the goals and values of the staff. In this role, the editor uses his or her special knowledge of the news operation to bargain for more resources or to win the cooperation of others.

Opinion leader. The editor has sources inside and outside the newspaper that others on the staff do not have. Leading newsmakers in the community may entrust the editor with information that is crucial to the development of major stories. These channels of information give the editor the status of an opinion leader within the newsroom. In addition, the editor's own respected position is such that his or her opinions have high value and often are effective in influencing the staff's attitudes or behaviors.

Listener. Editors who seem to be overwhelmed with paperwork and the pressure of producing a newspaper every day often diminish or ignore their role as a sounding board for ideas, suggestions, or problems. The editor who is a poor listener sets up a real barrier to effective communication. The staff reads a lot into these signs: the editor is too busy, the editor is not interested, the editor has a low tolerance for different ideas or opinions, the editor doesn't want to hear bad news, the editor doesn't care about me.

Barriers to Good Communication

Barriers to communication can be explained by physical, personal, and semantic reasons. Physical barriers, typically, are noise or distance. Personal barriers are of a psychological origin—our backgrounds, prejudices, and experiences can hinder listening efforts. Semantic barriers result when we give different meanings to the same words.

Communication problems often are only symptoms of other difficulties among people and groups in an organization. Following are some barriers to communication that can be especially troublesome to editors:

Interpretation. We read things into messages. We evaluate what others say to us—"What did he mean by that?" In his research on interviewing techniques of psychological counselors, psychologist Carl R. Rogers found that the tendency to evaluate what someone has said is the greatest barrier to effective communication because evaluation leads to defensiveness. Perception is not based on logic but experience.[7]

Edward T. Hall, in his pioneering work, *The Silent Language*, says the gestures, the tone of voice, the environment altogether, not to mention cultural and social refinements, cannot be dissociated from the spoken language. Without them, in fact, the spoken word has no meaning and cannot communicate. The silent language of behavior significantly affects how we see others, how they see us, and how we interact.[8]

Defensiveness. Defensiveness is a natural reaction to negative messages, yet we don't often think how defensiveness affects communication. Two editors attempting to defend their own actions will not communicate very well because neither will be listening to the other. Or, an editor might express frustration with a reporter by saying, "Your story was a mess. We missed an edition trying to fix it." The reporter is likely to respond, "The desk always complains about my copy, and when they rewrite it they screw it up." What chance is there for communication here? A better approach by the editor might have been, "Your story needed a lot of work on the desk this morning. Let's go over it and see what the problem was."

Fig. 4.2

CLOSE-UP

Following are some examples of distortion in the newsroom communications process.

What the editor said:	What the editor meant:	What the subordinate heard:
I'll look into hiring another person for the city desk as soon as I complete the budget.	We'll start interviewing for the job in about three weeks.	I'm tied up with more important things. Don't bother me with this problem now.

Fig. 4.2, continued

What the editor said:	What the editor meant:	What the subordinate heard:
Your performance was below par last year. I really expected more of you.	You're going to have to do better work, but I know you can do it.	If you screw up one more time, you're out.
Why did we allow the mayor to be an unidentified source in this story?	We should be careful about letting local officials use our news columns to make anonymous statements.	Don't use unidentified sources in local stories.
Can we do a backgrounder on the city's new downtown proposal?	We should take a good look at the downtown plan for the Sunday paper.	We better pull the city hall reporter off the council story and keep her overtime to get out a piece tonight on the downtown plan.
We had some late pages again today.	Let's find out what the problem is and get it fixed.	I don't care how many heads you bust, I don't want any more late pages.

Source: Adapted from Richard M. Hodgetts and Steven Altman, *Organizational Behavior* (Philadelphia: W. B. Saunders, 1979).

Distortion. Messages get altered as they are passed along communication channels. Distortion occurs when imprecise language is used, when information is misinterpreted, when social or status barriers exist, when information is condensed, or when the sender and receiver use different frames of reference. The editor may ask to see an advance copy of any stories mentioning the publisher, the intention being to tell the publisher so that he or she won't be surprised by the story. The city editor relays the editor's request this way: "The editor wants to check anything that's coming up on the publisher." And the staff hears it this way: "The editor wants to censor any stories about the publisher." You can see how misinterpretation caused this message to be distorted.

Omission. As a message is transmitted, one or more parts may be left out. Around the news desks, instructions are given briskly under the press of deadline and omissions are not uncommon. The news editor asks the copy desk to insert three new paragraphs in a story based on a wire update, but neglects to add that three graphs from the original story have to come out.

Distance. Physical barriers are necessary in most newsrooms, but they can prevent good communication. The managing editor who sits in the middle of the newsroom is easier to talk to than the one who stays in his or her office. Yet there are important reasons why a managing editor has an office and must use it. That means the managing editor must make a special effort to be in the newsroom and to be easily accessible in order to offset the barrier that his or her office presents.

Too much information. Editors can get overloaded with information if their subordinates fail to screen the amount of material presented to them. In planning the newspaper every day, the editor cannot read every available story. That is why wire-service budgets are an effective shortcut, telling editors much of what they need to know to plan the paper. The wire editor is a critical information control point, filtering out the less important stories and giving the editor a quick summary of the top stories to consider for page one.

Stereotyping. The tendency to categorize people—good-bad, union-nonunion, loyal-disruptive, self-starter–lazy—affects how we evaluate their messages. Editors who stereotype individuals will evaluate what they say based on these artificial classifications rather than the substance of the message.

Fear and insecurity. Editors and staffers talk frequently, but too often there is an underlying anxiety of what might happen to them if either is too candid. They do not always express their true feelings and this lack of openness, as it becomes part of the relationship, is a barrier to good communication.

Emotion. Good communication rarely occurs in the heat of an argument. A vigorous disagreement may be a healthy and honest outlet of feelings, but after a cooling-off period, an attempt should be made to resolve the issue rationally. It is the editor's responsibility to initiate a discussion that focuses on the facts and avoids finger pointing or personal remarks.

Improving Listening Skills

Listening is a powerful management tool; unfortunately, few people truly understand the importance of listening. As communicators, editors may be so intent on the effectiveness of their speech and the persuasiveness of their delivery that they fail to listen effectively. Bad listening habits such as those listed below are common to all of us and can minimize our listening ability.[9]

- Hop-skip-and-jump listening. The average person speaks at a rate of about 125 words per minute. We can listen at four times that rate. Rather than slow down listening speed, the poor listener's mind will wander, then rush back to the speaker. Soon, the listener has lost the drift of the conversation.

- Listening only for facts. The listener who concentrates on remembering just the facts may miss the real meaning of the message, which may be in voice inflections, facial expressions, and imagery used by the speaker.

- Faking attention. Many people are masters at acting as if they are paying attention when, in fact, they may be daydreaming and have no idea what is being said.

- Dismissing the subject as uninteresting. The person who decides that the speaker has nothing interesting to say is "tuning out" and thinking about more fascinating subjects.

- Reacting to the speaker. If the speaker is sloppily dressed and talks with a lisp, we may give a more critical reading to his or her message than we would if the speaker were natty and charming.

- Getting excited. A strong positive or negative reaction can change what we hear, taking a thought far beyond what was intended by the speaker.

- Tolerating distractions. Doodling, tapping fingers, and allowing others to interrupt the conversation are ways of showing disinterest in what is being said.

- Avoiding hard messages. When the subject is an uncomfortable one or difficult to face, the instinct is to tune out, to stop listening.

Fig. 4.3

CLOSE-UP

Thomas Gordon, author of several books on listening, says that most people respond to communication in one of the following ways:

Ordering, directing: "You have to . . ."
Warning, threatening: "You'd better not . . ."
Preaching, moralizing: "You ought to . . ."
Advising, giving solutions: "Why don't you . . ."
Lecturing, informing: "Here are the facts . . ."
Evaluating, blaming: "You're wrong . . ."
Praising, agreeing: "You're right . . ."
Name calling, shaming: "You're stupid . . ."
Interpreting, analyzing: "What you need . . ."
Sympathizing, supporting: "You'll be OK . . ."
Questioning, probing: "Why did you . . ."
Withdrawing, avoiding: "Let's forget it . . ."

Fig. 4.3, continued

Gordon suggests that any of these messages in response to communication can indicate nonacceptance, which in turn raises the risk that the person who initiated the message will feel defensive.

A more effective way of responding is what Gordon calls "active listening." This is a listening skill designed to help people solve their own problems, and it requires the listener to understand the content and feeling of what is being said.

For example, a reporter says to the city editor, "The deadline for this story is not realistic." The editor replies, "You feel you are being pressured to get the story done." With this reply, the editor is thinking about the problem from the reporter's perspective, checking the accuracy of what he or she perceived the reporter to have said.

Through active listening, Gordon contends, the editor can learn what the reporter means and how the reporter feels about the situation. By reflecting back to the reporter the sense of the statement, the editor is confirming that the two agree on the meaning of the message. As a result, the editor may be able to help the reporter see why the deadline is realistic and what can be done to meet it.

Source: Thomas Gordon, *Parent Effectiveness Training* (New York: Peter H. Wyden, 1970), 41–44.

The editor who is a good listener gathers valuable information, learns about coworkers, and strengthens his or her ability to motivate staffers or influence colleagues. Editors who develop good listening skills can also be effective counselors and mentors. Their willingness to listen sensitively to expressions of fear and anxiety can help a staffer as a person while building a strong bond with him or her as an employee. Listening is especially important to the success of a performance review in which the editor has an opportunity to counsel and motivate.

Following are some guidelines for better listening:[10]

- Look at the other person. This doesn't mean staring or looking only at their eyes. Looking toward the person who is talking is enough. This shows your concern or interest. It is widely known that failure to look at a person who is talking leads to suspicion and distrust.

- Listen to the entire message. The editor should be patient and give the speaker a full hearing. Don't interrupt. Don't jump to conclusions. If the staffer starts to wander, the editor can bring the conversation back on track with a question.

- Ask questions. That's the art of being a reporter, and it is as effective at drawing information from a coworker as from a news source. The editor's goal should be to master the details of the subject quickly and use questions to draw out facts and information the speaker does not volunteer.

- Think about the message. As the editor listens, he or she should review the main points in the message and draw on experience and background for understanding. Analyzing the speaker's point of view requires the editor to consider the unique qualifications and possible hidden agendas behind the message. Effective communication occurs when the editor understands the other person's position and needs.

- Look for nonverbal messages. Attention to nonverbal cues enables the editor to understand feelings as well as words. When verbal and nonverbal messages contradict, it is the nonverbal portion that must be examined to discover the real meaning of the communication. Credibility, trust, and status are communicated through nonverbal channels. Eye contact, facial expression, posture, and tone of voice are nonverbal cues that signal important information to a responsive listener.

- Hold back emotions. A good listener will hear out a speaker without interrupting or betraying anger, disappointment, suspicion, or other emotions. Little is to be gained through arguing or losing one's temper. The listener who reacts emotionally fails to hear what the other person is saying. All of the facts, figures, and logic the staffer presents will be lost on the editor who brings *emotional bias* to bear on the communication. Emotion also can come into play when the staffer thinks the editor is offering a personal criticism. A message that focuses on work or on performance and avoids personalities is less likely to encounter emotional resistance.

- Switch places. A staffer's perceptions are determined by needs, attitudes, emotions, and experience, which influence how the staffer will react to a message. If, for instance, a staffer has had an accuracy problem in the past and thinks the editor was not helpful in solving the problem, the staffer is likely to interpret fresh interest by the editor in accordance with previous experience.

Too often we tend to talk to people as if they are all the same instead of recognizing their individual differences. If we understand the personalities of the people we work with—if we can distinguish the high achiever from the people person, the analytical person from the idea person— and if we try to talk to these individuals on their own terms, we create a nonstressful situation in which communication can take place. In this way, staffers will react to information according to the roles in which they see themselves. A senior reporter will respond better to a message that acknowledges his or her special role on the staff. A beginning reporter who works hard and shows improvement wants to be dealt with on that basis rather than simply as a raw recruit.

- Be responsive. This is an essential principle for good listening and understanding. Responsive demeanor, posture, and facial expression will show that the editor is interested. Showing signs of hearing and understanding, such as an occasional nod of the head or standing or sitting attentively, can be effective. Giving oral responses to show understanding, such as an occasional "Um-mm" or "Uh-huh," also helps.

Fig. 4.4

CLOSE-UP

Participants at a workshop in effective listening were asked to think of the worst listeners they know and list their characteristics. Following are the traits they cited:

- Always interrupts.
- Jumps to conclusions.
- Finishes my sentences.

- Is inattentive, has wandering eyes and poor posture.
- Changes the subject.
- Writes everything down.
- Doesn't give any response.
- Is impatient.
- Loses temper.
- Fidgets with pen or pencil or paper clip.

The workshop members then were asked to think of the best listeners they know and identify their key traits:

- Looks at me while I'm speaking.
- Questions me to clarify what I'm saying.
- Shows concern by asking questions about my feelings.
- Repeats some of the things I say.
- Doesn't rush me.
- Is poised and emotionally controlled.
- Reacts responsively with a nod of the head, a smile, or a frown.
- Pays close attention.
- Doesn't interrupt me.
- Keeps on the subject until I've finished my thoughts.

Source: Robert L. Montgomery, "Listening Made Easy," *Nation's Business,* October 1981, 65–68.

ORGANIZATIONAL COMMUNICATION

Research has identified four communication networks that are effective in organizations: (1) the chain, (2) the wheel, (3) the circle, and (4) the star.[11] The diagrams in figure 4.5 depicting these networks enable us to give structure to the relationships that exist in the newsroom.

Communication Networks

Fig. 4.5.

This diagram shows the characteristics of four different communication networks.

Chain. The chain represents a communication pattern in which information flows up or down a formally defined chain of command. A message that travels from the publisher to the editor to the managing editor to the city editor to the staff would follow this pattern. Information that comes through the chain reflects a high centralization of power and authority. Accuracy of such communication is high if written, but low if spoken. Decisions can be made rapidly at the topmost levels, but the level of group satisfaction and group commitment to chain communication is low.

Wheel. Communication that follows this pattern is found on the various news desks where several reporters or copy editors report to one editor. There is a moderately high centralization of authority. Communication for simple tasks is fast; for complex tasks, it is slow. The wheel permits moderately fast decisions, but generally does not result in high levels of group satisfaction or commitment.

Circle. Task forces or committees communicate in a circular pattern. They are somewhat autonomous and therefore do not have centers of power or authority. When the members are talking together, the accuracy of the communication is high. When the members are isolated, the accuracy is low. Committees are slow to make decisions, but they produce high levels of group satisfaction and commitment.

Star. This communication network exists outside the formal organizational structure of the newspaper. It is essentially a grapevine in which information flows informally from a variety of channels. The *grapevine* has little authority, but is able to move messages rapidly with moderate accuracy and results in high group satisfaction.

Fig. 4.6

CLOSE-UP

Research indicates that effective communication techniques differ, depending on whether the information is moving up or down the chain of command. Following is a ranking of communication techniques, from high (1) to low (10):

Fig. 4.6, continued

Rank	Upward from Employee to Boss	Rank	Downward from Boss to Employee
1	Informal discussions	1	Small group meetings
2	Meetings with supervisors	2	Memos
3	Attitude surveys	3	Supervisory meetings
4	Grievance procedures	4	Mass meetings
5	Counseling	5	Letters sent home
6	Exit interviews	6	Bulletin boards
7	Union representatives	7	Pay envelope inserts
8	Formal meetings	8	Public address system
9	Suggestion boxes	9	Posters
10	Employee newsletter	10	Annual reports, media ads

Source: Adapted from Andrew D. Szilagyi, Jr., *Management and Performance* (Glenview, Ill.: Scott, Foresman, 1981), 384.

Internal Communication Systems

The basic systems of internal communication used by chain or company newspapers no longer give employees all the information they want and need. Specifically, the systems fall short for two reasons: (1) most newspaper jobs now require greater knowledge and coordination than in the past; and (2) as never before, employees not only insist on being kept informed, but also they want to provide feedback to management on the information they receive.

Fig. 4.7

CLOSE-UP

Dr. Craig Pinder, associate professor of organizational behavior at the University of British Columbia, worked with a group of executives from the *Vancouver* (British Columbia) *Sun* on employer-employee relations. In developing recommendations for the newspaper's staff, Pinder listed several barriers to communications at the newspaper:

- The role of information as currency. Information often does not flow in an organization because it has value as currency—particularly currency related to power. Superiors can hold power by not transmitting needed information to subordinates. Subordinates can undermine the power base of a superior by not passing on vital information.

- The increasing need for more and more information. The need to communicate increases as work becomes more complex and interdependency among work units grows. Ironically, information overdose can also occur. Then the recipient starts filtering information out of his or her consciousness.

- Generalized messages that attempt to reach everybody but reach nobody. Sometimes the message is too hard for some, too easy for others. In a differentiated organization like a newspaper, the need is for different messages for different audiences.

- Status differences between sender and receiver. The receiver of information doesn't seek clarification for fear of looking like a dummy. Or, clarification is not pursued for fear of revealing the boss to be a dummy.

- The variety of media used for communications. For some messages, the most appropriate medium is a memo or a letter; for others, the telephone; for still others, face to face; and for yet others, a combination of two or more media. Sensitivity to the appropriate medium is important.

- The pressure of time and stress as it relates to information. As you put more and more stress on an individual, the less he or she pays attention to peripheral clues related to other information—the less sensitivity, for example, to interpersonal relations.

- The sender's understanding of the message. Poor delivery and reception of information frequently result from the imperfect grasp the sender has of the message he or she is trying to communicate.

- The sender's view of the receiver. One individual's perception of another—too stupid, too poorly educated, too excessively educated—influences the way information is sent. This includes the "halo effect": "I like one thing about you; I therefore assume that all things about you are likable/positive/capable." Stereotyping and the halo effect may lead to incorrect assumptions and encourage barriers to communication.

- Nonverbal cues. Body English—the rolling of eyes, squirming, impatient finger tappings—may all contradict the oral message.

Fig. 4.7, continued

- Poor listening skills. The receiver with poor listening skills listens only to messages consistent with his or her set of beliefs.

- Confounding of related and associated messages. The third memo on a given subject gets thrown out—unread—because it looked the same as the earlier two.

- Views and suspicions held by receivers. "On the basis of past behavior, I think you're a liar/sneak/conniving power-grabber; therefore, nothing you tell me will I again believe."

- Autocratic leadership that doesn't desire subordinates to have full information. These bosses don't want to share responsibilities but want to co-opt subordinates. Subordinates perceive participation schemes as phony. Frustrated, the workers withdraw and refuse communication with bosses.

- Punishment for candor. This can be described as, "I really want to know what you think"—Pow!

- Lack of trust in the receiver's ability to deal with the information. "I won't tell you things because you'll blab them to everyone else." This immediately shuts down all communication.

- Role conflict. When one individual reports to multiple bosses, the outcome is inconsistency in message and stress.

Source: Malcolm F. Mallette, *How Newspapers Communicate Internally: Case Studies and Samplings from a Changing Workplace* (Reston, Va.: American Press Institute, 1981), 8–12.

Floyd Whellan, senior vice-president/human resources for the newspaper division of Harte-Hanks Communications, says employees "want a continuous flow of knowledge on the economic status of the company and business goals, but prefer that this information originate from their immediate superior. The corporatewide magazine is appreciated, but they really want to have closer communications from immediate supervisors whom they know and supposedly trust. We forget some of the good old standbys, which are still effective, like the Christmas party and the summer picnics."[12]

J. Edward Murray, a long-time newspaper editor and former publisher of the *Daily Camera* in Boulder, Colorado, says that good internal communication on newspapers requires two general ingredients: (1) a keen interest at all levels in what is happening in the newspaper profession, especially in useful ideas, innovations, and technology; and (2) an understanding of the art of communication—both speaking and listening—and a determination to practice the art.

Then, says Murray, you build an enthusiastic, friendly, tightly knit management team. The publisher sets the tone through keen interest in new developments, by routing new information to department heads and discussing trade news, and "by raising proper hell when there are communication breakdowns." Perhaps the most important single element of good communication, says Murray, is a firm faith in the highest ideals of newspapering. It tends to be both contagious and inspirational in communication.[13]

Fig. 4.8

CLOSE-UP

John McMillan, publisher of the *Salem* (Oregon) *Statesman-Journal*, thinks that the elaborate internal communications systems devised in large corporations are unnecessary and counter-productive at a small newspaper company. "I have my doubts about the need for employee hotlines and suggestion boxes on smaller newspapers—as long as the publisher has an open-door policy and moves about the business in an informal way with some frequency."

At his 63,000-circulation newspaper, McMillan uses several formal methods of communication: a weekly meeting with the top twenty-five supervisors; posting on all bulletin boards the minutes of intradepartmental meetings and the weekly meetings he holds with his seven division heads; a monthly house organ; letters from the publisher in paycheck envelopes every two weeks; an orientation for new employees that permits them to meet all division heads; a weekly meeting with night supervisors, on their work shifts; and meetings of all staffs with division heads at least once every two weeks.

Source: Malcolm F. Mallette, *How Newspapers Communicate Internally: Case Studies and Samplings from a Changing Marketplace* (Reston, Va.: American Press Institute, 1981), 5–6.

The complexity of internal communication systems increases with the size of the newspaper, simply because there are more people with whom to communicate and more management layers through which to filter the information. The larger the paper, the more opportunities for distortion and misunderstanding.

A few principles for developing good communication are common in any newsroom, irrespective of size. Creating a positive communication environment goes far beyond the communication principles themselves. It involves leadership styles, reward systems, job descriptions, performance-appraisal systems, and group interaction.[14]

Communication Channels from Staff to Management

If the editor is using the communication skills described in this chapter, the remaining link in a sound newsroom environment is to open channels from the staff to the management. This cannot be left to chance. It will not happen on its own. The editor has to seed the process. If employees think their ideas are valued and the editors care about their feelings and attitudes, a more positive *organizational climate* will result.

- Unless editors ask for ideas and demonstrate that the good ones will be used, the instances in which staffers volunteer their opinions and thoughts will be very selective. In a business where creativity is important, editors know the value of brainstorming. Reporters, copy editors, photographers, and artists should be encouraged to participate. In encouraging ideas to flow up from the staff, the editor should be sensitive to how the assistant desk editors respond. It is common for ideas to be more threatening to a new first-level supervisor, such as an assistant city editor, than to a senior editor. Yet reporters have more opportunities to pass along thoughts to the desk than they do to participate in a formal brainstorming session. The presence of a single editor on a desk who resists fresh approaches can damage the best intentions of the managing editor for a free flow of ideas.

- Meetings are a more formal way of stimulating communication up from the ranks. Meetings have a variety of purposes and the quality of feedback can differ. A meeting to announce a new policy is likely to result in much feedback, whereas a meeting to ask the staff to help shape a new policy will encourage a great deal of participation. Editors need to be sensitive to the idea that staffers may behave one way as individuals and another way as members of a group, as our earlier examination of group behavior demonstrated (see Chapter 2). It is more difficult for some to voice their true feelings in a meeting. As a result, the editor won't get accurate feedback. Still, meetings are a useful way to stimulate two-way communication.

- Finally, the editor needs to be prepared to follow up ideas with action. Staffers may think they are being listened to, but they want to see something happen. They want the editor to do more than hear them out; they want their ideas acted on. If staffers perceive that their ideas will go on the shelf, they will quickly lose interest and enthusiasm. An editor who invites ideas from the staff should be prepared to act on the good ones and explain that the others, though not implemented, were given serious consideration.

Meetings

In his years as managing editor of the *Times-Union* in Rochester, John Dougherty developed an effective style for limiting the length of meetings. Dougherty would listen to his editors for no more than five minutes, then turn his back on the group and start typing. Subordinates quickly learned to shape the discussion to fit his five-minute limit. Dougherty understood that meetings were necessary, but they also tended to waste time unless the leader imposed a discipline on the group.

In every newspaper organization, people come together in small groups for a variety of purposes. Some of the meetings, such as the daily news conference, have been long established and serve a practical purpose. Others are for solving problems or planning projects. Still others may seem to serve no purpose at all.

There are at least six functions that meetings can perform better than any other communication device:[15]

1. A meeting defines the team, the group, the unit. Those present belong to it; those absent do not.
2. A meeting is the place where the group revises, updates, and adds to what it knows as a group. Every group creates its own pool of shared knowledge, experience, judgment, and folklore. A great many plans are improved and sometimes transformed by the collective work of a committee.
3. A meeting helps every individual understand both the collective aim of the group and the way in which each member of the group can contribute to the group's success.
4. A meeting creates for its members a commitment to the decisions it makes and the goals it pursues. Once something has been decided, membership in the group entails an obligation to accept the decision, even for those who argued against it.
5. A meeting is very often the only occasion where the team or group actually exists and works as a group. It is the only occasion when the boss is perceived as the leader of the team rather than as the executive to whom individuals report.
6. A meeting is a status arena, a time when members get the chance to find out their relative standing in the group.

Most editors have learned from experience that a meeting of four to seven is the best size, with ten being tolerable and twelve the limit. Experience also suggests that the early part of a meeting is livelier than the end and that little of value is achieved after two hours. Research indicates that the best times for meetings are between 10 A.M. and noon and between 2 P.M. and 4 P.M. In conducting a meeting, the editor has several responsibilities dealing with both the subject and the people:[16]

- Start on time. There is only one way to ensure that a meeting starts on time, and that is to *start on time*. Latecomers who find that the meeting has begun without them soon learn the lesson.

- Control the talkers. Unfortunately, many people take a long time to say very little. If the editor conveys a sense of urgency, members of the group will recognize the need for brevity. If it is necessary to stop someone in full flight, the editor can pick up a phrase a subordinate has just uttered and ask someone else in the group to comment.

- Draw out the silent. The psychology of group behavior (see Chapter 2) suggests that most of those at a meeting will be silent most of the time. If the silence is a consequence of shyness or apprehension about the group's reaction to a suggestion, it is important for the leader to seek participation and then express interest and pleasure—although not always agreement—and encourage further contributions. If the silence suggests the group is hostile to the editor and to the process by which decisions are being reached, the editor can try to breach the group's detachment by probing and drawing out the feelings of the unfriendly individuals.

- Protect the weak. Disagreements in meetings are common, but if an argument gets out of hand, if one side suggests that the other has no right to contribute, preemptive measures are necessary. The editor can restore balance to the discussion by writing down a point made by the minority and referring to it later in the meeting.

- Encourage the clash of ideas. A good meeting is a crossflow of discussion and debate with the leader occasionally guiding, mediating, probing, stimulating, and summarizing while others thrash out ideas. The editor must be careful, though, not to promote a clash of personalities. Confrontation can be controlled through seating positions. Having members sit face to face across a table enhances opposition, conflict, and disagreement. Sitting side by side makes disagreements and confrontation harder.

- Watch for the suggestion-quashing reflex. If members of the group think that making a suggestion will provoke outwardly negative reactions or laughter, they will hesitate to speak up. Because suggestions are easier to ridicule than opinions and because they contain the seeds of future success, the editor must be prepared to discourage the tendency to put down someone who has an idea. The editor can take special note and show interest when someone makes a suggestion and can require the quasher to produce a better suggestion on the spot.

- Come to the senior people last. The editor is apt to get a wider spread of views and ideas by letting the junior members of the group start things off. Once the senior members, especially those with high authority, have their say, the others are likely to be inhibited.

- Close on a note of achievement. Even if the meeting ends with the issue unresolved, the editor can refer to progress or to a point that was settled as he or she closes the meeting.

NETWORKS

Networks are people talking to each other, sharing ideas, information, and resources—a communication system that creates linkages between people. Marilyn Ferguson, who has written extensively about the subject in her book, *The Aquarian Conspiracy*, describes networking as "conferences, phone calls, air travel, books, phantom organizations, papers, pamphleteering, photocopying, lectures, workshops, parties, grapevines, mutual friends, summit meetings, coalitions, tapes, newsletters."[17]

In his book, *Megatrends*, John Naisbitt says networks exist to "foster self-help, to exchange information, to change society, to improve productivity and work lives, and to share resources. They are structured to transmit information in a way that is quicker, more high touch, and more energy-efficient than any other process we know . . . Networks cut across the society to provide a genuine cross-disciplinary approach to people and issues. Whereas bureaucracies look like conventional organization charts, boxers arranged in some hierarchical order with the leader on top, networks are quite different . . . Structurally, the most important thing about a network is that each individual is at the center . . . What occurs in networks is that members treat each other as peers—because what is important is the information, the great equalizer."[18]

The informal communication systems in newsrooms are dominated by men for the simple reason that there are so many more of them. An outgrowth of the white male–dominated newsroom, the "old-boy network" is focused on control and, interestingly, provides few opportunities for men to share their feelings with other men. Generally, men have been socialized to deny the need to share their emotions and feelings. They are less likely than women to be comfortable with expressions of sensitivity or comfort or with acknowledging that they are vulnerable and in need of support.

The power of the male networks is diminishing as more and more women journalism school graduates are being hired for entry-level jobs and as women move ever more easily into middle- and senior-level management roles in the newsroom. Racial minorities are making progress, too, both in hiring and in moving into the ranks of editors, although less rapidly than white women.

As outsiders to the men's informal system, women and minorities need other sources of support, advice, and information. One of the most viable means of achieving this is through a network of other women or other minorities. An understanding of networks is based on knowledge of work groups (see Chapter 2). To a large extent, the dynamics of newsroom peer groups are present in the networks that emerge in response to the specific concerns of women and minorities.

James House, author of *Work Stress and Social Support*, identifies four types of support that networks can provide to individuals and that are important in moderating the effects of stress on the job:[19]

1. Emotional support. The sharing of feelings, trust, esteem, and concern may be the most important source of support in helping individuals handle stressful situations at work. High support from supervisors or coworkers typically is related to high performance, full participation, and increased commitment to the organization. Research shows that men emphasize gregariousness and similarity in their friendships while women emphasize assistance, reciprocity, and intimacy. Men often have difficulty offering emotional support to others and tend to interact with male friends in groups.

Women tend to interact in pairs. Women's networks are natural outgrowths of the female instinct to give support to those around them.

2. Appraisal support. Feedback and affirmation are important to success on the job, and networks can be a source of this kind of support. Women do not receive constructive criticism as often as men because the males who give feedback are not always sure how the women will respond. In addition, women do not ask for information about their performance as often as men do. Women tend to seek approval, not information. Networks can help women and minorities understand how to fit in and what it takes to get ahead.

3. Information support. Information is casually exchanged among coworkers and, under the rules of white-male dominance, women and minorities can be excluded. Men often are not aware, for instance, of how much information is passed on informally around the news desks, in the men's room, at the card table, on the tennis court, or over drinks. Women and minorities often feel shut out of these networks. In their own networks, women and minorities can build the social structure they may have been denied, as well as develop a pipeline for understanding the rules, regulations, and norms of the newsroom.

4. Instrumental support. A strong system of trust that is inherent in a network can help women and racial minorities, as well as men, overcome a natural hesitancy to solicit information, ask for opportunities, seek advice, or ask someone to intervene on their behalf. The network concept can put to rest the idea that asking for help is "using a connection." To the extent that reciprocity is available, the individuals in a network are more likely to feel comfortable asking for help, knowing that they will have opportunities to offer support in return.

As women and minorities recognize the value of all four types of support and as they make conscious attempts at networking, the power of white-male networks to control the life-style of the newsroom will gradually give ground.

Networks enhance the prospect of building relationships with people in the newspaper organization over and beyond those individuals seen in the course of the day's work. Individuals can use their networking skills to get to know those who may be important in making promotion and success in the next job possible.[20] A network of fellow staffers or fellow professionals also allows individuals to learn to give and take, to stay on top of trends in the newspaper field, to become visible to others, to appraise their skills, and to expand potential opportunities.

The old-boy network and the newer informal associations of minorities and women all share a common principle: They are based on trust. Trust is played out in several ways. It includes the sharing of confidences, fears, and anxieties, and helping identify bosses who are particularly supportive of women or minorities and who are good coaches. Trust means being able to depend on others for help, support, and advice. A willingness to risk dependence on others is strengthened when those in the group recognize that they are vulnerable individually and that their success as a network depends on consistency in supporting each other.

Women and minorities particularly find that the most useful networks stretch beyond the circle of fellow workers. Organizations such as the National Association of Black Journalists and Women in Communications offer important formal and informal contacts. In many communities, a women's network brings together women from a variety of professions to share information about problems, achievements, and strategies for advancing careers.

CHAPTER SUMMARY

Good communication is at the heart of newsroom performance. Effective communication contributes to common understanding and the quality of decisions editors make.

Communication is sharing information with others in terms of their own experiences. Perception is a key to communication, for we can perceive only what we are capable of perceiving.

One form of communication in the newsroom is communication between individuals. Interpersonal communication has four basic purposes: (1) to influence others, (2) to express feelings and emotions, (3) to exchange information, and (4) to reinforce the formal structure of the organization.

The editor has a number of roles in the communication process, which include acting as translator, informer, buffer, liaison, opinion leader, and listener.

Barriers to effective communication exist in all organizations. Some of the more common barriers include interpretation, defensiveness, distortion, omission, distance, overload, stereotyping, fear and insecurity, and emotion.

Listening is a powerful management tool. Effective communication is enhanced through listening skills, such as looking at the speaker, listening to the full message, asking questions, thinking about the message, watching for nonverbal cues, holding back emotions, being sensitive to the other person's position, and being responsive.

A second form of communication in the newsroom is organizational communication that flows up or down the newspaper's chain of command. In the newspaper company, communication follows a variety of patterns, the most common of which are the chain, the wheel, the circle, and the star.

An important factor affecting communication in the newsroom is the credibility of the editor. The editor can enhance the climate for good communication in the newsroom by seeking ideas, holding effective meetings, and demonstrating that good ideas are important by acting on the best ones.

Meetings can serve a variety of purposes in the newsroom. The editor should be aware of the needs best served by meetings and learn how to conduct productive meetings.

White males have dominated newsrooms and the informal networks within them, but women and minorities are discovering that they can have their own effective networks to exchange support and to help each other feel less alone. Specifically, networks offer four kinds of support to individuals: (1) emotional, (2) appraisal, (3) information, and (4) instrumental.

NOTES

1. Richard M. Steers, *Introduction to Organizational Behavior*, 2d ed. (Glenview, Ill.: Scott, Foresman, 1984), 257–58.
2. Peter F. Drucker, *Management* (New York: Harper & Row, 1974), 485–86.
3. Ibid., 487.
4. Henry Mintzberg, *The Nature of Managerial Work* (New York: Harper & Row, 1973), 171.
5. William G. Scott and Terence R. Mitchell, *Organization Theory: A Structural and Behavioral Analysis* (Homewood, Ill.: Irwin, 1976), 193.
6. Jerry L. Gray, *Supervision* (Boston: Kent, 1984,) 233–34.
7. Carl R. Rogers, *Counseling and Psychotherapy* (Boston: Houghton Mifflin, 1942), 151–58.
8. Edward T. Hall, *The Silent Language* (New York: Anchor Press, 1973), 34–59.
9. William G. Callarman and William W. McCartney, "Identifying and Overcoming Listening Problems," *Supervisory Management*, March 1985, 40–41.
10. Judi Brownell, "Listening: A Powerful Management Tool," *Supervisory Management*, October 1984, 36–39.
11. Everett M. Rogers and Rekha Agarwala-Rogers, *Communication in Organizations* (New York: The Free Press, 1976), 120–21.
12. Malcolm Mallette, *How Newspapers Communicate Internally: Case Studies and Samplings from a Changing Workplace* (Reston, Va.: American Press Institute, 1981), 6–7.
13. Ibid., 7–8.
14. Gray, *Supervision*, 247–49.
15. Antony Jay, "How to Run a Meeting," *Harvard Business Review*, March–April 1976, 44–45.
16. Ibid., 55–57.
17. Marilyn Ferguson, *The Aquarian Conspiracy* (New York: J. P. Tarcher, 1980), 62–63.
18. John Naisbitt, *Megatrends* (New York: Warner Books, 1984), 215, 219–20.
19. Reba Keefe and Christine Russell, "Working Connections," in *Organization and People: Readings, Cases, and Exercises in Organizational Behavior*, 2d ed., ed. J. B. Ritchie and Paul Thompson (St. Paul: West, 1984), 133–38.
20. Margaret Hennig and Anne Jardim, *The Managerial Woman* (New York: Anchor Books, 1977), 166–67.

5

Newsroom Supervisors

Supervising, managing, and leading are three essential functions of the editor-manager. Editors typically get their initial management experience as supervisors. Learning to understand and use the authority and responsibilities of supervision is the first essential step in acquiring the skills that can lead to higher management roles.

THE MANAGEMENT HIERARCHY

The newsroom has several layers of management. Starting at the top, the chief news executive may hold the title of editor or executive editor. On smaller newspapers, the managing editor may be the top news executive. The editor holding the top rank on the news staff generally reports to the publisher, who is the chief executive officer of the newspaper company.

The significance of the various editor titles can be confusing. The person with the title of editor may be the ranking news executive, or he or she may have authority and responsibility that are limited to the editorial page. On some papers, the editor outranks the executive editor; on other papers, the reverse is true. Or, if the executive editor runs the news department and the editor runs the editorial page and both report to the publisher, then neither outranks the other.

There are papers with an executive editor and a managing editor and no editor. There are papers with an editor and a

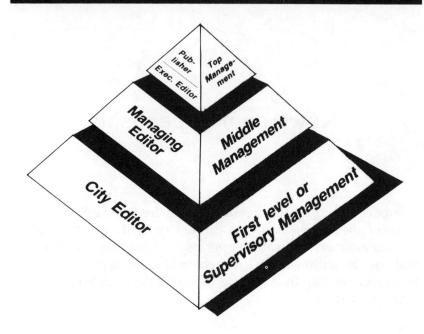

Fig. 5.1.

Managers are divided into three basic categories: top, middle, and first-level or supervisory management. These categories and the newsroom positions traditionally associated with them are shown in this illustration.

---

managing editor and no executive editor. On smaller papers, there may be but one senior news executive, whose title can be editor or executive editor or managing editor. The titles often are determined by the traditions of the newspaper or the wishes of the owner or publisher.

Top management. Whatever the title, the chief news executive is the most influential editor and is part of the top management of the newspaper. This editor is responsible for the overall management of the news department as well as carrying additional responsibilities to help meet the objectives of the newspaper company. In the latter role, the editor assists the publisher and cooperates with other members of the top-management team—advertising director, circulation director, production director, personnel director, and promotion director—in carrying out a plan to make the newspaper strong and successful.

Middle management. At the second level, known as middle management, titles again can be somewhat misleading. In a newsroom headed by an editor or an executive editor, the managing editor is part of middle management. Editors holding the rank of assistant managing editor also are part of middle management. This is true whether the managing editor is the top news executive (and therefore a member of top management) or one of the middle managers. It is important to remember that middle managers oversee the work of other managers.

First-level management. The third layer of management is called first-level or supervisory management. These positions include features editor, sports editor, news editor, business editor, city editor, photo editor, and chief artist or graphics editor. The main tasks of first-level managers involve the supervision and direction of reporters, copy editors, photographers, and artists.

Editors at each level—top, middle, and first-level—have the responsibility and the authority of managers. They carry out the five basic roles of management—planning, organizing, staffing, directing, and controlling—with those in top-management positions having greater responsibility and more authority than those in middle or first-level management.

SUPERVISORY MANAGEMENT

In this chapter, the principles of supervision and the situations used as examples will involve the city desk. The material can be applied easily to other desks or departments in the newsroom.

Every newsroom supervisor has a special kind of management challenge. Sports editors worry about ethics and travel

Newsroom Management Hierarchy

Fig. 5.2.

This diagram shows how the management structure is organized in a typical newsroom, with the chief news executive at the top and the levels of middle managers, supervisors, and staffers who report to the editor.

Fig. 5.3

CLOSE-UP

Tom Peters, coauthor of the best-selling book, *In Search of Excellence*, described his formula for supervisory excellence as "superior performance. That is a function, not of what management does, but what the average person does. The level of management responsible for the attitude and performance of first-line people is obviously first-line supervision."

Peters continues, "Supervisors must learn to be facilitators and cheerleaders, not cops and naysayers. You can order people to come to work, but you can't order them to be excellent in what they do . . .

"The biggest mistake managers make is forgetting that excellence comes from people who care, not from a good reporting system or other system of control . . .

"Being a facilitator means keeping the junk out of people's way, especially the silly bureaucratic rules. The supervisor's job is to bring people and resources together more rapidly than the Mickey Mouse regulations would allow in even the best of companies. The objective is to turn everybody into winners. You do that by showing it is possible to do the job well and that you appreciate it when it is done well."

Source: "Tom Peters' Formula for Supervisory Excellence," *Supervisory Management*, February 1984, 2–6.

---

budgets; their staffers tend to be sports junkies who work odd hours. Features editors typically supervise creative people and must be adept at managing writers with strong egos. Photo editors and graphics editors supervise creative specialists, some of whom were not trained as journalists. In the photo and graphics departments, the editors serve as brokers, interpreting the newsroom for the photographers and artists and explaining the work of photographers and artists to the newsroom.

The definitions of supervision are not always understood, as the editor might discover by posting a note calling a meeting of all supervisors. Many editors in the newsroom would wonder whether they should attend. And, some of the terms associated with supervision are misinterpreted; for example, if the city editor is the supervisor on the city desk, then the reporters are subordinates and the managing editor is a superior. These terms, *subordinate* and *superior,* often are mistaken as personal references or affronts to individual dignity. In behavioral science, however, they simply refer to *roles.*[1] The role of the reporter is subordinate to the role of the city editor; the role of the managing editor is superior to the role of the city editor. That is how *subordinate* and *superior* will be used here: as references to roles and role relationships, not people.

Fig. 5.4

CLOSE-UP

In the literature of newspaper journalism, the city editor is typically a stereotype, as characterized in this newspaper column by writer Jim Bishop:

"The city editor makes me think of the driver of the twenty-mule Borax team. He cracks the whip over his reporters because they are his eyes and his ears and, through them, he sees the city.

"His rewrite men are on the far side of his desk and, through their typewriters, they give him what he wants when he wants it.

"He sits behind a double-desk. His assistant, who probably will inherit his job, sits opposite. Between them are several telephones and no schoolgirl can keep them as busy as the men on the desk.

"The city editor and his assistant have direct wires to police headquarters, to the courthouse, to the prosecutor's office, the mayor's office, sometimes to the hospital.

"The city editor knows approximately what time the big trial of today will recess, who the witnesses are expected to be and, quite often, what they will testify.

"He knows who is on the skids at police headquarters and who, at this time, can do no wrong.

"He knows things about the mayor's private life that Mrs. Mayor doesn't know and, usually, he knows which men on his staff are paying alimony and how far behind they are.

"He knows the policies and politics of the publisher and, although the city editor may not subscribe to them, he will defend them, in print, to the death.

"He understands the weaknesses of his own men and he, above all others, knows it isn't always booze or women.

"From the moment a story breaks until it is locked into a page form, the city editor is on top of it.

"No matter how good he is, the city editor never stops worrying. His moment of truth comes each day when a boy comes in with the opposition newspapers.

"Always the city editor pretends to be casual about it. He continues to shout his orders as his eyes search page one for a good story which he hasn't got.

"When he doesn't see it, he begins to breathe. He turns to page two of the opposition, then page three. The weight lifts from his chest.

" 'Get my wife,' he says to the assistant. 'Tell her I'll be home for dinner.' "

Source: Jim Bishop, *Jim Bishop: Reporter* (New York: Random House, 1966), 105–7.

City editors hold an important and special position in American newsrooms. They are the center and the soul of the local news operation. Like the sports editor or the features editor or the business editor, they have the final responsibility for ensuring that the goals and plans of the senior editors are carried out.

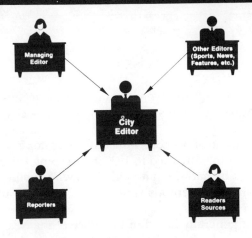

Fig. 5.5.

Common to most first-level supervisors, such as the city editor, is the time spent interacting with other people. This diagram shows the wide network of individuals who are typically part of the city editor's work day.

One editor described the city editor as "the crossroads of the newsroom, the center of the action, the person to see about just about everything that really matters at the paper, journalism's drill sergeant, the newsroom's third-base coach . . ."²

Many of the old-timers who ran city desks were first-class characters. Some were coldly efficient. Others were disliked around the office for the terror they struck in the hearts of staff members. Still others were loud and reckless with the facts. Many city editors were solid, competent, and great teachers who built outstanding reporting staffs. The newspaper stereotype has cast the city editor as a somewhat heroic but vulnerable figure who acted out his role in the manner of a tough guy. We see this in Stanley Walker's 1934 classic volume, *City Editor*, in the movies that play on "front-page" themes, and in the television characterization of Lou Grant.

In spite of the portrayal, it is unwise to generalize about city editors. Their role in the management of the newsroom has grown, although the city editor no longer has the almost unlimited authority and prestige that he exercised as recently as the 1940s (when city editors were almost always men).

Fig. 5.6

CLOSE-UP

In *City Editor*, an enduring commentary on newspaper life in the 1930s, Stanley Walker gave this portrayal of a famous city editor at the *New York Evening World*:

"The classic example of the cold, efficient city editor is, of course, the late Charles E. Chapin, who died in 1930 in Sing Sing Prison, where he had been sent after he had shot and killed his wife, Nellie. Today, men who develop traits and methods similar to his are said to be marked with the 'Chapin stigmata.'

"He was rather generally hated in the office of the *New York Evening World*, which he ruled with more power than most city editors have, but his professional ability was respected, and with good reason.

"Chapin had a cold, objective attitude toward his own work. 'I gave no confidences; I invited none. I was myself a machine, and the men I worked with were cogs. The human element never entered into the scheme of getting out the paper. It was my way of doing things. That it was not a bad way is proven by the fact that I stayed on the job for twenty years and was the highest salaried city editor on earth. I used to fire the boys for being late, or making up bum lies, or falling down on a story. But I never fired a man for being drunk or getting in a personal jam.'

"Chapin as city editor fired 108 men. He had one of the most brilliant staffs ever assembled, but he did not hire cubs, as some of the papers did, and train them. He let the other editors do the training, and then he would offer them so much more money that they would jump to the *Evening World*.

"He had no patience with amateurs, incompetents, or bunglers. He knew his job and expected the men to know theirs. He could spot a four-flusher at a great distance, and he prided himself on the variety of ways in which he fired men. Once a reporter was late telephoning a story. Chapin barked at him: 'Your name is Smith, is it? You say you work for the *Evening World*, do you? You're a liar. Smith stopped working for the *Evening World* an hour ago.'

"Chapin was a good but cantankerous judge of writing. He once fired a man for using the word *questionnaire*, which at that time had not been admitted to the dictionary.

"Chapin worked himself up by sheer nerve and ability, asking no favors and giving none. Whatever may have been wrong with this creature, so hard and so twisted, he was professionally competent, and probably would be today if he were alive and sitting at the desk of a metropolitan newspaper. Quite possibly, viewed as a machine, he was the ablest city editor who ever lived."

Source: Stanley Walker, *City Editor* (New York: Frederick A. Stokes, 1934), 4–8.

The jobs of all newsroom managers, including city editor-supervisors, include three basic elements:

1. *Authority.* This is the right to make decisions. To a certain degree, all newsroom employees have some authority. Photographers make decisions about which picture to shoot. Reporters make decisions about how to organize and write a story. Copy editors make decisions about which element in a story belongs in the headline. For newsroom managers, authority is the recognition that they have been empowered to direct the work activities of the people on the staff who report to them.

2. *Responsibility.* This is the obligation to direct the work of the staff. In a formal sense, it defines the types of activities that go with being city editor. To say that the city editor is responsible for the daily operations of the city desk means that any activity related to producing the local news report is the responsibility of the city editor.

3. *Accountability.* The idea of accountability ties together the concepts of authority and responsibility. In the newsroom, almost everybody answers to somebody. The reporter answers to the city editor. The city editor answers to the managing editor. In newspaper groups, the publisher of the local newspaper answers to a corporate officer. And the chief executive officer of the corporation answers to a board of directors. That's accountability. In theory, it requires everyone, including managers, to report to—be *accountable* to—a superior.

If the city editor fails to direct the staff effectively in covering the community and in preparing the local news report, this may indicate to the managing editor that the city editor has not exercised the authority or fulfilled the responsibility of the job. The managing editor's evaluation of the situation will be shared with the city editor and the two will discuss strategies for improvement. And while the city editor will be accountable to the managing editor for upgrading his or her performance, the managing editor will be accountable to the top editor or the publisher for the daily product of the city editor and the city-desk staff.

Fig. 5.7

CLOSE-UP

Nelson Poynter, the late editor of the *St. Petersburg Times* and *Evening Independent,* used to say to his young editors: "Despite what a lot of people think, I can't give you authority. I can make it available to you, but you have to take it. I can give an assistant city editor a title and a new desk and a raise and make the authority available. But he or she has to take it, show that he or she has it and is going to exercise it."

Source: Robert J. Haiman, interview with author, January 1984.

THE CITY EDITOR

Authority, responsibility, and accountability are elements of all managerial jobs. But, if that is true, then what distinguishes the city editor's role from that of the managing editor?

Both editors hold important positions in the newspaper's management hierarchy. As a first-line supervisor, the city editor is concerned only with the immediate responsibilities of the city desk. The managing editor or the executive editor is concerned with the larger picture; his or her range of authority, responsibility, and accountability includes the entire news department and, increasingly, companywide matters.

The city editor occupies the first level of management above the rank and file. Staffers supervised by the city editor—typically, reporters and copy editors—have no managerial authority themselves. City editors perform traditional managerial functions: Planning involves scheduling staffers and deciding which stories will be covered. Organizing may consist of assigning reporters to beats and delegating authority to an assistant city editor. Staffing is the city editor's opportunity to add new employees to the city-desk staff. Directing means communicating with the staff and providing leadership, both to individuals and to the city desk as a unit. Controlling focuses on getting the work done effectively and on time.

Common to most newsroom managers is the amount of time spent dealing with people. The city editor may spend more time on tasks that require technical skills—preparing news budgets, working with reporters, handling copy, keeping the future book, or preparing the overtime payroll—while editors in middle and top levels of management devote more of their time to conceptual matters such as planning and organizing.

Authority is the backbone of the city editor's role. Without it, the city editor is little more than a cheerleader who must rely on cunning or personal charm to get the work done. The legendary vision of the newsroom in which the city editor's word was law has changed somewhat. The authority of the city editor diminishes as top news executives come under pressure to control newsroom costs, to bring more women and minorities onto the staff, to initiate reporting projects that require close coordination with the advertising and production departments, and to

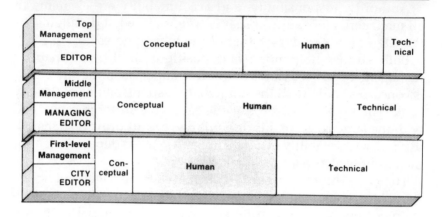

Fig. 5.8.

As an editor moves up in newsroom management, the work becomes more conceptual and less technical—and the demands for people skills remain strong.

prepare the staff for changes in the technology of electronic editing. In some cases, union contracts and government regulations have eroded the city editor's ability to discipline or dismiss staffers or to assign work.

The degree to which the city editor's authority may have been diminished, however, is not likely to have been accompanied by a lessening of responsibility or accountability. The managing editor continues to hold the city editor fully accountable for the city desk's mission. To be effective with somewhat less authority but full responsibility and accountability, city editors must rely more and more on the human skills of understanding and working with people.

The City Editor's Authority

The theory of supervision suggests that to be fully accountable for the performance of the city-desk staff, the city editor must be able to control or share in the control of the following:

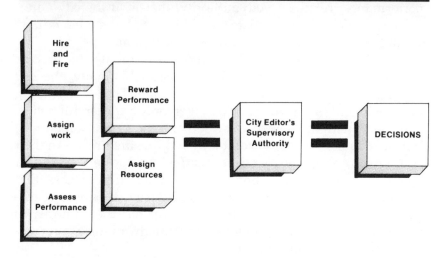

Fig. 5.9.

As a supervisor who is accountable for the performance of the city desk staff, the city editor must have authority. This diagram indicates the decisions that a city editor controls or shares in controlling.

The right to hire and fire subordinates. Every new city editor inherits the staff of his or her predecessor. It is not possible to clean house and start over—fairness, government regulations, and the counsel of the managing editor would prevent the city editor from dismissing the reporters and hiring new ones. The new city editor's challenge is to build on the existing staff and use each job vacancy as an opportunity to strengthen the paper.

It is important for the city editor to have a major role in the selection of new city-desk staffers. On many newspapers, the selection process involves a number of people. Candidates visit the newspaper and, under the supervision of the city editor, undergo an intensive routine of interviews, tests, and work assignments. Though the decision to hire a new reporter requires the approval of the senior news executive, the recommendation to hire comes first from the city editor and moves through other editor levels until it reaches the top editor's desk. In such a process, there is much discussion among editors. In most cases, the city editor, who will be accountable for the new reporter's performance, retains a veto authority; that is, if the city editor does not believe the candidate should be hired, the other editors are not likely to override that recommendation.

The city editor also has the authority to initiate the process that may result in discipline or dismissal. Normally, the city editor does not exercise this authority alone. The steps leading to punishment or termination are taken only after careful review of the facts with the newspaper's senior editors and, sometimes, its legal counsel. Under current laws, editors are limited in their authority to abruptly dismiss a staffer. A reporter is fired or asked to resign as the final step in a lengthy process that includes performance appraisals, goal-setting sessions, coaching, and regular feedback. The city editor has the authority to initiate the process, to monitor it, and finally, to make a recommendation to the senior editors.

Assignment of work. Every city desk is composed of a variety of talents. The mix includes gifted writers, skilled interviewers, thoughtful specialists, competitive deadline performers, solid all-around journalists, jaded veterans, eager beginners, and those whose ability or commitment is marginal. The city editor knows their strengths and weaknesses as well as anyone and should be the most qualified to assign these individuals to beats, to the rewrite desk, or to general assignment duty. On a major breaking story where the full resources of the city desk are needed, the city editor has the authority to pull reporters off their beats and assign them to special coverage.

If the authority to assign beats on the city desk was held by someone else—the managing editor, for example—the city editor's management of the staff would be less effective. The reporting staff would be confused as to who was in charge of the city desk and would question the city editor's authority. As a result, the city editor would continue to be accountable for the performance of the staffers, but could lack the authority to influence their work.

Rating performance. The city editor has the authority to assess the performance of each member of the city-desk staff. This may be the most underused of the city editor's authorities. Unless an evaluation program is introduced by the senior editors and becomes an operating practice in the newsroom, the city editor often avoids exercising this authority.

The right to assess performance is critical to the city editor's authority role with the staff. If reporters know that the city editor is casual about reviewing performance or that the managing editor does the appraisals, the city editor's influence on individual performance is lessened.

The authority to rate performance is tied to the city editor's authority to discipline or dismiss staffers. A reporter whose work is failing cannot be punished unless the city editor has discussed the failures with the reporter and given him or her a chance for improvement. A systematic, well-organized, and regular review of performance is especially crucial when a staffer's job is on the line.

Rewarding performance. The city editor has the authority to recognize differences in performance and to recommend that some staffers receive larger pay increases than others. Although senior editors must approve pay raises, the city editor has the authority to make the initial recommendations. If the city editor is able to exercise this authority, it will increase his or her influence with the staff.

Pay increases based on performance are called merit raises. The authority to recommend pay increases is tied to the authority to evaluate performance. Pay decisions by the city editor and the senior editors are more likely to be accepted as fair by the staff if the decisions are based on a thorough review of performance.

Under some union contracts, pay is negotiated on the basis of seniority or raises of equal amounts are given to everyone. The city editor's authority is diminished by each of these methods of pay increases. Reporters know they will receive the same increase as everyone else no matter how well they perform.

The newsroom budget and the newspaper company's policies are other considerations that affect the city editor's ability to influence the pay levels of the city-desk staff.

Assignment of resources. The city editor has the authority to assign physical resources. This control is important because access to resources affects the staff's productivity. A reporting staff's physical resources typically consist of desks, chairs, terminals, pens, notebooks, telephones, and the like. If a staff of ten reporters has only six desks and six terminals, the sharing of resources will cut into productivity.

While the city editor has the authority to assign resources, the amount of resources available to the city editor will be determined in the budgeting process. Even so, the city editor's voice counts. His or her recommendation to the top news executive that additional resources are needed may influence the decision to buy more desks and terminals. But other considerations come into play. The senior editor may include the city editor's recommendation in the news department's budget request. The publisher will review the request, balancing the newsroom's needs against the needs of other departments of the newspaper company, and finally deciding whether there are funds to purchase desks and terminals.

Once the budget is fixed, the city editor should have full authority within the limits of the budget. How well the city editor uses the resources provided by the budget then becomes one factor for which he or she is accountable.

The above outline of the city editor's authority is based on the traditional range of authority for supervisors.* The city editor's actual authority may differ, depending on a number of factors. Such influences may include what the senior editors expect from the city editor, the range of the city editor's skills and experience, and the relationship between the city editor and the managing editor. The fact remains, however, that if the city editor is to be held accountable for the performance of the staff, he or she must have the authority that has been explained here.

Potential city editors should get a clear understanding of what authority the job carries before agreeing to accept the responsibility. It is difficult to imagine a city editor being successful in a poorly defined role. The ambiguity that results when the city editor is unsure of his or her authority is highly stressful.

---

* For a more extensive description of supervision, refer to Jerry L. Gray, *Supervision* (Boston: Kent, 1984), and Warren R. Plunkett and Raymond F. Attner, *Introduction to Management* (Boston: Kent, 1983).

THE ASSISTANT CITY EDITOR

On a small newspaper, the city editor may be the only editor on the city desk. Larger papers have one or more assistant city editors who perform specialized tasks such as page layout, special projects, or suburban coverage as assigned by the city editor. The same structure applies to the other desks in the newsroom, depending on the size of the paper.

Assistant city editors often work directly with reporters in assigning stories and in processing those stories for publication. In all of their tasks, assistant city editors report to the city editor.

Assistant city editors can be delegated to assign work and they can participate in evaluating work, but their role in hiring, firing, assigning resources, and rewarding reporters is limited. They often defer the final choice in these matters to the city editor.

The limited authority of assistant editors can be understood by thinking of accountability as an upward spiral from the lowest- to the highest-ranking manager in the newsroom. It is a natural hierarchy in which the city editor, accountable for the work of the assistants, is inclined to make the key decisions or review decisions made by an assistant city editor. In some ways, assistant city editors could be viewed as consultants.

The role of the assistant city editor is useful because it relieves the city editor of some managerial duties; however, if the assistant city editor's role is not well defined, it can cause confusion. The city editor should make it clear whether the assistant city editor has authority only in selected areas or assists the city editor in all activities of the city desk. This can be tricky. The city editor must retain the real authority on the city desk, but authorize the assistant city editor to act for him or her.

How the assistant city editor's role is defined will affect the relationship between reporter and assistant city editor. For example, an assistant city editor may instruct a reporter to rework a story. The reporter argues that the story does not need changes. Does the assistant city editor have the authority to require the reporter to make changes, or does the reporter have the right of appeal to the city editor? Unless the roles have been clarified, both reporter and assistant city editor may be uncertain.

In most newsrooms, there are no written rules to answer the question, but the personal style of the city editor and the traditions of the newsroom may suggest that the city editor is free to assign any part of his or her supervisory duties to the assistant city editor. Thus, the reporter is expected to follow the instructions of the assistant city editor and then discuss the incident with the city editor after deadline. Or, style and tradition may suggest that the assistant city editor can call in the city editor as an arbiter.

Fig. 5.10

CLOSE-UP

Robert Haiman, president and managing director of the Poynter Institute and former executive editor of the *St. Petersburg Times,* recalls his first job as assistant city editor of the *Times* at age twenty-five:

"I can hardly think of anything that I did right. I was unjustifiably impressed with myself. I was not very well equipped to do the job and I fear I showed it.

"I was saved from certain disaster by two veteran reporters. Each took me out for a beer and told me in a fairly gentle but direct way how badly I was behaving.

"They both said that I needed to know a few things that my behavior indicated I didn't know. 'Almost all of the staff likes you. You don't have to whip us into line because we are ready to follow. We really want to do what you want us to do. So far you haven't done any editing on our stories that we think is wrong. You may think this is the most important job you have ever had in your life. It is not and if you will give us a chance, we'll help you be a success.'

"I was completely mortified and apologetic, realizing how I had been acting like an idiot, a self-important stuffed shirt, showing confusion and learning a lesson that probably every young second lieutenant has to discover: that there are a number of senior staff members who are your single best resource in running the group. Not only is there no shame in asking them for advice as to how the outfit runs, but it is almost essential to do that if you want to avoid giving everybody heart failure, including yourself."

Source: Robert J. Haiman, interview with author, January 1984.

Tradition and the city editor's style also will influence the handling of situations in which the city editor and the assistant city editor disagree. If the city editor reverses a decision made by the assistant city editor, it must be done in a way that avoids undermining the assistant city editor's role.

In spite of the limits of their authority, assistant city editors are considered part of first-level management in the newsroom. That perception becomes clouded in organized newsrooms where union contracts claim assistant city editors as part of the bargaining unit. In these situations, the assistant city editor's loyalties become torn between the management of the newspaper and the rank and file represented by the union.

The Assistant City Editor's Responsibility

Powerful forces tend to draw supervisors toward those they supervise. Most city editors and assistant city editors were once reporters. They carry a perception that reporters and city-desk editors come from a background that differs significantly from that of upper management, even though the managing editor, the executive editor, and even the publisher once may have worked as reporters and later as city editors.

It is not uncommon for assistant city editors to take an "us-against-them" stance in relation to the senior editors or the management of the newspaper company. This behavior is influenced by the size of the paper and the levels of responsibility in the newsroom. The tendency is for the editor at the lowest level of management and closest to the rank and file to be drawn back to former peers on the reporting staff. Those at the higher levels tend to relate more naturally to management.

Fig. 5.11

CLOSE-UP

The transition from reporter to assistant city editor is difficult for some. Phil Currie, who achieved that passage at the *Times-Union* in Rochester, says: "It is difficult for some reporters to subvert their ego. If they get right down to it and analyze it in their hearts, they love

Fig. 5.11, continued

seeing that byline on page one. They like being out, meeting the crowds. They like being seen on the hustings and known as a reporter. When you move to the city desk or any desk, you lose that. You become much more anonymous. Certain people can adjust to that. And certain people can't.

"Becoming an assistant city editor is a tough problem simply because you are going from being a pal to everybody you work with to being their boss. One of the interesting things I found when I moved from one to the other was that some of the griping was not justified. I suddenly understood a lot more about management. For example, a reporter would say, 'Geez, the city desk really screwed up my story today,' and I would see the story that reporter had handed in and I'd realize that the city desk didn't screw it up. It needed to be fixed.

"People who do move to the desk find that all of a sudden, they can have a lot more to say about what is going into the newspaper as city editor or later as managing editor than they could as a reporter. And they love that. But others don't think it offsets some of the grind that goes with it, including dealing with a lot more paperwork and, in some cases, with prima donna reporters."

Source: Phil Currie, vice-president/news, Gannett Company, Inc., interview with author, January 1984.

The self-interest of first-level supervisors bends them to the will of the senior editors. First, city-desk editors are professionals and should be committed to producing a first-rate newspaper. Second, they know they have to cooperate with the boss if they want opportunities for advancement and increases in pay. Third, city-desk editors recognize that they depend on the senior editors for the resources that help them get the job done. However comfortable the identity with their former peers in the reporting ranks may seem, the attraction of being part of management can be powerful, too.

The jump from reporter or copy editor to assistant city editor is a big one. The new assistant city editor quickly discovers there is more to the promotion than meets the eye. Becoming a member of the newsroom management team is complicated by the change in relationships with others on the staff. Everyone looks at the new editor in a different light. They expect more.

They will test the new editor. And they will watch to see whether he or she abuses authority or gets a swelled head or neglects those who helped make the promotion possible. Some may even want to see the new editor fail.

Reporters and copy editors who were peers now report to the new editor. Some may not be happy about that. Some may have wanted the job themselves. They may believe that the wrong person was chosen and will look for indications that the new assistant city editor can't handle the job. Those who wish for success also will be looking for signals on how to proceed. They'll want to know rather quickly if they can catch the new editor for an after-work drink or whether he or she can be trusted to share office gossip.

It is difficult for new assistant city editors to understand why they should distance themselves from the reporting staff. They want to hang on to their old ties for both social and professional reasons. They want to be the boss and yet maintain the closeness they enjoyed when they were one of the troops. They may be uncomfortable asking a reporter to rewrite a story or plug a hole in the copy. They are anxious about making a decision that may anger an old friend. Early in the game, a new assistant city editor may feel the need to apologize or defend the fact that he or she is now a boss.

After time, the assistant city editor begins to understand that he or she is in a position to affect the professional lives of those on the reporting staff. The assistant city editor can influence whether a reporter gets a raise, gets a new beat, gets more recognition, gets additional opportunities, or gets disciplined. That's career influence. It is a serious responsibility, and it demonstrates why the decision to become a supervisor carries the obligation to develop new and different relationships with former peers on the reporting staff.

The rules change with the other assistant city editors, too. Formerly superiors, they now are on the same level with the newcomer on the desk. The new editor consults with them instead of reporting to them. The senior assistant city editors may feel threatened because the newcomer has advanced while they have not. A few may fear that the new person is on a "fast track" and soon may be their boss. The new assistant city editor is likely to be challenged and tested to see whether he or she is up to the task.

The city editor is still the boss, but that relationship has changed, too. If the city editor pushed for the promotion, there may be high expectations for the assistant city editor to succeed, creating pressures for the new editor to demonstrate that the promotion was a good decision and to perform well in areas where he or she may not feel confident.

If the new editor can accept the idea that the change is irreversible and that newsroom relationships will never be what they were, then he or she can get on with the business at hand.

This is a time when it is difficult for the assistant city editor to reckon with his or her new role as part of the newspaper's management. It is critical to recognize quickly the obligation to act for the newspaper, to help carry out its plans and objectives, and to assist in the professional development of individuals on the staff. To do that effectively and successfully, a realignment of loyalties is clearly necessary.

CHAPTER SUMMARY

There are three levels of management in the newsroom: (1) the top news executive has overall responsibility for the operation of the news department and also is part of the newspaper company's top management, (2) middle managers are editors below the top level who supervise other managers, and (3) first-level supervisory managers are those who directly supervise workers.

The city editor, sports editor, news editor, features editor, business editor, photo editor, and chief artist or graphics editor are supervisors. They perform traditional managerial functions, but their authority, responsibility, and accountability are limited to their own desk or department.

These editors control or share in the control of hiring and firing, assigning work, rating performance, rewarding performance, and assigning resources.

Assistant city editors are key lieutenants on many city desks, but they are not supervisors in the full sense because their authority is limited.

New assistant city editors often find it difficult to distance themselves from their former friends and counterparts on the reporting staff. Equally difficult is the challenge of learning how to act for the company and recognizing that they have the responsibility to make decisions that can affect the careers of those they supervise.

NOTES

1. Jerry L. Gray, *Supervision* (Boston: Kent, 1984), 26.
2. Walker Lundy, "The City Editor Then: The Toughest Guy in the Joint," *The Bulletin of the American Society of Newspaper Editors*, March 1983, 14.

6

Newsroom Management Roles

As managers, editors perform a variety of functions, all concerned with making decisions and getting work accomplished. The functions of management draw on human, financial, and material resources. The editor's understanding of these functions is vital in developing a management style that will be both comfortable and effective.

THE EDITOR AS MANAGER

The five basic roles of management—planning, organizing, staffing, directing, and controlling—are carried out at each level of the newsroom organization. These roles are fundamental to all of the work that goes into the preparation of the daily news report and the management of the news staff.

The top news executive—the editor, executive editor, or managing editor—is responsible for developing the editorial mission of the newspaper. This includes the organization of the staff, the news policy, the major operational practices, and the standards for performance.

The top editor *plans* the budget and changes in news or feature content, *organizes* resources based on the budget plan, *selects and develops the staff* for the newsroom organization, *directs* the work of the staff through other editors, and *controls* performance through feedback, appraisal, and rewards. The editor shares with others his or her sense of the day's news, comments on individual stories, headlines, and photographs in the paper, and offers bits of intelligence that may help shape the paper's coverage plans. From time to time, the editor will be directly involved in planning or editing an individual story for publication.

On smaller papers, the managing editor (as the top news executive) not only handles all of the management responsibilities, but he or she also has a major hands-on role in the selection of stories, in the layout of page one, in editing difficult stories, in planning a reporting assignment, and in reviewing and editing stories for special projects.

On larger newspapers where the editor or executive editor is the top editor, the managing editor's responsibilities are traditionally those of a middle-level manager. These responsibilities center on translating the editor's broad objectives into daily routines for managing the staff and producing the news report. This managing editor is concerned with short-range plans for coverage and the flow of news into the paper.

First-line supervisors, such as the city editor, features editor, and sports editor, carry out the objectives of the editor by *planning* coverage of the news, *organizing* the staff to gather, write, and edit the news, consulting with other editors in *staffing* decisions, *directing* the activities of individual journalists in preparing the news report, and *controlling* the process through deadlines and a series of quality-control steps such as copy editing and page layout.

To be able to carry out the variety of responsibilities assigned to him or her, the editor-manager must first accomplish two specific tasks:

1. The editor's first task is to form a unified news staff out of a group of individual journalists and to create a whole news report out of disparate news stories, photographs, and illustrations. If we were to draw an analogy between a newspaper and a symphony orchestra, we would find that the editor is like the conductor: He or she is the interpreter whose energy, vision, and leadership influence the performance of individuals on the staff. And, as in the case of the conductor who hears the individual cellist as well as the full orchestra,

the editor recognizes the performance of each individual staffer along with that of the whole staff.[1]

In creating an effective news staff, the editor attempts to maximize individuals' strengths and minimize or neutralize their weaknesses. In so doing, the editor has to balance interests that often seem to be in competition: the journalistic standards of the staff, the economic goals of the newspaper, and the standing of the newspaper in the community. The editor's decisions and actions need to satisfy each of these interests. Satisfying one at the expense of another—for example, sacrificing a stable bottom line for uncontrolled expansion of newsgathering—weakens the whole newspaper.

2. The second task of the editor-manager is to keep the short-term and long-term goals of the news department in harmony with the goals of the rest of the newspaper. Management consultant Peter F. Drucker calls this keeping the nose to the grindstone while lifting the eyes to the hills.[2] The editor should know the mission of the newspaper for the next two to five years and be able to balance against that mission the day-to-day decisions on coverage and staffing. If it is the newspaper's long-term goal to add suburban readers and advertisers, for example, the editor must assess how this goal would be affected if suburban coverage were reduced because of vacancies on the staff. In this case, the editor must protect the immediate interest of getting the paper out short-handed while limiting the damage to the future goal of building strong support among suburban readers.

PLANNING

Planning involves thinking and looking ahead, anticipating the future, setting goals, generating ideas for improving the newspaper, and then making appropriate decisions. The planning process must be assertive, forward-looking, and creative, yet reflect pragmatic estimates of what is possible. Planning is the first management function because it establishes the foundation for the organizing, staffing, directing, and controlling that follow.

The questions to be answered in a plan are the same as those to be answered in the lead of a news story: what, when, where, who, why, and how? *What* is the goal, a statement of the objective—is it short-term or long-term? *When* is a matter of timing. *Where* concerns the place or places where the plans and planning will reach their conclusion. *Who* asks which people will perform the tasks essential to the plan. *Why* is the justification for the goal. *How* explains the steps to be taken in achieving the goal, including the cost.[3]

For the editor, a plan can answer such questions as: How will we cover the mayoral campaign? How can we improve headline writing? How can we target our life-style coverage to younger readers? How can we develop a special section for health and medicine? How can we justify a new front-end system?

If there were no plan, none of these projects could be accomplished without errors, waste, and delays. Having a plan does not eliminate problems, but it creates a framework for a thoughtful, efficient process in which full consideration is given to an idea before commitments are made. Planning creates a method of organizing resources and activities to give shape to an idea, provides guidelines for directing the work, and establishes a standard for measuring progress, an essential element in controlling work.

The editor's planning process should mesh with the objectives of the newspaper company. A plan to improve news content, while a worthy goal itself, must be tied to the objectives of the production department, the advertising department, and the circulation department, as well as the publisher. It is often the case, for example, that the editor's desire to create a special section cannot be fulfilled unless the advertising department can create enough additional revenue to pay for extra staff and newshole and the production department is able to configure the presses to handle another section.

Similarly, teamwork among editors is necessary in planning. If the managing editor develops plans that are not in line with those of the editor, the conflicting objectives that result can create tension, uncertainty, and inefficiencies. Ideally, the supervisory editors and the managing editor will help the editor devise the newsroom plan, recognizing its limitations and risks and sharing in the commitment to achieve success.

Planning gives editors the ability to adjust to unexpected changes rather than simply react to them. In preparing an annual newsroom operating budget, for example, the editor can plan how to cut newsroom costs if advertising lineage drops. This is called a contingency budget. It gives the editor a formula for efficiently reducing the newshole or cutting travel or keeping staff vacancies open in a way that minimizes the risks of long-term damage to the news product, and yet helps the publisher keep the bottom line stable in the face of lower advertising revenue.

Rarely is a plan created that is not changed at a later time. Changes sometimes result from miscalculations in the plan, but more often they are caused by a turn of events that forces managers to adjust the plan.

In the newsroom, as in any other operation of the newspaper, there are two kinds of planning: strategic and tactical.

Strategic Planning

A strategic plan involves the entire news operation or the entire newspaper and requires the involvement of individuals at various levels on the staff. The editor is responsible for setting the overall direction and tone of the plan, while at progressively lower levels, the managing editor and the desk editors develop the full details to execute the plan. As the plan moves down the line, the requirements for achieving the goal become more specific.

Peter F. Drucker defines strategic planning as the continuous process of making entrepreneurial or risk-taking decisions systematically and with the greatest knowledge of their prospects; organizing systematically the efforts needed to carry out these decisions; and measuring the results of these decisions against the expectations through organized, systematic feedback. Such planning is essential, whether long-range or short-range. A task rarely gets done unless it is organized and executed purposefully.[4]

Thought, analysis, imagination, and judgment are the qualities of strategic planning. As Drucker says, it is a responsibility, not a technique, and one that is entrepreneurial in spirit.

Drucker raises four points of caution about strategic planning:

1. It is not a box of tricks, a bundle of techniques.
2. It is not a prediction of the future.
3. It does not deal with future decisions, but with the preparation to make future decisions.
4. It is not an attempt to eliminate risk.[5]

Strategic planning requires analytical thinking that may result in committing resources to action. For example, a newspaper that is preparing to do readership research is engaged in strategic planning. The newspaper's publisher and other key executives are asking fundamental questions about the paper: Why are we losing circulation? What do we want to learn from our readers? How can we attract new readers without risking the loss of those we have? How can we target news content to selected reader groups? Would our readers prefer morning to afternoon delivery? Is poor circulation service driving away readers?

A thoughtful analysis of the newspaper's problems will be translated into a questionnaire. The results of the research will be analyzed further as the executives build a model for change and evaluate the costs against anticipated results. But whatever good information the research provides cannot be used to predict the future growth of the paper or forecast circulation trends. The executives can make reasonable guesses about what short-run circulation gains might result through content changes, more newshole, stronger promotion, earlier press times, more single-copy outlets, and better delivery service, but they cannot foresee the course of other events that might influence the life-styles and loyalties of newspaper readers over a longer period. They cannot predict turns in the economy, changes in mail rates that might strengthen or weaken shoppers and mailed advertisements, or new applications of cable-television programming and home computers that could influence long-term newspaper-buying habits.

So, the strategic planning role requires newspaper executives to address the challenge of being ready for the uncertainties of tomorrow. They must look at the results of their research and decide what variables they have to incorporate into their thinking, what options must be considered, what time spans are crucial, and what data from the research will help them make rational decisions now.

The executives will recognize that the great uncertainty of the future demands solutions that carry risks. The risks cannot be eliminated, so the key is to use the strategic planning process to select the *right* risks. Such a risk might be a decision to commit more money for targeting additional news sections to special reader groups, for hiring an agency to develop a promotional campaign, for using more color, or for improving subscriber services. The publisher would be betting (calculated though that bet may be) that a smaller profit in the short run would build a stronger reader and advertiser base in the long run.

Any commitment must be translated into specifics. Perhaps some things can be accomplished in the short run, but others will take time. Adding an op-ed page, for example, can be done rather quickly. On the other hand, the commitment to use more color in ads and news layouts may require the purchase of new offset printing presses to replace old letter presses. This plan may take a year or more to implement.

Tactical Planning

Whatever the time span, a goal must be pursued in a systematic, well-organized manner that will convert a plan into action. This is done through a tactical or operating plan. Tactical plans are used by lower-level units to determine how they must do the work and who will have the responsibility for doing it.

To add an op-ed page, for example, the responsibility and much of the work will fall on the editorial-page editor. The graphics editor may be asked to create an attractive package for the material, but the editorial-page editor will choose the columns and cartoons and establish a procedure for selecting material to be used on the page, including letters to the editor and longer pieces from local readers. The actual work of selecting the letters, editing the columns, and laying out the page can fall to the editorial-page editor or can be delegated to someone else.

City editors have tactical plans for a number of unusual news situations: storms, urban riots, plane crashes, etc. Tactical plans also spell out how the newspaper will continue to publish in the event of a power outage, fire, computer failure, or strike.

A tactical plan takes one of two basic forms: a single-use plan, put into operation for one specific purpose, or an ongoing plan. Within this framework, there is a variety of applications of tactical plans:[6]

- A program is a single-use plan. An example would be a workshop on libel law for the news staff conducted by the newspaper's counsel. When the workshop is completed and the editors believe that the goal of broadening the staff's understanding of libel has been satisfied, repeated workshops would not be needed.

    Some programs have a long life even though they have but a single use. An accuracy program, in which readers are queried about the accuracy of news stories involving them, might go on indefinitely if the editor's goal is to check routinely on accuracy.

- A budget is a single-use plan that usually has a life of about eighteen months—six months for planning and twelve months in which it is used to control newsroom operating costs. Once the budget year has ended, a new budget is put in force and the old one has no more value.

- A policy is an ongoing plan that provides guidelines for handling the news or for individual conduct. Policy statements are often broadly worded, pointing editors and staffers in a particular direction but allowing individuals to use their professional judgment in specific situations.

- A practice is a commonly accepted but unwritten way of doing things that becomes habit through repetition or tradition. An editor who routinely answers mail and phone calls from readers because it seems the right thing to do has developed a practice. Other editors may adopt that practice, even though no policy or memorandum suggests that they do so.

- A procedure is a set of step-by-step directions explaining how a task is to be performed. An editor preparing next year's operating budget may follow a procedure laid out by the publisher or the business office. Most newsrooms have a book of procedures explaining how to create and edit stories on the electronic editing system.

- A rule is a specific plan that attempts to control human behavior. For example, a style book is a collection of "do" and "don't" statements for correct usage—rules of style. Likewise, companies have rules that are designed to promote the safety or security of employees.

The Budget

The growth of large newspaper companies and the strength of other media organizations that are competing for advertising dollars and readers' time has made budgeting a necessary planning responsibility for newspaper executives. Editors no longer have the luxury of casually running the news department, spending whatever it takes to pay the staff and cover the news. Increasingly, editors are looking at the expense sheets with a sharp eye. They are under pressure from publishers who want to pare costs and increase profits.

Why have a budget? What are its values, aside from meeting the publisher's interest in controlling costs?

The operating budget is a valuable resource that helps editors make the most effective use of dollars for pay increases, travel, overtime, hiring, training, features, wire services, and other major expenses.

Budgets help set priorities. They help editors decide what is important and what is not so important. They give editors a tool for building vital improvements in the news operation for the coming year. In preparing a budget, editors discover that payroll is the most easily controlled newsroom cost.

Budgets help editors compete for operating dollars with other departments at the newspaper. The directors of advertising, circulation, production, and marketing are searching for every advantage in the budget game. Money for improvements and additions may no longer be there just for the asking, but may be available to the manager who can assemble the information to make a compelling justification of his or her plans. The budget process also is an opportunity for the editor to enlist the support of the publisher in setting a high priority for newsside improvements.

Obstacles to Planning

Like most managers, few editors are born with the ability to plan. Most come to their first management jobs as assistant editors with little background and little specific knowledge of planning. Often they do not know how to go about the process of planning, but with thoughtful guidance from a senior editor or with formal management training, most can learn how to plan.

Conceptual skills—the ability to analyze, to deal with ideas and concepts, to innovate—are a vital part of an editor's repertoire. Without this essential talent, planning may be a difficult barrier to overcome.

Planning is a demanding and sometimes frustrating exercise. Editors who are unable to manage their time find it easier to let other responsibilities intrude when they should be planning. They prefer to handle each situation as it comes up or to play it by ear. Fear of failure is another reason why editors have misgivings about planning, particularly if they have had no planning experience.

Some editors lack a commitment to planning. Their tendency is to react to situations rather than try to anticipate events through sound planning. Editors who permit short-term problems to overshadow long-term needs will have trouble preparing for the future. For example, if they allow the daily urgencies of the newspaper to delay the search for candidates or the training of a replacement for the city editor who is retiring in a year, they are sacrificing the long term for the short term.

Poor planning or a lack of planning can result from the subconscious wish of an editor to create crises. When a crisis develops, the editor is expected to make an immediate decision that will set things straight. Because the staff turns to the editor in a crisis, he or she feels needed and important. This tendency is found in editors who are insecure in their jobs. Their lack of confidence prevents them from developing plans and delegating responsibilities. In the absence of a strong, dependent relationship that is built through effective planning and delegation, the staff has no sense of direction. The result is crisis management and frustration for the staff.

A major barrier to effective planning is information that is out-of-date, inaccurate, or of otherwise poor quality. For example, editors who fail to maintain accurate records of the flow of news pages to the typesetter will be ill-prepared to meet the challenge of a production director who says the news department is missing deadlines. And, editors shirk their long-term planning responsibility when they accept the business office's budget projections without having their own data on the cost of running the news department for comparison purposes.

Editors erect yet another barrier to planning when they limit their focus to things they can control while ignoring the unknown. These editors plan newshole and overtime spending for only those events that have been scheduled, while failing to provide resources for the unspecified news events that are bound to occur every year.

Even if the editor has experience and conceptual skills, the demands of reflective, systematic planning are challenging. Newspaper work has about it an unrelenting pace characterized by activities that are brief, varied, and often disconnected. The editor's life is strongly oriented to action, and whatever planning goes on must be done in that context. The problems editors face often are complex and require ingenuity and creativity to resolve.

Successful Planning Principles

Editors who are successful planners rely on four principles:

1. Plans should be realistic. They should reflect a thoughtful assessment of the resources available and what can be achieved in a reasonable period of time. If plans are simply a product of the editor's wishful thinking or if they are too ambitious, there is little chance that they will be accomplished.
2. Plans should be specific. The details should inform superiors and subordinates of what is to be improved, how it is to be improved, what the improvement will cost, and how long it will take to achieve. Vague objectives are likely to be rejected by the publisher, and plans given to the staff with imprecise guidelines will create a sense of uncertainty among those assigned to carry out the plan.
3. Plans should have a deadline. A deadline provides a control for the editor and gives the staff a target for carrying out the plan.
4. Others on the news staff should participate in planning. In most cases, participation is useful because it draws on a reservoir of ideas and builds a commitment to the objectives of the plan. Participation also increases communication, the flow of information, and an understanding of the plan and its objectives by those who will have to carry out the details.

ORGANIZING

Organizing is the management activity that links the authority of managers to the work to be done. Four activities define organizing as a management role:[7]

1. Determining what work has to be done to achieve the objectives of the company.
2. Classifying the type of work and the groups of workers into manageable units.

3. Delegating appropriate authority and assigning work to individuals.
4. Designing a hierarchy of decision-making relationships.

A clear relationship exists between planning and organizing. The organization of the copy desk, for example, is determined by the editor's plan for smooth copy flow, editing of wire copy and local stories, and quality control through a slot editor. The copy desk must be organized with enough people and appropriate work schedules to meet the goals in the editor's plan. In other words, the plan for copy-desk organization is a tool of the newsroom management to achieve its goals for accurate, well-edited stories.

The importance of organization in the newsroom is better understood when one considers the variety of tasks performed and the way different news subjects and individual journalists are grouped. In a typical newsroom, there will be a news desk, a copy desk, a city desk, a business desk, a sports desk, a features desk, a photo department, and an art or graphics department. These desks and departments illustrate clearly how news is assembled and processed. Similarly, the organization of the newsroom clarifies and defines the tasks and responsibilities of staffers on each of the desks—something commonly called a division of labor.

In management theory, the typical newsroom organization would fit the definitions of both a functional approach—having separate operations for reporting, editing, photography, and art—as well as a product-line approach—where the product of the sports desk is different from the product of the copy desk or the photo department, but they all come together to form the news content of the paper.

This organization also facilitates coordination between and among desks. In the urgency of getting the paper out, there is little tolerance for confusion or obstacles. Interaction between the city desk and the copy desk is well understood although, from time to time, the editor may have to write guidelines or procedures to smooth the flow of work between the two desks or to keep differences of opinion from becoming a barrier to moving copy.

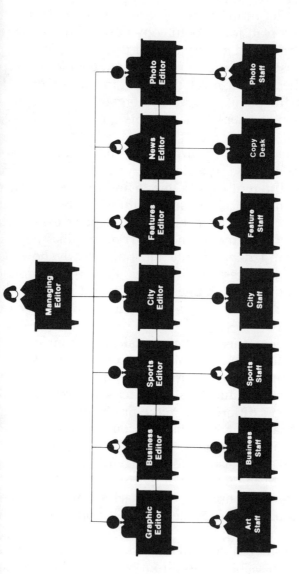

Fig. 6.1.

This diagram illustrates how authority flows from the managing editor to other editors and staffers in the newsroom. The desk editors are on the same organizational level and all report to the managing editor. The staffs reporting to each desk editor represent that editor's span of control.

The flow of authority from the editor to each of the news desks is achieved through a principle called unity of direction.[8] This principle calls for one authority figure for each major task. The editor is the authority figure for the managing editor. The managing editor is the authority figure for each of the desk editors. The features editor is the authority figure on the features desk who coordinates all plans and activities of the features staff.

Through the organization of desks and the unity of direction emerges a decision-making structure. This structure allows an effective flow of information and decisions up and down the chain of command.

Despite its traditional structure, the newsroom organization is not static. A number of influences have brought changes to the organization and created new relationships among the decision makers. Some examples include reader representatives or ombudsmen, desks to handle new sections, graphics specialists, and editors responsible for expanding computer applications. Rapidly changing technology will continue to influence the way newspapers are produced and will force editors continually to rethink the organization of the news staff.

On medium-sized and large newspapers, growth and change are reflected in the number of individuals carrying the title of assistant managing editor. There may be an assistant managing editor in charge of the Sunday paper, another for the daily newspaper, another for features, and another responsible for administration, who looks after budgets and coordinates evaluations, pay changes, job interviews, and travel planning.

This new mix of roles has introduced editors to different types of authority. Traditionally, the newsroom organization has been described as having a classic *line authority* relationship; that is, the relationship between the managing editor and each of the desk editors is a direct supervisory relationship. Line authority flows down from the editor to the managing editor to the desk editors to the reporters, copy editors, artists, and photographers.

The introduction of newsroom managers whose roles are advisory, such as an administrative assistant to the top editor, has added *staff authority* to the newsroom hierarchy. An administrative assistant does not exercise control over any news staffers or newsgathering activities. He or she is responsible for such tasks as preparing and managing the budget, gathering information, providing technical assistance, and advising the editor. Many of the editor's decisions are based on the input of an administrative assistant, but in the editor's absence, the assistant normally does not inherit the authority of the editor.

By itself, the news department is a line department. It is headed by a line manager, the editor, and is responsible for a major objective of the newspaper company. The advertising, production, and circulation departments also carry out line functions and are important cogs in the major mission of the newspaper company: publishing and delivering news and selling advertising at a profit.

Other departments at the newspaper provide assistance to the line departments and to each other, but they do not have a direct responsibility for the newspaper's major mission. Traditional staff departments include accounting, personnel, computer services, and public service, which serve special needs of the newspaper company by providing skilled support to the line departments. The expert advice of the computer specialists, for example, often is crucial to getting the paper to press on time.

STAFFING

People are a newspaper's most important resource, and the editor's skills in selecting individuals to be hired or promoted are critical to the newspaper's success. Staffing has a significant impact on the long-range character of the paper. If the editor handles the staffing responsibility poorly, then the staff will lack the talent and energy necessary to carry out effectively the editor's goals.

Staffing involves a series of steps designed to get the right people in the right positions. Many of the steps will be explored in detail in later chapters. Let's look at some basic principles of staffing now.[9]

Human resource planning. Changes in news content or in the technology necessary to produce the paper can require changes in the newsroom organization. A plan for pagination, for example, may include additional staff positions for page layout. The plan should indicate what skills will be needed to fill the page-layout positions. Effective human resource planning will ensure that the appropriate staff positions are part of the overall planning for pagination.

Recruitment. Recruiting to fill vacancies on the staff can be done in a variety of ways; for example, while candidates for most newsroom positions come from college journalism programs or from other newspapers, it is not unusual for prospective staffers who specialize in music or art or medicine to have limited journalism backgrounds. Their strength is in their knowledge of a specialty. Editors recruit these individuals believing they can be taught the basics of journalism.

Selection. Usually more than one candidate is interviewed in the search for the person whose credentials match a job's requirements. The steps in the selection process may include completing an application form; submitting a résumé and samples of work; interviewing, either by telephone or in person; testing; a work tryout; reference checks; and a physical examination.

Orientation. Integrating a new employee into the news staff begins with an introduction to the policies and rules of the newspaper. On small papers, the editor or the editor's secretary explains such things as pay practices, insurance and health benefits, work schedules, the performance-review program, vacations, and holidays. On larger papers, this task generally falls to the personnel department. Another dimension of orientation is the socialization that begins when an editor introduces the newcomer to others on the staff.

Training and development. These terms have different meanings in the shaping of a newspaper's staff. Training is building staffers' skills; for example, new reporters or copy editors receive training in the newspaper's style and procedures. And, from time to time, the editors may hold workshops to train staffers in dealing with libel, courtroom closures, and school budgets. Development is preparation for new responsibilities. An example of development occurs when a reporter works on the city desk as a vacation replacement or attends a seminar for city editors.

Performance appraisals. A sound program of reviewing work behavior is essential in developing a highly skilled staff. Performance reviews should be based on established standards and must include feedback to staffers.

Employment decisions. Flowing out of performance appraisals are decisions relating to pay, transfers, promotions, and terminations. Information generated by performance reviews builds a solid base for effective decisions by the editor that affect the professional standing of each news staffer.

Although the newspaper is part of private enterprise and its newsgathering and publishing activities are protected by the First Amendment, decisions about staffing are influenced by other laws. Laws governing equal employment opportunity and affirmative action aim to protect job applicants and employees from discrimination.

The Equal Employment Opportunity statutes prohibit employers from making hiring, promotion, or discharge decisions on the basis of race, color, religion, sex, age, or national origin.

Two kinds of discrimination are covered by the law: overt and covert. An editor commits overt discrimination by considering only male candidates for the position of sports editor even though women could do the job equally well. Covert discrimination occurs if the editor selects new staffers using results of written tests that have not been validated for minority candidates.

The federal definition of minorities includes the following groups:

Hispanics: Spanish-surnamed Americans.
Negroes: Blacks not of Hispanic origin.
Oriental Americans: Asians or people from the Pacific Islands.
American Indians: Natives of North America.
Eskimos: Alaskan natives.

These groups are protected under the EEO laws. Any part of the employment process that has an adverse impact on members of these groups is unlawful. For example, recruitment advertisements can no longer specify male or female; a company cannot rely on word-of-mouth advertising to attract minorities; preemployment inquiries not related to job performance are prohibited. Questions on sex, age, marital status, race, religion, national origin, type of military discharge, color of hair and eyes, height, and weight must be eliminated on applications and in interviews.[10]

Affirmative action requires an employer to make an extra effort to hire and promote members of minority groups. The idea behind affirmative action is to correct the effects of past discrimination. Many editors have affirmative-action goals that are designed to increase the numbers of women and minorities on their news staffs. These are voluntary goals, but often an editor's performance in hiring and promoting minorities is taken into account in determining the amount of his or her year-end bonus.

Fig. 6.2

CLOSE-UP

Following is a summary of federal laws that may influence how an editor carries out the staffing function:

Equal Pay Act of 1963	Prohibits sex as a basis for difference in pay for equal work.
Title VII 1964 Civil Rights Act	Prohibits discrimination based on race, color, sex, or national origin. Applies to private employers of fifteen or more employees.
Age Discrimination in Employment Act of 1967, amended in 1975	Prohibits age discrimination against people between the ages of forty and seventy.

Fig. 6.2, continued

Title I 1968 Civil Rights Act	Prohibits interference with a person's exercise of rights with respect to race, color, religion, sex, or national origin.
Vietnam Era Veterans Readjustment Act of 1974	Prohibits discrimination against disabled veterans and Vietnam-era veterans.
Privacy Act of 1974	Established the right of employees to examine letters of reference concerning them unless the right is waived.
Revised Guidelines on Employee Selection 1976, 1978, and 1979	Established specific rules on employment selection procedures.
Mandatory Retirement Age Act of 1978	Determined that an employee could not be forced to retire before age seventy.
Equal Employment Opportunity Guidelines of 1981	Prohibits sexual harassment when such conduct is an explicit or implicit condition of employment, if the employee's response becomes a basis for employment or promotion decisions, or if it interferes with an employee's performance. The guidelines protect both men and women.

Source: Warren R. Plunkett and Raymond F. Attner, *Introduction to Management* (Boston: Kent, 1983), 245.

DIRECTING

Directing is the function of getting work done by others in pursuit of the newspaper's goals. The editor's role in directing the work of the news staff involves two essential activities: delegation and decision making. These activities recognize that newsroom employees must be managed on an individual basis, that editors must know their subordinates on a personal level, and that the particular style of direction the editor adopts will influence the climate of the newsroom, the productivity, and the potential for motivation.

Delegation

The amount of work editors can accomplish is tied directly to the amount of work they delegate to others. Delegation is a power that enables the editor to multiply his or her abilities many times. In practical terms, delegation means investing another editor with the responsibility to make decisions. An editor is inefficient if he or she is making decisions that other editors are capable of making.

Two types of tasks can be delegated:

1. One is a task that is regularly performed in managing the newsroom; for example, the editor may delegate to the managing editor the responsibility for running the daily news meeting.
2. The other type of task that can be delegated is a special situation that occurs infrequently; for example, the editor may be expected to brief the publisher every morning on the play of stories on page one. This is a routine responsibility for the editor; but if the editor is going out of town for a day, he or she may ask the managing editor to brief the publisher. This is a one-time delegated responsibility that the managing editor surrenders when the editor returns.

The meaning of delegation is best understood when the concept of accountability comes into play. Two sets of mutual and equal responsibilities go with every act of delegation. First, a senior editor delegates a variety of tasks to others. In each case, the subordinate editor is accountable to the delegating editor for successful completion of the assignment. Second, the delegating editor remains accountable to his or her boss for the performance of subordinate editors. For example, the editor can assign responsibility for planning the Sunday paper to the managing editor, but the editor cannot be excused from blame if the managing editor fails to deliver a good product.

It is important to understand that assigning work to a subordinate is only part of the editor's obligation; the other part is the editor's responsibility for the final results. This rule holds true as the duty is delegated down the line. An assignment may go from the editor to the managing editor to the city editor to the assistant city editor. Each of these editors is obligated to his or her superior for the results, but only the top editor is accountable to the publisher.

Accountability can be clearly demonstrated in the case of the newspaper's publisher. The publisher usually is the delegate of a board of directors or a corporate executive. The publisher has the responsibility for increasing advertising and circulation sales and strengthening the news product. In turn, the publisher assigns specific responsibilities to key executives of the newspaper. Advertising performance is delegated to the director of advertising, circulation sales to the director of circulation, and the quality of the news report is the responsibility of the editor. Each of these executives is obligated to produce the results the publisher desires.

However, if the circulation director fails, it is the publisher who is accountable to the board or the corporate officer, not the circulation director. The publisher cannot say of the circulation director, "It's his fault; I'm blameless."

Accountability means the editor cannot safely pass the buck. For the editor who delegates as a way of shirking responsibility, the consequences are clear: Subordinates will develop a distaste for delegation and a lack of respect for the boss. By the same token, delegation is not an invitation to dump unpleasant tasks on others. Undesirable work that has to be delegated will create less resentment if interesting tasks are delegated as well.

How effective the editor is in performing the first task of delegation—setting the action in motion—will be influenced by style. If the editor simply turns a job over to others, the editor's role is reduced to that of an observer. The editor can be a manager only by working through others, only by insuring that subordinates are acting as an extension of the editor, only by staying well informed in order to protect his or her personal accountability and to be certain of the outcome.[11]

Keeping a hand in the work that has been spread among aides

does not mean supervising every detail. Self-discipline and periodic audits will keep the editor a safe distance from the work, but will enable him or her to make timely suggestions and corrections as well as influence the development of subordinates' abilities and talents.

The value of the editor's role as an auditor can be seen in the following steps of delegation:[12]

Previewing direction. The editor gives the managing editor a project: Develop a training program for summer interns. The editor asks for a memo by the end of the week outlining a plan of action. By this process, the editor can elicit the managing editor's interpretation of the assignment. The two can work out a strategy and a detailed plan that can be corrected or adjusted when necessary.

Questioning progress. This is the most informal and the most time-consuming style of delegation, but one that gives the editor the maximum grasp of what is going on. It requires the editor to go to the managing editor at appropriate stages in the development of the project. The editor needs to be deft in timing and to convey an attitude of friendly interest. The appearance of "checking up" is likely to injure the managing editor's self-confidence.

Requiring reports. The editor asks the managing editor to submit periodic memos on the progress of the intern training plan. This can be an efficient method of auditing because it saves time; however, the usefulness of a written update depends on the managing editor's ability to provide a crisp summary of developments reflecting his or her critical judgment of progress based on the measurements agreed upon by the two editors at the beginning of the project. The success of the periodic report will rest on both the managing editor's talents in developing the project and the editor's clarity in putting across the idea from the start.

Scheduling meetings. Setting future dates to review progress injects deadlines into the development of the plan and creates a forum in which corrections and adjustments can be considered.

In the intern training plan, a well-defined chronology may be important. The interns will be on the staff for ten weeks and a schedule of activities—such as a tour of the newspaper, sitting in on major board and council meetings, writing critiques, and meetings with key executives of the newspaper company—requires coordination with many individuals inside and outside the newsroom. Meetings to measure progress against the original plan improve the prospects that the training program will materialize as anticipated.

Setting deadlines. The delegation of a specific assignment should be accompanied by a realistic deadline. The pressure imposed by time—in this case, the arrival of the interns—finally overcomes all other obstacles to completing the project.

Checking results. Once the training of summer interns begins, it is important to audit the progress of the program. The real test here is in the self-discipline of the editor, since progress can best be measured firsthand. It requires the editor to be present during some of the training activities and to display a knack of showing interest, a temperament for making constructive suggestions, and a skill at leaving behind a sense of encouragement.

Assessing results. At the end of the interns' newsroom experience, the editor can begin to prepare for next summer's program by asking the managing editor to write a memo assessing the strengths and weakness of this year's training and suggesting changes or improvements. This will bring the task to an effective close, give the editor an opportunity to evaluate the performance of the managing editor in executing an important job, and prepare the editor for whatever accounting he or she must make to the publisher.

Following these steps of delegation permits freedom of thought and action, encourages development of talents by giving subordinates full and unrestrained authority, and limits the need for interruptions by the delegating editor.

In making a choice of a style of delegation, an editor is weighing time and effort needed to stay on top of a job against the value of a first-rate performance. The key is for the editor to determine when his or her intervention will produce maximum insight into a project.

On a major investigation, the editor may want to be present at the following points:

- developing the idea and assigning preliminary research;
- reviewing initial information and making story assignments, including photography and graphics;
- drafting an outline for what is to be written;
- reviewing the first drafts of the stories;
- preparing publication plans, including editing and packaging; and,
- reading page proofs.

At each of these points, the editor can audit progress and decide what amount of intervention is required. This is not always a harmonious process. What the editor finally chooses to do may be a matter of compromise, a matter of weighing the following considerations in reaching a solution:[13] How important is this job? What are the costs of imperfect final results? How much time or money will it take to make the maximum audit? Do I have this much time? Must I make the time available? Can I interrupt this project to make an evaluation? For how long? How important is the deadline for completion? How much faith do I have in the editor I have assigned to carry out this project?

If the job is so important that the editor cannot risk failure, then of course control is the primary objective. In the editing of a story where libel is a consideration, the involvement of the editor and the newspaper's lawyers is necessary—a time-consuming method of control that may delay publication, but which in the end will be a small price to pay for avoiding a mistake that could result in a libel suit.

A limiting factor in delegation is the exception principle.[14] Routine local news decisions are made by the city editor, but it is understood that when events take an unexpected turn, the managing editor is to be consulted. To make this process effective, the managing editor must make clear what the standard pattern is so that the city editor can recognize the exception when it occurs. This is commonly known as the "no-surprise" rule.

The advantages in effective delegation serve the middle-level and supervisory editors, the staff, and the newspaper company equally well.[15] These advantages can be summed up as follows:

Training and development. The best way of teaching people to handle responsibility is to give them some. Delegation is the path to providing hands-on experience. Responsibility can be delegated in bits, which allows a staffer to learn how to handle a new role in small steps rather than by the sink-or-swim method. The editor should monitor the staffer's performance and increase responsibility according to his or her progress.

Effective training, of course, requires time and can be done successfully only if the editor is willing to invest time by explaining the basic principles of the task, by patiently auditing progress, and by offering feedback. An editor sometimes shuns the chance to train a subordinate on the grounds that "I can do it better myself." Others lack the patience, are poor communicators, or don't understand how people learn. These short-sighted views fail to consider the time that will be saved once the subordinate learns the job.

Time for managing. If the top editor spends too much time on operational tasks—writing headlines or preparing the day's news budget, for example—managerial tasks will be neglected. As a result, the staff will be poorly managed. When the staff is not well managed, the editor continually finds fires to put out—and the more time spent fire fighting, the less time will be spent managing. This becomes a vicious circle, resulting in a crisis style of management. The editor may be flattered to be needed to put out the fires, but crisis management usually is a symptom of poor management. A benefit of being an effective delegator is that the editor will have more time for the management tasks that he or she alone can do or is best suited to do, which ultimately will make the editor a better manager.

Getting the job done better. No matter how strong the editor's operational skills, there are others on the staff who are more talented as copy editors or head writers. Some editors are reluctant to admit this and continue to sit on the rim at deadline. It may satisfy their egos to know they can still write a good headline, but there are broader ramifications. Subordinate editors may resent the idea that the boss doesn't trust them to write the page-one headlines and is, in effect, always looking over their shoulders. The top editor is missing an opportunity to train others to improve their skills.

In some newsroom specialties, such as graphics, subordinates are expected to achieve better results than the boss. Getting the job done better may also mean getting it done differently. No two editors would rework a story or lay out a page the same way, but whether or not this difference matters is closely linked to the editor's leadership style. Some editors equate being different with being wrong or incompetent. Autocratic editors are more likely to have difficulty with this. They have their own way of doing things and expect others to follow their lead. They are more easily disappointed with the work of a subordinate who tries different methods.

Fig. 6.3

CLOSE-UP

As a young managing editor at the *Akron Beacon Journal*, I had a tendency to rewrite major local stories. One afternoon, after reworking a series on county government, I described my feat to the editor, Perry Morgan, a gentle-natured man of the South.

"Why did you do that?" he inquired.

"Well, the series was pretty badly organized and I thought I could do the rewrite better than anyone else."

"You probably can. But that is not what I pay you to do. I pay you to train the reporters to do it right the first time and, when they can't, to train the editors how to fix it. If they come to depend on you to do the rewriting, they'll never learn how to do it right."

Improved communication. Effective delegation requires the editor to give clear instructions to subordinates, specifying what results are desired and what kind of feedback the editor expects. In this way, subordinates are able to learn more about the task and how it relates to the editor's overall objectives for the paper. This process increases the flow of information up and down the chain of command, and can improve the relationship between boss and subordinate. For example, an editor who is delegating the responsibility for closing the first edition fifteen minutes earlier should be prepared to explain why the change may help the circulation department sell more newspapers.

Job satisfaction. Effective delegation can have a positive impact on employee morale and motivation. Opportunities to learn on the job lead to feelings of increased responsibility and involvement. Delegating to a senior member of the copy-desk staff the responsibility for developing a series of advance obituaries on leading citizens—and emphasizing the importance of the assignment—will enhance the copy editor's feelings about the job. It will also provide an opportunity for the copy editor to bring the top editor up-to-date on the project through notes or brief conversations.

Subordinate editors sometimes resist accepting additional responsibility. This could happen because the boss may be one of those editors who makes things easy for subordinates by holding on to tasks that should be delegated to others. In addition to making the subordinate editors' lives easier, the top editor is creating a dependent relationship in which the other editors make the boss feel more important. A comfortable relationship in which there are few demands may seem to be quite satisfying, but in fact, both parties are being harmed. The subordinate editors are not developing properly and the top editor is spending too much time doing what others should be doing. For the top editor, the important distinction is between being helpful and being a crutch.

For some, resisting responsibility is the safest way to avoid punishment. The editor who roars at mistakes and strikes fear in the hearts of subordinates will find few risk takers on the staff.

Making mistakes is part of learning, and effective delegation carries the understanding that errors are human and often lead to greater growth and development in the job. Mistakes should not be ignored, but should be considered opportunities for the editor to teach, to discuss or demonstrate the correct way.

A new assistant city editor, promoted without training and expected to supervise effectively, may resist responsibility. The new editor may have no idea how to carry out delegated tasks. The senior editors may fail to recognize that proper training and information are needed; instead, they will begin to wonder whether they may have made a poor choice. Such an experience can leave the bewildered newcomer with little confidence. Early failure and criticism without training can lead to feelings of inadequacy—an unfortunate situation to which individuals with low self-esteem are particularly vulnerable. In the absence of success, they quickly begin to doubt their ability to do the job.

More experienced subordinates can resist responsibility with the explanation of being "overloaded." A lack of enthusiasm for additional tasks should prompt the editor to find out whether the subordinate actually is overloaded or a poor manager of time who needs help organizing his or her tasks.

Fig. 6.4

CLOSE-UP

In a survey of one hundred employees in various work settings, Robert Maidment, a professor of educational planning at the College of William and Mary, developed a list of insightful observations about delegation. Two of Maidment's comments seem to have particular application to the newsroom.

What does it mean when my boss doesn't select me for a particular job that I'm clearly qualified to do?

"Many supervisors and managers avoid delegating tasks because of a fear that the employee will perform the work better or that the subordinate will make a mistake or that some control over the employee will be lost or that prestige will be diminished or even that others

Fig. 6.4, continued

will think the boss isn't busy enough to justify his or her continued presence."

I've always wanted to ask my boss why he asks me to draft a set of recommendations and then completely ignores them.

"Nowhere is it written that a boss must act on a subordinate's advice. If, however, the task were assigned as busy work, the boss has no one to blame but himself or herself if the next delegated task is performed less enthusiastically or, worse, less competently. Even when a boss wants to compare his or her thinking on an issue with the employee, the issue of trust demands up-front clarification. If a manager has asked a subordinate for advice, it is important for that manager to explain why he or she has taken another approach to the problem, if that's the case."

Source: Robert Maidment, "Ten Reasons Why Managers Need to Know More about Delegation," *Supervisory Management*, August 1984, 8–10.

Following are guidelines for editors to consider in developing their own delegating styles:[16]

- Specify the results expected.
- Explain why you are delegating.
- Give the necessary authority to carry out the task.
- Let others know of the delegation.
- Display confidence in your subordinates.
- Delegate important tasks as well as trivial ones that have to be done.
- Set high standards, but don't expect that your subordinates will always do the task as well as you.
- Invite the participation of others in the delegation process. Don't be autocratic in your delegation style by simply ordering others to do things.
- Audit the work thoughtfully, but avoid the temptation to check up constantly to see how things are going.

- Be perceptive about the workload of your subordinates and avoid giving them responsibility for too much.
- Give credit for results achieved by subordinates.

Decision Making

In addition to delegating, making decisions is one of the editor's primary directing responsibilities. A decision is rarely a choice between right and wrong or good and bad. It may be a choice between "almost right" and "probably wrong." More often, a decision is a choice between two courses of action, neither of which is provably more nearly right than the other.[17]

An editor's approach to making a decision is not unlike that of a reporter working with a story idea. The germ of many stories is an opinion that an event or a situation is newsworthy. It is an untested hypothesis. The reporter tests the hypothesis by looking for facts and by seeking opinions and observations from sources. If the results of the reporter's work fit the hypothesis, there is a story. The angle the reporter comes up with may not match the hypothesis, but there is still a story, and often a better one than the original assignment suggested.

As in the genesis of a story, a decision begins with opinions, with untested hypotheses rather than facts. The editor's understanding of a problem and the choice to be made is enhanced by a diversity of opinions and a clash of ideas. Thoughtful comments from colleagues will help the editor discern all of the pertinent facts. Decisions facing a top editor are not made by acclamation; rather, the editor makes a decision after identifying several options from which to choose. If an editor fails to consider alternatives, this may suggest a closed mind.

The first rule of decision making is that one does not make a decision unless a disagreement exists. Alfred P. Sloan, Jr., longtime chairman of General Motors, is reported to have said at a meeting of GM executives, "Gentlemen, I take it we are all in complete agreement on the decision here." Everyone around the table nodded assent. "Then," Sloan continued, "I propose we postpone further discussion of this matter until our next meeting to give ourselves time to develop disagreement and perhaps gain some understanding of what the decision is all about."[18]

Disagreement simply provides the editor with two or more alternatives from which to choose. However, the choice will not be a decision unless there is an uncertainty about the course of action. If a decision is based on complete and full understanding of the alternatives, the choice will be obvious.

Making decisions means using judgment. In handling the news, this is called critical judgment. Its ingredients are intuition, experience, a strong sense of events, and a concern for fairness and balance. Editors use critical judgment to reduce to a manageable level uncertainty about the relative value of news stories. Given a blank news page and a budget, a dozen news editors would lay out a dozen different pages. Some stories might show up on every page, but many would not. These differences are the result of each editor's unique combination of the ingredients comprising critical judgment.

Inherent to the news editor's job is seldom having all the information necessary to make decisions about what goes on page one. Success in making a good call routinely depends on the intangibles of experience and intuition.

Decisions based on a full slate of information are called computational decisions.[19] Many of the decisions made at the supervisory level in the newsroom fit this description. The decision on how many columns of news will be in tomorrow's newspaper is controlled by a budget. The editor may decide to increase the size of the paper to handle a major story, but that decision is controlled by the knowledge that the paper can go up only in two- or four-page increments.

We can compute travel budgets, headline sizes, meeting times, and other elements of the news operation to reduce the number of unknown and uncontrollable factors. They present us with a set of fixed alternatives, which results in a programmed decision.[20]

The city editor supervising a group of reporters will give them a set of programmed decisions when covering the news, with freedom to chose among them. For example, the following are standard alternatives available to reporters:

- Cover the event firsthand.
- Interview participants and observers in person.
- Talk to participants and observers by telephone.
- Take information from a participant who wishes to remain anonymous.
- Obtain documents containing information about the event.

The editor typically allows the reporter to make decisions within these guidelines. The reporter has the freedom to suggest what kinds of information should be included and the order in which it should be organized in the story.

The editor sets the tone and focus for the newspaper, decides who will fill key editing slots, what wire services to buy, and how the operating budget will be used. These are unprogrammed decisions that will weigh heavily in shaping the character and the personality of the paper. The editor's judgment, of course, is controlled by the goals and objectives of the newspaper organization and by the legal constraints of libel and equal opportunity. Still, the editor's burden of making good choices on high-risk issues is great and explains, in part, why editors are paid more than city editors.

All decisions are made with some emotion. Programmed decisions, with all the facts available, are made more rationally than unprogrammed decisions where values and feelings are likely to come into play. Ideally, every decision reflects a blend of rational thinking and emotion.

However, a decision born of strong anger or disappointment often is an unwise decision. If the editor is upset by a sharply critical memo from the publisher, he or she should be cautious about rushing off to confront the publisher or going immediately to the typewriter to compose a vigorous reply. In this situation, applying the "hold-it" rule is the better part of valor. Better that the editor investigate the publisher's complaint, sleep on the information, and reply the next day. That is a good way of avoiding a decision the editor likely will regret later.

An issue that is always present for editors is the extent to which they should allow their associates to participate in decision making. Participation represents one method of decentralizing authority and influence throughout an organization. It is believed that participation can lead to improved decision quality, increased commitment of members to decision outcomes, and increased satisfaction resulting from involvement.[21]

The daily news meeting is an example of how an editor invites subordinates to participate in decision making. Rare is the editor who will read all the news budgets and dictate the content and display of each section in the paper. The spirit of the news meeting is that the editor trusts each subordinate to be on top of the news and to help decide the content mix through discussion, give-and-take, and compromise.

Research evidence supports the idea that managers invite more participation when the stakes are high and acceptance of the decision by subordinates is critical. Participation also is encouraged by relationships built on trust and where there is minimal conflict among subordinates. However, managers are less likely to include others when all the information to make a high-quality decision is present. Managers also tend to make decisions alone when the problem is well structured, when a solution is available that has been successful in the past, or when time is limited and immediate action is required.[22]

Other investigations have developed support for the belief that participative decision making contributes to greater satisfaction and cooperation, and less turnover, absenteeism, and job-related stress.[23]

Participation works because it clarifies the organization's needs and gives employees a fuller understanding of what is expected of them. It increases the probability that employees will work for rewards and outcomes they value. And it gives employees the feeling that they have more control over their own work.[24]

A decision is not a decision unless some action results; up to that point, it is at best a good intention. Peter F. Drucker, author of many books on management, suggests six steps to the decision-making process:[25]

1. Classify the problem. Is it a generic problem or a stray event? The answer to a fundamental problem has to be sought

through a rule, a principle, a procedure. The truly exceptional event can be handled only as it occurs. Planning coverage of the county budget hearing is a generic problem. Planning coverage of a one hundred–year flood is a unique event.

2. Define the problem. Once the problem has been classified as generic or unique, it is fairly easy to define what is pertinent or critical about the situation. If the definition is incorrect or incomplete, it will set in motion a series of actions that will produce a predictably wrong answer. Checking the definition against all available facts is the best safeguard.

3. Specify what the decision has to accomplish. Every decision has minimum goals, objectives, or conditions to satisfy. The boundaries of these specifications can shift as the nature of the problem changes. Newsroom copy-flow deadlines are the result of generic decisions aimed at satisfying the need to start the presses on time. If the computer fails and it is impossible to set type, the boundaries change. The goal then becomes one of devising a way to get the paper published, even if it is late coming off the press.

4. Seek a decision that is "right" rather than one that is "acceptable." A decision is typically the result of a compromise. The editor can distinguish between the right compromise and the wrong compromise by understanding how the specific boundaries might have changed. In an emergency created by a computer crash, the editor who recognizes that the goal is to publish the paper may agree to reduce the number of sections from four to two and print an edition carrying only the stories that had been set at the time the computer failed. That is a compromise—a right compromise—that gives up the editor's standing objective of a four-section paper containing the latest news, but protects the publisher's goal of delivering a newspaper to readers.

5. Build in the action to carry out the decision. Converting a decision to effective action usually is the most difficult and time-consuming part of the process, yet a decision will not become effective unless an action component is built in from the start. Using the above example, if the editor is in the

process of issuing instructions for restructuring the paper at the instant the computer is restarted, the staff will instantly go back to editing the paper under normal procedures. The decision to cut back the paper is not now a decision; it was only a good intention.

Converting a decision into action requires answering several questions: Who has to know of the decision? What action has to be taken? Who is to take it? The action commitment becomes doubly important when staffers have to change behavior, habits, or attitudes. The editor must make sure not only that the responsibility for action is clearly assigned, but also that the staffers assigned are capable of carrying out the work.

6. Elicit feedback to test the validity and effectiveness of the decision against the course of events. Reports, figures, and studies are the traditional ways editors test their decisions. This feedback enables the editor to measure the actual results against what he or she expected to happen.

Decisions are made by humans. They are, at best, fallible. Most decisions do not have long lives. The probability is high that the best decisions may be wrong and that the most effective ones eventually will become obsolete.

CONTROLLING

The last of the five management functions is controlling. This is the process by which the editor monitors each of the other functions of management. Without effective control systems, the editor may have little success in keeping the other goals of the news staff on target.

For the editor, the process of creating a control process is straightforward: The first step is to establish standards against which performance is to be measured; the second step is to measure performance against the standards; and the third step is to take action to correct performance that falls short of the standards. This is the heart of the performance-review process, which will be described in Chapter 10.

The editor can use a variety of controls in managing the news staff:

Prevention controls. This is another name for the job descriptions that exist for all newsroom jobs. The city editor's job description, for example, describes the work to be done, the authority, and the span of control, and clarifies the city editor's position in the newsroom hierarchy. Job descriptions help prevent duplication of effort and potential organizational conflict.

Diagnostic controls. A diagnostic control tells the editor what has gone wrong, but not why. The headline-count feature in the electronic editing system is a diagnostic control that shows the copy editor if the headline will fit. The monthly budget report is a diagnostic control that tells the editor how newsroom spending has deviated from the budget plan.

Feedback controls. Assessing a completed project so that lessons learned can be applied to similar tasks in the future is a feedback control. For example, the editor will ask the staff to help evaluate the newspaper's coverage of a local airplane crash. Though the feedback session cannot affect that story because it has already been published, it will help the staff be prepared to cover the next air disaster more effectively.

Generally, controls work only if the staff wants them to. The staff must be satisfied that the controls are fair and contribute to getting the work done. Too many controls or those that appear to be arbitrary can lead to frustration and a lack of motivation. A chief news executive who insists on approving—and often rewriting—every page-one headline is establishing a control that may be seen as unnecessary and unfair.

The news staff has a number of critical control points. In a way, each serves as a funnel to assure efficiency and quality in the flow of the news. All national and international news, for example, is screened and sorted by the wire editor. This is a critical control point that permits the wire editor to prepare for the news editor a manageable selection of top stories for the paper. Another control point is the slot on the copy desk through which all copy flows on its way to the typesetter. The editor in the slot cannot allow stories to become backlogged without risking a late press start. An editor looking for the cause of missed deadlines will focus on these critical control points where failure cannot be tolerated.

If the staff is not getting copy to the composing room on time, the editor will look for new or additional controls to solve the problem. If the slot editor is working effectively but the volume of copy reaching this control point on deadline is too great, the editor must weigh the cost of additional controls against the benefits they may deliver. For example, if the editor tells reporters to get their copy to the desk fifteen minutes earlier, some of the reporters may have to start earlier and thus require overtime for assignments later in the day. The editor then will have to decide whether the expense of additional overtime is justified by the need to get the paper out on time or whether a less costly way to solve the problem must be found.

The editor may discover that lack of information is one of the reasons the control point at the copy desk slot is not working well. Story lengths assigned by the news editor are not being passed on to the copy editors, so stories are coming to the slot editor longer than the space that has been budgeted for them. The slot editor cuts some of the stories and sends the rest back to the rim for trimming. The result is that the copy flow is slow. Recognizing that as the problem, the editor can tighten controls for assigned story length.

Good controls rely on information that is timely as well as accurate. A significant story breaking on edition time means that the editors have only a few minutes to decide whether to hold the presses or increase the press run. The editor making these decisions needs to get from his or her subordinates a succinct description of the story and an accurate update on the effect of holding the edition for ten minutes.

Controls are more effectively implemented on smaller newspapers than on papers with several management layers where the flow of authority is complex or overlapping. One control should not lead to another; rather, the idea is to refine the various control procedures to reduce complexity, confusion, and duplication of effort.

CHAPTER SUMMARY

There are five basic roles of management: (1) planning, (2) organizing, (3) staffing, (4) directing, and (5) controlling. Each of these roles plays a significant part in the management of the newsroom.

As a planner, the editor channels creative energy and practical judgment into looking ahead. The plan he or she creates sets the foundation for all that follows. Strategic planning involves long-range goals and a course of action to achieve those goals. Tactical plans center on short-term goals and often are the action agendas that help the newspaper achieve its strategic plans.

The operating budget is a valuable planning tool that helps editors make the most effective use of the dollars available to them.

Obstacles to planning can be overcome by relying on four principles: (1) plans should be realistic, (2) plans should be specific, (3) plans should have a deadline, and (4) others on the staff should participate in planning.

Organizing links the authority of the editors to the work that must be done. It involves determining what has to be done, classifying the work, assigning the tasks and delegating the authority, and creating relationships for decision making. Line authority describes the traditional relationship in the newsroom organization in which authority flows down through the levels of management. Staff authority is advisory, generally involving a specialist who advises the editor on administrative or budgetary matters.

People are the most important resource in the newsroom; thus, an editor's skill at staffing has a significant impact. Getting the right person in the right job is crucial to developing the long-range character of the newspaper. Staffing involves several steps: human resource planning, recruitment, selection, orientation, training and development, performance appraisals, and employment decisions. Many decisions about staffing are influenced by federal Equal Employment Opportunity laws.

Directing as a management role has two distinct activities: delegation and decision making. The editor's skill in delegating work to others influences the amount of work he or she is able to do. As an effective delegator, the editor will consider the following steps in assigning work and auditing performance: previewing direction, questioning progress, requiring reports, scheduling meetings to review the work, setting deadlines, and checking and assessing results. Decision making, one of the editor's primary responsibilities, is not a matter of choosing right from wrong, but of making a rational choice among alternatives.

Controlling requires editors to set standards for performance, measure performance against those standards, and follow up with actions that will correct deviations from the standards. In order to be effective, controls need to be accepted by the staff. They must also be accurate, timely, and easily understood, and they should focus on the critical control points of the newsroom.

NOTES

1. Peter F. Drucker, *Management* (New York: Harper & Row, 1974), 398–99.
2. Ibid., 399.
3. Warren R. Plunkett and Raymond F. Attner, *Introduction to Management* (Boston: Kent, 1983), 98–99.
4. Drucker, *Management,* 125–26.
5. Ibid., 123–24.
6. Plunkett and Attner, *Introduction to Management,* 102–4.
7. Ibid., 176–77.
8. Ibid., 178–79.
9. Ibid., 240–42.
10. James Ledvinka and Robert Gatewood, "EEO Issues with Preemployment Inquiries," *The Personnel Administrator* 22 (February 1977): 22–26.
11. James C. Harrison, Jr., "How to Stay on Top of the Job," in *Executive Success: Making It in Management* (New York: John Wiley & Sons, 1983), 440.
12. Ibid., 442–43.
13. Ibid., 447–48.
14. Jerry L. Gray, *Supervision* (Boston: Kent, 1984), 356.
15. Ibid., 358–59.
16. Ibid., 366.
17. Drucker, *Management,* 470.
18. Ibid., 472.

19. Gray, *Supervision*, 380–81.
20. Ibid., 382–83.
21. Richard M. Steers, *Introduction to Organizational Behavior*, 2d ed. (Glenview, Ill.: Scott, Foresman, 1984), 286–87.
22. Victor H. Vroom and Philip W. Yetton, *Leadership and Decision Making* (Pittsburgh: University of Pittsburgh Press, 1973), 10–31.
23. Steers, *Introduction to Organizational Behavior*, 286.
24. Ronald J. Ebert and Terence R. Mitchell, *Organizational Decision Processes: Concepts and Analysis* (New York: Crance, Russak, 1975), 262–63.
25. Peter F. Drucker, "The Effective Decision," in *Executive Success: Making It in Management* (New York: John Wiley & Sons, 1983), 464–75.

7

Leadership and Power

Leadership is the third function of management. Combined with supervising and managing, it completes the newsroom management structure. Leadership and management are not synonymous, but without leadership skills, managers cannot function effectively. Knowledge of the principles of leadership and its companion—power—is essential to the editor's understanding of the entire management process.

THE NATURE OF LEADERSHIP

What is leadership? Some see leadership as an enigmatic quality that is associated only with great people involved in the drama of power and politics. Such a view of leadership contrasts sharply with the mundane, practical, yet important realization that leadership is really influencing work that other people do.[1]

Thus, a basic definition of leadership is: influencing others to achieve willingly rather than because they are required to or because they fear the consequences of failing to achieve.

Following are other definitions of leadership:

"Leadership is interpersonal influence exercised in a situation and directed, through the communication process, toward the attainment of a specialized goal or goals."[2]

"Leadership is influencing people to follow in the achievement of a common goal."[3]

"Leadership is the relationship in which one person, or the leader, influences others to work together willingly on related tasks to attain that which the leader desires."[4]

"[Leadership is] the influential increment over and above mechanical compliance with routine directives of the organization."[5]

The distinction between management and leadership is significant. Management is working with and through others to accomplish organizational goals, while the broader concept of leadership involves using influence to establish an atmosphere conducive to achievement. Some editors who are skilled at carrying out the management roles of planning, organizing, staffing, directing, and controlling may lack the ability to influence the staff toward strong performance. Among the ranks of reporters, copy editors, artists, and photographers are individuals whose leadership qualities are easily recognized. Although their roles are informal, they are clearly successful in influencing their peers in the work group and, sometimes, the management of the newspaper.

The work of Peter Senge, assistant professor of management at Massachusetts Institute of Technology, focuses on the ability of leaders to create a vision. A true leader creates a vision, communicates that vision in such a way that others will make a commitment to it, maintains the course when obstacles arise, and designs the organizational structure to focus the efforts of employees toward accomplishing the vision.[6]

Fig. 7.1

CLOSE-UP

In their best-selling book, *In Search of Excellence*, authors Thomas J. Peters and Robert H. Waterman, Jr., characterized leadership this way:

"Leadership is many things. It is patient, usually boring coalition building. It is the purposeful seeding of cabals that one hopes will result in the appropriate ferment in the bowels of the organization. It is meticulously shifting the attention of the institution through the mundane language of management systems. It is altering agendas so that new priorities get enough attention. It is being visible when things are going awry, and invisible when they are working well. It's building a loyal team at the top that speaks more or less with one voice. It's listening carefully much of the time, frequently speaking with encouragement, and reinforcing words with believable action. It's being tough when necessary, and it's the occasional use of naked power—or the 'subtle accumulation of nuances, a hundred things done a little better,' as Henry Kissinger once put it."

Source: Thomas J. Peters and Robert H. Waterman, Jr., *In Search of Excellence* (New York: Harper & Row, 1982), 82.

In any discussion of leadership, the question is raised whether leaders are born or made. Classic research in 1948 that attempted to determine whether leaders' traits are inborn identified three characteristics generally thought then to be found in leaders:[7]

1. Height. Leaders tended to be taller than average.

2. Intelligence. Leaders tended to be rated higher on IQ tests, verbal fluency, overall knowledge, originality, and insight.

3. Initiative. Leaders tended to show high levels of energy, ambition, and persistence.

The research found no clear relationship between leader success and characteristics such as emotional stability or extraversion. Inherent personal qualities, such as intelligence, were thought to be transferable from one situation to another. Because all individuals did not have high intelligence or initiative or other leader qualities, only those who possessed these attributes were considered potential leaders. Thus, the leader-is-born idea, when carried to its logical conclusion, discounted the value of training individuals to assume leadership positions.[8]

The trait approach to leadership, which was studied for fifty years, ultimately failed to produce one personality trait or set of qualities that could be used to differentiate between leaders and nonleaders.[9] Research emphasis shifted in the early 1950s toward the idea that leadership is a dynamic process that changes from situation to situation. Studies at the University of Michigan and Ohio State University led to similar conclusions: Effective leader behavior was found to be multidimensional, suggesting that effective leaders exhibit different behavior in different situations.

The studies at Ohio State used the Leader Behavior Description Questionnaire to describe how leaders carry out their activities. As the data were analyzed, two distinct behaviors emerged:[10]

1. *Consideration.* Behavior that reflects friendship, mutual trust, respect, and warmth in the relationship between leaders and followers.

2. *Initiating structure.* Behavior that centers on establishing well-defined rules and procedures, patterns of organization, and channels of communication.

As they studied leader behavior, the Ohio State researchers concluded that these two behaviors—consideration and initiating structure—were separate and distinct, and that the behavior of a leader could be a mix of both. In other words, the leader who found time to listen, who was willing to make changes, and who was friendly and approachable (consideration) also could be effective in assigning tasks, asking workers to follow standards and rules, and telling them what is expected of them (initiating structure).

In the 1920s and early 1930s, a popular theory emerged that *authoritarian leaders* were concerned with tasks while *democratic leaders* were concerned with relationships; that is, leaders influence their subordinates in one of two ways: They can tell their subordinates what to do and how to do it, or they can share their leadership responsibilities with subordinates by involving them in the planning and execution of the task. These ideas were linked to Douglas McGregor's Theory X and Theory Y (see Chapter 3). The authoritative leader's behavior was based on the assumption that the power of leaders is derived from the position they occupy and that people are innately lazy and unreliable (Theory X). The democratic style assumed that the power of leaders is granted by the group and that people can be basically self-directed and creative at work if properly motivated (Theory Y).[11]

Fig. 7.2

CLOSE-UP

Robert Tannenbaum of the University of California at Los Angeles and Warren H. Schmidt of the University of Southern California showed that a broad range of leader styles can be found between the authoritarian leader at one end of the spectrum and the democratic leader at the other.

They noted that the manager often is in an uncomfortable state of mind, not quite sure how to behave. There are times when the manager is torn between exerting "strong" leadership and "permissive" leadership. Sometimes new knowledge pushes the manager in

Three Categories of Leadership Behavior

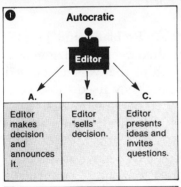
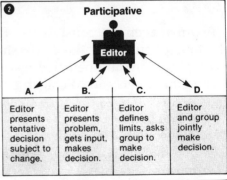

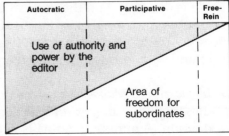

Fig. 7.2, continued

one direction while experience pushes in another direction. The manager is not sure whether inviting a group decision is really appropriate or merely a device for avoiding his or her own decision-making responsibility.

The illustration titled "Three Categories of Leadership Behavior" shows the range of leadership behaviors available to managers, as identified by Tannenbaum and Schmidt. Each type of action is related to the degree of authority exerted by the boss and to the amount of freedom available to subordinates in reaching decisions. The actions shown on the extreme left in the diagram characterize the manager who maintains a high degree of control, while those shown on the extreme right characterize the manager who releases a high degree of control.

This model of leadership behavior illustrates how the editor's role changes when using autocratic, participative, or free-reign leadership behavior.

Source: Robert Tannenbaum and Warren H. Schmidt, "How to Choose a Leadership Pattern," *Harvard Business Review,* May–June 1973, 163.

MANAGERIAL GRID

Two management consultants, Robert R. Blake and Jane S. Mouton, popularized the leadership theory emphasizing task accomplishment and personal relationships that was developed in the Ohio State and Michigan studies. They used those concepts in their managerial grid, an idea that became the basis for a best-selling book and for the teaching of leadership in management development programs.[12]

On the managerial grid, five management behaviors are plotted from the interplay of tasks and relationships. Concern for people is illustrated on the vertical axis and concern for production on the horizontal axis. Five different styles are on the grid, one style positioned in each quadrant and a fifth in the center. Blake and Mouton describe the managerial behaviors this way:

1. *Impoverished Management–1,1. (lower left)* This represents a dissatisfied manager with little concern for people or production. A minimum effort is necessary to keep the managerial job. In the case of a newspaper editor employing this

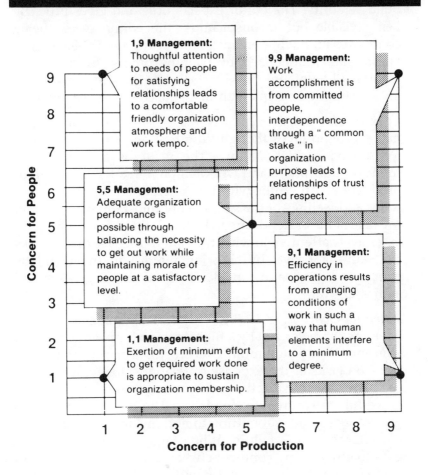

Fig. 7.3.

The managerial grid plots five management behaviors according to the individual manager's concern for people and concern for production.

Source: Adapted from Robert R. Blake and Jane S. Mouton, *The New Managerial Grid* (Houston: Gulf Publishing, 1978).

style, the key motivation is to stay in the system and not "rock the boat" by doing enough to preserve the job and build seniority. The editor expects little and gives little. By being visible but inconspicuous, the editor avoids being controversial, having enemies, or getting fired. Mistakes or failures are rationalized by blaming others. By not being emotionally entangled with tasks or people, the editor avoids coming to grips with inadequacies and inabilities.

2. *Country Club Management–1,9. (upper left)* This represents a manager who gives thoughtful attention to people's needs for satisfying relationships. The result is a comfortable, friendly atmosphere and work tempo, but a low concern for production. An editor with this orientation thinks the attitudes and feelings of the staff are of utmost importance, and because of his or her desire to be liked, the editor tends to be excessively attentive to what the staff thinks. He or she seeks the staff's approval by showing interest in them and by being good, kind, and considerate. The editor's greatest fear is disapproval.

3. *Authority-Obedience–9,1. (lower right)* This management behavior is characterized by a high concern for production and efficiency, but a minimum concern for workers. Managers focus on tasks at the expense of relationships with employees. An editor with this orientation would strive to be powerful, to control, to dominate. The editor is driven to win, to master all, submitting to nothing and no one. His or her greatest fear is failure. When failure occurs, the blame goes to others. Any conflict between people and production is resolved at the expense of people. Such an editor affirms McGregor's Theory X.

4. *Organization Man Management–5,5. (middle point)* The manager who takes this middle-of-the-road position places a moderate emphasis on concern for production and people. The lack of a strong commitment to either results in adequate production and satisfactory levels of morale. This editor wants to look good and to be "in" with the staff. Being popular means taking on characteristics, including whatever

is fashionable or trendy, that will make friends. The editor is superficial in his or her own convictions and is cautious to avoid self-exposure. Prevailing opinions become the opinions of this editor. The ability to back and fill, to shift, to twist and turn and yet stay with the the majority is important. The editor wants to avoid looking bad, and when unsuccessful, he or she experiences shame. The fear of being excluded by colleagues can cause anxiety.

5. *Team Management–9,9. (upper right)* This represents the manager with high concern for both production and people. Work is accomplished by committed people whose belief in a common stake in the organization leads to relationships based on trust and respect. An editor with this orientation desires to make a contribution to corporate success, coupled with the commitment to involve others. These values promote voluntarism, spontaneity, openness, and responsibility shared with others in accomplishing clear and challenging goals. For the editor, a sense of gratification, enthusiasm, and excitement results from making an important contribution. In failure, the editor is likely to feel self-defeat, disappointment, and discouragement. He or she may be disturbed or uneasy, faced with self-doubt about his or her capacity to meet future problems successfully.

Blake and Mouton say that a number of conditions can influence which managerial style will become dominant: the company in which the editor is employed, the particular situation the editor has to deal with, the editor's values about working with people or getting results, and the editor's personality. Thus, editors may have a managerial style that is consistent for most situations, but they also can move to a backup style if a situation demands it. For example, an editor who uses logic and reason (9,9) with a reporter who makes repeated errors of fact may decide to get tough and demand an improvement in accuracy (9,1).

In spite of the need to adopt a backup strategy occasionally, Blake and Mouton argue that there is "one best way" to manage—team management (9,9). They contend that the pragmatic concepts of leadership stressing flexibility to deal with different situations result in little more than "seat-of-the-pants management."

CONTINGENCY THEORY

A popular contemporary theory dealing with the tendency of leaders to adapt to situations was advanced in 1967 by Fred Fiedler at the University of Illinois. In his contingency theory, Fiedler challenged the idea of a "best" style of leadership, proposing instead that leadership involves selecting the most effective style for a particular situation.

Fiedler identified three factors that characterize any situation in which a leader operates:[13]

1. *Leader-member relations.* The degree to which the leader is accepted by the group. This is measured in respect, confidence, and trust. An editor who is highly rated in these areas should be able to exercise influence over subordinates.
2. *Task structure.* The nature of the work. A structured job is one in which everyone knows precisely what to do. An unstructured job would have complexity, variety, and room for creativity. If extreme examples of a structured job would be an assembly-line worker and an unstructured job a research scientist, the variety of tasks performed by newspaper journalists could be plotted at a number of points on the task-structure spectrum.
3. *Position power.* The power base from which the manager operates. In the newsroom, the editor has the strongest power base. He or she possesses a great capacity to use rewards and punishments. In contrast, the range of power held by a first-level supervisor such as an assistant city editor is limited, for example, by the lack of authority to reward and punish staffers.

An example of the Fiedler model would suggest that in a newsroom where the editor is trusted and respected and the task structure is moderate, the editor is in a position to be an effective leader. This capacity for leadership exists because everyone knows what to do, yet there is an abundance of variety and room for creativity, and the editor's position gives him or her the power to hire, fire, promote, and give pay increases.

PATH-GOAL THEORY

The path-goal theory of leadership is concerned with ways in which a leader can influence a subordinate's motivation, goals, and attempts at achievement. It suggests that a leadership style is effective or ineffective on the basis of how the leader influences the work goals or rewards of subordinates and the paths that lead to successful goal accomplishment.[14]

To understand the path-goal theory, we need to recall the expectancy theory of motivation (introduced in Chapter 3) in which a staffer's motivation is influenced by the importance of the reward, the possibility that the desired outcome can be accomplished by performance, and how much effort is required to achieve the reward. The path-goal theory contends that a leader can influence these perceptions of rewards and can clarify what employees have to do to achieve the rewards.

Robert J. House, who advanced the path-goal theory, proposed that if subordinates are performing highly structured tasks, the leader will be most effective by building a relationship that is supportive and by not emphasizing guidance and direction. This is based on the conclusion that routine tasks are inherently less satisfying and a source of frustration and stress for subordinates.[15] A supportive editor might introduce an important dimension in the work life of staffers doing routine tasks. The more highly structured tasks in the newsroom that might suggest this approach to leadership are copy editing, night rewrite, and the preparation of calendars and sports agate pages; for example, the reporter handling night rewrite might be assigned a special reporting project.

For staffers such as beat reporters who perform relatively unstructured tasks, the path-goal theory proposes a leadership style that is high on task behavior and low on relationship behavior. The unstructured nature of reporting, for instance, may be more satisfying to some than the structured work of copy editing because the changing nature of the news adds a variety to the work of reporters that copy editors typically don't have. Therefore, editors would be inclined to give a copy editor a pat on the back while exhibiting more direct behavior in guiding a reporter's activities.

House and a colleague, Terence R. Mitchell, advanced the idea that subordinates are motivated by the leader's behavior. In this way, the leader is able to influence a staffer's perception that a goal is attractive and point out the paths available to reach goals.[16] The path-goal theory is summed up in two points:

1. Leader behavior is acceptable and satisfying to staffers to the extent that they view such behavior as either an immediate source of satisfaction or the path to future satisfaction.

2. Leader behavior will improve staffers' efforts if it links effective performance with what gives them satisfaction and if the leader is supportive of their efforts to achieve goals.

The editor adopting a path-goal style of leadership would, for example, link performance reviews with merit pay and promotions, thus demonstrating to the staff how performance can be instrumental in achieving desired rewards.

SITUATIONAL LEADERSHIP

Up to this point, leadership theory and research have not been very helpful to practitioners. The material is difficult to understand and much of it is impractical for the modern manager. For the most part, it suggests that there is no magical formula for leaders.

Research in leadership has moved toward the idea that each situation is different and, to be effective, a leader must be able to diagnose situations sensitively and then adapt his or her behavior. Situational leadership was developed in the 1970s by Paul Hersey and Kenneth H. Blanchard and is used for manager training at the Center for Leadership Studies in Escondido, California.

Following are some definitions that are at the core of situational leadership:[17]

Task behavior. The extent to which the leader engages in guidance and direction, spelling out the duties and responsibilities of an individual or group. This includes telling people what to do, how to do it, when to do it, where to do it, and who is to do it.

Relationship behavior. The extent to which the leader engages in communication with one or more people. This includes listening, encouraging, facilitating, providing clarification, and giving emotional support.

Readiness. How well a person performs a particular task. Readiness, or maturity, depends on the knowledge, experience, and skill a person brings to the job, and his or her confidence, commitment, and motivation to accomplish a task. In assessing readiness, the leader is dealing with demonstrated ability and willingness, not potential.

Leadership Styles

The emphasis in situational leadership is on the behavior of the leader in relation to subordinates. What is important is how the editor appears in the eyes of the staffers. The editor may think of himself or herself as caring and sensitive, but if the editor is perceived by others as tough and dictatorial, that perception is the one that will affect staff behavior. How the leader is seen by others is known as leadership style.

A variety of leadership styles is needed to adapt to the different situations or problems a leader encounters. Managers use both task behavior and relationship behavior to influence their subordinates.

Four leadership styles are found in the situational leadership model, shown here in a quadrant:[18]

Leader Behavior

PROVIDING SUPPORTIVE BEHAVIOR → Relationship Behavior (Low to High)
PROVIDING DIRECTIVE BEHAVIOR → Task Behavior (Low to High)

③ Share ideas and facilitate in making decisions...
High Relationship / Low Task

② Explain your decisions and provide opportunity for clarification...
High Task / High Relationship

④ Turn over responsibility for decisions and implementation...
Low Relationship / Low Task

① Provide specific instructions and closely supervise performance...
High Task / Low Relationship

Fig. 7.4.

The definitions in this grid, developed by Paul Hersey and Kenneth H. Blanchard, are at the heart of understanding situational leadership.

Source: Adapted from Paul Hersey and Kenneth H. Blanchard, *Management of Organizational Behavior*, 4th ed. (Englewood Cliffs, N.J.: Prentice-Hall, 1982).

1. *Style 1.* This leadership style is characterized by above-average amounts of guidance and direction and below-average amounts of relationship behavior.

   Newsroom example: The city editor takes control of the newsgathering following a plane crash at the airport. The first-edition deadline is thirty minutes away and there is little time to explain instructions or ask reporters whether they have questions. The city editor is very directive. Instructions are issued without explanation. Copy is edited briskly, with no time for discussion about the lead or the writing style. A Style 1 editor tells individual reporters or the staff what to do, when, where, how, and with whom to do it.

2. *Style 2.* This leadership style is characterized by above-average amounts of both task and relationship behavior.

   Newsroom example: The city editor is sending a reporter to the state capital to do a special report on mental health. Before the reporter leaves, the city editor explains the assignment. The editor suggests several angles to be developed and gives the reporter the names of agencies to be visited and officials to be interviewed. The reporter asks several questions and, by the time the meeting ends, has clarified most of the uncertainties about the assignment. A Style 2 editor provides guidance and direction, but also offers opportunities for explanation and clarification.

3. *Style 3.* This leadership style is characterized by above-average amounts of relationship behavior and below-average amounts of task behavior.

   Newsroom example: A new reporter is going out on her first major assignment. The city editor is confident she will do well and spends a few minutes talking with the reporter and offering encouragement before she leaves the building. The reporter asks the editor for suggestions. The editor replies, "Just do your best." After the reporter has written the story, the city editor goes over the experience with her, providing an opportunity for discussion. The Style 3 editor offers encouragement and promotes discussion, but does not provide direction or make decisions.

4. *Style 4.* This leadership style is characterized by below-average amounts of both task behavior and relationship behavior.

Newsroom example: A new copy editor is having trouble learning the codes for fitting and setting headlines on the electronic editing system. He asks the slot editor for help, but the slot editor says he can't take the time. The copy editor continues to struggle and eventually becomes frustrated. The slot editor ignores the copy editor's pleas for help. The Style 4 editor provides little direction and low amounts of communication and supportive behavior.

Readiness or Maturity Levels

The editor's choice of a leadership style is influenced by the readiness or maturity of the staffer. The idea of assessing worker maturity ties into the motivation research of David McClelland at Harvard (see Chapter 3). McClelland said that achievement-motivated people have certain characteristics in common: the capacity to set high but obtainable goals, the concern for personal achievement rather than the rewards for success, and the desire for feedback on how well they are doing in the job rather than how well they are liked by the boss.[19]

Readiness, or maturity, as defined by Hersey and Blanchard, has two facets:

1. *Job maturity.* The ability to do something. It concerns knowledge and skill. Reporters who have high job maturity have the knowledge, ability, and experience to carry out their assignments without direction from others.

2. *Psychological maturity.* The willingness or motivation to do something. Reporters with high psychological maturity think responsibility is important. They have self-confidence and good feelings about their responsibilities. They are self-starters and do not need encouragement from editors to get the work done.

There are four levels of readiness in the situational leadership model:[20]

1. *Readiness Level 1.* The staffer either is unable and unwilling or unable and insecure.

   Newsroom example: A new reporter needs to learn to how to understand a school budget, but may be unable and lacks the commitment and motivation to learn; or, the reporter may have no confidence in his ability to understand figures.

2. *Readiness Level 2.* The staffer lacks the ability, but is motivated and making an effort, confident as long as the leader provides guidance.

   Newsroom example: Having coaxed the school board treasurer into giving him a crash course on school finances, the reporter still is unable to write a budget story without help from the desk. But the reporter is working hard and starting to feel confident as long as an editor is there as a backup.

3. *Readiness Level 3.* The staffer has the ability to perform the task, but either is not willing or is too insecure to use the ability.

   Newsroom example: The reporter is now able to understand and report on school finances, but finds the subject boring and is unwilling to pursue stories about the budget. Or, having failed so often in attempting to write a budget story, the reporter is nervous and apprehensive about future assignments concerning school finances, even though he understands the process.

4. *Readiness Level 4.* The staffer has the ability to perform, likes doing the job, and is confident he can do it successfully.

   Newsroom example: After covering four school budget hearings, the new reporter finds covering school finances an interesting challenge and is confident that his stories are well written.

Leader Behaviors

Situational leadership teaches that the leader has to consider each situation, including the maturity levels of staffers, to understand which leadership style is appropriate. In their model,

Hersey and Blanchard suggest relating the four different levels of readiness to the four basic leadership styles, a match that results in the following leader behaviors:[21]

Telling. This behavior is appropriate when attempting to influence low levels of readiness. It is called "telling" because the editor gives clear, specific directions. The editor is defining roles and telling staffers what, how, when, and where to do the assignment. It emphasizes direct behavior. This style of supervision has the highest probability of being effective with staffers at a low maturity level. Too much supportive behavior with staffers at a low maturity level may be seen as permissive, easy, and, most significant, as rewarding poor performance.

Selling. This behavior is appropriate when attempting to influence low to moderate levels of readiness. It is called "selling" because the editor is providing direction and guidance to compensate for the staffer's lack of ability, as well as support and communication to reinforce the staffer's willingness and enthusiasm. Through communication, the editor tries to get the staffer to accept the desired behaviors. Staffers at a low to moderate readiness level usually will go along with a decision if they understand the reason for the decision and if the editor also offers some help and direction.

Participating. This behavior is appropriate when attempting to influence moderate to high levels of readiness. It is called "participating" because both editor and staffer share in providing guidance and direction. The editor needs to take the first step by offering support of the staffer's efforts to use his or her abilities. A supporting, nondirective participating style has the highest probability of being effective with staffers at a moderate to high maturity level. The editor and the staffer share in decision making. The main roles of the editor are to assist and to communicate.

Delegating. This behavior is appropriate when attempting to influence high levels of readiness. It is called "delegating" because the editor turns over the responsibility for decision making and implementation to the staffer. This style provides little direction or support and it has the highest probability of being effective with staffers at a high maturity level. Even though the editor still may identify the problem, the responsibility for carrying out the assignment is given to mature staffers. They are permitted to run the show and make decisions about how, when, and where. In the newsroom, this is what happens when the editor delegates to the city editor the responsibility for running the city desk.

It is clear from the strategies proposed in situational leadership that as staffers develop in their jobs, as newcomers grow and gain experience and ability, the editor must respond by decreasing control over their work and giving them increased autonomy. As reporters are able to do more on their own, the relationship with the editor becomes increasingly one of trust and confidence.

When a staffer's strong performance leads to promotion, the editor will have to change leadership behavior to accommodate the individual's inexperience in the new position. The staffer who required little supervision as a reporter will need more support and direction from the editor initially as he or she learns to be an assistant city editor.

The level of maturity in the newsroom can also affect the style of communication the editor selects. Maturity may determine the amount of distracting information the staff can tolerate—information that can divert attention and energy away from the essential tasks of getting out the paper—or the manner in which the editor conveys the information. Potentially distracting information may be news of a drop in advertising lineage, a hiring freeze, or a cut in news space. Rumors can be distracting. So can antimanagement memos circulated by newsroom union leaders. The psychological maturity of the staff suggests whether it can absorb these messages and get on with the work or whether the messages will distract staffers, causing them to chatter, take sides, and be less productive. An editor who utilizes strong group leaders (see Chapter 2) to help convey information can counterbalance the tendency of an immature staff to overreact to information.

Fig. 7.5

CLOSE-UP

How are managers different from leaders? Abraham Zaleznik of the Harvard Business School assessed some of the fundamental differences between leaders and managers.

	Managers	*Leaders*
Attitudes toward goals	Impersonal, if not passive. Goals arise from necessity, not desire.	Active in shaping goals. Influence moods, evoke images and expectations.
Conceptions of work	Focus on process, not substance. Flexible in use of tactics. Act to limit choices.	Develop fresh approaches, open issues for new options. Create excitement at work.
Relations with others	Prefer to work with people. Avoid solitary activity. Give attention to how things get done. Low level of emotional involvement. Reconcile differences. Seek compromises. Establish balance of power. Send signals, not messages. Play for time.	Relate intuitively and empathetically. Interested in what events and decisions mean to people. Attract strong feelings of love and hate.
Sense of self	Conservators and regulators of existing order with which they identify and gain rewards.	Feel separate from their environment. Do not depend on membership, work roles for for identity.

Source: Adapted from Abraham Zaleznik, "Managers and Leaders: Are They Different?" in *Executive Success: Making It in Management* (New York: John Wiley & Sons, 1983), 126–33.

POWER

Rosabeth Moss Kanter, author and sociologist at Yale, describes power as "America's last dirty word—it is easier to talk about money than it is to talk about power. People who have it deny it. People who want it do not want to appear to hunger for it. People who engage in its machinations do so secretly."[22]

More than most other work groups, newspaper journalists are exposed to power—the power of the institutions and the elected officials they cover, as well as the power that resides in the daily newspaper. The power of the press is the focus of a continuing debate in this country. Richard Nixon saw the power of the press as ". . . primordial. It sets the agenda for public discussion . . . It determines what people will talk and think about—

Fig. 7.6

CLOSE-UP

Numerous definitions of power are found in the literature of management and organizations. The most familiar comment on power is the great epigram by Sir John E. E. Dalberg, the first baron of Acton and a British historian. Lord Acton wrote that "power tends to corrupt and absolute power corrupts absolutely."

English philosopher Bertrand Russell defined power as "the production of intended effects."

A. J. Grimes noted that "what legitimizes authority is the promotion or pursuit of collective goals that are associated with group consensus. The polar opposite, power, is the pursuit of individual or pluralistic goals associated with group compliance."

Mary F. Rogers of Providence College pared the definition of power to simply "the potential for influence."

Sources: John Emerich Edward Dalberg-Acton, letter to Bishop Mandell Creighton, 5 April 1887; Bertrand Russell, *Power* (London: Allen and Unwin, 1938), 35; A. J. Grimes, "Authority, Power, Influence, and Social Control: A Theoretical Synthesis," *Academy of Management Review* 3 (October 1978): 725; Mary F. Rogers, "Instrumental and Infra-Resources: The Bases of Power," *American Journal of Sociology,* 79, no. 6 (1973): 1418–33.

an authority that in other nations is reserved for tyrants, priests, parties, and mandarins . . . When the press seizes a great issue to thrust onto the agenda of talk, it moves action on its own."

Most journalists would not recognize the Nixon definition of power in their actions as reporters or editors. Journalists are not without real power, but as Theodore H. White argues, "[The press] is not an institution consciously and consistently dedicated to accumulating and exercising control over other institutions or over people's lives. It is, in fact, rarely consistent and often unconscious about the power it does have."[23]

It is common to think of power as evil, to equate it with exploitation and corruption. We fear being manipulated. We know the anger and frustration of having our lives or our careers reordered as a result of the use of power by someone else.

In a sense, perhaps, our view of power has been shaped by experiences in our own lives and by the negative focus on public power in the news. Yet, as an instrument of management, power is necessary. Its dynamics can be positive and useful; indeed, without power, we cannot accomplish very much. Power is a critical element in effective newsroom management. No power means no authority; no authority means no discipline; no discipline means newsroom order and systems are difficult to maintain. Editors should not hide the fact that they have power and that they will use it.

Where does power come from? First, from the editor's access to the support, resources, and information necessary to get the work done. Second, from the ability of the editor to gain cooperation. Hersey and Blanchard identify seven bases of power or potential means of successfully influencing the behavior of others:[24]

1. *Coercive power.* Based on fear. A leader who uses coercive power attempts to induce compliance through the threat of punishment, such as undesirable work assignments, reprimands, or dismissal. Staffers who work hard because they fear being yelled at or ridiculed in the newsroom by the editor are submitting to coercive power.

2. *Legitimate power.* Based on the position held by the leader. Normally, the higher the position, the higher the legitimate

power tends to be. A leader with legitimate power influences others because it is recognized that, by virtue of position in the organization, the leader has the right to expect that his or her suggestions will be followed. Legitimate power is another name for authority. It does not depend on the leader's relationship with others; the staff will carry out the editor's request simply because he or she is the boss.

3. *Expert power.* Based on the leader's possession of expertise, skill, and knowledge, and others' respect for those proficiencies. A leader high in expert power is seen as possessing the expertise to assist others. The resulting respect leads to compliance with the leader's wishes. The editor who once worked as a reporter in a Washington bureau knows that his or her opinions on government and political news will be highly valued on the news desk. Staffers who have little or no authority but who possess a specific skill or ability that others need are more powerful than their position or title would indicate. A staff assistant to the editor, for example, acquires power out of the ability to understand the budget and to move through the newspaper's bureaucracy the approval of pay increases, new hires, and promotions.

4. *Reward power.* Based on the leader's ability to provide rewards for other people who think that compliance with the leader's wishes will lead to positive incentives such as pay, promotion, or recognition. If the editor can establish a strong link between performance and reward, he or she will have a greater power to influence better work than the editor whose reward power is limited because pay is based on a labor contract.

5. *Referent power.* Based on the leader's personal traits. A leader with strong referent power generally is liked and admired by others because of his or her personality. These appealing or charismatic qualities help define the editor's reputation and enable him or her to influence others.

6. *Information power.* Based on the leader's possession of or access to information that is perceived as valuable by others. The editor is in the know, in both the formal and informal

sense. Information allows the editor to influence subordinates because they need the information the leader possesses. Some editors withhold information from staffers, knowing that the staffers cannot make their own decisions because they do not have all the information they need. In this way, the editor uses the dynamics of information to become more powerful.

7. *Connection power.* Based on the leader's connections with influential or important people inside or outside the organization. The editor's power increases if he or she has close contact with a sponsor, such as the publisher or a corporate news executive; a peer network, such as the advertising or production directors; or powerful and prestigious members of the community.

Is there a "best" power base? Research suggests it is not possible to generalize, that leaders may need various power bases depending on the situation.[25] Studies show that expert and legitimate power appear to be the most important reasons for worker compliance, but that power based on personal traits (referent power) tends to be strongly and consistently related to subordinate performance and satisfaction.

Hersey and Blanchard propose applying the uses of power to situational leadership in the following ways:

- Coercive power is often necessary in a "telling" style of leadership.
- Legitimate power is influential among those with moderate levels of maturity where a "selling" or participative management behavior is effective.
- Expert power works with highly mature staffers who can respond to a "delegating" style.
- Reward power can influence workers with low to moderate levels of maturity where a "selling" style is effective.
- Referent power works among those with moderate to high levels of maturity where a "participating" style is effective.

- Information power helps motivate workers with above-average maturity where "participating" and "delegating" styles are effective.

- Connection power influences those at the lower maturity levels where a "telling" or "selling" style is effective.

Fig. 7.7

CLOSE-UP

Richard E. Neustadt of Harvard, in his study of presidential power, wrote, "Roosevelt had a love affair with power in that place [the White House]. It was an early romance and it lasted all his life . . . He wanted power for its own sake; he also wanted what it could achieve. The challenge and the fun of power lay not just in having, but in doing. His private satisfactions were enriched by public purposes and these grew more compelling as more power came his way . . .

"It is not information of a general sort that helps a President see personal stakes; not summaries, not surveys, not the bland amalgams. Rather . . . it is the odds and ends of tangible detail that pieced together in his mind illuminate the underside of issues put before him. To help himself he must reach out as widely as he can for every scrap of fact, opinion, gossip, bearing on his interests and relationships as President. He must become his own director of his own central intelligence."

Source: Richard E. Neustadt, *Presidential Power* (New York: Signet, 1964), 147, 154–55.

Good editors want power; that is, they have a high need for influencing people, not for personal gain, but to benefit the newspaper. The discipline and control the editor exercises in the use of power will significantly influence the staff's perception of the editor.

Everyone wants to work for an editor who has clout. It is simply easier to accomplish more for the news staff when the editor is in a position of power. When the staff recognizes that its editor can get things done, the staff, in turn, is likely to be more highly motivated.

Powerful as the position of editor may be, there are limits to that power. The limits tend to be controlled by two factors:

First, the editor may allow his or her power to erode. This can happen in a number of ways, but the most common cause of power erosion among editors is the failure to make decisions. The staff counts on the editor to act, to decide. For example, an editor may be faced with decisions such as whether to run a controversial series, or whether to replace an unproductive city editor, or whether to chose between two candidates for a staff vacancy. If the editor vacillates and gives the impression of indecision, the editor is surrendering the perception that he or she has the power to decide, the power to act. Once the power base is eroded, the effectiveness of the editor's leadership suffers.

Second, the editor's power may be eroded by the publisher. If the editor does not know when to consult the publisher and when to act alone and if, as a result, the publisher reverses a decision made by the editor, the staff may see the editor as powerless.

In the newsroom management hierarchy, there are different levels of power in the same way there are different levels of authority.

At the supervisory level, the desk editors and assistant desk editors have the authority to require the compliance of the staff. Their exercise of authority is backed by legitimate power. In most cases, these editors have expert power, information power, and connection power working for them. They have little reward power. They often are required to explain and administer practices or policies they had no hand in shaping. How much clout they have is determined by other editors. If the top editor manages by fear or keeps a tight rein on subordinate editors—either out of concern for their ability to do the job right or as a result of the editor's own insecurity—the desk editors will have little power. In newsrooms where staffers are represented by a union, the rank and file may have sources of power to buffer the effects of the desk editors' power. Such counterpower can be another factor in the relative powerlessness that desk editors often feel.

Desk editors tend to act out their powerlessness by becoming turf-minded.[26] They create islands within the newsroom, setting themselves up as the only ones who can control professional standards and judge their own work. Sports departments are noted for this tendency. Their disdain for the newsroom's senior management may be expressed, for example, in a subtle refusal to support the managing editor's efforts to publish more stories about participant sports. The remedy for this is twofold: (1) the managing editor should take an active interest in the sports department, demonstrating his or her interest in the sports report and knowledge of the games and players being covered by the sports staff, and (2) the managing editor should require the sports editor to be a regular participant in planning and strategy sessions for the news department. Such moves tend to make the desk editor—the sports editor in this case—feel less powerless, less turf-minded, and more a part of the managing editor's team.

At every level of the newsroom organization, political platforms allow for the expression of individual interests and motives through which people can develop their careers. The ability to move to the high editing posts depends on the accumulation of power. In this way, power allows individual interests to be transformed into activities that influence other people.[27] For example, the city editor who wants to build a power base to promote his or her ambition to succeed the managing editor might have a facility for mixing with the movers and shakers in the newspaper's primary circulation area. By working these contacts for good story ideas—which are then shared with the managing editor and other desk editors, and often with the publisher—and by creating the impression in the community that he or she is the person to see at the paper, the city editor is using a special interest to accumulate power that can lead to larger responsibility.

People cannot get the power they want just for the asking. They enter into a competition, vying for the scarce opportunities that occasionally are available at the top of the newsroom management pyramid. The politics of power is especially evident when a retirement is announced and several months may elapse before a successor is named. In this situation, it is no longer possible to keep ambition at bay. Rival camps emerge to support the main contenders. The risk, of course, is that the "winner" will gain power at someone else's expense.

The following definition relates the concept of power to the concept of *politics:* "If power is a force, a store of potential influence through which events can be affected, politics involves those activities or behaviors through which power is developed and used in organizational settings. Power is a property of the system at rest; politics is the study of power in action. An individual, subunit, or department may have power within an organizational context at some period of time; politics involves the exercise of power to get something accomplished, as well as those activities which are undertaken to expand the power already possessed or the scope over which it can be exercised."[28]

Like power, political activity should not be viewed as bad. Many of the political activities undertaken by editors are in the best interest of the newspaper as a whole. This may take shape, for example, in the building of coalitions with other department heads of the newspaper company to challenge a traditional or outdated policy or practice.

Organizational behavior, as it applies to the newsroom, can become political rather than rational under the following situations:

Scarcity of resources. Politics surface when resources are scarce and decisions must be made about who gets what. In the newsroom, a reduced travel budget would cause the sports editor, city editor, features editor, and business editor to become political in trying to claim their "share."

Ambiguous decisions. When a decision is not clearly defined and leaves room for interpretation, it also leaves room for political maneuvering. When the editor makes a programmed decision, such as the choice of a new city editor, there is little room for maneuvering. But if the editor announces a 5 percent increase in the newshole without specific details as to how it will be used, important questions are left unanswered, thus inviting each desk to lobby for a major piece of the additional news space.

Ambiguous goals. Similarly, when the goals of the editor or the publisher are ambiguous, there is more room for politics.

Organizational change. Change of ownership of the newspaper, appointment of a new editor, and efforts to restructure a news desk or create a new content section are invitations to all to join in the political process.

If the editor acquires power by means that are essentially political, it is important to develop strategies that will enable the editor to keep that power. Depending on the situation, several tactics are effective.[29]

In preparing to argue for additional reporting positions on the staff, the editor can make *selective use of information* that will help convince the publisher to give approval. One of the simplest ways to influence a decision is to *control the agenda,* insuring that whatever the issue, it will be considered on the editor's terms. Sometimes the editor can gain an advantage by *using an outside expert.* Often the experiences of other editors or other newspapers in a similar situation will help make the editor's case. Finally, the editor can effectively increase power by *building coalitions and alliances* with other units of the newspaper company. Others in the coalition may be competitors for resources, but there may be enough at stake for all parties to agree on a course of action.

THE PACE OF MANAGEMENT

In spite of the voluminous literature on leadership and the variety of definitions and theories to explain it, there is neither a unified point of view about it nor a clear understanding of the phenomenon.

Criticism of the research is that it tends to focus quite narrowly on the relationship between the leader and the group and fails to take into account the nature of managerial work.[30] The hectic pace of managerial work is aggravated by the manager's relative lack of control over it. In one study, managers initiated only 32 percent of their contacts with others at work. And of all contacts with others, 93 percent were arranged on an ad hoc basis.[31]

Because there are so many activities in a day and so little uninterrupted time, the practitioner of a formal leadership role must be "proficient at superficiality"—that is, adept at handling quickly those encounters and decisions that do not require deliberation. Training models that advocate "rational" decision strategies make sense, but they are extremely difficult to implement because they tend to ignore the crunch of the pace and the breadth of the activities. The work is demanding and largely reactive. Activities that require little time and are relatively routine may postpone other activities that are ambiguous and have no routine solution. As a result, more important decisions may be made by default.[32]

The pace of managerial work has been described as unrelenting and capricious, the job never-ending, and its practitioner often guessing, reacting, never sure of success and never able to say there is nothing else to be done. The work of managers is characterized by brevity, variety, and fragmentation.[33]

The nature of the editor's job, then, seems to require a leadership style that includes shifting gears as situations change, forming creative viewpoints, acting quickly on simple problems, setting up mechanisms for feedback to help get a fix on newsroom problems, and using social skills, rewards, and punishments to control the newsroom organization.

CHAPTER SUMMARY

Leadership, together with supervising and managing, completes the newsroom management structure. Leadership is a broader concept than management, relying on the ability of individuals to influence the behavior of others.

Early leadership studies abandoned the idea that leaders could be identified by such personal characteristics as height, intelligence, and initiative. Later studies focused on such leader behavior as relationships between leaders and followers and on the rules and patterns of the organization and the channels of communication.

Several models of leadership have been developed for the training of leaders. One is the managerial grid, which is based on the idea that the best leadership style results from a concern for both production and people.

The contingency theory deals with the tendency of leaders to adapt to situations, and the path-goal theory is concerned with ways in which a leader can influence a subordinate's motivation, goals, and attempts at achievement.

The situational-leadership model shows how a leader's behavior is guided toward one of four styles by the amount of direction needed by subordinates, by the leader's relationship with subordinates, and by the maturity or readiness levels of subordinates. This combination of factors determines one of four leadership behaviors: (1) telling, (2) selling, (3) participating, or (4) delegating.

Power is a handmaiden to leadership and a necessary instrument of management. Research has identified seven bases of power: fear, position, expertise, rewards, personality, information, and connections.

Politics in the newsroom is simply power in action. Political behavior is increased by a scarcity of resources, by decisions or goals that are ambiguous, and by change. Editors can increase their power by building alliances and coalitions.

The most enlightened concept of leadership is one in which the editor's skills and human insights are used to enhance the development of individual skills. The pace of management requires a leadership style that includes shifting gears as situations change, forming creative viewpoints, acting quickly on simple problems, setting up mechanisms for feedback, and using social skills, rewards, and punishments to control the newsroom organization.

NOTES

1. Abraham Zaleznik, "Managers and Leaders: Are They Different?" *Harvard Business Review,* May–June 1977, 6.
2. Robert Tannenbaum and Warren H. Schmidt, "How to Choose a Leadership Pattern," *Harvard Business Review,* May–June 1973, 162–68.
3. Harold Koontz and Cyril O'Donnell, *Principles of Management,* 2d ed. (New York: McGraw-Hill, 1959), 435.
4. George R. Terry, *Principles of Management,* 6th ed. (Homewood, Ill.: Irwin, 1972), 458.
5. Daniel Katz and Robert L. Kahn, *The Social Psychology of Organizations,* 2d ed. (New York: John Wiley & Sons, 1978), 528.

6. Peter M. Senge, "System Dynamics and Leadership" (Paper presented at the 1980 International Conference on Cybernetics and Society, Cambridge, Mass., 10 October 1980).
7. Ralph Stogdill, "Personal Factors Associated with Leadership: A Survey of the Literature," *Journal of Psychology* 25 (1948): 35–71.
8. Paul Hersey and Kenneth Blanchard, *Management of Organizational Behavior*, 4th ed. (Englewood Cliffs, N.J.: Prentice-Hall, 1982), 83.
9. Eugene E. Jennings, "The Anatomy of Leadership," *Management of Personnel Quarterly* 1, no. 1 (Autumn 1961): 2.
10. Richard M. Steers, *Introduction to Organizational Behavior*, 2d ed. (Glenview, Ill.: Scott, Foresman, 1984), 334–35.
11. Hersey and Blanchard, *Management of Organizational Behavior*, 85.
12. Robert R. Blake and Jane S. Mouton, *The New Managerial Grid* (Houston: Gulf, 1978), 9–17, 41, 58–59, 75–76, 95.
13. Fred E. Fiedler, "Style or Circumstance: The Leadership Enigma," *Psychology Today*, March 1969, 38–43.
14. Warren R. Plunkett and Raymond F. Attner, *Introduction to Management* (Boston: Kent, 1983), 333.
15. Hersey and Blanchard, *Management of Organizational Behavior*, 135–36.
16. Robert J. House and Terence R. Mitchell, "Path-Goal Theory of Leadership," *Journal of Contemporary Business* 3, no. 4 (Autumn 1974): 81–97.
17. Paul Hersey, *The Situational Leader* (Escondido, Calif.: The Center for Leadership Studies, 1984), 29–31.
18. Ibid., 34–37.
19. David C. McClelland, *The Achieving Society* (Princeton: Van Nostrand, 1961), 221–38.
20. Hersey, *Situational Leader*, 46–49.
21. Ibid., 62–63; and Hersey and Blanchard, *Management of Organizational Behavior*, 153–54.
22. Rosabeth Moss Kanter, "Power Failure in Management Circuits," in *Executive Success: Making It in Management* (New York: John Wiley & Sons, 1983), 249.
23. Theodore H. White, *The Making of the President 1972* (New York: Atheneum, 1973), 245–50.
24. Hersey and Blanchard, *Management of Organizational Behavior*, 178–79.
25. Walter E. Natemeyer, "Situational Leadership, Perception, and the Impact of Power," *Group and Organizational Studies* 4, no. 4 (December 1979): 418–28.
26. Kanter, "Power Failure in Management Circuits," 256.
27. Abraham Zaleznik, "Power and Politics in Organizational Life," in *Executive Success: Making It in Management* (New York: John Wiley & Sons, 1983), 268–69.
28. Jeffrey Pfeffer, *Power in Organizations* (Marshfield, Mass.: Pitman, 1981), 7.
29. Steers, *Introduction to Organizational Behavior*, 322–23.

30. Morgan W. McCall, Jr., "Leaders and Leadership: Of Substance and Shadow," in *Technical Report No. 2* (Center for Creative Leadership, January 1977), 12.
31. Henry Mintzberg, *The Nature of Managerial Work* (New York: Harper & Row, 1973), 49.
32. Henry Mintzberg, "The Manager's Job: Folklore and Fact," in *Executive Success: Making It in Management* (New York: John Wiley & Sons, 1983), 416–17.
33. Michael M. Lombardo, "Looking at Leadership: Some Neglected Issues," in *Technical Report No. 6* (Center for Creative Leadership, January 1978), 5–6.

8

Styles of Management

Editors who are familiar with the conventional wisdom of management and leadership realize that the theories don't always fit neatly with their own behavior. To a large extent, this is explained by editors' individual differences and the fragmented nature of the work they do. The theories of management and leadership can be effective for editors who understand their own strengths and weaknesses, who learn to cope with their inner conflicts, and who recognize the patterns of behavior they present daily to the staff. What emerges is a *management style*.

MOVING FROM THEORY TO STYLE

So far, our attention has been fixed on theories and concepts. We have been thinking of newsroom management in terms of work groups, of ideas to explain motivation, of the planning, organizing, staffing, directing, and controlling elements of management, and of various approaches to leadership.

The editor may not be comfortable attempting to incorporate the theories and concepts of management into a working lifestyle characterized by long hours, fragmented activity, talking, and listening. It is not the editor's nature to recall instantly the ideas of Maslow or McClelland or the formulas of situational leadership when thinking through a problem. The editor's management style is more likely to emphasize informality and the flexibility to react to situations rather than a structured quality.

For example, when a fire in the press room damages all but one of the newspaper's press units and the editor has to cut the size of the paper and advance deadlines, is this planning, organizing, staffing, directing, or controlling? At best, these elements of management define the roles the editor will carry out in handling this emergency. How effectively the editor performs these roles will be greatly influenced by his or her management style.

Fig. 8.1

CLOSE-UP

Henry Mintzberg, professor of management at McGill University in Montreal, points out four myths or folklores about the manager's job that, he says, do not bear up under careful scrutiny of the facts:

Folklore 1. The manager is a reflective, systematic planner.

Fact. Study after study has shown that managers work at an unrelenting pace, that their activities are characterized by brevity, variety, and discontinuity, and that they are strongly oriented to action and dislike reflective activities.

Folklore 2. The effective manager has no regular duties to perform.

Fact. In addition to handling exceptions, managerial work involves performing a number of regular duties, including ritual and ceremony, negotiations, and passing along important information from outside the company.

Folklore 3. The senior manager is at the apex of the organization and needs to have a formal information system to provide knowledge of everything that is going on in the company.

Fact. Managers strongly favor an informal, conversational style of communication. They rely heavily on telephone calls, meetings, and talks with individuals.

Folklore 4. Management is, or at least is quickly becoming, a science and a profession.

Fact. The managers' programs—to schedule time, process information, make decisions, and so on—remain locked deep inside their brains and are no more scientific than human instinct and judgment. Even though the computer, so important for specialized work, is gaining wider use among executives, there still is a heavy reliance on sharing and acquiring information by word of mouth.

Source: Henry Mintzberg, "The Manager's Job: Folklore and Fact," in *Executive Success: Making It in Management* (New York: John Wiley & Sons, 1983), 416–20.

SEEING OURSELVES

The editor's ability to develop an effective management style is influenced by two factors: First, the editor's understanding of the nature of work behavior—that is, the full range of theories and concepts we have explored so far. As this knowledge is absorbed, it sharpens the editor's instinct for recognizing behavior patterns and their probable causes, for reacting to situations, and for identifying a range of choices and deciding which choice to pursue. Second, the development of an effective management style is influenced by the editor's capacity for self-examination.

Our sense of self is shaped by all of our life's experiences. William James, in *The Varieties of Religious Experience,* suggests that individuals who have encountered many difficulties, whose lives have been marked by continual struggle, will have a different world view, a different personality, than people who move through life at a smooth and easy pace. The experiences of our lives and the way we deal with those events help us shape what is called a self-image. Our impressions of ourselves can be characterized through a string of adjectives—smart, witty, disorganized, demanding, kindly, misunderstood, savvy, timid, well-intentioned, chatty, affectionate, honest, shrewd, prompt, stingy, and so on.

We see ourselves in several roles—editor, spouse, parent, colleague, boss, subordinate, and social companion, for example. Conflicts can arise as a result of the responsibilities that accompany each of these roles. If we see the demands rising in our job as editor, if we spend more time at the office or work at home on weekends, then our role as spouse or parent suffers. Consequently, conflict arises between our self-image as an editor and our self-image as spouse or parent. We may be meeting our standards on the job but falling short at home. We attempt to cope with such a situation by assuring ourselves that we are doing our best while ignoring the tension and guilt that may be developing because the job is getting more attention than the family.

How we see ourselves often is critically different from how others see us. Many editors who failed in their jobs have been fired, eased out, or moved laterally. The official explanation, issued to help the unsuccessful editor save face and make the transition as easy as possible, rarely comes close to the real reason for the change. Unless the editor is willing to engage in honest introspection, he or she may never recognize that at the root of the setback was an unrealistic self-appraisal. It was a failure to grasp the disparity between the editor's self-view and what the publisher thought about the editor's performance. The editor may have clung rigidly to a style of newspapering that had been successful for years whereas the publisher was looking for an editor who could adapt to a new, broader management role reflecting the changes in newspaper publishing.

Accurate self-appraisal and self-image are important by-products of performance reviews (see Chapter 10). An honest, realistic assessment of one's own work is the first step in developing insight into work behavior and performance, which can lead to motivation and goal achievement.

While the self-concept is important in understanding human behavior in general, it becomes critically so in understanding manager development, where changes in behavior are the objective. As a matter of psychological fact, a change in behavior on the job, for better or for worse, means a change in self-concept. If we examine ourselves and others critically, we will see that changes in behavior are constant. Some managers encounter difficulties as a result of their inability to detect change in their own behavior and from fuzzy thinking behind such comforting, though fallacious, notions as, "You can't teach an old dog new tricks."[1]

Fig. 8.2

CLOSE-UP

Lyman W. Porter and Edwin E. Ghiselli contrasted the differences in self-perceptions between a group of middle managers and a group of top managers. Top managers, they found, perceived themselves as capable, determined, industrious, resourceful, sharp-witted, enterprising, sincere, sociable, pleasant, dignified, sympathetic. Middle managers discerned themselves as discreet, courteous, practical, deliberate, intelligent, calm, steady, modest, civilized, patient.

Porter and Ghiselli noted that "top managers see themselves as the 'dynamic brains' of the organization. Their role is one of thinking up new things to do, new areas to enter, new ways of accomplishing things. They are action-oriented idea men. Middle management people, on the other hand, seem to see themselves as filling a role that could be called the 'backbone' of the organization. Their chief forté is that they provide the careful, thorough investigation of ideas and plans that is necessary before these can be put into extensive use. They lend the stability to the organization that is necessary for it to function over an extended period of time."

Source: Lyman W. Porter and Edwin E. Ghiselli, "The Self Perceptions of Top and Middle Management Personnel," *Personnel Psychology* 10, no. 4 (Winter 1957): 400, 402.

Resistance to change is natural. Changes that may affect an individual's complex instinctive qualities—attitudes, habits, drives—are most likely to be resisted. This is a phenomenon encountered when an aggressively competitive reporter is promoted to assistant city editor, a position that requires the individual to acquire the ability to develop insight and be cooperative. The former reporter instinctively retains the drive to surpass others. If he or she senses that the new need for insight and cooperation conflicts with the deep and natural instinct for competition, the editor will resist developing the new skills. However, if the new assistant city editor sees that the need for insight and cooperation will be enhanced by natural competitive skills, the resistance will diminish and mature growth will occur.

There is an important link between self-concept and growth,

both of which come from within. Because an individual's self-image bears directly on his or her confidence, motivation, drive, ambition, and interest in learning, growth is less likely to occur when one's self-concept is weak or negative. No one can tell others how to grow, but through effective counseling, evaluation, and goal setting, individuals can learn to understand themselves and strive to move in the best direction.

Growth does not proceed in clear-cut, logical steps. Sometimes it occurs in inexplicable spurts; at other times, it evolves with agonizing slowness. Real learning can be so deeply unconscious that no overt behavior change shows up for a long time. Psychological regressions may even occur, as when a veteran reporter makes an unexplained error that might typically be found in the work of a beginning-level reporter. The process of growth is a nebulous, multifactored, fluid, dynamic process, often astounding, and usually only partially controllable. The process of personal growth takes place in a series of steps:[2]

Self-examination. If we were to attempt a systematic analysis of what happens when growth in a manager occurs, we would start with self-examination. This begins with a feeling that tells us something isn't quite right or that gives us an inkling that our behavior should be different in some respect. Self-examination is what happens when a golfer sees a videotape of his or her swing or when a reporter is forced to compare a rewritten and edited version of a story with the original. The function of self-examination is to lay the groundwork for insight, without which no growth can occur. Insight is the "Oh-I-see-now" feeling that must, consciously or unconsciously, precede change in behavior. Insights—real, genuine glimpses of ourselves as we really are—are reached only with difficulty and sometimes with real psychic pain, but they are the building blocks of growth.

Self-expectation. As we examine ourselves, we may discover things we do not like and may wish to change. A desire to correct shortcomings affects our self-expectation. We create new demands and challenges for ourselves. Theologians say that recognition of sin must precede salvation. Psychologists say that if we accept the fact that we have a problem, then we are ready to find a solution.

Changing self-expectation. There is no best way to shift from the recognition that we should be different to actually changing our self-concept. What can be done on the job is for the superior to point up constructively a subordinate's needs for growth. The emphasis here is on the word *constructive,* which means helpful, insightful ideas. Another source of insight is a spouse or close friend. Those closest to us have a way of sensing when we need to be reminded that our self-images have become distorted. In fact, anything that enables the individual to get a new perspective—reading, observing, studying, going to conferences, attending meetings—can provide personal insight; and out of insight comes change in self-expectation.

Self-direction. We can master our own destiny only if we take charge of our own development. Nothing can be done by others to make us grow; we grow only as we want to and as our own insights enable us to.

It is clear that many development programs miss their mark at this point. They make the assumption that exposure to experiences or people or books or courses is enough to produce growth. This is not so. Development programs effect change in us only as we reach out and take something—a bit of wisdom, a new idea, a new concept—that stretches us and gives us an answer to our own problems. We might say that just as learning is impossible without motivation, so real executive development is impossible unless the executive seeks it. Moreover, the strength of our desire is stronger if we seek development because we want to develop than if we are merely trying to please the boss or do what is expected of us. Fundamentally, this is the age-old problem of motivation. Executives grow because they derive their strength, desire, and drive from inner, unachieved goals, and from the satisfactions of self-realization.

A number of dilemmas are posed for editors by their roles of power and authority. Training and instinct cause us to externalize conflicts and dilemmas. If we are immobilized by a difficult problem, we are apt to look outside for an explanation; we may blame a lack of authority or incompetent subordinates. The tendency to attribute failure to someone or something else is what psychologists call *projection.* But often the source of these troublesome situations can be found within the individual. Unless personal conflicts are resolved, the inner discord will affect behavior on and off the job.

Abraham Zaleznik, professor of social psychology of management at the Harvard Business School, has suggested that executives can bring problems under more rational control by separating inner conditions from those on the outside. That separation is not easily achieved, but it is crucial for the exercise of leadership. Zaleznik has identified two types of inner conflict that are prevalent among executives:[3]

1. *Status anxiety.* This refers to dilemmas frequently experienced by those at or near the top of their organization. When an individual achieves success and recognition at work, a change occurs within that person as well as among relationships with associates. The bright young comer suddenly is seen as a threat. Peers appear more cautious. There is tension between the responsibilities of newly acquired authority and the strong need to be liked. Sometimes the executive will play down authority and try to be the "nice guy." This is called status stripping, where the individual tries to discard symbols of status and authority in exchange for the continued affection of associates. Sooner or later, however, attempts at status stripping fail.

    Another side of status anxiety has to do with the desire to be near sources of power and to be accepted and understood by the boss. This can lead to excessive and inappropriate dependency, in which the subordinate has a lack of autonomy and the superior thinks he or she is being leaned on too hard for support. Status anxiety also is generated by the fear of aggression and retaliation from the boss, an experience that can lead to feelings of loneliness or detachment.

    A constructive approach, Zaleznik notes, recognizes that all work involves aggressive energy, demanding a kind of give-and-take where much is at stake and where it is impossible for everyone to be right all of the time. The executive who can develop a position, believe in it, support it to its fullest, and then back down when necessary is a strong person.

Zaleznik cautions against equating the virtue of humility with executive behavior that appears modest, uncertain of a stand, and acquiescent toward others—behavior that frequently is feigned modesty to avoid becoming a target.

2. *Competition anxiety.* This kind of inner conflict refers to those dilemmas generated while climbing to the top. There are two patterns of competition anxiety: the fear of failure and the fear of success. The fear of failure is present when an individual lacks a strong sense of identity, is short on self-esteem, and tends to quit rather than face confrontations that might result in failure. Instead of risking failure, he or she opts for anonymity. Fear of failure can be resolved only when the person is able to examine and understand how competition works, judge its basis in reality, and make rational changes in behavior.

The fear of success occurs when an individual fantasizes that his or her success came at the expense of someone else. A prominent pattern is one in which an individual strives hard to achieve a goal, but just when the goal is within reach, the person sabotages himself or herself. In sports and politics, this is called snatching defeat from the jaws of victory.

Zaleznik's research points to the following suggestions for managing inner conflicts:[4]

- Understanding our own motives. Everyone would like to think that his or her inner world is populated by only the socially acceptable drives and wishes, but this is not so. Equally human feelings include rivalry, dislike, rebelliousness, anger, and contempt. Awareness of how one is reacting in a situation and acceptance of negative feelings are beneficial and permit more flexibility in thinking and action.

- Establishing a firm sense of identity. Knowing who one is and who one is not—the sense of autonomy and separateness—permits a freedom of action and thinking so necessary for leadership.

- Maintaining a constancy of response. Behavior that constantly shifts is confusing to associates. Subordinates are entitled to a sense of security that comes from a pattern of reasonable continuity in the responses of the boss.

- Becoming selective in activities and relationships. While gregariousness and participation in many activities at work are of great value to executives, of greater importance is selectivity. The ability to say "no" without the sense that one has lost esteem can save the executive from a costly emotional energy drain.

- Learning to communicate. Resolving conflict, both internal and external, depends on communication: First, developing a keen awareness of one's own reactions; and second, making opinions and attitudes known without wasteful delays.

HOW OTHERS SEE US

The dynamics of self-image are not the only factors that help forge different management styles. To subordinates, the editor's style is what the staff perceives rather than how the editor thinks he or she behaves. This is a difficult concept to accept. Editors have to learn to recognize what impression they are creating in others. Unfortunately, such feedback is difficult to obtain, for subordinates often are reluctant to be honest with the boss on this subject.[5]

Sensitivity or T (Training) Group, developed in 1947 at Bethel, Maine, attempts to help individuals learn how others perceive their behavior. T Group is based on the idea that a number of individuals participating as learners in an unstructured situation will develop working relationships with each other and will discover a great deal about themselves by learning how others in the group see them. Individuals may learn about their own motives, feelings, and strategies in dealing with other persons. They also learn of the reactions they produce in others. As participants learn to analyze their behavior, they become more sensitive to human interaction. They learn to control relationships with others.[6]

Fig. 8.3

CLOSE-UP

Critics of sensitivity groups say that the training is designed to change individuals, not necessarily change the environment in which they work. When individuals return from sensitivity training and attempt to use what they have learned, they often find their co-workers unwilling to accept it or, even worse, what they have learned may not be appropriate for the situation back home. An alternative is to bring the training to the staff.

Within weeks after I joined the Rochester, New York, *Times-Union* and *Democrat and Chronicle* in 1977, a committee of female staffers brought me a petition describing a pattern of sexist attitudes they perceived among male editors. The committee and I met to discuss the issues and agreed to bring in an "outsider" for sensitivity training.

We selected Jayne Vogan, a psychologist from the State University College at Brockport, New York. Vogan began a series of lively meetings that involved everyone in both newsrooms—230 individuals in all. We described the sessions as training in communications, but they were clearly focused on sensitivity with the intent of changing behavior. The experience was successful because everyone was involved, because the editors were able to learn how others perceived their behavior, and because it was plain to the staff that continued sexist behavior would not be tolerated.

The staff is a crucial factor in any management situation, not only because subordinates individually accept or reject the leader, but also because as a group they actually determine whatever personal power the leader will have.

Victor H. Vroom, in a doctoral dissertation at the Carnegie Institute of Technology in Pittsburgh, suggests that the effectiveness of a leader is dependent to a great extent on the style of the individual workers.[7]

If the editor wants to influence a change in the behavior of a subordinate editor, it may be necessary for the editor temporarily to adapt to the behavior of the subordinate. For example, a newly promoted managing editor inherits a city editor who is accustomed to close supervision, who shuns responsibility, and who routinely bucks questions to the editor for decisions. If the editor wants the city editor to take more responsibility and to operate with less supervision, the change cannot be expected to take place overnight. The editor will have to tolerate the city editor's behavior for the short term and work with him or her to develop a different style over time. To demand an instant change in style would create confusion, anger, and resentment on the part of the city editor.

STYLE AND EXPECTATIONS

Behavior of managers in an organization results from the interaction of style and expectations. In the newsroom, expectation is defined as what staffers think they should do in their jobs and what they think their superiors, subordinates, and peers should do in theirs. If newsroom assignments are well defined and widely understood, then there will be shared expectations; that is, each individual will perceive accurately and will accept his or her own role and the roles of others.

Some editor jobs are defined by expectations. For instance, in supervising the more structured and routine jobs on the copy desk, the slot editor occupies a position that leaves little room for expression of individual style. Much of the slot editor's concern is focused on adherence to style of grammar and usage, accuracy of facts, and length of stories. Little innovative behavior by copy editors is tolerated on those points, although flair and creativity with headlines is encouraged. While the slot editor may not have a Theory-X attitude (see Chapter 3) about copy editors' motivation, he or she may strike a decidedly Theory-X style in running the desk—that is, close supervision and a "firm-but-fair" approach to dealing with others. On the other hand, fewer specific expectations are attached to the role of city editor, allowing for more latitude in expressing an individual style of operation and encouraging more innovative behavior from the reporting staff. Consequently, the city editor's style is likened more to a Theory-Y approach, with less close supervision and more room for the expression of individual differences and talents.[8]

An editor's style emerges over time from experience, education, training, and internal forces. At least four internal forces influence a manager's style:[9]

1. The manager's value system. How strong is the manager's belief that individuals should have a share in making the decisions that affect them? The strength of the editor's convictions on this question will influence whether he or she will be more democratic or more autocratic in management style. The editor's behavior also will be influenced by the relative importance he or she attaches to organizational efficiency, personal growth of subordinates, and company goals. If the editor's values are centered on organizational efficiency and goals, the style will tend to be oriented more toward decision making at the top. If personal growth of subordinates is important, the editor will be inclined to share the decision-making responsibilities.

2. Confidence in subordinates. Editors differ greatly in the amount of trust they have in others, and this carries over to the particular employees they supervise. They are likely to make a sharp-eyed assessment of the knowledge and competence each staffer has with respect to a problem. A central question the editor often asks is, "Who is best qualified to deal with this problem?" In situations where the editor may have more confidence in his or her own capabilities than those of subordinates, the editor may handle the situation himself or herself. If the editor's values tend toward the growth of subordinates, he or she will delegate the responsibility, expecting that it will contribute to enlarging the capacity and experience of key associates.

3. Personal leadership inclinations. Some editors seem to function more comfortably and naturally as highly directive leaders. Resolving problems and issuing instructions come easily to them. Other editors operate more comfortably in a team role where they are continually sharing many of their functions with subordinates. A consequence of the team role, however, is that these editors tend to subdue the urge to decide in favor of delegating the responsibility to others.

4. Feelings of uncertainty. The editor who releases control over the decision-making process thereby reduces the predictability of the outcome. Some editors have a greater need than others for predictability and stability. They dislike ambiguity and are uneasy about being accountable for decisions they have delegated and cannot control fully. The editor's tolerance for ambiguity will influence the style he or she develops for dealing with problems.

Qualities possessed by the editor's subordinates—the managing editor and various desk editors—also provide keys to help the editor decide how to manage. Like the editor, subordinates are influenced by many personal variables. Each of these editors also has a set of expectations about how the boss should act. The better the editor understands these factors, the more accurately he or she can determine what kind of behavior will enable subordinate editors to perform most effectively. The editor can permit subordinates greater freedom if the following conditions exist:[10]

- Subordinates have relatively high needs for independence. This is a quality likely to be found among newspaper editors at all levels.

- The subordinates have a readiness to assume responsibility for decision making; that is, they view additional responsibility as a reflection on their ability rather than simply a case of a superior editor passing off tasks. Here the editor can make individual distinctions based on such factors as experience, initiative, and personal ambition.

- The subordinates have a relatively high tolerance for ambiguity. Such a tolerance seems to go well with an instinct for the freedom to take an assignment and develop it. Subordinates with a low tolerance for ambiguity may be frustrated by an open-ended assignment and may yearn for clear-cut direction.

- The subordinates are interested in the problem and think it is important.

- The subordinates understand and identify with the goals of the editor and the newspaper.
- The subordinate editors have learned to share in decision making. Individuals who have come to expect strong leadership and centralized decision making and then are suddenly confronted with a request to share more fully in deciding are often upset and confused by the experience.

The editor's view of subordinates is influenced by natural assumptions about human nature. The editor's Theory-X or Theory-Y instincts can determine how much control or freedom the editor gives to staff members, depending on whether the editor thinks them basically lazy, unreliable, and irresponsible, or creative and self-motivated.

Fig. 8.4

CLOSE-UP

Every editor's management style and self-image of that management style are different. For some, style is a highly personal, instinctive behavior. For others, style is wedded to proven management systems and theories. Following is a collection of musings from editors about their management styles:

"My management style was born in self-defense when, at age twenty-five, I became city editor of the *Nashville Tennessean* and realized I had no idea what I was doing. Having no credentials to direct anyone, I took the coward's way out and asked the staff what I should do. It worked. This same 'let's-all-get-together-and-do-my-job' approach has stayed with me through several positions for which I've been similarly unprepared."

James D. Squires
Editor
Chicago Tribune

"Get the right people in key jobs under you and it's almost impossible to fail. Have the wrong people there and it is impossible to succeed. When you have the right people, pay attention to their real needs—as professionals and as human beings. Listen, even if you have other things to do. Be sure they understand their talent and their labor are

Fig. 8.4, continued

critical to success. If they need help, make giving it your first priority. Almost as important as people is a sense of time and direction. Don't ignore tomorrow's paper but devote prime time to planning and working for a better future."

Larry Jinks
Vice-President
Knight-Ridder Newspapers

"My style involves a lot of persuasion and teaching, a little like preaching and occasionally behaving like a DOUBLE S-O-B (that's 'boss' spelled backwards). I try to get everyone involved in a team effort, taking a positive approach to whatever problem we're dealing with. I try to be quick with criticism and just as quick with praise. I can be very patient, especially on big things; it's the little things that trigger my temper."

Marjorie Paxson
Publisher
The Daily Phoenix
Muskogee, Oklahoma

"Style is not an acquired skill. It's genetic. The management styles we've got—for better or for worse—are the ones we were born with. Style is a function of personality; it's not easy to change either one. I'd call my management style Celtic Contemporary—an approach that combines the best of St. Patrick and Brendan Behan. Under this style, it's important to have an office big enough for a conference table. If people hold a lot of meetings in your office and staffers use it for interviews and to eat lunch and watch TV and to call their friends, then you've solved the problem of access. After all that, you haven't got an office, you've got a day room—and that's good. This style requires instant availability and undivided attention for problems of alienation, personal finance, domestic turmoil, career and/or identity crises, and afflictions based on the real or imagined fear that the copy desk is out to get you. Like most other editors I know, I'd rather edit than manage. But both editing and managing are vital, and good management is really nothing more than the soft side of editing."

Neal Shine
Senior Managing Editor
Detroit Free Press

Source: "Musings from Editor-Managers on Their Management Styles," *The Bulletin of the American Society of Newspaper Editors,* May 1981, 5–7.

HOW EDITORS THINK

When we talk about what editors do, a number of clichés come to mind. Editors "take the long view," they "look at the big picture," they are "in charge of the overall operations of the newsroom." However trite these descriptions might seem, they do offer an insight into the capacity of individuals who become editors.

After years of study, behavioral scientists have concluded that the workings of the executive mind are distinctive. Elliott Jaques, director of the Institute of Organization and Social Studies at England's Brunel University, offers a concept he calls "the time frame of the individual."

Jaques's research indicates that individuals vary radically in the length of the time periods in which they can analyze, organize, and work through problems. For some of us, it is tough to figure out what to do today and in what order. Others—those with executive-type minds—can see a long way. They can identify the steps necessary for a move that may take years to complete. They are able to envision the consequences of each step and then take measures to set the organization in motion.[11]

Newspaper examples of this long-range executive vision are seen in A. M. Rosenthal's plan to develop special weekly sections in the *New York Times* and Allen Neuharth's concept for a national newspaper that became *USA TODAY*. Executive editor Rosenthal introduced the weekly sections one at a time, beginning in 1976 with "SportsMonday." By 1978, "ScienceTimes," "Living," "Home," and "Weekend" also were in place. Their appearance transformed the *Times* and contributed to a dramatic upsurge in the newspaper's advertising lineage. At Gannett, chairman Neuharth and a group of executives began brainstorming *USA TODAY* in 1980. The newspaper was introduced in September 1982, and Neuharth made public a schedule that projected advertising and circulation growth and that anticipated a profit for *USA TODAY* by 1987.

Jaques said that over a lifetime, a person typically becomes capable of handling progressively longer time frames. Most of the population is never capable of more than a three-month time span; a smaller group is able to envision an entire year, and so on. The significance of this is Jaques's additional finding that companies have a natural structure wherein most jobs can be classified according to the time frames in which the employees are required to operate. On the news staff, for example, reporters generally work in time frames of one day to one week. The city editor must be able to organize things for the next month. The managing editor has to plan for the next year. The editor and other top executives are called on to cast their minds ahead for a year or more in charting the directions of the newspaper. This ability to look far into the future, much sought after in executives, is called vision.

Jaques thinks that time frame is the best indicator of the broader mental capabilities that psychologists call *cognitive power*. Cognitive power is not the same as IQ. It reflects not raw brainpower, but how someone's perception and thinking are organized, how they operate. An individual able to work with a time frame of up to one year is capable of something called *reflective articulation*—the ability to stand back from what is going on, form ideas about it, and then manipulate these ideas.[12]

Siegfried Streufert, a psychologist at the College of Medicine at The Pennsylvania State University, says senior managers display a greater capacity for what he calls *differentiation*. Streufert's conclusions come from the results of complicated decision-making exercises he has administered to executives and others of approximately the same intelligence. He finds that successful managers can see distinctions between similar-appearing phenomena better than lay people, and that managers are more prone to consider the same fact from a different perspective, including someone else's point of view.[13]

Yale psychology professor Robert Sternberg has done research suggesting that managers have an ability for *selective decoding*— that is, the executive brain can quickly sort the relevant from the irrelevant. This ability gives them an edge in recognizing and defining a problem where others see only a jumble of business as usual. Daniel J. Isenberg, a professor at the Harvard Business School, suspects that managers may, in fact, pay less attention to isolated pieces of information than others do. The big thinkers have learned that it is more effective to spend their time putting everything together, including dredging up from memory solutions to past problems to see how they might shed light on the problem at hand.[14]

ANALYZING PROBLEMS

A manager's thought processes have a direct relationship to his or her ability to solve problems and make decisions rationally. Close observation has shown that even experienced managers are likely to be very unsystematic when dealing with problems and decisions. A hit-and-miss style often produces decisions based on erroneous conclusions, suggesting that the decisions also may be wrong.[15]

In any newsroom situation, the analysis of a problem can be separated into these five steps:

1. Defining the problem. Like every issue reported in the news columns, each problem has more than one side, more than one point of view. Before beginning to diagnose a problem, the editor should get the full picture and consider the situation from the points of view of those who are affected.

2. Outlining the task. After hearing all of the arguments, the editor's job is to set aside the competing interests and decide what the focus of the investigation will be. If the issue is late copy on the city desk, the editor may focus on how to fix the problem rather than establishing who is at fault.

3. Spotting the distinction. With the relevant facts and full opinions on the table, the editor's job is to see the flaw in the copy-flow system that no one else recognized.

4. Seeking the cause. Having spotted the flaw, the editor now must identify the cause, a process that may require an on-site investigation and some probing among the leading actors.

5. Fixing the problem. Finally, it is the editor's responsibility to devise a remedy for the problem of late copy, explain the solution to his or her subordinates, and follow through to see that the change is implemented and that it is effective.

The editor is particularly suited to problem solving of this kind because of the ability to step back from the work, understand what is going on, and form ideas about it. These steps are facilitated by the ability to see distinctions between similar-appearing types of information and the tendency to consider the same fact from different perspectives.

PARTICIPATIVE MANAGEMENT

A participative or democratic style of management is based on Douglas McGregor's Theory-Y assumptions about people (see Chapter 3). Editors express this style by delegating authority to subordinates, by involving them in decision making, by trusting them to handle responsibility, and by exerting little direct control over their behavior. The editor's underlying belief is that staffers and subordinate editors have a lot to contribute and he or she creates a climate in which these contributions can be stimulated.

Research indicates that groups that have democratic bosses tend to have higher morale. Specifically, participation in decision making leads to increased satisfaction, especially when decisions are important to employees' jobs and when employee participation is authentic.[16] Another series of studies on managerial decision-making styles produced evidence that managers tend to be more participative when the quality of the decision is important and when acceptance of the decision by subordinates is critical for its effective implementation. This research also suggested that managers tend to be more participative when they trust their subordinates to focus on organizational rather than personal goals and when conflict among subordinates is minimal.[17]

Participative decision making takes place at the daily news meeting, where editors from each news department discuss their story budgets. The managing editor often runs the meeting. Give-and-take and informal banter typically are part of the process of deciding the lead stories for each section of the paper. A participative-style managing editor will offer suggestions, but will allow subordinate editors to make most of the decisions on story play. Only a sharp disagreement around the table or a strongly held opinion by the managing editor requires him or her to make the call.

Why does participation work? A partial answer is that it helps staffers understand more fully what is expected of them, it increases the likelihood that employees will work for rewards and outcomes they value, it heightens the effects of peer pressure on behavior, and it enlarges the amount of control employees have over their own behavior.[18]

However, it is wrong to assume that an editor who is comfortable with a democratic style will take every decision to subordinates for participation. The editor tends to be selective about participation. Quick judgments about the news sometimes have to be made without consultation. Larger decisions involving choices of key subordinates often are made by the top news executive alone. But if the following conditions are present, the editor is safe in concluding that participation may be effective:

- The decision must be important to subordinates.
- Subordinates must be given time for full participation.
- Subordinates must be qualified to participate by virtue of experience, knowledge, or creative talents.
- Subordinates must be given complete information about the problem.

Unless these conditions can be met, the process is likely to dissolve in frustration. Staffers will think they are being manipulated and the editor will conclude it was a waste of time.

A common misconception about democratic leadership is that, in the process, the editor will allow subordinates to vote on a decision. That is a political perception of democracy that does not exist in the decision-making environment of the newsroom. Indeed, if the editor took a vote, he or she would be abdicating the role of the boss. The editor remains accountable for any decision forged by the group and, therefore, must retain the right to make the final call. The idea of a majority of one is played out at many newspapers when the editorial board meets to decide its political endorsements. It is not uncommon for the majority of the editorial board—generally the editorial-page editor and staff—to vote for one candidate and the editor or publisher to cast a single but deciding vote for another.

When the editor is looking at a problem and trying to decide whether to ask others to help, several factors may influence the strategy:[19]

- The editor is not an authority on the problem.
- The group has knowledge the editor needs to solve the problem.
- A critical factor is acceptance of the decision and the successful implementation of the plan.
- Resistance to the decision is anticipated.
- Staffers who will be asked to carry out the decision are skilled and motivated.
- The editor is confident that he or she can "sell" the idea and get the participating staffers to "buy" the plan.
- The editor is unsure about the strength of his or her power base.

In the examination of the phenomenon of participation, researchers have discovered a tendency in which the group's effort to concur becomes so dominant that it overrides any realistic appraisal of alternative courses of action. This concept is called groupthink and it resulted from studies of high-level governmental policy decisions regarding U.S. involvement in Korea, the Bay of Pigs, and Vietnam. The analysis found numerous examples in which the group norms favored improved morale at the expense of critical thinking. In these studies, seven primary symptoms of groupthink were identified:[20]

1. Illusion of invulnerability. Group members often reassure themselves about obvious dangers, become overly optimistic and willing to take extraordinary risks.

2. Rationalizing. Group members tend to discount warning signs and other types of negative feedback that could lead to a reconsideration of the course of action being planned.
3. Illusion of morality. Group members often believe in the inherent morality of the group, causing them to ignore the ethical or moral consequences of their decisions.
4. Stereotyping the opposition. Group members often characterize leaders of opposition groups in such harsh stereotypes as to rule out any need to negotiate with them on differences of opinion.
5. Self-censorship. Group members often use self-censorship to avoid deviating from what appears to be a group consensus. As a result, they tend to minimize to themselves the seriousness of their doubts.
6. Illusion of unanimity. Self-censorship encourages the development of the illusion of unanimity, the assumption that everyone holds the same opinion.
7. Controlling information. Victims of groupthink often appoint themselves as "mindguards" to protect the leader and other members of the group from adverse information that may cause conflict in the group over the virtue of a certain course of action.

Fig. 8.5

CLOSE-UP

Following is a collection of self-study questions for editors who are interested in looking at themselves and their management styles. There are no right answers, only useful answers that result from honest self-examination:

1. Where do I get my information, and how? Can I make greater use of my contacts? In what area is my knowledge weakest?
2. What information do I share with my staff? With my editors? How important is this information to them? Do I keep too much infor-

Fig. 8.5, continued

mation to myself because sharing it is time-consuming and inconvenient?

3. Do I tend to act before information is in? Or do I wait so long for all the details that opportunities are lost and I become a bottleneck?

4. What pace of change do I ask the staff to tolerate? Is change disruptive in my newsroom? Do I give full consideration to the long-term impact of change on the newspaper?

5. Am I sufficiently well-informed to pass judgment on proposals from my editors? Could I leave the final choice to them more often? Do we have problems because my editors make too many decisions independently?

6. What is my vision for the newspaper? Are these just loose ideas in my mind? Should I articulate them as a guide for others on the staff?

7. How do my subordinates react to my managerial style? Am I sensitive to the powerful influence my actions have on them? Do I find a good balance between encouragement and pressure? Do I stifle initiative?

8. Is there any system to my time scheduling? Or do I just react to the pressures of the moment? Do I concentrate on one type of function at the expense of others because I find it more interesting? What times of the day or week am I most efficient?

9. Do I overwork? What effect does my workload have on my efficiency? Should I force myself to break the pace of my activity?

10. Am I too superficial in what I do? Can I really shift moods as quickly as my work patterns require? Should I attempt to decrease the amount of fragmentation and interruption in my work?

11. Am I a slave to the action and excitement of being an editor so that I don't give as much attention to issues and problems that need my attention? Should I be more reflective?

12. Do I know how to make the most of written communication? Do I rely excessively on face-to-face communication? Do I spend enough time in the newsroom? Are my meetings well-planned and efficient?

Source: Adapted from Henry Mintzberg, "The Manager's Job: Folklore and Fact," in *Executive Success: Making It in Management* (New York: John Wiley & Sons, 1983), 480–84.

DEVELOPING A MANAGEMENT STYLE

Individuals who occupy the position of top news executive vary widely in the way they use the authority of their office. Differences in basic instincts about people, ideas, and things dictate the rich diversity of styles in the newsroom leadership of U.S. newspapers.

Most human-behavior experts, wary of correlating personality traits with executive performance, acknowledge that personality does play a critical role in determining how a manager's job will

Fig. 8.6

CLOSE-UP

A clear illustration of how personality influences leadership style is offered by Richard E. Neustadt of Harvard University in his study of presidential power. Neustadt contrasted the styles Franklin Roosevelt and Dwight Eisenhower in their responses to the problem of power in executive relations.

Of Roosevelt, Neustadt wrote: "The first task of an executive, as he evidently saw it, was to guarantee himself an effective flow of information and ideas . . . Roosevelt's persistent effort therefore was to check and balance information acquired through official channels with information acquired through a myriad of private, informal, and unorthodox channels and espionage networks. At times he seemed almost to pit his personal sources against his public sources . . . His favorite technique was to keep grants of authority incomplete, jurisdictions uncertain, charters overlapping. The result of this competitive theory of administration was often confusion and exasperation on the operating level; but no other method could so reliably insure that in a large bureaucracy filled with ambitious men eager for power, the decisions, and the power to make them, would remain with the President."

Of Eisenhower: His "use of men tended to smother, not enhance, the competition roused by overlapping jurisdictions. Apparently this was intentional . . . Eisenhower seemingly preferred to let subordinates proceed upon the lowest common denominators of agreement than to have their quarrels—and issues and details—pushed up to him."

Source: Richard E. Neustadt, *Presidential Power* (New York: Signet, 1964), 149–50, 153–54.

be handled because so much of the job involves discretionary dealings with people. The job is often a reflection of the personality of the individual holding the editor's job; the job description is secondary.

In his best-selling book, *In Search of Excellence,* Thomas J. Peters emphasizes a management style he observed at Hewlett-Packard. He calls it "Managing By Wandering Around." It is a brand of leadership that puts the manager in touch with employees and customers.[21]

Management By Wandering Around—or MBWA—is natural to many editors. They prowl the newsroom, checking the news budgets, looking over page proofs, discussing page-one play, passing along a story idea, holding an ad hoc meeting with two or three subordinates, kibitzing with staffers about sports, politics, and the weather. It creates a high degree of informal communication. That's the key. And it gives the editor an opportunity for what Peters calls "the art of naïve listening"—hearing raw impressions, picking up on the staff's agenda, getting the real message.

In one view of how personality types dictate management style, Leonard R. Sayles, professor of business administration at Columbia University's Graduate School of Business, developed the following breakdown:[22]

- Rigid and simplistic. Managers with rigid and simplistic personalities are described as "frustrated engineers" who view management as simply making correct, deductive decisions. To these managers, everything is either "right" or "wrong." They are baffled and distressed when problems turn out to have large gray areas. These managers go by the book and yearn for a clear-cut answer to every problem. They want consistency and unity. Subordinates who ask challenging questions or push for change are thought to be disloyal.

- Adversarial. Managers who think it is a dog-eat-dog world see themselves surrounded by individuals and systems that are dishonest and untrustworthy. Adversarial managers see themselves as "jungle fighters" in which their chance for survival depends on getting their enemies before their enemies get them. Their day-to-day lives consist of building alliances and proving their power. They base decisions on the potential impact on personal power, visibility, and influence.

- Super-sales-oriented. Managers who seek to win by super-salesmanship usually are highly articulate and able to dominate in a one-on-one situation. They learn that shrewd, pressuring tactics will gain them enough concessions to get the job done. As forceful talkers, they can overwhelm their more reticent colleagues, but over time, this builds resentment and encourages backlash.

- Compromising. For these managers, most problems do not have a right answer. There is no perfect truth, only partial answers. They believe in giving a little to get a little, splitting many disputes down the middle. They are skilled at negotiation and trade-offs.

- Creative. These managers have highly developed problem-solving skills and they can resolve complex situations creatively. They have found methods for reaching their goals that enable others to attain theirs as well. They understand the need to work through the organization and are open to different ways of doing things.

Whatever the personality mix of the manager, certain characteristics are thought to be common to all successful leaders. The clues to watch for include: the ability to manage stress, the readiness to view themselves as expendable, the capacity to concentrate, and the willingness to act as mentors for younger leaders.

The question of an editor's style comes around finally to the idea of expectation. We see it in the theme of George Bernard Shaw's play *Pygmalion*, where one person, by effort and will, can transform another person. In the world of newspapers, many successful editors play Pygmalion-like roles in developing subordinates and in stimulating their performance. Those editors treat their subordinates in a way that conveys an expectation for higher performance.

J. Sterling Livingston of the Harvard Business School has documented in a number of cases the effect of expectation as the centerpiece of management style. The results of his research reveal:[23]

1. What a manager expects of subordinates and the way he or she treats them largely determines their performance and career progress.

2. A unique characteristic of superior managers is their ability to create high performance expectations that subordinates fulfill.

3. Less effective managers fail to develop similar expectations, and as a consequence, the productivity of their subordinates suffers.

4. Subordinates, more often than not, actually do what they think they are expected to do.

The editor can communicate expectations in a number of ways. In a one-on-one discussion with a staffer or a subordinate editor, it is difficult to mask expectations. The editor's body language, posture, tone of voice, and choice of words all suggest, however subtly, what the editor expects. If the editor talks expansively and positively about an assignment, sets a demanding standard, and expresses confidence, the staffer has no doubt of the editor's high expectations. The staffer is likely to make a great effort to satisfy the editor's expectation. If the editor is indifferent, that message too will be transmitted, however unintentionally, and will influence the quality of work that results.

Clearly, the editor's expectations must be realistic and not simply the result of wishful thinking or an overrated confidence in the staff. If staffers are driven to reach for unattainable or unrealistic goals, eventually they give up trying and settle for performance that may actually be lower than they are capable of achieving.

The editor's expectations cannot be sustained unless there is a broader foundation of support that can be understood by the staff. This is where the traditions and the standards of the newspaper come into play. There will be a common understanding of the editor's expectations in any newsroom where the editor has established standards against which the staff's performance will be measured. The staff knows that its rewards will be determined by the success in meeting the standards. Within the framework of these standards, the editor is able to translate high expectations into specific guidelines for individual assignments.

The editor who understands self and expectations can become a truly superior manager. Over time, these two key qualities give the editor greater confidence in his or her ability to make strong choices for subordinates, to develop the talents and skills of subordinates, and to express clearly to them what is expected and how they will be managed.

CHAPTER SUMMARY

An editor's management style is highly individualistic. It is the combination of management theory with personality, self-perception, and experience. The theories and concepts of management help the editor carry out job responsibilities effectively within the framework of his or her working life-style and internal makeup.

The ability to develop a realistic self-image is necessary before growth and maturity in the job can occur. Critical self-examination leads to setting high goals and taking charge of one's own development.

The editor's real style is how the staff perceives it rather than how the editor perceives it. Sensitivity training has proved effective in helping leaders understand how their followers view them.

An editor's management style is influenced by his or her value system, confidence in subordinates, personal leadership instincts, and capacity for dealing with uncertain situations.

Like most executives, top editors tend to have the ability to plan and organize tasks over long time frames, to stand apart from a problem and form ideas about it, to spot distinctions in situations that appear similar, and to separate the relevant from the irrelevant.

In analyzing problems, the editor is likely to follow these five steps: (1) define the problem, (2) outline the task, (3) spot the distinction, (4) seek the cause, and (5) fix the problem.

A democratic, or participative, style of leadership is most effective when subordinates have strong needs for independence, when they are ready to assume responsibility, when they have a high tolerance for ambiguity, and when they identify with the editor's goals. Participative management tends to increase the morale and satisfaction of workers, particularly when the shared decisions are important and when employee participation is authentic.

Researcher Leonard R. Sayles defined several personality types that help shape management styles: rigid and simplistic, adversarial, super-sales-oriented, compromising, and creative.

The editor's expectations are an important part of his or her management style because they directly influence the level of performance of individuals on the staff. Successful editors create high but realistic performance expectations.

NOTES

1. Paul J. Brouwer, "The Power to See Ourselves," in *Executive Success: Making It in Management* (New York: John Wiley & Sons, 1983), 17.
2. Ibid., 22–26.
3. Abraham Zaleznik, "The Human Dilemmas of Leadership," *Harvard Business Review*, July–August 1963, 14–18.
4. Ibid., 18–19.
5. Paul Hersey and Kenneth Blanchard, *Management of Organizational Behavior*, 4th ed. (Englewood Cliffs, N.J.: Prentice-Hall, 1982), 128–29.
6. Leland P. Bradford, Jack R. Gibb, and Kenneth D. Benne, *T-Group Theory and Laboratory Method* (New York: John Wiley & Sons, 1964), 1–2.
7. Victor H. Vroom, *Some Personality Determinants of the Effects of Participation* (Englewood Cliffs, N.J.: Prentice-Hall, 1960), 70–74.
8. Hersey and Blanchard, *Management of Organizational Behavior*, 126–27.
9. Robert Tannenbaum and Warren H. Schmidt, "How to Choose a Leadership Pattern," *Harvard Business Review*, May–June 1973, 163–64.
10. Ibid., 116.
11. Walter Kiechel III, "How Executives Think," *Fortune*, 4 February 1985, 127.
12. Ibid., 128.
13. Ibid.
14. Ibid.

15. Perrin Stryker, "Can You Analyze This Problem?" *Harvard Business Review*, May–June 1965, 73.
16. William G. Scott and Terence R. Mitchell, *Organization Theory: A Structural and Behavioral Analysis* (Homewood, Ill.: Irwin, 1976), 85–86.
17. Victor H. Vroom and Philip W. Yetton, *Leadership and Decision Making* (Pittsburgh: University of Pittsburgh Press, 1973), 82–83.
18. Ronald J. Ebert and Terence R. Mitchell, *Organizational Decision Processes: Concepts and Analysis* (New York: Crance, Russak, 1975), 263.
19. Jerry L. Gray, *Supervision* (Boston: Kent, 1984), 299–300.
20. Irving L. Janis, "Groupthink," *Psychology Today*, November 1971, 43–46, 74–76.
21. Thomas J. Peters and Robert H. Waterman, Jr., *In Search of Excellence* (New York: Harper & Row, 1982), 122–23.
22. Leonard R. Sayles, *Leadership: What Effective Managers Really Do . . . and How They Do It* (New York: McGraw-Hill, 1979), 219.
23. J. Sterling Livingston, "Pygmalion in Management," *Harvard Business Review*, July–August 1969, 82.

9

Understanding Individual Potential

Journalists view themselves as creative people whose work requires critical judgment, a strong sense of events, and the ability to act quickly. The individual talents that journalists bring to their tasks are shaped by a variety of experiences, life-styles, values, personalities, and motivations. For the editor, creating a work environment that is free and open, that encourages innovative work, and that enables staffers to share the public commitment and responsibility of the newspaper requires a delicate balancing act. The editor must have a sophisticated understanding of how individuals work, how their personalities and experiences influence their values, and how their imaginations can help generate satisfying and productive work. These management functions are enhanced by the editor's own interest in discovering and formulating ideas for solving problems.

CREATIVITY

Although there are no substitutes for knowledge, analysis, and energy, creativity is clearly an integral part of the work of journalists.

Creativity is sometimes thought of as a gift bestowed upon certain individuals that enables them to produce creations of genius. Although creativity is typically associated with artists—sculptors, painters, composers, novelists, and poets—it is not limited to the arts and artists. Inventiveness and innovation flower in all individuals and in all organizations. In the broad view, a creative person is one who generates new and different ideas, designs, theories, and works of art in ways that are not amenable to explanation.[1]

Research on creativity began with Sir Francis Galton, an English scientist and cousin of Charles Darwin. Galton's studies in the latter half of the nineteenth century pursued genius, and his pioneering work—suggesting that heredity is a greater influence on genius than the social environment—led to other investigations of exceptional intelligence and creativity. Yet, creativity remains an elusive concept. Even today, there is no general agreement on how to measure, how to elicit, or how to develop creativity.

Attempts to define creativity often include the words *discovery, originality, innovation, invention, inspiration,* and *idea.* But, is it creativity when a copy editor turns a dull lead into a compelling one and tops it with a sharp headline? Is it creativity when a graphic artist produces a striking illustration that precisely captures the mood of a story? Or when a reporter translates a long interview into a well-crafted story? Or when a managing editor devises an effective solution to a complex personnel problem?

These are all creative activities. They are examples that suggest most of us are creative, but they also help show that some individuals are demonstrably more creative than others. While it is often difficult to recognize creative people until they have proven themselves to be so, there are some characteristics that seem to be shared by most creative people:[2]

- Fluency. The ability to generate and articulate a large number of different ideas rapidly. A highly creative person will have a rich flow of ideas.

- Originality. The quality of producing unusual or atypical answers to questions, responses to situations, or interpretations of events.

- Flexibility. The ability to move easily from one frame of reference or one approach to another. Flexibility is associated with broad interests and exposure to many ideas, with a willingness to examine a problem from different angles, and with a respect for differing points of view.

- Tolerance of ambiguity. The ability to be comfortable with situations in which the questions are not clearly defined, the methods are unfamiliar, the resources are not all in hand, and the rules are not in order.

- Playfulness and humor. Qualities that many believe are hallmarks of high creativity. There is a relationship between humor and creativity since both require the ability to see things outside the normal pattern. Creative people like to play with ideas and combine them in unlikely ways.

- Strong work ethic. The instinct for showing strong curiosity and for being positive, enthusiastic, and optimistic about their work. Creative people are intrigued and captured by problems. They are likely to be motivated by the appeal of the problem. More than others, they tend to become immersed in the project and are apt to work longer and harder without external pressures or incentives.

- Independence. The tendency to create their own standards and to be less concerned with what others think. Independent people are self-disciplined and display self-confidence in attacking new or unfamiliar problems.

- Nonconformity. The lack of concern with making a good impression on others. Nonconformists see themselves as "different." They also tend to belong to fewer organizations than others.

Donald W. MacKinnon of the University of California at Berkeley describes the creative personality as one of "openness to his own feelings and emotions, a sensitive intellect, and understanding self-awareness and wide-ranging interests, including many which in the American culture are thought of as feminine."[3] MacKinnon studied architects, whom he thought of as highly creative and inclined to have positive opinions of themselves. He found their self-images to include being inventive, determined, independent, individualistic, enthusiastic, and industrious. He characterized the less creative architects as more concerned with being virtuous, of good character, rational, and sympathetic to others.

While sharing common characteristics, creative workers also

have some common needs. High among them is the need for recognition, for ego gratification. Creative people want to control their work. They want an atmosphere and a management style that encourage professional development. And they want the freedom to think creatively about their work.

The Creative Process

Gardner Murphy, a psychologist and director of research at The Menninger Foundation, identified four stages to the creative process: (1) the long immersion of the sensitive mind in a medium that gives delight and fulfillment; (2) the acquisition of "storehouses full of experiences" which are consolidated into patterns; (3) the sudden inspiration drawn from the storehouses of experience; and (4) the "hammering out," the sifting and testing, the critical evaluating and perfecting of the creative work.[4]

Abraham Maslow, originator of important theories of motivation (see Chapter 3), stressed improvisation and inspiration rather than the finished product in his studies of creativeness. He drew a distinction between *primary creativeness* (the inspirational phase) and *secondary creativeness* (the working out of the inspiration). "I am very certain," Maslow wrote, "that many, many people have waked up in the middle of the night with a flash of inspiration about some novel they would like to write, or a play or a poem or whatever, and that most of these inspirations never come to anything. Inspirations are a dime a dozen. The difference between the inspiration and the final product—for example, Tolstoy's *War and Peace*—is an awful lot of hard work, an awful lot of discipline, an awful lot of training . . . and throwing away first drafts and so on. The virtues that go with the secondary kind of creativeness, the creativeness which results in actual products, in the great paintings, the great novels, in the bridges, the new innovations, and so on, rest as heavily on other virtues—stubbornness and patience and hard work—as they do upon the creativeness of the personality."[5]

Maslow described the inspirational phase of creativity as the time when a person "loses his past and his future and lives only in the moment. He is all there, totally immersed, fascinated and absorbed in the present, in the current situation, in the here-now, with the matter-in-hand."

This tendency to become lost in the present is familiar to many of us. It is an almost mystical experience in which we are absorbed in a task and are unaware of anything else, including the passage of time. Being completely absorbed in one's work can produce a peak experience. A fascination with the task results in high levels of concentration and often high levels of productivity and satisfaction. This phenomenon can be compared to a long-distance runner's feeling of rapture, described as the "runner's high."

The creativity that results in good newspaper work has important preconditions—one is knowledge; another is experience. An editor who has a bright idea is simply combining previously unconnected ideas. To do this effectively, one must possess knowledge, which is the result of education and experience. For example, we would not expect an editor to create a more effective way of controlling local expenses without some knowledge of budgeting and the activities of the reporting staff.

In the newsroom, before there is writing or editing, there is thinking—the invention of an approach to gathering information or laying out a news page or writing a story or a headline. Many approaches to writing a news story are possible. Each is the unique result of how the reporter or the reporter and editor together view the story.

In a little volume called *Newsthinking*, journalist Bob Baker says the thought process that all reporters go through before they strike the first computer key "is an intense examination of those moments in which you make your facts fall into place. This is newsthinking, where the genius of great writers—their creativity, their imagination, their willingness to take risks—unfolds."[6]

Just as every story is different, so too is everyone on the staff—no two reporters are alike as they weave information, perception, logic, and organization into a story. The creative edge that some reporters possess is played out in a complex meshing of concentration, analysis, flexibility, and writing ability.

Within the standards of good journalism, there are rules for style and deadlines, but there are no intellectual guidelines that restrict the mind in processing the news. There are no rules to limit the reporter in the pursuit of an angle that will make the story different, perhaps better. That is the difference between the structured and the unstructured elements of handling the news. It explains the normal tensions of the newsroom that rise when the creative aspects of writing and editing clash with the structure of the news operation and its emphasis on deadlines and page flow.

Behavior in the newsroom often is based on rules, past practices, policies, systems, and techniques. Systematic learning influences our approach to writing a news story or laying out a news page, and what is learned becomes part of the tradition of how we produce the newspaper. As such, this behavior can be a barrier to innovation and to brainstorming in search of better ways.

Another inhibiting factor to creativity is that any new idea threatens an old one. It fosters the prospect of change and stimulates feelings of inadequacy in those who did not think of the new approach and who recognize that the successful innovator may claim more power.[7]

Students of creativity argue that a vigorous tradition of freedom of thought and inquiry is essential to the continued renewal of both individuals and organizations. They observe that the innovator has always been a threat to the status quo and is viewed as a disruptive force.[8]

Every organization has to maintain its internal stability and can tolerate only a limited amount of internal dissension. This explains why, in many companies, virtue is more likely to be rewarded than creativity.[9] By contrast, editors tend to tolerate—indeed, encourage—more inventiveness and originality. Witness the unceasing efforts of city editors to prod reporters to use descriptives, to be more selective with quotes, to give the lead a compelling spin, and to strive for clarity.

Managing Creativity

For the editor, creativity is linked to the management of ideas. In an environment that is strongly oriented toward producing a full news report each day, the editor quickly recognizes that creativity must have one crucial quality: It must have value. It must generate something meaningful, something useful for the newspaper.

To contend with the challenge of the fast-moving changes and new technologies in communication, editors will need vision and skill in generating and manipulating ideas. Melvin Anshen of the Columbia University Graduate School of Business calls this "the skill of the great philosophers—the ability to universalize from here and now to everywhere and always. If it is true that top executives in the years ahead are going to be tested above all by their ability to manage ideas, then they are going to have to understand what it means to think like philosophers and develop skill in doing it."[10]

The education, training, and selection of future editors must recognize that the special ability to translate ideas into action will tolerate no second-rate minds or even first-rate minds that are narrowly oriented. It is true, as British philosopher Alfred North Whitehead wrote, "The vitality of thought is an adventure. Ideas won't keep. Something must be done about them."[11]

Editors are faced with the challenge of promoting creativity and providing an atmosphere where "wild and crazy ideas" can flower and be examined, but within the constraints imposed by deadlines and other realities of newspaper publishing. Staffers with a talent for discovery must know that the editor is willing to let them seize and develop ideas that excite their curiosity. Not every idea will fly, of course; but when possible, staffers should be given working time to follow an inspiration to a conclusion. Besides encouraging innovation, the editor will be inviting the questioning, probing, doubting, and restlessness that accompany creative activities.

Such an atmosphere is what Gardner Murphy calls the setting for the *habit of creation*. Creative insights come more and more frequently to those who have had them before and who have worked their ideas through into adequate expressions of the creative drive. Studies of inventors suggest that "creativeness may become a habit of perceiving, ruminating, catching a point through analysis, rearranging, trying out. Some of this undoubtedly is constitutional, but the records of the inventors seem to to offer convincing evidence that learning to create is as dominant a fact in the sphere of practical things as it is in poetry and music. Since learning to create, like all learning, is intimately dependent on a personal context, we cannot speak of creativeness as isolated from the rest of life, once a beginning is made. In every mind there are widening regions of creativeness if once the spark has been allowed to generate the fire. We can speak, therefore, of the development of a personality 'slanted' toward creativeness and maintaining this slant—and slanting more and more determinedly—unless pushed violently back into some other slant through adverse circumstances."[12]

Maslow describes a type of creative individual—whom he calls a "lone wolf"—who is apt to get ground up in an organization, apt to be afraid of it, and apt to work off in a corner alone. He sees the managing of creative people as being a little like trying to reconcile the revolutionary with the stable society because "the people I've studied are essentially revolutionary in the sense of turning their backs on what already exists, and in a sense of being dissatisfied with what is now the case."[13]

The presence of staffers who have a highly developed habit of creating does not mean the editor lets go of management functions or dismisses behavior that is out of step with the norms of the newsroom. Research focusing on scientists in industry shows that the scientists perform more effectively if there is frequent communication than if they are isolated. In these studies, reported by Rensis Likert of the University of Michigan, the best performance is attained when the scientist has considerable control over his or her work, including the setting of goals, and when this control is combined with free access to someone in authority. Likert suggests that the potential of younger subordinates is best developed by a boss who can maintain close interest in their work without dominating it.[14]

Additional research among scientists indicates that workers with high levels of freedom and autonomy in their work are not necessarily better performers than those without autonomy. In other words, creativity needs direction and support. Without guidance, creative instincts may be frustrated because innovation may not be brought to a satisfying or productive conclusion.

The idea that every organization should have a vigorous tradition of free thought and inquiry and a capacity for self-renewal becomes a critical influence on individual creativity within the organization. Thus, if a newspaper is blind to its own faults or is given to rationalizing those defects, it will not be likely to investigate forms of self-criticism, brainstorming, and the use of outside consultants for activities that could lead to renewal and growth, such as market and readership research. And it will not make effective use of staffers whose ideas challenge the status quo.

How can the editor control the activities of the staff within established patterns and rules and still nurture creativity? One answer is that if an idea is good and if it works, then any rule it breaks may not be worth preserving. Another answer is for an editor to look more closely at how creative powers are being used. Are editors equipped to provide literate, refined criticism of writing or do they fall back on a string of clichés such as "nice piece" or "reads well"? A talented reporter working for a shallow-thinking editor faces a long and lonely struggle to discover and correct the weaknesses in his or her writing.

A thoughtful editor can spare a reporter disappointment by sharing a personal comment—perhaps a sentence in a memo that offers advice on a dilemma the reporter may feel but cannot articulate. Guidance on selective use of quotes, on effective transitions, on a tendency to reach for dramatic words, on how to give effective shape to uninhibited, impulsive ideas, or on how to develop discipline will help the reporter concentrate on getting his or her writing under control.

The conditions for creativity in the newsroom require some special characteristics, but essentially they are identical to those required for good management:

- Providing communication that is based on frequency, openness, and clarity.
- Giving feedback that is timely and that encourages the continued search for creative solutions. Performance is enhanced if staffers have an opportunity to listen to colleagues who may think differently.

- Being able to talk with the boss. This is a positive influence that contributes support, feedback, and resources for creative efforts.
- Participating in goal setting. This can lead to challenging, realistic targets, particularly when the process of defining objectives is done with free access to someone in authority.
- Emphasizing a low level of supervision. Creative staffers are best encouraged by a supervisor who maintains a close interest but does not dominate the staffer's work. Too much supervision can lead to resentment.
- Encouraging participation in decision making. This gives staffers ownership in decisions affecting them and can increase motivation. The confidence imparted by the knowledge that their opinions are valued can encourage staffers to open their creative channels.
- Providing freedom to try new ways of performing tasks. A skillful editor will manage creative problem solving so that staffers have no fear of failure.
- Exerting a moderate amount of pressure. Staffers can get lost in the process of creating and need the discipline that an editor can impose through deadlines and routine editing controls.
- Encouraging the flow of ideas. The creative environment begins with the top editors, who welcome ideas from every level and who establish a philosophy that new ideas are not threatening.

LIFE-STYLES

Two books published in the late 1970s and early 1980s looked at values and life-styles in the United States. *The Nine American Lifestyles* by Arnold Mitchell of the Stanford Research Institute draws on research in an attempt to explain who we are and where we are going.[15] In *The People Puzzle,* author Morris Massey, owner-director of a consulting firm in Boulder, Colorado, argues that our life-styles and values were shaped by the era in which we were born and by the dramatic events in the outer world during our first ten years of life.[16]

What Mitchell and Massey offer is another dimension for editors to consider in understanding themselves and the journalists they manage. Mitchell says that the most compelling reason for knowing about our values and life-styles is that they tell us so much about who we are. "People's life-styles say a good deal about where we are going, and they help explain such practical, diverse questions as: why we support some issues and oppose others; why some people are strong leaders and others weak; why some people are economically brilliant and others gifted artistically—and a few are both; why we trust some people and are suspicious of others." Mitchell's definition of *values* is "the entire constellation of a person's attitudes, beliefs, opinions, hopes, fears, prejudices, needs, desires, and aspirations that, taken together, govern how one behaves."[17]

Mitchell observes: "For the most part, we try to mold our lives to make our beliefs and dreams come true. And in our attempts to reach our goals, we test ourselves again and again in diverse ways, and in doing so we grow. With this growth comes change, so that new goals emerge. In support of these new goals come new beliefs, new dreams, and new constellations of values. Some unusual people grow and change many times throughout their lives. Others change hardly at all with the decades. Most experience one or two periods when what is most important, most compelling, most beautiful shifts from one comprehensive pattern to another. These are the times when a person's values change—and life-styles are transformed."[18]

Mitchell's ideas and terms were drawn from many sources. We can recognize, for example, the influence of Maslow's needs hierarchy on Mitchell's value and life-style definitions. Mitchell separates life-styles and values into four groups which are then subdivided into nine life-styles. These groups are characterized as follows:[19]

1. *Need-driven groups: Survivors and Sustainers.* These two groups are very different, but Survivors and Sustainers share the burden of being poverty-stricken so that their lives are

driven by need. *Survivors* tend to be despairing, depressed, withdrawn, mistrustful, rebellious about their situation, lacking in self-confidence, and finding little satisfaction in any aspect of their lives. *Sustainers* are angry, distrustful, rebellious, anxious, combative people who feel left out of things—but, unlike the Survivors, they have not given up hope. Sustainers mistrust the system and have little confidence in leaders. Their life problem is less merely to survive than to secure and sustain hard-earned gains, and if possible, to move ahead to a better life.

2. *Outer-directed groups: Belongers, Emulators, and Achievers.* This is a huge, highly diverse category that includes about two-thirds of the adult population. The common denominator is that outer-directed people respond to signals from others, that they conduct themselves according to what they think others will think. *Belongers* are traditional, conforming, conservative, "moral," and nonexperimental. *Emulators* are intensely striving people, seeking to be like those they consider richer and more successful than they are. *Achievers* are the driving, driven people who have built "the system" and are now at the helm.

3. *Inner-directed groups: I-Am-Mes, Experientials, and Societally Conscious.* These groups are so named because the principal driving forces of their lives are internal, not external. Their sensitivity to their own feelings makes them sensitive to others and to events around them. Many are active in social movements, while others express their concerns more privately, such as in artistic pursuits. As a group, the inner-directeds are highly self-reliant and notably indifferent to social status. Money is of little importance to them. The actions of the *I-Am-Mes* mark them as energetic, enthusiastic, daring, and seeking the new. The *Experientials* seek direct, vivid experiences. For them, it is not things that count, but emotion. As a group, the *Societally Conscious* are successful, influential, mature. They believe in simplicity, in living in harmony with nature, that small is beautiful, and that everyone should help solve society's problems.

4. *Outer- and Inner-directed group: Integrateds.* Maturity, balance, and a sense of what is fitting are prime characteristics of this group. The *Integrateds* view each life-style as equally good, powerful, useful, and needed; each is simply different and appropriate in its own place. They tend to be open, self-assured, self-expressive, keenly aware of nuances and shadings, and often possessed of a world perspective.

Morris Massey's research is aimed at building a model that describes why people behave as they do. He focuses on the one thing that is common to all people: a value system. The process of value formation begins at birth and is programmed during the first twenty years of life, with the first ten years being especially significant. Once those values are established and behavior patterns are set, it becomes harder to change behavior. The pivotal element in Massey's model is the period of time in which individuals acquired their values. One's personality may differ markedly from the personalities of others, but each individual fits more or less into his or her own generational cluster. People respond to common patterns of life—the way they live, spend their money, use their time, function in their jobs, raise their children, respond to religion, and enjoy themselves. Values are influenced by such forces as family, school, religion, and the media. Massey offers these snapshots on formative periods in recent history:[20]

1930s. For people whose values were formed in the 1930s, the major experience was the Great Depression. Massey suggests that as these individuals grew up, the things they did without as children become critical. The things they grew up with they accept, reject, take for granted, or ignore. During the depression, economic security was important. People did without a lot of things. The 1930s was a time of heroes, traditional values, and "good, clean living." That generation is now security-oriented. Money is a motivator.

1940s. This was a time of turbulence, of World War II. The nation was galvanized to win, united as never before; the commitment to win was the major motivation for this generation. Important social change began. With Rosie the Riveter, women entered the work force in large numbers. Kindergartens mushroomed and the schools began to influence values at an earlier age. Adolescence became a cult. Teenagers were catered to commercially as never before.

1950s. Everything changed in the 1950s. Those who had their values formed during this period were to become substantially different from any previous generation. The good life arrived and its focus on gratification of one's desires—affluence, indulgence, permissiveness, money—became the motivation for this generation. Television hit the scene. So did Dr. Spock. Nearly 60 percent of U.S. families had moved into the middle class. Mass production led to mass consumption. The suburbs grew and the ultimate goal for many was to be well adjusted. The worker whose values were formed in the 1950s is characterized as a team player, part of a corporate structure.

1960s. In no other decade did values experience such dramatic shifts and changes, making the value programming of the 1960s difficult to analyze. People experienced a world in direct conflict with the stable era of the previous decade. Civil rights, the idealism of John Kennedy, the Vietnam War, and civil disobedience were seminal influences for those whose values were formed in these years. A new morality was expressed in dress, behavior, language, and the Pill. Change was a major motivation for this generation, and indeed, the 1960s saw the greatest changes in the shortest period of time—political, legal, economic, social, and commercial.

1970s. In the 1970s, there were seemingly endless reasons for feeling frustrated—inflation, pollution, crime, the continuing war in Vietnam, the stock market, the generation gap, immorality, riots, traffic, racism, skyjacking, and bumper stickers that insulted everyone. Nothing seemed to be working right. Nothing seemed to hold still. It was a time of confusion that centered on values—personal issues versus public issues. Campus demonstrations, Watergate, abortion, the ERA, religious upheaval, inflation, sexually active youngsters, the splintered family, and a new yearning for the past left scars on the generation that got its impact during these years.

For managers, the thrust of Massey's value analysis is to look at another person, know what was happening in the world when he or she was at age ten, and use that knowledge to help understand the individual. Realistically, we can look at people as part of a group. An editor dealing with a fifty-five-year-old copy editor and a twenty-five-year-old reporter doesn't need to know exactly what happened to each during value programming. But it is useful to know that the fifty-five-year-old and twenty-five-year-old may hold different generational values. Understanding those influences allows the editor to communicate, motivate, and interrelate more effectively. The values of blacks, Hispanics, Indians, Asian-Americans, and other minority groups were formed in the same way, but obviously many of their values are different from those of individuals who grew up in the mainstream.[21]

Out of the generational clusters, Massey has identified four broad categories of value differences: (1) traditionalists, (2) in-betweeners, (3) challengers, and (4) synthesizers. Look for patterns between Massey's clusters and the groups identified by Mitchell.

Traditionalists. People whose values were formed between 1930 and 1940 fit into a traditional mode. They are programmed with values expressed in statements, beliefs, customs, and legends that have been handed down mostly unchanged from generation to generation.

In-betweeners. Those who were programmed from the late 1940s to the late 1950s are the in-betweeners. This group was caught in the middle. It doesn't know which way to go. Members of this group hold the traditional orientation, but have also encountered a large number of new values that swept in during the 1950s. This is a pivotal group that can communicate with earlier and later generations.

Challengers. This is a rejection-oriented generation that formed values between 1960 and the early 1970s. They challenged the older generation, rejecting many traditionalist values and institutions. They believe the greatest resource is people as opposed to technology, money, things, and politics. The challengers can't be ignored. They are the baby boomers and there are a lot of them.

Synthesizers. The youngest group, being programmed in the 1970s and early 1980s, may be thought of as synthesizers. They are unique because of the information coming at them from the three older generations. The traditionalists tell them to beware, pay attention, become conservative. The challengers tell them not to listen, the world is fouled up, everything has gone wrong. The in-betweeners give conflicting directions. The synthesizers, Massey says, are emerging as a skeptical but concerned, even conservative, group.[22]

The utility of *life-style research* lies in its capacity to help editors understand the personalities of individuals on the newsroom staff. It is no easy matter to match people to their jobs in a way that will contribute to their satisfaction and productivity and enable editors to retain the most gifted and creative individuals.[23]

VALUES

Values make a profound difference in the life of an individual. They determine the depth of our commitments, the integrity of our relationships, the degree of energy we put into our work, and the level of gratification we get from success.

Staffers and editors basically have very similar value systems. The management task in the newsroom typically does not require editors to give attention to colliding values. The wise newsroom manager will recognize that newspeople are more similar than they are different. Adversarial relationships result more from differences in style than from differences in values. One of the editor's tasks in motivating staffers is to bring out the values that already exist in newspeople.

Journalists are keenly aware of the values ascribed to their craft. To some, journalism is a calling. Journalists honor codes of ethics because honesty and integrity matter, and it is important to them that readers think well of their behavior as journalists. Editors and staffers are sensitive to the idea of avoiding conflicts of interest. Newspapers hire lawyers to help protect the staff's relationships with sources.

Sources are important to the newspaper's value system in another way: Reporters and editors fuss over the meaning of words and the accuracy of quotes. They are, by nature, competitive. They value the intellectual challenge of the work. They need the feeling of being essential to the success of the newspaper. They worry about credibility and the image that journalists are arrogant and elitist. Journalists need to know that sources recognize and acknowledge the role of journalism and its practitioners.

These values are shared, quite often, by newspaper organizations. In many cases, such values are bound up in the history and traditions of the newspaper and become ingrained in the individuals on the news staff. Many will agree with the idea that a newspaper inevitably comes to take on the personality of its leader—owner, editor, or publisher. The values of the leader become the values of the newspaper.

In Akron, through four decades, no one doubted that what the *Beacon Journal* stood for was what John S. Knight stood for. At the *St. Petersburg Times,* a former staffer who had had a brief contact with Nelson Poynter said, "I came to really get a strong sense of his commitment to excellence, his editorial independence, his courage to develop an editorial philosophy that was in conflict with most of his readers. I came to admire Poynter's concern for excellence on every level and his absolute passion for journalism, for what he called a 'sacred trust.' "[24]

On Martha's Vineyard, the weekly *Vineyard Gazette* is seen as being a lovingly crafted paper that conveys a powerful sense of place, carrying on the values of its longtime editor, Henry Beetle Hough. In Louisville, the Bingham family is proud of the fact that, except for a small profit, most of the revenues are plowed back into the paper. Family patriarch Barry Bingham, Sr. "wants to be known as the leader of a great newspaper and not necessarily a greatly profitable one." As a result, the *Courier-Journal* over the years has developed a reputation for taking the larger view of things—regional, national, and even international perspective on issues—and for providing generous financial support for its editorial efforts.[25] That legacy remains, in spite of differences in the Bingham family that forced the sale of the *Courier-Journal* and the *Louisville Times* to Gannett in 1986.

The values of Jack Knight, Nelson Poynter, Henry Beetle Hough, and Barry Bingham are important, not because they are different from those of working journalists, but because they are symbols of the values that journalists share.

As the essence of a company's philosophy for achieving success, values provide a sense of common direction for all employees and guidelines for day-to-day behavior. If employees know what their company stands for, if they know what standards they are to uphold, then they are much more likely to make decisions that will support those standards. They also are more likely to feel as if they are an important part of the organization. They are motivated because the life of the company has a meaning for them.[26]

In their book, *Corporate Cultures,* Terrence E. Deal and Allan A. Kennedy found that successful companies place a great deal of emphasis on values. In general, these companies share three characteristics:[27]

1. They stand for something—that is, they have a clear and explicit philosophy about how they aim to conduct their business.
2. Management pays a great deal of attention to shaping and fine-tuning these values to conform to the economic and business environment of the company and to communicating the values to the organization.
3. These values are known and shared by all the people who work for the company—from the lowliest production workers right through to the ranks of senior management.

The values and beliefs of an organization indicate what matters are to be attended to most assiduously—such things as tight cost controls or customer service or longer-term strategy. Values also play an important role in determining how far one can rise within an organization.[28] If the newspaper's overriding ethic is excellence in the news report and in sound management systems, journalists who share those values and demonstrate the ability to produce results with them are the ones most likely to be successful.

Deal and Kennedy suggest that *shared values* act as an informal control system that affects performance in three ways:

1. Managers and others throughout the organization give extraordinary attention to whatever matters are stressed in the corporate value system.
2. Down-the-line managers make marginally better decisions, on the average, because they are guided by their perception of shared values.
3. People simply work a little harder because they are dedicated to the cause.

A study, published in 1983, of nearly 1,500 executives and managers provides evidence that shared values between the individual and the company are a major source of both personal and organizational effectiveness. The research found that when managers' values are compatible or congruent with the values of their companies, both their personal lives and their approach to their jobs are healthier. Specifically, when there are shared values between managers and their organizations, the results are:[29]

- Greater feelings of personal success. Managers who share in the values of the organization are more likely to think that they will fulfill—or already have reached—their life's ambition.
- Stronger feelings of organizational commitment and loyalty. At all levels, those who think they share the organization's values are more certain that they will be with the company in three years. Commitment to the organization and its values increases as one is promoted and receives greater responsibility.

- Clearer perspectives on ethical dilemmas. Managers who share the company's values are much more certain that the organization is guided by highly ethical standards. They also are much more likely to resign rather than carry out an action they think is unethical. They are more likely to view their colleagues as being concerned about ethics, whereas workers who don't share the company's values are more likely to be cynical about the ethical concerns of their colleagues and the organization.

- Lower levels of work/home stress. The cost of having values that are incompatible is high, both to the individual and the organization. Managers who don't share the company's values think that the demands of the job and the anxiety of the job cause much of the stress in their personal lives. They think that the job prevents them from spending as much time with their families and friends as they would like. They also report that the job is less satisfying than other interests in their lives.

- Greater commitment to organizational goals. Those who share the goals of the company give greater importance to these goals. They particularly give higher value to effectiveness, productivity, reputation, morale, profit, and stability.

- Higher regard for others who have a stake in the organization. Managers who share the same values as their organization consider stockholders, owners, and customers as being more important than those whose value sharing is low.

- Different perceptions of important personal qualities. Older managers and those in more senior positions are more likely to be high in value sharing. This suggests that the acquisition of shared values may be a developmental process. Interestingly enough, gender and educational level do not seem to influence the value sharing. Whatever the size or location of the organization, managers are in solid agreement that what they value most in their colleagues is honesty, responsibility, competency, imagination, and rationality.

The values that provide meaning and direction for a corporation also can be associated with its downfall. In his role as a recruiter for Gannett, Phil Currie, vice-president/news, has interviewed hundreds of journalists who had just seen their newspapers fold. In those interviews, Currie learned about values that led to failure: deadlines that were too early to report the scores of the local baseball team's night games; an editor who didn't know some of his people well enough to give them a recommendation; newspapers where the Guild was in control of the newsroom; newspapers in large cities with few minorities on the staff; and many instances where staffers expressed feelings of lethargy and indifference.[30]

The values of journalism are more sharply defined than ever today, reflecting an increasingly sophisticated expectation of what newspapers should be doing and how journalists should behave. But those values are less likely to be shared by the individual journalist and his or her newspaper. The buying and selling of newspapers and the emergence of big media companies are influencing a shift of loyalties among individual journalists from the newspaper for which they work to the values and standards of journalism as a craft.

Our examination of values and the reasons for the increasing mobility among young journalists suggests a serious consequence for newspaper companies. More and more, the bright, educated, and introspective men and women coming into journalism are choosing where to work on the basis of the newspaper's ability to provide significant, creative, and satisfying work. Without a doubt, the values of journalism are important to them. To the extent that they are shifting their allegiance from newspaper values to journalism values generally suggests that many of them are ambiguous about the commitment of their newspaper to the ideals they hold. Ambiguity is the consequence when a newspaper does not back up public statements about its commitment to excellence with the resources to achieve such excellence. Ambiguity is the result when journalistic values seem to be compromised by decisions that reflect only the economic interests of the newspaper.

Fig. 9.1

CLOSE-UP

A major study at Indiana University reveals a notable shift in lifestyles and values of newspeople between 1971 and 1983. The survey was conducted by David H. Weaver, Richard G. Gray, and G. Cleveland Wilhoit of the Indiana University School of Journalism. Their data are compared to a 1971 study at the University of Illinois by John W. C. Johnstone, Edward J. Slawski, and William W. Bowman.

Following are some of the most striking differences:

- The size of the journalistic work force increased 61 percent during the 1970s, with the greatest percentage of growth in radio and television.
- U.S. journalists in 1982–83 were younger and more of them were female than in 1971. Minority journalists were younger on the average than nonminorities.
- More journalists are leaving the field after age forty-five than in 1971, primarily because of low salaries.
- There has been a significant gain in the proportion of women journalists employed in U.S. media during the 1970s. Overall, the proportion of women journalists has increased from about one-fifth in 1971 to about one-third in 1982–83, and this proportion is likely to grow, given the 60 percent enrollment of women in U.S. journalism schools.
- The largest increases in the percentages of women journalists have occurred in the broadcast field.
- There are proportionately fewer blacks, Hispanics, and Jews in U.S. journalism in 1982–83 than in 1971, although the actual numbers are up somewhat. This finding suggests that although efforts to recruit and retain women journalists in U.S. news media have been successful, such efforts with regard to minorities have been ineffective.
- Politically, many more journalists place themselves in the middle of the scale than in 1971, and significantly fewer put themselves on the right. This suggests that U.S. journalists as a whole are

becoming more centrist, not more leftist as some researchers have argued.

- Journalists working for the more prominent media organizations are more likely to be left of center politically, as was true in 1971, but the difference between them and other journalists is not as great as it was in 1971. This contradicts other findings that predict that the next generation of U.S. journalists is likely to be more to the left than is the current generation.

- The typical beat and general assignment reporter in the United States is thirty-one years old with eight years experience, three of which are with their present employer.

- Supervising editors are about thirty-five years old, much younger than the 41.5 age in 1971. Typically, they have twelve years experience, five years in their present job. Twenty-eight percent of supervisors are women.

- The Indiana team asked 1,001 journalists to identify those who had been influential in shaping their ideas on journalism ethics: 88 percent identified "newsroom learning" as extremely or quite influential, 72 percent said "family upbringing," and 61 percent said "a senior editor."

Sources: David H. Weaver, Richard G. Gray, and G. Cleveland Wilhoit, "Major Findings From a Survey of American Journalists, 1982–1983" (Indiana University, 1984); John W. C. Johnstone, Edward J. Slawski, and William W. Bowman, *The News People: A Sociological Portrait of American Journalists and Their Work* (Urbana, Ill.: University of Illinois Press, 1976).

DESCRIBING OURSELVES

Research by Judee and Michael Burgoon of the University of Arizona provides an arresting self-image of newspaper journalists that is important for newsroom managers as well as those concerned with how they relate to their readers.

The Burgoon research was first published in 1982 as part of the Newspaper Research Project sponsored by the American Society of Newspaper Editors and the Newspaper Advertising Bureau. Their findings are based on responses to a seventeen-page questionnaire by 489 working journalists at all levels of responsibility at ten newspapers and interviews with 187 journalists at the participating newspapers. The newspapers in the study were the *Day* of New London, Connecticut; the *Morning News* and *Evening Journal* of Wilmington, Delaware; the *Independent* and *Daily Mail* of Anderson, South Carolina; the *Tampa Tribune;* the *Plain Dealer* of Cleveland; the *Wichita Eagle and Beacon;* the *San Diego Union;* and the *Wenatchee* (Washington) *World.* The staff of the *Lansing State Journal* participated in a pilot test for the project.

The Burgoons' report to the newspaper industry identified important groups of journalists who are insulated from the public and who substitute communication with coworkers for communication with the public. The Burgoons analyzed the issue further and uncovered some intriguing qualities about U.S. newspaper journalists.

All respondents described certain characteristics about themselves. The Burgoons interpreted these self-descriptions and classified each respondent as either high or low on communication with the public and high or low on communication with other journalists. This created four communicator types:[25]

1. *Isolates.* Those with limited community contact and limited contact with other journalists. They communicate with neither the public nor their colleagues. This was the largest group; 29 percent of those interviewed so identified themselves. The isolates are relative newcomers to the industry; they have been at their newspaper a short time. They are more dissatisfied with their jobs. They are more likely to have nonsupervisory jobs: reporters, copy editors, photographers, columnists. They tend to be unsure about their future mobility and are slightly more likely to be found on newspapers with more than fifty-thousand circulation. They see themselves as dissimilar to their readers, read their own newspaper less thoroughly, and read fewer magazines and professional journals than others.

2. *Externals.* Those with considerable community contact but limited involvement with coworkers; 22 percent of the respondents fell into this category. The externals have been in

the industry longer and at their present location longer than others. They are primarily in nonsupervisory jobs, are least likely to have been promoted or given merit raises recently, are older than the average, and expect either no upward mobility or that they will leave newspaper work. The externals are more likely to see themselves as similar to their readers. They read more magazines but fewer professional journals than others.

3. *Fast-trackers.* Those with a great deal of interaction with coworkers but very little with the community; 22 percent were so classified. The fast-trackers are relatively new to newspaper work. They have been at their present location the least amount of time. They tend to be more satisfied with their jobs, are more likely to hold supervisory jobs, and are more likely to have been promoted or given merit raises recently. The fast-trackers are younger and expect to move up in the organization. They read fewer magazines but more professional journals and see themselves as dissimilar to their readers.

4. *Talkers.* Those who have a lot of contacts with both the community and coworkers; 27 percent of those interviewed placed themselves in this category. The talkers have been on newspaper jobs longer and at their present location somewhat longer than the rest. They are more satisfied with their jobs and are more likely to be in supervisory roles. They are likely to have been promoted and given merit raises and they expect to move up. They read more print media than others and see themselves as more similar to their readers than do others.

Taken together, the isolates (young staffers) and the fast-trackers (young editors) made up 49 percent of the study. They are the individuals most likely to be insulated from their public. The Burgoons attributed the insularity phenomenon to two factors:

1. The first is that younger journalists are more likely to have arrived recently at a newspaper. They have had little time to

establish social contacts beyond those with other journalists and have had less time to become acquainted with the community. If younger journalists continue to be mobile, to move because of low salaries or the lure of a larger market, it is likely that the pattern of low integration into the community will continue. If this development results in distancing the newspapers from their readers, it also contributes to diminishing the loyalty of staffers to the newspaper and its values.

2. The second factor is advancement. The Burgoons' data indicate that newspaper organizations reward those who are well connected in the newsroom. Young journalists with career aspirations may realize that cultivation of contacts with other journalists is beneficial; they spend their social time with coworkers at the expense of contacts with nonjournalists.

The Burgoons suggest that the isolation of the fast-trackers from the community may be especially troublesome for the newsroom organization. Because so many of the fast-trackers are supervisors, their decisions on story assignments, story play, and news policy may suffer from lack of knowledge of the community.

Michael Burgoon has identified what he calls the "three epoch of journalism," which add an important dimension to our understanding of the four self-selected groups of journalists in the study.[32]

1. The first epoch is that of the *craftsmen*. Journalism provided an outlet for these people who were interested in writing. Their rewards were based on their ability to communicate in writing, and they were willing to work for low pay at jobs that offered them this opportunity. They were motivated by accuracy, composition, and everything else associated with the word. Today, they tend to be the senior members of the staff.

2. The second epoch is that of the *social change agents*. They came into newspaper work in the 1960s and early 1970s when our

society was changing. They weren't word people. They were sociologists who were going to use their roles on the newspaper to help make people's lives better.

3. The third epoch is that of the *organizational politicians*. They do not have a great love of the language nor do they want to change society. They are looking for a job. They are young journalists who are talking to each other but not to their readers, and who are going to be running the newsrooms of the future. They are more interested in succeeding within the organization. Burgoon sees them somewhat cynically as "business-school washouts"—many of them wanted to go into business or law but couldn't. They are attracted to newspapers because there they see a clear path to success. For them, the work is a challenge rather than a commitment or a calling.

The groups identified in the Burgoon research are easily identified, but not exclusive. Many journalists entering their first newsroom jobs more typically fit the description of the wordsmith or the sociologist than the organizational politician.

In his stereotype, Burgoon sees the younger managers, the fast-trackers, as being more optimistic, more likely to think that the newspaper organization with which they are associated is good. The successful ones often find themselves in a role where they must manage the sociologists, whose nature it is to be cynical and to think that the newspaper organization they work for is bad.

This sets up a puzzle for editors: how to manage staffers from the three epochs. Individuals from each epoch—the wordsmiths, the sociologists, and the organizational politicians—are motivated differently and are seeking different satisfactions from newspaper work.

The basic management themes that have been woven into our discussions of the roles and strategies of the editor should provide the clues for dealing effectively with these diverse staffers: recognize individual differences; create fair and effective systems for feedback, pay, and promotion; draw on individual strengths; encourage innovation; set demanding and challenging goals.

CHAPTER SUMMARY

Although often thought of in an artistic context, creativity is a vital element in every newsroom. Editors need to be skilled in the management of ideas and in encouraging vision to meet the challenges in an era dominated by swift technological changes in communication.

Gardner Murphy identified four stages in the creative process: (1) immersion of the sensitive mind in a medium that gives delight and fulfillment, (2) acquisition of experiences, (3) sudden inspiration, and (4) perfecting the creative work.

Abraham Maslow distinguishes between two kinds of innovation: primary creativeness (the inspirational phase) and secondary creativeness (working out the inspiration). Creativity is enhanced by our ability to become lost in the present, totally absorbed in a task and unaware of anything else.

Requisite to the editor's management of ideas are providing good communication, giving feedback, being available to subordinates, allowing subordinates to participate in goal setting, emphasizing low supervision, encouraging participation in decisions, providing freedom to try things, exerting moderate pressure, and encouraging the flow of ideas.

The life-styles and values of individuals are shaped by the era in which they were born and by dramatic events in the world during their early years. Life-style research is an attempt to explain who we are and where we are going.

Values determine the depth of our commitments, the integrity of our relationships, the energy that goes into our work, and the satisfaction we get from it. The values of individual journalists are often influenced by the character and the traditions of the newspapers they work for. However, many younger journalists seem to be shifting their value orientation from their newspapers to the ideals of journalism generally.

When individual managers and their companies share values, the managers discover that both their personal lives and their approach to their jobs are healthier.

Judee and Michael Burgoon's research on newspaper journalists resulted in four communicator types: (1) isolates, (2) externals, (3) fast-trackers, and (4) talkers. They also identified three epics of journalism: (1) craftsmen, (2) social change agents, and (3) organizational politicians.

NOTES

1. Albert Shapero, *Managing Professional People* (New York: The Free Press, 1985), 190.
2. Ibid., 196–202.
3. Donald W. MacKinnon, "The Nature and Nurture of Creative Talent," *American Psychologist* 17, no. 7 (July 1962): 485, 488.
4. Gardner Murphy, *Human Potentialities* (New York: Basic Books, 1958), 129–31.
5. Abraham H. Maslow, *The Farther Reaches of Human Nature* (New York: Viking Press, 1971), 59–61.
6. Bob Baker, *Newsthinking: The Secret of Great Newswriting* (Cincinnati: Writer's Digest Books, 1981), 1–2, 160–61.
7. Harry Levinson, *The Exceptional Executive* (New York: New American Library, 1968), 206.
8. John W. Gardner, *Self-Renewal* (New York: Harper & Row, 1963), 71.
9. Levinson, *Exceptional Executive*, 207–8.
10. Melvin Anshen, "The Management of Ideas," *Harvard Business Review*, July–August 1969, 100.
11. Alfred North Whitehead, *Dialogues of Alfred North Whitehead* (Westport, Conn.: Greenwood Press, 1954), 100.
12. Murphy, *Human Potentialities*, 141.
13. Maslow, *Farther Reaches of Human Nature*, 81–82.
14. Rensis Likert, "Conditions for Creativity," *Management Review* 51, no. 9 (September 1962): 70.
15. Arnold Mitchell, *The Nine American Lifestyles* (New York: Macmillan, 1983).
16. Morris Massey, *The People Puzzle: Understanding Yourself and Others* (Reston, Va.: Reston, 1979).
17. Mitchell, *Nine American Lifestyles*, vii.
18. Ibid., 3.
19. Ibid., 4–24.
20. Massey, *People Puzzle*, 52–172.
21. Ibid., 174–75.
22. Ibid., 177–80.
23. For further discussion of life-styles and life cycles, see Daniel J. Levinson, *The Seasons of a Man's Life* (New York: Ballantine Books, 1978) and Gail Sheehy, *Passages* (New York: E. P. Dutton, 1976).
24. Roy Peter Clark, interview with author, 20 January 1984.
25. B. G. Yovovich, "A Long-Revered Paper Ponders Its Future," *Advertising Age*, 30 January 1984, M-46.

26. Terrence E. Deal and Allan A. Kennedy, *Corporate Cultures* (Reading, Mass.: Addison-Wesley, 1982), 21–22.
27. Ibid., 22.
28. Ibid., 31.
29. Warren H. Schmidt and Barry Z. Posner, *Managerial Values in Perspective* (New York: American Management Associations, 1983), 12–15.
30. Phil R. Currie, "The Journalism of Mismanagement," *The Bulletin of the American Society of Newspaper Editors*, April 1984, 26–28.
31. Judee K. Burgoon, Michael Burgoon, David B. Buller, and Charles K. Atkin, "Communication Practices of Journalists: Insularity from the Public and Interaction with Other Journalists" (Manuscript, University of Arizona, 1984).
32. Judee K. Burgoon and Michael Burgoon, interview with author, 25 February 1984.

10

Rating Performance

Objective rating of the work of individual journalists is a keystone in effective newsroom management. Performance appraisals can be powerful tools to help editors motivate the staff, encourage self-development, select candidates for promotion, make decisions about pay, identify weak performers, take disciplinary action, and improve newsroom effectiveness. When performance-appraisal systems can help with these management functions, editors will find that they have more time to devote to other responsibilities.

PERFORMANCE REVIEWS IN THE NEWSROOM

A performance review is a formal way of giving feedback, one of the oldest management techniques. Centuries ago, the slaves and convicts who helped build the early roads of Italy got immediate feedback on their work. Positive feedback came from seeing how their labor was shaping the finished roadway. Negative feedback was the lash of the whip from Roman soldiers who judged them to be lazy or sloppy in their work.

In American business and industry, performance appraisals have been standard practice in many companies since the 1930s. Before the 1960s, performance evaluations were designed primarily as tools to control employees. Early appraisal programs used employees' past performance to help management make decisions about salary, promotion, discharge, or retention. In the 1960s, management broadened the scope of performance appraisals, adding the additional focuses of goal setting, improving the quality of the individual's work life, planning, productivity, and job satisfaction.[1]

It wasn't until the late 1970s, however, that the need to evaluate formally the work of newspaper journalists was taken seriously. There are two reasons why editors have been slow to adopt rating systems:

1. Editors experience normal resistance and anxiety at the thought of confronting employees regarding their performance. It is difficult for editors to sit in judgment of staffers. As Douglas McGregor explained, ". . . Managers are uncomfortable when they are put in the position of playing God. The respect we hold for the inherent value of the individual leaves us distressed when we must take the responsibility for judging the personal worth of a fellow man. Yet the conventional approach to performance appraisal forces us not only to make such judgments and to see them acted upon, but also to communicate them to those we have judged. Small wonder we resist."[2]

   Editors do not easily overcome this inherent resistance, even when the publisher or the senior editor plays a forceful hand and initiates a program requiring editors to rate members of their staff.

2. Another reason for editors' reluctance to undertake employee rating systems is the challenge of appraising the work of creative people. Professionals have long resisted being rated. Doctors, lawyers, college professors, and journalists believe that their work defies traditional measures and definitions. In the professionals' view, the education, experience, and talents required in their work set them apart from traditional workers and traditional methods of measuring performance.

In the past, personnel directors of newspapers, as a rule, did not have enough information about the requirements for strong performance in the newsroom to design effective appraisal systems. Editors, for their part, lacked knowledge of management systems. They were not prepared by experience or training to create effective rating programs on their own. In the absence of a performance-review program, editors were left to make important decisions about pay, promotions, and dismissals based on "instinct" and random observation. "Instinctive" decisions about people may be influenced by such subjective elements as emotions and personal bias.

In the 1970s, publishers and senior editors came to understand that an objective appraisal of a staffer's behavior on the job can serve the needs of the newspaper company as well as those of the individual journalist.

PERFORMANCE APPRAISAL AND THE LAW

The ideal of objective evaluations helping both the journalist and the newspaper has taken on a significant new complexion as a result of laws designed to protect workers from the adverse effects of unfair appraisals.

The government's interest was established in Title VII of the Civil Rights Act of 1964. Title VII approved the use of "professionally developed ability tests" for employment decisions, provided the tests did not discriminate on the basis of color, race, religion, sex, or national origin. Congress assigned the responsibility for enforcing Title VII to the Equal Employment Opportunity Commission.

No cases involving newspapers have produced major court decisions affecting performance appraisals. However, other industries have been engaged in lawsuits that have led to decisions by the United States Supreme Court that are important in helping us understand how to interpret the limits the law places on uses of performance appraisals.

Brito v. Zia Company (1973)

In this case, the Supreme Court found that Zia, a manufacturing company in New Mexico, had violated Title VII by laying off several employees with Spanish surnames on the basis of low performance-appraisal scores. The company failed to demonstrate that its performance-review system was related to important work behavior in the jobs for which the employees were being evaluated, the Court said. Instead, the evaluations were based on the best judgments and opinions of supervisors, ". . . but not on any identifiable criteria based on quality or quantity of work on specific performance that were supported by some kind of record."[3]

Alfred Brito, a fifty-six-year-old laboratory technician with high seniority, said he had been fired because of his age. The company defended the discharge on the basis of poor work, unsatisfactory attendance, and attitude. Brito demonstrated that he had never been told his work was unacceptable and that he had received regular pay increases. He won his job back, along with back pay and legal costs, because his personnel file contained no evidence supporting the company's reason for firing him.

Wade v. Mississippi Cooperative Extension Service (1974)

The Supreme Court found the Mississippi Cooperative Extension Service guilty of discrimination based on a complaint filed by a black employee, Charlie F. Wade. What the company called an "objective appraisal of job performance" was, in the view of the Court, based on ratings by supervisors of such general characteristics as leadership, public acceptance, attitude toward people, appearance, grooming, personal conduct, outlook on life, ethical habits, resourcefulness, capacity for growth, mental alertness, and loyalty to the organization. Said the Court in its opinion, "As may be readily observed, these are traits which are susceptible to partiality and to the personal taste, whim, or fancy of the evaluator. We must then view these factors as presently utilized to be patently subjective in form and obviously susceptible to completely subjective treatment."[4]

Albemarle Paper Company v. Moody (1975)

The company in this case, Albemarle Paper Company, used performance appraisals as the criteria to validate selection tests used in hiring. The Supreme Court ruled that the company had failed to conduct a systematic job analysis to identify the critical elements of a job. Instead, Albemarle, a North Carolina paper manufacturer, had used undefined rankings of employee performance to validate the selection tests. To make matters worse, employees were ranked against one another without regard for the fact that they were doing different jobs. In deciding the case brought by an Albemarle employee, Joseph P. Moody, the Court said, ". . . there is no way of knowing precisely what criteria of job performance that supervisors were considering, whether each supervisor was considering the same criteria—or whether, indeed, any of the supervisors actually applied a focused and stable body of criteria of any kind."[5]

1978 Civil Service Reform Act

The government's role in performance appraisals grew with the passage of the 1978 Civil Service Reform Act. Section 430 of the act deals specifically with the establishment of performance-appraisal systems for federal employees. The act is noteworthy for journalists because it provides sound guidelines for performance appraisals. Following are some of the highlights of the act:

- Employees should participate in establishing performance standards.
- Standards must be based on critical elements of the job. These elements must be defined in writing and employees must be advised of them before the appraisal.
- An employee's appraisal must be based on performance of the critical requirements of the job.
- Appraisals must be conducted in writing at least once a year.

Although the legal reach of the 1978 Civil Service Reform Act is limited to agencies of the federal government, it is not unlikely that the courts eventually will apply the same standards to private industry.

Federal guidelines and court decisions may seem to raise obstacles for editors setting out to design their own performance-appraisal programs. But the wisdom of Congress and the courts should not be disregarded. The courts, especially, have provided valuable clues for designing appraisal systems that are fair and yet not too limiting.

The courts favor job-performance standards that are based on an examination of the actual job requirements. The courts take the view that a performance-appraisal program should be rational; that is, it must be designed for specific purposes that are reasonable and clearly identified and it must demonstrate that the objectives of the program can be achieved. The courts have not dictated what type of program or what techniques are most acceptable, yet they appear to favor programs that are systematically administered. This reflects a concern for equitable treatment of all groups of employees and a concern for regular, recurring appraisals as a matter of routine management practice.[6]

CREATIVE WORKERS AND PRODUCTIVITY

Measuring productivity in the newsroom is an elusive concept because the nature of the work defies measurement in the traditional sense. There is no orderly method of gathering and writing the news. The reporter works by watching and talking, by checking out tips and acting on hunches, by meeting sources in restaurants and corridors, by scouring records and talking on the telephone. The writing process is highly personal. The search for a lead is a ritual that may begin with a fresh cup of coffee or a cigarette and may continue with a trip to the water cooler, the pencil sharpener, or the nearest window.

The remarkable thing about this process is that it is at once thoughtful and punctual. Such is the concentration and discipline of mind that the assigned story arrives at the desk on time.

American business leaders have long been fascinated by the phenomenon of productivity. Economic forecasters consider productivity in preparing their predictions about the strength of the economy. Their view is that steady gains in productivity are translated into a rising standard of living, increases in the gross national product, a low inflation rate, increases in wages, profits and investment, and a strengthening of American industry's international competitiveness.[7]

Technology has made possible extraordinary growth in productivity in the production departments of daily newspapers. Not many years ago, the composing room was highly labor-intensive. Typesetters, printers, proofreaders, and stereotypers performed thousands of individual tasks each day in preparing pages for the press. Today, computerized editing and typesetting have eliminated most composing room jobs. Once the copy leaves the newsroom, it takes far fewer man-hours—and thus, a smaller payroll—to produce a newspaper page. These gains in productivity have contributed handsomely to the growth in newspaper profits. And this explains, in part, why some publishers continue to search for a similar method of increasing productivity in the newsroom. By contrast, the introduction of electronic editing has not improved newsroom productivity in the traditional sense. News copy can be written and edited with greater ease and converted to type more quickly, but those efficiencies do not translate into major reductions in the workload of newspaper journalists.

Fig. 10.1

CLOSE-UP

Examples of industrial-style productivity efforts in newsrooms are rare. In one case in 1964, the management of the *Cincinnati Enquirer* hired Alexander Proudfoot Company, a Chicago management consulting firm, to conduct time studies and recommend more efficient work schedules. Proudfoot had assured *Enquirer* executives that it could save the newspaper big money. That summer, young men wearing dark suits and wristwatches sat in the *Enquirer* newsroom, watching, taking notes, and asking questions.

"They kept talking to me endlessly about newsroom operations, about which they knew nothing," says Ralph L. Holsinger, the managing editor. "They had the idea that there was some standard time for the writing of a news story—that you would spend a certain component of time in the morgue, a certain amount of time on the telephone, a certain amount of time interviewing and at the typewriter, and the

Fig. 10.1, continued

result would be a story. In fact, they would ask me, 'How many phone calls does it take to write a news story, how many times do you have to go to the library?' "

It quickly became evident to the staff that the way Proudfoot was going to save money was to fire people. Morale fell. Top staffers left the paper. Proudfoot set up a scheduling program that required a full-time clerk to keep track of when stories got to the desk, when they left the desk, and when they went to the composing room. As the date approached for implementing the program, Holsinger was asked to draw up the list of people to be fired. After two sleepless nights, he presented the list to the executive editor. "I was told to put my name at the top because I was out of sorts with the project and I would have to go," says Holsinger, now a professor of journalism at Indiana University. "The system lasted practically no time at all. It was unworkable. It caused more delays than it eliminated."

Sources: "March of the Proudfoot," *Newsweek*, 22 February 1965, 54–55; "Efficiency in Cincinnati," *Time*, 22 February 1965; Ralph Holsinger, conversation with author, September 1984.

The eighteenth-century idea that productivity is a better utilization of resources to give the greatest output for the smallest effort has moved beyond the sphere of the manual laborer and taken on broad new meanings.

Peter F. Drucker believes that the greatest opportunities for increasing productivity are to be found in "knowledge work" and especially in management. He sees managers, researchers, planners, designers, innovators—the people who are lumped together by the accountants as "overhead"—as the most productive resource.

A primary task of management in the decades ahead will be to make knowledge productive. The basic capital resource, the fundamental investment—but also the cost center of a developed economy—is the knowledge or creative worker who puts to work what he or she has learned in systematic education; that is, this worker uses concepts, ideas, and theories. One thing is clear: Making knowledge productive will bring about changes in job structure, careers, and organizations. Managing knowledge work and knowledge workers will require exceptional imagination, exceptional courage, and leadership of a high order.[8]

Fig. 10.2

CLOSE-UP

The *Mesa* (Arizona) *Tribune* designed a system that attempts to measure the productivity of the news staff. The number and length of stories published each month are recorded on a computer. Comparisons of individual productivity are printed and given to the staff. Max Jennings, the editor, devised a measurement based on the square pica: ten thousand square picas equal one standard broadsheet newspaper page. "We chose the square pica as a measurement tool," Jennings explained, "because we had to measure in square something and it's easier to measure in square picas than it is in square inches or square millimeters."

Jennings likes the system because it "produces discussions based on facts instead of impressions. I don't have to argue with my city editor over whether local news production has decreased in the last few months. We know exactly how much has been produced and by whom. Now, we simply analyze the problem or the success instead of speculating on what it really is. It creates healthy peer pressure. Reporters who are not producing half as much as others seem to go to work once they find out. Most of the laggards are surprised, I think."

Sources: Max Jennings, speech to California Publishers Association, San Diego, California, 10 February 1984; correspondence with author, 23 February 1984.

CHARACTERISTICS OF GOOD NEWSROOM APPRAISAL SYSTEMS

Peter F. Drucker's vigorous statement leaves little room to doubt the limits of performance appraisals: "An employer has no business with a man's personality. Employment is a specific contract calling for specific performance and for nothing else. Any attempt of an employer to go beyond this is usurpation. It is immoral as well as illegal intrusion of privacy. It is abuse of power. An employee owes no 'loyalty,' he owes no 'love,' and no 'attitudes'—he owes performance and nothing else . . . Management and manager development should concern themselves with changes in behavior likely to make a man more effective."[9]

Several approaches to evaluations have been adopted by newspaper editors. Each can give valid results if care is taken in the design of the program so that objective appraisals can be achieved. An effective evaluation program should be designed with the following points in mind:

- The evaluation should be job related. It should cover only those aspects of the work that are important to success on the job. For newspaper reporters, for example, a performance review should focus on gathering information, developing sources, producing enterprise stories, and writing accurate stories. The behavior expected of reporters in executing these skills should be clearly explained in writing. Personality traits, race, sex, and judgments about attitude are not job related.

- Definitions of what will be rated and how it will be rated should be as clear and detailed as possible. Vague or broad generalizations can lead to personal and inaccurate interpretations by the staffer and the evaluating editor. For example, if reporters are going to be rated on tightly written stories, the newspaper's evaluation program should carry a written statement explaining what writing tight copy means: "Stories are succinct and written to the appropriate length. Leads are crisp and to the point. Reporter keeps story tight without losing interesting essential elements. Irrelevant material is eliminated. Word selection is economical, never using several words or a phrase when one word will do."

- Performance should be measured against a standard. For example, the newspaper's standard for meeting daily deadlines may be: "The reporter meets daily deadlines with complete, accurate, well-written stories requiring minimal editing. It is unnecessary for editors to supervise efforts to meet deadlines." That is the standard against which a reporter's performance in meeting deadlines is measured.

- Editors should be able to observe the work on which a reporter is being rated. A common task for reporters is writing stories. From reading and editing those stories, editors can observe whether a reporter is meeting the standard for accuracy or enterprise or completeness or story organization. Editors cannot "see" attitude; therefore, measures of attitude do not belong in a performance review.

- Evaluations should be objective. They should be designed to eliminate opportunities for evaluating editors to inject their personal points of view. Subjective judgments about performance can lead to distortion. If a performance-appraisal program is objective, several editors could evaluate a single reporter's work and find that their ratings were consistent.

- The performance being reviewed must be documented. A successful appraisal system depends on examples of good and poor work. This suggests that newspaper editors should routinely place copies of notes or summaries of important decisions concerning performance in a reporter's file. During an annual performance review, the editor must be able to present examples of a reporter's work to support points of praise and criticism.

In stating explicitly what behavior is expected, a performance-appraisal system can serve as a contract between the newspaper and the journalist. In an effective program, the feedback combines with two other important responsibilities: counseling and training. In a large sense, these three responsibilities form the basis for a variety of major decisions concerning the staffer's career at the newspaper.

Following are six reasons why an effective performance-review system is essential to good newsroom management:

1. Motivation. Our study of motivation (see Chapter 3) suggested that feedback is a key to better performance. High achievers, for example, need frequent feedback. Without formal performance reviews, each staffer is left to make assumptions about the quality of his or her work. Often, the perceptions of the staffer do not match those of the editor. There is a gap between what the editor expects and what the staffer thinks the editor wants. When no effort is made to recognize, reward, and reinforce good work, it is harder for

the staffer to continue striving for excellence. Some will be driven by pride or by the belief that they can build a strong clip file and get a job on another newspaper. But many will say, "Why try hard when no one seems to notice?" Weak performers will sense that their work is not going well, even in the absence of feedback. They will become frustrated because they don't get guidance. These staffers seldom leave the paper; rather, they lower expectations and settle into mediocrity.

2. Staff development. In a well-designed performance-review program, editors can help staffers analyze their strengths and weaknesses, assess their potential for growth and change, and create strategies that may lead to new opportunities. These are key elements in building a strong staff as well as in satisfying the needs of individual staffers for setting and reaching goals.

3. Promotion decisions. An important responsibility for the editor is selecting other leaders in the newsroom. In some cases, the decision is easy. More often, however, the editor recognizes there is no single outstanding candidate. The choice must come from among two or three candidates who appear equal in ability and potential for leadership. Performance appraisals can give the editor an accurate record of each candidate's work and can reveal important clues to help the editor make a choice. For example, which candidate performed better in the skills such as communication that are common to newspaper journalists? Which candidate responded better to the need to overcome problems or to the challenge of meeting goals for personal growth on the job?

4. Pay increases. Journalists are concerned about the fairness of their pay. They want to be assured that decisions about pay are based on the quality of their performance and on their value to the newspaper. They want their pay levels to be generally equal to those of others on the staff whose performance and value are similar to theirs. They are not as concerned with comparisons of pay at other businesses in the community or at newspapers in other cities. The perception of equity is most effectively supported by linking raises

with an objective review of performance. Regular performance appraisals create a carefully documented base for making decisions about pay. Appraisals allow the editor to convey to the staffer that his or her new pay level is the result of objective managerial judgment.

5. Weeding out poor performers. Not everyone on the staff will succeed. Some will fail. It is the responsibility of the editor to spot the poor performers and help them improve. If the problems persist, the editor faces the difficult task of terminating the staffer. A successful discharge is tied to how carefully the editor can document the staffer's failing performance. Fundamental to this process is a regular evaluation in which a record of unsatisfactory work is established and the staffer participates in setting short-term goals for improvement. The review gives the editor an opportunity to explain the consequences of continued poor work.

6. Helping editors do their jobs. One consequence of solving staff problems is that it helps make the editor's job easier. The problems of individual staffers also become the editor's problems. Common difficulties for reporters—the story-organization problem, the late-copy problem, the incomplete-story problem, the write-too-long problem—will be reflected in the quality of the newspaper and, ultimately, in judgments about the editor's performance. These problems consume the editor's time and energy that might be better spent planning enterprise reporting projects or counseling staffers or meeting with readers. A performance appraisal can be a powerful tool in helping correct a staffer's problems and freeing the editor for more productive tasks.

TECHNIQUES FOR PERFORMANCE APPRAISAL

Many forms of performance appraisals have been developed in business and industry. In fact, within a single company, a variety of techniques may be used. The existence of so many different approaches and techniques may be explained by management preference or the needs of individual work groups, suggesting that there is no agreement on the best way to evaluate performance.[10]

Following is a summary of the five most commonly used performance-review systems. Some of these techniques have been adapted for newsroom use.

1. Narrative appraisals. These are ratings in which the editor writes an open-ended essay on a staffer's performance. This approach relies on job descriptions or role analysis. The job description is usually the editor's idea of what a staffer should do, and the staffer's work is rated against that job description. Some narrative appraisals are expressed in a question-and-answer format: "Does the reporter meet deadlines? Yes or no." "Is the reporter's copy accurate? Yes or no." Unless the job descriptions are carefully drawn and are clearly job related, narrative appraisals can be subjective and can unfairly emphasize personal qualities rather than job performance.

2. Checklists. Several kinds of checklists are used for employee appraisals. One is a list of tasks. A reporter's checklist might include these tasks: "Writes accurate stories." "Follows stylebook." "Communicates with editors." "Meets deadlines." The editor places a checkmark next to each item that the reporter performs satisfactorily. Another checklist would rate qualities such as initiative, relationships with others, and dependability. A third kind of checklist would be a forced choice in which the reporters on the staff are ranked from best to worst. Checklists are commonly used for routine tasks such as clerical or technical jobs and have little effective application to newsroom work.

3. Critical incidents. The editor takes note of good and bad performance and uses that information as a basis for periodic review. The idea is to develop a continuing record of specific incidents of on-the-job performance rather than to appraise total performance periodically.[11] The critical incidents on which ratings are based may not reflect the major responsibilities of the job. Competent, routine work by a reporter can be overlooked in favor of a few incidents the

editor may have observed and recorded in a memo. Often, the editor's tendency is to take note of mistakes or problems. Critical incidents may be more effective in improving performance than for documenting an evaluation.

4. Goal setting. This is a popular rating technique in which the staffer and the editor agree on goals against which the staffer will be rated. While it is clearly job related, goal setting tends to emphasize improvements that are directly measurable and does not represent a full picture of the staffer's performance. For a reporter, goals might include an increase in the number of enterprise reporting projects completed or a decrease in the number of errors or in the number of times stories have to be rewritten. (Goal setting in this sense should not be confused with Management by Objectives, which will be discussed in Chapter 11.)

5. Rating scales. Rating scales were introduced in 1963 as the Behaviorally Anchored Rating Scale (BARS).[12] They have gained in popularity because they concentrate on the employee's performance and have proven highly reliable; however, because they require a great amount of time and effort to implement successfully, rating scales are not widely used. Their strength is that they are built on standards of performance. The standards represent detailed expectations describing what is required for the job to be done well. A worker's performance is then measured against the standards. Enlisting the help of the staff in writing the standards is a key to developing a successful appraisal program based on rating scales.

DESIGNING RATING SCALES FOR NEWSPAPER JOURNALISTS

The use of rating scales in the newsroom has several important advantages over other forms of appraisal. Rating scales can be tailored to measure the performance requirements for each newsroom position. Participation by the staff insures that the performance measures will be designed by those who will be rated by them rather than be influenced by the opinions of outsiders. The idea of using standards of excellence to measure performance provides a comprehensive picture of the newspaper journalist's job. The result is that staffers are required to focus on the aspects of the job that are critical to success for the individual and, as a result, for the newspaper.[13]

The model for our discussion was developed in 1982 for the staffs of the *Times-Union* and *Democrat and Chronicle* in Rochester, New York, by Christine D. Landauer, director of personnel for the Gannett Rochester Newspapers, and me.

Until then, a program of regular evaluations had been in place in our newsrooms for about five years, using a combination of checklists and narrative appraisals. There was little consistency in the ratings. The appraisals often were subjective. Lacking standards for newsroom tasks, editors tended to rely on their instincts about what was important and what was not. Some editors were influenced by impressions of a staffer's attitude or motivation or personality. These impressions weighed significantly in the ratings.

Setting Standards

The idea of rating scales was attractive because it allowed us to set measurable standards of excellence for all newsroom jobs: reporter, copy editor, supervising editor, photographer, and artist.

We began with teams of editors. We talked about the work that journalists do and asked the editors to define the basic tasks. "They write accurate stories," the editors said. "They meet deadlines." "They develop sources." "They write headlines." "They tighten copy." Then we asked the editors to tell us how the best people on the staff did this work. On deadlines, for example, they said the best reporters deliver complete, accurate stories on time and they don't have to be pushed by the editors to meet deadlines.

As the editors talked, they discovered there were specific, measurable levels of excellence that separated the top staffers from the others. It also became clear to them that they were looking at performance as a product of behavior rather than personality or attitude.

The notes from these meetings were translated into proposed written standards. In the case of deadlines, for instance, the standard was defined this way: "Meets daily deadlines with complete, accurate, well-written stories requiring minimal editing. It is unnecessary for editors to supervise efforts to meet deadlines."

Fig. 10.3

CLOSE-UP

A classic newsroom management problem is the tendency for editors and staffers to see the demands of a job differently. This leads to misunderstandings, sometimes subtle, over newsroom practices. For example, it is common for reporters to regard deadlines as a matter of beating the clock. Get the story to the desk on time and the deadline has been met. For editors, being on time is only part of it. If a story that moves to the desk at deadline is poorly organized or contains errors or needs heavy editing, the editor would say that the reporter missed the deadline. These misunderstandings dissolve when there is a written standard that defines meeting the deadline as producing complete, accurate, well-written stories delivered to the desk on time.

We wrote thirty-eight standards for reporters and arranged those standards under four headings: Accuracy, Reporting, Writing, and Communication. As our work progressed, it became clear that written standards would enable us to measure several things:

- The frequency of desired behavior. How often, for example, did the reporter meet the deadline?
- The staffer's own initiative in displaying the desired behavior. Did the reporter learn the newspaper's deadlines and try to meet them without having to be reminded to do so?
- The frequency of errors. How often did the reporter miss a deadline?

- The staffer's ability to correct and not repeat errors. If the reporter missed the deadline, was he or she likely to correct the mistake or repeat it?

- The amount of supervision required. How often did the editor have to intervene to make sure the reporter met the deadline?

Selecting Rating Levels

Once the standards are written, it is necessary to select rating levels for them. This can be done in a number of ways. An effective but time-consuming approach is to create separate rating levels for each standard.

Following is the basic standard for Spelling, Stylebook, and Typos and the rating levels developed for it:

The Standard: Copy is free of spelling errors and typos, even when submitted on deadline. Copy follows stylebook.

The Ratings:

Outstanding: Meets the standard, with rare exceptions.

Commendable: Usually meets the standard. When errors occur, they usually are made under pressure of deadline. Errors are not repeated once they are pointed out.

Acceptable: Meets the standard more often than not. Occasionally submits copy that contains spelling errors or typos or that does not follow stylebook. Deadline pressure is not necessarily a factor. Errors usually are not repeated once they are pointed out.

Marginal: Frequently fails to meet the standard. Often submits copy containing spelling errors or typos or style errors, even in stories not written under deadline pressure. Errors are often repeated, even after they are called to the reporter's attention.

Unacceptable: Rarely meets the standard. Most copy submitted contains errors in spelling or style and contains typos. Errors persist despite coaching from editors.[14]

The advantage of having a rating level written for each standard is that it provides a highly reliable way to grade performance. However, it is an imposing task to write separate rating levels. An effective and more manageable approach is to use common rating levels. Following is an example:

Clearly outstanding: Meets the standard with rare exceptions. Works effectively on his or her own and requires very little supervision. Errors are not repeated.

Exceeds position requirements: Usually meets the standard with little supervision. Occasionally requires minor guidance from an editor, but once this is given, works effectively on his or her own. Makes immediate improvements when problems are pointed out and seldom repeats errors.

Meets position requirements: Meets the standard more often than not. Generally requires some guidance and direction from editors, but works effectively once this is given. Occasionally repeats an error or fails to correct a problem but generally shows improvement after counseling.

Below position requirements: Frequently fails to meet the standard. Often needs the help of editors to work effectively and frequently is unable to do so on his/her own. Often makes errors and fails to correct problems, even after counseling. Slight improvement shown, but it is not consistent.

Inadequate: Rarely meets the standard. Requires close supervision and cannot work effectively without it. Repeats errors and fails to correct problems, even after counseling. Seldom shows improvement.

Not applicable: Not required in present assignment.

The evaluation form for rating an employee's performance has two sections. In the first section, the staffer's performance is rated against the standards, with the editor placing a checkmark in a box indicating the rating level for each standard. Beneath the rating boxes is ample space for the editor to comment on the ratings. Editors are expected to document examples of strong

Text continues on page 302

SAMPLE RATING FORM FOR A REPORTER

REPORTER PERFORMANCE REVIEW

NAME _____
DEPARTMENT _____
JOB TITLE _____
GRADE LEVEL _____
ANNIVERSARY DATE _____
TIME IN PRESENT ASSIGNMENT _____
REVIEW PERIOD _____
NEXT EVALUATION _____

☐ Annual
☐ Six-month
  (new hire)
☐ Six-month
  (new assignment)
☐ Other

© Copyright 1984, Gannett Rochester Newspapers, a subsidiary of Gannett Co. Inc.

ACCURACY

	OUTSTANDING	COMMENDABLE	ACCEPTABLE	MARGINAL	UNACCEPTABLE	NOT APPLICABLE
Spelling, stylebook, typos	☐	☐	☐	☐	☐	☐
Attributing information to sources	☐	☐	☐	☐	☐	☐
Factually accurate information	☐	☐	☐	☐	☐	☐
Verifying identities, addresses	☐	☐	☐	☐	☐	☐
Using best possible source	☐	☐	☐	☐	☐	☐
Calling errors to editor's attention	☐	☐	☐	☐	☐	☐
RATING/ACCURACY:	☐	☐	☐	☐	☐	☐

EDITOR'S COMMENTS:

REPORTING

	OUTSTANDING	COMMENDABLE	ACCEPTABLE	MARGINAL	UNACCEPTABLE	NOT APPLICABLE
Gathering information	☐	☐	☐	☐	☐	☐
Approach to routine stories	☐	☐	☐	☐	☐	☐
Suggesting and developing story ideas	☐	☐	☐	☐	☐	☐
Producing enterprise stories	☐	☐	☐	☐	☐	☐
Developing sources	☐	☐	☐	☐	☐	☐
Depth, perspective, insight	☐	☐	☐	☐	☐	☐
Research	☐	☐	☐	☐	☐	☐
Awareness of the news	☐	☐	☐	☐	☐	☐
Community awareness	☐	☐	☐	☐	☐	☐
Legal awareness/sense of fairness	☐	☐	☐	☐	☐	☐
Judgment	☐	☐	☐	☐	☐	☐
Coverage of beat/assignment	☐	☐	☐	☐	☐	☐
News of minorities	☐	☐	☐	☐	☐	☐
Following stories	☐	☐	☐	☐	☐	☐
Suggesting picture and graphic ideas	☐	☐	☐	☐	☐	☐
Meeting daily deadlines	☐	☐	☐	☐	☐	☐
Meeting long-range deadlines	☐	☐	☐	☐	☐	☐
Managing time	☐	☐	☐	☐	☐	☐
RATING/REPORTING:	☐	☐	☐	☐	☐	☐

EDITOR'S COMMENTS:

WRITING

	OUTSTANDING	COMMENDABLE	ACCEPTABLE	MARGINAL	UNACCEPTABLE	NOT APPLICABLE
Organizing story	☐	☐	☐	☐	☐	☐
Recognizing important story elements	☐	☐	☐	☐	☐	☐
Copy tightly written	☐	☐	☐	☐	☐	☐
Word selection	☐	☐	☐	☐	☐	☐
Writing under deadline pressure	☐	☐	☐	☐	☐	☐
Writing style	☐	☐	☐	☐	☐	☐
Grammar	☐	☐	☐	☐	☐	☐

RATING/WRITING: ☐ ☐ ☐ ☐ ☐ ☐

EDITOR'S COMMENTS:

COMMUNICATION

	OUTSTANDING	COMMENDABLE	ACCEPTABLE	MARGINAL	UNACCEPTABLE	NOT APPLICABLE
Working with editors to develop stories	☐	☐	☐	☐	☐	☐
Working with editors to improve stories	☐	☐	☐	☐	☐	☐
Using feedback for development	☐	☐	☐	☐	☐	☐
Working with other staff members	☐	☐	☐	☐	☐	☐
Keeping editor informed	☐	☐	☐	☐	☐	☐
Contact with the public	☐	☐	☐	☐	☐	☐
RATING/COMMUNICATION:	☐	☐	☐	☐	☐	☐

EDITOR'S COMMENTS:

This rating represents the conclusion of your editors on your overall performance. A number of factors influence this rating. Some factors in your performance are more critical than others to your success as a journalist. Other factors may rank high only because, in the judgment of your editors, there is a need for immediate improvement.

In addition, your overall performance rating can be influenced by experience and by the relative degree of difficulty in the specific job you are performing. In no case is your overall performance rating determined by averaging the functions or categories.

	OUTSTANDING	COMMENDABLE	ACCEPTABLE	MARGINAL	UNACCEPTABLE
OVERALL PERFORMANCE RATING:	☐	☐	☐	☐	☐

EVALUATING EDITOR'S SUMMARY:

The space below is available if you wish to respond in writing to this performance review. The spirit of performance reviews recognizes that differences of opinion about one's performance can exist. We believe that differences can be presented constructively, professionally and without risk.
YOUR COMMENTS:

PERFORMANCE DEVELOPMENT

Here are areas where, in the judgment of your editors, you can improve your performance.

☐ Improvements identified as Priority A are considered essential to meeting minimum acceptable standards. Immediate and serious attention is required. Your editor will state on the form the period of time you will have to correct any such deficiencies. Failure to make such improvements carries the warning that your continuing employment may be in question.

☐ Improvements identified as Priority B are those that will contribute to raising your performance from an acceptable level to one which is outstanding or commendable.

☐ Improvements identified as Priority C are those that would fine-tune already excellent performance.

☐ Improvements identified as Priority D are those that can help you to be considered for larger responsibilities or new opportunities.

IMPROVEMENTS   **PRIORITY**

SIGNATURES

Your signature indicates that you have read this performance review and have discussed it with your evaluating editor.

EVALUATING EDITOR _____ DATE _____

MANAGING EDITOR _____

YOUR SIGNATURE _____

Text continued from page 293
and weak performance. A summary rating is given for the standards; for reporters, these ratings are grouped under the headings Accuracy, Reporting, Writing, and Communication. Then the editor is asked to give the staffer an overall rating. There is a full page for the staffer to respond to the editor's appraisal. The spirit of performance reviews recognizes that differences can exist about one's performance. Staffers are invited to address those differences "constructively, professionally, and without risk."

The second section of the review form focuses on performance development and career development. Performance development relates directly to problems or opportunities arising from the staffer's rating. Here the editor can recommend improvements to correct unsatisfactory work or improvements that could contribute to a higher rating at the next evaluation, that could fine-tune already excellent performance, or that could help the staffer be considered for expanded responsibilities or new opportunities. Editor and staffer can give priorities to the improvement goals listed. In addition, if failure to improve is likely to lead to termination, the editor employs a tool known as progressive discipline. This begins with a verbal or written warning that continued failure to perform up to standards may lead to disciplinary action, including dismissal. (Progressive discipline is discussed in greater detail later in this chapter and in Chapter 15.)

Career development gives the staffer an opportunity to indicate what assignments he or she may be interested in now and in the future, and allows the editor to comment on how realistic these goals are.

THE APPRAISAL PROCESS

Standards based on the work behavior of the top staff members can serve several purposes in the newsroom. These standards can be a statement of quality, a guide to excellent journalism. They can be shared with readers as objectives for what the staff tries to achieve each day. They can become the basis for reward and punishment. They can be powerful tools for teaching and development. They can encourage staffers and editors to try creative approaches to handling the news. They can help clear up subtle misunderstandings between editor and staffer over newsroom practices.

Fig. 10.4

CLOSE-UP

In a typical libel action, a plaintiff may be hard-pressed to demonstrate what the appropriate standards of newsgathering are. As a result, it is difficult, quite often, to prove that the staffer or the newspaper has breached those standards. If a newspaper establishes performance standards that express its goals for excellence in journalism, does that also establish a legal standard against which the newspaper can be held? If, in a libel case, a staffer or editor does not act in strict accordance with the standards in the performance-review manual, will the plaintiff's case be enhanced? This is a point of concern for editors and lawyers, for in any serious libel case, some violations of the standards almost certainly will have occurred. The issue has not been tested. What the lawyers counsel for now is to make it clear in a manual of performance standards or ethics standards that they are "objectives" rather than a code of conduct to be followed in all situations.

To the editor falls the responsibility for making a well-designed performance-review system work. It is a process in which the top editor must convince the rest of the staff that evaluations are fundamental to improving individual performance.

Performance reviews are not a sometime thing, to be done annually and then forgotten for twelve months. To be effective, feedback on good and poor performance and guidance for making improvements have to be part of the editor's routine. How well an appraisal program is handled adds an important dimension to the editor's role.

As a rule, most performance reviews are done annually. Newcomers to the staff may be evaluated after three or six months. Staffers whose work is rated low may be reviewed every three months or more often. Continuing attention to staff

Fig. 10.5

CLOSE-UP

To insure that feedback is seen as a high priority, every supervisor should be rated on a standard for "evaluating the staff." Here's how that that responsibility might be defined:

The editor routinely assesses the work of staff members, using specific, measurable, and observable standards as a basis for appraisal. The editor always knows how members of his or her staff are performing, consistently provides feedback on both good and poor performance, and offers guidance for making improvements. Staff members have no reasons to be unsure how they are doing or to be surprised by results of performance reviews.

Continuing attention to staff members' performance results in the collection of detailed profiles which are used as a basis for formal performance reviews. Reviews show understanding of job requirements and professional standards. Conclusions about a staff member's performance are fair, reflecting a thoughtful, balanced examination of all factors involved. The editor accurately identifies problem areas and offers suggestions for improvements and meets deadlines for evaluations. Evaluation discussions are conducted in a positive, constructive manner. The editor seeks to help the staff member understand the basis for his or her ratings and to reach an agreement on performance levels and necessary improvements.

Source: Robert H. Giles and Christine Landauer, *Gannett Rochester Newspapers Performance Review Program* (Rochester: Gannett Rochester Newspapers, 1984).

members' performance results in a collection of detailed profiles that are used as the basis for formal performance reviews. The feedback habit helps editors quickly become aware of problems, accurately assessing the source and not being misled by symptoms. By reacting immediately to unsatisfactory performance, the editor can work with the staffer to determine and set into motion the proper solution. Feedback also assures the staffer that his or her annual performance review will contain no surprises. Both the problems and the strong points of performance will have been mentioned previously and the appraisal interview will be a restatement of items familiar to both editor and staffer.

Memos, notes about conversations with the staffer, and work samples—all of which are collected throughout the rating period—become the basis for the editor's written appraisal of the staffer's performance. Which editor is responsible for preparing the appraisal form and conducting the evaluation interview may depend on the size of the staff. On smaller papers, the managing editor may do every performance appraisal. On larger papers, the evaluating editor is more likely to be a department head—city editor, features editor, news editor, sports editor, business editor, graphics editor, or photo editor.

On the city desk, for example, the city editor would confer with the assistant city editors in preparing a performance review. Because the assistants are more often in daily contact with staffers, their judgment is vital.

Self-Appraisals

While the editor is completing the evaluation form, the staffer also is preparing for the performance review by completing a self-appraisal form.

The purpose of the self-appraisal is fourfold: (1) to help the staffer prepare for the evaluation interview; (2) to help the editors give full consideration to specific accomplishments in the staffer's job; (3) to help the staffer call the attention of the editors to situations that may have affected the staffer's performance; and (4) to help the editors assist the staffer in improving performance and preparing for new opportunities.

The theory of self-perception advanced by D. J. Bem in 1972 supports the belief that individuals are capable of making realistic appraisals of themselves. According to Bem, we determine our own attitudes by observing our own actions in the same way we ascribe attitudes to others by observing their actions.[15]

Studies at General Electric indicated that workers who participated in a self-appraisal were less defensive regarding the formal performance review. Discussions following self-appraisal often resulted in improved performance. Low-rated employees were more likely to show an improvement in performance following a self-review discussion.[16]

Other studies suggest additional benefits from combining a self-appraisal with a performance review conducted by the supervisor:

- A self-appraisal forces the worker to focus on what is expected in the job.
- The supervisor learns how the employee perceives the job responsibilities, performance on the job, and problems in carrying out the work.
- Self-appraisals help clarify differences of opinion between the employee and the manager regarding job requirements and job performance.
- Self-appraisals serve as effective tools for stimulating self-development because workers are encouraged to think about their strengths and about specific goals.
- Self-appraisals are especially effective where the employee is working in isolation or possesses a rare skill because such employees often have more information than anyone else about their own work behavior.[17]

Weighed against these pluses are a few disadvantages. Studies have indicated that employees who may resist self-appraisals are likely to be new on the job, have had little experience with performance reviews, or demonstrate a low need for independence.

On a self-appraisal form for journalists, the staffer would be asked to respond to the following statements and then return the completed form to the evaluating editor before the evaluation interview:[18]

- Since my last performance review, I have achieved the following specific accomplishments in my present job:
- Since my last performance review, I have demonstrated these significant areas of strength in my present job:
- Here are some specific areas in which I would like to develop further:

- Here are some things I would like my editors to keep in mind in reviewing my performance:
- Here are some things that would make my job more effective and satisfying:

The statements are posed in neutral, nonthreatening language. The tone is designed to encourage the staffer to use the self-assessment form as an opportunity to think about both current performance and career development. Clearly, the self-appraisal can serve as a good starting point for the performance discussion between staffer and editor.

THE EVALUATION INTERVIEW

The crux of the performance-review process is the interview. Here the staffer and the editor come together to talk about the staffer's work. The setting should be private and the editor should schedule as much as ninety minutes for a full, unhurried, candid discussion of performance and development. The idea is to clarify, to motivate, to direct, and to build strategies for improvement and for new career opportunities. The editor reads the staffer's self-appraisal form and the staffer reads the performance-review form. The interview must focus on performance and work behavior rather than personality or attitude. The editor's responsibility is to lead the discussion in a calm, productive way.

Fig. 10.6

CLOSE-UP

It is not uncommon for staffers to express feelings of alienation about performance appraisals. Robert Unger, national correspondent for the *Kansas City Times,* stated the case for the newsroom skeptics as a panelist at a meeting of the Associated Press Managing Editors:
"I think written evaluations are an absolute, utter waste of time. For one thing, any editor who has to wait a year to get said what's on his mind ought to be doing something else for a living. And if you've got to wait from January to January to say what you think about an

Fig. 10.6, continued

individual reporter or writer or copy editor, then you've got a problem in management. This [evaluations] is something that happens hour by hour, day by day, week by week, month by month, all the way through, if you are doing it right."

The other panelist, Leonard Pardue, then managing editor of the *Louisville Times,* responded: "Let me agree with you on that. The evaluation shouldn't be a surprise. A person should know what is coming because of the kinds of conversations you would have had all along the way. And if somebody has fallen down on the job and they first learn about that in the evaluation, then you have screwed up."

Unger: "If they know what is coming, then why are you doing it?"

Pardue: "You've got to get it on the record."

Unger: "OK. That's an important point from a reporter's point of view. You got to get it on the record. Why do you have to get it on the record? It's nothing that is going to do me any good."

Pardue: "I don't suppose you've ever complained about a paper that didn't deal with its problem reporters?"

Unger: "One of the reasons you have these crazy evaluations is to deal with your problem reporters, so that when the time comes that you have to give him or her the heave-ho, you have a shovel with which to do it . . . So you wonder why these things start out with a negative connotation from the people on your staff. Well, they are negative. Now the point is, I see no reason why you shouldn't evaluate people like that; by that I mean people you have some question about. You could spare the newsroom a hassle, you could spare your department heads a lot of time wasted on these pieces of trivia if you would admit to yourselves that certain people—people who have been with you five years and have been excellent employees—just don't need to be subjected to this nonsense. And if, at the end of six months, somebody's been a real screwup, then you call him in and you say, 'We've decided that you now are going to be subjected to the evaluation process again.' That sends him a pretty good message."

Pardue: "What you question is whether there is any value to it for somebody who is doing a good job. I think there is a way to make it useful and valuable. Anybody needs to be thinking about how he or she can do better. What new challenge, what new growth opportunity exists for that person? And that ought to be the subject of a discussion."

Unger: "Why are you waiting six months to tell me that? Tell me today. Let's go out and have a beer. I'll buy."

Source: Robert L. Unger and Leonard Pardue, "Performance Appraisals" (Workshop at the Associated Press Managing Editors Convention, Louisville, Kentucky, 3 November 1983).

There are three types of evaluation interviews: (1) tell-and-sell, (2) tell-and-listen, and (3) problem solving.

The *tell-and-sell* approach draws heavily on the editor's ability to convince the staffer of the validity of the appraisal. It is a one-way communication that may succeed if the staffer has a deep respect for the editor. More likely, the interview will end in an argument. Tell-and-sell conveys an attitude that the boss knows best and that the staffer is encouraged to be a "yes man."

In a *tell-and-listen* interview, the editor explains any problems concerning the staffer and then listens to the staffer's response. Recognition that the editor is actively listening and conveying an understanding of the staffer's feelings makes this a highly satisfying approach for the staffer. The two-way communication can produce a strong improvement in motivation, but no goals are set during the meeting.

In *problem solving*, the editor's role is to be a supporter and a helper rather than an evaluator. This approach emphasizes participation by the staffer in discussing performance and resolving problems. As performance is reviewed, the editor indicates a willingness to share responsibility for problems. The discussion is probing but nonthreatening. As the staffer's defenses and anxieties drop, the editor can seize the opportunity to move the interview toward goal setting.

These three methods of appraisal reviews should not be viewed as separate interviews themselves, but as different strategies that might be used in the same interview. The editor might change from one approach to another as the situation requires.

There is a vast literature providing guidance to managers in the skills of conducting performance-review discussions. Following are one company's guidelines:[19]

- Review what has been achieved since the last review and examine reasons for successes and failures.

- Stimulate and discuss ideas about what can be done to improve results achieved.

- Help the individual analyze personal performance and underlying factors affecting performance, such as skills and

knowledge, job structure, standards, and resources available.
- Strengthen the individual's commitment to the job.
- Learn about the individual's interests, goals, and long-range career plans and help the individual relate these to the current job.
- Strengthen the understanding between manager and individual and foster an open line of communication.
- Discuss and resolve specific anxieties, uncertainties, or misapprehensions affecting job-performance plans and directions for future career development; outline specific activities in support of these plans and directions.
- Seek feedback from the individual on how well you have managed.

GOAL SETTING

Development of the theory of goal setting began with laboratory experiments in which individuals were given goals for a variety of tasks. The tasks were simple ones, such as assembling toys, brainstorming, or adding columns of numbers. The experiments demonstrated that those who were assigned difficult goals consistently performed better than those who had easy or moderate goals. From these experiments in 1968, Edwin A. Locke, a psychologist at the American Institutes for Research, concluded that incentives, such as praise, feedback, participation, and money, lead to an improvement in performance only if they cause the individual to set specific, hard goals. Research indicates that goals affect performance because they compel the worker to focus on performance deficiencies that must be corrected in order to reach the goal, to put forth effort in proportion to the goal, and to work more persistently at achieving hard goals than easy ones.[20]

Gary Latham and Kenneth Wexley, in their useful book, *Increasing Productivity Through Performance Appraisal*, suggest tak-

Rating Performance 311

ing into account the following points when linking goal setting to performance appraisal:[21]

- Setting specific goals leads to higher performance than adopting an attitude of "do your best."
- Participation in goal setting is important to the extent that it leads to the setting of higher goals than when goals are assigned unilaterally by superiors. Participation does not necessarily lead to greater goal acceptance than when goals are assigned by a supportive manager. However, employee understanding of how to attain the goals may be increased as a result of their participating in the goal-setting process.
- Given goal acceptance and employee ability, the higher the goal, the higher the performance. However, the goal should be reasonable. Employees will not accept goals that are unreasonable, nor will they get a sense of accomplishment from pursuing goals that are never attained. People with low self-confidence or ability should be given more easily attainable goals than those with high self-confidence and ability.
- Performance feedback is critical for showing employees how they are doing relative to the goals, maintaining the employees' interest in the goals, revising goals, and prolonging effort to attain the goals.
- If employees are evaluated on their overall level of performance rather than goal attainment, they will continue to set high goals regardless of whether the goals are attained. If employees are evaluated on goal attainment regardless of the difficulty of the goal, they are likely to set low goals or reject hard goals imposed by supervisors.
- There must be some latitude for the individual to influence performance. This is particularly true for newspaper journalists whose work styles are individualistic and flexible.

These principles are basic to goal setting in connection with newsroom performance reviews. The concept of Management by Objectives, which will be discussed in Chapter 11, is a form of goal setting, too, but it is important to note the difference:

Goal setting focuses on behavior and requires counseling and coaching, while MBO is related to individual achievement above the requirements of the job.

Goal setting as part of the newsroom performance appraisal has two parts:

1. Performance development. Steps to help the staffer improve performance in his or her current job.
2. Career development. Steps to prepare the staffer for the next two or three years and for longer-range ambitions.

Performance development and career development are discussed at the end of the evaluation interview, after the staffer and editor have completed their examination of the performance ratings.

Performance Development

A discussion of performance development is clearly within the framework of the review of performance. The editor indicates specific areas where improvement is needed or where further development of skills is possible.

Following are four kinds of performance development that may be considered:

1. Improvements considered essential to meeting minimum acceptable standards. These address problems with performance that require immediate and serious attention. The editor and the staffer work out a program for correcting each deficiency. This may include tips that could lead the staffer to better work, suggestions to improve the staffer's concentration or awareness of the newspaper's standards, or regular meetings with an editor to review the staffer's progress. The editor sets a date by which the staffer is expected to have shown improvement in correcting the unsatisfactory work. Another performance review is scheduled for that time. The editor also may tell the staffer that failure to make improvements could lead to termination.

2. Improvements that would help lift the staffer's overall rating to the next highest level. The editor and the staffer together work out strategies that might raise the staffer's overall rating. An editor and a reporter may agree, for example, that the reporter will attend a writing workshop and that the editor will critique the reporter's stories each week.

3. Improvements that would fine-tune already excellent performance. The idea here is for the editor to help the staffer find additional ways to grow and stretch in his or her current job. A city hall reporter, for instance, may tackle a reading list and attend seminars on urban problems.

4. Improvements that would help the staffer qualify for consideration for expanded responsibilities or new opportunities. The editor may suggest special training, additional enterprise reporting projects, or working as a vacation fill-in on the city desk.

Career Development

Career planning is the process of setting individual career objectives and devising activities to achieve those objectives. While this process is largely a private, personal activity driven by the journalist's initiative and ambition, the editor has an important role in helping the staffer define career goals and in creating opportunities to reach those goals. The performance-appraisal interview is an appropriate time to talk about the staffer's career. When career planning follows the discussion about performance, a sense of reality is created in which the staffer's career prospects can be candidly assessed.

Many journalists are reluctant to disclose their ambitions to the boss. They would not dare to venture uninvited into the managing editor's office to say, "Someday I'd like to have your job. Will you help me figure out how to do that?" A career discussion in an appraisal interview opens the way for the staffer to make that statement without risk.

In the career-development section of the evaluation form, there are questions for both staffer and editor. The staffer answers these questions:

- Do you prefer to continue in your current assignment?
- What other assignments would you be interested in during the next one to three years?
- What would you like to be doing in your job three or more years from now?

The editor answers these questions about the staffer:

- Would you encourage the staffer to pursue the career goals outlined above?
- If the staffer is interested in a different position, is he or she ready to be considered now, expected to be ready in one to two years with additional preparation, or unlikely to be considered?

The editor and the staffer then list skills and knowledge the staffer might need to meet his or her career goals, along with a plan for acquiring these proficiencies.

To be effective, career planning must have the backing of the newspaper management, the participation and support of the editors, and the serious thinking and analysis of individual staff members. The newspaper must be willing to invest its resources for training, seminars, college courses, travel, and other experiences that will enrich the professional lives of its most talented journalists. Successful career planning results from coaching, counseling, evaluation, and self-examination. The idea is to motivate staffers to help themselves. The outcome will be largely up to the staffer. There may be some intangibles that influence what happens, but in the main, the issue will be decided by whether the staffer can summon the energy, the commitment, and the will to achieve the goals.

BEHAVIOR AND ATTITUDE

It is common to hear editors describe apparent troublemakers on the staff this way: "Wexler has a bad attitude" or "Morelli has an attitude problem."

All of us have attitudes about our jobs, about things that happen to us, about people we meet. Those attitudes influence our behavior.

Attitude has been defined as a predisposition to respond in a favorable or unfavorable way to objects or persons in one's environment. Three assumptions are at the heart of this definition of attitude: (1) while the consequences of an attitude can be observed, the attitude itself cannot. We do not see attitudes; we may only assume that attitudes exist and speculate about their causes. What we can observe is the behavior that results from attitudes; (2) an attitude toward a person or object can range from very favorable to very unfavorable—we like something or we dislike something; and (3) attitudes influence behavior. People behave according to how they feel.[22]

While it is important for editors to understand the nature of attitudes, supervisors are not qualified to evaluate attitudes or to draw conclusions about performance based on their perception of a staffer's attitude. Editors often attempt to deal with what they would define as "an attitude problem," but what they should focus on is behavior on the job. Performance-appraisal programs should only evaluate behavior that can be observed, measured, and changed.

Attitude may influence behavior, as when a reporter believes his or her job is dull or routine or lacking in opportunity for advancement. The reporter's attitude is likely to reflect job dissatisfaction. That attitude can be translated into behavior that may include poor performance or absenteeism.

Attitudes are formed for a variety of reasons. Some attitudes help people adjust to their work environment. In the first days on a new job, a reporter's attitude may be shaped by such things as the presence or absence of attention from the editors, support systems, rewards and benefits, praise and criticism. Attitudes can provide an ego defense, protecting staffers and editors from acknowledging basic truths about themselves. For example, a staffer's negative attitude about an editor may be traced to feelings of inferiority or frustration over a lack of advancement. Or, an editor's negative attitude about a staffer may be the result of feeling threatened or challenged or the need to feel superior. The editor and the staffer may not be able to admit to themselves the true nature of their feelings, so they project their negative thoughts to others to maintain their own attitude of superiority.

Attitudes also allow people to demonstrate what type of person they think they are and to express their central values. By saying, "It is my newspaper, right or wrong," an editor is making an effort to portray clearly how he or she perceives the editor's role in the organization. And, attitudes help explain and organize an otherwise chaotic world. People need standards or frames of reference for understanding and interpreting people and events around them. Attitudes help supply these standards.[23]

The editor's own point of view influences his or her judgments about a staffer. An editor might have a talented, effective reporter who does not put work above all else. This staffer may be reluctant to work overtime or may resist a call-in on Sunday to cover a breaking story. He or she has declined invitations to move from reporting to an assistant city editor's job. Thus, the editor makes a value judgment about this staffer: lacking in ambition, unmotivated, doesn't care. The editor may let those thoughts about "attitude" cloud an understanding of the staffer's true level of performance.

Common traits of the staffer with a "bad attitude" are typified by the staffer who argues with editors, who doesn't like direction, who is uncooperative. The staffer engages in heated, extended, unresolved conflict with editors. Making a change in a story causes conflict. Suggesting a different approach causes an argument. Indicating that the story is not as good as it might be triggers an outburst.

If the evaluation focuses on the staffer's uncooperative attitude, the result is likely to be more conflict and argument. If the staffer is unwilling to look at his or her work objectively, it is unlikely that the staffer would be willing to consider the editor's view about his or her attitude. However, staffers can be guided to understand how the things they say and do in the newsroom can affect their performance. An editor might recall the number of times stories were held from the paper unduly because the editor and the reporter could not agree on the proper approach. Or the times the reporter missed deadlines or created tension for others in the newsroom who observed his or her argumentative behavior.

Correcting the problem begins with addressing the unacceptable behavior that has been observed by explaining how it affects the staffer's performance rating and his or her prospects for advancement. For example:

- Argumentative behavior interferes with the process of getting the story written, especially on deadline.
- This behavior creates tension for others in the newsroom because the arguments go beyond professional disagreement.
- This behavior interferes with the staffer's professional development. The staffer is not able to take full advantage of the guidance offered by editors and the opportunities that may result from learning to consider other points of view or to try new approaches to writing stories.
- The sum of these behaviors is that the staffer is not sufficiently productive. Continued unacceptable behavior can affect pay increases and opportunities for advancement and, in serious cases, can lead to discipline.

RATING ERRORS

No appraisal system will work effectively if the evaluating editors make errors of judgment that are based on bias, distortion, or inaccuracy. These errors can occur in a systematic manner as editors observe and evaluate the behavior of staffers. What makes the errors so difficult to correct is that the editors usually are unaware of them. When they recognize the errors, editors frequently are unable to correct them. The unfortunate result can be an employee who is inappropriately retained, promoted, demoted, transferred, or terminated.[24] Training is essential to help evaluating editors understand the potential for such errors.

Following are some of the most common rating errors:

Halo effect. When an editor makes an inappropriate and inaccurate generalization about an aspect of a staffer's work and applies it to other factors in the staffer's job performance. For example, if a reporter is a poor speller, the editor may conclude that the staffer's overall performance is poor. Or, if the reporter consistently turns in stories with crisp, sparkling leads, the editor may incorrectly assume that the rest of his or her work is first-rate.

Similar-to-me. When editors tend to judge more favorably those staffers they perceive as similar to themselves. Sources of similarity are many and often can be traced to closeness in background or attitude. Why does this effect occur? We tend to like and to think more highly of those whom we perceive to be like us; the similarities are flattering and reinforcing. This effect may be acceptable in social situations, but it is an error when making appraisals on the job because it can lead to charges of discrimination as well as the assignment of tasks to the wrong people.[25]

Common associations for newspeople that might cause an editor to make the similar-to-me error in rating a staff member include having graduated from the same journalism school, having worked together for a wire service, belonging to the same club, playing tennis or jogging together, participating in the same amateur theater group, or coaching Little League teams.

Negative and positive leniency. When the editor is either too hard or too easy in rating staffers. An editor who is too easy may raise unfairly the expectations for raises, promotions, or new and challenging assignments. An editor who is too tough is seen as unreasonable or excessively demanding. The staffer may grow weary of the struggle, concluding that no matter what is done, the editor cannot be satisfied. Research indicates that workers do not like bosses who are unreasonably difficult and do not respect those who are too easy in their ratings.[26] In either case, the employee is likely to lose motivation and may feel the need to seek other employment.

Contrast effects. When the editor compares a staffer with other staffers rather than rating him or her against the requirements of the job. This may result in a staffer's being rated higher than is deserved because, when compared to the rest of the staff, the work is better, even if it falls short of standards. Or, a beginning reporter on a staff of veterans may get a low rating because he or she does not perform at the level of the older hands.

Contrast effects are particularly troublesome in performance appraisals because of the deeply imbedded assumption by many personnel people that the distribution of ratings should resemble a normal or bell-shaped curve. To rate automatically on a curve is not only in violation of the 1978 Civil Service Reform Act, it also is unfair. People should be evaluated on the degree to which they fulfill the requirements of their jobs, not on how well they perform relative to other people.[27]

First impression–last impression. When the editor makes an initial favorable or unfavorable judgment about a reporter and then ignores later evidence that suggests the overall performance level is different from that indicated by the first impression. For example, a reporter joins the staff and, because of summer-vacation absences, is pressed into coverage of a major story. The reporter is on page one three times the first week and the editor is impressed. Later, the reporter is assigned to cover suburban towns. The performance is spotty. But when it is time for a six-month evaluation, the editor vividly recalls the reporter's solid page-one stories the first week on staff and the reporter gets high marks. The theory holds, as well, when a reporter makes a strong impression just before a performance review is due. That impression can offset months of mediocre or outstanding work.

Central tendency. When the editor wants to play it safe by rating a staffer close to the midpoint even though the performance clearly deserves a higher or lower rating. An average rating covers the editor in the event the staffer does either extremely well or does poorly in the future. Such a rating also is easier to explain to the boss.

PERFORMANCE APPRAISALS AND DISCIPLINE

During the nineteenth and early twentieth centuries, employers believed they had an undisputed right to fire workers for any reason whatever. The common law of the day supported that view. The property rights of ownership and the personal liberty of the employer to run his business as he saw fit were at the heart of this belief.

In recent years, unions, civil-service systems, and protective labor laws have sharply limited the ability of an employer to dismiss workers. The language of union contracts prohibits discharges except for "just cause," and unions are obliged to represent workers who want to appeal their dismissal. In government, workers are protected by civil-service rules which state that employees cannot be fired without substantial evidence.

More than 60 percent of the American work force is nonunion and nongovernmental, and these employees draw protection from laws which prohibit employers from discriminating against workers on the basis of age, sex, race, or national origin. The legal doctrine known as "employment at will" considered employees to be working with the consent of the employer, so workers have had little recourse to contest firings. In 1984, bills were proposed in six states aimed at protecting workers who do not belong to unions from unjust dismissals.[28] The legislation was invited by multimillion-dollar judgments won by workers who convinced juries that they were discharged without good reason. Of thirty-two such cases in California between 1980 and 1982, seventeen were decided in favor of the discharged workers. Six of the workers walked away with combined awards of more than $600,000.

The interest of fairness and the activity of the courts make a strong argument for developing a thoughtful, orderly, and reasonable process for determining whether a worker should be discharged. Effective controls for terminating newsroom employees can be anchored with the performance-review system and a technique known as progressive discipline.

Progressive discipline generally occurs in four steps: (1) oral warning, (2) written warning, (3) suspension, and (4) dismissal.

The following case will show how performance appraisals and progressive discipline were used to resolve the problem of a veteran staffer whose work was unsatisfactory.

Harry had worked for the newspaper for twenty-two years. He was a gifted writer, a skill that earned him the science beat and later an assignment on the business desk. But his inability to get facts straight and his lack of enterprise forced the editors to take those beats away from him. In recent years, he had been doing routine jobs around the city desk: night rewrite, obituaries, general assignment. During that time, his performance was rated as "marginal" or "unacceptable." Harry's editors wanted to bring the issue to a head: either his work improved or he left the paper. It was unfair to the rest of the staff to let Harry stay if his performance continued to be unsatisfactory. The editors recognized that the newspaper was responsible for tolerating Harry's poor work for so many years. Also, they were not eager to confront Harry, for he was a surly fellow who had little to say.

Harry was due for his annual performance review in February. The editors decided they would tell him that unless his work improved, he was in danger of losing his job. The publisher and the newspaper's lawyers were consulted. It was agreed that the first warning would be oral, that a plan to help Harry improve would be developed, and that another evaluation would be scheduled in three months.

In the February evaluation interview, the editors reviewed with Harry the problems with his work: factual errors, inability to get information, problems with story construction, reluctance to communicate with editors. He was praised for examples of graceful writing and for turning in copy that was clean and free of typos. His overall rating was "unacceptable."

Under the Performance Development heading of the evaluation form, Harry's editors listed the improvements he needed to make. They outlined a plan to review his work weekly. At the end of the meeting, Harry was told that if his work did not improve, his continuing employment might be in danger.

Two months later, Harry told the city editor he would not continue to meet weekly with the editors to talk about his work. He characterized the meetings as "demeaning and unprofessional." The managing editor joined the discussion, and as the meeting ended, Harry agreed to resume the critiques.

In May, Harry's three-month performance appraisal showed no improvement. His editors restated the goals for improvement and told Harry that the weekly reviews of his work would continue. Another performance review would be held in thirty days. This time, the city editor put Harry's warning in writing: "You have thirty days to improve your performance to at least an acceptable level in all of the categories we have discussed. Failure to do so may result in your termination."

During the next thirty days, Harry's work continued at the same level. Following the performance-review interview, Harry met with the editor. They reviewed the history of Harry's employment and discussed the problems that might cause him to lose his job. The editor suspended Harry without pay for two weeks. Following the suspension, Harry would have two weeks to begin to show improvement. If he failed, he would be fired.

After the suspension, Harry wrote a story that contained an error. Harry learned of the error from a source soon after the story was published. He did not mention the error for two days, until an editor asked him about it—an oversight that the editors judged to be a serious breach of professional ethics. At the end of the second week, the editors met to review Harry's case. They agreed there was no reason not to fire him. The newspaper's lawyer reviewed the performance-appraisal records and the progressive disciplinary steps the editors had taken. The lawyer said the editors' case was well documented and the newspaper had a reasonable protection against an age-discrimination suit.

On Harry's last day at the newspaper, he met with the editor. They reviewed his work history. The editor handed Harry a letter explaining why his employment was being ended. In consideration of his long service with the company, Harry was allowed to resign.

In this case, the newspaper was able to terminate a senior employee whose work performance was below standard and who demonstrated no inclination to improve. The newspaper was successful because the editors were able to present to Harry a level of performance to be achieved, because they were fair in working with him and giving him an opportunity to improve, because they documented his failures, and because they carefully followed the steps in progressive discipline.

TRAINING EDITORS TO RATE THE NEWS STAFF

Editors cannot be expected to conduct effective performance appraisals without training. Such a program should be available to every new supervisor. Training sessions can be led by the editor or the personnel director. An effective program can be completed in three or four hours. The discussion leader can use case studies to introduce problems that may be encountered during performance appraisals.

The following five points should be emphasized in performance-appraisal training:

1. Understanding the newspaper's policies. In a training session, the discussion leader can begin to build support for the concept of performance appraisals by helping the new supervisor understand the reasons for evaluations and the newspaper's policies for rating performance; that is, performance reviews are designed to:

   - Indicate the editor's awareness of a staffer's abilities and strong points in job performance.
   - Point out areas in which weaknesses are noted and improvement is expected.
   - Set goals for development and advancement.
   - Help evaluate staff members for salary increases and promotions.
   - Provide a documented basis for termination, if necessary.
   - Require the editor to develop procedures for routinely appraising the work of staff members.
   - Provide a format in which editor and staff member meet to discuss performance and goals.

Such a discussion will underscore each supervisor's responsibility to become skilled at evaluating. Editors will begin to make the connection between failures by staff members and weak leadership and communication by editors. The leader also can describe the consequences of poorly done evaluations: grievances, lawsuits, and problems with morale, motivation, and productivity.

The training leader should give a step-by-step explanation of the performance-appraisal process: who prepares performance reviews, who contributes to them, who writes them, who reviews them, who leads the appraisal interview. It is important for each editor to understand his or her role. In all cases, the top editor should have an opportunity to review the written evaluation form before it is given to the staffer.

2. Understanding the standards on which staffers will be rated. No matter what approach the newsroom-appraisal system follows—narrative, checklists, goals, rating scales—there is a theory supporting it that needs to be explained. If standards similar to those described in this book are used, the editor needs to be intimately familiar with them and understand that they are statements of how the work should be done. The training leader can explain the critical role of standards in the rating process and can turn the discussion to the value and meaning of standards.

Fig. 10.7

CLOSE-UP

The practice of journalism in the United States, with its vigorous pursuit of truth and vigilant protection of the First Amendment, has given rise to traditions that are passed from generation to generation of journalists. Some of those traditions shape the character of a newspaper. They also reflect the newspaper's standards.

A. M. Rosenthal, executive editor of the *New York Times*, told an audience at the American Society of Newspaper Editors, "We have no written standards. You have to refer to the character of the *New York Times*. If he doesn't know it or she doesn't know it by the time he becomes an editor or she becomes as editor, then we have a problem. The character of the *New York Times* is that the history and the tradition determine the standards. We spent a long time—many years, really—bringing people to understand what our standards are. And obviously there is never total agreement but there is a sense of character."

Source: A. M. Rosenthal, "The News in the News Business" (Panel discussion at the American Society of Newspaper Editors Convention, Denver, Colorado, 10 May 1983).

3. Understanding how to use performance appraisals to motivate staff members. As we have learned, motivation plays a large part in determining how well members of the news staff perform. As a result, motivation is at the heart of the evaluation process. Editors can use the performance appraisal, particularly its goal-setting features, to motivate staffers. The link between motivation and improving the work of poor performers is especially important. Specific goals that are difficult but attainable consistently lead to better performance.

   The training leader can coach editors on the basics of motivation that were described in Chapter 3. Particular emphasis should be placed on creating strategies to help staffers improve and on learning how to reward staffers immediately for examples of better performance.

4. Understanding rating errors and how to minimize them. The training leader can review the common errors in appraisals: halo effect, similar-to-me, negative and positive leniency, contrast effects, first impression–last impression, and central tendency. The point can be stressed that a performance appraisal is not an attitude appraisal. It is the staffer's behavior on the job and not the staffer as an individual that is being rated. The training can attempt to reduce the possibility of error, keeping in mind that the whole process of performance review involves human judgment.

5. Understanding how to conduct an appraisal interview. The training leader can explain the types of interviews—tell-and-sell, tell-and-listen, and problem solving—and can stress

such other elements of an effective interview as being candid, being prepared to discuss all elements of a staffer's work, being a good listener, and using the interview as an opportunity to help motivate the staffer.

The training leader can use role playing as a way to give editors a chance to try their hand at the complexities of the evaluation interview. The other editors can critique and comment following the role play.

Following are some suggestions to consider in planning a strategy for an appraisal interview:

- Be specific. Use examples. Be able to document praise and criticism. Tie examples to your major points.

- Avoid reference to attitudes. Attitudes are personal; they cannot be observed and they may not have anything to do with work behavior.

- Criticize the work, not the person. Say, "The writing in this story is unclear" rather than "Your writing is unclear." This keeps the criticism from being personal.

- Define the problem. Make sure you and the staffer agree on what needs to be fixed. Explain and clarify.

- Avoid absolutes. Words such as *all, none, always,* and *never* are imprecise and easy to refute. They reduce the effectiveness of praise or criticism.

- Don't exaggerate. State the praise or criticism as it is. Don't embellish or pad.

- Don't praise everything. Even if all the ratings are outstanding, save some praise for another time.

- Be aware of your own biases. Don't let your personal feelings about the staffer intrude. Deal only with the quality of the work.

- Share responsibility. Part of the burden for the staffer's failure falls on the editor. A mature editor will let the staffer know this.

- Avoid comparisons with other staffers. This is an unfair way to evaluate. The staffer is likely to resent an attempt to compare him or her with someone else on the staff.
- Ask questions to get information. Don't ask questions that are designed to confirm what you believe or to test the staffer.
- Share your own feelings about the interview. If you are at an impasse, say so. If the staffer is making you angry, say so. If you are encouraged by the staffer's response to ideas for improvement, say so.
- Be succinct. A good point is often lost in an overkill of words.
- Soften the tone, not the message. The content of criticism will be understood more clearly if it is delivered in an even tone of voice.
- Don't make assumptions. Ask for explanations and clarifications.
- Don't criticize when you are angry. You will say something you will regret.
- Avoid feeling defensive. Work through the tendency to feel defensive by eliciting more information and by separating yourself from the problem.
- Draw on the staffer's strengths. Use your motivation skills to explain how the staffer's strong points can help solve his or her problems.
- Listen, listen, listen. Being a good listener is one of the most important skills of a good editor.

RATING THE BOSS

The idea that evaluations of editors by the news staff can be valuable to individual editors, and thus to the newspaper, has not been widely tested. Such a program, in which reporters, copy editors, photographers, and artists would rate their supervisors, has a single purpose: to assist in developing the management skills of the editors.

Limited research from nonnewspaper companies is available to suggest the potential, the limits, and the problems of appraisals by subordinates.

Exxon instituted a program in 1959 called "Rate Your Supervisor." The ratings were anonymous. Each supervisor was given a computer printout showing the average of his or her rating by workers. In addition, there was a comparison of how the supervisors were rated relative to each other. Exxon reported three major findings from the program:[29]

1. Twenty-five percent of the subordinates said they saw lasting changes in their supervisors as a result of the rating program.
2. Eighty-eight percent of the supervisors said they had tried to change their behavior after receiving the report of how they were rated by their workers.
3. Sixty percent of the supervisors and subordinates agreed that productivity had increased as a result of the program.

In 1974, the Weyerhaeuser Company took the Exxon program a step further. A comparison was made between the ratings of subordinates and supervisors for a group of foremen in one of the company's divisions. Where there were large discrepancies, management investigated the reasons. Frequently, the cause was a personality conflict between the individual and the supervisor.[30]

The Weyerhaeuser foremen were able to analyze the results and use low ratings given them by workers to build stronger communication links. The foremen discovered that some low ratings focused on things they could change. They made those changes and explained them to the workers. The foremen also saw areas where change required cooperation from workers. Through discussion and help from the workers, many of those changes were achieved.

Moreover, the foremen also saw that some of the criticisms

were for things they could not change, and they used that as an opportunity to explain the rationale for their inability to bring about change.

There are several potential advantages to a program of supervisor appraisal by workers:[31]

- Workers begin to view problems through the eyes of their supervisor.
- The supervisor begins to see concerns from the perspective of the worker.
- Increase in productivity and job satisfaction often results within two or three months.
- The supervisor can take the results of worker ratings to his or her boss and explain what has been done to maintain or improve the ratings.

In their writings on productivity and performance appraisals, Gary Latham and Kenneth Wexley have identified potential problems with subordinate appraisals. They note that "some subordinates may perceive the process as threatening. They may feel that their supervisor will reprimand them for an honest, unfavorable appraisal. This is why anonymity is critical for increasing the likelihood of accurate ratings."[32]

Richard Morano, a management consultant in Rochester, New York, was instrumental in developing a process for changing management style. The starting point for that change, he contends, is an honest assessment of a manager's current behavior by people who are familiar with it. To provide this assessment, Morano led the development of a questionnaire based on forty-four specific management behaviors. Employees are asked to use the questionnaire on a voluntary basis to assess their manager's style. The results are tabulated and made available to each manager. Morano emphasizes that the purpose of the questionnaire is not to rate the performance of managers, but to give them the feedback they need to assess and improve their current management style.[33]

The work of newspaper editors requires a blend of technical skills and management skills. The editor's performance review should make that important distinction. In considering an assessment of editors by staffers, the focus should be on management skills.

Using Morano's model, I designed a questionnaire listing twenty editor behaviors. The questions are asked in terms of effectiveness. Staffers are asked to measure editor effectiveness on a series of management skills. There are three possible rating levels for each question: usually effective, sometimes effective, and not effective.

The questionnaires are completed anonymously and returned directly to the editors being rated. Participation by staffers is voluntary. Their anonymity is assured. The objective is for the editor to use information obtained from the questionnaires as a guide in helping him or her understand how to improve interaction with the staff to achieve more effective management.

Following are the questions for an editor's rating program:

Using three possible rating levels—usually effective, sometimes effective, not effective—how would you rate your editor's effectiveness at:

1. Utilizing your skills and individual strengths?
2. Establishing a climate of openness and trust?
3. Encouraging you to express your ideas?
4. Encouraging you to speak about your concerns?
5. Listening to your ideas and concerns without interrupting?
6. Demonstrating knowledge, understanding, and concern about your needs?
7. Providing information that affects your ability to perform assignments?
8. Involving you in discussions about your work?
9. Understanding your workload?
10. Providing appropriate direction concerning your workload?
11. Discussing with you the objectives and problems of your assignments?

12. Allowing you to complete your assignments with support but not interference?
13. Providing regular feedback on assignments that you handled well?
14. Providing regular feedback on assignments on which you could have improved your performance?
15. Adjusting his or her management approach to meet your individual needs?
16. Considering your opinions in making decisions that affect your work?
17. Seeking your commitment and support for changes that affect you?
18. Discussing your strengths and areas for improvement?
19. Working with you to improve your performance?
20. Providing opportunities for you to develop beyond your present capabilities?

CHAPTER SUMMARY

A performance review is a formal way of giving feedback. The 1978 Civil Service Reform Act and court decisions arising from Title VII of the Civil Rights Act of 1964 provide sound guidelines for the design of performance-appraisal systems.

The performance of creative workers is difficult to assess because the nature of the work defies measurement in the traditional sense. Journalists think of themselves as creative people because their work requires critical judgment, a strong sense of events, and a capacity to act quickly, often under deadline pressure. The innovative character of newspaper work is highly personal and requires editors to create a newsroom environment that is open and conducive to creative approaches to the handling of the news.

A good newsroom appraisal program should be job related, define the work to be rated, measure performance against a standard, assess observable performance, and document results with objective evaluations. For editors, an effective performance-review system can be a key to good management, an important tool for motivation, staff development, promotion decisions, pay increases, weeding out poor performers, and helping editors do their jobs.

There are five commonly used types of performance reviews: (1) narrative appraisals, (2) checklists, (3) critical incidents, (4) goal setting, and (5) rating scales. Rating scales are especially effective because they evaluate performance against measurable standards of excellence. Key steps in designing rating scales for the newsroom are setting standards and selecting rating levels.

The editor holds the responsibility for effective performance reviews. Feedback leading up to the annual performance review must be given routinely. The staffer may be invited to complete a self-appraisal form, a process that helps the staffer focus on what is expected in the job and gives the editor insight into how the staffer perceives the job.

The crux of the performance-review process is the interview. Three basic methods of conducting such an interview are: (1) tell-and-sell, (2) tell-and-listen, and (3) problem solving. The interview must focus on the work, not on the staffer or the staffer's personality.

Goal setting is the part of the evaluation process that helps the staffer improve performance in his or her present job and plan for the steps leading to career advancement. Goals should be reasonable and attainable, but not too easy. The goal-setting part of the evaluation is an opportunity for editors to motivate staffers.

A staffer's attitude may influence his or her behavior, and while editors must understand the nature of attitudes, supervisors are not qualified to evaluate attitudes or to draw conclusions about performance based on their perceptions of a staffer's attitude.

Five types of rating errors are common in evaluations. These errors are: (1) halo effect, (2) similar-to-me, (3) negative and positive leniency, (4) contrast effects, (5) first impression–last impression, and (6) central tendency.

Appraisals can be effective in documenting the performance

of staffers who may have to be dismissed. Editors should develop a strategy, known as progressive discipline, which includes efforts to improve performance and follows these steps: oral warning, written warning, suspension, and termination.

Training programs for editors who will be expected to rate staffers should stress understanding of the newspaper's policies, the standards on which the staff will be rated, how appraisals can be used for motivation, how to minimize rating errors, and how to conduct an effective interview.

A process for the staff to rate the boss should focus on the boss's management skills.

NOTES

1. Evelyn Eichel and Henry E. Bender, *Performance Appraisals: A Study of Current Techniques* (New York: American Management Associations, 1984), 11.
2. Douglas McGregor, "An Uneasy Look at Performance Appraisals," *Harvard Business Review,* May–June 1957, 89–94.
3. Gary P. Latham and Kenneth N. Wexley, *Increasing Productivity through Performance Appraisal* (Reading, Mass.: Addison-Wesley, 1981), 24–25.
4. Ibid., 25–26.
5. Ibid., 26.
6. James W. Walker, *Human Resource Planning* (New York: McGraw-Hill, 1980), 221–22.
7. "The Revival of Productivity," *Business Week,* 13 February 1984, 92.
8. Peter F. Drucker, *Management* (New York: Harper & Row, 1974), 32–33.
9. Ibid., 424–25.
10. Walker, *Human Resource Planning,* 204.
11. Ibid., 208.
12. Eichel and Bender, *Performance Appraisals,* 43.
13. Latham and Wexley, *Increasing Productivity,* 179.
14. Robert H. Giles and Christine D. Landauer, *Gannett Rochester Newspapers Performance Review Program* (Rochester: Gannett Rochester Newspapers, 1984).
15. Daryl J. Bem, "Self-Perception Theory," in *Advances in Experimental Social Psychology,* ed. Leonard Berkowitz (New York: Academic Press, 1972), 1–62.
16. Latham and Wexley, *Increasing Productivity,* 81–82.
17. Ibid., 82.

18. Robert H. Giles and Christine D. Landauer, *Self-Appraisal Form* (Rochester: Gannett Rochester Newspapers, 1985).
19. Walker, *Human Resource Planning*, 213–15.
20. Latham and Wexley, *Increasing Productivity*, 120–21.
21. Ibid., 126–27.
22. Richard M. Steers, *Introduction to Organizational Behavior*, 2d ed. (Glenview, Ill.: Scott, Foresman, 1984), 419.
23. Ibid., 423–24.
24. Latham and Wexley, *Increasing Productivity*, 100.
25. Ibid., 103.
26. Ibid., 104.
27. Ibid., 101.
28. Roger Gillott, "Six States Proposing Strictures on Companies' Right to Fire Workers" (Associated Press, 25 June 1984).
29. Latham and Wexley, *Increasing Productivity*, 89.
30. Ibid., 89–90.
31. Ibid., 92.
32. Ibid.
33. Richard Morano, "Strategy for Changing Management Style," in *Human Resource Management* (Rochester, N.Y.: Xerox Corp., 1981).

11

Pay, MBO, and Other Rewards

Management of the pay program is an important and often difficult responsibility for the editor. The editor and publisher together attempt to build a pay system that is fair, that recognizes the need to reward individuals differently based on performance, and that is competitive in the marketplace and realistic in relation to the company's profit and ability to pay.

One of the tasks of the publisher, the editor, and the other top executives of a newspaper company is to mesh the goals of individuals with the goals of the organization. An approach that has been used successfully by newspapers is a participative program known as Management by Objectives. In addition to fostering teamwork and linking the efforts of the individual and the newspaper, MBO can be a source of additional income for newspaper executives, usually in the form of a bonus.

WAGES AND SALARIES

Pay is one of the most important subjects in the field of management. It is a means of providing income for employees and a cost of doing business to the employer.

Most of the theories of motivation (see Chapter 3) consider money to be a factor for motivation. Maslow and Herzberg saw pay as a basic need that had to be satisfied before workers could be motivated by the work itself. In McClelland's achievement theory, high achievers are not motivated by money, but see it as an important measurement of success. Adams, in the equity theory, observes that money is an important element when people compare their own work situation with that of others to determine the relative balance. In both the goal-setting theory and the expectancy theory, the role of money as a value is significant in the motivation equation.

As these theories suggest, pay has two important roles: It provides the means to buy material necessities and it is an important symbol. For some, money represents security; for others, it symbolizes success. Experience with Management by Objectives demonstrates that money can be an incentive when tied to achievement.

The movement for the development and adoption of sound principles and practices of wage and salary administration started in the 1920s and 1930s. It expanded greatly during and immediately after World War II and, in the 1950s, became more mature.[1]

"Wage and salary administration" is the term used to describe a system of policies and methods of employee compensation. Activities that may be included in a wage and salary administration program are job evaluation, development and maintenance of wage ranges, wage surveys, wage incentives, wage changes, profit sharing, merit pay, and control of payroll costs.

Wage is the term commonly used for compensation for employees who are paid by the hour. The amount of an hourly employee's weekly paycheck fluctuates according to the number of hours actually worked. *Salary* applies to earnings that are uniform from one pay period to the next, regardless of the number of hours worked. There is a status distinction between the two terms. *Salaried* often implies white-collar, professional, administrative, and professional employees. *Wage earners* are hourly or nonsupervisory employees. In the newsroom, nonsupervisory staffers—reporters, copy editors, artists, photographers, secretaries, and news assistants or clerks—make a weekly wage and are paid time and a half for hours beyond the regular work week. Supervisors and middle- and top-level managers are on salary and are not paid for overtime work. This distinction is blurred to some extent in many newsrooms because both salaried supervisors and nonsupervisory wage earners may receive full pay if they are absent for such reasons as sickness or the death of a family member.

Federal and state laws affect wage and salary rates and structures. The Fair Labor Standards Act of 1938 provides for a minimum wage. Congress periodically raises the minimum wage to reflect increases in the cost of living. Nearly all employees in private business and industry are covered by this law. The Fair Labor Standards Act also establishes rules for overtime pay. The Equal Pay Act of 1963 was passed as an amendment to the Fair Labor Standards Act. The intent of Congress was to end the practice in some companies of paying women less than men for the same classifications of work by prohibiting discrimination in wage payments on the basis of sex. The Equal Pay Act permits merit-pay plans that recognize a difference in levels of performance within a job range.[2] Other federal laws that regulate pay practices include Title VII of the Civil Rights Act of 1964, which requires that compensation be nondiscriminatory, and the National Labor Relations Act, which provides that employers must bargain collectively with representatives of a union that is certified as the employees' bargaining agent.

The Fair Labor Standards Act authorizes the Department of Labor to investigate questions of compliance to these laws. The Labor Department normally investigates in response to a complaint by an individual worker or by a union, but it may investigate a company's compensation practices even if no complaint has been filed. In the event of a violation, the Labor Department also supervises the payment of unpaid wages or unpaid overtime.

The law is specific on how overtime is to be paid. It prescribes forty hours as the maximum number of hours employees are required to work during any work week without overtime pay. In some newsrooms, the work week is less than forty hours. Under some union agreements, for example, the standard work week is thirty-seven and a half hours and overtime is paid for any work beyond that.

The normal overtime rate is figured as time and a half. Under union contracts, double-time pay is common for overtime work on Sundays and holidays.

Certain newspaper employees may be exempt from some of

the provisions of the Fair Labor Standards Act. The law defines three categories of employees whose salaries are not affected by the overtime provisions:

1. *Executives.* These employees qualify for an exemption from overtime pay if they meet the following criteria: The employee's primary duty—that is, 50 percent or more of his or her time—is the management of a company or one of its departments or subdivisions; the employee customarily directs the work of at least two other employees and has the authority to hire and fire or make effective recommendations concerning the status of employees. In the news department, the jobs that normally would fall under this exemption would be editor, executive editor, managing editor, assistant managing editor, chief photographers, photolab supervisors, and desk editors such as city editor, features editor, sports editor, business editor, and news editor, and the assistant editors under their supervision.

2. *Administrative employees.* This category typically includes assistants to executives or other administrators, staff specialists who perform functional as opposed to purely supervisory duties, and employees who work on special assignment. Generally, executive secretaries and staff assistants to the senior editors are covered by this exemption.

3. *Professional employees.* This category is most frequently subject to inquiry and interpretation because it seems to draw distinctions among reporters. Employees eligible for professional exemption must spend at least 50 percent of their time in work requiring scientific or specialized study of the type customarily acquired in college or graduate school. Employees also may be exempt professionals whose primary duties are "original and creative work in a recognized field of artistic endeavor. The work must depend primarily on the invention, imagination, or talent of the employee." Sales employees are exempt under this definition.

The classification of journalists as professionals has been of considerable interest to newspaper management since the Fair

Labor Standards Act was first enacted. Soon after the law was passed in 1938, a federal appeals court established the general rule that ordinary reporters and editors are not professionals because they are not members of the "learned professions" and few of them have attended specialized schools of journalism. Although most reporters and editors have journalism degrees today, the rule still stands.

However, the Labor Department's Wage and Hour Division recognizes that certain types of writers and photographers might satisfy the definition of a professional. In a bulletin issued by the Wage and Hour Division in 1975, it was stated: "Exemption for newspaper writers as professional employees is normally available only under the provisions for professional employees of the 'artistic' type. Newspaper writing of the exempt type must, therefore, be 'predominantly original and creative in character.' Only writing which is analytical, interpretive, or highly individualized is considered to be creative in nature. Newspaper writers commonly performing work which is original and creative . . . are editorial writers, columnists, critics, and 'top-flight' writers of analytical and interpretive articles.

"The reporting of news, the rewriting of stories received from various sources, or the routine editorial work of a newspaper is not predominantly original and creative in character and must be considered as nonexempt work. Thus, a reporter or news writer ordinarily collects facts about news events by investigation, interview, or personal observation and writes stories reporting these events for publication or submits the facts to a rewrite man or other editorial employees for story preparation. Such work is nonexempt work. The leg man, the reporter sent out under specific instructions to cover a murder, fire, accident, ship arrival, convention, sports event, etc., is normally performing duties which are not professional in nature within the meaning of the regulations."[3]

In 1962, the Labor Department clarified the status of newspaper photographers. Its opinion was that, generally speaking, photographers doing routine work would not be exempt from the Fair Labor Standards Act. It also noted that there might be situations where a specialty photographer might be exempt. Such a photographer would spend most of his or her time on work in which "artistic effect" is the prime characteristic and in which the photographer uses to a considerable degree artistic talents, creativity, discretion, and judgment.

Fig. 11.1

CLOSE-UP

The question of whether newspaper reporters, photographers, and nonsupervisory editorial employees can be classified as professionals has been tested in a federal district court in Concord, New Hampshire. The case involves a suit brought by the U.S. Department of Labor against the *Concord Monitor*. The outcome could affect more than sixty thousand newsroom employees whose pay is not governed by a union contract. Under a long-standing interpretation of the Fair Labor Standards Act, most nonsupervisory newsroom employees must be paid for overtime hours at a rate one-and-a-half times the regular wage. Employees designated as professionals are exempt from this regulation.

The suit was filed in 1981, charging that the newspaper had capitalized on "the product resulting from long, long hours of work of ambitious young reporters, editors, and photographers without paying them the overtime benefits" that the *Monitor* "knew full well were required by law."

The newspaper's publisher, George Wilson, says the issue is that reportorial work has radically changed since the Labor Department regulations went into effect in the 1940s. Wilson maintains that the ability, credentials, training, and skills of reporters have improved profoundly since then. He contends that reporters should have the same "professional designation as employees with either an artistic bent or learned background." Musicians, actors, cartoonists, and radio and television announcers are within the "artistic" and "creative" definition acceptable to the Labor Department. Accountants, nurses, teachers, and medical technicians also are "professionals," because of their academic training.

Groups representing journalists, including the Newspaper Guild, fear a ruling that favors the *Monitor* could have an effect on the thousands of newsroom employees at nonunion daily newspapers nationally.

Sources: "Suit Studies the Wages of Journalism," *New York Times,* 20 July 1986.

The status of newsroom employees under the Fair Labor Standards Act is of additional interest to editors because of what is known as *compensatory time*. It often is the preference of staffers and editors that overtime be compensated by additional time off rather than by overtime pay. This is compensatory time. Staffers like to put together blocks of time for a long weekend or extra days off at the end of their vacation. Editors see compensatory time as a way of cutting the payroll dollars that would otherwise go into overtime payments.

While compensatory time is permitted, there are clear limits under the law. If the company uses a biweekly payroll system, compensatory time may be offered for overtime but the time off must be taken during the same week as the overtime was worked. The comp time must be given as time and a half. For example, if an employee works four hours overtime and wants to take time off instead of receiving overtime pay, he or she is due six hours comp time by the end of the work week.

Accruing comp time beyond the work week in which it was earned is illegal. Newspapers that permit this practice are inviting an investigation by the Department of Labor, say lawyers who specialize in wage-hour law. However, attitudes toward compensatory time for workers in private industry may be influenced by a 1985 law affecting public employees. The law permits time-and-a-half compensatory time for workers who put in overtime and provides, specifically, that some classifications of employees can accumulate up to 480 hours of comp time before they must be compensated in cash.

Professionals are not bound by these restrictions and may, at the discretion of the editor, accumulate chunks of extra time off in return for working longer hours.

Overtime is one of the most difficult expenses to control. Because news happens at unexpected times and in unexpected ways, it is not always possible for a reporter to seek advance approval of overtime. If a staffer works overtime without the advance approval of an editor, the newspaper still must pay time and a half. Editors may wish to establish a policy to help them manage overtime and control its costs. Such a policy might include the following points:

- Overtime is a valuable resource for the news staff. It must be used carefully and with good judgment.
- Overtime must be approved in advance by an editor, typically the staffer's immediate supervisor.
- For those times when a news emergency occurs and there is no opportunity to obtain advance approval of overtime, the supervising editor will explain the situation to the editor.
- The supervising editor should be the sole judge of whether a situation actually is a news emergency and requires overtime.
- Staffers who abuse the policy by working unauthorized overtime may be subject to discipline.

Payroll is the largest single cost for newspaper companies. In addition to wages and salaries, payroll costs include extras or fringes such as sick pay, medical and hospital insurance, life insurance, vacation pay, and pension plans. It is not uncommon for additional benefits to add as much as 35 percent to the cost of wages and salaries.

The highly labor-intensive nature of newspaper publishing explains why publishers are concerned about controlling payroll costs, why they give careful attention to planning the budget, and why they sometimes appear unusually tough-minded in examining the editor's proposals for pay increases or hiring new staffers.

A publisher putting together a compensation program would have the following objectives in mind:

- Attracting competent personnel. Pay is only one factor considered by a candidate for a staff position; however, it is the most easily compared. It also is the element over which the newspaper's management has the most control.
- Retaining qualified personnel. Many factors explain why a staffer decides to remain with the newspaper or to seek a new opportunity. Job satisfaction and opportunities for personal growth and advancement are perhaps the most important considerations. Pay is always a key factor in that bal-

ance. The newspaper's pay structure must be competitive—not only in the local market, but also with other newspapers of its size—and fairly administered. In addition, the newspaper must be able to demonstrate to its employees that this is the case.

- Providing rewards for good performance. Staffers must see a clear relationship between performance and rewards. They must be satisfied that their pay is based on performance and that the system allows for higher than average pay increases for outstanding work. Merit-pay programs and incentive bonuses based on periodic performance appraisals are effective ways of linking pay to performance.
- Keeping the best reporters on the beat. In any newsroom, a few top staffers typically will become editors, but most will not. Those reporters, copy editors, and others should be rewarded for their special skills and should not be faced with the choice of becoming an editor just to make more money.
- Providing incentives for individual development. The key is for the staffer to understand that the best way to get a better assignment or more responsibility—and thus more money—is to master the present job. Feedback and goal setting are important parts of this process.
- Recognizing long service. The news staff benefits from having a core of senior staffers whose high-quality work, stable influence, and knowledge of the community are of great value. A compensation program should recognize that the worth of seniority goes beyond pins and other symbols of service.

Fig. 11.2

CLOSE-UP

The adequacy of pay levels for newspaper journalists has been the subject of serious study and intensive debate.

College journalism deans warn that the "best and brightest" students are not choosing careers in journalism and a factor in their

Fig. 11.2, continued

decisions is the pay practices of newspapers. The Education for Journalism Committee of the American Society of Newspaper Editors contends that low starting salaries present a serious obstacle to getting journalism students interested in newspaper careers.

Studies by the College Placement Council of Bethlehem, Pennsylvania, and by the Placement Services at Michigan State University support the contention that entry-level salaries on newspapers are substandard. Research by Paul V. Peterson, a journalism professor at Ohio State University, shows that the percentage of journalism graduates taking newspaper jobs has declined.

John Morton, a newspaper analyst with the New York securities firm of Lynch Jones & Ryan, observes, "Despite the pay, the newspaper industry has always attracted some notably talented people and produced its share of distinguished journalists, successful executives, and industry leaders. Still, except for those driven few, newspaper work is not so attractive a career for ambitious people as business, engineering, and a number of other occupations."

A number of factors affect newspaper pay levels, including the size of the newspaper, its geographic location, the pay scales of nearby competitors, and the market demand. To some extent, starting salaries may reflect the law of supply and demand; that is, there are more graduates looking for newspaper jobs than there are jobs to be offered.

In larger markets, newspaper pay is more competitive, both at the starting and at the experienced levels. Competition also is a factor. In Dallas and Detroit, for example, the intense competition for circulation leadership has influenced the growth in newsroom salaries.

Research at Indiana University's School of Journalism suggests that more young people are leaving newspaper work for other fields. The dominant reason they are leaving is salary and fringe benefits. On the other hand, the successful achievers in newspapers—publishers, senior editors, columnists, and top reporters—seldom leave the business for advertising, public relations, or some other career.

There are four major annual surveys of newspaper salaries. The oldest and largest is the Inland Daily Press Association's Wage and Salary Survey. The Dallas Morning News Compensation Survey covers mainly editorial employees and is limited to newspapers of more than 100,000 circulation. The Los Angeles Times survey focuses on the pay for management and supervisory positions. The Kansas City Star and Times study covers newspapers with circulation from 50,000 to 300,000.

Sources: Margaret Genovese, "Editors, Educators Lament Low Starting Salaries," *presstime*, February 1985; Clark Newsom, "Wages," *presstime*, August

1984, 6–9; John Morton, "Journalism Doesn't Pay," *The Quill*, July–August 1984, 15; David H. Weaver, Richard G. Gray, and G. Cleveland Wilhoit, "Major Findings from a Survey of American Journalists, 1982–1983" (Indiana University, 1984).

JOB EVALUATION

Job evaluation is a system for determining the relative money value of jobs within an organization. It involves the analysis of jobs for the purpose of writing job descriptions and specifications. Each job is rated and those ratings are converted to wage ranges.

The first attempts at job evaluation were begun by the Chicago Civil Service Commission in 1909. By the late 1940s, job-analysis programs became widespread in industry as management recognized the need for an orderly and logical means for explaining to labor unions how it arrived at wage-rate decisions.[4]

Many editors are unfamiliar with the process of job evaluation. At newspapers where the newsroom wage ranges are based on job evaluations, that analysis usually is done in the personnel department based on information provided by the editor.

Five steps involved in a job analysis are:

1. *Job description.* A statement of the duties, responsibilities, and job conditions.

    Following are two examples of job descriptions:

    Day city editor. This position has responsibility for assigning stories. The editor checks the morning and previous day's newspapers to insure that running stories are covered and updated. The editor maintains the future file, drafts assignments for reporters as they begin work, follows up on notes or phone calls left overnight, and prepares a news budget for the morning news meeting. The editor edits copy as it is written during the day, directs the work of all reporters on duty, and leaves the night city editor with a local news budget and a memo on the status of all stories in progress.

Copy-desk chief. This position is responsible for directing the work of the copy desk, which edits and sets all local and wire copy and pages. The copy-desk chief supervises copy editors on the rim, distributing work and then checking it. He or she provides training for copy editors and evaluates their performance. The copy-desk chief is the arbiter of style in the newsroom. The copy-desk chief is responsible for maintaining a copy flow to meet deadlines for all editions of the paper. The copy-desk chief checks pages laid out by news editors, paying particular attention to the accuracy, clarity, and fairness of headlines. The copy-desk chief returns stories to assigning editors on the city desk for further work if the stories cannot be edited to the standards of the newspaper. The copy-desk chief is the gatekeeper responsible for maintaining the newspaper's standards for writing, headlines, accuracy, fairness, and good taste, and who may take whatever steps are necessary to insure that stories set in type meet those standards.

2. *Job specification.* A statement of the human qualities—preparation, training, experience, and independent judgment—required for the job.

3. *Job rating.* The job description and the job specification are evaluated and a relative value or score is assigned to each job. Job ratings reflect job worth and value of similar positions in the marketplace. For news staff jobs, a variety of ratings is possible; for example, there may be one grade for entry-level reporters and another for experienced reporters. If newsroom employees are represented by a union, the terms of the contract will influence the number of job ratings.

4. *Money allocation.* Based on the job rating, pay scales or ranges are established for each job classification or job title, such as reporter, copy editor, or photographer. Where there is a union, pay scales are negotiated for members of the bargaining unit; otherwise, management sets the pay ranges. Pay ranges for most newsroom supervisors and managers are established by the publisher.

5. *Employee classification.* All employees are classified under the proper job title, based on the work they perform.

Job evaluation provides a formal basis for a newsroom pay plan in which differences in pay are based on experience, performance, responsibility, and job conditions. It also is a foundation for establishing wage ranges that are competitive, for responding to complaints about pay, and for informing staffers about the procedures used to determine wage levels.

MERIT PAY

Merit pay is a concept that requires managers to recognize distinctions in performance. In most pay-for-performance plans, all employees receive a base pay raise and, for those who qualify, merit pay is added to the base.

Merit-pay systems are widely used in business, although not always successfully. The prevailing criticism is that decisions about pay reflect opinions rather than concrete measures of performance.

Establishing a merit-pay program is difficult. There are two critical challenges to be met:

1. A performance-appraisal system (see Chapter 10) must first be developed. The editor must be able to defend the evaluation process as fair, free of bias, and a true measure of performance. A performance-appraisal system in which work behavior is measured against standards of excellence can become the foundation on which a merit-pay program is built.
2. The performance review must be linked to pay raises. The editor must be able to demonstrate that, within the context of the newspaper's salary-administration plan, pay is awarded on the basis of performance. Under the equal employment opportunity guidelines, pay practices can be challenged if it is suspected that the pay levels for women or

minorities are less than those for white males doing the same jobs and having comparable experience.

Pay ranges can help editors develop a pay strategy that recognizes both experience and performance. For example, the lower third of the range would be appropriate for those recently hired, recently promoted, or performing below standard. The middle third of the range would reflect the current market value of the job and is appropriate for fully qualified, experienced staffers who are performing at or above performance standards. The upper third of the range is reserved for truly outstanding staffers.

Pay increases in a merit system should be based on performance, but must fall within the limits of the ranges. A staffer whose performance clearly exceeds the standards should be considered for merit increases annually, generally on the anniversary of his or her employment or the date he or she began the current job assignment.

To make a merit-pay system effective, the editor must be willing to take an uncompromising stand on poor performers. They must be denied pay increases and be given opportunities to improve their performance. Failure to improve means no pay increase. This practice enhances the value of merit pay for top staffers. Consider its effect in a payroll budget in which the increase in wages is 5 percent. Rather than give a 5 percent raise to everyone, a merit-pay plan would allow the editor to spread the money this way: 6 to 8 percent for the outstanding performers; 3 to 4 percent for the average performers; and 1 percent or less for the poor performers.

Contracts between the newspaper and a union normally contain experience steps and a negotiated annual increase for staffers. During their first two to six years on the paper, new staffers move to the next experience level each year and are guaranteed a pay increase. Once a staffer reaches the top of the experience scale, or journeyman level, the amount of annual increase is determined by the union contract. Most management-union agreements acknowledge the company's right to award merit pay.

Fig. 11.3

CLOSE-UP

Contracts between newspapers and unions representing newsroom employees historically contain wage provisions calling for annual pay increases to be paid across the board. Pay is based on experience and job classification. "Journeymen" reporters, copy editors, artists, and photographers receive the same pay increase. There is no consideration of performance. The reality of merit pay in most management-union contracts is that once payroll dollars have been budgeted for the increases required by the contract, there is little left for merit.

This pattern is changing somewhat. The explanation is that individual journalists see themselves more as creative workers who should be rewarded on the basis of how well they use their individual talents. Additionally, editors are developing stronger management skills and are demonstrating a greater sense of fairness in hiring, promoting, and evaluating. Staffers may be more willing to trust editors to administer a merit-pay plan and, as a result, union negotiators are showing a willingness to discuss merit-pay plans.

At the *Times-Union* and *Democrat and Chronicle* in Rochester, New York, the Newspaper Guild participated in the evolution of a performance-review program and a merit-pay plan. After the evaluation system had been in place for a year, the Guild was asked to agree to a one-year trial in which decisions on pay would be tied to results of performance reviews. Two levels of pay were proposed. The first, termed "work history," would go to everyone on an annual basis. In spirit, it replaced the across-the-board increase the Guild had traditionally negotiated. Those whose performance was rated "outstanding" or "commendable" would receive merit pay in addition to work history.

During the year's trial, Guild officers monitored the system of performance and pay. At the end of the trial, the Guild membership concluded that there was value in linking performance with pay. The union voted to include both programs in the contract.

In a later negotiation, the Guild accepted a plan to put more money into merit pay by agreeing that staffers whose work was rated substandard would no longer receive a "work-history" increase.

In a merit-pay program, it is common practice to delay a decision on pay until after the editor and the staffer have discussed performance in an evaluation interview (see Chapter 10). The focus of the appraisal interview should be performance and goal setting. Anticipation that the editor will end the interview by disclosing details of the staffer's raise may distort the agenda. Moreover, the discussion of the staffer's performance may alter the editor's thoughts about the raise. When the evaluating editor has an opportunity to review with the managing editor the details of the performance-appraisal discussion, the decision on pay is likely to be fairer and more realistic.

If a staffer is performing below standard, the editor can stretch out the interval between pay increases. The editor and the staffer may agree on goals for improvement and may decide to review progress in three months. If the staffer has shown improvement and is working up to standard, a pay increase can be considered at that time. Unless required by a newspaper's agreement with a union, a salary increase every twelve months should not be expected unless performance justifies it.

MANAGEMENT BY OBJECTIVES

The concept of Management by Objectives was introduced by Peter F. Drucker in the early 1950s. In his book, *The Practice of Management,* Drucker observed, "What the business enterprise needs is a principle of management that will give full scope to individual strength and responsibility and at the same time will give common direction of vision and effect, establish teamwork, and harmonize the goals of the individual with the commonweal. The only principle that can do this is Management by Objectives and self-control."[5]

Drucker's idea was popularized in the 1960s, largely through the efforts of George Odiorne, director of the Bureau of Industrial Relations at the University of Michigan. Odiorne's definition of MBO is, "A process whereby the superior and the subordinate managers of an enterprise jointly identify its common goals, define each individual's major areas of responsibility in terms of the results expected of him, and use these measures as guides for operating the unit and assessing the contribution of each of its members."[6]

MBO, as Odiorne envisioned it, is especially suitable for professional and managerial employees and can extend as far down the hierarchy as first-line supervisors. He suggested that MBO could help overcome many of the chronic problems encountered by those who manage professionals and managers by measuring their contribution through the achievement of goals that are valued by both individuals and the organization.[7]

The common elements of Management by Objectives are:

- Formulation of clear, concise, and realistic goals.
- Development of action plans to achieve the goals.
- A systematic monitoring and measuring of progress.
- Amendments to the plan, when necessary, to achieve the desired results.

Management by Objectives provides a way to identify common goals and organize the effort of the staff to achieve those goals. While the theories of goal setting (see Chapters 3 and 10) and MBO are closely linked, MBO has many different and useful purposes: It makes managers plan. It focuses management efforts on carrying out plans. It helps managers reach personal goals. Because an editor's conscious goals influence his or her work behavior, the setting of goals that are consistent with the publisher's objectives is the essence of Management by Objectives.

Harry Levinson of the Harvard Business School argues that in managing the MBO process, top executives underplay the importance of personal goals. He says they fail to consider such questions as: What do individual managers want and need from work? How do their needs and wants change from year to year? How do organizational objectives and the role of the individual relate to those needs and wants? No goals will have significant incentive power if they are forced choices unrelated to an individual's underlying dreams, wishes, and personal aspirations.[8]

Such a conflict between personal goals and organizational objectives might occur, for example, if the editor were a journalist of strong ideals committed to giving readers a high-quality news report every day, but who was thought of by the publisher as only an instrument for holding down costs. Or, in the MBO planning stage, there may be disagreement between publisher and editor over whether the editor's goals are truly compatible with those of the newspaper company. Such a conflict can arise if the editor wants to hire additional reporters to staff a special section but the publisher thinks the newspaper's projected revenues won't support the cost. Tact and skill are necessary to discuss goals openly and candidly and to reach agreement on objectives that are important to both the editor and the newspaper company.

Other evidence suggests that supervisory behavior is a factor in whether an MBO program can be successful. A boss who assigns goals or limits the choices of goals and who treats the performance-appraisal process as a hostile experience will diminish individual performance. Studies of high achievers (see Chapter 3) show that workers perform better when they have specific goals and high levels of feedback. Performance also is enhanced by anticipation and anxiety over an evaluation of one's progress against goals. Other research has suggested that while goal-setting techniques often lead to improved performance, this performance at times is achieved at the expense of personal satisfaction. Where goals are seen by managers as being too rigid, the credibility of the program itself may be jeopardized, leading to poor effort and performance.[9]

Odiorne thought that the greatest area for improvement in MBO was in encouraging goals that demanded innovation and creativity. "No manager should be permitted to set goals for his position on the presumption that the status quo was good enough. The solution of perennial problems, or the introduction of new ideas to achieve better results than are presently being attained, should be insisted upon during the goal-setting process."[10]

Objectives can be linked to routine job responsibilities, but may call for innovative or creative achievements, such as development of new products, systems, or programs. They may focus on problems, such as reduction of excessive employee turnover, or they may be concerned with personal development—acquiring additional knowledge, skills, and experience that will improve performance.[11]

Creative goal setting can be divided into two categories: *extrinsic creativity* (the introduction of new ideas from the outside) and *intrinsic creativity* (the discovery of new ways to do the present job).

Not every newspaper task will lend itself to extrinsic creativity. The development of a performance-review program based on standards and rating scales (see Chapter 10) is an example of introducing a new idea taken from a concept developed by psychologists.

Intrinsic creativity is more common to newspaper work. Efforts to improve news coverage, story content, and packaging are ideas simply meant to enhance present jobs. Good ideas get around rather quickly in the newspaper business. An innovation that works at one paper will be borrowed and tried at others.

MBO is a results-oriented way of managing. Goals typically are set by identifying areas of individual responsibility that are considered important to the organization, then defining key targets or goals and the results for each.[12] For example, the editor may recognize that the training of first-year reporters is an important responsibility. The editor's MBO plan would include programs to achieve the goal of a well-trained reporting staff.

For an editor to be motivated to achieve a goal, two things are necessary: (1) the editor must participate in setting the goal, and (2) he or she must understand why the goal is important and what the benefit will be for accomplishing the goal. Advocates of MBO acknowledge that when an MBO program fails, the most likely explanation is that the top executives neglected to involve managers in setting goals, to obtain their commitment to the goals, and to make success a high priority.

Fig. 11.4

CLOSE-UP

Management by Objectives has created an industry of its own: books and articles, graduate theses, and consultants who have prospered by explaining and implementing MBO.

In its basic framework, MBO is not complicated. Any child who has

Fig. 11.4, continued

ever set a goal would understand the idea. Following are two hypothetical MBOs for a ten-year-old:

Goals	Action Plans
1. Improve batting average to at least .350.	1. Batting practice two nights a week.
	2. Wind sprints daily to beat throws to first base.
2. Save at least $100 for a new bike by July 4.	1. Find an additional lawn to mow.
	2. Wash family car every Saturday.

Few ten-year-olds are this well organized. Fewer still will achieve their goals without constant reminders. And the rewards, while tangible, are difficult to keep in mind. But the concept is valid because the goals are measurable and achievable, worth attaining, and easy to understand.

Source: Edward N. Baron, director of training and development, Gannett Company, Inc., "Management by Objectives," August 1984.

Nearly twenty years after MBO became popular, Odiorne observed that MBO was not as effective as it should be. He listed three reasons: (1) MBO requires changes in the way things are done; (2) many knowledge workers enjoy "winging it," preferring to adjust their goals as they gain knowledge instead of working to advance goals required by the MBO; and (3) many people don't know how to make MBO work. They understand the theory but are deficient in implementing its technique.[13]

In reviewing the research, Odiorne found that where the objectives are financial, MBO has persisted; where nonfinancial goals are involved, it is easier to operate in a more traditional way. The basic workings of MBO are easier to see and are more easily accepted when the work centers on plans and problem-solving goals. The idea that a face-to-face discussion or group participation method of goal setting is essential in MBO hasn't been nearly as well accepted.[14]

The difficulty of developing and maintaining an effective MBO program that centers on ideas, creativity, and intuition may explain why editors were the last group of newspaper executives to adopt Management by Objectives. Generally, MBO was not introduced in newsrooms until the mid-1970s—several years after editors' counterparts in advertising, circulation, production, and business were setting goals and earning bonuses for their successes. The initial reaction of many editors was that MBO was simply a device to serve the bottom line and nothing more. Editors who took MBO seriously found that MBO goals often resulted in important improvements in the newspaper.

Editors and MBO

An effective performance-appraisal program (see Chapter 10) includes the setting of short- and long-term goals for every member of the news staff. These individual goals work best, however, when they can be linked with the editor's overall objectives so that everybody on the staff is pulling in the same direction.

Goal setting as part of an annual review focuses on individual improvement. Such goals serve the objectives of the newspaper in the sense that any improvement in individual performance contributes to the overall quality of the newspaper. There is no monetary reward attached specifically to these individual goals, yet successful achievement may influence a staffer's pay if the newspaper recognizes performance in setting pay levels. And, of course, a staffer who is committed to setting and reaching individual goals will achieve personal growth that may lead to an opportunity for greater responsibility.

Generally, an MBO program is limited to the top editors on the newspaper—those at the level of editor, executive editor, and managing editor. On some papers, MBO reaches down to first-level supervisors—city editor, sports editor, news editor, features editor, graphics editor, photo editor, business editor, etc. The idea is that anyone responsible for major plans or significant numbers of people can benefit from MBO.

The ideal MBO process is designed to:[15]

- Measure and judge performance.
- Relate individual performance to organizational goals.
- Clarify both the job to be done and the expectations of accomplishment.
- Foster the increasing competence and growth of the subordinate.
- Enhance communications between superior and subordinate.
- Stimulate the subordinate's motivation.
- Serve as a device for organizational control.

The publisher's or editor's major role in MBO is to ask specific questions that will channel a subordinate's thinking toward a constructive analysis of the problem and a creative goal. If, for example, the managing editor is working with the city editor in examining why four new reporters hired in the past year are not doing well, the managing editor might ask the following questions to arrive at possible explanations:

What are the specific areas where the reporters' performances are below standard? Are their basic language skills satisfactory? Have they acquired bad habits since joining the staff? Are they getting regular feedback from their supervisors? Are they able to manage their time effectively? Has their relationship with others in the reporting peer group influenced their performance? Did we overestimate their skill levels when we hired them? Did we investigate their performance in school and in other jobs as carefully as we should have? Did we overlook any warning flags in the interviewing and hiring process? How can we use their strengths to overcome their weaknesses? What specific steps should be taken immediately? What steps should follow?

The ultimate solution may be a special training program for the four reporters. The questions posed by the managing editor during the examination of the problem will have made clear the major criteria for setting up the training program as a goal and for evaluating the city editor's performance in meeting the goal.

Creating an MBO Plan

There are three stages to an MBO program for newspaper editors:

1. In the planning stage, the editor and his or her subordinates agree on the results to be accomplished. MBO is part of a process of setting priorities, of deciding what the news department and the rest of the newspaper will try to achieve during the next year. It is an opportunity to strive for changes and improvements that will result in a better newspaper.

    There should be nothing in the editor's MBO plan that is routine, that is a normal part of the job. Meeting deadlines is not an appropriate MBO goal. Getting the paper to press on time is a necessity. The editor should not receive a bonus for that kind of achievement. However, the editor may propose revising the page flow to enable the copy desk to handle more late news on deadline. There is stretch in that kind of a goal.

    An MBO plan is written on a standard form. In some MBO programs, five or six well-developed goals will be sufficient. In others, editors are asked to have a longer list of specific, detailed goals that represent an intricate statement of their objectives for the year.

    The editor should state each goal, describe the change or improvement that is anticipated, explain how it will be accomplished, and provide a timetable for completion of each part of the MBO plan. In developing each goal, editors should ask themselves these questions: What do I want to accomplish and why? How will I know when the goal is achieved? When will I do it? Is this goal a stretch or is it part of my basic responsibility as a manager? Editors should review their own MBO with skeptical eyes, giving the goals the same close scrutiny they would give the editing of a major investigative story.

    The editor carries the news department's plans into meetings with the publisher and other department heads. This encourages a face-to-face examination of each executive's plans and contributes to what is known as "TNC," Total Newspaper Concept. This means that the publisher, the editor, the advertising director, and other managers pool their ideas and resources to improve the newspaper. The editor's goals recognize the advertising director's need to sell and market the newspaper and the circulation director's obligation to get each day's editions to readers on time. Likewise, the goals of other department heads acknowledge the value of a strong and credible news report.

2. In the second stage of an MBO program, the goals are carried out. The idea is that individuals will work harder to carry out the plans because they helped create them. The publisher will review the editor's progress periodically, usually every three months. At some newspapers, this review offers an opportunity to adjust goals or to add new ones. For example, if the editor's plan to begin zoned weekly editions is delayed for reasons beyond the editor's control, the editor may propose adjusting or killing the goal. Or, if in midyear the editor gets an idea for developing a minority internship program with the local high schools, the publisher may agree that it should be added to the editor's MBO.

3. In the third stage, the editor's performance is reviewed. This is when the results are measured against the objectives. The review typically occurs a year after the MBO plan was put into effect. The publisher and the editor discuss the results—why part of the plan may have succeeded or why part may have fallen short of the goal. The publisher grades the editor's performance, and that grade becomes part of the consideration for the editor's executive incentive or bonus.

In some newspaper companies, the editor is accountable to a corporate boss in addition to the newspaper publisher for the planning, execution, and review of his or her MBO plan.

Knight-Ridder was one of the first newspaper companies to include editors in Management by Objectives. James K. Batten, president of Knight-Ridder, describes the company's practice as "principally a bottom-up" kind of process, but it also is a forum to reinforce the overall goals of the company. "It should not be Knight-Ridder deciding that thus-and-so ought to happen and here is your MBO. It ought to be just the reverse of that with the understanding that Knight-Ridder has certain broad objectives that will be in the minds of the people who are reviewing the draft MBO and suggesting refinements and fine-tuning. But the point is that it's basically a bottom-up process when it works well."[16]

In addition to providing the basis for the editor's year-end bonus, MBO has these benefits:

- The editor is held accountable for his or her goals.
- The goals are specific and they lead to specific results.
- The goals require above-normal effort.
- The goals are measurable.
- The goals are limited in time, generally one year.
- The goals are realistic and attainable; not too easy, not too hard.
- The goals encourage planning and control.
- The goals force the editor and the publisher into a closer working relationship.

Fig. 11.5

CLOSE-UP

What makes a good MBO? Ivan Jones, director of personnel research for Knight-Ridder Newspapers, offers these examples of newsroom goals:

- Produce a new typographic scoreboard for the sports page.
- Increase the number of qualified black professionals on the staff by a net of two.
- Produce a plan for repackaging the Sunday newspaper so the news sections are better organized.
- Develop a plan for coverage of significant conventions in the city.

Fig. 11.5, continued

- Establish consistent weekly reports on important state legislation and activities of legislators from our metropolitan area.
- Complete a policy and procedures guide, a style book, and a VDT users' manual.
- Refine the orientation program for new staff members.

Source: Ivan Jones, "Getting on Target with MBOs," *The Bulletin of the American Society of Newspaper Editors,* May 1981, 10–11.

The impact of the MBO process on the editor's management style can be significant. Editors find they are forced to plan, to step back from the day-to-day routine to think about the future. They recognize that they are accountable for producing results rather than just managing activities. And when they put their minds to it, they discover that they can create new ways of doing things.

Editors of small and large newspapers can benefit equally from the MBO process. On smaller papers, the editor is so involved in directing the daily news report that there is little time for planning and the other functions of managing. MBO has the particular advantage of requiring these editors to engage in planning.

Batten says, "If you don't have a clear vision in your mind about interim and long-term goals and have them written down, then the nature of this business is that it sucks you into it and keeps you there until 11:30 at night, exhausted. You may have made the paper a little bit better for tomorrow, but you may have blown it in terms of the top editor's responsibility to move the paper forward in a methodical, clear way."[17]

Editors going through the MBO process for the first time are often surprised by the amount of time it takes to do it right. Discussing ideas, documenting goals, coordinating the roles of the news staff or of other departments, and laying out realistic timetables are complicated and demanding tasks.

As they identify goals, editors should consider any variables that may be beyond their control. The means for achieving goals should be within the editor's span of responsibility and authority. For example, in preparing a goal for the newsroom that relies on the coordinated efforts of the advertising department or the production department, the editor should be aware of what can happen in the other departments over which he or she has no control.

In writing an MBO plan, the key is to prepare a detailed description of the goal and the action plan. Following are examples of MBO goals in which the original ideas were improved by adding details that made them more measurable:

	Goal	Action Plan
Original:	Improve television coverage. By May 1.	Redesign and rename TV book, add listings daily and Sunday.
Revised:	Improve packaging and content of daily and Sunday TV coverage to include cable listings. By May 1.	Redesign and rename Sunday TV book. Create television grid with sixteen channels, including cable. Add summaries of television movies. Use sixteen-channel grid daily with spot color. Develop "Best Bets" column for daily TV page.
Original:	Improve orientation program for new staff members. By October 1.	Give new staffers understanding of company policies, newsroom practices, and community history.
Revised:	Expand and improve orientation program for new staff members. By October 1.	Arrange tours of all departments within first week on the job. Schedule meetings with personnel department to review benefits. Introduce to publisher. Meet with managing editor to discuss style book, other newsroom practices. Arrange meetings with city historian.

The Incentive Bonus

The editor's success in meeting MBO goals is assessed at the end of the year and may help determine the size of his or her bonus. The bonus, or executive incentive, is in addition to the editor's salary. Management by Objectives is an incentive system that is tied to the profit performance of the newspaper as well as improvement in management and the newspaper itself. For example, if the editor achieved his or her MBO goals but circulation and advertising revenues fell short of the plan, the editor's bonus may not be as large as if the profit picture were better.

The incentive bonus recognizes two factors about the roles of the publisher, editor, and other top newspaper executives. First, these executives bear the same risks as the owners. At many family-owned newspapers, the top executives are the owners and they share in the benefits of ownership. But at many newspaper companies, some of them publicly owned, the top executives assume the risks of ownership without the benefits, without the rights to share in the profits. Second, the rewards of top executives must stimulate them to manage the company with as much zeal and enterprise as if they were the owners.

How important is money in an MBO program? "Very," says Ivan Jones, director of personnel research for Knight-Ridder. "Managers cannot be motivated when they have no advance knowledge of who will receive payments or on what basis payments are calculated. MBO provides an excellent means to tie compensation to performance . . . money, after all, gets everyone's attention."[18]

The editor's bonus for meeting MBO goals can be as much as 40 percent of his or her salary. Putting part of an executive's total compensation "at risk" provides an incentive for achievement. In a similar way, a person in sales can earn commissions on top of his or her base salary.

Batten explains that at Knight-Ridder, the level of bonus payments for most editors is tied both to the economic progress of the individual newspaper and to the editor's success in meeting his or her goals. "Nobody is expected to get one hundred points out of one hundred. The assumption is that the goals ought to have a lot of stretch in them. There ought to be some that you just aren't able to bring off because it is not intended to be a softball sort of program to begin with.

"We agreed that we would keep our basic salary ranges for editors competitive and not count on MBO money to bail them out. In terms of the overall compensation of an editor, the MBO is a significant part, but equity is not intended to depend on a smashing big bonus at the end of the year. 1982 was a rough year and the bonuses were pretty meager. Yet, in most cases, we had our salary scheme in such shape that people were still fairly paid."[19]

Following is an example of a commonly used scale for measuring the performance of executives against their MBO plan:

Rating	Appraisal	Definition
0–2	Change needed	Clearly unable to achieve objectives.
3–4	Below standards	Tried but did not achieve primary goals.
5–6	Commendable	Did a solid job and achieved desired results.
7–8	Superior	Clearly exceeded what was expected.
9–10	Exceptional	Rare performance; counted among the few extraordinary producers.

Under this form of performance assessment, a manager who has met objectives and who has done what is expected of a qualified, experienced person in the assigned position would be rated in the 5–6 range as meeting standards.

There is a tendency for the distinction between salary and bonus to blur over time. This occurs when the bonus comes to be regarded as automatic and a routine, predictable part of compensation. If this is allowed to happen, the implication is that the goals become pro forma. Editors go through the motions of striving to achieve goals, taking for granted that the bonus money will be paid regardless of their effectiveness.

Byron Harless, a former senior vice-president of Knight-Ridder and an architect of its MBO approach, suggests that MBO too often is seen simply as a way of delivering money to people.

When the focus is too much on the mechanics of the goals and the rewards, what gets lost is the extraordinary value of MBO as a planning tool and a source of innovation for the newspaper.

Why MBO May Miss the Mark

Following are some traps editors and publishers can fall into when preparing MBO programs for the year ahead:

- Being blind to reality, either through excessive loyalty to the newspaper or an intense commitment to a particular idea. Newspaper executives need to allow for their own biases. A hard-nosed assessment of the market potential or of the capacity of subordinates will help them avoid goals that can't be reached.

- Confusing cause and effect. If the afternoon paper's circulation is slipping, for example, the editor and publisher may conclude that the cause is to be found in content when the real explanation is a dramatic shift in the demographics and the life-styles of readers.

- Failing to consider elements beyond the editor's control. Lack of advertising support may be the explanation for the editor's failure to reach the goal of developing a special business section. It is not the editor's fault, but the editor does not get the bonus money, either.

- Generalizing from bad examples. After phone calls from friends about two obits the newspaper missed, the publisher may conclude that the staff is doing a poor job of handling obituaries. As a result, the publisher may require the editor to set up a program for improving the paper's reportage of deaths in the community.

- Setting goals that really aren't goals. The editor may propose a goal of meeting with his or her subordinate editors weekly.

That isn't a goal; it is an activity. Only if the meetings are geared toward a specific result would they qualify as a goal.

- Setting goals that are too high or too low. If the goals are too low, they don't challenge; if they are too high, they frustrate.
- Treating MBO as a paperwork exercise. If the editor thinks of goal setting as something required by the publisher or by the corporation, the result is likely to be that MBO will measure nothing and motivate no one.
- Writing a plan and then filing it away. MBO won't mean much if the list of goals is kept out of sight and is not reviewed periodically.
- Setting goals that are not measurable. Many of the ideas put forth by editors can't be quantified. For example, a change that has an aim of "improving quality" is not readily measurable and is difficult to assess unless the editor provides a standard against which the improvement can be gauged.

"MBOs have a tendency to lose their effectiveness after four or five years unless top management is determined not to let that happen, unless top management insists that MBO continues to be done and to be done right," says Knight-Ridder's Batten. "People learn the system and the rhythm of the thing. They run through the obvious agendas that they had in mind, even though they were not accumulating them for this [MBO] purpose. After a while, people begin to say, 'Gee, I've already run through the things you can do.' We believe that unless you really stay on the case, there is a tendency for the quality to erode."[20]

An expectation about MBO that has not been generally fulfilled is that it would lead to participative management. While MBO has involved many staffers in the planning process, it has not brought about an equalization of power between those in charge and those in subordinate positions. It is a program that remains largely in the hands of the editor and the publisher. In the newsroom, MBO requires participation of many editors, but it has not altered the basic management system, which remains a top-down kind of management. The editor is in charge and may invite active consultation from others, but he or she retains a strong influence on the shape and direction of all newsroom MBOs.

The short-term nature of MBO—goals that can be achieved within a year—ignores long-term planning and the value of developing programs for the next three to five years of the newspaper's life. Long-term planning is done, but typically achievement is more difficult to measure and it does not have the incentive of well-defined rewards.

CHAPTER SUMMARY

Pay is one of the most important subjects in the field of management. It has two important meanings for workers: (1) it provides the means to buy material necessities, and (2) it is an important symbol.

Wage refers to the compensation of employees who are paid by the hour. Salary refers to compensation that is uniform from one pay period to another, regardless of the number of hours worked.

The Fair Labor Standards Act of 1938 established regulations for the minimum wage, overtime, and equal pay. The most important of these rules for editors is overtime and the law's interpretation of compensatory time, or time off in lieu of overtime pay. Comp time can be substituted for overtime pay if it is offered at the rate of time and a half and taken during the same week in which the overtime is earned.

Job evaluation is a system for determining the relative money value of jobs within an organization. Five steps involved in a job analysis are: (1) job description, (2) job specification, (3) job rating, (4) money allocation, and (5) employee classification.

Merit pay is a concept that requires managers to recognize distinctions in performance. Establishing a merit-pay program requires two important steps: (1) developing an effective performance-review program, and (2) linking performance appraisals to pay raises. The evaluation program will help the editor document the level of performance upon which merit pay is based.

Management by Objectives is a concept that attempts to link the goals of individual managers with those of the organization. It was introduced by Peter F. Drucker in the early 1950s and popularized through the writings of George Odiorne.

MBO is a common management practice in most newsrooms, most effectively applied to professional and managerial employees. It is a way of identifying common goals and organizing the effort of individuals to achieve those goals. MBO is generally implemented in three stages: (1) planning, (2) carrying out the goals, and (3) reviewing performance.

MBO is closely linked to the ideas of motivation and goal setting. If an individual participates in setting the goal, if the goal is compatible with his or her own ambitions, and if there is a reward connected with achievement of the goal, the individual will be motivated to strive hard to succeed.

MBO measures results rather than activities. In the ideal MBO program, employees are evaluated on how successful they were in reaching their goals. In most MBO programs, an incentive bonus is the reward for achievement of the goals.

In planning MBO goals, managers should be aware of potential traps: intense commitment to particular ideas that can blind them to reality, confusing cause and effect, failing to consider elements beyond the manager's control, generalizing from bad examples, and setting goals that are too high, too low, or not readily measurable.

NOTES

1. Dale S. Beach, *Personnel: The Management of People at Work*, 3d ed. (New York: Macmillan, 1975), 641.
2. Ibid., 650.
3. *An Overview of Wage and Hour Laws as They Apply to Newspapers* (Reston, Va.: American Newspaper Publishers Association and Newspaper Personnel Relations Association, 1979), 11–12.
4. Beach, *Personnel*, 652–53.
5. Peter F. Drucker, *The Practice of Management* (New York: Harper & Row, 1954).
6. George Odiorne, *Management by Objectives: A System of Managerial Leadership* (New York: Pitman, 1965), 55–56.
7. Ibid., 55.

8. Harry Levinson, "Management by Whose Objectives?" in *Harvard Business Review on Management* (New York: Harper & Row, 1975), 60.
9. Richard M. Steers, *Introduction to Organizational Behavior*, 2d ed. (Glenview, Ill.: Scott, Foresman, 1984), 175–76.
10. Odiorne, *Management by Objectives*, 113.
11. Anthony Raia, *Managing by Objectives* (Glenview, Ill.: Scott, Foresman, 1974), 48–50.
12. James W. Walker, *Human Resource Planning* (New York: McGraw-Hill, 1980), 188.
13. George Odiorne, "MBO in the 1980s: Will It Survive?" *Management Review*, July 1977, 39–40.
14. Ibid., 40.
15. Levinson, "Management by Whose Objectives?" 55.
16. James K. Batten, interview with author, 13 March 1984.
17. Ibid.
18. Ivan Jones, "Getting on Target with MBOs," *The Bulletin of the American Society of Newspaper Editors*, May 1981, 9, 11.
19. Batten, interview.
20. James K. Batten, interview with author, 16 August 1985.

12

Managing Change in the Newsroom

Managing change is an important part of every editor's job. Nearly everything the editor does is concerned in some way with implementing change. Making over page one, creating a new section, introducing a merit-pay program, hiring a new staffer, promoting a reporter to assistant city editor, planning for pagination, switching beats on the city desk—each of these activities requires knowledge of how to manage change effectively.

In planning and introducing change, the editor will call on his or her knowledge of motivation, group dynamics, leadership, human behavior, and communication. To be an effective manager of change calls for diagnostic skills, strategies for planning and implementation, and the ability to adopt the most effective leadership style in directing change.

UNDERSTANDING CHANGE

The newspaper is a daily record of change in our society. The news columns are filled with stories of change: elections, obituaries, discoveries, negotiations, new products, sports scores, crime, weddings, new laws and regulations, inventions, prices, fashions, trials, market trends, and much more.

Simultaneously, newspapers find themselves assaulted by change: rapidly changing technology, constitutional and legal questions involving libel, personal privacy, and the First

Amendment, challenges from readers about accuracy and fairness, new problems of style and semantics—is it *Miss, Mrs.,* or *Ms.?*—and the growing commitment to hire and promote women and minorities.

As common as it is, as familiar with it as journalists are, change quite often is accompanied by stress, argument, subtle undermining, foot-dragging, needless internal politics, and a loss of time and money.

Resistance to change is not irrational; it stems from legitimate concern. What will change mean to me? is the first question everyone wants answered. How change is accepted will depend on individual perceptions. A change may not be threatening, but if people perceive that it is, they will behave accordingly.

Change may represent a great opportunity, but it is never without its losses—loss of the past, loss of an important relationship, loss of routines, comforts, or traditions that were important. Whatever the outcome, change means that things will never be quite the same again.

For a newspaper, change can originate from outside or inside the organization. External changes might include competition, a swing in the economy, shifting social or cultural values, technology, and government laws and regulations. Internal sources of change might include different policies or procedures, a new publisher or editor, increased expectations for job performance, a strike, or improvements in the pay or benefits system.

Fig. 12.1

CLOSE-UP

In her book, *The Change Masters,* Rosabeth Moss Kanter observes that incentives for enterprise in a company stem from a "climate of success."

"First, there is emotional and value commitment between person and organization; people feel that they 'belong' to a meaningful entity and can realize cherished values by their contributions. There is a sense of uniqueness and joint-ness that is supported by a feeling of being a member as much as being an employee. Hence, there is usually more innovation in organizations with more job satisfaction . . .

"The second related 'intangible' incentive is the company's culture: whether the company's culture pushes 'tradition' or 'change.' . . . Most people seek to be culturally appropriate, even the people leading the pack. There is thus more impetus to seek change when this is considered desirable by the company.

"Pride in company, coupled with knowing that innovation is mainstream rather than counterculture, provides an incentive for initiative. A feeling that people inside the company are competent leaders—that the company has been successful because of its people—supports this.

"Individual esteem plays a role, too. There is much evidence that success breeds success. Where there is a 'culture of pride,' based on high performance in the past, people's feelings of confidence in themselves and others go up. They are more likely to take risks and also to get positive responses when they request cooperation from others. Mutual respect makes teamwork easier. Thus, high performance may cause group cohesion and liking for workmates as well as result from it; pride in the capacity and ability of others makes teamwork possible."

Source: Rosabeth Moss Kanter, *The Change Masters* (New York: Simon and Schuster, 1983), 149–50.

The editor's environment for initiative is great, if only because the nature of the job invites it. The job of editor carries a broad charter: It is ambiguous, nonroutine, and provides the autonomy to get action going without the publisher's specific approval.

One of the requirements for successful change at a newspaper is stability. While one part of the operation is changing, other parts must be able to remain steady for a while. Indeed, some parts of the news operation will need to work without much attention. For example, a staff that has been asked to install and test an electronic editing system and learn to use it must be confident that sufficient time will be given to make the transition and that, in the meantime, the managing editor won't attempt to reorganize the city desk.

Another dimension to stability is continuity of staff. Change that requires participation depends on communication and relationships. The pace is disrupted when the players are changing because of promotion or turnover.

In a newspaper company, change or innovation typically takes place in three waves: (1) identifying and defining the problem, (2) building coalitions, and (3) mobilizing resources and individuals to put an idea into effect.

1. Identifying the need for change. The process of change begins with identification of the problem. The skills used in diagnosing a problem are, in a broad sense, the skills of reporting. The editor listens, observes, gathers information, asks questions, looks at things from different angles, and interprets data. Specifically, the editor wants to know what actually is happening in a particular situation, what is likely to happen if no change is made, what is the ideal, and what are the restraints that may block a movement from the actual to the ideal.[1] At the same time, the editor may be "planting seeds"—dropping a hint here and a kernel of an idea there, looking to see who picks up on the idea and helps develop it.

   In gathering information, the editor also is sizing up the political situation, figuring out who has stakes in the status quo and who can become allies in supporting and selling a project for change.

   For example, the editor may observe that the city desk is not organized to give regular feedback to inexperienced reporters. If the situation continues, the reporters may acquire bad habits and may not develop the skills they need. Their experience on the job is different from their expectations and they will become frustrated. The editor envisions a change in the city desk editors' daily routine that would overcome the problem, and he or she assesses the resistance that such a change might encounter. In this diagnosis, the editor is seeking to identify the discrepancies between what is actually happening and the ideal.

   Kurt Lewin, a pioneering social psychologist at the University of Iowa, developed a technique known as *force field analysis*, which is useful in visualizing situations that are in need of change.[2] Lewin says that in any situation, there are both driving forces and restraining forces that influence any change. *Driving forces* are those that are pushing to initiate change and keep it going. Pressure from an editor, incentive earnings, and competition from other individuals on the staff or from other news organizations are examples of driving forces. *Restraining forces* act as reins on the driving forces. They resist change. Apathy, hostility, low motivation, and poor performance are examples of restraining forces.

An equilibrium exists, according to Lewin, when the driving forces and the restraining forces are in balance. Improvements in performance and in the content of the paper result when the driving force is stronger than the restraining force.

Initiating stronger driving forces is a challenge that often faces a new editor. As a newcomer, the editor has to size up what may be going for him or her in planning changes—the driving forces—and what may be going against him or her—the restraining forces. An editor who attempts to start making changes without understanding these forces is asking for trouble.

If the editor's analysis shows that the driving forces outweigh the restraining forces, it is possible to push hard for change. If the conclusion is that the restraining forces are stronger, the editor has this choice: give up the change effort for now and concentrate on neutralizing the restraining forces, or convert the restraining forces to driving forces.

Fig. 12.2

CLOSE-UP

Kurt Lewin's research on change drew the attention of the United States government during World War II. At the time, meat was rationed, and scarce ration stamps were required to buy the choice cuts of meat: roast, steaks, and chops. Other cuts of meat, such as liver, tongue, brain, and heart, were not rationed, but people showed little interest in buying them.

Lewin, who was a professor at the University of Iowa, was asked to research this question: Was it possible to get housewives to change their meat-buying habits and to start using the nonrationed products?

In his experiments, one group of housewives listened to lectures that linked the problem of nutrition to the war effort, that emphasized the

Fig. 12.2, continued

vitamin and mineral value of the nonrationed meats, and that explained recipes. Only 3 percent of the women who heard the lectures served any of the nonrationed cuts of meat at home.

A second group of housewives participated in discussions about food, nutrition, and the war effort. The women were asked for ideas. What could they could do to assist in the war effort? Following these discussion sessions, 32 percent of the women served at least one of the previously avoided meats.

What had happened that made one group more responsive to change than the other? Lewin's analysis suggested that the differences were influenced by:

- The degree of involvement of people in the discussion and decision.
- The motivation in actually being a party to the decision.
- Group influence and the support of others in reinforcing the decision to try the nonrationed meats.

Source: William Dyer, "Planned Change," in *Organization and People: Readings, Cases, and Exercises in Organizational Behavior,* 3d ed., ed. J. B. Ritchie and Paul Thompson (St. Paul: West, 1984), 384–85.

---

2. Building coalitions. The second step in introducing change or innovation is creating a team and getting others to sign on, finding peers to act as cheerleaders, and getting blessings for the change from the top. What is critical is "not only the quantity but the source of the power tools that are gathered, and this is why broad coalitions are important," writes Rosabeth Moss Kanter in her book, *The Change Masters.*[3]

Kanter describes *coalition building* as a process that resembles a zigzag more than an orderly progression up the chain of command. The first step involves clearing the idea with an immediate boss, explaining the idea, and later updating the boss on its status. This step requires only the boss's tacit acceptance that the innovator will attempt to develop the idea, build support, and come back with evidence to convince the boss that the change should be implemented.

Kanter identified a common pattern of support seeking

that occurred after approaching the boss and that went lower rather than higher in the organization. She found that innovators used a variety of analogies to describe this process: "Making cheerleaders," or lining up supporters in advance of formal approval; "tin cupping," or begging for involvement; and "loading the gun," or lining up the ammunition. Potential collaborators were approached individually, giving them a chance to influence the project and giving the innovator the maximum opportunity to sell it. The innovator also avoided putting uncommitted people together where they might discover common doubts or opposition to the project.

Once the idea has been planted, the bargaining begins. The innovator promises payoffs from the project in exchange for support. The innovator has two forms of reassurance to offer: his or her skill in persuasion, which comes as a result of having done enough homework to have the right answers, and spreading the risk, or making sure there are enough supporters lined up so that their very presence indicates the likelihood of success in selling the idea and distributes the responsibility for implementing the change among a larger group.

Kanter says the coalition is still unformed and tentative until the final step in the process takes place: getting the "blessing" of higher-level officials. At this point, the innovators are likely to skip levels in the chain of command and go up as high as necessary to gather the ultimate support and resources needed for the project. Of course, the enterprising manager has to know *who* at the top executive level has power on this issue. With promises of support and resources, the innovator can begin to make specific plans for going ahead with the project.

For example, an editor who wants to start a special business or sports section will try to forge a coalition with the directors of advertising, production, and marketing before seeking the approval of the publisher. Studies of innovations that fizzled after bright starts show that a critical factor was the connections between the department initiating the innovation and outside departments. Innovations are easier to achieve, of course, when they can be conceived and implemented with total autonomy in the newsroom. They are much less vulnerable to resistance when they don't depend on cooperation from circulation, production, or advertising.

3. Putting an idea to work. As the action phase begins, the innovator switches roles from composer or creator to conductor. A large number of additional players may become involved at this point. The stage may be quite crowded as the project-team workers are assembled and forged into an operating entity. Most often, the action players are subordinates. The editor brings them together, gives them briefings and assignments, pumps them up for the extra effort, seeks their suggestions and ideas, and promises them a share in the rewards.

At this point, opposition or resistance tends to take a passive form: criticism of specific details, foot-dragging, slow response to requests, or arguments in favor of shifting resources to other projects. Kanter identifies a number of tactics that innovators use to disarm opponents during the action phase: waiting it out, wearing them down, appealing to larger principles, inviting them in, sending emissaries to smooth the way and plead the case, reducing the stakes, and warning the critics.

Fig. 12.3

CLOSE-UP

In 1981, Reg Murphy became publisher of the *Baltimore Sun*, a newspaper with a rich tradition as a reporter's paper. Murphy, a former editor in Atlanta and San Francisco, found himself with few allies on the staff and in a city with established reportorial and reading habits. Following are some things he remembers from his early efforts to bring change to the *Sun*:

- Go slow. What seems like a tortoise pace is a hare's hop to the inmates of the institution.
- Enlist townsfolk. Sports people love good sports sections. Even

proper matrons like personality profiles. Color graphics are enticing to just about everybody.

- Establish committees. Forget the gobbledygook about government-by-committee; a strong internal group will protect your backside from the snipers. The group also will work for quality every time.

Source: Reg Murphy, "Recipe for Change in a New City and a New Job," *The Bulletin of the American Society of Newspaper Editors,* April 1984, 31–32.

THE EDITOR'S APPROACH TO MANAGING CHANGE

An editor's philosophy of change should encompass three elements: (1) trust, (2) organizational learning, and (3) adaptiveness.[4]

1. Trust is essential in all organizations. People would rather follow individuals they can count on, even when they disagree with them, than people they agree with but who shift positions frequently. Reliability, or what is sometimes called constancy, is a major determinant of trust. A boss who writes memos containing exaggerated and inaccurate statements that are written in an abusive and threatening tone and who then seems calm and reasonable in face-to-face meetings is behaving in an inconsistent, unreliable manner that will destroy the trust of subordinates.

    Creating an environment where trust can be nurtured is vital to editors seeking to deal effectively with change. Research shows that trust between employees and managers is the most important factor in having an effective, well-functioning organization.

    Like all people, managers behave according to their assumptions of how the world works. It can be a kind place or a cruel place. Louis D. Barnes, professor of organizational behavior at the Harvard Business School, describes mistrust as "so subtle, so prevalent, and yet so unproductive that it can create a destructive atmosphere."

    Barnes identifies "three harmless assumptions" that can lead to mistrust:

(1) The first assumption is when "either/or" thinking dominates choices and decision making. Typically, managers narrow their alternatives to such options as act or react, expand or retrench, reward or punish. Such thinking not only limits the options, but it also encourages people to become emotionally attached to a choice and to see it either as good or bad. "We set up alternatives as adversaries and turn them into unions versus management, blacks versus whites, government versus business, theory versus practice, and us versus them," Barnes says. "It is easier to take a firm position and act as if us or them, right or wrong, good or bad were the major real-life options."[5]

(2) Barnes's second assumption is that "hard" drives out "soft" and routine work drives out nonroutine work. Managers who feel the need to defend their positions rely on hard facts rather than soft feelings, hard numbers rather than soft words, specific steps rather than abstract possibilities. This results in short-term action rather than long-term planning and tell-it-like-it-is statements rather than speculative explorations.

Barnes concludes that either/or thinking can easily lead a person to a hard-nosed, buccaneer management style. Doubt is turned into action, which stirs the hearts of those who idolize such uncompromising figureheads as General George Patton or John Wayne's macho cowboy characters. As many editors know, in most tough-guy contexts, it can be very difficult to appear soft.

(3) The third assumption is "nice guys finish last"—an attitude that helps contaminate the other two, Barnes thinks, because it holds that the world is a dangerous place where a person must adopt a position of pervasive mistrust to survive. Barnes says that a boss's attitude of noncaring will be reciprocated, not surprisingly, by key subordinates. As a result, the basis for any organizational trust is likely to disappear.

Trust is important for both effective performance and high satisfaction. When explaining behavior in their companies, managers may gloss over the crucial role of trust and fall back on more convenient explanations, such as personality differences and the boss's actions.

Two essential elements must be present for trust to develop between managers and employees: a sense of adequacy and personal security. Adequacy refers to an employee's feeling of being valuable to the organization. Personal security is the degree to which each employee thinks that he or she can be openly honest and candid about personal observations without risk of retaliation on the part of management or others. A high degree of trust between managers and employees can lessen the employees' fear of change.[6]

2. The second factor in a manager's philosophy toward change is how the manager and the organization integrate new ideas into the established system. This concept, known as organizational learning, is a key element in developing a sound philosophy of change.[7]

A manager can view organizational learning in one of two ways:

(1) In the first view, the organization has a set way of doing things and the manager sees no alternative to that course. If things are not being done according to company standards, adjustments are made to get performance in line. There is little flexibility and, as a result, the organization has more difficulty adapting to change.

In such a situation, change typically is forced from the top down. Top executives might decide on a change and, with little assistance or warning, order middle managers to pick up the pieces and make the new system work. This creates an atmosphere of uncertainty and insecurity that immobilizes managers rather than stimulating them to innovate. Unexpected change causes some individuals to focus their energies on simply coping with change and keeping up with new developments, and inhibits others who have to know where things stand before taking action.[8]

(2) In the second view of organizational learning, change is seen as acceptable if there is a difference between the way things are supposed to be and the way they actually are.

Change is made easier if it is approached with the idea of determining which behavior is best for meeting organizational goals.

3. The third element relative to change is a managerial commitment to being prepared for change before the actual need for it. Managers who are adaptive rather than reactive will minimize wasted energy and make the best use of time in a situation where change is required. This philosophy enables a manager to approach the need for change with a broad, overall perspective.

ORGANIZATIONAL CHANGE

Larry E. Greiner, a specialist in organizational development at the University of Southern California, has outlined the pattern of successful change in organizations such as a newspaper or a newsroom. Common approaches to introducing changes in organizations include unilateral action at one extreme and sharing the responsibility for change and delegating that responsibility at the other extreme.[9]

Typically, unilateral action comes by decree. This form of introducing change has its roots in centuries of practice within the military and government bureaucracies. It is essentially a pronouncement made by the leader in a memo, a lecture, a policy statement, or an oral command.

If change by decree fails, then a second approach, change by replacement, is attempted. In this instance, those at the top conclude that the organization's problems are the fault of a few strategically placed individuals and that replacing them will bring about sweeping and basic changes.

A third kind of unilateral change is to alter the structure of the organization to fit individuals—by restructuring jobs, for example.

Sharing the power for introducing change is expressed in two ways. One way is group decision making, where the problem is defined at the top but lower-level groups are free to develop alternative solutions to the problem. The second way of introducing change is group problem solving in which both the definition and the solution of the problem are left to the group. In this approach, most of the responsibility for defining and acting on problems is turned over to subordinates.

Dynamics of Organizational Change

	STIMULUS on the Power Structure		REACTIONS of the Power Structure
Phase 1	Pressure on Top Management		Arousal to Take Action
Phase 2	Intervention at the Top		Reorientation to Internal Problems
Phase 3	Diagnosis of Problem Areas		Recognition of Specific Problems
Phase 4	Invention of New Solutions		Commitment to New Courses of Action
Phase 5	Experimentation with New Solutions		Search for Results
Phase 6	Reinforcement from Positive Results		Acceptance of New Practices

Fig. 12.4.

The pattern of successful change in organizations was plotted in studies by Larry E. Greiner at the University of Southern California. In each of six phases of change identified by Greiner, the stimulus on the power structure leads to reactions by the power structure.

Source: Adapted from Larry E. Greiner, "Patterns of Organizational Change," *Harvard Business Review,* May–June 1967, 121–30.

In Greiner's model, there are six phases to organizational change:

Phase 1: Pressure and arousal. The publisher or the editor senses pressure for change, and the reactions to that pressure are felt throughout the newspaper's power structure. If top management agrees that change is necessary, their support for the actions to be taken is critical. Thus, the pressure for change creates an arousal to take action.

For example, a newspaper's declining circulation may bring the publisher under pressure from advertisers. The publisher may sense that the ground is beginning to shift under the foundations of the newspaper, that the pressure brought by advertisers reflects on his or her own capabilities. The publisher may react to being put on the spot by making a commitment to discover the cause of dropping circulation and to make changes that will reverse the trend.

Phase 2: Intervention and reorientation. While strong pressure may arouse the publisher, it does not provide automatic assurance that top management will successfully identify the problems or take the correct action to solve them. There is a tendency to rationalize about problems, to blame groups or events beyond the control of the newspaper's management. In many cases, an outsider, such as a consultant, is selected to make an objective appraisal of the organization and its problems.

The most common service provided by a consultant for a newspaper is conducting readership research. The results of interviews with readers or advertisers and the consultant's interpretation of these interviews prepare the publisher and the top executives of the newspaper for the third stage of Greiner's model.

Phase 3: Diagnosis and recognition. This phase involves gathering and analyzing information about the problem. A shared approach to change is evident because subordinates are invited to learn the results of the consultant's research and to offer ideas for change. It is evident to all that top management is willing to change, that important problems are being acknowledged and faced up to, that topics once considered taboo can now be discussed openly, and that ideas from lower levels are being valued by top management.

Phase 4: Invention and commitment. Once problems are recognized, it is another matter to develop effective solutions and to get a full commitment to solving the problems. There is a natural tendency to try to solve problems with old methods. Successful changes require intensive searches for creative solutions. The emphasis here should be on collaboration and participation by large numbers of people.

With the results of the readership research in hand, the editor and the newsroom task force in our example can put together ideas for changes in content and coverage designed to win back readers.

Phase 5: Experimentation and search. This phase allows for temporary and controlled testing of both the problem's diagnosis and its treatment. It is a time for reviewing proposed solutions in terms of cost, additional resources, and potential results. An atmosphere of tentativeness exists in which lower-level managers are concerned with whether top management will support their recommendations.

The editor and staff in our example prepare prototypes of new sections for the paper. They review them with the publisher and test them among selected groups of advertisers and readers. Based on this outside input, the sections are modified and revised.

Phase 6: Reinforcement and acceptance. When changes improve performance of the organization, they become permanent and standard procedures. Success through this process leads to acceptance of change by the members of the work group.

Once the new sections and other improvements have been launched, the staff continues to work with them, making adjustments and striving to sustain the quality. If the new sections are successful in drawing new readers to the newspaper, the publisher will continue to invest the resources necessary to support the sections and the staff will accept the changes.

Fig. 12.5

CLOSE-UP

Shortly after purchasing the *Philadelphia Daily News* in 1970, Knight-Ridder Newspapers sent Rolfe Neill in as editor. Some years later, J. Montgomery Curtis, a Knight-Ridder vice-president and former director of the American Press Institute, asked Neill how he went about taking over.

"Enter the city as a guest and behave as one. Be exceedingly curious, travel widely, talk little, listen deeply, compliment that which appeals to you, and temporarily temper disagreeable opinions. Make no public pronounciamentos. Promise nothing but hard work and columns that are hospitable to all points of view.

"Make no sudden changes. When a publication swerves, it unsettles readers who were satisfied with the course traversed yesterday. Gradualism is as important in publishing as in any enterprise I know.

"Beware all panaceas. If a simple solution would have done it, likely the problem would have been solved ere you arrived. Resist as you would a highway robber that overpowering urge to make over all that you have inherited. The paper was coming out before we took over so let it continue in its natural gait. Everything has a rhythm. Never disturb a rhythm until you understand its tempo."

Source: Rolfe Neill, letter to J. Montgomery Curtis, 27 February 1974.

CHANGING INDIVIDUAL BEHAVIOR

Being a *change agent* is one of the many roles of a newspaper editor. The function of a change agent is to make it possible for subordinate editors and staffers to recognize the need for change and to help initiate change.

Organizational changes implemented by the editor—for example, new sections, introduction of performance reviews, fresh leadership on the city desk—usually bring change to the working lives of individual staffers. Some changes may alter routines; others may mean more work, a change of responsibility, and a gain or loss of control.

The editor also must be a change agent in dealing with the newsroom staff. The editor's prime concerns are strengthening individual staffers' skills and knowledge and improving their work behavior. The editor's understanding of motivation (see Chapter 3) and performance reviews (see Chapter 10) are critical elements in working effectively with staffers to develop their talents and overcome their weaknesses.

Changes in a staffer's knowledge are the easiest changes to make. Experience on the job, reading books and articles, and attending training seminars will strengthen a staffer's knowledge.

Changes in individual behavior are more complicated and time-consuming to effect. These changes involve emotions, attitudes, and experiences with other leaders, as well as customs, mores, and traditions that have developed over many years.

Working with an individual staffer to change behavior involves four steps: (1) awareness, (2) understanding, (3) acceptance, and (4) change.

1. *Awareness.* A staffer cannot begin to change until he or she becomes aware of the problem. This is the "Ah-ha" experience when the light bulb goes on and the problem becomes clear.

   For example, the features editor may not be able to delegate work, thinking he or she can get more done by doing the work alone. He or she will not consider assigning tasks until becoming aware that the failure to delegate is a problem. The editor can help the features editor recognize the consequences: he or she works longer hours, routine tasks take time that should be spent planning or working with writers, staffers are not able to get prompt feedback on their work.

2. *Understanding.* Once the features editor is aware of the problem, the next step is learning about delegation. Many managers don't delegate effectively because they don't understand the principles of delegation. In this case, the editor can help the features editor turn the old way of doing things into a new concept of delegating.

3. *Acceptance.* Having become aware of the problem and understanding what must be done, the features editor now must accept responsibility for the change. The features editor

Fig. 12.6.

The process of change can be understood by examining each of four steps: awareness, understanding, acceptance, and change.

Source: Adapted from Bob Marsenich, "How to Teach the Steps of Change," *Training*, March 1983, 62–63.

---

knows that he or she has the power to make the change, and it must become his or her intention to do so.

4. *Change.* As soon as the features editor knows that he or she has the ability to respond to the need to delegate, a move into the final step of the process—change itself—will follow naturally.

Editors who are dealing with the need to change individual behavior have a choice of two styles: participative change and directive change.[10]

Participative change. This change cycle begins when the editor shares with the staffer or another editor information about his or her performance or a different assignment. The staffer or editor is made aware of the need for change in performance through routine feedback and regular performance reviews. Changes in assignment generally come as a result of months or years of monitoring performance.

Collaboration between editor and staffer in monitoring performance is likely to lead to a positive reaction and commitment to proposed changes. An editor is more likely to be successful in bringing about change through participation if he or she has personal power—that is, power based on information, expertise, and personality (see Chapter 7).

Directive change. This change style is imposed on individuals and the organization. In some cases, directive change comes from the publisher or the newspaper corporation, as when an announcement is made regarding a change in medical benefits, the introduction of Management by Objectives, or the selection of a new editor. Directive change is common in fast-moving news situations where an editor orders changes on page one to accommodate a developing story.

A direct or coercive change style occasionally is appropriate with individuals on the news staff. Those who are less ambitious or highly dependent or not willing to take on new responsibilities unless forced to do so might prefer a directive approach. Editors who wish to make changes using a directive approach need significant position power—that is, legitimate power, connections, and the authority to reward and punish (see Chapter 7).

Research shows that most individuals will accept the need to learn new skills, to update their knowledge, or to take on new assignments. But most employees also resent pressures to change behavior that reflects their attitudes about the job or the management. Consequently, as we learned in Chapter 10, it has been found easier to change skills, knowledge, and behavior than to change attitudes.

Research also shows that unless the attitudes supporting behaviors can be influenced, changes in behavior will not take place or will be temporary at best. Individuals will conform to management demands when managers are watching, but they will regress to old habits and patterns of behavior when managers are absent.[11]

Kurt Lewin developed a useful model that shows how lasting changes can be brought to individuals as well as to organizations. Lewin's model has three phases: (1) unfreezing, (2) change, and (3) refreezing.[12]

1. *Unfreezing.* The editor sees a problem in a staffer's behavior. The troublesome behavior is contributing to poor performance and conflict. The editor confronts the staffer, explaining the behavior that has been observed and the problems it is causing. The editor seeks to convince the staffer that a change is necessary and suggests ways of overcoming the problem. The editor may bring pressure on the staffer to make him or her feel uncomfortable and dissatisfied with the present behavior.

2. *Change.* When the staffer's discomfort level rises high enough and when the editor offers incentives to change, the staffer will begin to look for ways to reduce the tension in his or her life. The staffer will start to question present motives and patterns of behavior. This is the appropriate time for the editor to offer support or a role model to help the staffer adopt new patterns of behavior. Once new performance levels begin to emerge, they must be supported and reinforced in order to be lasting.

3. *Refreezing.* The editor recognizes and rewards the staffer's new patterns of behavior. Any changes that create new problems are identified and discouraged by starting the cycle over with the "unfreezing" phase. The original pressures that created discomfort and tension are relieved. The staffer's new attitudes and the behaviors they support become part of his or her work habits and routines.

RESISTANCE TO CHANGE

An important key to guiding the staff through change is the ability to analyze the reasons why people resist change. Author Rosabeth Moss Kanter has distilled a list of the ten most common reasons managers encounter resistance to change:[13]

1. *Loss of control.* How people greet change is influenced by whether they feel in control. To most individuals, change is exciting when it is done *by* them; it is threatening when it is done *to* them. Most people want and need to feel in control of the events around them. Consequently, the idea of "ownership" is a cornerstone of participative management. It means that if people have a chance to participate in decision making, they will feel better about the decisions. Giving people opportunities for involvement can help them become more committed to the change in question. Participation is important because it demonstrates that the employees are assumed to be capable enough to suggest new ideas to the company when there is a problem or a need for change.

2. *Excess uncertainty.* Not knowing enough about what the next step is going to be makes comfort impossible and makes change seem dangerous. Managers who do not share enough information with their employees about what is happening at every step of a change process and about what they anticipate happening next are inviting resistance. Change requires faith that the new way will indeed be the right way. If the leaders themselves do not appear convinced, then others will not budge. Information counts in building commitment, especially by using step-by-step devices such as timetables and milestones.

3. *Surprise, surprise!* People are easily shocked by decisions or requests that are announced unexpectedly. Their first response is resistance. Companies frequently make this mistake when introducing organizational changes. They wait until all decisions have been made and then announce them to an unsuspecting staff. People often react to such announcements by feeling threatened by the change and defending against the new way or undermining it.

4. *Giving up old habits.* Change requires people to become conscious of and to question familiar routines and habits. A great deal of work in organizations is habitual: Our offices or desks are in the same place, we have systems for handling expense forms, there is a pattern of getting stories typeset by deadline. Imagine how upsetting it would be if the furniture in the newsroom were rearranged every day or if we had to contend with new deadlines for each day's paper. We would feel uncomfortable and would need to expend additional physical and emotional energy just to deal with the routine aspects of the job. When a change is being introduced, it is important for managers to limit alterations to other routines or habits. Commitment to change is likely to be stronger if it is presented as a continuation of tradition.

5. *Loss of face.* People are certain to resist change if accepting it means admitting that the way things were done in the past was wrong. Nobody likes to lose face or feel embarrassed in front of their peers. But sometimes making a commitment to a new procedure, product, or program carries with it the implicit assumption that the old ways must have been wrong. This can put all the adherents to the old ways in the uncomfortable position of either looking stupid for their past actions or being forced to defend them—and thereby arguing against any change. Commitment to change is ensured when past actions are put in perspective; that is, the old procedures were apparently the right thing to do then, but now times are different. This way people do not lose face by accepting change; in fact, just the opposite happens. They look strong and flexible. They have been honored for what they accomplished under the old conditions, even if it is now time to change.

6. *Concerns about future competence.* Anxiety about the ability to be effective after the change is another source of resistance. Can I do it? How will I do it? Will I be successful under the new conditions? Do I have the skills to operate in a new way? These concerns may not be expressed out loud, but they can result in finding reasons why change should be avoided. It is essential to make sure that people feel compe-

tent and that there is sufficient training and education available so that they can master what they need to do. Employees need a chance to practice new skills or actions without feeling that they are going to look foolish to colleagues and peers. Positive reinforcement is more important in managing change than it is in managing routine situations.

7. *Ripple effects.* Changes inevitably send ripples beyond their intended impact. Sometimes they disrupt other plans or projects, even affecting personal and family activities that have nothing to do with the job. Anticipation of those disruptions can cause resistance to change. Change masters look for the ripples and introduce the change with flexibility so that personal and company plans can go through a transition period rather than face an abrupt change. That kind of sensitivity helps get people on board and makes them feel committed rather than resistant to the change.

8. *More work.* One reasonable source of resistance stems from the fact that change can simply mean more work. The effort it takes to manage things under routine circumstances is multiplied when things are changing. Changes require more energy, more time, and greater concentration. Members of project teams creating innovation put in a great deal of overtime on their own because of the demands and the lure of creating something new. If people do not want to put in the effort, that is reason to resist change. They need support and compensation for the extra effort to move from resistance to commitment.

9. *Past resentments.* The cobwebs of the past can get in the way of the future. Anyone who has ever had a gripe against the organization is likely to resist the organization's telling them that they now have to do something new. An uneasy truce based on avoiding confrontations can come undone when you ask for change. Unresolved grievances from the past rise up to entangle and hamper the change effort. Sweeping away the cobwebs of the past is sometimes necessary for overcoming resistance to change. As long as people remain aggrieved, they will not go along with what the company wants.

10. *Facing a real threat.* This may be the most reasonable of all the points of resistance: Sometimes the threat posed by the change is a real one. Sometimes change does create winners and losers. Sometimes people lose status, clout, security, or comfort. Managing change means recognizing these political realities. It is important to avoid pretense and false promises. Those who are going to lose something should hear about it early rather than having time to worry and to infect others with their anxiety or antagonism. If some are going to be let go or moved, it is more humane to make those changes quickly. There is a relief in knowing one's destiny, even in learning that what they have feared is true. There is also the anxiety of recognizing that change may mean success for others.

Resistance to change, says Kanter, is not irrational. It stems from valid and understandable concerns. Managers who can analyze the sources of resistance are in the best position to invent solutions to it—and to manage change smoothly and effectively.

Fig. 12.7

CLOSE-UP

Robert Haiman, president and managing director of the Poynter Institute, recalls a time in the early 1980s when, as executive editor of the *St. Petersburg Times,* he was concerned about inroads into newspaper readership being made by television.

"They were going to layer cable on top of network television and then layer specialty service on top of that. Editors worried whether we were going to be devoured by the electronic monster. I started looking hard at television. It occurred to me that newspaper editors sort of put down television. Maybe I ought to look at television more critically. Maybe they do some things better than we do. I finally persuaded myself that one of the things that television might know more about than newspapers was the weather. I concluded that the *St. Petersburg Times* grossly underreported the weather and that we should do something about it.

"At that time, there were many other unmet needs at the paper. I was fairly sure that if I suddenly announced that we were going to add a full-time weather reporter, there would be a substantial outcry from people who thought we had greater needs.

"My plan was to get the managing editor and the city editor, over a period of some months, to come up with the idea themselves. I started talking about the weather. I started emphasizing. I started praising good jobs that we would do on weather coverage. I didn't miss an opportunity to talk about how important weather is. Over a period of two or three months, a half-dozen people among the editor ranks were sensitized to the issue.

"At one point, Andy Barnes, the managing editor, and Mike Foley, the city editor, came to me with the dilemma of a very good editor on the news desk who wanted to become a reporter. Their suggestion was to make him a weather reporter. And I said, 'I hadn't thought of that, but it's a great idea.'

"Some people might say this was a protracted way to accomplish that. I thought it would have a much better chance of success if the idea came out of the newsroom rather than out of my office."

Source: Robert Haiman, interview with author, 19 January 1984.

MAKING CHANGE WORK IN THE NEWSROOM

In spite of the legitimate reasons for resisting change, there are many reasons why people are willing to accept change and may even be eager for it:

- The change may be their choice. The reporter who has been pressing for the opportunity to become an assistant city editor will be grateful for the challenge and will eagerly accept the change.
- The change may satisfy a need. Journalists who want to control their own work and be in charge of their own destiny often approach change as an opportunity to reach their personal goals.
- The change may be for the better. It may resolve a long-standing conflict or correct an irritating situation.

Participation is a commonly used strategy to bring about effective change, but it is not without potential problems.

One question for the editor to consider in planning change is at what stage to bring the staff into the process. When major change emanates from the publisher or the editor, the overall objective often is not debatable and certain elements of the change also may not be debatable. For example, if the publisher decides to shift publication of the newspaper from an evening to a morning cycle after examining the facts and consulting with key department heads, that change is not debatable. When the staff is told of the decision and invited to participate in planning the change, there is little room to debate the basic decision. The editor has no authority to compromise.

In this example, the appropriate time to involve the staff is after the research and other factors have been considered and after the decision has been made to switch to a morning publication. Bringing staffers in earlier in the process would not be appropriate because they do not have the information or the broad experience from the advertising, circulation, and marketing sides to make helpful suggestions. And without a plan to discuss, their tendency to resist would be greater. The proper time for the staff to become involved is when the editor begins planning how to implement the change. This is when the editor gives the staff a full report on the decision behind the change and presents the task ahead as an opportunity and a challenge.

Fig. 12.8

CLOSE-UP

The most potentially traumatic changes facing newspaper journalists in the 1980s are mergers and changing publishing cycles. When the staffs of a morning and evening paper are merged into one or when an evening paper becomes a morning paper, the human element is one of the key factors in the success of the change.

Newspaper managers frequently direct their energies to working out the details of the change, neglecting the anxieties and concerns of the staff. New roles and assignments, deadlines and copy flow, reorganization of news desks, press starts, and promotion tend to get more attention than the staff's legitimate desire for information and sensitive attention to what the changes mean.

Failure to address individual needs will result in a lessening of trust in the newspaper's management.

Data gathered from mergers in industrial corporations suggests that the primary long-term employee reactions are the following:

Depression. The feeling that the company no longer is prosperous.

Uncertainty. A reaction that leads to less risk taking.

Disillusionment. A loss of belief in the company's image of caring for its employees.

Editors and publishers who want to cushion the impact of major change should be prepared to address the following questions that naturally arise:

What are the reasons for the change? Why is it necessary?

What does the newspaper company expect to gain from the change?

How shall the news staff operate while the change is taking place?

What changes are planned in the structure and life-style of the newsroom?

Will any present jobs or responsibilities be eliminated or changed? Who will keep their present titles and who won't?

How will the change affect individual staffer's chances for promotion?

Source: Arlyne J. Imberman, "Human Element of Mergers," *Management Review,* June 1985, 35–37.

One strategy for helping staffers live with change is called transition training.[14] The core of this idea is to help people release their grasp on where they have been and grab hold of where they want to go or where they must go. Transition training is different from skills training or technical training in that it deals more directly with the human components of change: values, attitudes, beliefs, perceptions, emotions, language, and behavior.

There are two kinds of transition training:

Cultural transition training is needed when the organization is changing. It would be appropriate where the staff of an afternoon newspaper was preparing to change to a morning publishing cycle. A program would be designed with the goal of helping the staff focus on the different culture that exists in the newsroom of a morning paper—perceptions, news values, schedules, routines. The idea would be to make the staff sensitive to a new life-style, one that represents a change in both their personal and professional lives, and to enhance the likelihood of a successful change.

Personal transition training is needed when people are changing roles within the organization. Here the emphasis is on assisting staffers to adapt to new roles on the newspaper. Orientation programs for new editors would acquaint them with their responsibilities as supervisors as well as help them examine the value of finding and working with a mentor, building a network for peer support, and understanding the dynamics of the larger newspaper organization.

The change from staffer to editor is a profound one for most journalists. Those making this change need help in paying attention to the transition period itself: building new attitudes and perceptions, examining values and emotions, letting go of old relationships and friendships and building new ones, and dealing with a situation in which one may be, temporarily, ineffective.

USING COMMUNICATION TO HELP IMPLEMENT CHANGE

Although the staff often is brought in on a planned change only after the basic decisions have been made, the fact remains that very few things are secret in any organization. It is likely that news of a pending change will not long remain confidential but will run rampant through the networks of informal groups at the newspaper (see Chapter 4).

Withholding information tends to increase anxiety and resistance. This is a difficult problem for executives. Secret, confidential planning may be necessary, but it has negative consequences. Rumors may start before planning has reached a point where the employees should and can participate. Providing partial information can increase tensions. Unfortunately, there is no clear-cut rule on when communication with employees should begin in the change process.[15]

Because of their influence in the newsroom, peer-group leaders (see Chapter 2) can play an important role in implementing change. If the editor can gain their cooperation and commitment, informal group leaders may help reduce substantially the resistance to change in the newsroom.

The best method of winning the support of informal leaders is to involve them in the planning of the change. Once involved, their commitment will be greater. The informal leader also can anticipate problems that may be encountered and may suggest ways of revising plans or building in trade-offs. This approach is not without its traps. If there is low trust between editor and the leader of an informal newsroom peer group, the group leader may feel the editor is trying to manipulate him or her, which could lead to increased resistance. To avoid this, the editor should view the informal leader as a resource, a person who has ideas that can be obtained only through participation in the change. If the editor is able to gain the commitment of the informal leader, then—and only then—can the editor utilize the group leader's influence.

CHAPTER SUMMARY

Managing change is a central part of every editor's job. Initiating and implementing change calls on the editor's understanding of many of the elements of behavioral science, including motivation, group dynamics, leadership, human behavior, and communication.

The editor has to deal with changes originating from outside the organization—competition, the economy, social changes, technology—and from the inside—staff changes and different practices or policies. The ambiguous, nonroutine, and autonomous nature of the editor's job provides a strong environment for initiative.

Change in an organization usually takes place in three steps:

(1) identifying the need for change, (2) building coalitions, and (3) mobilizing resources and individuals to put an idea into effect. In analyzing a problem, the editor may consider the forces driving for change and the forces restraining change, a technique known as force field analysis.

The editor's philosophy of change should encompass three elements: (1) trust, which is based on a sense of adequacy and personal security; (2) organizational learning, how new ideas are integrated into an established system; and (3) adaptiveness, the ability to make the best use of time and energy in a situation where change is required.

Organizational development specialist Larry E. Greiner developed a model for organizational change that has six phases: (1) pressure and arousal, (2) intervention and reorientation, (3) diagnosis and recognition, (4) invention and commitment, (5) experimentation and search, and (6) reinforcement and acceptance.

Individual changes should focus on work behavior. The editor's understanding of motivation and performance reviews are crucial in dealing with changes in individual behavior. The most effective individual changes are those in which the staffer participates. Working with an individual staffer to change behavior involves four steps: (1) awareness, (2) understanding, (3) acceptance, and (4) change.

Editors have a choice of two styles for implementing change: (1) participative change or (2) directive change.

There are many reasons for individual resistance to change. These may include loss of control, excess uncertainty, surprise, giving up old habits, loss of face, concerns about future competence, ripple effects, creation of more work, past resentments, or fear of loss of status, clout, or security.

An important part of the editor's job is to overcome resistance to change. Some strategies for achieving this include staff participation, keeping the staff informed, and creating a climate in which change is expected. Communicating with peer-group leaders may help reduce the resistance to change.

NOTES

1. Paul Hersey and Kenneth Blanchard, *Management of Organizational Behavior*, 4th ed. (Englewood Cliffs, N.J.: Prentice-Hall, 1982), 267.
2. Kurt Lewin, "Frontiers in Group Dynamics: Concept, Method, and Reality in Social Science; Social Equilibria and Social Change," *Human Relations* 1 (June 1947): 5–41.
3. Rosabeth Moss Kanter, *The Change Masters* (New York: Simon and Schuster, 1983), 221–31.
4. Warren R. Plunkett and Raymond F. Attner, *Introduction to Management* (Boston: Kent, 1983), 413–14.
5. Louis D. Barnes, "Managing the Paradox of Organizational Trust," *Harvard Business Review*, March–April 1981, 107–18.
6. Plunkett and Attner, *Introduction to Management*, 413.
7. Ibid., 413–14.
8. Kanter, *Change Masters*, 84–85.
9. Larry E. Greiner, "Patterns of Organizational Change," *Harvard Business Review*, May–June 1967, 126–29.
10. Hersey and Blanchard, *Management of Organizational Behavior*, 273–74.
11. Plunkett and Attner, *Introduction to Management*, 418.
12. Lewin, "Frontiers in Group Dynamics," 5–41.
13. Rosabeth Moss Kanter, "Managing the Human Side of Change," *Management Review*, April 1985, 52–56.
14. Richard A. Richards, "Learning to Live with the Owl," *Training*, September 1983, 50–53.
15. Jerry L. Gray, *Supervision* (Boston: Kent, 1984), 500–501.

13

Managing Conflict in the Newsroom

Conflict in the newsroom is inevitable. It is natural for editors and their subordinates to disagree on issues, goals, and perceptions. Conflict can arise between the individual and the newspaper, between or among individuals, between groups and individuals, or between groups and the newspaper company. Yet conflict in itself is neither good nor bad; it is the consequences that can be damaging if conflict is poorly managed or is allowed to continue. If editors learn to manage conflict, the attainment of individual and organizational goals is more likely. The starting points in this process are understanding why conflict occurs and developing effective strategies for managing it.

THE NATURE OF CONFLICT

Just how important the topic of conflict is to newspaper editors can be seen in the results of an American Management Association survey of managers in a variety of fields. The survey found that the amount of time spent dealing with some form of conflict ranged from about 18 percent for top managers to about 26 percent for middle managers. These managers said that the presence of conflict was an important part of their organizational lives. They ranked dealing with conflict equal to or slightly higher in importance to such other basic management responsibilities as planning, communication, motivation, and decision making.[1]

For newspaper editors, the percentage of time spent dealing with conflict may be considerably higher. Conflict is inherent in any discussion of the news. There are elements of conflict in the daily news meeting, page-one conference, editorial board meeting, and in the dialogue between reporter and supervising editor over the content or structure of a story.

Moreover, skill in handling conflict is one of the qualities that is a predictor of an individual's success as an editor, even though it is not always identified as a specific management skill. The editor who can build a team that values hard work and cooperation and that finds the work satisfying probably is effective as a manager of conflict.

In certain instances, conflict can be more productive than harmony. It can bring forth ideas, fresh interpretations, and imaginative alternatives. It can stimulate innovation and change. It also can contribute to the motivation of individuals who need to excel and who will push themselves in pursuit of a goal. If conflict between individuals leads to an airing of differences and an easing of tensions, a more stable relationship may result.

An editor's philosophy about conflict will influence how he or she deals with conflict situations.[2] One approach is known as the traditional view of conflict. The editor who takes this view sees conflict as unnecessary and harmful to the newsroom. This editor fears conflict and tries to avoid it or eliminate all evidence of it. When conflict occurs, the editor thinks he or she has failed because the conflict was not prevented.

A second attitude is a behavioral view of conflict. The editor recognizes that conflict is common because of the nature of people and organizational life and because of the competition for resources. This editor expects conflict, but anticipates that the conflict will be harmful, although he or she recognizes that occasionally conflict turns out to be positive.

A current philosophy, the interactionist view of conflict, considers conflict to be inevitable and even necessary in organizations. An interactionist editor sees the challenge as managing conflict so that the outcome is positive.

THE SOURCES AND PROCESS OF CONFLICT

Seven specific sources of conflict typically are present in the newsroom:[3]

1. *Shared resources.* A limited resource that must be shared by the staff may be a source of conflict. For example, if newshole is tight, there may be disagreement over the allocation of space. Or, conflict can arise if there is a shortage of VDTs and reporters must wait their turn to write stories.

2. *Goals.* Individuals may have goals that are different from those of the newspaper. This could occur when the editor's goal of strengthening the paper by adding staff and newshole comes in conflict with the company's profit goals.

3. *Perceptions and values.* Individual value systems and perceptions may differ, leading to conflict. A reporter who prizes time with the family may be in conflict with the city editor who pushes the reporter to work long hours and weekends. Because the reporter's value system is different from that of the editor, the editor may think the reporter lacks commitment and is lazy.

4. *Role requirements.* Role conflict can occur at every level of the organization. The sports editor may think the baseball writer's role is to be at the ballpark every possible minute and to hang around the locker room and the after-hours spots with the players. The writer may take a more detached view of the assignment, thinking that keeping an arm's length from the team will permit more balanced coverage. Or, the publisher may see the editor as a hands-on boss who is in the middle of the action, whereas the editor may think he or she is more effective delegating the work while concentrating on problem solving and planning. In each instance, there is a basis for conflict.

5. *Nature of the work.* Inequity in workloads or in rewards can be a source of conflict. If one assistant city editor pushes hard ten hours a day and another is able to get away for lunch and head for home after eight hours, the comparative workloads

may be out of balance. The inequity may be further magnified if their pay is equal. The potential for conflict exists.

6. *Individual styles.* People have different styles and approaches to dealing with work and with other people. An editor who is aggressive and combative will tend to have a conflict with an associate who is reflective and cautious.

7. *Ambiguity.* Uncertainty over responsibility is a certain cause of conflict. If the slot editor and the city editor both think they have authority to put stories in the paper or hold them out, conflict is bound to occur when the editors disagree over whether a story is ready to be published.

The process of conflict generally occurs in four stages: (1) frustration, (2) conceptualization, (3) behavior, and (4) outcome.[4]

1. In the first stage of conflict, individuals or groups are frustrated because their goals are blocked. The frustration can be traced to anything a group or individual cares about. Typically, factors contributing to frustration, and thus conflict, may include performance goals, promotions, pay raises, power, scarce economic resources, rules, and values.

2. In the second stage, the parties to the conflict attempt to understand the nature of the problem. They begin to conceptualize what they want and what their opponents want, and what strategy each side will employ in resolving the conflict. This phase involves problem solving and developing strategies.

3. The third stage in the model is actual behavior. Having come to grips with the problem and decided on a strategy, the parties then attempt to move toward a resolution.

4. The final stage is the degree of satisfaction each side achieves with the outcome of the conflict. If one party is not satisfied or is only partially satisfied, the seeds of future discontent are sown. A later episode of conflict is likely.

This model suggests why effective action by managers aimed at achieving both quick and satisfactory solutions to conflict is vital. Failure to eliminate sources of conflict invites new conflicts.

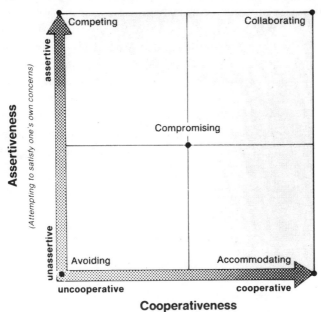

Fig. 13.1.

This model suggests two dimensions to the resolution of conflict: assertiveness and cooperativeness. If one's own concerns are paramount, the likely choice will be a degree of assertiveness. If satisfaction of the other party's concerns is paramount, the choice will involve cooperativeness. Compromising and collaborating are seen as midpoints between the two.

Source: Adapted from Kenneth W. Thomas, "Conflict and Conflict Management," in *Handbook of Industrial and Organizational Behavior*, ed. Marvin D. Dunnette (New York: John Wiley & Sons, 1976).

It is interesting to note what studies concerning conflict suggest about the decisions people make about their opponents. Among five possible styles of dealing with conflict—competition, collaboration, compromise, avoidance, and accommodation (see fig. 13.2)—executives thought of themselves as using collaboration or compromise most often to resolve conflict. Typically, they described their opponents as using a competitive style almost exclusively. In other words, executives underestimated their opponents' concern for satisfying both sides. They viewed them as uncompromising while giving a flattering self-portrait of their own willingness to satisfy both sides in a dispute. In portraying themselves as "reasonable," the executives used these phrases to describe their behavior: pointed out, asked for, advised, suggested, explained, recommended, informed, described, and so on. Their opponent's behavior was described with phrases that suggested arbritrariness and unreasonableness: demanded, refused, ordered, disagreed, said it couldn't be done.[5]

Fig. 13.2

CLOSE-UP

A major task in developing a strategy for resolving conflict is deciding what kind of action to take. In one model developed by psychologist Kenneth W. Thomas, five different approaches are possible:

Approach	*Situation*
1. *Competing:* forcing behavior; win/lose.	a. When quick, decisive action is vital.
	b. On important issues where unpopular actions, such as cost cutting or discipline, need implementing.
	c. On issues vital to company welfare when a person knows he or she is right.
	d. Against people who take advantage of noncompetitive behavior.

Approach	Situation
2. *Collaborating:* confronting disagreements, problem solving to find solutions.	a. To find a solution when both sets of concerns are too important to be compromised. b. When the objective is to learn. c. To merge insights from people with different perspectives. d. To gain commitment by incorporating concerns into consensus. e. To work through feelings that have interfered with a relationship.
3. *Compromising:* horse trading, proposing middle-ground positions.	a. When goals are important, but not worth the effort or potential disruption of more assertive behavior. b. When opponents with equal power are committed to mutually exclusive goals. c. To achieve temporary settlements of complex issues. d. To arrive at expedient solutions under time pressure. e. As a backup when collaboration or competition is unsuccessful.
4. *Avoiding:* withdrawal, buck-passing, failure to take a position.	a. When an issue is trivial or when more important issues are pressing. b. When one perceives no chance of satisfying his or her concerns. c. When potential disruption outweighs the benefits of resolution. d. To let people cool down and regain perspective. e. When gathering information supersedes immediate action. f. When others can resolve the conflict more effectively.

Fig. 13.2, continued

Approach	Situation
	g. When issues seem symptomatic of other conflicts.
5. *Accommodating:* attempting to soothe the other and seek harmony.	a. When a person finds that he or she is wrong, thus allowing a better point of view to be heard or to learn or to show reasonableness.
	b. When issues are more important to others. This results in satisfying others and maintaining cooperation.
	c. To build support for later issues.
	d. To minimize loss when one is overmatched and losing.
	e. When harmony and stability are especially important.
	f. To allow subordinates to develop by learning from their mistakes.

Source: Kenneth W. Thomas, "Toward Multidimensional Values in Teaching: The Example of Conflict Behaviors," *Academy of Management Review* 2 (1977): 487.

CONFLICT AND INDIVIDUALS

Conflict can produce a variety of emotions, such as anxiety, fear, and anger. When there seems to be no satisfactory way to reduce those feelings, we rely on our *defense mechanisms.*

The concept of self-image is at the heart of our defense mechanisms.[6] When conflict threatens self-image, there are at least two ways to dissipate the threat. First, we can change the self-image so that it moves into harmony with whatever is causing the difficulty. For example, if the city editor challenges a reporter on a fact in a story and the reporter recognizes that, indeed, an error was made, the reporter can resolve the threat to his or her self-image by acknowledging the error. The second way of dealing with a threat to self-image is to be defensive. This occurs when the reporter denies that an error was made or

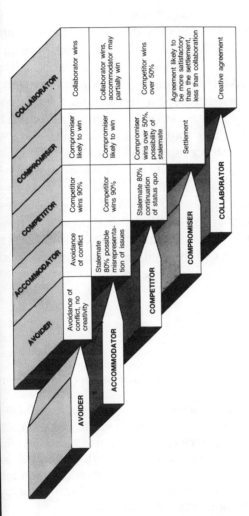

Fig. 13.3.

This model, developed from studies by Kenneth W. Thomas, illustrates the likely outcomes from each of five approaches to resolving conflict. By understanding how other parties will attempt to resolve conflict, the individual can select the mode that seems appropriate in each situation.

Source: Adapted from J. Patrick McMahon, "The Maturity Factor: Adding Insight to Your Conflict Training," *Training*, November 1983, 57, 59-60.

attempts to reject or distort the editor's criticism. Such distortion may be conscious or unconscious. In this way, the reporter maintains the integrity of self-image.

Defense mechanisms may reduce the awareness of the threat, but they seldom affect the cause of the threat.[7] In a situation where the sports editor feels threatened because the managing editor is critical of his work, the sports editor defends himself by placing the blame on the boss. In his mind, he assembles a list of instances where he thinks the managing editor overreacted or was unfair or held him responsible for things that were beyond the sports editor's control. These rationalizations will reduce the intensity of the threat that the sports editor feels, but they will not stop the managing editor from thinking the way he or she does about the sports editor. Soon the sports editor will have to justify his defensive reactions to himself. He may do this by saying the boss is "out to get him." Each of these defenses—denial, rejection, and distortion—will require further justification and further defense. In time, the sports editor will have built up deep layers of defense that will have to be uncovered if he is to understand the cause of his performance problems.

Fig. 13.4

CLOSE-UP

Defense strategies can be grouped into three categories: aggressive, compromise, and withdrawal:

Aggressive defense mechanisms include those reactions by which we directly or indirectly attack the source of the threat to our self-image. Typical aggressive behavior includes fixation, displacement (attacking a person or object other than the source of the threat), and negativism.

Compromise allows us to make satisfactory adjustments when faced with an undesirable situation. Compromise reactions include compensation, identification, projection, and rationalization.

Withdrawal offers a variety of ways in which we can remove ourselves—physically or psychologically—to reduce a threat to our self-image. Examples include fantasy, regression, repression, apathy, and flight.

These defense mechanisms are normal. They should not be seen as either good or bad. We use them to protect ourselves from threat and to maintain our self-image. It is important to recognize that these defense mechanisms exist and that they are powerful influences on our perceptions, attitudes, and behavior.

Following are examples of common defense mechanisms as they might be seen in the newsroom:

Aggressive Strategies

Fixation. An editor is upset because his or her opinion was not sought in changing headline style. To protest, the editor continues to use the former headline style.

Displacement. After being rebuffed by the managing editor, the city editor displaces his frustration by sharply rejecting a simple request from an assistant city editor.

Negativism. The features editor, unhappy at having to serve on a special projects team, picks apart every suggestion that is made in the meetings.

Compromise Strategies

Compensation. A reporter who never advanced very far in the newsroom hierarchy becomes the zealous, hard-working president of the newsroom union.

Identification. An assistant to the editor takes on the vocabulary and mannerisms of the boss.

Projection. An unsuccessful assistant city editor subconsciously would like to block the rise of others and projects this trait to others by thinking that they are out to "get him."

Rationalization. A staffer pads mileage statements or meal receipts because "everybody does it."

Reaction formation. A staffer who has not been promoted reacts by exhibiting traits that are the opposite of his true feelings. He may overdo the defense of the boss and may vigorously uphold company policies.

Withdrawal Strategies

Conversion. A disabling headache keeps the features editor off the job after a pet project has been rejected.

Fantasy. A daydream in which an assistant city editor corrects the city editor's mistake and is acknowledged by the managing editor to be the real leader on the city desk.

Fig. 13.4, continued

Regression. The editor has been blocked in the quest of a goal and becomes absorbed in clerical or technical duties more appropriate for subordinates.

Repression. An assistant city editor forgets to tell the city editor the circumstances of a missed assignment.

Resignation, apathy, and boredom. A staffer who receives no praise or encouragement no longer cares about doing a good job.

Flight or withdrawal. A staffer who is constantly rejected or criticized by the editor is pushed toward being a loner and ignores any friendly gestures that are made.

Sources: Stanley K. Fitch, *Insights into Human Behavior* (Boston: Holbrook Press, 1970), 261–72; Timothy W. Costello and Sheldon S. Zalkind, "Psychology in Administration: A Research Orientation," *Journal of Conflict Resolution* 3 (1959): 148–49.

WORKING WITH DIFFICULT PEOPLE

Every editor has encountered hostile readers, unfriendly co-workers, indecisive bosses, and subordinates who are excessively agreeable but do nothing. They are a troublesome minority, but a challenge, nevertheless.

Abrasive employees also require special attention from the editor. These individuals tend to be impatient, domineering, and frustrated. They usually are intelligent and bring valuable skills to the organization, yet they dominate conversations and point out mistakes made by others. They can cut through to the heart of a problem, but their manner turns others off.

Researchers suggest that in spite of their apparent confidence, abrasive people usually suffer from low self-worth. They have strong needs for affection and approval.

Psychologist and consultant Harry Levinson suggests the following approaches to handling an abrasive subordinate:[8]

- Recognize a hunger for attention. Underneath their harsh outercoat, abrasive people want to be liked and cared for—especially by the boss. They want to be applauded for good work.

- Initiate contact. When an abrasive subordinate is putting forth a strong effort, the editor should express his or her appreciation or respect for the work and the individual's qualities.

- Avoid arguing. Because they frequently challenge or debate positions, abrasive subordinates can easily push the editor into an argument. When this happens, the editor should explain that he or she is not interested in arguing about the issue, but that a calm discussion would be welcome.

- Be firm. The editor should not try to convince an abrasive subordinate that he or she is wrong and the editor is right. Even if there is proof that the subordinate is wrong, he or she wouldn't accept it. The editor should emphasize what is thought to be best for the news department's goals.

- Control anger. It is natural that an abrasive subordinate will irritate the editor. When that happens, the editor should not fire back. Rather, the editor should explain that he or she is trying to see the other side of the issue but that the subordinate's manner is annoying. The editor should be honest in explaining the consequences of continued arguing or other unacceptable behavior.

- Be patient. Abrasive subordinates did not develop their personality traits overnight. They will not change overnight. They may be as frustrated with their behavior as the editor is. The editor should look for small improvements in the subordinate's behavior and reinforce those changes. The editor should be specific in describing behaviors that are abrasive. Patience should not be endless, however. If no improvement is shown after a reasonable period, the editor may have to consider discipline for insubordination.

Fig. 13.5

CLOSE-UP

Robert Bramson, a management consultant, has studied difficult behavior among managers and workers. He has concluded that any

Fig. 13.5, continued

work force is divided roughly into three parts: 10 percent are troublemakers, 70 percent are unable to cope with troublemakers, and 20 percent are not bothered by troublemakers. He has identified patterns of behavior that seem to be most disruptive or frustrating:

Hostile-aggressives

Behavior: These are people who try to bully and overwhelm by bombarding others, by making cutting remarks, or by throwing tantrums when things don't go the way they want.

Response: The basic strategy in coping with them is not to rise to the bait. Stand up to the bullies but avoid a fight. Get them to sit down, try to be friendly, and state your view forcefully. Smoke out the snipers and then focus on problem solving. Let the tantrum run its course, meet in private, and show that you take them seriously.

Complainers

Behavior: These are individuals who gripe incessantly but who never try to do anything about the problem because they feel powerless or because they refuse to bear responsibility.

Response: Listen carefully. Don't agree with or apologize for their charges. State facts without comment. Move to problem solving.

Silent and unresponsive

Behavior: Their style is to respond to every question or plea for help with a "yep," a "no," or a grunt.

Response: Ask open-ended questions. Do not talk during lulls in the conversation. Stay on the subject. Set another meeting if the person won't open up.

Superagreeables

Behavior: They often are personable, funny, and outgoing. In the presence of an editor, they are reasonable, sincere, and supportive. But they don't produce what they say they will. Or they act contrary to the way they have led the editor to expect.

Response: Work hard to bring out the reasons for their failure to perform. Listen for messages in humor. Let them know you value them. Be ready to negotiate and compromise.

Negativists

Behavior: When a project is proposed, they are bound to object. Typically, they say, "It won't work" or "It's impossible." All too often they effectively deflate any optimism for the project.

Response: Make optimistic but realistic statements about past successes with similar problems. Don't try to argue them out of their pessimism. Discuss problems thoroughly. Be ready to take action on your own.

Know-it-all experts

Behavior: These are the superior people who believe, and want others to recognize, that they know everything about anything worth knowing. They are condescending, imposing, or pompous, and they will likely make others feel like idiots.

Response: State facts or alternatives as descriptively as possible. Offer "experts" a way to save face. Deal with "experts" alone when possible.

Indecisives

Behavior: Those who stall major decisions until the decision is made for them. They can't let go of anything until it is perfect, which means never.

Response: Make it easy for them to tell you what is delaying the decision. Listen for clues to the problem. If issues surface, help resolve them. Stress plusses of the plan. Give support after decision seems to have been made.

Source: Adapted from Robert M. Bramson, *Coping with Difficult People* (Garden City, N.Y.: Anchor Press, 1981), 25, 41, 68, 84, 97, 111, 128, 157.

GIVING CRITICISM

Few people are comfortable giving or receiving criticism. When we are criticized, our self-esteem is threatened. Editors may be reluctant to criticize others for fear of hurting their feelings, losing their affection, or having to deal with their anger and pain.

Criticism is usually thought to be entirely negative, focusing only on faults. However, if criticism is viewed as a form of communication, it can be used as a way of leveling with staffers and subordinates. It is frank talk that should contain valuable information, guidance, and direction for overcoming problems. Editors are expected to deal honestly and openly with subordinates and staffers. Being direct and frank should be part of the editor's managerial attitude.

The key points to keep in mind when giving criticism are similar to those recommended for editors during a performance-appraisal interview (see Chapter 10): criticize in private; be specific; avoid reference to attitudes; criticize the work, not the person; define the problem; avoid absolutes; don't exaggerate; be aware of personal biases; share responsibility for the problem; avoid comparisons with other staffers; ask questions to get information; be succinct; soften the tone but not the message; don't make assumptions; don't criticize when you are angry; avoid feeling defensive; draw on the staffer's strengths; and listen, listen, listen.

While following these suggestions won't make criticism easier to give or to receive, this approach will focus on solving a problem, it will create an atmosphere in which a frank exchange of information and feelings is possible, and ultimately, it can enhance the respect both parties have for each other.

Employees who want to be candid with management encounter several barriers to that communication. Many individuals think they cannot speak honestly about the company or about a situation in the newsroom without risk. There is the perception that disagreeing with the boss may block a promotion or an opportunity. Management often is perceived as not being interested in the problems or the views of individual employees.

It is true that some managers stifle criticism and frank expression of opinions because they think it makes them look bad in the eyes of their superiors. Or, the boss may be moody and unpredictable, so individuals are reluctant to stick out their necks and speak up. In some organizations, the culture suggests that employees should defer to the boss and do what they are told without comment. The boss may be seen as a poor listener with a closed mind. Speaking up may be considered a waste of time and energy with the risk of creating antagonism.[9]

Editors can encourage subordinates and staffers to be frank with them by rewarding those who are honest and who suggest ideas, by strengthening the channels of communication within the management hierarchy, by being available so that when employees have a problem they know they will be heard, by reading nonverbal behavior and initiating contact when it appears that an employee has a concern to discuss, and by being sensitive to employees.

From time to time, the staff or an individual on the staff may be upset by a decision made by the editor. Occasionally the editor will encounter a staffer who is hostile, who is boiling with anger, who rushes up with fists clenched and fire in the eyes. Following are some things to remember when that happens: Back off. Give the staffer room to walk around and vent the anger. Keep your hands off an angry person. Encourage him or her to unwind. Offer a cup of coffee or a soft drink. Show concern and interest. Give some nonverbal feedback that may comfort the person and reduce stress. If the staffer continually interrupts, the editor can either be attentively silent, or pause and try again using different wording. Take notes as the staffer talks about the problem. Hold all distractions—no phone calls, no interruptions. As the staffer's anger is spent, move the discussion to dealing with the problem. If the staffer continues to be hostile and angry, the editor should break off the meeting, stating a need for time to think things over. If, after several attempts at discussing the problem, the editor finds that the staffer remains hostile and angry, it may be useful to invite a third party to intervene and help defuse the emotions.

STRATEGIES FOR RESOLVING CONFLICT

As we come to understand that conflict is not unusual and that some conflict can be good both for the organization and the individual, there are formal strategies to consider for managing conflict.

Approaches to resolving conflict that have not proven to be effective include nonaction—do nothing, ignore the problem, and maybe it will go away; or, the editor may acknowledge the problem and say that it is "under study" or that "more information is needed." Another ineffective strategy is to set up a complicated process for resolving conflict. Here, due process is intended to be long and complicated, a tactic to wear down a dissatisfied employee. Editors also attempt to reduce conflict through secrecy, the logic being that controversial issues decided in secret can be carried out with a minimum of resistance. This a "what-they-don't-know-won't-hurt-them" strategy.

Each of the above strategies is ineffective at solving conflict. The long-term effect of each is to initiate or increase distrust of management.

To some extent, the best way to respond to conflict is to use the situational approach, where the editor adapts a specific style depending on the situation or the individuals involved. A useful framework in which to consider this approach is based on the situational-leadership ideas of Paul Hersey and Kenneth Blanchard (see Chapter 7). Their thesis is that the effective manager will assess the work maturity level of an employee or a group of employees to determine the most appropriate action in various situations.

Applying this theory to conflict, an employee's *conflict maturity* would be determined by how he or she perceives and reacts to a number of factors concerning self, other parties in the conflict, the work environment, and the nature of the conflict.[10] The maturity factors that influence the choice of a particular conflict-handling style include the employee's emotional levels, skill levels, clarity of goals, interpersonal relationships, attitudes toward power and authority, concern for formalities, norms or traditions, self-image, and fear of punishment or coercion.

By giving attention to the maturity of the parties in a conflict on each of these points, it is possible to determine the likely outcome when one conflict-handling style is matched against another.

Following are four general strategies for reducing conflict:[11]

1. *Problem solving.* This may be the most straightforward approach to conflict. Editors attempt to identify the nature of the problem, consider alternatives, and select the most appropriate option. Problem solving works when the problem

can be looked at objectively and when there is a willingness to cooperate in working out a solution. For example, if the editor and the staff are planning zoned coverage of neighborhoods, everyone is likely to be seeking the same end. The problem of how to accomplish the plan can be looked at carefully and objectively. The solution usually will satisfy most of the participants.

2. *Persuasion.* With this technique, one party attempts to convince another to change its mind or to agree to cooperate with a proposed solution. Personality is thought to have a close link with an individual's persuasive powers. In one study, a person with high credibility was more easily able to persuade others to change their opinions. Those who are most easily influenced tend to be individuals who are high in authoritarianism—that is, those who are most comfortable being told what to do and how to do it.[12]

Most of us are unaware of how we go about persuading others. The language of persuasion is diverse and complicated. Popular books on influencing others give contradictory advice. Some advocate assertiveness, others stealth, others reason and logic. Can they all be right? Studies of business managers who told how they attempted to influence their subordinates, peers, and superiors at work revealed three basic persuasion strategies—hard, soft, and rational.[13]

The hard strategy involves ordering another person to do something and threatening to give an unsatisfactory performance rating if the order is not carried out, or getting higher management to back up the order. The soft approach is carried out by acting humble while making the request or by making the person feel important and especially well qualified for the task. The rational approach includes trade-offs—you do this for me and I'll do something for you—and explaining the reason for the request.

Influencing others is a social act, and whether any of the three strategies is effective depends on the perception of the individual the manager is trying to persuade. Whatever the strategy, it is no good if the other person doesn't accept the request or doesn't agree to accept the proposed opinion or idea. The basis for selecting a strategy is often explained as using what feels right.

Managers in the study explained the circumstances in which they chose a soft, hard, or rational tactic. The hard tactics were used when the manager had the advantage, when resistance was anticipated, when the target's behavior violated social or organizational norms. Soft tactics were employed when the manager was at a disadvantage, when resistance was anticipated, or when the manager would benefit from achievement of the goal—act nice if you want a favor. Rational tactics were used when neither party had an advantage, when resistance was not anticipated, or when the goal would help both the manager and the organization.

Objectives and power positions were significant. If the goals were clear and if the manager had sufficient power, the choice of persuasive behavior was toward the rational strategy. Reason and logic were found to be particularly useful when the manager wanted to persuade the boss to accept an important idea.

3. *Politics.* Politics is a fact of life and can be an effective vehicle for getting things done in an organization, particularly when conflict is involved. Using politics as a strategy in resolving conflict rests on the idea that power is distributed among parties. A manager brings politics into play by attempting to accumulate enough power to control a decision. This is often done through building coalitions—pulling together individuals or small groups that support the manager's position and increase his or her ability to influence a decision.

4. *Bargaining.* Negotiation is conferring with another to arrive at a settlement. Conferring—which suggests openness, objectivity, respect—is the key to creating the right attitude about bargaining. Bargaining is effective where both parties have something to offer and are willing to give and take. It focuses on arriving at a solution that offers something to all parties in the conflict. Everyone sacrifices somewhat and everyone benefits, with no clear winner—that is the ideal spirit of bargaining, but it is not always carried out that way. In labor-management negotiations, for instance, the strategy

of both sides is to win by forcing the other party to make important concessions.

Negotiating an agreement in which both sides benefit and which neither could have accomplished alone often is done within the following framework:[14]

- Acknowledge the other position. Negotiating does not require that both parties have equal rank or that they like each other. It does demand a willingness to recognize that there may be another point of view and to be ready to listen as well as to talk.
- Agree on the aim of the negotiation. Before the bargaining can begin, the issue has to be defined and a general idea of the objectives and dimensions of the solution must be present. If the editor is going to negotiate the newsroom budget with the publisher, the first step is to understand the bottom line costs and profit expectations for the next year.
- Know the facts. Being well versed in all aspects of the subject is critical. Nothing turns off a negotiation quicker than the remark, "Let me get back to you on that." This indicates a lack of interest or a failure to do the necessary homework. In negotiating a newsroom budget, the editor should be thoroughly familiar with every part of the newsroom operation and the related costs. To indicate uncertainty or lack of knowledge weakens the editor's negotiating position.
- Set the limits. Research suggests that twenty to thirty minutes is the limit for intense concentration on any subject being negotiated. After that, minds begin to wander. Frequent breaks or changes of topic and a realistic time limit can keep the discussions on target and in perspective.
- Gain the other person's trust. No matter how logical and factual your position may be, it will be worthless if your credibility is doubted. Good faith begins with symbols such as eye contact, hand shakes, and good manners, and is maintained by honesty. Trust also is shaped by the individual's track record. The editor's credibility with the publisher

on the budget, for example, will be influenced by how well the current year's newsroom budget is being managed. Trust is often absent in labor-management bargaining, leading to such tactics as bluffing and stalling.

- Pick areas of mutual interest and agreement. Finding a point of agreement or a common ground where meaningful negotiations can begin is an important early step in resolving differences. In negotiating the budget, the editor and the publisher might agree on areas where newsroom spending can be tightened and areas where growth or additional investment is required.

- Start and end on a positive note. The tone of negotiation must be positive. This applies both to what is discussed and how it is discussed. If you have something negative to say, try to phrase it in a constructive way or preface it with a positive statement. This helps prevent defensive reactions and promotes affirmative thinking.

- Be aware of what you are saying and doing. People sometimes become so intent on watching, listening, or speaking to others that they fail to heed themselves. Words, body language, voice tone, and inflection have many meanings and can help or hurt the message you are trying to convey. Humor is especially troublesome because it can easily be interpreted as flippancy or sarcasm.

- Maintain a question/answer exchange. The heart of any negotiation is the ongoing dialogue during which negotiators attempt to discover each other's feelings, understandings, attitudes, prejudices, and objective views of reality. Asking specific, open-ended questions and probing areas of conflict help in separating actual from fancied needs, in isolating the real obstacles, and in identifying which approach to use in obtaining agreement.

- Stay on the subject. If the topic is so complex that the discussion keeps going off on tangents, break it into more manageable segments and handle each separately before going on to the next. If the segments can be organized so that one builds upon another, the goal can be approached logically and repetition can be avoided.

- Develop proposals and compromises. Start by resolving small differences and build from there. Develop proposals and compromises in which everyone wins something. Concede minor points that your counterpart considers important. Swap concessions until a partial or total resolution of the larger issue is reached. Should a deadlock occur on one topic, move on to another issue and resolve that one. Often, agreement in one area softens disagreement in another area and triggers ideas that lead to settlement.

- Handle objections with tact. The negotiation process is not a debate where the aim is arguing and scoring points. To focus on winning is to force the other person to be defensive and to maintain a rigid position to save face. If an objection is raised that is rational, accept it and proceed to other points that may be more favorable to your views. If the objection is irrational, acknowledge it temporarily and move on to other topics that may help the other person to see that the objections he or she raised were based on false fears and doubts.

- Summarize each topic. Frequent summaries ensure that everyone is proceeding in the same direction and will ultimately reach the same destination. The summaries need not be formal, but they do need to spell out results. A recap should include points of disagreement as well as concessions, compromises, and conclusions.

- Don't give up. Hang in there, even when hope for an agreement seems to be waning. Negotiations are cyclical. What is steadfast today may be open to change tomorrow. People resist change, and that is what bargaining is all about. Given time to rethink their positions and adjust to new ideas and situations, people often soften their rigid postures. As former New York Yankee catcher Yogi Berra once said about the game of baseball, "It's not over until it's over."

Fig. 13.6

CLOSE-UP

The basic strategy that people take toward negotiation has been defined as "Win-Lose," an approach that has four basic outcomes: (1) I Lose–You Win, (2) I Lose–You Lose, (3) I Win–You Lose, and (4) I Win–You Win.

1. *I Lose–You Win* comes from a fear of confrontation. The permissive manager, fearful of engaging in a dialogue, sacrifices his or her needs and goals in favor of those of the opponent. This strategy of avoidance suppresses the symptoms and produces a leadership vacuum that will have to be filled by someone else.
2. *I Lose–You Lose* is a compromise that costs all parties a goal or need to satisfy the other's demands. This "Pollyanna" treatment of conflict assumes the problem is solved. Instead, the symptoms once again are suppressed. Hostility and resentment arise from unmet needs and a leadership vacuum begs to be filled.
3. *I Win–You Lose* means that I dominate and can impose a solution in any test of wills. A manager who selects this style also tends to suppress the symptoms of the problem and create hostility and resentment.
4. *I Win–You Win* is the result of rational problem solving that works toward mutually acceptable goals. It is a form of confrontation that deals with the causes of the conflict rather than the symptoms and works toward meeting needs rather than discounting them. This strategy leads to cooperation, not only in solving the present problems, but also in dealing with future problems.

Source: Donald H. Weiss, *Managing Conflict* (New York: American Management Associations, 1981), 67–68.

TEAMBUILDING

Building trust through a management-development process known as teambuilding is a more formal way of preparing editors to handle conflict. Teambuilding means dropping facades, being one's self, and learning to level with people and to allow them to level with you. It means being nondefensive, talking straight, and facing the truth about one's behavior. It means being willing to risk changing to improve working relationships.

That definition of teambuilding comes from Dolly King, manager of training and development for the *Charlotte Observer* and a consultant for KPC Management Consulting Services. She conducted her first teambuilding program in 1982 to help a group of metro editors who were forming a new management team. She also helped merge the staffs of the *Charlotte Observer* and the *Charlotte News*.[15] Since then, King has conducted teambuilding programs for the *San Jose Mercury-News* and for other newspaper organizations and other businesses.

King begins a teambuilding program with a confidential "needs-assessment" interview. The concerns of the editors in the program form 60 to 70 percent of the agenda for the teambuilding sessions. In the first program in Charlotte, the editors wanted the following issues to be addressed:

- Building trust among five talented but different personalities.
- Learning how to move from a competitive, territorial desk to one based on cooperation and collaboration.
- Learning to communicate candidly with each other.
- Giving and seeking feedback regarding behavior.
- Discussing how much of their lives they were willing to give to the *Charlotte Observer*.
- Learning to treat reporters with fairness and consistency.
- Learning how to motivate reporters and how to help them feel valued and nurtured.
- Learning how to address problems of productivity, particularly staffers who are not performing up to par.
- Looking at ways to design career-development plans for middle-level editors and for reporters who want to become editors.

King and the editors held six sessions away from the newspaper building. Each session lasted three and one-half hours.

1. The first session focused on self-awareness. "I believe personal and professional effectiveness is directly related to how well we know ourselves, the kind of clarity we have about ourselves, and what kind of impact we have on those we deal with," King says.

   The editors got personal feedback from an exercise known as the Myers-Briggs Personality Type Indicator, which was designed in 1943 by Isabel Briggs Myers and Katharine C. Briggs. The answers help show how individuals look at things and how they go about deciding things. There are no right or wrong answers to the questions.

   The preferences measured by the Myers-Briggs exercise are extroversion/introversion, sensing/intuition, thinking/feeling, and judgment/perception. Everyone uses each of these characteristics, but one usually is preferred and better developed. Following are some of the key words associated with the pairs of preferences:

   Extroversion/Introversion: active-reflective, people-privacy, breadth-depth

   Sensing/Intuition: details-patterns, facts-innovations, practical-imaginative

   Thinking/Feeling: head-heart, impersonal-personal, analyze-empathize, cool-caring

   Judgment/Perception: organized-flexible, deadlines-discoveries, plan-wait

   Sixteen personality types are measured by the Myers-Briggs Personality Type Indicator. Each personality type has its own strengths and weaknesses and each type has a value in giving an organization a mix and diversity of personalities.

   The Myers-Briggs Personality Type Indicator helps make several important points: Editors don't need to know everything; they don't have to be all things to all people; they have certain strengths that others don't have; they should not be threatened by someone else's competency and skill, but should embrace their own strengths because they, too, have something unique to offer.

2. From the self-awareness exercise, King moved the editors toward building trust. "An atmosphere of trust is necessary so that working relationships, creativity, and productivity can flourish. Trust allows employees to give information about themselves, to admit how they feel, to say what they think, to drop facades," King says.

To set the stage for building trust, King asked the editors to complete another exercise, the Johari Window Model, which shows how willing individuals are to give and receive feedback. The editors completed a diagram that had two scales: one to measure the tendency to give feedback, the other the tendency to seek feedback. Lines were drawn connecting the points on the scales. The result was four quadrants that represented specific aspects of the individual's personality.

The upper left-hand corner is called the "Arena." It represents things that you and others know about yourself. The upper right-hand corner is the "Blind Spot," the things you don't know about yourself but others are aware of. The lower left quadrant is the "Facade," the hidden area. It represents the things you know about yourself that others don't because you do not allow them to. The lower right quadrant is the "Unknown." It represents the unconscious, the things both you and others do not know about yourself.

In the ideal window, according to the Johari Window Model, the Arena quadrant dominates. This represents a communication style in which behavior is open and aboveboard and in which there is little need for others to interpret your meanings.

King used the Johari Window Model to help the editors understand that to work effectively, facades had to come down through self-disclosure and blind spots had to be

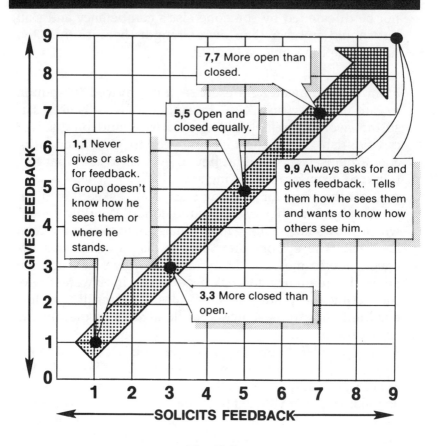

Fig. 13.7

The relationship of points on this grid demonstrates how the willingness of individuals to give and receive feedback influences their ability to deal with conflict. The grid is an adaptation of the Johari Window Model, developed by psychologists Harrington V. Ingham and Joseph Luft.

Source: Adapted from Harrington V. Ingham and Joseph Luft, *Group Processes: An Introduction to Group Dynamics*, 3d ed. (Palo Alto, Calif.: Mayfield Publishing, 1984).

reduced by being receptive to feedback. Once these changes are made, lines of communication can be opened.

3. King got the editors to talk about themselves through an expectations exercise in which each editor identified what he or she wants and needs from the others, what each does well, and what each needs help with. Sheets of newsprint were taped on walls and participants wrote down their ideas for each person.

It was difficult for the participants to open up for this exercise, King said. "Teambuilding requires a lot of truth telling. In every group, people have been afraid initially. But the process has worked every time."

In the middle of this exercise, an assistant managing editor leaned across the table and said to the editor: "You bulldoze people. In your determination to get something done, you run over people. You take friends who are trying to help you and you knock them aside. You consider someone who raises a question disloyal. So, as a consequence, no one will say anything."

The revelations, the editor wrote later, were often painful, but he thought it the most valuable exercise in twenty years of newspapering.

One of King's roles during the exercises was to keep the participants safe. "The truth can be told gently. I require gentleness. Not once has anyone ever been attacked or hurt. I assure people of this before we begin."

Once the communication barriers began to crumble, King was able to lead the editors in candid discussions of changes and additions that would improve the metro desk.

MANAGEMENT-UNION CONFLICT

Collective bargaining is the term used to describe the interaction between managers and unions. It is essentially adversarial, although the nature of the interaction differs from company to company. Collective bargaining has given a formal framework to conflict and confrontation. It is limited as well as protected by rules, accepted practices, and laws; that is, the rights of management and the union, the security of workers, and the power each side can use in its relationship with the other are clearly defined.

John T. Dunlop, a Harvard professor and Secretary of Labor under President Gerald Ford, describes the three groups in the collective-bargaining process as "actors": (1) managers and their hierarchy within the company; (2) workers and their hierarchy of organized representatives; and (3) regulators who play specific roles. The regulators, who generally are brought in by the other actors, can represent the government or private agencies.[16]

Three independent agencies of the executive branch of the federal government have a role in the management-union process:[17] (1) the National Labor Relations Board, (2) the Federal Mediation and Conciliation Service, and (3) the Department of Labor.

The National Labor Relations Board (NLRB) was established under the Wagner Act in 1935. It is responsible for administering the basic federal law governing management-union relations. The NLRB has broad authority to investigate charges that a company or a union has violated the law. In cases where efforts to gain voluntary compliance fail, a trial examiner is appointed by the NLRB to hear the evidence. If a controversy persists beyond the trial examiner's ruling, the case may be reviewed and decided by the full NLRB.

The Federal Mediation and Conciliation Service was created by the Taft-Hartley Act of 1947. It works through the voluntary cooperation of management and unions, and its mission is to assist management and unions in reaching collective-bargaining agreements. A mediator is most likely to be called at a difficult point in the bargaining when the parties are on the verge of an impasse or a strike. The mediator is neutral. His or her role is to listen, to assess the other actors as well as the issues, and to find a formula that will extract the parties from untenable positions or that will resolve the dispute.

The Department of Labor's main activity is in the field of protective legislation and in research. It is the president's official liaison to organized labor and to employers in their collective-bargaining capacity.

A nongovernmental agency that helps resolve management-union conflict is the American Arbitration Association, a private, nonprofit organization. The role of an arbitrator is to determine the outcome of a dispute over the interpretation of a contract between management and union. Collective-bargaining agreements traditionally provide for a process by which disagreements over the rights and duties spelled out in the contract can be settled. If one party thinks the other party is violating the rules, it files a grievance. A group of union officers, known as the grievance committee, and company representatives meet to discuss the alleged violation. If they cannot settle the dispute, they call in a third party—the arbitrator.

The arbitrator must be impartial and fully familiar with the issues and the law. Quite often, arbitrators are lawyers or members of college faculties. The arbitrator schedules a hearing, listens to the evidence, asks the two sides to file briefs, and then makes a decision that is binding on both parties. The arbitrator's power derives from the agreement of management and union to abide by the arbitrator's decision. Although arbitration has demonstrated its usefulness, it also is costly, slow, and cumbersome.

The traditional perception of management-union relations is one based on conflict and confrontation. That view is reinforced by news stories detailing strikes, picketing, public statements about disagreements at the bargaining table, lawsuits, NLRB rulings, and open criticism of wages, fringes, and featherbedding practices. In reality, the two sides share a major common concern: the welfare of employees.

There is a variety of reasons why employees join unions. The most common are:[18]

Better bargaining position. Individual employees acting on their own generally have little bargaining power in dealing with the company. This is becoming less true in many newsrooms where merit-pay programs and the tendency of editors to recognize differences in performance have given individual newspaper staffers an increasing ability to bargain effectively for themselves.

Fair and uniform treatment. Employees often join unions to secure fair treatment. Favoritism, discrimination, and capricious management behavior are the kinds of situations that cause employees to organize or to join unions. They look to the union to eliminate unfair management practices.

Economic security. Procedures for layoffs, job reclassifications, discipline, and pay increases are spelled out in the agreement between management and union. Because the contract usually prevents management from acting impulsively or without cause, employees think that their personal economic security is strengthened.

Alienation. Employees attempt to organize a union or join one because they have a sense of alienation from the company. The alienation may result from the behavior of individual supervisors or managers toward employees, or it may be caused by company practices that deprive employees of a feeling of belonging. Failing to provide feedback and failing to have a formal system for dealing with employee complaints are two common causes of alienation. Union membership offers a satisfactory means of achieving the recognition that management fails to provide or of gaining a sense of participation that management has not offered.

Which staffers are eligible for membership in a newsroom union is determined by the agreement between the newspaper company and the union. Generally, all nonsupervisory employees—that is, reporters, copy editors, photographers, artists, news assistants, and clerks—are covered by the contract. In some cases, the agreement also includes first-line supervisors, such as assistant desk editors. Although assistant desk editors may not be supervisors in the full sense because they do not have the minimum levels of authority (see Chapter 5), it is a contradiction to expect assistant desk editors to be at once a boss and a member of a union. In this situation, a supervisory editor is faced with conflicting loyalties—he or she must choose between obligation to the company and obligation to the union and its members.

Fig. 13.8.

CLOSE-UP

About 20 percent of U.S. newspaper journalists belong to a union. Most of those belong either to The Newspaper Guild, which is affiliated with the AFL-CIO, or to unaffiliated associations known as company unions.

Five big locals—New York, San Francisco–Oakland–San Jose, Washington-Baltimore, Toronto, and the Wire Service Guild—account for well over a third of the Newspaper Guild's enrollment. The union has some 150 contracts in the United States and Canada.

After its founding in 1933, the Guild was caught up in the drama of the rise of industrial unionism in the United States, a development that took place against the backdrop of the Great Depression of the 1930s. It was a tumultuous period highlighted by massive organizing campaigns, strikes, picket-line violence, and bitter rivalries between the craft unions of the American Federation of Labor and the new Congress of Industrial Organizations.

For the Guild, the ferment was intellectual and political as well as economic. The early newsroom enthusiasts in the union were confident they could become involved in a burgeoning movement without undermining the detachment their jobs required.

Over the years, the Guild's focus has been economic. It has been influential in improving wages, benefits, and working conditions for newspaper journalists. But its role and its influence in the modern, noneconomic issues of journalism have been limited.

"Where the Guild lost its way," wrote A. H. Raskin, the long-time labor writer for the *New York Times*, "was in failing to recognize that its status as an organization of journalists imposed on it an obligation to be as concerned with the advancement of professional quality as it is with pay scales and improving fringe benefits and working conditions . . . Increasingly, the Guild has tended to seem an irrelevancy in the newsroom."

The Guild has not demonstrated that it is equipped to cope either with the rise of giant communications companies or with the onrush of technology that has dramatically changed the way newspapers are published.

Source: A. H. Raskin, "The Once and Future Newspaper Guild," *Columbia Journalism Review*, September–October 1982, 26–34.

In addition to eligibility, management-union agreements control whether an individual has a choice about joining the union. Under some contracts, the newsroom is known as a union shop or closed shop. The publisher is required to make union membership a condition of employment. Where there is no union-shop clause, staffers can choose whether or not to join the union. Staffers who elect not to join are covered by the provisions of the contract and are entitled to the same benefits and protections as dues-paying members.

For editors and publishers, the most important principle underlying a collective-bargaining agreement is what is known as *management rights*. It is based on the premise that management inherently possesses total freedom and discretion in running the company. Whenever the company makes a concession to union demands, it is giving away part of the rights that inherently belong to management. Whatever remains after those concessions continues to be management rights. Three specific management rights cannot be conceded: (1) freedom to select the business objectives of the company, (2) freedom to determine the uses to which the material assets of the enterprise will be devoted, and (3) power to discipline for cause.[19] "Cause" normally means insubordination or a failure to perform that can be documented over a period of time.

Over the years, publishers at some newspapers have let some important controls slip away. In the production departments, for example, publishers negotiated away their rights to determine how many printers or pressmen were needed to get out the paper and to introduce freely new production equipment and processes. As a result, unions became very powerful and publishers could not make the decisions needed to operate efficiently.

Once management rights had been negotiated away, publishers discovered that it was nearly impossible to win them back at the bargaining table. Surrendering the right to control work practices and the size of the work force was a contributing factor in the failure of newspapers in New York in the 1960s. During the 1970s and 1980s, publishers have been successful in reclaiming some management rights through negotiation with unions, but at a very high price.

Management rights alone do not make an editor-manager. The rights reinforce the editor's role. The editor's effectiveness is enhanced by managerial use of the delegated rights and the power and authority derived from them. Editors who plan the operations, organize the work flows, and assign the work, who direct and coordinate activities and control results, are carrying out the accepted functions of a manager. In performing this role, the editor acts for the newspaper organization.[20]

With a full understanding of management rights and a willingness to use them, an editor can manage an organized newsroom effectively and with a minimum of conflict. The editor's ability to build a good relationship with the union's leadership will be helped by taking the following points seriously:

- Know the contract. Understand fully what can and cannot be done under terms of the management-union agreement. Ignorance of such contract provisions as staff scheduling can cost penalty pay and result in inefficient use of manpower. Continued abuse of the rules can lead to grievances and arbitration.
- Uphold the contract. Respect the contract and make sure that all other newsroom supervisors and managers honor the agreement. Willingness to live by the agreement is important in building trust with union members.
- Respect the union's position. Get to know the union leaders. Don't use ridicule or sarcasm in dealing with them. Remember that staffers have a right to accept or reject union representation in an environment that is free from threats, coercion, intimidation, or surveillance.
- Respond promptly to grievances and complaints. Protect the company's position while listening carefully and responding fairly to the issues presented by union representatives.
- Ask for help. Many issues raised by the union may require interpretation of the law or may involve issues that the editor is not trained to handle. Contract language may be ambiguous and may invite different interpretations. In

many cases, the agreement may have been negotiated by a company representative other than the editor. Don't hesitate to ask for help in absorbing the language as well as the spirit and intent of the contract, or to request that the company's negotiator or lawyer be present in meetings with union representatives.

The management right that is most difficult for editors to employ in an organized newsroom is the power to discipline. Although staffers are protected both by the contract and by labor laws, editors have full power to discipline or dismiss individuals for just cause (see Chapter 10).

Two common reasons for discipline are insubordination and poor performance. In either case, the editor has considerable freedom to act. The key is for the editor to support a decision to discipline with a well-documented case. Except in an instance where insubordinate behavior is so outrageous—such as a staffer's physically assaulting an editor—that immediate dismissal is required, the best approach is for the editor to build a reasonable case for discipline through regular performance reviews. Once the staffer's behavior indicates that some action by the editor is required, an effective technique is progressive discipline. It generally occurs in four steps: (1) oral warning, (2) written warning, (3) suspension, and (4) dismissal (see Chapter 10). The editor should give the staffer up to six months to change his or her behavior before moving to the next step of progressive discipline. In addition, the editor should be prepared to give the staffer consistent feedback and direction aimed at overcoming problems with work behavior. Progressive discipline is fair to the individual staffer and also puts the editor in a strong position to defend any discipline against objections by the individual or the union.

CHAPTER SUMMARY

Conflict, ranging from individual to group conflict, exists in every newsroom. Conflict is not inherently bad. In the newsroom, it is a common element in handling the news and often leads to improving story selection and strengthening individual stories.

Some specific sources of conflict typically present in the newsroom are: shared resources, goals, perceptions and values, role requirements, nature of the work, individual styles, and ambiguity.

The process of conflict generally occurs in four stages: (1) frustration, (2) conceptualization, (3) behavior, and (4) outcome.

In individuals, conflict can produce such emotions as anxiety, fear, and anger. These feelings are reflections of how conflict threatens our self-image. When faced with conflict, we can work through our differences or we can be defensive. Three common defenses are: (1) denial, (2) rejection, and (3) distortion.

Working with difficult individuals can be handled most effectively by recognizing a hunger for attention, initiating contact, avoiding arguments, being firm, controlling anger, and being patient.

When it is necessary to give criticism, the editor should view the process as a form of communication. Being direct and frank should be part of the editor's managerial attitude.

Four general strategies for reducing conflict are: (1) problem solving, a straightforward approach that looks at the problem, weighs alternatives, and selects the best one; (2) persuasion, an attempt to convince someone to change his or her mind; (3) politics, using power to build coalitions in support of an idea or a position; and (4) bargaining, conferring with another to arrive at a settlement.

Teambuilding is a training process that seeks to prepare editors to handle conflict more effectively by creating lines of communication among team members. Editors learn to level with others, "talk straight," drop facades, face the truth about their behavior, and be willing to risk change to improve working relationships.

A source of formal conflict that editors encounter is through interaction with a newsroom union. Management-union relations are basically adversarial and develop through collective bargaining and through complaint procedures such as grievances and arbitration. The relationship between management and union is governed by laws, rules, and accepted practices.

NOTES

1. Kenneth W. Thomas and Warren H. Schmidt, "A Survey of Managerial Interests with Respect to Conflict," *Academy of Management Journal*, 1976, 315–16.
2. Stephen Robbins, *Managing Organizational Conflict* (Englewood Cliffs, N.J.: Prentice-Hall, 1974), 12–14.
3. Warren R. Plunkett and Raymond F. Attner, *Introduction to Management* (Boston: Kent, 1983), 425–26.
4. Richard M. Steers, *Introduction to Organizational Behavior*, 2d ed. (Glenview, Ill.: Scott, Foresman, 1984), 489–90.
5. Kenneth W. Thomas and Louis R. Pondy, "Toward an Intent Model of Conflict Management among Principal Parties," *Human Relations* 30 (1977): 1089–1102.
6. Steers, *Introduction to Organizational Behavior*, 492–93.
7. Chris Argyris, *Personality and Organization* (New York: Harper & Row, 1957), 41–44.
8. Harry Levinson, "The Abrasive Personality," in *Harvard Business Review on Human Relations* (New York: Harper & Row, 1979), 232–33.
9. Walter D. St. John, "Leveling with Employees," *Personnel Journal*, August 1984, 55.
10. J. Patrick McMahon, "The Maturity Factor: Adding Insight to Your Conflict Training," *Training*, November 1983, 57, 59–60.
11. James G. March and Herbert A. Simon, *Organizations* (New York: John Wiley & Sons, 1958), 129–31.
12. Carl I. Hovland, Irving L. Janis, and Harold H. Kelley, *Communication and Persuasion* (New Haven: Yale University Press, 1953), 25–36.
13. David Kipnis and Stuart Schmidt, "The Language of Persuasion," *Psychology Today*, April 1985, 42–46.
14. Robert W. Goddard, "Negotiation: How to Win by Forgetting about Winning," *Training*, March 1984, 34, 37.
15. Material for the section on teambuilding was taken from the following sources: Dolly King, interview with author, 15 April 1985; "Teambuilding Unifies Employees by Building Trust," *Pennsylvania Newspaper Publishers Association Press*, November 1984, 8; Dolly King, correspondence with Frank Quine, American Press Institute, 31 March 1983; "Teambuilding: Painful, but Valuable, Lesson in Management," *The Bulletin of American Society of Newspaper Editors*, June–July 1984, 16–17; and Katharine C. Briggs and Isabel Briggs Myers, *The Myers-Briggs Personality Type Indicator* (Palo Alto, Calif.: Consulting Psychologists Press, 1976).
16. John T. Dunlop, *Industrial Relations System* (New York: McGraw-Hill, 1958), 7–8.
17. Edwin F. Beal, Edward D. Wickersham, and Philip K. Kienast, *The Practice of Collective Bargaining*, 5th ed. (Homewood, Ill.: Richard D. Irwin, 1976), 131, 209, 413, 419, 421.

18. Don Caruth and Harry N. Mills, Jr., "Working toward Better Union Relations," *Supervisory Management*, February 1985, 7–8.
19. Beal, Wickersham, and Kienast, *Collective Bargaining*, 253, 275–76.
20. Ibid., 279–80.

14

Stress and Survival

Stress—it's a word likely to come up in any conversation about newspaper work. Stress is a modern metaphor, one we use to describe whatever makes us feel uncomfortable. Job-related stress affects all of us. Although prolonged stress can lead to burnout, the stress of covering a great story or putting together a compelling front page can be invigorating and stimulating. On the other hand, unrelieved stress can lead to physical and emotional health problems. Stress is a major cause of absenteeism, turnover, low productivity, and employee unrest. Sound management practices can eliminate many of the serious effects of stress. For editors to recognize what steps can be taken to help themselves and members of the staff cope with stress, it is important that they understand the nature of stress in the newsroom.

DEFINING STRESS

Hans Selye, a pioneering endocrinologist and father of stress research, gave stress its modern meaning as a "nonspecific" response of the body to any demand upon it. Each demand requires the body to adapt. Whether the situation is pleasant or uncomfortable is not important. What matters is the intensity of the demand to which the body must adjust or adapt.

We can win a Pulitzer Prize and, the next month, lose a parent to cancer. The nature of the two events—joy and sorrow—is

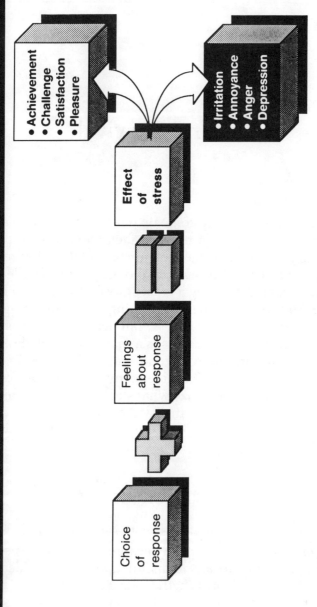

Fig. 14.1.

The effect of stress on individuals is influenced by two human reactions: the choices made in response to a stressful experience and the feeling about those choices. These choices can lead to "good" stress or "bad" stress.

completely different, but the effect on the body—forcing it to adjust to a new situation—is the same. Each sets in motion a chain of events that includes a rise in blood pressure, heightened senses, increased energy, and other physical reactions.

Millions of years ago, the stress mechanism helped primitive men and women survive. It prepared them for action, to fight back against animals or other primitives. Had they been paralyzed by fear when faced with danger, these people would have been destroyed. But when fear was combined with aggressive feelings, it helped them survive. It was a physical response to a physical threat.

The stressful situations we encounter today don't often carry a physical threat. Instead, what typically is threatened is our security, our self-esteem, or our emotional sense of well-being. But the body's reaction is just the same: Striking changes are set in motion. Digestion stops. Blood is shunted to the brain, which is highly alert, and to muscles, which are tensed for action. The heart pounds. Blood pressure increases. The skin becomes cool and clammy. From the nervous system, a message goes to the adrenal glands to secrete a hormone called epinephrine, more commonly known as adrenaline. This is the "juice" that increases heart action, supplies extra glucose to serve as fuel for the muscles, and relaxes and enlarges the airways so that more air can reach the pituitary gland at the base of the brain. The pituitary gland responds by causing the thyroid and other glands to pour out their hormones. This instantaneous mustering of the forces of body and mind completes the physical preparation for dealing with the stressful situation.[1]

Walter Cannon, a physiologist at Harvard University in the 1920s, initiated the study of what goes on when stress occurs. Cannon called it the "fight-or-flight" response.[2]

The options for coping with stress today are the same as those for prehistoric people. We can fight, perhaps by confronting the boss over a decision with which we disagree. We can flee by withdrawing, passively accepting the decision. Or, as is often necessitated by the realities of the modern world, we can adapt by adjusting to the new situation and making the best of it.

In each choice, Cannon suggested, the human body seeks *homeostasis*. It tries to maintain a balance, which is necessary for a healthy life. When stretched beyond its normal shape or function, the body makes great effort to return to normal limits at the earliest possible time.[3] Physical or emotional health problems are likely to occur when stress upsets the balance for extended periods of time.

In 1956, Selye concluded that the human response to stress followed a fairly consistent pattern, which he called the *General Adaptation Syndrome*.[4] This syndrome consists of three stages. The first, the alarm stage, is the body's reaction to the first sign of stress. Following the initial shock, the body moves into the second stage, resistance. In this stage, the choices Cannon observed—fight, flee, or adapt—come into play. Whatever the choice, the body is attempting to return to a condition of homeostasis. If a balance returns, the body's physical reaction to stress will disappear. If the stress condition continues long enough, however, the body's capacity to deal with it becomes exhausted. In the third stage, exhaustion, the individual's defenses wear away and he or she experiences a variety of stress-related illnesses. It is the third stage that presents the greatest threat to individuals and, as a result, to organizations.[5]

ELEMENTS OF STRESS

Henry Babcock, a Harvard psychiatrist, distinguished three forms of tension that are often related but caused by different situations. These forms of tension are:[6]

1. Tensions arising primarily from inner conflict, such as a neurosis. This form is closely connected with what psychiatrists call anxiety. The individual usually is not aware of the cause. It serves no constructive purpose. It hinders the creative process. And it is beyond the power of most managers to deal with.

2. Tensions arising primarily from external factors. This form of stress may be created by hurdles in the organizational structure, by management goals, and by similar obstacles, such as loss of control, that interfere with the satisfaction of an individual's drives and desires.

3. Tensions arising primarily from a need to be creative. Individuals with a gifted mind and special talents need an environment in which to play out their creative nature. Tensions for these individuals may accompany the demands of a virtuoso performance, such as leading a crucial meeting. Or, the tensions may be those which accompany and sustain mental creativity, having more of an intellectual nature, such as reporting and writing a long story on a complicated subject or analyzing a difficult newsroom management situation. This form of tension is most helpful when there are no other forms of tension are present.

For many years, there was an assumption that stress was something to be avoided. The public was told that stress was taking a heavy toll on the individual's well-being, and that they should slow down, relax, escape the stressful environment. A popular remedy was popping antistress pills such as Valium and other prescription medications.

More recent studies have put forth a different theory: Stress can be good for you. There is value to certain kinds of tension. It is, in fact, a crucial part of life that contributes to production and satisfaction. An editor who feels in control of his or her life can channel stressful energy into achievement.

There are three basic factors that determine the effect stress has on us: (1) environment, (2) vulnerability, and (3) stressors.

Environment

The environment is the setting and frame of mind in which the editor works. When the environment is good, it provides a balance that helps the editor cope. When it is bad, the environment becomes a source of stress rather than an aid in coping with stress. Examples of the editor's environment include how the editor feels about his or her job at the moment, relationships with the boss and the staff, the newspaper company's values and policies, the range of the editor's authority and control, and the way in which each of these relates to the editor's personal values.

Outside the office, family and close friendships are part of the environment that influences the amount of stress an editor experiences.

A major influence on the nature of an editor's environment is the level of commitment to the job, challenge from the job, and control over the job that editors think they have. In a 1983 questionnaire survey of 902 newspaper editors and their spouses, sponsored by the Associated Press Managing Editors to examine the effects of stress on the health of newspaper editors, large numbers of the editors who responded reported positive feelings about commitment, challenge, and control. Another important element in the editor's environment is the match between personal values and the ability to satisfy those values at work.

Following are statements that at least 70 percent of the editors in the APME survey said were true about their jobs:

- My job involves being faced with criticism of my newspaper or of my staff from readers and news sources.
- The accuracy of my newspaper and other newspapers influences the public perception of my newspaper.
- My job involves making important decisions.
- I am not satisfied that my newspaper is as good as it should be.
- I am interrupted by phone calls and by unscheduled visits from staffers, news sources, and readers.
- My job involves important responsibility to readers to make the right decisions about news coverage.
- Mistakes in my newspaper contribute to public distrust of the press.
- My job involves thinking about tomorrow's paper before today's is published.
- There is a sense of urgency about my tasks as an editor.
- My job involves working under the pressure of a deadline.
- My job is highly visible and this increases the pressure I feel to produce good newspapers.

- There is more work than I can complete in a normal working day.

- My job involves implementing decisions with which I disagree.

- The public nature of my work as an editor means that my spouse/family is exposed to criticism of the newspaper or my work more frequently and to a greater degree than the spouse/family of executives in other fields.

Each of these points represents an important part of the editor's environment.

Vulnerability

The second factor in the stress equation—vulnerability—determines the effect of stress on the editor. Here we must move from the editor's management role to examine the editor as an individual. One's personality, physical and psychological makeup, and preparation for unexpected events and the intensity of change are among the factors that influence vulnerability to stress.

Following are five indicators that can help the editor assess his or her vulnerability to stress:

1. *Life change.* Early in this century, Adolph Meyer, a physician at Johns Hopkins University, kept life charts on his patients. From these charts, he found that his patients tended to become sick when clusters of major changes occurred in their lives.

   Beginning in 1949, Thomas Holmes, a professor of psychiatry at the University of Washington School of Medicine, drew on Meyer's work. He listed events that seemed to trigger illnesses such as colds, rashes, stomach upset, and tuberculosis. While the symptoms were diverse, they had one thing in common: a change in life pattern. Holmes concluded that people can get sick when something happens that requires them to adjust or adapt.[7]

   In 1972, Holmes and Richard Rahe, a navy captain and head of the stress medicine division at the Naval Health

Research Center in San Diego, developed a scale that can be used to predict the likelihood that an individual will experience a stress-related illness.

On the Holmes-Rahe scale (see fig. 14.2), each life event carries a number value related to the intensity of feeling associated with the change. For example, death of a spouse carries a value of 100 and is more likely to increase the risk of illness than such events as a change in financial status or an outstanding personal accomplishment.[8]

Fig. 14.2

The Holmes-Rahe Life Event–Stress Scale

Rank	Life Event	Stress value
1	Death of spouse	100
2	Divorce	65
3	Marital separation	65
4	Jail term	63
5	Death of a close family member	63
6	Personal injury or illness	53
7	Marriage	50
8	Fired at work	47
9	Marital reconciliation	45
10	Retirement	45
11	Change in health of a family member	44
12	Pregnancy	40
13	Sex difficulties	39
14	Gain of new family member	39
15	Business adjustment	39
16	Change in financial state	38
17	Death of a close friend	37
18	Change to different line of work	36
19	Change in number of arguments with spouse	35
20	Mortgage or loan for major purchase	31
21	Foreclosure of mortgage or loan	30
22	Change in responsibilities at work	29
23	Son or daughter leaving home	29
24	Trouble with in-laws	29
25	Outstanding personal achievement	28

Rank	Life Event	Stress value
26	Spouse begins or stops work	26
27	Begin or end school	26
28	Change in living condition	25
29	Revision of personal habits	24
30	Trouble with boss	23
31	Change in work hours or conditions	20
32	Change in residence	20
33	Change in schools	20
34	Change in recreation	19
35	Change in church activities	19
36	Change in social activities	18
37	Mortgage or loan for small purchase	17
38	Change in sleeping habits	16
39	Change in number of family get-togethers	15
40	Change in eating habits	15
41	Vacation	13
42	Christmas	12
43	Minor violation of the law	11

Source: L. O. Ruch and Thomas H. Holmes, "Scaling of Life Change: Comparison of Direct and Indirect Methods," *Journal of Psychosomatic Research,* 1971, 15.

Holmes and Rahe suggest using this scale as an early warning system to estimate risk of illness. Totals above 300 indicate that the likelihood of having an accident or becoming ill is 79 percent greater than usual. Totals from 200 to 300 indicate that the likelihood of becoming ill or having a major accident is 51 percent greater than usual. Totals from 150 to 200 indicate that the likelihood of having an accident or becoming ill is 37 percent greater than usual. Totals under 150 indicate that the individual is living in a calm and stable environment and is less likely than average to become ill or have an accident.

The life events on the Holmes-Rahe Scale show that stress is not limited to negative change but can also be associated with positive experiences such as promotion, personal achievement, or marriage.

2. *Personality.* The research of two San Francisco cardiologists, Meyer Friedman and Ray Rosenmann, suggested that there

is a link between personality characteristics and the likelihood of heart attack. The most common explanation for heart attack is a condition known as atherosclerosis, in which fatty deposits narrow the channels of the arteries that feed the heart muscle. The blockage prevents blood from reaching the heart. Research has established a number of risk factors that are likely to bring on heart disease: smoking, excess weight, lack of exercise, a family history of heart problems, high blood pressure, and high levels of cholesterol.

Yet, physical factors alone do not provide the complete answer. Evidence of high blood pressure or high cholesterol is not always present in heart patients. Research has demonstrated that stress can be a major influence. In the 1940s, Karl and William Menninger of the Menninger Clinic in Topeka, Kansas, were among the first psychiatrists to study the personalities of patients suffering from heart disease. They noted that many of their patients appeared to be aggressive, but kept their aggressive tendencies under the surface.

A decade later, another psychiatrist, Flanders Dunbar, examined a large group of coronary patients and found them to be hard-driving individuals who were single-minded in seeking refuge in work. Dunbar also concluded that these individuals had less interest in sports, more frequent illness, and less sexual satisfaction than noncoronary patients.[9]

Friedman and Rosenmann made a strong case for the importance of behavior and personality in coronary heart disease. They described two major types of personality: Type A and Type B. They found that high-risk heart patients—Type A people—displayed the following characteristics:[10]

- Chronic and severe sense of time urgency.
- Constant involvement in multiple projects subject to deadlines.
- Persistent desire for recognition and advancement.
- Excessive competitive drive.
- Neglect of all aspects of life except work.

- A tendency to take on excessive responsibilities—the feeling that "only I can handle it."

- Explosiveness of speech and a tendency to hasten the pace of normal conversation.

Individuals who fall into the Type-B pattern are described as serious but easygoing, able to enjoy leisure, and with no feelings of being driven by time. Most people tend to be a mix of the two types, with either Type-A or Type-B characteristics being dominant.

Paul Rosch, president of the American Institute of Stress in Yonkers, New York, says that people with Type-A personalities engage in a chronic, continuous struggle against circumstances and people and perhaps even themselves: "The Type A individual has become addicted to his own adrenaline and unconsciously seeks ways to get those little surges." He suggests that journalists work better under deadline pressure because they think that their bodies will give them a boost of adrenaline for increased energy and performance. "They are very competitive. They know that promotion is based on performance."[11]

In 1980, Friedman added some new insights into Type-A behavior. Based on his continuing research, he wrote that Type-A behavior is exhibited by people who are unable—or unwilling—to evaluate their own competence, to see themselves realistically. "Such people prefer to judge themselves by the evaluations of those whom they believe are their superiors," he reported. "And to enhance themselves in others' eyes, they attempt to increase the quantity—but rarely the quality—of their achievements. Their self-esteem becomes increasingly dependent on the status they believe they achieve." Hoping to achieve a satisfactory sense of self-esteem, such people "incessantly try to increase the sheer quantity of their achievements. And it is this chronic and incessant struggle to achieve more and more in less time, together with a free-floating but covert and usually well-rationalized hostility, that make up the Type-A behavior pattern."[12]

In research at the University of Texas, psychologist David C. Glass noted that by raising levels of cholesterol in the bloodstream, stress can make a heart attack more likely. In addition, stress causes a rise in blood pressure so that blood passing through the arteries under high pressure increases the likelihood of tears in the arterial walls, around which fatty deposits can form. In his studies, Glass found that in Type-A men, blood pressure rises sharply when hostility is aroused. Moreover, the blood-clotting process in Type-A men is significantly faster than that of others, increasing the likelihood that a vessel-clogging blood clot may form. Glass also found that in Type A's, the push to achieve leads them to press their bodies to the limit. They ignore or deny their body's fatigue in the struggle to attain their goals.[13]

A 1984 study by Meyer Friedman of more than eight hundred men who had suffered heart attacks demonstrated that counseling to reduce characteristics of Type-A behavior can cut in half their chances of suffering another heart attack.[14] However, a three-year study of 516 heart patients, completed in 1985, suggested that there was no link between Type-A behavior and heart disease.[15] The point here is that while the Type-A theory as a basic concept is valid, the idea is not quite as simple as just Type A–Type B. There are variations and shadings that have produced controversial and contradictory results.

How can we identify Type-A individuals? Dr. Rosch cautions that any attempt to assess Type-A coronary-prone behavior is difficult without a structured, aggressive, probing interview in which the questions asked may arouse emotions in the interviewee. Questionnaires designed to identify Type-A behavior are "notoriously inaccurate" because many Type A's really are unaware of their reaction patterns or will deny them on such questionnaires.[16]

Fig. 14.3

CLOSE-UP

In a 1983 Associated Press Managing Editors Association study, editors were asked to respond to a checklist of values, personality traits, and expressions of self-image. Within that list were several items that are associated with Type-A behavior. Following are those characteristics and the percentage of editors who said they fit the description:

- I am productive. I get things done. (89 percent)
- I enjoy competition and want to win. (81 percent)
- I am irritated when something is not done correctly. (74 percent)
- I hate to wait. (69 percent)
- I try to do several things at once. (67 percent)
- I try to get things done as quickly as possible. (65 percent)
- I need recognition from my boss and my peers. (60 percent)
- I have ambitious goals. (50 percent)
- In the last few years, I have not used all my vacation time. (42 percent)
- I become impatient with others who are less creative or intelligent than I. (39 percent)
- I am usually the first one finished eating a meal. (39 percent)
- When others speak slowly, I try to rush them along by finishing the sentence for them. (31 percent)
- I tend to talk fast. (30 percent)
- I feel compelled to tell others about myself. (17 percent)

Source: Robert H. Giles, *Editors and Stress* (Rochester: Gannett Rochester Newspapers, 1983), 25.

3. *Values.* Another important indicator to help editors assess their vulnerability to stress is values. In the 1983 APME survey, editors were asked to rank their values. Those that were most important were a sense of accomplishment, family security, and self-esteem. The values that were ranked as least important were an exciting life and spiritual development. If the important values are threatened, the editor's vulnerability to stress increases.

4. *Fears.* Fears are common to most of us. Some fears are personal and focus on health or family situations. Others

reflect uncertainty about our professional skills or our capacity to compete for top jobs. Fears often point to the areas of greatest vulnerability. They often generate anxiety or a diffuse, unpleasant, vague feeling of apprehension. Individuals are more likely to be affected when stress occurs in those areas where their fears are strongest.

The editors in the APME survey identified the following as their major fears:

- Being locked in and unable to freely change my way of life. (39 percent)
- Not having enough money. (38 percent)
- Declining physical capabilities, illness. (33 percent)
- I have no major fear. (24 percent)
- Messing up my personal life. (22 percent)
- Not being able to cope with the demands of my job. (19 percent)
- Finding out I'm not as good an editor as I thought I was. (19 percent)
- Others finding out I'm not as good an editor as they thought I was. (14 percent)
- Not advancing fast enough. (14 percent)
- Lack of recognition. (11 percent)

5. *Stages of life.* Two books, *The Seasons of Man's Life* by Daniel Levinson and *Passages* by Gail Sheehy, suggest that there are periods of life during which adults may commonly experience special changes, crises, and concerns.[17]

   During these transitional periods, people tend to reexamine themselves, their relationships, their goals and achievements, their values and responsibilities. These periods of self-examination quite often are intense, difficult, and painful. The conclusions that are reached and the decisions as to what to do determine, to a large extent, whether the transition from one stage of life to the next will be made successfully. The length of the transitional periods is unique to each individual. They can extend over several months or be as long as a year or two.

Following are the age ranges that have been identified in research and the changes that can be anticipated:

- Entering the adult world. This period occurs between ages twenty-two and twenty-eight, when we enter the adult world with all of its responsibilities and rules. It is the time when we make a commitment to a career, cultivate the capacity for intimacy, and establish ourselves as unique individuals. During this period, it is important to strike a satisfactory balance between the adventure of exploring the new world we are entering and the need to create a stable life structure that involves being more responsible and making something of our lives.

- Age-thirty transition. This period extends from about age twenty-eight to age thirty-three. This is when we question whether we have made the right decisions about our careers, our relationships, our commitments, and our values. We discover that life is for real. Stresses occur around age thirty that are associated with the feeling that our present life structure is unsatisfactory, yet we are uncertain how to change that structure. In our jobs, we worry about why we do not seem to be getting ahead as rapidly as some of our peers and we question our ability to succeed.

- Midlife crisis. This is the most widely discussed and, for many, the most difficult of the transitional periods. It occurs between ages forty and forty-five. Our life structure again comes into question. We sense for the first time that we are mortal. We compare what we are with what we had hoped to be. We look closely at relationships, especially marriage and the family, and we think critically about the level of satisfaction that we draw from them. For men particularly, this examination comes at a time when wives and children are reaching outside the family, developing new interests and new relationships of their own.

  In the midlife crisis, we reflect on our professional values and goals. It is common to be dissatisfied with being middle-level managers and working for someone else. We want to be our "own man" or our "own woman." We want to make our own decisions. At this time, we begin to make choices and set priorities. More than a few of us decide to make a change—in our life's work, in our life-style, in our life's relationships. A strong influence during the midlife crisis is that the physical effects of aging begin to show. We are increasingly concerned about illness, about physical and emotional well-being, and about sexual dysfunction.

- Age-fifty transition. This period normally lasts from age fifty to fifty-five. We begin to accept ourselves with all our strengths and weaknesses. Survivors of the midlife crisis often find the age-fifty transition the happiest and most rewarding period of their lives. There is a greater tolerance and acceptance in relationships with spouses and lovers. The rewards of close relationships are felt more keenly. For those who did not resolve the midlife crisis, however, the age-fifty transition can be a time of crisis; despair and failure are felt with greater intensity. Levinson suggests that it is not possible to get through middle adulthood without having at least a moderate crisis in either the midlife transition or the age-fifty transition.[18]

- Late-adult transition. This period occurs between ages sixty and sixty-five, and it prepares us for the era to come. We focus on the immutable process of aging and make important decisions about how we will live the rest of our lives. It is a period of significant development and represents a major turning point in the life cycle.

If we look at the period of our lives that we call middle age—beginning at about age thirty-five and going on until we come to terms with ourselves—it is a peak time in our careers. These are the years when experience and maturity make possible a full flowering of achievement. For those in the ranks of editors, middle age represents the years when they discover how much they can achieve, how high they can go. If the reality is that they have reached their zenith, it also can be a time of crisis.[19]

The newspaper business has changed so that the average age when men and women can think of becoming an editor is decreasing. The stereotype of the fifty-five-year-old, silver-haired city editor has given way to a new pattern in which journalists in their late twenties are rising to important positions of command. This increases the competitive pace. The age span between the first newspaper job and the prospect of becoming an editor has narrowed. And as the pressures for achievement increase, the pain of defeat becomes more devastating.

As we look at the management pyramid in the newsroom, there is only one top job, a few at the next level, and a few more at the level below that. As the choices are made to fill those vacancies, many men and women who yearned to be selected experience defeat. No matter how well they appear to take it, these individuals suffer setbacks that are threatening and stressful.

It is particularly painful to be disappointed at middle age and to discover that the system that selects leaders no longer has as much regard for age or seniority. Compounding such disappointment is the growing awareness of declining physical capacities. Thus, an assistant managing editor, upon learning that he or she will not achieve the goal of becoming managing editor, may experience a mixture of feelings. It may occur to the assistant managing editor that the current position will be the height of his or her attainment, that what was sought was only partly won. There may be anger, both toward one's self for failing to achieve the goal of becoming managing editor and toward the organization that demanded the sacrifices along the way and then awarded the plum to someone else. Even for the successful middle-aged editor, there is the bittersweet recognition that one can no longer have youth and achievement at the same time.

The higher the stakes and the more intense the competition, the greater the motivation to hold one's place and the more threatening young rivals become. Yet, for the editor moving along in middle age, there is the conflicting need to prepare rivals to succeed him or her and ultimately to give way to them.[20] These situations contribute to the commonplace crisis that occurs in middle age.

Typically, those who are middle-aged and in middle management will feel a sense of discontent if they look ahead and see no opportunities for promotion, if they think that they are not consulted, or if they don't know what is going on.

Stressors

The third factor in determining stress reactions, stressors are the situations that occur in our lives that are perceived as being stressful. For example, each of the items on the Holmes-Rahe scale is a stressor.

In the APME stress questionnaire, a broad range of situations was listed and editors were asked whether any of them occur in their jobs and private lives. Specifically, editors were requested to point out which stressors made them feel annoyed, frustrated, concerned, depressed, guilty, angry, or fearful. For editors who may be vulnerable for physical or emotional reasons, these stressors can increase the likelihood of illness.

Following are situations in which some editors acknowledged feeling negative stress:

- The expectations of my staff and the demands of my boss often conflict.
- My job involves implementing decisions with which I disagree.
- I receive assignments without sufficient people and resources to carry them out.
- The newspaper does not back up its commitment to journalistic excellence with the resources necessary to carry out that commitment.
- My boss yields to influential pressure from outside the newsroom, which sometimes results in decisions that compromise my news judgment.
- My journalistic values are compromised by decisions that reflect only the economic interests of the newspaper.
- I am not satisfied that my newspaper is as good as it should be.

- Mistakes in the paper contribute to public distrust of the press.
- Unimportant tasks take up my time; as a result, I am not able to concentrate on the important tasks.
- It is difficult to stay on top of my responsibilities as an editor.
- My job involves being faced with criticism of my newspaper or my staff from readers and news sources.
- I am interrupted by phone calls and by unscheduled visits from staffers, news sources, and readers.

We can see in these stressors some of the classic situations underlying frustration for editors: role ambiguity, lack of control or authority, role conflict, poor management, too much work, responsibility for people and for the image of the newspaper, and company politics.

Balancing the Elements of Stress

The sets of circles in figure 14.4 illustrate how the three elements of stress—environment, vulnerability, and stressors—interact.

In the first example, environment, vulnerability, and stressors—each represented by a circle—are under control. The editor is satisfied with the job, has a comfortable relationship with the boss, is proud of the newspaper, and has a good home life. The environment is supportive and under control. The editor is sound physically and emotionally, and thus not vulnerable. The stressors the editor experiences—pressure of deadlines, deciding how to play the news, feeling a sense of urgency about the work, being visible and under pressure to produce good newspapers, dealing with problems of accuracy—tend to be stimulating and challenging. As a result, these stressors are not harmful.

Let us imagine, however, that in the last year, the editor has been promoted, has stopped smoking, took out a big mortgage to pay for a new house, and has a child starting college. The editor is forty-five years old and was told recently that he has

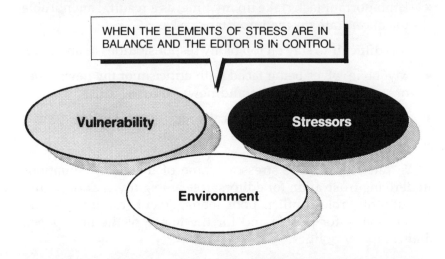
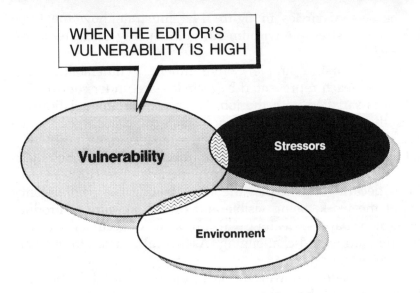

Fig. 14.4

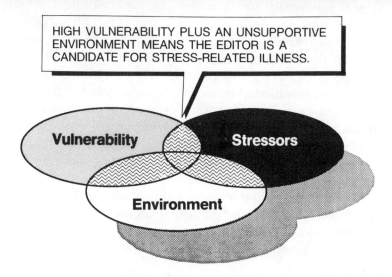

Fig. 14.4, continued

slightly elevated blood pressure. Just last month, the editor's mother died and left him a large estate. Suddenly, the editor's vulnerability is high. In the second example, the circle representing vulnerability is enlarged and begins to overlap the circles representing environment and stressors. At this point, the editor has a slightly higher risk of harm from additional stress.

In addition, the editor has been told to cut the newshole and freeze newsroom hiring. The publisher has required the editor to abide by decisions that were in conflict with the editor's own strongly held principles. The editor's environment is no longer as supportive. The new demands for cutbacks and the publisher's "meddling" are negative stressors. The circle representing stressors begins to grow. Taken together, the increased vulnerability, less supportive environment, and negative stressors—shown by the overlapping circles in the third example—make the editor a prime candidate for stress-related illness.

SOURCES OF STRESS AT WORK

Work is inherently stressful. A wide variety of jobs is found to produce tension, pressure, and strain. Journalists think of their work as being particularly stressful, but so do people in many other lines of work. In a study for the National Institute for Occupational Safety and Health, 130 occupations were surveyed. Those identified as being most susceptible to occupational stress were manager, secretary, foreman, waitress/waiter, office manager, inspector, and clinical lab technician. The low-stress jobs were farm laborer, maid, craft worker, stock handler, heavy-equipment operator, college professor, and personnel worker.[21]

In a study of executive stress for the American Management Associations, 2,659 top- and middle-level managers were asked to identify causes of stress among a variety of possible sources. The managers agreed on four leading causes:[22]

1. Excessive workload and unrealistic deadlines.
2. Disparity between the executives' goals and levels of achievement.
3. The company's "political" climate.
4. Lack of feedback on job performance.

Clearly, the stressful situations that occurred most often and with the most intensity involved work demands and time pressures. Among middle-level managers, a common sore spot was lack of decision-making authority commensurate with their responsibilities.

Fig. 14.5

CLOSE-UP

Darrell Sifford, a columnist for the *Philadelphia Inquirer,* was recalling in a magazine piece the kind of pressure he encountered as executive editor of the *Charlotte News:*

The message that blurted from the police radio monitor was partly garbled, but the urgency of the voice was unmistakable:

"I think we got one down . . . and it don't look good!"

It was 12:30 P.M., twenty minutes before deadline, and we had what we sensed was a major catastrophe—a downed jetliner, with a possible heavy loss of life.

I checked with the managing editor and the city editor. Then I called the composing room and the press room: "We've got to hold."

In less than a minute, the circulation director called: "What do you mean—we got to hold? Dammit, I want those papers off on time! They can watch it on television."

The telephone rang again. It was a reporter at the airport: "It's really bad. Good God. I've never seen anything like it."

The composing room foreman called: "I need some copy. I can't set it if I don't have it."

The press room foreman wanted to know when he could expect the last page. The circulation director called back to make sure that I fully understood what he had said.

The managing editor asked simply: "What do you want me to do?"

Yes, that's pressure . . .

Source: Darrell Sifford, "Take 2 Aspirin and Call Me," *Quote Unquote—The Editor's Magazine,* May–June 1983, 47.

In 1979, the Associated Press Managing Editors Association sponsored a survey of newspaper editors and their spouses. The 650 editors and spouses who responded identified the following situations as being particularly stressful for newspaper editors:[23]

- Time. The constant pressure of deadlines keeps the clock always in mind.

- Always being responsible. Carrying the responsibility for every line in the newspaper means that the editor may never be able to feel completely "free," even though he or she is physically away from the office.

- Striving for excellence. The pressures that editors put on themselves are stressful—pressures that reflect the editor's ideals and standards, pressures that come from following the instinct to push for the next challenge.

- Rarely being satisfied. Editors are their own worst critics.

- Accuracy. In the minds of readers, the credibility of newspapers is closely linked with accuracy. The editor is aware that the newspaper is being read in homes throughout the community where any errors are visible for all to see. Accuracy is seen as a measure of the integrity of the newspaper and its staff.

- Managing people. This is an "executive stress," recognizing that newspaper people are a different breed who are creative, independent, and sometimes difficult to control.
- Leadership. Having the title and the authority means that the editor may be viewed by the staff with mixed feelings. Moreover, once at the top, the editor finds that it is more difficult for staffers to share information and be direct with him or her. They tend to assume the editor knows what they want.
- Confrontation. Dealing in a direct way with problems may cause anger among individuals or groups in the newsroom.

Fig. 14.6

CLOSE-UP

As more and more newspapers switch from an evening to a morning publishing cycle, more and more newspaper journalists are working at night.

For some, working nights is attractive. There is usually more freedom from close supervision and office intrigues. The working atmosphere is casual. There is less traffic to and from work. Many A.M. staffers think they have more elbow room working at night. And for many, there is premium pay for working nights.

But night work has its own stresses, particularly for those who are being introduced to an after-dark life-style.

Poor sleep can result from a change in the body's natural twenty-four–hour rhythm and from noise and interruptions while trying to sleep during the day. Loss of sleep leads to increased fatigue, gastrointestinal complaints, and inefficiency. Increased divorce rates and excessive drinking are commonly associated with night work.

Source: Adapted from "The Lonely World of Night Work," *Fortune,* 15 December 1980, 108–14.

The Editor's View of Stress

How a newspaper editor looks at stress can determine whether the effect is positive or negative. The benefits of healthy tension in the newsroom are several. It can speed development in the sense of learning and understanding. It can stimulate imagination and performance. It can spur the individual to be vigilant and to engage in self-examination and self-appraisal—qualities in an editor that can energize the entire staff.[24]

Following are factors that influence the editor's view of stress:[25]

- Perception. The way we see events, and not the events themselves, can create stress. Situations that are seen as highly stressful for some may have no effect on others. For example, in the 1983 APME survey, 80 percent of the newspaper editors said that working under the pressure of deadlines was stimulating and challenging or something they had learned to handle. But 3 percent of the editors said deadline pressure made them frustrated or angry or fearful.

- Commitment. A deep commitment to the ideals of journalism or to the goals of an individual newspaper lessen the tendency of newspaper editors to feel high levels of stress. In the 1983 APME survey, 88 percent of the editors said they were "highly committed" to their jobs.

- Challenge. Editors who are challenged, interested, and stimulated by their jobs are less likely to experience stress. Editors who think that their abilities are not being used well are more likely to suffer ill effects from stress. However, editors who may be challenged but who also report being overwhelmed by the volume and complexity of their work—and who work long hours and experience unrelieved stress as a result—risk physical or emotional damage.

- Control. Feelings of being in control of the job and of having sufficient authority and resources to fulfill responsibilities are important reinforcements that lead to a positive reaction to stress. Editors who report a lack of authority or an uncertainty about their range of command are more inclined to say that they are distressed about their jobs.

- The nature of stress. Editors reported that the more important the situation, the stronger the response to stress. The loss of a job, for instance, carries long-term consequences and creates stress that is more deeply felt than that resulting from getting beat on a story.

- Frequency and duration of stress. The human body acts like a spring, bouncing back after being under stress. However, if the pressure happens too often or lasts too long, the body will begin to fail, much as a spring loses its elasticity. Whether or not illness results from stress is influenced by whether there is time to relax between periods of heavy stress. Unless the body can rebuild its reserves of energy and emotional balance, it cannot continue to work free from harm. Stress that is unrelieved leads to burnout.

- Simultaneous stress. There is a cumulative effect when several sources of stress are at work at once. A series of disagreements with the publisher and a need to cut the newsroom budget and discipline a staffer, plus a serious problem at home—all coming one on top of another—increase the risk of illness.

- Change. Change is a major source of stress. When combined with the stress of life's routines, change can increase vulnerability to physical or emotional illness. An editor who, in the period of one year, changes jobs, separates from his or her spouse, inherits money from the estate of a parent, and sends the youngest child to college has experienced four major changes. While these events are both happy and sad, it is the combined effect of the changes that can put the editor at risk.

- Familiar stress. Situations that are familiar and that we have learned to cope with tend to be less stressful than an unexpected challenge or an event that causes anxiety based on earlier failure. For example, because they are familiar to editors, daily deadlines tend to be less stressful than the unexpected failure of the electronic editing system.

- Physical and psychological makeup. Stress can cause physical and psychological reactions. High blood pressure, heart disease, ulcers, and stroke are conditions that can result from stress. Research shows that people who are physically fit are less likely to suffer symptoms of stress-related illness than people who are in poor physical condition.

  Psychological reactions to stress spring from our unconscious and are the result of personality, attitudes, and self-image. Editors in the 1983 APME study seemed less likely to bear the scars of stress if they saw themselves in a positive light, if they had a sense of humor, if they thought they were competent and capable, and if they thought they were responsible for their lives.

- Values. When personal values and job values are in harmony, there is less risk of damage from stress. When personal and job values conflict, there is greater potential for health problems.

Fig. 14.7

CLOSE-UP

The sources of organizational stress can be quite varied and sometimes difficult to identify. Following is a group of the most common stressors that can lead to problems for the individual and the company:

Stressor	Corrective Action
Job misfit	Relocation or transfer. Training to build specific skills. Education to increase aptitude and ability.
Role conflict	Communication to give the staffer a clear picture of the company's conception of his or her role. Training to build skills for fulfilling that role.
Role ambiguity	Communication to explain the nature of the job and the company's expectations of the staffer.
Role overload	Training to build skills to overcome incompetence. Education to develop time management programs to deal with time pressure.

Fig. 14.7, continued

Stressor	Corrective Action
Fear	Training to help develop skills and build confidence. Counseling to help the staffer understand and deal constructively with underlying fears.
Working conditions	Counseling to help the individual deal with behavioral problems such as feelings of isolation. Communication to help staffer understand justification for work processes and how he or she fits into those processes.
Relationships	Training in teambuilding. Counseling to deal with personality conflicts and social isolation. Improve communication to help supervisors and subordinates relate more effectively to each other.
Alienation	Counseling to help staffer deal constructively with his or her feelings. Communication to provide ways for participation and involvement.

Source: Charles R. Stoner and Fred L. Fry, "Developing a Corporate Policy for Managing Stress," *Personnel*, May–June 1983, 73.

STRESS AND TECHNOLOGY

In recent years, the newspaper business has gone through intense changes. The process of producing newspapers has been altered dramatically. We have gone from an era of manual typewriters, editing by pencil, and setting stories by Linotype machines to an era of electronics and computers. In many ways, our newspapers are better. Stories can be prepared for publication faster and with fewer typos. In the bargain, the editor has assumed more responsibilities. The editor has taken from the composing room the responsibility for typesetting and proofing reading. Electronic editing systems, the emphasis on color, graphics and packaging, and the advent of pagination mean that editors have had to change their thinking about how they handle and present the news.

In addition to learning new tasks, the editor has the added responsibility for helping plan and select new editing systems and for training and guiding the staff in new ways of getting out the paper. The demands of the new equipment and the feeling of being tied to a computer terminal have given rise to a new layer of stresses for the editor and the staff. The demand for computer literacy means that top editors suffer from the same anxieties and fears about computerization as do reporters and copy editors.

Staffers are quick to notice how drastically the computer changes their jobs. The stress this causes is further aggravated by the reality of introducing a new system in the newsroom. The newspaper still has to get out every day, so there can be no letup in productivity while the staff learns and adapts to the new system. Additionally, editors have a limited idea of how to manage the introduction of computer technology. They tend to become so caught up in the promise of the speed, power, and flexibility of the system that they forget how much change individual staffers are confronting.

In many situations, the way staffers are taught to interact with the computer virtually guarantees what has come to be called *technostress*. Some key points that can help reduce this kind of stress are worth noting:

- Staffers should participate in deciding how the new system will be designed and used.
- Computers should be introduced with appropriate notice and preparation, including plans for training.
- The training schedule should acknowledge the fact that all employees are not capable of learning to use new technologies at the same rate.
- Workloads cannot be maintained at traditional levels while people attempt to master new tasks and procedures.
- Computers cannot solve such problems as labor tension, poor morale, or falling productivity.

These were lessons drawn from the first experiences of introducing computers into newsrooms during the late 1970s and early 1980s. They can apply to the new round of training that will accompany pagination and second-generation editing systems.

Once a system is introduced, the process of adaptation begins in earnest, and with it come several potential sources of stress.[26]

Higher mental workloads force workers to pay close attention to immediate jobs and overlook creative alternatives. This is particularly crucial in working with news copy. It is the likely result when staffers are not comfortable or confident in working at the "tube" or when the complexity of codes and editing commands creates mental overload and fatigue.

The rapid, instant access of the computer distorts the staffer's own sense of time. Studies have shown that any computer response time longer than one and a half seconds leaves the user impatient. As deadline approaches, more staffers attempt to use the computer to scroll through news budgets and to hyphenate and justify copy. When the response time slows, experienced users are stressed by the computer's apparent slowness. They tap their fingers on the desk, shuffle papers, and take deep breaths—acts that reflect the stress of waiting.

Another source of stress is that the system seems to have distant, centralized, and unyielding control over our jobs. The computer is programmed with precise rules as to who is allowed access to which files and who can monitor whose work. Passwords are assigned and special access codes distributed among top editors. Productivity is governed by the health of the computer. If the computer is slow or if it crashes at a crucial moment, the speed of our work is taken from our control. We become more and more dependent on the machine. We tend to blame the computer for some of our problems.

Closely related to the question of control is the frustration that is bred of computer malfunction. The reality of the computer's capability often is unequal to the expectation it kindles. The newsroom front-end system is introduced with glowing assurances that it will make our jobs easier. What we hadn't counted on were the frustrations that accompany computer malfunctions—a crash or a system that operates at half-speed. Frustration over its fallibility doesn't reach full force until age causes the system to demonstrate a maddening capacity for crankiness and undependability.

The computer in the newsroom is not a labor-saving device. Newsroom layoffs are not a natural consequence of the addition of front-end systems. The process of preparing the news report still remains highly labor-intensive. In fact, in many cases, even more staffers are needed because the use of computers has shifted to the newsroom many responsibilities formerly performed by the production department.

Because computers will play an increasingly dominant role in the processing of news, publishers and top editors must guard against pushing into the background the needs and the frustrations of the people using the new technology. Sound policies must include good communication, staff participation in selection and training, a willingness to invest in equipment that is reliable, efficient, and easy to use, an understanding of the limits of the technology, a thoughtful redefinition of jobs, the development of a genuine learning environment for new equipment, a transition phase that reflects a concern for those using the equipment, a program that challenges individuals to push for excellence, and a concern for the well-being of the staff.

Fig. 14.8

CLOSE-UP

Typically, reporters and editors point to each other as major sources of job-related stress. In the following passages, Ken Tucker, a popular-music critic for the *Philadelphia Inquirer*, and Linda Hasert, the newspaper's popular-arts editor, explore the origins of such stress.

Editor-Induced Stress: A Reporter's View

Many people think that only bad writers need editors. People who work for newspapers, however, know that the only writer who doesn't need an editor is dead.

In an ideal world, editors help writers achieve that balance between clarity and style that constitutes good newspaper prose. In the real world, writers think that editors exist primarily to screw up their copy.

As a writer, I admit that we can be paranoid about this—I know of one writer who chose to have his piece killed before he'd allow an editor to modify one sentence in a two thousand–word feature. On the

Fig. 14.8, continued

other hand, perhaps that's not paranoia at all; maybe it's just self-respect and an honest disagreement with an editor that the piece needed the slightest bit of tinkering.

Which leads me to the first sort of editor who inflicts intense stress upon a writer: the Slasher, whose compulsion it is to change copy for the sake of changing it—to demonstrate that an editing job has occurred. Writers come to recognize a Slasher very quickly, and many take defensive measures to avoid the Slasher's rapier-pencil . . .

Another stress-inducing sort of editor might be called the Condescending Co-Conspirator. The CCC's favorite sentence, uttered seconds before some amusing detail or enriching wordplay is excised from the text, is, "I know what you're saying here, but our readers will never understand what you're getting at." This attitude—phrased in such a way as to make the writer a partner in condescension: We're smart, but they're all TV animals out there—can escalate to alarming proportions . . .

If a writer begins to think his or her editor will go only for the most obvious stories, the temptation is to grind out the obvious stories, with self-contempt the principal sort of stress induced . . .

Most writers will tell you, though, that the only thing worse than waiting for an editor to get to your story is the editing session itself. Some editors use the editing session to discourse at length upon the subject you've just let blood over for a week. These editors are frequently the ones who decided how the story should come out the day it was assigned . . .

If any complaint about editors from writers is universal, though, it's the poignant one about editors' commonplace urge to expunge from stories any trace of the writer's thoughts, personality, or sense of humor. In this, however, editors have those damnable word processors on their side. Why do you think they call it a "Delete Character" key?

Ken Tucker

Reporter-Induced Stress: An Editor's View

Newsroom stress is probably inevitable. Deadlines, long hours, tender egos—no wonder reporters and editors drive each other crazy. Sometimes, though, the sheer perversity and variety of reporters' stress-inducing techniques make an editor wonder if there's not a conspiracy.

Some are as simple as a single sentence. "Oh, I thought the

copydesk would check that," or "I had so much good stuff I just thought I'd write it all and let you cut . . ."

Mostly, however, stress is caused less by the actual problems than by their unrelenting predictability. I gird myself for the telephone call to the arrogant columnist whose next-day piece I'm killing because it's too much like a recent feature . . . An important story is assigned to a general assignment reporter whose capabilities fall far short of the task and who I know I'll have to rewrite . . . A reporter wants to know why Photo decided hers was the story it didn't have time to shoot . . . A slow writer brings the copydesk, operations desk, and composing room down on my head . . . Crucial clips are lost . . . Turf wars ignite . . . Stories with holes come back too late to fix . . . These are the things of which editors' stress is made.

To fight stress, we bitch among ourselves about this reporter and that reporter. We develop a stance—part compromise, part bravado, part authority, part bluff. When it all works together with a sense of humor, confrontation is defused and we congratulate ourselves on our "management style." Some souls, myself included, even enjoy the process.

However, when things go less smoothly or the problems seem endless, instinct gets temporarily hijacked by stress. Should I turn up the compromise and turn down the bluff? Resort to authority and cease all negotiations? And, hey, what happened to the fun I used to have in this job?

Linda Hasert

Source: Ken Tucker, "Editor-Induced Stress: A Reporter's View," and Linda Hasert, "Reporter-Induced Stress: An Editor's View," *The Bulletin of the American Society of Newspaper Editors*, December–January 1983, 6–7.

WORKAHOLICS

Excessive devotion to work and an aggressive, achievement-oriented, frequently hostile, and chronically rushed approach to living define the characteristics of the workaholic. When workaholics get into management—and they often do—the behavior patterns they bring to their management role can be divisive. The workaholic's style and the obligations of a manager are a contradiction in terms. A manager sets priorities, delegates responsibility, is patient in gaining the commitment of others and in negotiating objectives, and establishes reasonable deadlines. The workaholic manager is determined to do everything. He or she has little patience with others, works unending hours to make up for others' perceived lack of commitment, sets arbitrary deadlines, and applies pressure to assure compliance. The eighteen-hour-a-day workaholic boss breeds stress. Others are expected to follow the pattern of arriving early and leaving late, but because most people can't do this, resentment, antagonism, and stress result.[27]

Companies need dedicated employees who put in long hours and love attention to detail; however, this may not necessarily be the person to be in charge. High energy should not be confused with brainpower. Workaholics are best kept out of management roles. Their energy should be focused on tasks, not the management of people.

It is important to note that there is a clear difference between the editor who is in charge of starting a new section and works long hours to get the project rolling, and the hard-charging editor who always seems to be in the office. The entrepreneurial editor knows that after a brief, intensive focus on a new project, it is possible to step back and turn the finished product over to others on the staff.

STRESS AND THE FAMILY

Among the challenges to success and happiness among newspaper editors, none is so difficult and so potentially pervasive in its effects as that of maintaining a proper balance between life at the office and life at home. For the editor, the spouse, and the children, the challenges can include questions of dual careers, obligations of parenthood, the impact of promotion (particularly if it means the family has to move), the handling of success, the trauma of job loss, or the failure to achieve.

The editor and the spouse as a couple are an important part of the editor's environment. Their relationship can have an effect on how the editor deals with stress. When the editor and the spouse agree about the importance of the editor's career—and the responsibility and commitment that go with it—an environment exists that is supportive and helps the editor cope with pressure.

The personal cost of reaching one's career goal can be tremendous. In a 1980 survey conducted by the *Wall Street Journal* and the Gallup Organization, 780 chief executives were surveyed about their work attitudes, the kinds of personal sacrifices they made to get to the top, and the ways they cope with job pressures. Eighty percent said that their family lives had suffered because of their careers. The regret mentioned most frequently was too little time spent with family. Some spoke of failing to provide enough parental guidance and feeling guilty about neglect. Others said they missed getting to see their children grow up. More than one in ten said that serious family problems had resulted from their work situations. It was clear to these executives that the long hours and regular absences had put a strain on their families.[28]

A 1983 study of elementary and secondary public school teachers in Michigan measured the effect of work overload and interrole conflict. The researchers, Denise M. Rousseau of the Kellogg School of Management at Northwestern University and Robert A. Cooke of the College of Business Administration at the University of Illinois at Chicago, found the effect of family roles on physical strain among working people to be complex.[29]

Their study of teachers suggests that the demands of family roles affect strain in three ways. First, as individuals marry and have children, they are subject to increased conflict as their nonwork roles change and become increasingly demanding. Second, in the role of parent and spouse, the individual has a lower tolerance for high demands at work. Third, there is a positive effect of the family roles. Once the individual has adjusted to the demands of the job and the expectations of the family, the presence of spouse and children is related to physical well-being.

Rousseau and Cooke suggest that the support to be found in the family can be particularly meaningful when the working spouse holds nontraditional sex-role attitudes and is willing to share child-rearing and housework activities.

The 1983 survey for the Associated Press Managing Editors Association isolated the two central conflicts in the personal lives of editors: family obligations and competing commitments with their spouses.[30]

Responses to questions about family life indicated that editors think that the demands of their jobs interfere with their personal lives. They feel it to a much greater degree than do their spouses, and their reaction is likely to be stressful. The responses suggested that editors are more likely than their spouses to feel uneasy about the family situation and to show a stronger awareness of the effects their jobs can have on family life. Spouses, on the other hand, were more inclined to say that they can handle the disruptions in family life that are caused by the editor's job.

The two-paycheck family is now the rule rather than the exception. And whether the second spouse works merely for additional income or whether it is a two-career family, the question of competing commitments is significant. In the APME survey, the following basic themes were identified as resulting from the spouse's experiences and attitudes as a member of a newspaper family:

- Spouses said that the demands of the editor's job conflicted with the demands of the spouse's outside interests. In cases where there was conflict, spouses said that their commitments must yield to those of the editor.

- Spouses said that the demands of their commitments were equal to the editor's demands and that it was difficult for them to meet both the commitment to a job and the obligations as an editor's spouse.

- Despite their outside commitments, spouses carry the primary responsibility for the operation of the home—a responsibility that editors do not share because of the demands of their job.

- Editors said that the spouse's commitments outside the home were as important to the spouse as the editor's commitment was to the editor, and that this created conflict.

- Spouses said that their activities outside the home were limited by the editor's job. They are more likely to be annoyed by this than editors think they are.

The traditional support system is rapidly disappearing. The family may no longer have a primary focus on the success of the editor's work—an ethic that demanded major family sacrifices and routine adjustments in schedules in the interest of the editor's career.

The APME research shows that while the spouse has been able to deal more effectively with the nontraditional family, the editor is having trouble with it. Male editors tend to feel guilty when their jobs take them away from family obligations because their traditional role has been to be in control and to be the guardian.

In the APME survey, the percentage of single editors was too small to provide a valid cross-sample. The absence of a support system traditionally represented by the family, however, is an important factor in assessing the single editor's vulnerability to stress. Many single editors have friends and other relationships that provide appreciation and support as well as conflicting demands.

Fig. 14.9

CLOSE-UP

Barrie Greiff, who developed and taught a course at the Harvard Business School called "The Executive Family," says the irony is that "businessmen look very seriously at what they do—at work. They plan their production, marketing, and financial strategies . . . But when it comes to their marriage, they assume that 'things will work out'—as though some miraculous god will descend from the heavens and take care of them.

"I don't expect executives to give up one aspect of their lives for another. But what they can do is try to develop some perspective in terms of what's happening to them, to look and think about the implications of various critical crossroads in their lives. It's putting the same degree of planning or organization or strategy to work in their

Fig. 14.9, continued

home lives that they do in their business lives. The people who do that have a better handle on what's going to happen to them, so they have fewer problems. It's technically known as primary prevention—trying to resolve problems before they occur."

Greiff suggests the following checklist for survival in an executive family:

- Maintain open communication with one another. Supply booster shots of recognition, love, and concern.
- Recognize that terms such as *success, goals,* and *objectives* are fluid ideas subject to change at different stages of life.
- Try to recognize early problems: Don't play the ostrich game.
- Be adaptable: Life is full of compromise.
- Learn to use your third eye and third ear: If your intuitive sense tells you something's important, pay attention—and follow up.
- Learn to explore inner space: Know yourself, be aware of the effects of loss and gain, intimacy and distance in your life.
- Develop a sense of "unlonely aloneness": Learn to enjoy spending time by yourself doing the things you enjoy.
- Develop multiple satellites, things outside your direct sphere of work that give you pleasure—and options.
- Learn to anticipate inevitable life crises and conflicts. Don't always ask, "Why me?" One can always ask, "Why not?"
- In your personal auditing, ask yourself, "Who am I? What do I want? Is it realistic? Am I achieving it? If not, why not?"
- Develop refueling techniques: A successful marriage isn't a chance phenomenon—it's an active process characterized by creative reciprocity.

Source: James Morgan, "The Executive Family," *TWA Ambassador,* November 1975, 16–18.

THE EFFECTS OF STRESS

The effects of stress can cover a broad range of reactions—excitement, satisfaction, challenge, frustration, distress, and illness. The idea that stress is not always harmful has been the focus of much of the stress research of the 1970s and early 1980s. The decision makers—the men and women in high-powered, high-pressure executive positions considered to be highly susceptible to stress because of the nature of their work—turn out not to be as threatened by stress as it once was thought.

In a 1977 study of 259 executives at Illinois Bell Telephone Company, Suzanne Kobasa, a psychologist at the University of Chicago, found that certain people seemed to be particularly able to handle stress. She described them as "hardy" people and said that their health was not affected no matter how intense their job pressures or how ominous their family history. Kobasa concluded that if people felt a sense of purpose, showed a strong commitment to their work, viewed change as a challenge and not a threat, and thought that they were in control of their lives, they were not adversely affected by stress.[31]

Results of the 1983 APME survey showed that situations described by editors in the 1979 survey as highly stressful were not always harmfully so. Such newspaper stresses as the urgency of handling the news, working under deadlines, and managing people were stimulating and challenging to most editors.

The majority of newspaper editors in the 1983 survey reported few ill effects from the stress of their jobs. They seemed to fit the contemporary definition of managers who were in good health, who worked in a supportive environment, and who thrived on the challenges of their jobs. However, a strong minority of the editors—39 percent—said they had experienced a health problem they thought was the result of job-related stress. Another 10 percent said they had experienced a health problem but were unsure whether it was related to the stress of the job. High blood pressure was the effect mentioned most often by editors who thought that there was a strong relationship between stress and their health problems. Next came ulcers, heart disease, arthritis, alcoholism, asthma, cancer, drug abuse, and stroke.

In addition, many other editors reported an inability to sleep, feelings of constant fatigue, heartburn, muscular soreness, and frequent headaches, and they said they were drinking or smoking more. All of these are early signs that warn us our defense against stress is wearing down.

Are these numbers significant? Is it alarming that 39 percent of the 544 editors responding to this survey said that their health problems resulted from job stress? The answers are limited. There is no research from other industries against which to measure the responses of newspaper editors. But it is clear that the situations editors said caused them negative stress are the types of situations that scientists have connected with illness.

Paul Rosch of the American Institute of Stress, who helped evaluate the results of the APME research, said that for editors, harmfully stressful situations seemed to fall into two categories: (1) those in which editors said they no longer had the control they once had or thought they should have, and (2) situations in which editors could not take pride in what they were doing.

Lack of control is well established as a major contributor to harmful stress. The question of control and the question of pride seem to be bound up in such issues as whether there is too much attention to the bottom line, whether publishers and newspaper companies are committed to the same standards of journalistic excellence that editors say they are committed to, and as a result, concern about whether the newspapers are good enough.

Both the healthy editors and those with stress-related illness reported that, for them, the most intense levels of stress came from dealing with the boss and the company. The editors reported more serious stress when they thought the company placed greater emphasis on profit than on quality and quantity of the news report, when the company allowed business judgments to interfere with treatment of the news, or when the company did not provide sufficient resources to match its public commitment to excellence.

The editors who reported stress-related health problems were more likely to have strained relationships with the boss, to have questions about their control and authority, and to think that they are not privy to important information and decision making. These concerns seemed to reflect the changing nature of newspaper management, in which the editor is expected to carry on in the best traditions of journalistic excellence but also is expected to share the responsibility for the newspaper as a "profit center."

Editors with health problems also found the time pressures of the job to be more intense, frequent, and annoying. They reported stressful reactions to unimportant tasks taking time from important tasks, pressure to work every minute with little time to relax, interruptions from phone calls and unscheduled visitors, and paperwork and administrative details that take up too much time.

Both groups of editors reported that managing people is among the least stressful elements of their jobs as newspaper editors. Differences that set them apart are that editors with health problems were more likely to say that the staff does not share their journalistic values and that the staff does not understand the pressures on the editor. In addition, editors with health problems were more inclined to think that the expectations of the publisher and the staff were in conflict and that it was not possible to be completely open and candid with the staff.

Fig. 14.10

CLOSE-UP

How do individual editors react to stress? Following are the coping mechanisms of seven editors:

I try to avoid stress by being as open as I can. But sometimes openness fails, and the situation is not under my control. If I feel under stress, I go for a walk through the downtown area or a park within a block of our building.

William Hilliard
Executive Editor
The Oregonian

The most damaging stress results from minor problems. I try to avoid as many of these as possible by controlling those items I can control. For instance, I delegate decisions on minor issues. I give myself plenty of time to handle tasks—plenty of time to go to the airport—so I won't wind up pressured at the last minute. It is important to keep my sense of humor along with my ability to laugh at myself. Stress is contagious, spreading to those you work with, so

Fig. 14.10, continued

relaxation is important. For me, this can be anything from golf to handball to novels.

> Ralph Looney
> Editor
> *Rocky Mountain News*

After a week of angry readers' calls, budget memos from the publisher, computer-system crashes, and complaints from the staff about newshole, nothing helps ease stress like attacking a tree with a chain saw. I work out my chain-saw aggression on a small farm that I bought after moving to Iowa. The farm is my escape, where, depending on my psychic needs at the time, I can sit by a pond and listen to the frogs croak, or feverishly assault an innocent oak or hickory with the saw . . . There is no telephone and no television, and, more important, no newspaper at the farm. There are no deadlines when you are sitting on the grass, under a walnut tree, listening to the woodpecker hammer on a hollow branch. I smoke a pipe, drink a beer, and watch the swallows fly in and out of the barn. The farm is a burial ground for stress.

> James P. Gannon
> Editor
> *Des Moines Register*

I get up every day at 5:15 A.M. and vomit. Then, most mornings, I play squash. After that, I go to work. And work. On really bad days I put on my two-feather headdress.

> Donald H. Forst
> Editor
> *Boston Herald*

Get angry—or vent my anxiety in some way, even crying sometimes. Or play tennis. Or have a long talk. Or go sailing. Or go skiing. Or take a long walk. Then, try to focus on the exact problems, decide which problems I can do something about and which I can't, forget about what I have no control over, make a list of what steps I'm going to take to solve the problems I do control—then take the steps.

> Nancy Woodhull
> Senior Editor
> *USA TODAY*

I take a lot of aspirin. But that's not a method of handling stress I recommend. I would be better off if I jumped up and down, pounded the desk and shouted. But I don't. I present what I hope is a placid countenance and try to help reason prevail. The result: tension, headache, aspirin. When the aspirin doesn't work, I go sailing.

> Waldo Profitt
> Editorial Director
> *Sarasota Herald-Tribune*

I once asked an old-time city editor how he handled the pressure without getting ulcers. "I don't get ulcers," he bellowed. "I give 'em." I can't recommend that technique. But after experience in three of the nation's most competitive markets—Philadelphia, Dallas, and Denver—I do have this suggestion to override stress: planning.

> Will Jarrett
> Executive Editor
> *Dallas Times-Herald*

Source: "How Seven Editors React to Stress," *The Bulletin of the American Society of Newspaper Editors*, December–January 1983, 16–17.

Burnout

Burnout results from unrelieved stress. During World War II, the military called it battle fatigue. That was the devastating effect of exhaustion and a sense of futility experienced by soldiers who were in combat for long periods of time or by bomber crews who flew daily missions without relief.

Managers who work under severe pressure in people-oriented jobs for long periods of time with little support and limited gains are prime candidates for burnout. Burnout is likely to result from situations that:[32]

- Are repetitive or prolonged.
- Engender enormous burdens on the managers.
- Promise great success but make attaining it nearly impossible.

- Expose managers to risk of attack for doing their jobs, without providing a way for them to fight back.
- Arouse deep emotions—sorrow, fear, despair, compassion, helplessness, pity, and rage.
- Exploit managers but provide them little to show for having been victimized.
- Arouse a painful, inescapable sense of inadequacy or guilt.
- Leave managers feeling that no one knows, let alone cares about, what price they are paying, what contribution or sacrifice they are making, or what punishment they are absorbing.
- Cause managers to raise the question "What for?"—as if they'd lost sight of their purpose for living.

After people have expended a great deal of effort—intense to the point of exhaustion and often without visible results—a special phenomenon occurs: They feel angry, helpless, trapped, and depleted. They are burned out. This experience is more intense than what is ordinarily referred to as stress. The major defining characteristic of burnout is that people can't or won't do again what they have been doing.

Herbert J. Freudenberger, a New York psychoanalyst, defined burnout after observing fatigue among mental-health workers. Freudenberger observed that burnout is followed by physiological signs, such as the inability to shake colds and frequent headaches, and such psychological symptoms as quickness to anger and a suspicious attitude about others.[33]

Christina Maslach of the University of California at Berkeley, a pioneer in research on burnout, emphasizes that burnout symptoms are frequently found among people who spend considerable time in "close encounters."[34] First-level supervisors and middle-level editors are continually working with peers and subordinates in the newsroom, suggesting that these editors, perhaps, are more vulnerable to burnout than the editor or executive editor. These supervisors and middle-level editors must cope with a variety of personalities and talents. Most frustrating are the tasks of managing the least able, the suspicious, the strong egos, the malcontents, the rivalrous, and the depressed. Continuing interaction with staffers who have these traits requires the editor to deflect their hostility, resolve conflicts, set priorities, hold the staffers to the editor's standards, and seek ways to help them become motivated.

People suffering from burnout generally demonstrate the following characteristics: chronic fatigue, anger at those making demands on them, self-criticism for putting up with the demands, cynicism, negativism, irritability, a sense of being besieged, and hair-trigger display of emotions. Other destructive types of behavior accompany these feelings: inappropriate anger at subordinates and family, withdrawal from those whose support is most needed, walling off home and work completely from each other, diffuse physical symptoms, efforts to escape the source of pressure through illness, absenteeism, drugs or alcohol, increased use of psychological escape such as meditation or biofeedback, increasing rigidity of attitude, and cold, detached, and less emphatic behavior.[35]

A twenty-year study of a group of middle managers disclosed that many of them who had few prospects of promotion were tolerating unhappy marriages, narrowing their focuses to their own jobs, and showing less consideration to other people. Despite outward sociability, they were indifferent to friendships and often were hostile. They had become rigid, had short fuses, and were distant from their children. Personality tests disclosed that these managers had a higher need to do a job well for its own sake than did most of their peers. They initially had a greater need for advancement as well, although this declined over time. They showed more motivation to dominate and lead, and less to defer to authority than other managers. While they could still do a good day's work, they could no longer invest themselves in others and in the company.[36]

The definitions of burnout among executives and managers suggest that newspaper editors who have an intense need to achieve and who don't reach their goals can become hostile to themselves and to others. They tend to limit their efforts and channel them into more defined work tasks. If, at times like these, editors do not increase their family involvement, they are especially likely to approach burnout.

The top management of newspapers can take steps to keep managers out of situations in which they are likely to burn out. The following precautions can help:[37]

- Recognize that burnout does happen.
- Recognize when people are overdoing it, when they are working excessively long hours.
- Make sure there is a systematic way of letting people know that their contributions are important.
- Encourage people to take a breather, to walk away from the desk for fifteen minutes between editions.
- Make sure that people take the vacation time they have earned.
- Help staffers establish long-term objectives and priorities.
- Provide ways in which people can express such emotions as anger, disappointment, helplessness, futility, defeat, and depression.
- Defend publicly against outside attacks on the newspaper or individual staffers.
- Provide training in management, technology, and journalistic skills to refresh and reinvigorate staffers.
- Encourage an atmosphere in which closeness and support can be cultivated between and among individuals on the staff.

MANAGING STRESS

The key to managing stress is keeping it in balance. The importance of balance was demonstrated in 1908 in experiments by Robert M. Yerkes and John D. Dodson of the Harvard Physiologic Laboratory. They showed that as stress increases, so do efficiency and performance—but only to a certain level. If stress continues to increase, performance and efficiency decrease. Yerkes and Dodson plotted their findings on a curve. Low performance at the beginning and the end of the curve represented, respectively, an absence of stress or an excess of stress. The top of the curve measured the point at which stress and energy produced peak performance. Their work became known as the *Yerkes-Dodson Law*.[38]

What can be done to reduce job-related stress? A number of answers can be suggested. Some important buffers against stress are internal. They come from inside us and represent the highly individual ways we cope with stress. Other keys to reducing stress are found in the environment around us: our company, our boss, our family, and our friends.

Individual Coping Strategies

Each of us is equipped with the ability to resist threats to our well-being. Our reactions to threatening experiences are expressed in a wide range of individual responses. The classic defense mechanisms such as repression, denial, isolation, and rationalization rely heavily on avoidance and blocking information about the threat.

We can get some insight into the extent of our coping resources by considering how people react to severe physical injury. It is thought that the coping behavior seen in response to injury helps explain how many of us react to the threat of emotional trauma, such as job-related stress.

Clinical research has concluded that many patients are remarkably resourceful in the face of a catastrophic situation. Specifically, patients who recovered from injury showed the ability to keep stress within manageable limits, to maintain a sense of personal worth, to restore relations with friends and family, to seek information that would help them understand the nature of their illness and the prospects for recovery, and to adopt a personally valued and socially acceptable life-style after maximum physical recovery has been achieved.[39]

Self-awareness is an important key to defusing stress. Each of us has an inner voice that reports silently, making us conscious of our environment and continually assessing our limits, our behavior, our ability to cope with potential problems. By consciously listening to these internal reports, we may discover that we are overreacting to a threat or that our subconscious assessment of our ability to cope is too pessimistic.

If we listen to these internal messages, we can interject a soothing thought that might ease the feeling of frustration. For example, if the mayor is tied up in a meeting and his secretary won't put your phone call through, the inner voice is likely to be talking impatiently about "those long-winded politicians" and computing how much time you have to get the story done. This is the time to tune in on those worrisome messages and say, "I don't like waiting to get a quote from the mayor, but there is nothing I can do about it so I might as well relax."

During a tense situation, talk reassuringly to yourself and praise yourself for what you accomplished rather than scold yourself for poor preparation or performance. And afterward, luxuriate in the relief that the burden has been lifted. These are steps that help you control your life rather than letting it control you.

What distinguishes the more successful copers from the less successful ones? A study by John M. Rhoads, a professor of psychiatry at Duke University School of Medicine, revealed the following clues: Long hours of work are not harmful if the work is enjoyed and provides freedom of time and judgment. The ability to postpone thinking about problems until it is time to deal with them is a striking quality found among healthy, successful executives. Strong interests outside of work and a sense of humor were regarded as crucial attributes.[40]

Other studies of executives successful in coping with stress have convinced some experts that what many such executives have in common is an awareness of the stress potential, sensitivity to their own reactions, and a capacity to find appropriate responses. They are able to decide what is worth worrying about and what is not. They share the load by effectively delegating tasks to others. They set priorities and establish goals to achieve their most important objectives. They are realistic about perfection. When the tension begins to build, they talk and blow off steam. They know when to take a break, when to withdraw from the situation for a while. When they go home, they do not take the problems of the job with them. And they engage in physical exercise as an aid in releasing tension and building health.

Professional and personal relationships may be among the most useful weapons against the stress of the job. Social support provides the additional resources and assistance that can help individuals cope with stress. An individual can draw on a good support system for information, for feedback, for help, and for empathy, care, love, and trust.

Organizational Coping Strategies

Because the editor has more control over the working environment in the newsroom than do individual subordinates or staffers, he or she has more influence on the level of stress in the newsroom. How the editor views the job and copes with stress inevitably filters throughout the newsroom. An editor who is highly stressed cannot expect the rest of the staff to be immune from the tension he or she creates. The editor also has more opportunities than others to contribute to the reduction of work-related stress.

Some important new research, however, goes beyond the obvious—that the boss has power over how one feels. The findings suggest that the boss can be a crucial defense against stress, which has strong implications for management styles. The key factor is not so much the personality of the boss as it is his or her approach to subordinates as they struggle to handle their problems.[41]

Michael Lombardo, a behavioral scientist at the Center for Creative Leadership in Greensboro, North Carolina, says that bosses most effective in helping employees cope with stress tend to use the following approaches:

- They give employees tools to solve their problems, but do not do it for them.

- They shield the staff from irrelevant problems.

- They suggest putting problems aside for a while or they ask questions that will force the staffer to think about problems in new ways.

One study emphasizes the powers of a skillful boss in protecting employees against the physical and psychological ailments associated with stress. The research, by Suzanne Kobasa and Mark Pucetti, psychologists at the University of Chicago, showed that employees who were under considerable stress as a result of widespread policy and organizational changes but who thought they had their bosses' support suffered half as much illness in a year as those who thought that their bosses were not behind them.[42]

In a study of 357 Defense Department employees at Air Force bases in the Middle West, the single problem that correlated with higher levels of cholesterol—a major risk factor in heart disease—was having a boss who was too bossy. One of the researchers, William Hendrix, a professor of management at Clemson University, said, "Such a boss is a stickler for the rules, more concerned with details like whether employees are on time than with the larger picture of how productive they are. He goes strictly by the book, not letting employees stretch the rules, even if it would mean they were more effective."[43]

In helping manage stress in the newsroom, the editor should keep firmly in mind the values and goals of the newspaper and his or her responsibilities as a top executive. In this sense, tension has implications that cannot be overlooked: Editors should acknowledge that the presence of tension in the newsroom is natural and that the difference between management values and the values of individual journalists or groups in the newsroom may contribute to the normal levels of tension.[44]

A number of management skills that have been examined in other chapters of this book are effective in reducing stress in the newsroom. Among them are:

- Regular performance appraisals that are fair, fully documented, and based on standards, and that focus only on work behavior (see Chapter 10).

Stress and Survival

- Improvement of the selection and placement process (see Chapter 15) so that candidates who are hired or promoted are able to perform the assigned tasks satisfactorily.
- Training for staffers and supervisors to improve individual skills and reduce the stress of learning a new task or assignment (see Chapter 15). The objective is to enliven and enrich the individual but not overwhelm him or her.
- Greater participation in designing management processes and in preparing special news projects (see Chapter 12). Editors who invite participation tend to be high achievers, confident in the abilities of their subordinates and not threatened if others get in the act.
- Teambuilding to establish greater trust and cohesiveness among editors (see Chapter 13). Teambuilding results in stronger support systems for individuals.
- Open communication to keep the staff informed about what is happening in the newsroom and in the newspaper company that affects their work (see Chapter 4). With greater knowledge, role ambiguity and conflict are reduced.
- Goal setting to help staffers grow in their jobs and establish objectives can increase satisfaction and commitment and, in the balance, reduce stress (see Chapters 3 and 10).
- Encourage staffers to exercise, to keep a balance in their lives, to relax, and to take scheduled days off and vacations. Regular exercise that involves at least thirty minutes of sustained effort three times a week contributes to the body's ability to combat the physical effects of stress.

SUBSTANCE ABUSE

Substance abuse in many forms is a problem in the newsroom. Alcoholism continues to be a primary concern, even though the old stereotype of the drunk reporter being propped up to write a story and then passing out on the desk is no longer in vogue. Addiction and abuse of both prescription and illegal drugs have affected life inside the newsroom as they have life in the community.

Whether the result of stress or other factors, the consequences of increased drug usage are causing employers to establish programs to help employees with drug-dependency problems. Employee-assistance programs are expected to become a standard among media companies and in other industries. The programs attempt to address two concerns among employers: First is the concern for individual employees who are suffering from drug dependency; second is the threat of liability if drug-related accidents or deaths occur in the workplace.

Editors who are faced with the dilemma of what to do when a staffer appears to have a substance-abuse problem often are unsure what steps to take. Following are some guidelines:

1. The primary focus must be on performance. If a staffer is showing symptoms, such as high absenteeism or erratic behavior, those are signals for the editor to initiate a conversation.

2. The editor is not qualified to make a diagnosis. The discussion should focus on work behavior. The editor should take special care to avoid any language or tone that would suggest the employee is being accused of drug use. And while the editor should avoid probing into the staffer's private life, it is appropriate for the staffer to be invited to talk about any outside pressures or problems that may be affecting performance.

3. If the editor suspects that there may be a drug or alcohol problem, the staffer should be asked to get medical help. A doctor can counsel the staffer, if necessary, on how and where to get assistance in treating substance abuse. The doctor also can help the editor understand what problems the staffer may be facing and what steps can be taken to begin rehabilitation.

TIME MANAGEMENT

Managing time is an essential principle in any approach to reducing stress. Good time management means analyzing what needs to be done, setting priorities, determining the best and most effective way to do the job, focusing on the most important aspects of the job, and eliminating things that waste time.

Time is irreversible and irreplaceable. It is a resource that can be invested in achievement but one that cannot be replenished. To waste time is to waste life. To master time is to make the most of life.

Time is a commodity in our lives, a preoccupation that is built into our culture and our language. Most of us wear watches. Clocks and electronic time-and-temperature signs remind us that the day is ticking away. Work in the newsroom is scheduled according to deadlines. Editors tell us that time pressures related to both their professional and personal lives are stressful. We speak of taking, losing, gaining, wasting, stealing, and killing time.

Time is an important control on our behavior and, as a result, it is a stressor that can trigger anxiety. The stress stems from feelings of too much to do, of guilt for not having accomplished more, of boredom from lack of challenge, and of anger from interminable delay. For each of us, there is a well-defined sense of urgency within which we can work effectively and gain a sense of accomplishment. Although time stress creates the same physical effects as other stressors, it has its own mental aspects. When the demands of time get out of control, we feel desperate, trapped, miserable, and helpless. Often a free-floating hostility accompanies the struggle against time.[45]

There are three kinds of management time: (1) time to accomplish tasks the boss requires, (2) time to handle requests from peers and subordinates, and (3) time to do those things the manager initiates. Tasks imposed on the editor by the boss and the staff carry penalties if they are not done. These demands can be managed, but they are not to be ignored. The manager's strategy becomes one of increasing the amount of discretionary time to do the things he or she initiates.

The "monkey-on-the-back" analogy is appropriate in underscoring the value of assigning, delegating, and controlling as part of good time management.[46] The analogy, adjusted to a newsroom setting, goes like this: The city editor walks up to the managing editor and says, "We've had another problem with

Charlie. Three more late stories and we found a major error in yesterday's page-one piece." At this point, the managing editor knows enough to get involved but not enough to make a decision. He says, "Let me think about it."

Before this exchange between the city editor and the managing editor, the monkey was on the city editor's back; afterward, it was on the managing editor's. The city editor has imposed time on the managing editor to think about a solution to the problem of a slow and inaccurate reporter. In accepting the problem, the managing editor has taken back responsibility from a subordinate and promised a progress report. And to emphasize the transfer of responsibility, the city editor will stick his head in the managing editor's office the next day and ask, "What do you think we ought to do with Charlie?"

Let's suppose that the managing editor kept the monkey on the city editor's back with a parting comment, "Send me a memo with your recommendations on what to do about Charlie." The city editor dutifully writes the memo and sends it off to the managing editor. Where is the monkey now? On the managing editor's back. And the longer the managing editor takes to consider the city editor's recommendation, the more frustrated the city editor will become.

The care and feeding of "monkeys" require that the managing editor leave with the city editor all problems and decisions that are appropriately the responsibility of the city editor. By reducing time-consuming assignments imposed by subordinates, the managing editor will increase the value of his or her own management time.

To get started in managing time, the editor should consider the "ABC" priority system. Take all of the items on the desk and make three piles. Mark one pile "A" for those things that have to be done immediately. Mark the second pile "B" for those things that are important but don't have to be done right away. Mark the third pile "C" for those things that have a low priority and can be done anytime. Get to work on the "A" pile. This will help make the best use of your time.

Getting control of time begins with organizing work and giving priorities to the most important tasks:

- Each day make a "to-do" list, starting with the items in the "A" pile.
- Block out chunks of time for major projects. Control interruptions during these critical periods by accepting no visitors and no phone calls.
- Let subordinates know there are certain times each day when you don't wish to be interrupted and certain times when anyone is welcome.
- Identify your internal prime time—when you do your clearest thinking—and allocate this time to the top priorities.
- Postpone shorter projects until you have started longer ones.
- Delegate as much as you can. Keep the monkeys on someone else's back.

CHAPTER SUMMARY

Stress is an inevitable part of the jobs of journalists. Stress takes its meaning from the pioneering work of Hans Selye, who defined stress as a "nonspecific" response of the body to any demand upon it. The demand can be sad or joyful, but the effect on the body is the same: It must adjust to a new situation.

Studies by Walter Cannon of what takes place when stress occurs led to the "flight-or-fight" explanation. Whether the stress is physical or emotional, we have three choices concerning how to respond: (1) we can fight, (2) we can flee, or (3) we can adapt.

Selye concluded that the human reaction to stress has three steps, which he called the General Adaptation Syndrome. The alarm stage is the first sign of stress. The resistance stage is when we choose to fight, flee, or adapt. The exhaustion stage is when our defenses wear away and we experience stress-related illness.

Henry Babcock identified three forms of tension caused by different situations: (1) inner conflict, such as a neurosis, (2) external factors, such as the company or the boss, and (3) tensions arising from the need to be creative.

Three basic elements determine the effect stress has on us: (1) environment, (2) vulnerability, and (3) stressors.

The environment can include how we feel about our job, relationships with boss and staff, and the authority and control we have.

Vulnerability is determined by one's personality, physical and psychological makeup, and preparation for unexpected events. Indicators that can help the editor assess his or her vulnerability to stress are life changes, which can predict stress-related illness using the Holmes-Rahe scale; personality (Type-A individuals who are aggressive and hard-driving and Type-B individuals who are low-key and relaxed); values; fears; and stages of life.

Stressors are the situations that occur in our lives that are perceived as being stressful.

When the three elements of stress—environment, vulnerability, and stressors—are in balance, we are not likely to become ill as a result of job-related stress. If the environment is less supportive or if our vulnerability increases, the elements are no longer in balance and we are candidates for stress-related illness.

The four leading causes of stress at work are: (1) excessive workload and unrealistic deadlines, (2) disparity between the executives' goals and levels of achievement, (3) the company's "political" climate, and (4) lack of feedback on job performance.

Stress can have positive or negative effects, depending on the editor's view of stress. Factors that influence how the editor looks at stress include: perception, commitment, challenge, control, the nature, frequency, and duration of the stress, physical and psychological makeup, and values.

Another source of stress at work comes from changes involving new technologies. Technostress refers to stress that results from interacting with the computer.

Workaholics are individuals who show excessive devotion to work and are aggressive and achievement-oriented, with a chronically rushed approach to living. A workaholic boss breeds stress when others are expected to follow in his or her pattern of work.

Stress affects the family when demands of the editor's job come into conflict with the demands of the family. The effects of stress can cover a broad range of reactions—excitement, satisfaction, challenge, frustration, distress, and illness. Burnout results from unrelieved stress. Victims of burnout often feel angry, helpless, trapped, and depleted.

Many important buffers against stress are internal. They represent the highly individual ways we deal with stress. Self-awareness is a key to coping with stress. Being in touch with ourselves, learning to relax and take time off, exercising regularly, developing outside activities, and having a sense of humor are all part of individual coping strategies.

The boss is an important element in helping individual employees cope with stress. Many of the traditional management skills are important in helping create a working environment that is nonstressful.

Substance abuse can be a problem in the newsroom. Editors should approach such a situation as a problem with performance and should not make personal accusations.

Managing time is an essential practice in any approach to reducing stress. Good time management means analyzing what needs to be done, setting priorities, determining the best and most efficient way to do the job, focusing on the most important aspects of the job, and eliminating things that waste time.

NOTES

1. Henry Babcock, "Talent and Tension" (Comments during a panel discussion at the Fifth Annual Human Relations Forum, sponsored by the Connecticut Mutual Life Insurance Company, 24 October 1963).
2. Robert M. Yerkes and John D. Dodson, "The Relation of Strength of Stimulus to Rapidity of Habit-Formation," *Journal of Comparative Neurology and Psychology* (1908): 459.
3. Walter B. Cannon, *Bodily Changes in Pain, Hunger, Fear, and Rage*, 2d ed. (New York: Appleton, 1929), 27.
4. Richard E. Winter, *Coping With Executive Stress* (New York: McGraw-Hill, 1983), 40–41.
5. Alan A. McLean, *Work Stress* (Reading, Mass.: Addison-Wesley, 1979), 18.
6. Robert H. Giles, *Editors and Their Families* (Rochester: Gannett Rochester Newspapers, 1979), 21.

7. Winter, *Executive Stress*, 50.
8. Thomas H. Holmes and Richard H. Rahe, "Social Readjustment Rating Scale," *Journal of Psychosomatic Research* 11 (1967): 214.
9. Winter, *Executive Stress*, 61, 64–65.
10. Meyer Friedman and Ray Rosenmann, *Type A Behavior and Your Heart* (New York: Knopf, 1974), 53–79.
11. Robert H. Giles, *Editors and Stress* (Rochester: Gannett Rochester Newspapers, 1983), 25.
12. Meyer Friedman, "Type A Behavior: A Progress Report," *The Sciences*, February 1980, 10–11, 28.
13. David C. Glass, "Stress, Competition, and Heart Attacks," *Psychology Today*, December 1976, 65–67.
14. Jane E. Brody, "Modifying Type A Behavior Reduces Heart Attacks," *New York Times*, 7 August 1984, C1.
15. Robert B. Case, Stanley S. Heller, Nan B. Case, and Arthur J. Moss, "Type A Behavior and Survival after Acute Myocardial Infarction," *New England Journal of Medicine* 312, no. 12 (21 March 1985): 737–41.
16. Giles, *Editors and Stress*, 68.
17. Daniel J. Levinson, *The Seasons of a Man's Life* (New York: Ballantine Books, 1978); and Gail Sheehy, *Passages* (New York: E. P. Dutton, 1976).
18. Levinson, *Seasons of a Man's Life*, 62.
19. Harry Levinson, "On Being a Middle-Aged Manager," *Harvard Business Review*, July–August 1969, 2–3.
20. Ibid., 6.
21. Hans Selye, *The Stress of Life* (New York: McGraw-Hill, 1956), 4–13.
22. Richard M. Steers, *Introduction to Organizational Behavior*, 2d ed. (Glenview, Ill.: Scott, Foresman, 1984), 508.
23. "How to Deal With Stress on the Job," *U.S. News & World Report*, 13 March 1978, 80–81.
24. David W. Ewing, "Tension Can Be an Asset," *Harvard Business Review*, September–October 1964, 74–75.
25. Giles, *Editors and Stress*, 9–10.
26. Craig Brod, *Technostress: The Human Cost of the Computer Revolution* (Reading, Mass.: Addison-Wesley, 1984), 42–52.
27. Jack Falvey, "The Workaholic Boss: An 18-hour-a-day Menace," *Wall Street Journal*, 10 May 1982.
28. Frank Allen, "Chief Executives Say Job Requires Many Family and Personal Sacrifices," *Wall Street Journal*, 20 August 1980.
29. Denise M. Rousseau and Robert A. Cooke, "Stress and Strain from Family Roles and Work-Role Expectations," *Journal of Applied Psychology* 69, no. 2 (1984): 252–60.
30. Giles, *Editors and Stress*, 63–65.
31. Suzanne C. Kobasa, "Stressful Life Events, Personality, and Health: An Inquiry into Hardiness," *Journal of Personality and Social Psychology* 37, no. 1 (January 1979): 3–10.

32. Harry Levinson, "When Executives Burn Out," *Harvard Business Review*, May–June 1981, 75–76.
33. Herbert J. Freudenberger, "Staff Burn-out," *Journal of Social Issues* 30, no. 1 (1974): 159.
34. Christina Maslach, "Burn-out," *Human Behavior*, September 1976, 16.
35. Levinson, "When Executives Burn Out," 76.
36. Douglas W. Bray, Richard J. Campbell, and Donald L. Grant, *Formative Years in Business* (New York: John Wiley and Sons, 1974), 93–128.
37. Herbert J. Freudenberger, "5 Ways to Short-circuit Burn-out," *Health*, April 1982, 51; and Levinson, "When Executives Burn Out," 78–81.
38. Ari Kiev and Vera Kohn, *Executive Stress: An AMA Survey Report* (New York: AMACOM, 1979), 21–23.
39. David A. Hamburg and John E. Adams, "A Perspective on Coping Behavior," *Archives of General Psychiatry* 17 (September 1967): 277–78.
40. Winter, *Executive Stress*, 173–74.
41. Daniel Goleman, "Boss Seen as Best Buffer against Stress," *New York Times*, 31 January 1984.
42. Suzanne C. Kobasa and Mark Pucetti, "Personality and Social Resources in Stress Resistance," *Journal of Personality and Social Psychology* 45, no. 4 (1983): 839–50.
43. Goleman, "Boss Seen as Best Buffer against Stress."
44. Ewing, "Tension Can Be an Asset," 76–77.
45. E. M. Gherman, "Win Your Battles with the Clock," *Nation's Business*, March 1982, 20–22.
46. William Oncken, Jr., and Donald L. Wass, "Management Time: Who's Got the Monkey?" *Harvard Business Review*, November–December 1974, 76–78.

15

Hiring, Training, and Promoting

The people who work for a newspaper are its most important resource. They represent the crucial difference between average performance and excellence. Many of the problems encountered in the management of the newsroom are "people problems" that can be traced to decisions made in hiring and in promotion. The choices of who joins the staff and who will be the editor-managers can have enormous impact on the quality of the daily news report. Complementing good selection in hiring and promotion is management's commitment to training, or teaching that sharpens individual skills, and development, the coaching that sets the foundation for future opportunity.

THE HIRING PROCESS

Hiring may be the most important function an editor performs. The editor's own success or failure will be influenced by the caliber of the newsroom staff. In preparing to fill a staff vacancy, the editor must answer several questions: What is the job that is to be filled? What is the job description? (See Chapter 11 for a detailed discussion of job descriptions.) What qualities and skills should the new staffer have? How can the best candidates for the job be recruited? The answers to these questions must relate specifically to the job, assuring that no candidates for the position will be excluded for reasons such as age, race, personality, beliefs, or attitudes.

Since the passage of the Civil Rights Act of 1964, employers have made progress toward eliminating discrimination in hiring, but it has made the process more complex and time-consuming. The editor should be familiar with federal laws that may influence how he or she carries out the hiring function. The most important of these statutes, which are more fully explained in Chapter 6, are:[1]

- Title VII of the 1964 Civil Rights Act.
- Title I of the 1968 Civil Rights Act.
- Equal Pay Act of 1963.
- Age Discrimination in Employment Act of 1967 and the amendments passed in 1975.
- Vietnam Era Veterans Readjustment Act of 1974.
- Revised Guidelines on Employee Selection of 1976, 1978, and 1979.
- Mandatory Retirement Age Act of 1978.
- Privacy Act of 1974.
- Equal Employment Opportunity Guidelines of 1981.

Research suggests that if talent of marginal quality is hired, marginal performance will result. The probability is low that poor performance due to limited talent can be improved by management techniques or development programs. In a 1975 study measuring the performance of technical professionals in an industrial laboratory, little change in performance was noted over nine years. Those who were judged to be "high" performers in the initial assessment were found to be "high" performers in the second assessment nine years later. The same results were recorded among "low" performers. There was little movement from the "low" category to the "high" category.[2]

Editors should remember that a staffer's quality of performance persists through time. Hiring a reporter with marginal skills or apparent deficiencies and hoping for improvement is an approach that has little chance of success.

The hiring process consists of seven steps: (1) recruiting, (2) measuring the candidate's qualifications, (3) interviewing, (4) the tryout, (5) testing, (6) the selection decision, and (7) orientation. Each of these steps must be accomplished successfully to assure that a newcomer to the staff is well qualified and is given an introduction to his or her job that will increase the chances of a satisfactory experience and a strong performance.

Recruiting

Recruitment is an unending task. Most newsroom staffs typically have at least one vacancy that editors are seeking to fill. Editors must discipline themselves to allow time for interviewing and coordinating the other elements of the hiring process.

In the 1920s and 1930s, editors tended to fill reporting and copy-editing positions from among those applicants who walked in the door or sent unsolicited résumés. Few of these candidates had college degrees. They could be hired cheaply and fired easily if they didn't work out. Today, editors cannot dismiss staffers indiscriminately. Good management practice and the law require editors to document poor performance and to give staffers opportunities to improve before termination can be considered. As a result, editors are examining applicants' qualifications more carefully and are making a greater effort to hire staffers who can succeed.

Editors have become more aggressive in their recruiting strategies. Some advertise job vacancies in publications such as *Editor & Publisher* or through the placement offices of journalism schools. Campus visits by recruiters seeking talent for internships as well as full-time positions are common. Many papers have established informal ties with faculty members at nearby journalism schools and liberal arts colleges. These contacts and occasional campus visits give a paper early opportunities to consider the top graduates.

Small liberal-arts colleges may not have journalism programs, but they do have talented students who work on the school paper and develop strong writing skills through English courses. These students tend to major in subjects such as history, economics, science, government, or prelaw, all of which are important to newspaper work because of the range of reporting beats today.

Fig. 15.1

CLOSE-UP

More journalism school graduates go to work for newspapers and wire services than any other media-related field. The Dow Jones Newspaper Fund charts the career choices of journalism graduates annually. In its 1985 survey, the fund reported that only 22 percent of journalism graduates were news-editorial majors. Of that group, 42.5 percent took jobs with newspapers and wire services. Of the remainder, 16 percent went to work in other media fields, 8 percent went to graduate school or found nonmedia jobs, and 8 percent were unemployed.

Source: "1985 Survey of Journalism Graduates" (Dow Jones Newspaper Fund).

Good copy editors are hard to find. The top editing students are in great demand. Enterprising editors overcome the shortage of desk candidates by looking in their own communities for teachers, free-lance writers, staffers at suburban weeklies, and people not active in the job market who have a background in writing.

Large dailies generally require daily newspaper experience—sometimes as much as five years—before they will give serious consideration to a candidate. These papers fill vacancies by hiring staffers from other newspapers or by promoting young people who have served apprenticeships as news assistants or news clerks. Summer internship programs open doors to many bright and industrious young journalists who are able to parlay summer jobs into offers of full-time work when they graduate. The bidding for prize talent is intense and competitive, resulting in increased opportunities and, in some cases, high starting salaries.

Many editors rely on their instincts and their experience to guide them in the hiring process. These customary practices alone, however, may not deliver the rate of success that every editor seeks. More effectual hiring decisions will be made if the newspaper establishes criteria to aid in recruiting and selection. What is the editor looking for in a new staffer? What should the editor expect of him or her?

Editors should look for at least six qualities when considering a job candidate:[3]

1. Capability for high technical performance. This is the sine qua non for newsroom staffers. Journalistic competence must come before all other considerations; if it is lacking, other qualities cannot compensate. For freshly minted journalism graduates, judgment of their competence must focus on the basic skills: reporting and writing or editing. For experienced journalists, a demonstration of their competence can best be found in their previous work record. For beginners and experienced journalists alike, competence is influenced by such qualities as commitment, curiosity, judgment, energy, integrity, resourcefulness, and an awareness of the news.

2. Ability to enhance the staff's performance. Does the candidate share with the editor and the staff similar moral values, work ethic, and sense of events? Will his or her goals fit with the newspaper's goals? Will the potential hire interact easily with the rest of the staff? Does the candidate offer skills or experience the staff needs? Does the chemistry seem right? Will the person be a problem? The newsroom has a broad tolerance for individuality, yet the editor should recognize when a job candidate is likely to exhibit behavior that will upset colleagues, anger news sources, or make disproportionate demands on editors' time. The tryout can be a key to recognizing whether the candidate is likely to achieve a good fit with the rest of the staff.

3. Willingness to take initiative. Newspaper work depends to a great extent on the self-direction of individual staffers. The editor needs self-starters on the staff because he or she cannot directly control the details of all of the reporting or editing in progress. The city editor's span of control may be

as few as two or three reporters or as many as one hundred, depending on the size of the newspaper. An efficient city desk depends on staffers who have the ability and the motivation to initiate work and to carry it through without the constant direction of an editor. The presence of an incompetent staffer on the desk can reduce to one the editor's span of control if the editor gives that person undue attention at the expense of others.

4. Potential for development. In assessing job candidates, it makes good sense to look for people who have the potential for growth beyond the immediate tasks for which they are being considered. Not everyone wants to be an editor or should be an editor, of course, but everyone on the staff should have the capacity for improving his or her professional skills and effectiveness. Selection of staffers with this in mind will reduce the number of occasions when the editor has to face the painful task of dealing with an employee who has reached a plateau or who has neither the ability nor the drive to move ahead.

5. Retainability. Employee turnover is expensive. In addition to losing the investment the newspaper has made in the staffer who leaves, recruiting and hiring a replacement incur extra costs—travel, lodging and meals during a tryout, moving expenses, and the time editors and staffers spend during the interviewing process. Is there such a thing as an optimum turnover rate? That depends on the quality of the staff at the time. If the staff is weak, turnover presents an opportunity to hire better-qualified replacements.

Turnover is common, no matter how good or how large the paper. The turnover rate is influenced by the transient nature of young journalists who move from paper to paper seeking broader challenges and responsibilities. Some have their sights set on working for major metropolitan papers, and they will make several moves to get to such a newspaper. Others will move because the opportunity looks richer somewhere else. Still others will leave because they don't like the life in a particular community or they don't feel good about the newspaper or they think they are not being challenged enough in their jobs.

It is difficult to predict during the job interview how long a potential hire might stay with the paper. Nevertheless, retainability is an important quality. Journalists who are willing to put down roots and make a commitment to the newspaper bring stability to the staff and a sense of community to the paper that is valued by readers and news sources.

The hiring interview can bring forth clues that might indicate the likelihood that the newspaper can retain a potential staffer. The editor can probe for a sense of whether the candidate is just looking for a job or is genuinely interested in the paper, whether geography matters, whether it is important to be close to his or her hometown, and what the candidate's longer-term ambitions are.

6. Creativity. Editors place a high premium on creativity, and they use the hiring process to seek candidates who are creative in the belief that such individuals will bring an important dimension to their newspaper. Although creativity is difficult to identify (see Chapter 9), evidence of it can be found in past performance and in any discussion in which the candidate is asked to talk about ideas.

Measuring the Candidate's Qualifications

How can the editor tell whether a candidate meets the above criteria? It is important that the hiring process include a step that will give the editor a detailed summary of a candidate's capabilities, characteristics, and experience. This information can be obtained from the application form and résumé, which should provide: (1) enough biographical information to permit the editor to decide whether the applicant meets minimum requirements for the job; (2) indicators such as references and previous experiences that may suggest whether the candidate merits serious consideration; and (3) biographical and experience data that will help assess performance on the job and the likelihood of success if hired.[4]

In addition, the editor may ask the candidate to write a professional autobiography. Such a statement offers a revealing portrait of the applicant's writing style, work and life experiences, thoughts about the future, and how the candidate thinks about himself or herself. Finally, the editor may send the candidate several issues of the newspaper and invite him or her to write a memorandum commenting on the writing, headlines, editing, story selection, and graphics.

The *reference check* is a common practice in evaluating candidates for newsroom jobs. A 1959 study of 109 applicants for professional jobs with the U.S. government found some correlation between references from supervisors or acquaintances and actual performance. The same study suggested there was no correlation between performance and recommendations from personnel officers, coworkers, and relatives.[5]

The applicant usually will be asked to list two or three references on the application form. It is natural for job candidates to list only references who will give positive information. The editor should make a thorough check of the references, including those volunteered by the candidate and others of the editor's choosing.

Editors should be careful of the traditional practice of telephoning a friend at another newspaper to get a reading on a candidate. If an unsuccessful applicant learns that an unfavorable reference was given, potential legal action may result. Yet, the spoken communication, with its pauses, inflections, and intonations, is revealing. An editor who shares a trust with a colleague at another newspaper often is willing to be candid about the performance of a former staffer. The editor describing the work of a former staffer whose performance was weak tries to balance two obligations: One is to be honest with the other editor, and the second is not to prevent the former staffer from getting another chance. In trying to strike this balance, the editor must also avoid creating a liability for the newspaper.

Invasion of privacy in seeking reference information has been the subject of court cases. Many newspaper companies, eager to avoid wrongful claims, advise managers to refer all outside inquiries about former employees to the personnel department.

Increasingly, the practice in personnel is to provide only job title and dates of employment.

Interviewing

The interview is a vital part of the hiring process. Indeed, for many, it is the primary method for evaluating candidates. Authorities on interviewing consider it to be a social situation affected by what is at stake—a job—and by the perceptions the editor and the candidate have of each other and of the task at hand. The purpose of the interview is twofold: (1) to help determine the suitability of the candidate for the job and (2) to give the job-seeker an opportunity to assess the newspaper as a place to work.

The editor should not fail to recognize that hiring is a two-way proposition. An individual's decision to accept a job represents a major change in his or her professional life and personal lifestyle. In this sense, the individual's decision to take a job can be more critical to him or her than the editor's decision to offer a job is to the newspaper.

The interview should be regarded as subjective—as an art, not a science. Because hiring decisions made by the editor are based on opinion, and opinion is subject to bias and prejudice, the interview obviously has limitations. An applicant being interviewed for a job may behave in an unnatural manner out of anxiety or out of a desire to impress the editor. Such behavior may have a disproportionate effect on the editor.

Two types of interviews are appropriate in assessing candidates for newsroom jobs: planned and patterned.[6] The *planned interview* is the one most familiar to editors and job applicants. Basically, it is a long, in-depth conversation in which the editor invites the candidate to talk freely about his or her education, experience, goals, and attitudes toward newspaper work. The discussion typically takes a number of detours that allow the editor and interviewee to talk about ideas or tell newspaper stories. The editor may probe for clues that would indicate the applicant's potential for success or failure on the job. The planned interview often is an opportunity for the editor to provide information about the newspaper, the nature of the position, pay, and advancement. It also is a good time to address expectations so that the candidate gets a realistic view of the task and of the potential for advancement. In their eagerness to impress a top candidate, editors should be careful to avoid giving an unrealistic portrayal of life in the newsroom or of the opportunities for advancement. This can result in expectations that are likely to go unfulfilled and that can quickly result in a disillusioned new staffer.

The *patterned* or *standardized interview* is based on a comprehensive questionnaire. Patterned interview forms list a number of detailed questions that seek to get at every relevant bit of information about the background, knowledge, attitudes, and motivation of the job applicant. The patterned interview is not commonly used by editors. Interviewers using the patterned form usually are well trained in interviewing techniques, which may explain why studies reveal good results with this method.

In the interview, the editor wants to help the applicant feel trusting and confident. Establishing rapport is best achieved by showing interest in the candidate and in the candidate's educational or newspaper experiences. Creating a relaxed atmosphere will help the applicant be spontaneous in his or her responses.

The editor's questions can be expressed in a directive or a nondirective style. *Directive questions* are those for which there are explicit answers. They are used to gather specific information the editor needs to evaluate the candidate. For example: "What are your impressions of our newspaper?" "Why are you interested in leaving your present job?" "What are your career goals?" "What books have you read recently?" *Nondirective questions* are more general and give the candidate some latitude in answering. They are valuable in indicating how the applicant's mind works and how he or she sorts and explains information. For example: "Tell me about your current and previous bosses." "What kind of people are they?" "Has your job performance ever been appraised?" "How were you assessed?" "Tell me about the most difficult story you've done." "What is the most satisfying part of your present job?" "What is the most frustrating part of your job?" "Describe a time when you felt ineffective and tell me why you felt that way."

The editor needs to be aware of several potential pitfalls in the job interview that can influence the selection decision:

- The halo effect (see Chapter 10). This occurs when the editor allows a single characteristic of a candidate to influence his or her overall judgment about the person. The influencing characteristic may be something the editor likes or dislikes, such as dress or personal manner.
- Failing to listen. This is a common weakness. Inexperienced interviewers tend to do most of the talking, leaving the job candidate to do the listening.
- Rejecting biases. The editor should be aware of his or her own biases and prejudices and discard them when evaluating a candidate.
- Assuming confidentiality. Hiring interviews are confidential. This is more binding on the editor than on the job applicant, largely out of concern for laws that seek to prevent discrimination in hiring. The editor should say nothing in an interview that he or she would not say to anyone else at any other time.
- Communicating feelings about the candidate. The editor may be enthusiastic about an applicant and may give the impression that the job is going to be offered to him or her. However, if a better candidate comes along later, the editor will have instilled bad feelings in the first applicant because of the unrealistic expectations that were created.
- Comparing applicants with others. Job candidates should be evaluated on their own merit and on their own performance record.
- Forming stereotypes. Editors form stereotypes of the characteristics needed for the job and apply those stereotypes in assessing applicants. The most common stereotypes are made on the basis of group membership, particularly race, sex, and age.

Fig. 15.2

CLOSE-UP

Editors can unwittingly commit a discriminatory act through thoughtless or insensitive questions during the hiring process. Numerous court decisions have drawn distinctions between acceptable and discriminatory inquiries. Following are examples of both kinds of inquiries.

	Acceptable Inquiry	*Discriminatory Inquiry*
Name	Additional information relative to change of name or use of an assumed name or nickname necessary to enable a check on applicant's work records.	The fact of a change of name or the original name of an applicant whose name has been legally changed.
Birthplace and residence	Applicant's place of residence. Length of time at applicant's current residence.	Birthplace of applicant or applicant's parents. Requirement that applicant submit birth certificate or naturalization or baptismal record.
Creed and religion	None.	Applicant's religious affiliation. Church, parish, or religious holidays observed by applicant.
Race or color	General distinguishing physical characteristics such as scars.	Applicant's race. Color of applicant's skin, eyes, hair, etc.
Photographs	None.	Photographs with application. Photographs after application but before hiring.

	Acceptable Inquiry	Discriminatory Inquiry
Age	If hired, can you furnish proof of age?	Date of birth or age of applicant except when such information is needed to avoid interference with the operation of any retirement, pension, or employee benefit program.
Education	Academic, vocational, or professional education and the public or private schools attended.	
Citizenship	Are you in the country on a visa that would not permit you to work here?	Any inquiries about whether applicant intends to become a U.S. citizen.
National origin and ancestry	None.	Applicant's lineage, ancestry, national origin, or nationality. Nationality of applicant's parents or spouse.
Language	Language applicant speaks or writes fluently.	Applicant's mother tongue. Language commonly used by applicant at home. How applicant learned to read, write, or speak a foreign language.
Relatives	Names of relatives already employed by the newspaper. Name and address of person to be notified in case accident or emergency. Name or address of any relative of applicant.	

Fig. 15.2, continued

	Acceptable Inquiry	Discriminatory Inquiry
Military experience	Military experience of applicant in U.S. armed forces. Whether applicant has received any notice to report for active duty.	Applicant's military experience in other than U.S. armed forces. National Guard or Reserve units of applicant. Draft classification or other eligibility for military service. Dates and conditions of discharge.
Organizations	Applicant's membership in any union, professional, or trade organization. Names of any service organization of which applicant is a member.	All clubs, social fraternities, societies, lodges, or organizations to which the applicant belongs other than trade, professional, or service organizations.
References	Names of people willing to provide professional or character references for applicant. Names of people who suggested applicant apply for a position with the newspaper.	The name of the applicant's pastor or religious leader.
Sex and marital status	Maiden name of applicant.	Sex of applicant. Marital status of applicant. Dependents of applicant.
Arrest record	Number and kinds of convictions for felonies.	Number and kinds of arrests.
Height	None.	Any inquiry about height of applicant, except where it is a bona fide occupational requirement.

Source: Carole A. Carmichael, "What Employers Are Allowed to Ask on Employment Application and in Interviews," *Chicago Tribune,* 3 July 1977.

A 1971 study based on interviews at thirty-three metropolitan Cincinnati firms employing one thousand or more showed that 90 percent of those hiring would offer a job to individuals on the basis of an interview, even if negative information were received from other sources.[7]

Other research suggests common tendencies and influences in the use of interviews to make hiring decisions:[6]

- Interviewers are quite consistent in the way they rate an interviewee. When reinterviewing the same person or listening to a tape recording of the original interview at a later date, their ratings are about the same.

- Structured interviews—that is, ones in which a set list of questions is used—yield fairly consistent ratings of the same individuals by different interviewers. However, if each interviewer uses a different set of questions, their ratings of the same candidates differ substantially.

- If different interviewers conduct unstructured interviews and have no prior information on the candidates, they generally come up with quite different ratings of the same interviewees. In other words, reliability among raters is low.

- Although the interview has a low validity in predicting job success, encouraging results have been obtained using the team approach. In the team method, three or four interviewers sit as a panel to interview applicants. The team method also is used when applicants are interviewed separately by a number of people who then compare judgments to arrive at a group decision.

- The attitudes and biases of interviewers heavily influence their ratings of job candidates.

- Interviewers tend to be influenced in their judgments more by unfavorable than favorable information. They tend to search for negative data. Experiments have shown that it is easier to induce shifts in ratings toward rejection than toward acceptance.

- Interviewers tend to arrive at their decisions to accept or reject a candidate fairly early in an unstructured interview.

The Tryout

The tryout is a standard part of the hiring process at many newspapers and is an opportunity to observe job candidates at work. A 1980 survey of forty-one small and mid-sized newspapers found that 39 percent of the editors use tryouts lasting a week or less in assessing job candidates. The expectations of the editors and the tasks given to applicants during tryouts varied. In some cases, the editors exposed the candidates to a rigorous workout to test their skills. Others said the candidates were expected to "help out" in the newsroom, to "do some interviews, write some obituaries, and answer the phones." Some editors asked applicants to write a critique of the newspaper or the newsroom operation. What did editors expect of applicants during a tryout? Some indicated they wanted the candidates to show "independence." One editor said applicants should "think, ask questions, and show creativity." Others were more interested in how quickly the applicant "learned our system" or "fit in." Some editors wanted to observe personal traits or get a sense of how ambitious the candidates were.[8]

In a tryout, reporting candidates are assigned stories to cover and write. Candidates for the photo staff go on picture assignments and work in the darkroom. Copy-editing applicants edit stories and write headlines. In addition, some newspapers find that giving a test to copy editors—to measure proficiency in usage, grammar, spelling, and punctuation—focuses on the candidate's skills and shows areas where help is needed.

The tryout provides a check against the quality of work an applicant presents in the clip file. The comparison indicates whether the spark in the clips is genuine or whether it might have been edited into the stories by a copy editor. A tryout at an unfamiliar paper in a new town is stressful and some allowance should be made for that. Nevertheless, a tryout will allow the editor to observe important work qualities: energy, resourcefulness, the ability to gather information, use the library and ask questions, and a facility for writing with accuracy.

Testing

The hiring process at some newspapers includes written tests. One broad definition of a *test* is a systematic procedure for comparing the behavior of two or more people.[9] Most tests used in the hiring process are objective in the sense that the candidate's score is not influenced by the opinions of those evaluating the test results. When used properly, tests can play an important role in a largely subjective process.

The field of testing for selection and promotion appears simple but is deceptively complex. Any program that attempts to evaluate aptitude, achievement, and motivation should be administered by a psychologist or someone who has been trained in the use of tests. The effective use of tests requires using the results as an adjunct to skillful interviewing. Test scores may be properly interpreted in the context of other information about the individual.[10]

Psychologists have done so much work in developing tests that the testing field has almost become their special province.[11] The following terms will help editors understand the meaning and uses of psychological tests in hiring and promoting:

Standardized test. A test for which a uniform procedure has been established to administer and score it.

Norms. A raw score has no meaning until it is compared with a reference group or a norm group. For example, the raw score of a reporter candidate will be compared to the test scores of reporters who have previously taken the test.

Reliability. A reliable test is one that yields nearly the same score when an individual takes it more than once.

Validity. This is the degree to which the test actually measures what it is intended to measure. To be valid, a test must be job-related and it must predict success on the job.

Predictive validation. A comparison of test results to determine whether the high scorers on the tests also are high achievers on the job.

Concurrent validation. The degree to which test scores relate to the performance of employees already on the payroll.

Content validation. A comparison of how well the content of the test questions relates to the subject matter being measured.

A test can be reliable and not valid; that is, a test may be good at consistently measuring some trait or behavior, but the trait or behavior may not correlate with performance required on the job. On the other hand, a valid test is, by definition, reliable.

Two types of tests most commonly given to newsroom candidates are measurement tests and psychological tests. *Measurement tests* are used for skills such as writing, editing, language knowledge, and awareness of events. For example, if the editor wants to test a reporting candidate's vocabulary, he or she uses a test with a representative set of words. Whether the test adequately measures the applicant's ability to define words depends on the number and the nature of items in the sample. If the test were composed entirely of journalistic terms, it probably would not provide a valid estimate of the candidate's vocabulary range.[12]

A *psychological test* is essentially an objective and standardized measure of a sample of behavior. These tests measure personal characteristics, such as aptitude, motivation, and achievement. For most jobs, a psychological test is helpful in hiring, job assignment, transfer, promotion, or termination.

A variety of tests is available to measure an individual's capacity to learn or do particular kinds of work. Some widely used tests have been validated for certain occupational groups, such as supervisors or managers. In cases where a newspaper company has developed a testing program, those tests are validated for specific newsroom jobs. The following general categories of tests can be used for newsroom selection and promotion:

- Aptitude tests attempt to measure intelligence, job-related intellectual aptitudes, decision-making competence, analytical thinking, mental alertness, ability to learn, judgment, and interpersonal skills.

- Achievement tests measure what an individual has learned. Specifically, an achievement battery might include measurements of one's knowledge of spelling and grammar, vocabulary, copy editing, story construction, news events, and supervisory principles and practices.

- Personality tests measure personality traits and areas of interest. Personality tests typically measure such tendencies as self-sufficiency, introversion-extroversion, dominance-submission, sociability, objectivity, emotional steadiness, assertiveness, hostility, and other factors.

  In a "projective" personality test, a candidate would be asked to project his or her own interpretations of various nonstructured situations. Both the style and content of the individual's reactions provide insight into his or her beliefs, attitudes, and behavior.

Fig. 15.3

CLOSE-UP

Knight-Ridder, Inc. has one of the most extensive psychological testing programs in the newspaper industry. Knight-Ridder executives and editors say the tests have contributed to the diversity of personality types and to the strength of the top and middle-level executives throughout Knight-Ridder newspapers.

Byron Harless, who developed the Knight-Ridder program, was introduced to the newspaper business while working as a psychologist in Tampa, Florida. In 1951, Nelson Poynter, concerned about high turnover at his newspapers, the *St. Petersburg Times* and *Evening Independent*, hired Harless to help strengthen the management selection and promotion programs.

"At the time," Harless remembers, "we had seven hundred different companies that were working with my firm, but no newspapers. I began to take the techniques that were available and applied them to the newspaper, particularly at the management end. We did job analyses, we ran everybody through a program of interviewing and testing, comparing an individual to what we were looking for and measuring his or her success against that. The tests that we use today

Fig. 15.3, continued

are, in most instances, measuring the same types of things that we were attempting to measure then."

In the 1960s, Harless was hired by Knight Newspapers and began to build the present Knight-Ridder program. He was a senior vice-president of the company for many years before retiring in 1983, and has continued to serve Knight-Ridder as a consultant.

Harless says all psychological tests have some limitations "because you can't measure all of the factors to my satisfaction that I think ought to make up a good executive. I don't think we have an instrument to measure empathy. I happen to think that empathy is one of the key factors in a good executive. We can observe it, over time, and we can determine whether an individual has it. But I don't know how to measure it and I don't know how to teach it.

"To determine whether a person really wants to manage or not is another difficult area to measure through testing. People can say, 'Yes, I want to manage. I want to get things done through people. I get a big satisfaction out of watching people improve.' But will they really do that on the job? I don't think there are very many people who can delegate a task, see others do it well, and get a gut reaction of satisfaction from it.

"We have to rely on more traditional and classic techniques—picking up clues through some of the personality evaluation measurements—to determine whether people really want to manage. Personality characteristics are still difficult to measure objectively. The reliability of the results is no better than the practitioner that's doing the assessment."

Does Knight-Ridder have a higher level of success in picking good people by using the tests than a newspaper that does not?

"I am confident we have averages well above the 95 percent success rate," says Harless. "We have employed some people who didn't perform as well on the tests. Based on their performance record and the hiring editor's satisfaction that these people had something to offer, I've encouraged the editor to hire them anyhow. Our success rate is not as high as when they meet all the criteria, but we don't lose them all, either. I don't think we need to do all the things we do just to hire an individual. But if we are going to tie in the personal development of that individual, then we need to do what we are doing, because we are really taking a career in our hands and trying to do everything we can in the future to help that person grow and develop."

Source: Byron Harless, interview with author, 13 March 1984.

The idea of using psychological tests for newsroom jobs has received limited acceptance. Development of a testing program requires a strong commitment at the top levels of the newspaper company. The individual in charge of the program should be a psychologist or a specialist in personnel management. Creating a testing program involves several steps: analyzing jobs to identify characteristics necessary for success, selecting a group of tests, administering the tests to a selected group of people, establishing criteria for job success, analyzing results, and deciding how the tests will be administered. Putting together a professionally run, valid, and reliable testing program is time-consuming and expensive.

There is a good reason for the resistance to testing programs among journalists. Byron Harless, a psychologist and the architect of Knight-Ridder's testing program, explains why editors are difficult to bring into a testing program: "They are more critical. They are more suspicious. They feel that their jobs are different, that they are unique among the line management and professional jobs in the company. I don't have any problem with that. In fact, I consider it a good challenge."[13]

Following are guidelines for the use of tests in the hiring and promoting process:[14]

- Tests should be used only as a supplement to other parts of the selection process such as interviews, assessment of previous performance, and reference checks. Even a full battery of tests will provide only a small sample of a person's total pattern of behavior.

- Tests are more accurate at predicting failures than successes.

- Tests are most useful in picking from a larger group of people a smaller number who are most likely to succeed on the job.

- To be of any value, a test must be validated in one's own organization and for the job with which it is to be used. It is necessary to validate the test before any degree of confidence can be placed in its ability to predict successful job performance.

- Test scores should not be considered precise measures of the characteristic being measured. The tests are not so accurate that a candidate with a score of 92 can be considered emphatically better qualified than another with a score of 90.

- The relationship between a test score and job success is not always linear; that is, if several applicants score well on a test, those with the very highest scores are not necessarily a better choice than those scoring slightly lower.

The single most important recent development in employment testing has been the involvement of the federal government in defining adequate testing procedures as a consequence of the Civil Rights Act of 1964. The goal of that law was to end the economic isolation of women and minorities by prohibiting discrimination in employment practices on the basis of race, color, religion, sex, or ethnic origin. The imposition of guidelines and the hundreds of testing cases that have been litigated attest to the vigor of the government's interest in employee selection procedures as a major focus of the drive to eliminate discrimination in U.S. society.

The salient fact about the use of ability tests is that blacks, Hispanics, and native Americans do not, as a group, score as well as white applicants as a group. Basically, a test is considered to be biased if it excludes more than 20 percent of a minority group protected by the Equal Employment Opportunity Commission. When candidates are ranked according to test scores and when test results are a determinant in employment decisions, a comparatively large percentage of blacks and Hispanics are screened out.

As long as minority groups continue to have a relatively high proportion of less-educated and more-disadvantaged members than the general population, test scores will reflect this. Even highly valid tests will have an adverse impact. It is important to remember, however, in making the leap from test results to job performance, that making a prediction of job success is a matter of probabilities; any individual might prove the prediction wrong. Guidelines for Employee Selection Procedures, issued by the EEOC in 1970, set demanding standards for the evidence needed to demonstrate that a test is valid. A major point is that an organization must justify the use of any assessment procedure that has an adverse effect on the hiring or promotion of minority workers. The guidelines emphasize that a test should be validated for each minority group with which it is used.[15]

The Selection Decision

This is the time to compile and evaluate what has been learned about each candidate as a result of reference checks, interviews, and tests, and to read clip files and consider the work done during the tryout. As the editors assess the candidates, they are looking for the signs of a winner, for the traits that are linked to success. Their decision to select one candidate over the others may rest on such inner qualities as a positive attitude, determination, mature behavior, strong motivation, aptitude, and intelligence. The top editor will discuss with his or her key associates the results of each step of the hiring process, along with impressions about the candidates. Out of this review may come the decision to offer the job to one of the applicants.

Involving editors and other staffers in the interviews, giving the candidate a good workout, and making a thorough check of past performance will lessen the possibility of hiring someone who happened to make a good first impression but who wasn't qualified.

The terms of the offer and the timing are influenced by competitive factors and by prevailing wage levels paid by the newspaper. The hiring offer should be made in writing. It should contain all pertinent information, such as starting date, amount of pay, vacations, hospitalization, and other benefits, as well as a description of the new staffer's duties and responsibilities. An offer is not an employment contract. It is simply a written statement of what the paper will deliver and what the individual will deliver. It is best to review hiring notes with the legal or personnel department prior to preparing the hiring offer.

Orientation

The socialization of newcomers into the newsroom is a process that requires the attention of the editor. Typically, new staffers enter the newsroom alone, where they encounter an organization that has its own systems, traditions, and pace of activity. The individuals they meet are established insiders. For some newcomers, the experience can be overwhelming.

Initially, socialization will result in changes in the newcomer as he or she adjusts to the newsroom environment and learns the practices and procedures of the newspaper. The new staffer will become part of a formal work group (see Chapter 2), such as the city desk. He or she will also connect with one or more informal groups in the newsroom.

Two important goals for the newspaper during the new staffer's first days on the job are: (1) to give the newcomer a warm welcome so that he or she will feel comfortable as soon as possible, and (2) to provide information about the newspaper's practices, policies, and resources.

Orientation often begins with the personnel department, where paperwork to put the new employee on the payroll is handled and where details of benefits, savings or stock plans, and payroll deductions are explained. Some newspapers give a new staffer copies of the employee handbook, information sheets, the ethics code, performance-appraisal forms, deadlines, and statements of the newspaper's operation and philosophy. The new staffer needs to know how he or she fits into the newsroom organization and such mundane details as where the restrooms and snack and drink machines are located. When appropriate, maps and other information about the city and assistance in finding housing are offered.

One of the most far-reaching purposes of an orientation is to explain expectations—what is expected of the new staffer, what he or she can expect on the job, and what it takes to get ahead. This will temper any unrealistic impressions the candidate may have picked up during the interview and tryout.

In the flush of being recruited for a job, a candidate may embellish impressions beyond what was actually said by an interviewer. The editor may paint a bright picture of life in the newsroom, and in talking about the candidate's goals, the editor may emphasize opportunities for advancement. The point is that strong performers get ahead, but the candidate often misses that important link between performance and promotion. This misunderstanding can lead to an unrealistic expectation of how quickly the new staffer will move along. An explanation of how performance will be assessed, how raises are earned, and what the general pattern of progression has been in the newsroom will clarify the avenues of opportunity. Even though the newspaper may be a good place to work and the opportunities abundant, a new employee whose expectations are unrealistically high may be disappointed. If the new staffer is allowed to begin work with unrealistic expectations of what lies ahead, then the seeds of disillusionment and potential turnover have been sown.

Following are eight steps that should be included in a new employee orientation program:[16]

1. Introduction to the newspaper. Introductions are simply a matter of explaining what the newspaper is, where it has been, and where it is going. The key is to make the new staffer feel good about the company and to begin to share in feeling a part of the company.

2. Review of policy and practice. This will vary from newspaper to newspaper, but it must include information about performance standards, performance appraisals, probationary periods, and ethics codes.

3. Review of benefits and services. The idea is to communicate what is provided and at what expense: health and life insurance, holidays, leaves of absence, educational reimbursement, sick pay, security, pensions, car-use policy, mileage, and out-of-town travel reimbursement. Additionally, services that the staffer might not think of as benefits should be explained: food service, medical care, credit union, discounted classified ads, ID cards, telephone system, parking, and social or recreational services.

4. Benefit-plan enrollment. Benefit forms should be explained so that the newcomer understands what options are available. The employee should be encouraged to discuss benefit-plan options with his or her spouse before making a commitment.

5. Completion of employment documents. These include payroll withholding, emergency information, employment agreements, equal employment opportunity data, and other relevant material.

6. Review of the newspaper's expectations. This discussion, generally with an editor, covers the new staffer's responsibilities, including details of the assignment, relationships with supervisors, schedules, motivation, and commitment.

7. Setting of employee expectations. What can the new staffer expect if he or she meets the newspaper's standards? Details should be provided on training and development, scheduled pay reviews, working conditions, opportunity for advancement, and counseling.

8. Introductions. The new staffer should meet fellow workers, get a tour of the newspaper plant, and be introduced to the job. A good way to let the staff know that a new hire has come aboard is to post a note and his or her photograph on the bulletin board.

THE PERSONNEL DEPARTMENT

It is uncommon for the news department and the personnel department to seek each other's cooperation. The perception among editors typically is that personnel directors don't understand news people and are not qualified to assist in selection or promotion. Personnel directors, on the other hand, tend to see editors as being careless about personnel management practices and reluctant to seek assistance from the personnel department.

At newspapers where this adversarial relationship is giving way to cooperation, editors are discovering that the personnel department can assist them in a number of ways. Pat Renfroe, manager of personnel relations for the American Newspaper Publishers Association, suggests three areas in which news and personnel can work together:[17]

1. Screening job applicants. The personnel department can assist editors by screening either the job applicants or their

résumés. Editors concerned that the personnel department might miss the really talented reporters should understand that the personnel department can eliminate the people who lack the basic skills or experiences expressed in an editor's job requisition or job description. The personnel department also can give the candidates an explanation of benefits, medical coverage, moving costs that the company might pay, and working conditions.

At the start of the hiring process, the editor should spend some time explaining to the personnel director his or her special needs and the way he or she likes to manage. Once the initial screening is done, the responsibility for the interviewing becomes the editor's. No personnel director wants to make the final hiring decision for any manager. The idea is to save the editor time initially, allowing him or her to see the best candidates and to make the final hiring decision.

2. Reference checks. Editors should use the personnel department to conduct reference checks. Personnel departments know how important these checks are and can do them thoroughly and legally. If particular information is needed, make sure the person doing the reference check knows that.

Editors have all sorts of acquaintances and, hence, preferences on the best people to talk with. It may help editors feel more comfortable relinquishing this task if they review with the personnel staff those questions usually asked by editors in a reference check and the reasons for them. That way, the editor will have all the information he or she needs for a wise and long-term hiring decision.

3. Conducting a legal interview. Don't put the newspaper in jeopardy. If the editor is not certain of everything that should be known to conduct an interview legally, a personnel professional can help. For instance, does the editor know enough about Title VII of the Civil Rights Act of 1964 and the Age Discrimination in Employment Act to avoid asking—directly or indirectly—questions that would make the newspaper vulnerable? How about others on the staff?

The personnel department can also collaborate in other areas: performance appraisals and the documentation needed before firing, for example.

TRAINING

No matter how successful the hiring and orientation of new staffers, little is gained without a positive climate for learning in the newsroom. This is particularly true for newcomers who are in entry-level jobs or who have one or two years' daily newspaper experience.

Training is the building of skills and knowledge a staffer needs to improve performance in his or her job. Training is different from *development*, which is preparing a staffer for a job at a higher level. The link between training and development is that the staffer who improves skills and grows in his or her current position becomes a prime candidate for development programs that prepare individuals for larger responsibilities.

In a newsroom where the editors have established a good training climate, the following qualities generally are apparent:[18]

- Staffers are accepted for what they are. Effective training uses people's natural skills, abilities, and aptitudes in developing them to fit the needs of the newsroom organization.

- The editor-trainer is seen as a helper, not an evaluator. The best trainers are those who can help people learn in a supportive manner. Judgment about competence can inhibit the learning process. Many editors have difficulty being good trainers because their roles require them to evaluate performance as well.

- Mistakes are accepted as natural. Part of the learning process is making mistakes. If mistakes are punished or ridiculed, progress will be slower and the training will become drudgery. Risk taking is part of creativity. Fear of punishment when new approaches don't work stifles fresh thinking.

- Employees are encouraged to learn and develop. Without a strong, positive signal from the editors about learning, staffers will think the newspaper cares little about their personal advancement and growth. Some will remain in dead-end jobs and blame the newspaper for it. Others will seek new jobs.

- Training is part of the newsroom routine. The newspaper may offer specific training programs, such as writing seminars, from time to time, but the development of individual staffers is a daily responsibility for the editors.

Understanding a staffer's ability to improve on the job will be helped by recalling Edwin A. Locke's theory of goal setting (see Chapter 3). Locke identified a relationship between an individual's intentions or goals and subsequent behavior. Satisfaction with job and supervisor is linked to work performance. The supervisor can enhance satisfaction by helping the staffer pursue his or her goals. Training as a path to goal achievement is one kind of satisfier the supervisor can make available to the employee.

Fig. 15.4

CLOSE-UP

Roy Peter Clark, former writing coach for the *St. Petersburg Times* and now associate director of the Poynter Institute in St. Petersburg, talks of the "collaborative relationship" between editor and reporter as being at the heart of the newsroom teaching process.

Clark's convictions about how good writing is developed are based on what he has learned in the classroom as well as the newsroom. "What teachers do to students' writing is that they give assignments and they correct mistakes. The paper comes back filled with red ink. They are never asked to do anything else. There is no contact. There is no dialogue. There is no conferencing. The extension goes from the classroom to the newsroom. And editors wonder why people never grow or why people keep making the same mistakes.

"A reporter for the *Washington Post* told me the thing that she loved most about Shelby Coffey, the paper's managing editor, was that they had a terrific relationship and it was based on the fact that she would often hand in a flawed story. And she knew it was flawed. And she knew that he knew it was going to be flawed, too. But he had enough confidence in her that if there was something wrong with the story, she could fix it. She said that was the center of their relationship, part of collaborative editing."

Clark talks about how editors can leverage their time so that in a few

Fig. 15.4, continued

minutes they can get an important point across to a reporter. "I've got a teacher who teaches writing every day. I work with her. She teaches eighth grade. And she has 170 students. And she has them write every day. The question is: How does she manage it? She's learned from conferencing. She's learned how to conduct a two-minute conference, which helps the student take the next step in the story. But then, she doesn't spend her time correcting all those mistakes. She assumes that once she has identified the problem in a story, it is the writer's responsibility to change it.

"We have to depend on newspapers to be like teaching hospitals, given the way the newspaper business has changed and given the fact that journalism education is so different from legal education or medical education. We can't expect people to come into the newsroom knowing everything they need to know. That's why I believe so strongly in professional education. I think it is at the heart of how newspapers can improve themselves."

Source: Roy Peter Clark, interview with author, 20 January 1984.

Training is based upon the learning process. The principles associated with learning have been scientifically developed, and training in the newsroom should be based on these principles:[19]

- Hands-on experience is the most effective way to teach newsroom skills. Group discussions, reading books and articles, and watching others are useful in the learning process, but actual improvement in skills comes through experience. Editors should combine coaching of writing or reporting techniques with opportunities for the staffer to practice.

- Learning should occur in small bites. An editor helping a new staffer with story organization can break the learning process into many parts: writing leads and transitions, quoting sources, recognizing important story elements, selecting the appropriate words, eliminating irrelevant material, and selecting the right style for content, tone, and mood.

- Learning should have targets. Training goals should be challenging but not too difficult. Breaking the process into small parts will permit mastery of individual objectives within reasonable time frames. Providing feedback increases the value of reaching goals.

- Positive reinforcement is important. The editor should adopt a coaching style that is as positive and encouraging as possible. The editor's role is to help. Mistakes are normal. Encouragement makes the training a positive experience.
- Learning is influenced by expectations. The editor should explain clearly why new skills are important, how they will relate to the staffer's performance evaluation, and whether they can lead to larger opportunities.

Effective training can help the editor manage his or her own time. Staffers who continue to deliver copy that is too long or too late or incomplete command disproportionate amounts of the editor's time simply to clean up the stories for publication. Training staffers to correct those shortcomings eventually will free the editor for other important tasks.

How long should it take a staffer to learn a specific skill? That depends on the individual. No standards exist for training time in newsroom skills, but editors should keep in mind the two principles of the human *learning curve:* (1) the more complex the job, the longer the learning curve, and (2) positive reinforcement is needed more frequently at the beginning of the training to help the staffer overcome feelings of insecurity and frustration.

Although the editor's role as a trainer should emphasize coaching rather than evaluating, it is useful at the start of training for the editor to initiate a thorough assessment of the skills that need to be learned. The editor may ask the staffer for a written self-evaluation in which the staffer would suggest areas for improvement and outline ideas and goals for the training. The editor should evaluate the staffer's skill levels and discuss the details of the training program.

Some common errors in training staffers include expecting too much too quickly, failure to recognize individual differences, punishing those who don't learn quickly, calling attention to mistakes in a way that can be observed by staffers who have mastered the tasks, and failure to provide follow-up training.

Fig. 15.5

CLOSE-UP

Some of the most difficult training challenges involve the transition from reporter to assistant city editor. Experience on the reporting staff does little to prepare one for the tasks of being an editor.

New assistant city editors struggle with the question of how much or how little editing they should do. Some editors think they should leave their "stamp" on everything that crosses their desk. They fiddle with leads and organization. They pepper the reporter with questions. Often this results in a story that grows to an unrealistic length as the reporter attempts to answer the questions, only to have the story kicked back to the reporter for shortening. Other new assistant city editors rewrite story after story, robbing the reporter of his or her own voice without adding anything to the story.

New editors, unsure of their authority or insecure personally, may defer too much to the reporter's judgment and the reporter's writing, making changes hestitatingly or only when compelled to. Other assistant city editors are blind to the need to correct stories. They approach their role as expediters rather than as potential readers.

New editors also struggle with their style of telling the reporter that the story needs work. How should the changes be made? Some editors can't resist the impulse to do it themselves. They think this will show the reporter how it should have been done. Others return the story to the reporter, knowing that the reporter will learn more by doing.

The training process for a reporter who has demonstrated the ability and desire to become a supervising editor should begin on the copy desk. On the copy desk, the reporter will learn about style and about the production side of the newsroom. More importantly, it is on the copy desk that the reporter can make the transition from a writer of news stories to an editor of news stories. There the reporter will discover the indispensable quality of a good editor: the willingness to act on his or her own judgment about stories. If this judgment is sound, the transition to city desk supervisor can be made without great difficulty.

Source: Lawrence K. Beaupre, executive editor of the Westchester Rockland Newspapers, correspondence with author, 10 January 1985.

MENTORS

The vocabulary of mentoring is revealing: *coach, guide, supporter, educator, godfather, champion, role model, guardian angel;* and *protégé, successor, heir apparent, fair-haired boy, clone, crown prince, crown princess.* The words suggest not only the nature of the relationship but also the potential problems. Mentoring is a classic example of individual development that takes place outside the normal chain of command in the newsroom. At its best, it is spontaneous, informal, and personal.

An editor's initial judgment of a person is crucial. Prime candidates usually have demonstrated a commitment to the newspaper, strong performance, a willingness to learn, a tendency to be challenging but not argumentative, and have set high expectations for themselves.[20]

Fig. 15.6

CLOSE-UP

Howell Raines, deputy Washington editor of the *New York Times*, wrote about his mentor/protégé relationship with Richebourg Gaillard McWilliams, a teacher of literature and composition at Birmingham-Southern College:

"He influenced me more than any man I have known other than my own father. He helped shape my choice of careers and the standards of professional performance and personal honor by which I judge people to this day. In short, he was my mentor, and since his death in February [1986], I have been reflecting on the union of spirit that exists between mentor and protégé. A young man cannot will a relationship with a mentor. It must emerge from the flow of two lives, and it must have the reciprocity of a good romance. The adulation of the younger man must be received with a sheltering affection that, in time, ripens into mature respect between equals. Carried to full term, it is a bond less profound but more complex and subtle than that between father and son, a kinship cemented by choice rather than biology. There will be no one else like Richebourg McWilliams in my life, nor would I want there to be."

Source: Howell Raines, "A Mentor's Presence," *New York Times Magazine,* 20 July 1986, 46.

Mentoring works well only when there is mutual respect and an honest exchange of information. A mentor and a protégé are something like a parent and a child. The parent attempts to teach the child suitable behavior that will enable him or her to get ahead in the world. The child will try to develop an individual personality and every so often will feel the need to strike out on his or her own. And so it is with a mentor and a protégé. The mentor will encourage the development of an individual style and will not be disappointed if it is different from his or her own style. A protégé will test how far he or she can go and what the limits are.

When the mentor is not the protégé's immediate supervisor, conflicts can arise. If the managing editor is mentor to an assistant city editor, for example, the managing editor must be alert to the possibility that the assistant city editor might try to use the relationship to gain an advantage over his or her supervisor, the city editor. In this situation, the city editor might think that his or her authority and control are being undermined. Moreover, the managing editor should avoid making demands on the assistant city editor that conflict with the demands of the city editor. The managing editor must make clear to the protégé that his or her role as mentor is to counsel and advise and not to second-guess or overrule the city editor.

There are two points to consider when the mentor is the protégé's immediate supervisor, as, for example, when the managing editor acts as mentor to the city editor. First is the risk of creating resentment among other editors who hold the same rank as city editor, such as features editor, news editor, or sports editor. Second is that the managing editor's responsibility for evaluating the city editor's performance and setting his or her salary may make it difficult to establish the closeness a mentor-protégé relationship requires.[21]

While mentor-protégé relationships are common among men, they are of special interest to women and racial minorities who recognize them as a way to learn and grow that does not depend on the male-dominated structure of the newsroom. Getting ahead depends on ability and performance, of course, but it also is a political process, and having a mentor can be useful to individuals who may not have easy access to the normal newsroom networks.

As mentors and protégés, men and women often do not anticipate the chemistry that results from the of sharing ideas or the same professional interests. Body language and eye contact during the courting stage in a romantic relationship are similar to the body language observed between people who are stimulated by an idea. When a man and a woman relate to each other in a way that the mind remembers as being sexually oriented, it is normal for observers in the newsroom to suspect that the relationship has a romantic connotation. For some, this may be the easiest way to explain another's success.

Rumors and innuendo can be minimized if protégés and mentors in cross-gender relationships are careful to keep their work strictly on a business level. The editor's choice of a protégé who is clearly outstanding also will diminish the tendency of others to perceive ugly overtones.

Another source of resentment can be the impression that a staffer has been "chosen" as an heir apparent and that there is no need for that individual to continue to perform at a high level or for others on the staff to aspire to the position for which the protégé appears to have been selected. The "crown-prince (or crown-princess) syndrome" is best managed when the editor insists that the basis for continued counsel and assistance to the protégé is strong performance on the job.

Any mentoring relationship carries the risk that, over time, a protégé may advance beyond the editor. This turn of events can be disconcerting, and its possibilities should be considered by the editor before any mentor-protégé relationship is initiated. The editor's self-concept and an honest appraisal of his or her own promotability will influence how such a promotion of a protégé might be accepted. It is a high compliment to a mentor for the newspaper organization to recognize a protégé by promoting him or her to increasingly challenging positions. But is that enough balm for a bruised ego?

What happens if, after time, the relationship doesn't work, if the mentor is disappointed in the growth of the protégé and concludes that, in spite of the careful consideration given to the selection, it was a poor choice? If the editor must end the relationship, the most graceful and helpful way is to act quickly by explaining the reasons to the protégé.

Fig. 15.7

CLOSE-UP

Looking back over their formative years as journalists, many successful reporters and editors recognize individuals who made important contributions to their growth. As a young staffer working assignments in Albany, Washington, and Saigon for the *New York Times*, R. W. Apple, Jr. learned from some of the newspaper's most distinguished and well-known correspondents and editors:

"There were many along the way who helped me. Charlie Mohr very much taught me my career as a foreign correspondent. Harrison Salisbury taught me my trade as a national correspondent. They were mentors of mine, as was Scotty Reston, who was kind of a father to us all, in a lot of ways.

"The characteristic common to them is very obvious, perhaps ridiculously obvious. Every single one of them either was or had been a world-class reporter. Harrison was superb, a very different kind of reporter. Scotty, midwestern, Presbyterian, moralistic to his core, a very intuitive reporter and writer, not cerebral at all. Salisbury was equally midwestern, but ascetic and very intellectual.

"While Scotty was warm and loving, Harrison was always a burr, always saying to you, when he was the national editor, 'I am going to give you this assignment, even though you are not up to it.' Charlie Mohr was always a colleague in my case, always leading by example, always willing to do twice as much work as you did.

"Another quality all of them had—and I think this is quite important—all of them were willing to take time with you, a quality that I see passing out of the business to an astonishing degree. I wonder about a lot of my colleagues now. How do they think they got where they are, that they just learned it by themselves? I don't find many people having much time for youngsters."

Source: R. W. Apple, Jr., interview with author, June 1984.

SELECTING AND DEVELOPING EDITORS

Promotion possibilities in the newsroom are limited in the sense that there are few top jobs to go around, yet the demand is great for journalists who want to manage others and who have the talent for it. Norman Isaacs, former chairman of the National News Council and former executive editor of the *Courier-Journal* and *Louisville Times*, says that choosing newsroom leaders is "journalism's biggest problem: How deep and careful is the checking on those selected to move into the pipeline that so often leads to directing editors? . . . I keep restudying the problem because everything in journalism depends on its leaders."[22]

The idea of the newspaper editor as a buttoned-down corporate manager is repugnant to many editors. They continue to see themselves as shirt-sleeve editors with a passion for news. They relish the independence their position gives them and they resist taking on the responsibilities of a manager.

Changes in the newspaper business since the 1960s have placed new demands on editors, and more changes in the years ahead will place a premium on men and women who can be both talented editors and sophisticated managers. Increasingly, they will have to be involved in profit planning, marketing strategies, career development, and staff assessment, as well as the decisions of how to play the news.

The terms *management development* and *succession planning* are not synonymous, but they are related because management development is most often the major focus of a succession plan. A succession plan involves identifying candidates for promotion and establishing that the candidates are prepared to step in when needed. As individual newspapers and newspaper companies grow and mature, they face an increased need for a more systematic process of defining future management requirements, identifying candidates to fill those roles, and matching the two.

A 1981 survey by the American Newspaper Publishers Association found that of 529 newspapers responding, 26.8 percent said they had a formal management-development program that systematically identified management personnel and provided training and growth opportunities for them.[23]

Implicit in a commitment to develop newsroom managers is a high degree of support from the senior management of the company. Training, educational experiences, short-term assignments, and assessment of talent are part of the company's investment in management development.

Beyond the interest of senior management in a systematic development program, editors at every level of the newsroom can list reasons for having a successor in mind. An editor is more promotable if a competent replacement is ready to move in. Identifying and developing a successor does not mean the editor is ordaining an heir; rather, it is simply the best way of insuring that the work will go on uninterrupted.

Development for middle-level editors can be accomplished informally as the editor explains the special demands of his or her job, delegates a few responsibilities, and shares knowledge about budgeting, communications, dealing with the boss, giving performance appraisals, and making decisions about news content or staff.

One of the keys to management development is the individual's development as a person. The aim is to enable an individual to develop his or her strengths to the fullest extent and to find personal achievement. No one can motivate an individual toward self-development; that motivation must come from within.

The starting point for management development is an assessment of what the individual does well, what he or she can do well, and what limitations need to be overcome. Such an appraisal should be a joint effort, involving both the individual and his or her manager.[24]

An editor preparing a development plan for a subordinate would begin by looking at how the individual is performing in his or her current position. The editor should compare the results actually attained with those that should have been attained. If a significant difference can be seen between the expectations and the actual performance, that difference should be considered a training need. Any developmental plan should be delayed until the individual is fully competent in his or her current job. The editor should be prepared to discuss what may have prevented the subordinate from meeting the standards; for example, if the subordinate has problems with delegation, the editor can describe situations in which the subordinate performed tasks that should have been delegated to others.

If the subordinate is meeting the standards in his or her job, the first step in building a development plan is to decide what the subordinate needs to know or do to prepare for higher level managerial positions; for example, what learning and what experiences are necessary to prepare the subordinate to succeed the editor?

In putting together a development plan, the editor should decide what he or she can do to help prepare the subordinate for advancement, what the company can do, and what the subordinate must do himself or herself. Following are some possible developmental activities:

- Individually tailored special assignments.
- Involvement in capital appropriations and budgeting.
- On-the-job coaching by a supervisor.
- Short-term experience in other departments.
- Attending departmental or staff meetings.
- Working as acting department head when the boss is on vacation.
- Representing the boss at departmental or staff meetings.
- Participating in hiring interviews and performance-appraisal interviews.
- Reading books and articles on management.
- Being a mentor to a high-potential employee.
- Attending a management-development seminar.
- Serving as chair of a special task force on an issue of special importance to the paper, such as studying news content and recommending improvements or analyzing the impact of pagination on copy-desk staffing.

The brainstorming and planning that go into a management-development program are generally discussed by the editor and subordinate in an interview. At the end of such a meeting, the editor should reemphasize what the subordinate has done well, summarize where things stand in connection with the subordinate's future, review plans for improvement, avoid unrealistic commitments, arrange follow-up meetings, and provide reassurance and support. Part of the meeting should include establishing that the subordinate's goals are consistent with the editor's plan for the subordinate. After all, not every successful subordinate wants to become managing editor or editor.

Fig. 15.8

CLOSE-UP

In preparation for a speech on management to a Canadian editors group in 1979, Richard B. Tuttle, then managing editor of the *Democrat and Chronicle* in Rochester, New York, asked five newspaper editors and a psychologist specializing in management development this question: "What five characteristics do you look for when evaluating an employee's potential for promotion to a supervisory job?"

In their responses, the most important quality was listed first.

Judgment—knowing what questions to ask and what to do with the answers.

The ability to handle people well.

Maturity.

A sense of humor.

Technical skills.

John L. Dougherty
Managing Editor
Rochester Times-Union

The capability of using resources—personnel, time, professional knowledge, and skill.

Ability to react to unforeseen events.

Ability to plan—to set objectives and achieve them.

Problem solving—how well the employee can recognize a problem, analyze it, and solve it.

Decision-making capability—speed, quality, and follow-through.

>Byron Harless
>Psychologist and Senior Vice-president
>Knight-Ridder Newspapers

Judgment.

Professional skills.

Unusual command of interpersonal skills—communications talent.

Energy.

Sensitivity.

>Larry Jinks
>Editor
>*San Jose Mercury News*

Ego control—how much can you leave people alone to do their jobs and still be the boss?

Supportive personality.

Technical ability.

A willingness to challenge conventional wisdom.

Command presence—does the person look and act like a leader?

>Kurt Luedtke
>Executive Editor
>*Detroit Free Press*

Managerial aptitude—a sensitivity and understanding of people.

Desire and motivation.

Leadership qualities.

Creativity.

Ambition.

>Paul Poorman
>Editor
>*Akron Beacon Journal*

Fig. 15.8, continued

A basic commitment to the newspaper—a professional to the bootstraps.

A willingness, an eagerness to learn every aspect of the business.

Ability to deal and communicate well with people.

Ability to critique an operation—to be able to sit back and take a broad view of the product and then convey the criticism in a constructive way.

Human concern—knowing and caring about people and their problems, and the ability to help solve those problems when appropriate.

>John Quinn
>Senior Vice-president
>Gannett Company, Inc.

Many large newspaper companies have management-development programs. For small groups or independent newspapers, succession planning can be more difficult. The choice and training of future managers is more likely to fall exclusively to the local editor or publisher because they have fewer resources to call on in succession planning. Moreover, editors at smaller papers must commit more of their time to editing the paper and managing the staff. Consequently, there is less time for developing and executing a thoughtful development program.

Training and Development Opportunities outside the Newspaper

In addition to the training and management development that can be done on the job, a growing variety of training and development opportunities are available to the newspaper industry. Two of the best known and most respected are the American Press Institute in Reston, Virginia, and the Poynter Institute for Media Studies in St. Petersburg, Florida.

The Southern Newspaper Publishers Association Foundation in Atlanta, Georgia, offers about twelve midcareer education seminars annually on public issues and newsroom operations. The American Newspaper Publishers Association conducts sessions for managers from all parts of the newspaper operation.

Fig. 15.9

CLOSE-UP

In assessing the performance and the potential of a subordinate for a higher-level job, it is important for the editor to base his or her judgments on behaviors that can be observed and behaviors that are important to managerial success.

Following are some "managerial" behaviors that can be observed:

Impact. Ability to create a good first impression, to command attention and respect, to show an air of confidence, and to achieve personal recognition.

Communications skills. Effectiveness of expression in individual as well as group situations. Ability to make a persuasive, clear presentation of ideas and facts. Ability to express ideas clearly in writing and to organize and present material in a convincing manner.

Problem solving. Effectiveness in seeking out pertinent data, determining the source of a problem, and making a sound judgment. Ability to reach logical conclusions based on evidence at hand and to decide whether the evidence is sufficient or more is needed.

Planning and organizing. Effectiveness in planning and organizing one's own activities and those of a group.

Delegation and control. Effective use of subordinates. Understanding when a decision can best be made. Appreciation of needs for control. Maintenance of control over a group or a resource, such as the budget.

Creativity. Ability to develop or recognize imaginative solutions to news and management situations.

Energy. Ability to be self-starting and to achieve a high activity level.

Stress tolerance. Stability of performance under pressure and under opposition.

Tenacity. Tendency to stay with an important problem or line of thought until the matter is settled or reduced to the point where it should be postponed or dropped.

Leadership. Acting to seek leadership opportunities. Effective and at ease in role of leader. Actions based on own convictions rather than a desire to please others. Willingness to take responsibility for decisions.

Fig. 15.9, continued

Sensitivity. Skill in perceiving and reacting with sensitivity to the needs of others. Empathy. Willingness to listen and to understand feelings as well as words.

Personal motivation. Importance of work in personal satisfaction. Demonstrated desire to achieve at work. Interest in advancement. Interest in prestige and status.

Flexibility. Ability to modify behavioral style and management approach to reach a goal.

Decisiveness. Readiness to make decisions or to render judgment.

Source: Jim Wells, director of training, Knight-Ridder Newspapers Institute of Training, Miami, Florida (Seminar handouts, January 1984).

One of its programs, "Leadership in the Newsroom," is a management-development workshop.

The Knight-Ridder Institute of Management Training in Miami, Florida, draws primarily from Knight-Ridder employees. Other newspaper companies, such as Harte-Hanks and Gannett, give training workshops and management-development seminars for selected employees. These programs last from a few days to two weeks. The participants work together, eat together, and drink together. Journalists find these seminar experiences to be hard work, great fun, and professionally stimulating. The opportunity to share ideas and "talk newspapers" is highly invigorating.

Newspaper-development experiences on university campuses last from several months to a full academic year. The Gannett Center for Media Studies at Columbia University in New York City focuses on development opportunities for individual scholars and journalists. Three well-known midcareer programs are the Nieman Fellowships at Harvard University, the John S. Knight Fellowships at Stanford University, and the Journalists in Residence program at the University of Michigan. The Newspaper Management Center for minorities, founded by the Institute for Journalism Education, combines a month of classwork at Northwestern University's Kellogg School of Management with extensive field experience at newspapers. Some newspaper groups send promising executives to advanced management programs at Harvard Business School and at other universities.

As an industry, newspapers have just begun to adopt modern management and supervisory techniques. Understanding human behavior in the workplace, strategic planning, the art of listening, internal communications, performance evaluations, and disciplining will get broader attention in the 1980s and 1990s.

NONPROMOTABILITY

Not every staffer who aspires to be city editor or managing editor will succeed. Not enough of those jobs exist to satisfy everyone's ambition. And, as every editor realizes from time to time, ambition exceeds the reach of some staffers. Nonpromotability is not a subject that is easily discussed. The editor doesn't like the task of giving a middle-aged assistant city editor the message that he has gone as far as he can go, and the assistant city editor doesn't want to hear the editor's opinion that his career advancement is blocked.

Few journalists are so introspective or self-aware that they can see the early signs of nonpromotability. Instead, the reality sneaks up. Often, the first time the warning signs are visible is when a younger, less experienced colleague begins to draw the attention of the editors and eventually gets a promotion.

The process of nonpromotability is thought to have three phases: (1) onset, (2) development, and (3) fixation.[25] The *onset* stage occurs during the first five years of a career, often on the second job. The staffer comes to recognize his or her place within the pecking order. Comparisons with others who are competing for advancement lead to certain questions: Am I as smart as they? Do I work harder? Do my boss and peers like me any better? Am I accomplishing more? Am I politically adept at maneuvering for advantages? How does my work compare with that of others?

When answers to the above questions indicate that the competition has the upper hand, the staffer has entered the *development* stage of nonpromotability. The possibility that he or she will not advance develops rapidly between years five and ten of a career. At this stage, job switching is common. The same questions that were asked during the onset phase apply in the development stage. The staffer's answers to these questions often are reinforced by performance appraisals and the frequency or amount of pay increases.

In the *fixation* stage, most staffers are aware that their career aspirations will never be attained. This phase can begin when the individual is in his or her thirties and last until the final preretirement years. In the fixation stage, energy has waned and behavior can be marked by hostility, bitterness, or indifference. Questions that help confirm that an individual has passed into the fixation stage are: Is my next career step certain? Have I accumulated detractors during the past years? Are there any blemishes on my performance record? Do I work as hard now as I used to? Do I enjoy my job as much as I did in past years? Has my rate of learning and development decreased? Am I as concerned about the future as I have been? Do others who are important to my career act as if they are still considering me for future opportunities?

Insidious as it is, the impact of realizing that one's career is blocked can be softened. Editors can help provide insight into why it has happened. Full exposure to the problem enables the individual to deal with the situation candidly and rationally. He or she can devise whatever emotional defenses will help in surrendering to the idea that one's hopes and dreams are out of reach.

The editor's role in counseling a staffer who is nonpromotable is anchored in the appraisal process (see Chapter 10). Daily feedback and, to a larger extent, annual performance reviews are the appropriate settings to give the staffer a realistic measure of where he or she stands. The annual evaluation provides an opportunity for frank discussion about career objectives. The editor should be honest in relating performance and progress to ambition. If the editor encourages a modest performer to think the city editor's job is possible, an unrealistic expectation is created. When the staffer eventually faces the reality of nonpromotability, one of the natural defense mechanisms will be to get angry with the editor who gave false encouragement.

In most cases, effective appraisals remove doubts about promotability. The staffer knows how he or she is doing and what improvements are necessary. If the items listed under "areas for improvement" are the same year after year, it will be clear why no promotion is likely.

Counseling a staffer whose career is reaching an impasse requires sensitivity and special considerations, especially if he or she has been a hard worker and a striver who doesn't have the talent to go further. The editor should be prepared to give a thoughtful, complete, and caring evaluation of the staffer's work. A realistic picture of the staffer's fitness for larger roles and the competition for them should set the stage for the editor and the staffer to consider alternatives. The editor's objective should be to help point the staffer toward an assignment that is challenging and satisfying. It might be a redesign of his or her present job, a different role in the newsroom, an opportunity somewhere else in the newspaper company, or a decision to move to another paper or to another line of work.

TURNOVER

Turnover is a bittersweet experience for the editor. When a good staffer leaves, the editor feels disappointed and begins to ask searching questions about what went wrong or what could have been done to make the departing staffer more content and satisfied in his or her job. Often, no satisfactory answer can be found. For many journalists, there comes a point in their careers when it is time to move on. The most talented among them may think they have done all that they want to do at the paper. They have achieved their goals and they need to find new challenges. At small and medium-sized newspapers, the departure of able journalists for richer opportunities is part of the rhythm of the newsroom. In a sense, it is satisfying to editors that someone they helped shape and nurture is sought by another newspaper. It is no small compliment to these editors that larger papers raid their staffs because of the editors' reputation for hiring and training well.

Employee turnover is one of the most widely studied topics in organizational behavior. Several models of the turnover process have been proposed, and the research suggests that employees typically make conscious decisions to leave their jobs.

In a 1967 study by Allen J. Schuh of the Naval Aerospace Medical Institute at Pensacola, Florida, intelligence tests, aptitude tests, and interest inventories were found to be good predictors of turnover. Schuh examined test scores of twenty-three thousand applicants for jobs such as secretary, factory worker, factory foreman, salesperson, bus driver, telephone operator, and service representative. This study also found employees who remained in their previous jobs for longer periods were inclined to show higher satisfaction in their present jobs.[26]

In a 1980 study of two hundred clerical and service workers at a midwestern hospital, it was found that the causes of turnover and absenteeism were independent. Personal characteristics—age, tenure, sex, and education—were found to be significantly associated with absenteeism, but not with turnover. Prior work experiences—attitudes toward the organization, satisfied expectations, job challenge, organizational dependability—were significantly associated with turnover, but not with absenteeism.[27]

In one model tracing the steps leading to turnover, the starting point is an employee's evaluation of his or her existing job.[28] The evaluation leads to a conclusion about whether or not the job is satisfying. If the employee finds the job unsatisfying, he or she may think about looking for another job. Thoughts of quitting, however, force the employee to face the reality of searching for and accepting a new job—cost, sacrifice of seniority and pension benefits, inconvenience, loss of friends, change in life-style, value of spouse's employment, and uncertainty of change. If the employee concludes that the cost of leaving is too high, he or she may decide to remain. If the cost seems reasonable, then the search for alternatives will begin. If an alternative is found, the employee then compares that opportunity to the present job and decides whether to stay or leave. This model is based on a rational decision-making process and does not consider the fact that some individuals act impulsively in the face of job dissatisfaction or a fresh opportunity.

If a newsroom is well managed—that is, if expectations are

realistic, if feedback and regular performance appraisals are part of the routine, if opportunity and pay are based on performance—then the editor will be able to differentiate between two kinds of turnover: high performers and low performers. A high turnover rate among the poor performers is desirable, but the editor should look for reasons why the hiring process failed.

On the other hand, turnover can be positive. It allows the editor to hire staffers who are more skilled and motivated. It opens up avenues of promotion for the strong performers who remain. It reduces entrenched conflict by eliminating situations in which the opposition of individuals or groups is disruptive.[29]

In attempting to strengthen the commitment of the most talented staffers, the editor should remember that the best performers have the highest standards and are more susceptible to feelings of discontent. These individuals' commitment can be increased by demonstrating that the management of the newspaper is interested in them. The editor can serve as a mentor, giving the staffer special guidance, counsel, and experience. Top staffers should be fairly rewarded for their performance. The editor must be alert to signs of boredom and remember that the best people need to be continually challenged. They need opportunities to stretch and grow. Temporary reassignment or cross-training can offer invigorating learning experiences that reinforce management's interest in and commitment to an individual's future. One of the strongest enticements for a valued associate is for the editor to share some of his or her power. This is more than delegating tasks. It means relinquishing some responsibilities with no strings attached. It means informing others that this person is authorized to speak for the editor in certain matters.

DISCIPLINE

Disciplining an employee through suspension or dismissal is not a pleasant task. Few editors enjoy it. Many are reluctant to confront a severe problem. They put off acting because they are uncertain whether they have documented the need for discipline, because they don't want to stumble into a legal problem, because they are sensitive to the feeling of the individual staffer, or because they dislike confronting someone with the decision that his or her employment is ending.

Although discipline must be administered sensitively and carefully, the editor must not allow feelings or emotions to cloud the responsibility to act. Firing is a last resort, and the editor should first consider offering the staffer several alternatives: transfer, demotion, resignation, or retirement. Editors should think through the disciplinary process so that if it comes to discharge, the editor is able to say to the staffer, "You know what is coming. You have discharged yourself."

Disciplinary action is taken when a staffer's conduct or performance is not what it is reasonably expected to be. Conduct refers to violation of work rules or practices, or behavior that may be insubordinate. Performance refers to problems in the quality of work. The editor's decision about discipline is linked to the staffer's record. Typically, if it is the first time inappropriate behavior has been observed, the editor's response will be different than if such behavior has occurred before.

In administering discipline, the editor must be aware of the obligation to preserve the interests of the newspaper and protect the rights of the individual. A sound policy for administering disciplinary action will avoid short-run expediency and will result in decisions that can stand a test before an arbitrator or a judge (see Chapter 10). The principle underlying both our legal system and the fundamental beliefs of journalists is that an individual is presumed innocent until proven guilty. This applies to discipline cases in the newsroom. The burden is on the editor to demonstrate that the worker is guilty of inappropriate conduct or poor performance. If the editor's disciplinary action is challenged and doubts are present in the mind of an arbitrator or a judge, the employee tends to get the benefit of the doubt.

Consistency is a management principle that is too easily ignored. Management cannot discipline one employee for one offense and ignore the same offense committed by another employee. This kind of inconsistency is most likely to occur in the absence of standards for performance and professional conduct and in the failure of management to act on a day-to-day basis as problems occur.[30]

The standard approach to discipline is a procedure known as *progressive discipline* (see example in Chapter 10). It involves four steps: (1) an oral warning, (2) a written warning, (3) suspension from the job, and (4) discharge. At each step in the disciplinary process, the employee should have an opportunity to explain or defend himself or herself. The employee has the right to have a union representative at such a meeting.

The oral warning should be given at the first instance of misconduct or when a pattern of performance problems shows up. In either case, the warning should be given with counseling. The editor must meet in private with the staffer to point out the problem, listen to the staffer's explanation, outline the required behavior, and set a date to review performance.

If a written warning is necessary, a copy should be added to the staffer's employment record. The warning note should be reviewed with the staffer in a private meeting. The circumstances should be discussed, goals for improvement should be agreed upon, and a date for review set.

When the problems persist and a suspension may be necessary, the editor should inform the publisher and seek the advice of the personnel director, the newspaper's labor-relations representative, or the newspaper's legal counsel. Discipline at this level is a specialized matter and authoritative advice is required. The editor may wish to act promptly to avoid giving the impression of condoning an offense, but it is sufficient to tell the staffer at this point that disciplinary action may be taken and an investigation is under way.

A staffer should not be suspended without a hearing. An employee who is a member of a bargaining unit has the right to be represented in a disciplinary meeting by someone from the union. Nonunion employees are not entitled to be represented in a disciplinary hearing. The editor should be assisted by another editor and by a counselor who knows labor and personnel law. The purpose of a suspension hearing is to discuss the facts and hear the employee's explanation. At the conclusion of the hearing, the editor should promise the staffer a decision within a day unless significant additional investigation is needed.

There may be mitigating factors that would suggest a lesser

penalty than suspension, of course. But whatever the decision, it should be in writing and should be given to the staffer in a private meeting. The editor's memorandum should review the incident or the pattern of poor performance, the staffer's explanation, the results of any investigation, the disciplinary decision, the requirements for future conduct, and the consequences of failure to correct the problem. If the decision is to suspend, the amount of time off the job without pay usually is from one day to two weeks, depending on the seriousness of the problem.

The final step in the progressive discipline process is discharge. The same care and preparation that went into the suspension decision are required for discharge. At this point, the objective is to get the individual off the payroll and out of the newsroom as quickly as possible. The editor has some options in doing this. Some individuals will offer to resign, preferring not to have a firing on their employment record. To those who do not offer to resign, the editor may suggest that option. The editor may also offer extra pay or continued health insurance as a severance settlement along with an agreement not to give the staffer a poor reference if the employee will resign and give the newspaper a release of all claims the employee might later bring against the newspaper. In preparing such an agreement, the editor should always consult legal counsel.

In cases of gross misconduct, the first two or even three steps may be bypassed. Gross insubordination, dishonesty, or a gross violation of journalistic ethics may call for immediate discharge.

Editors who are responsible for discipline typically receive little direction in how to approach it and what attitude to have about it. As a result, two common behavior patterns emerge: (1) the editor assumes the role of a punishing parent and treats the staffer as an offending child, or (2) the editor assumes the role of prosecutor and judge and the staffer is the accused.[31] Neither approach is effective in correcting behavior or assessing the need for discipline.

Some suggested approaches for handling discipline include:

- The discipline problem is the employee's to solve. The editor cannot "make" the staffer perform; only the employee can do that.

Hiring, Training, and Promoting   553

- The employee must understand that continued poor conduct or poor performance may lead to discharge.
- The employee must understand that under similar circumstances, any staffer would be treated in the same manner.
- The discipline process should make it clear that the focus of the discipline is on job behavior and not on the staffer personally.
- The process should make clear that the discipline is based on observed behaviors and not on such subjective characteristics as attitude.
- Once the employee understands the policies or the standards to be met, he or she makes the choices about behavior and assumes the risks.
- Discipline should be aimed at improving performance, not exacting punishment.

CHAPTER SUMMARY

The hiring process, one of the key responsibilities of the newspaper editor, includes seven separate but related steps: (1) recruiting, (2) measuring the candidate's qualifications, (3) interviewing, (4) the tryout, (5) testing, (6) the selection decision, and (7) orientation. The editor is involved in managing and coordinating all elements of this process.

In recruiting and assessing job candidates, the editor is particularly interested in several basic qualities: technical skills, a good fit with the staff, initiative, potential for development, retainability, and creativity.

In checking references and interviewing candidates, editors are bound by laws that seek to eliminate discrimination in hiring.

The interview is frequently the key to the hiring process. Many hiring decisions are based on impressions gained during the interview, yet research casts doubt on the reliability of the interview as an indicator of how well an individual will perform on the job. There are two types of interviews: (1) the planned interview, a long, in-depth conversation in which the candidate is invited to talk freely on a number of topics, and (2) the patterned interview, based on a list of set questions.

The tryout is an opportunity to observe the applicant at work. Although it is a stressful experience for most candidates, the tryout offers a realistic look at their ability to work effectively with newsroom assignments.

Two kinds of tests may be used in the newsroom hiring process. Most common is the type that measures skills, such as editing, writing, knowledge of events, and use of the language. Other tests measure personal characteristics such as aptitude, motivation, and achievement. In either case, tests should be used only as a supplement to other elements of the selection process.

Following the selection decision, once the new hire is on staff, his or her introduction to the job is important. The newspaper's responsibilities during orientation include helping the newcomer feel welcome and providing information about employee benefits and the newspaper's practices, policies, and resources.

The newspaper's personnel department can offer assistance to the editor in screening job applicants, conducting reference checks, and conducting a legal interview.

Training and development are both part of a strategy to improve the work of individuals and provide opportunities for larger responsibilities. Training is the building of skills and knowledge in the present job. Development is preparing a staffer for a job at a higher level. Editors looking for staffers with managerial potential pay special attention to such behaviors as impact, communication skills, problem solving, planning and organizing, delegation and control, creativity, energy, stress tolerance, tenacity, leadership, sensitivity, motivation, flexibility, and decisiveness.

Mentoring is a classic example of individual development that takes place outside the normal chain of command in the newsroom. An editor who serves as a mentor often selects as a protégé a staffer who demonstrates unusual potential. The mentoring process is, at its best, spontaneous, informal, and personal. Mentoring has been of special interest to women and minorities because it offers ways to learn and grow that do not depend on the white male–dominated structure of the newsroom.

A succession plan involves identifying candidates for promotion and establishing that the candidates are prepared to step in when needed. In addition to developmental activities at the newspaper, there are training and development opportunities outside the newspaper, such as seminars and advanced management programs.

Facing the prospect of nonpromotability is painful, both for the staffer and his or her supervisor. Arriving at an honest decision that one's career may be at a dead-end requires introspection, self-awareness, and honesty on the part of the individual and support from his or her editor. Nonpromotability comes on in phases. Editors should be aware of its onset and be prepared to counsel the staffer.

Turnover is a frequent concern of editors for which there often is no satisfactory answer. However well the newsroom is managed, staffers will leave for other opportunities. When turnover involves marginal performers, their leaving gives editors an opportunity to strengthen the staff.

Occasionally, editors are faced with the need to discipline staffers. Discipline should be done with sensitivity and care. Essentially, there are four steps in a process known as progressive discipline: (1) oral warning, (2) written warning, (3) suspension, and (4) dismissal. The editor must be able to document an individual's failure of performance or conduct that resulted in the discipline.

NOTES

1. Dale S. Beach, *Personnel: The Management of People at Work*, 3d ed. (New York, Macmillan, 1975), 275–76.
2. Raymond L. Price, Paul H. Thompson, and Gene W. Dalton, "A Longitudinal Study of Technological Obsolescence," *Research Management* 18 (November 1975): 22–28.
3. Albert Shapero, *Managing Professional People* (New York: The Free Press, 1985), 5–8.
4. Ibid., 11.

5. Howard W. Goheen and James N. Mosel, "The Validity of the Employment Recommendation Questionnaire in Personnel Selection," *Personnel Psychology* 12, no. 2 (1959): 297–301.
6. Beach, *Personnel*, 278–79.
7. Desmond D. Martin, William J. Kearney, and G. D. Holdefer, "The Decision to Hire: A Comparison of Selection Tools," in *Business Perspectives* (Southern Illinois University, Spring 1971), 11–15.
8. Ron Smith, "Employment Screening Procedures: Tests and Tryouts," *Journalism Research Journal* 5, no. 2 (1980–1981): 29–30.
9. Lee J. Cronbach, *Essentials of Psychological Testing*, 2d ed. (New York: Harper & Row, 1960), 21.
10. Anne Anastasi, *Psychological Testing*, 5th ed. (New York: Macmillan, 1982), 3–4.
11. Beach, *Personnel*, 252.
12. Anastasi, *Psychological Testing*, 22–23.
13. Byron Harless, interview with author, 13 March 1984.
14. Beach, *Personnel*, 253–54.
15. Alexandra K. Wigdor and Wendell R. Garner, eds., *Ability Testing—Part I: Uses, Consequences, and Controversies* (Washington: National Academy Press, 1982), 119, 143.
16. Ronald E. Smith, "Employee Orientation," *Personnel Journal*, December 1984, 48.
17. Patricia P. Renfroe, "A Personnel Manager Tells Editors: 'We Can Help You if You'll Let Us,'" *The Bulletin of the American Society of Newspaper Editors*, October 1983, 23.
18. Jerry L. Gray, *Supervision* (Boston: Kent, 1984), 339–40.
19. Ibid., 340–41.
20. Matthew J. Henneck, "Mentors and Protégés: How to Build Relationships that Work," *Training*, July 1983, 37.
21. Ibid., 41.
22. Norman Isaacs, "'Journalism's Biggest Problem' Is Choosing Newsroom Leaders," *The Bulletin of the American Society of Newspaper Editors*, June 1985, 3.
23. Patricia P. Renfroe, "Succession: Grooming Replacements Should Be Company Policy," *presstime*, March 1984, 6.
24. Peter F. Drucker, *Management* (New York: Harper & Row, 1974), 426.
25. Edward Roseman, *Confronting Non-Promotability: How to Manage a Stalled Career* (New York: AMACOM, 1977), 4–5.
26. Allen J. Schuh, "The Predictability of Employee Tenure," *Personnel Psychology* 20 (1967): 133–52.
27. Daniel G. Spencer and Richard M. Speers, "The Influence of Personal Factors and Perceived Work Experiences on Employee Turnover and Absenteeism," *Academy of Management Journal* 23 (1980): 567–72.
28. William H. Mobley, "Intermediate Linkages in the Relationship between Job Satisfaction and Employee Turnover," *Journal of Applied Psychology* 62 (1977): 238.

29. Richard M. Steers, *Introduction to Organizational Behavior*, 2d ed. (Glenview, Ill.: Scott, Foresman, 1984), 474–75.
30. Beach, *Personnel*, 607–8.
31. Daniel Cameron, "The When, Why, & How of Discipline," *Personnel Journal*, July 1984, 39.

16

Managing Upwards

Like all newspaper employees, every editor has a boss, and managing upwards by establishing a mutually satisfying relationship with one's superior is a critical factor in determining the editor's success or failure. At most newspapers, the top boss—the chief executive officer—carries the title of publisher. How to be a good subordinate is a part of the management art that is frequently neglected. Managing that relationship is as vital as managing the relationship with those under the editor's command. Being a successful subordinate can be difficult when the leadership style of the publisher causes the editor to feel demeaned, blocked, unappreciated, bored, or intimidated. Thus, the subordinate's choice is between chafing at the leadership style or adopting strategies that may transform the relationship.

UNDERSTANDING THE BOSS

During a decade of studying top management at some fifty private and public organizations, Chris Argyris of the Harvard Graduate School of Education observed several leadership characteristics among chief executive officers:[1]

- Most chief executives have three characteristics in common: They are articulate, competitive, and persuasive. They also compete vigorously for attention, excel in one-upmanship, and encourage win-lose competition.

- CEOs are more competitive than other executives. They unconsciously encourage conformity and discourage risk taking among their subordinates.

- The win-lose style of competition is an outgrowth of the chief executive's own leadership style. CEOs claim to value vice-presidents who, like themselves, are articulate, persuasive, competitive, and willing to speak their minds. They think that this "fit" between their own and their subordinates' leadership styles creates a self-reinforcing system.

- The vice-presidents who are articulate and competitive report, however, that they do not always speak their minds. The stronger the win-lose style within the top executive group, the more carefully they measure and plan their statements. At the same time, they try to disguise their caution because success within their organizations depends on a show of forcefulness.

Argyris found that most of the CEOs in the study were genuinely interested in people and wanted to create an environment within the company that would stimulate both organizational and human development. But most of the CEOs were not prepared, either through educational background or executive training programs, to act consistent with their values. The vice-presidents who recognized the wide gap between theory and behavior also understood that their bosses did not wish to discuss the discrepancy, so the vice-presidents chose to play it safe and to act as if the inequities did not exist.

If the CEO values frankness, why do the vice-presidents choose to be cautious? The reason given most frequently, Argyris reports, is to protect the boss: "If he really knew his impact, he would be upset." Second to that is the desire to protect the organization. Third, vice-presidents want to protect themselves.

"The CEO experiences an easy ambivalence when confronted with reactions to his behavior," Argyris said. "He is proud of being perceived as dynamic, intense, and aggressive, yet disturbed by reports that his vice-presidents consider him 'overpowering' and 'difficult to deal with.' He is particularly disturbed because he believes that he has chosen subordinates who are not easily intimidated."

Away from subordinates, however, the chief executives interviewed by Argyris said they understood the problems caused by their leadership and readily admitted that a successful leader is not likely to allow others in the organization to duplicate his or her style. These CEOs realized that by setting tight managerial controls (especially financial) and by making highly detailed plans, they may unwittingly have encouraged dependency, submissiveness, and lack of initiative among subordinates.[2]

The successful subordinate is a keen observer of the boss's operating style—that is, how the top man or woman gets work done and changes made. The editor knows from his or her own experience that managing at the top levels of an organization can be enormously difficult and that no single approach works consistently. By watching the boss carefully, the subordinate can learn to distinguish between effective and ineffective styles.

Executives who consistently accomplish a lot are notably inconsistent in their manner of attacking problems. They continually change their focus, their priorities, their behavior patterns with others, and their own "executive styles." An analysis of the activities of managers in thirty-one case studies suggests that those who are high achievers are self-disciplined and careful analysts of individual situations. It is these skills that permit them to be inconsistent in personal and managerial style.[3]

The successful achievers in these case studies know when to get into fine details in one situation and stay at the strategic level in another. They delegate in some cases and take a highly hands-on approach in others. They communicate orally with some colleagues and in writing with others. They analyze some problems in great depth while they move with abruptness and intuition on others. They talk a great deal or are suddenly rapt listeners. They are able to perceive differences between one situation and another—an absolute necessity for a successful boss. In doing so, they are applying the ideas of situational leadership (which was explained in Chapter 7). Less successful managers in the same study were found to have several persistent and predictable patterns: the tendency to "wing it," inappropriate attention to details, attention to details without a plan, no handle on priorities, not moving fast enough, lack of boldness, nerve, and self-confidence, tolerance of ineffective subordinates, and failure to seek advice or help.[4]

THE PUBLISHER

Typically, the chief executive officer of the newspaper is the focal point of power and responsibility for managing operations, creating a *unilateral organization*. Although titles in the newspaper business are varied and ambiguous, the publisher is the chief executive officer at most newspapers. Some publishers carry dual titles, such as "president and publisher" or "editor and publisher." In some newspaper groups, the publisher of the local newspaper is akin to the head of a division or a subsidiary. He or she normally reports to a corporate officer in another city and lacks the authority and autonomy of the publisher of an independent newspaper.

By contrast, some newspapers operate with two executives in charge: a general manager and an editor, each of whom has a separate jurisdiction. The editor has authority over the news and editorial operations. The general manager has authority for advertising, circulation, production, personnel, marketing, promotion, public service, and other nonnews departments of the newspaper. The general manager and the editor govern through consensus. If they are unable to resolve a difference of opinion, they can turn to their corporate counterparts for assistance. The *bilateral organization* is used in the Scripps-Howard Newspapers, the Booth Newspapers of Michigan, and in some Knight-Ridder newspapers.

In a 1981 study, John Kaufman, an assistant professor of communications at California State University at Fullerton, compared bilateral and unilateral newspaper administrative structures.[5] His hypothesis was that a newspaper run by a general manager and an editor will have a "healthier living system" than one with a publisher in charge. In Kaufman's definition, a newspaper's living system is the strength of the working relationship among the departments of the newspaper, the degree of cooperation in resolving interdepartmental disputes, and the effect of a human environment that encourages motivation and high efficiency. Kaufman was testing ideas proposed by Rensis Likert, director of the Institute for Social Research at the University of Michigan. Likert advocated group-oriented management in which the cooperation and shared goals of senior managers were enhanced by the competence, motivation, and general effectiveness found in a human organization. Likert characterized highly productive organizations as having tightly knit social systems and as being run by people who understand one another's roles and their relation to the overall mission of the company.[6]

In his study, Kaufman selected the *Grand Rapids Press* in Michigan as a model of the bilateral concept and the *Dayton Daily News* in Ohio as the unilateral newspaper. His research produced no evidence that the bilateral newspaper administration promotes a healthier living system. Indeed, he concluded that there is evidence that a publisher-led newspaper is to be preferred. Kaufman found that the administrative structure led by a publisher at the *Daily News* more closely approximated the group-oriented style of management advocated by Likert than did the bilateral structure at the *Press*.

Fig. 16.1

CLOSE-UP

The following account of the death of the *Washington Star* in 1981 underscores the crucial relationship between publisher and editor in the success or failure of a newspaper:

"Time Inc.'s most basic imprint on the *Star* was documented each day in opposite corners of its editorial page, although few readers ever noticed it. In the upper left corner, in small, boldface type, was the name of the editor, Murray J. Gart; in the bottom right, in exactly the same sized type, was the name of the publisher, George W. Hoyt.

"As editor and publisher, the two men commanded separate but equal realms of the paper, as do the editor and publisher of each of Time's enormously successful magazines. Time's executives consider the separation sacred; they refer to it as 'church and state.' But for 'church and state' to work smoothly at a newspaper, the editor and

Fig. 16.1, continued

publisher must have a close working relationship, based on mutual trust and respect.

"That was not the case at the *Star*, where Gart and Hoyt were no closer than were their names on the far corners of the editorial page.

"Gart often hurled obscenities when talking to his deputies about how 'dumb' he considered Hoyt to be. Hoyt complained to his production staff that Gart stockpiled gripes 'like hand grenades, and then lobbed them over the wall.' The two men developed such mutual hostility that at times they communicated only through go-betweens, most often through associate editor Sidney Epstein. James R. Shepley, who was *Star* board president as well as the president of Time Inc., often had to step in to mediate minor disagreements that had mushroomed into major standoffs, particularly over the paper's problem-plagued computer system, which was maintained by Hoyt's production staff.

"Their clear contempt for each other exacerbated the *Star*'s ills in its dying years, executives on both sides of the editor-publisher wall agree. And the situation was all the more harmful because of the many innovations under way—zoned editions, special morning edition, a third editorial page, new layout designs, and more—all requiring smooth coordination between the editing and publishing sides of the paper."

Source: Dale Russakoff, Ron Shaffer, and Ben Weiser, "Bitter Feud Erupted at Time's Star; Bitterness on Bridge of Sinking Ship: Church and State Dissolved in Acrimony," *Washington Post*, 17 August 1981.

In the examination of the editor-publisher relationship that follows in this chapter, the editor is the highest-ranking person with full-time responsibility for the news operation at the paper, and the publisher is the person to whom that editor reports. The key elements that are relevant in the dealings between editor and publisher also can be applied to other subordinate-boss relationships, such as assistant city editor to city editor, sports editor to managing editor, or managing editor to executive editor.

The greatest power in the newspaper is wielded by the publisher. His or her decisions can have a great impact on the tone and quality of the news report as well as on the newspaper's business, marketing, and service practices. The underlying editor-publisher relationship is an important part of the publisher's power structure. This relationship must be based on mutual trust and respect because of the publisher's need for the editor to participate and cooperate in the overall business strategy of the newspaper.

Edwin A. Lahey, an able and irreverent reporter for the old *Chicago Daily News* and later the Knight Newspapers Washington Bureau, once said that all he ever demanded of his publisher was that he be solvent. It was Lahey's way of saying that the publisher should concentrate on making the profit and stay out of the newsroom. With few exceptions, newspapers in Ed Lahey's time—from the 1940s through the mid-1960s—were locally owned, and the publisher was likely to be a businessman rather than someone who had risen from the editorial or advertising ranks of the paper.

The publisher's interest and influence today extend far beyond the business office. Whatever the background of the publisher, he or she gives attention to all phases of the newspaper and strives to keep all of its operations in balance.

Fig. 16.2

CLOSE-UP

As the 1984 presidential election campaign came to a close, the fifteen-member editorial board of the *Miami Herald* voted two to one to endorse Walter Mondale. *Herald* publisher Richard Capen overruled the editorial board and instructed the newspaper's editors to write an editorial endorsing President Reagan. The incident was widely reported and offered a glimpse at how a publisher and an editor interacted in a disagreement over editorial policy.

Capen said he overturned the editorial board because "I couldn't live with an endorsement that I couldn't defend. As publisher, I have the ultimate responsibility to defend what we do more than anyone else . . . Sometimes when you lead, you have to act decisively, even if it ruffles some feathers."

Herald editor Jim Hampton reacted by offering his resignation. "My first inclination was to just quit outright. But you don't win by walking away from the table."

Capen tore up the resignation letter and suggested that Hampton

Fig. 16.2, continued

use his Sunday column to state his own position and to explain to readers how the endorsement decision was reached. Hampton accepted the idea. Capen also wrote a column that Sunday discussing his reasons for endorsing Reagan.

Many readers who called or wrote to the *Herald* said they particularly appreciated the chance to learn about the internal decision-making processes at the newspaper.

Source: Andrew Radolf, "Editorial Controversy in Miami," *Editor & Publisher,* 10 November 1984, 9–10.

In a 1983 study for the American Society of Newspaper Editors, Philip Meyer, a former newsman and professor of journalism at the University of North Carolina, examined the relationships between editors and publishers and how they work together to set and enforce ethical standards on daily newspapers. Although the focus of the study was ethical behavior, the findings offer a broader picture of the basic interaction between editor and publisher.

The attitudes measured in the survey indicate that the publisher who has a hands-off policy toward the editorial side is not the type most preferred. Instead, editors are more comfortable with a publisher constructively involved in the newsroom. Meyer labels this sort of publisher the Statesman and says that he or she is more likely than other publisher types to suggest major investigations, to demonstrate by selective use of praise or criticism what the editor should do, to participate in discussions about reporting assignments on occasion, and to be seen frequently in the newsroom. The Statesman does all this without succumbing to the temptation to seek special handling of stories for those with economic clout or social connections.[7]

In addition to the Statesman, Meyer described three other basic types of publishers, according to their operating styles: the Partisan, who intervenes in the newsroom only to obtain favored treatment for friends or advertisers; the Politician, who intervenes to help make improvements to the paper as well as to obtain favored treatment for friends or advertisers; and the Absentee, who does not intervene at all.[8]

The survey provided three measurable signs that the Statesman runs a more ethical newspaper than the publisher who studiously avoids the newsroom:

1. Evidence that decisions are made on a case-by-case basis with freedom from knee-jerk responses. Many ethical abuses are not the result of an absence of rules but are due to rules being applied too rigidly.
2. Mutual respect between editor and publisher. Editors and publishers know ethical behavior when they see it, and they like each other for it.
3. High staff morale. Newsroom people need "psychic income" as much as any other kind, and nothing ruins morale as quickly as the perception that the newspaper is being run without regard for moral values.

On each of these counts, Meyer reports, the Statesman publisher comes out ahead. The Statesman has the happiest newsroom, the greatest respect from editors, and tends not to make knee-jerk or visceral responses to specific dilemmas.

Other findings of Meyer's study observe differences between editors and publishers in addressing fundamental issues at the newspaper:[9]

- Editors and publishers tend to agree on the substance of most ethical issues. They are much less likely to agree on how to resolve those issues or even on who at the newspaper should help resolve them.
- News-editorial people tend to be suspicious of money and its power. The publisher is more likely to evaluate expenditures in instrumental terms—that is, money is a tool, and one uses it as efficiently as possible.
- The idea of codifying ethical principles, while popular overall, is most accepted among publishers who are least likely to get their hands dirty with real-life application of those codes.

- The staff is much more likely than the editor to see the publisher as a bad influence in the newsroom.

Each relationship between publisher and editor is unique. It is influenced by the personalities and interests of the two individuals, and is affected by the newspaper's traditions and the nature of its ownership. If the relationship is to be productive, it must be nurtured by mutual regard and frequent discussions.

In the preface to a small volume called *The Editorial Page*, Katharine Graham, publisher of the *Washington Post*, described her relationship with the newspaper's editorial-page staff: "The making of the editorial page really begins with the hiring process, and with the criteria that are applied with respect to the writers as well as the editors. For the editors, this means a certain measure of compatibility, as well as the obvious professional attributes . . . I attend editorial conferences whenever possible—sometimes (and ideally) about once a week, though there may be long intervals when other business pre-empts my time. At those meetings I like to engage in the discussions on the same basis as everybody else—talking when I think I can make a contribution, and deferring to others in areas in which they are better informed. If my presence on these occasions is inhibiting or overpowering or even faintly chastening, the evidence cannot be found in silence, and still less in deference. A certain irreverence, toward all things, is perhaps the prevailing spirit—which is how it ought to be."[10]

It usually is the editor's prerogative to make the final judgments on the selection and display of the news as well as on such matters as hiring, promotion, and pay increases. In most cases, the editor-publisher relationship works well as long as the "no-surprise rule" is observed. This means that the editor will spare the publisher the experience of opening the newspaper and finding an investigation of a local bank, a major shift of editorial-page policy, or the announcement of key promotions on the news staff about which the publisher had not been consulted or apprised.

The partnership between publisher and editor thrives on the fulfillment of expectations. The following are things the publisher might expect the editor to know or do and ways in which the editor and publisher might interact:

- Understand the newspaper's role. As a community institution, the newspaper has a role in the lives of its readers. What is that role? How does the newspaper serve that role? Does the newspaper open its pages to all points of view? Who is the newspaper reaching? How do the newspaper's traditions fit into its contemporary role? The publisher and the editor should share a mutual understanding of the newspaper's role.

- Know the community. The editor must have a sense of what and who make the community tick. What's on readers' minds? What is the local agenda? What are the community standards? Who are the leaders? Who are the power brokers? Who are the powerless?

- Have a commitment to excellence. The editor should never be satisfied with today's paper. There are always things that can be done better. The push for improvement is continual. It begins with the editor and is ingrained in the staff.

- Cultivate ideas and initiate change. The editor routinely plants ideas for interesting projects and changes. He or she frequently engages the publisher in a dialogue about what may be ahead and about what needs to be done as a way of laying the groundwork for change. If a newspaper is not improving, then it is falling back. There is no standing still. The editor may not have all the bright ideas, but he or she is responsible for creating an environment that encourages improvement. Once those ideas bubble up from the staff, the editor must find ways to nurture the ideas and put the best of them to work for the paper.

- Set standards. The staff and the community should know what the editor's standards are, both for ethical conduct and for excellent performance. These standards must become part of the newsroom routine. The editor should encourage the publisher's awareness of and support for newsroom standards.

- Be sensitive and sensible. Although the editor has the power to publish information that can affect the lives of individuals and institutions in the community, that power should be used in a restrained, sensitive, and sensible manner. The editor's aggressive instincts for rooting out wrongdoing and corruption should be balanced with a care that such reporting does not victimize the innocent.

- Strive for an alliance. Don't freeze the publisher out of the decision-making process, but don't invite the publisher to make decisions that belong to the editor. The publisher is reassured when the editor offers information and seeks advice and counsel. These acts let the publisher know that his or her opinion and position are valued. When the editor listens hard for the publisher's viewpoint, it becomes unnecessary for the publisher to initiate a larger, hands-on role in the news operation just to maintain a presence. The editor's sensitivity to the publisher's mood will suggest how to mix the good news with the bad and when to hold some of the bad news for another time. Even though the publisher may show displeasure—usually nonverbally—at hearing bad news, he or she needs to know about failures as well as successes.

- Deal in solutions, not problems. When the editor takes a problem to the publisher, the editor also should be prepared to explain how he or she expects to solve it. One of the keys in building a solid alliance between editor and publisher is for the editor to be able to demonstrate that he or she can creatively and competently take some of the load off the publisher. An editor who is on top of his or her responsibilities and who initiates actions to fix problems quickly will earn the boss's respect. If the editor has strengths that the publisher lacks and can use those talents with diplomacy and sensitivity, it will go a long way toward winning the boss's trust and respect.

- Initiate feedback. Communication is vital to the partnership of editor and publisher. In addition to discussing problems, ideas, and solutions and following the no-surprise rule, the editor's ability to communicate with the publisher can have other important effects. Casual conversation about life in the newsroom or about news stories can be an effective way to teach a publisher who has little background in news. It helps make the publisher sensitive to why the news staff does what it does. For the publisher who is a former news hand, keeping in touch in this way is simply informative and fun.

Taking special note of the publisher's accomplishments and complimenting him or her is another way the editor can use feedback to give the publisher a message. Some publishers are not good communicators. They give vague instructions. They express dissatisfaction through innuendo instead of direct statements. For some publishers, this is a matter of style. For others, it may be a question of self-confidence. Whatever the case, the editor needs to be alert to subtle messages, to respond to ambiguous comments with direct ones, and to be consistent in his or her style of working with the publisher.

Fig. 16.3

CLOSE-UP

As publisher of the *Cincinnati Enquirer*, Gary Watson observed that any editor who wishes to prosper must practice the art of dealing with the boss: "This doesn't require bowed head and bended knee. Rather, the successful manager understands and works at improving the relationship."

Following are Watson's thoughts on the "care and feeding" of publishers:

1. Be sure that your perception of your job agrees with your boss's perception. You may be doing a great job, but it may be the wrong job as defined by your publisher. Periodically, check signals. Don't wait for the boss to initiate the conversation. It's your career; you start the discussion.

2. Make your management style complement the boss's style. The styles needn't be identical, but they should be complementary. Your success will depend, in part, upon your ability to be part of a

Fig. 16.3, continued

team. If your style is too different from your publisher's, think about changing yours—fast. The boss's style is what got him or her the big job, and it's unlikely to change.

3. When you succeed, the boss succeeds. We all love to bask in the reflected sunshine of a job done well—by someone else.

4. Anticipate, anticipate, anticipate. Learn what the boss expects and get the job done before being asked. The boss's confidence is essential to your success.

5. Solve problems. The publisher has enough to do without spending time dealing with problems that should be dealt with at your level. If a problem must be considered by the boss, propose more than one solution. Give the boss some options, but don't create a situation in which the only response is "no."

6. Be a knowledgeable advocate for the staff. When a staff member is right, be a strong supporter. But when a staff member is wrong, don't go down in flames out of a misplaced sense of loyalty. The boss will begin to question your judgment and your abilities. Don't be an excuse-maker for the staff.

7. Don't forget whose team you are playing on. You can't have it both ways; you can't be for and against the boss. Work within the established rules. If you find the environment intolerable and unchangeable, find a new team you can play on.

Source: Gary Watson, "The Care and Feeding of the Boss," *Gannetteer*, July 1985, 3.

SUBORDINATE POWER

Editors and other newspaper executives, as a group and as individuals, have power over the publisher. Subordinate power comes in many forms and can, when used effectively or collectively, put the boss at a relative disadvantage. Following are examples of subordinate power[11]:

- Possessing skills that are difficult to replace quickly or easily.
- Having specialized information or knowledge that is important and that others do not have.

- Good personal relationships, which make it difficult to reprimand or replace a subordinate without incurring the anger of other key employees and managers.

- The importance to the boss's agenda of the position a subordinate holds, in which the performance of the subordinate can have a major impact on the performance of the boss.

- Interdependencies between a subordinate's job and other key jobs, which make the boss indirectly dependent on the subordinate.

IF THE BOSS IS DIFFICULT

A 1983 study of highly successful executives in three large industrial corporations revealed that fifty-eight of the seventy-three executives had had experiences with intolerable male bosses. The most frequently mentioned complaint was the lack of integrity—lying, failing to keep their word, absence of trust. The easiest to spot and the hardest to cope with were those who were described as "dictators, little Napoleons, or martinets"; they take offense if anyone else makes decisions or stands out in any way.

The researchers—Michael M. Lombardo, Morgan W. McCall, Jr., and Ann Morrison of the Center for Creative Leadership in Greensboro, North Carolina—identified four patterns of behavior among the executives with impossible bosses:[12]

1. Most of the executives understood that the boss is the boss. They kept on working for him, trying to adapt to his ways, seeking to understand and predict his next move. They recognized that changing the boss was a long shot and that changing themselves to improve the relationship was a better possibility.

2. The men also came to realize that the adversity created by a difficult boss necessitated transitions that are painful but essential for growth. When faced with the reality that their own version of rationality would not prevail, these executives avoided the temptation to become cynical and worked

through the problem to a more pragmatic view of the complexity and chaos of business life.

3. The executives also learned the value of patience in dealing with adversity. They devised strategies for coming to terms with events beyond their control. For example, they learned how to deal with conflict and how to disagree without destroying a relationship. Some discovered that nothing could improve the relationship. For them, the strategy became one of reminding themselves that they work for the company, not the boss, or of simply learning to live by the boss's rules.

4. Finally, the executives discovered that they could learn to manage things better by watching someone else manage them wrong. Some clarified their ideas about the responsibility of managers. Others refined their notions of how subordinates should be treated.

From their negative experiences with difficult bosses, thirty-six of the executives drew positive guidelines for their own managerial philosophies: Give people recognition for what they accomplish. Give people responsibility, a chance to show what they can do. Look below the surface to understand people's actions. Accept your own responsibilities.

On the more immediate question of how to get along with an intolerable boss, the executives offered a few guidelines:[13]

- Keep searching for common ground. Don't take the easy way of blaming everything on the boss. Remember that top management's evaluation of how you handle the situation may hinge on how hard you try to improve it. Coping with adversity will reveal a quality of many successful executives: composure under stress.

- Try modifying both your behavior and the boss's. Maybe he doesn't realize he's intolerable. Perhaps he has an intolerable boss, too. Or, in his eyes, your behavior may make you the intolerable one.

- If all strategies fail, leave the job. No one should remain in a truly intolerable situation, especially if basic integrity and principles are being compromised.

As discussed in Chapter 14, research shows that the most intense levels of stress editors experience came from dealing with the boss and the company.[14] Editors reported more serious stress when they thought that the company placed greater emphasis on profit than on the quality of the news report, or when the publisher allowed business judgments or friendships to interfere with treatment of the news. In these situations, editors reported that they were concerned about the degree of control they had over their responsibilities. Often, the concern over control manifested itself in harmful stress.

No less than editors, publishers have personality quirks. Little things they do on occasion drive editors "up the wall." Editors tolerate their publishers' behavior because, despite the quirks, the overall behavior is acceptable, or even better than acceptable. But what happens to editors when the publisher seems to be all quirks, when there is no in-between? The publisher's behavior can be contagious and it can have a devastating effect on the editor and other key subordinates of the newspaper.

The top subordinates of an eccentric publisher are drawn together by a particularly close bond and tend to lose touch with reality. In psychiatric literature, the powerful influence of an eccentric leader together with a break in reality among the leader's close subordinates is known as *folie à deux*. An example is the behavior of the subordinates of J. Edgar Hoover, the late director of the Federal Bureau of Investigation. Hoover viewed his directorship as infallible, and subordinates soon learned that dissent equaled disloyalty. No whim of Hoover's was considered too insignificant to be ignored. If it originated from Hoover, a trivial, unimportant, and even unclear order caused subordinates to take some form of calculated action. The subordinates were said to understand that they should expect trouble if they did not take the directive seriously. As a result, these directives often assumed lives of their own.[15]

When *folie à deux* occurs in organizations, conflict becomes stifling, creativity is discouraged, and distrust becomes the prevailing attitude. Affected managers react to emergencies by withdrawing or finding scapegoats instead of taking realistic actions. Corrective action for an editor might include these steps: First, establish a trusting relationship as a way of helping the "eccentric" publisher understand that his or her assumptions are invalid. Second, the editor should monitor what the publisher is susceptible to by critically appraising values, actions, and interpersonal relationships. Third, solicit the help of interested parties who might be influential in helping correct the problem. Fourth, foster a healthy work climate as a buffer against irrational behavior.[16]

Fig. 16.4

CLOSE-UP

The seventy-three executives at three major U.S. corporations who participated in research by Michael M. Lombardo, Morgan W. McCall, Jr., and Ann Morrison at the Center for Creative Leadership in Greensboro, North Carolina, identified several types of intolerable bosses. These types are:

- Snakes-in-the-grass. The most frequently mentioned failing is the lack of integrity. Bosses of this type lie, fail to keep their word, employ their authority to extort confidential information, and then use that information to a subordinate's disadvantage. Generally, they just can't be trusted.
- Dictators. The dictators, little Napoleons, or martinets are not dismayed by a string of mistakes, and take offense if anyone else makes decisions or stands out in any way. Of the intolerable types, they are both the easiest to spot and the hardest to cope with. They simply sit on people.
- Heel-grinders. "They treat others like dirt," one man said. They belittle, humiliate, and demean those beneath them, showing their insensitivity in many ways. A popular sport for heel-grinders is raking people over the coals in front of a group.

- Egotists. These blowhards know everything, won't listen, and parade their pomposity proudly. One boss plays a ruthless game in which he brings up a seemingly insurmountable problem and then disparages every solution proposed. When his subordinates run out of ideas, he presents them with the solution he had in mind all along.
- Dodgers. These bosses are unable to make decisions and shirk responsibilities whenever possible. They have never heard of the saying, "Lead, follow, or get out of the way."
- Incompetents. Bosses in this group don't know what they are doing and won't admit it. They are prime examples of the Peter Principle, individuals who have risen to the level of their incompetence.
- Detail drones. They go strictly by the book, delight in detail, and love to make big issues out of little ones.
- Slobs. Their personal habits, appearance, or prejudices are intolerable to others.

Source: Michael M. Lombardo and Morgan W. McCall, Jr., "The Intolerable Boss," *Psychology Today,* January 1984, 47.

TRUST

Like all executives, newspaper publishers exhibit human qualities that provide clues to help the editor understand what type of individual he or she is working with. Some publishers are difficult and unpredictable, and no amount of insight will lessen the editor's burden. Others are effective, sensitive executives who are able to create a partnership with their editors.

Trust is the ultimate quality in the relationship between editor and publisher. Although trust itself has no shape or form, its presence or absence is a critical force. Trust is a delicate property in human relationships. Influenced far more by actions than by words, trust takes a long time to build, but it can be destroyed very quickly. Even a single action—perhaps misunderstood—can have powerful negative effects. It is the perception of the other person and his or her actions, not the objective reality, on which trust is based. Such perceptions are profoundly influenced by emotions: needs, anxieties, guilt, expectations, and hopes. Mutual trust and open communication are closely interrelated. Open communication helps prevent misperceptions of actions, but inconsistencies between words and actions decrease trust. Openness clearly involves genuineness and honesty.[17]

A soundly run newspaper organization, of course, builds a reputation around reader trust and advertiser trust. Trust is the inherent virtue behind the business practices and the news and editorial practices of successful newspapers.

A key ingredient in the relationship between editor and publisher is trust. Based on mutual respect for personal and professional values, a trusting relationship allows freedom of action and thought, encourages supportive behavior and honest exchange of information, and enables both individuals to maintain their personal sense of worth and importance. The editor must recognize that there is a difference between liking a person and respecting him or her as a manager and a boss. A bond of respect can be the basis for a successful relationship even if personal affection is lacking.

Fig. 16.5

CLOSE-UP

When an editor concludes that a decision by the publisher to cut the staff is unacceptable, one of the editor's options is to quit. That was the choice made by Charles W. Bailey in October 1982, following the announcement that twenty-eight editorial staff members would be dropped from the *Minneapolis Star* and *Tribune*.

"This is a very serious mistake and one that will have grave consequences for the newspaper," Bailey told his staff of 230 reporters, editors, photographers, artists, and other newsroom employees. Bailey, a thirty-two–year veteran of the *Tribune* and its editor for ten years, said the reductions would make it "difficult to maintain, let alone improve" the paper's quality. Under the circumstances, he said, it would be "unthinkable to remain in any capacity," and his departure was "the only way to meet my obligations to my craft, my colleagues, and my own conscience."

A few weeks later, in his farewell column to the readers of the *Star* and *Tribune,* Bailey offered the following reflections about the role of the editor in a modern newspaper company:

"I think there are some new threats to the independence and public utility of newspaper editors. One of these is the growing tendency to encourage, in fact require, editors to become businessmen—to be part of a 'management team,' to concentrate on things that involve business rather than journalistic concerns. Now I know that an editor has to be aware of where the money comes from, but I don't think most editors are especially qualified in matters of business and finance. And even if they were, I don't think they should spend much of their time and energy on such matters.

"They have more important things to do. There will always be plenty of people around to tell a publisher how he can do things more cheaply, more profitably, less controversially. He needs someone to explain, from time to time, why things have to be done more expensively, less profitably, and in ways that create rather than avoid controversy. Editors love to play this role, but if they weren't there, publishers would need to invent somebody to play it. And I have come to believe that to the extent that editors pretend they are businessmen, they reduce their ability to do the things only they can do."

Sources: Jonathan Friendly, "Minneapolis Newspaper Editor Quits in Protest Over New Staff Cuts," *New York Times,* 8 October 1982; "Bitter Ending: An Editor Walks Out," *Time,* 18 October 1962, 101; Charles W. Bailey, "Point of View," *Minneapolis Tribune,* 7 November 1982.

In his studies at the University of Michigan's Institute for Social Research, Rensis Likert asked supervisors and managers sets of questions to measure attitudes within their companies. Many of those questions related to trust. Following are Likert's questions that seem particularly to focus on the matter of trust between editor and publisher:[18]

- To what extent does your boss convey to you a feeling of confidence that you can do your job successfully? Does he or she expect the "impossible" and fully think you can and will do it?
- To what extent is your boss interested in helping you to achieve and maintain a good income?

- To what extent does your boss try to understand your problems and do something about them?
- How much is your boss really interested in helping you with your personal and family problems?
- How much is your boss interested in training you and helping you learn better ways of doing your work?
- How much does your boss help you solve problems constructively—not tell you the answers, but help you think through your problems?
- To what extent does your boss see that you get the budget, equipment, and other resources you need to do your job well?
- To what extent is your boss interested in helping you get the developmental training that will assist you in being promoted?
- To what extent does your boss try to keep you informed about matters related to your job?
- How fully does your boss share information with you about the company, its financial condition, earnings, and plans?
- Does your boss ask your opinion when a problem comes up that involves your work? Does he or she value your ideas, seeking them and endeavoring to use them?
- Is your boss friendly and easily approached?
- To what extent is your boss generous in the credit and recognition given to others for their accomplishments and contributions rather than seeking to claim all the credit?

The interactions suggested in these questions will readily show whether the boss's behavior is supportive. In a trusting relationship, both editor and publisher know that one will not take advantage of the other. The editor will be confident of putting his or her status, job, or career into the publisher's hands. A managerial relationship that is authentic and open can be limited, of course, by organizational attitudes toward emotion. Moreover, power relationships—that is, those in which there is a boss and a subordinate—create a situation in which genuine openness is unlikely. The vulnerability of the subordinate—in this case, the editor—places some limits on the degree of openness possible. Yet even with these limits, there can be a climate of mutual trust and support that encourages a genuine respect for differences, whether in ideas, knowledge, attitudes, interests, or special skills.

CHAPTER SUMMARY

Research into the behavior of chief executives suggests that although they are genuinely interested in people and want to create a climate that fosters development, they are not prepared to develop behavior in others that matches their values.

At most newspapers, the chief executive officer is the publisher, an individual with responsibility and authority over all departments. The publisher wields the greatest power in the newspaper. Some newspapers use a bilateral management in which a general manager and an editor have separate jurisdictions and govern by consensus.

Research indicates that the type of publisher editors are most comfortable with is the one who is constructively involved in the newsroom. This type of publisher suggests major stories, uses selective praise and criticism to demonstrate what the editor should do, occasionally participates in discussions of stories, and is seen in the newsroom.

The publisher's expectations for the editor include understanding the newspaper's role, knowing the community, having a commitment to excellence, cultivating ideas and initiating change, setting standards, being sensitive and sensible, striving for an alliance with the publisher, dealing in solutions rather than problems, and initiating feedback.

Subordinates have power over the publisher when they possess skills that are difficult to replace quickly or easily, when they have specialized information or knowledge that others do not have, when they have good personal relationships with others at the newspaper, and when the performance of the subordinate can have a major impact on the performance of the boss.

Research among successful executives with difficult bosses reveals that these executives acknowledge that the boss is the boss, that the adversity of these relationships can lead to growth, that patience is important, and that there is much to be learned from watching someone else make mistakes in managing people.

Trust is a key ingredient in the relationship between the editor and the publisher. Trust is an intangible quality that depends on actions and that deals with needs, anxieties, guilt, expectations, and hopes. Mutual trust and open communication are closely related. A trusting relationship respects personal and professional values, allows freedom of thought and action, encourages supportive behavior and honest exchange of information, and enables both editor and publisher to maintain their personal sense of worth and importance.

NOTES

1. Chris Argyris, "The CEO's Behavior: Key to Organizational Development," *Harvard Business Review,* March–April 1973, 42.
2. Ibid., 43.
3. Wickham Skinner and W. Earl Sasser, "Managers with Impact: Versatile and Inconsistent," *Harvard Business Review,* November–December 1977, 140.
4. Ibid., 141–42.
5. John A. Kaufman, "Effectiveness of Bilateral and Unilateral Newspaper Administrative Structure," *Newspaper Research Journal* 2 (1981–1982): 54–64.
6. Rensis Likert, *The Human Organization* (New York: McGraw-Hill, 1967), 1–10.
7. Philip Meyer, "News Side and Business Side: Getting Us Together," *The Bulletin of the American Society of Newspaper Editors,* July–August 1983, 26–27.
8. Philip Meyer, *Editors, Publishers, and Newspaper Ethics* (Washington: American Society of Newspaper Editors, 1983), 45.
9. Meyer, "News Side and Business Side," 27.
10. Laura Longley Babb, ed., *The Editorial Page* (Boston: Houghton Mifflin, 1977), 5–6.
11. John P. Kotter, *Power and Influence: Beyond Formal Authority* (New York: The Free Press, 1985), 82.
12. Michael M. Lombardo and Morgan W. McCall, Jr., "The Intolerable Boss," *Psychology Today,* January 1984, 46–47.

13. Ibid., 47.
14. Robert H. Giles, *Editors and Stress* (Rochester: Gannett Rochester Newspapers, 1983), 16.
15. Manfred F. R. Kets de Vries, "Managers Can Drive Their Subordinates Mad," *Harvard Business Review,* July–August 1979, 125–26.
16. Ibid., 128.
17. Douglas McGregor, *The Professional Manager* (New York: McGraw-Hill, 1967), 163–64.
18. Likert, *Human Organization,* 48–49.

17

The Changing Face of the Newsroom

Beginning in the early 1980s, values in the workplace started taking on a new dimension, causing a shift from independence to interdependence and reshaping the old American ethic of rugged individualism. The demand for intellectual strength and for technical and analytical abilities remains high, but today's competent managers also are expected to acquire the additional skills of a new-style management. Described in terms of collaboration and interpersonal relationships, these updated values reflect the fact that women and racial minorities are assuming larger roles in management. The result is a blending of the concern for tasks (long viewed as a characteristic of white male managers) with the concern for people (a trait associated with women and minorities).

THE NEW MANAGERIAL COMPETENCIES

In 1972, a revealing study of forty midcareer corporate officers and their wives showed the effect of masculine reticence and aloofness on the executives' home lives. Fernando Bartolome, author of the study and a professor at the Harvard Business School, said, "The American male business executive is, in my opinion, a man caught in a stereotype. He is limited by a role definition obliging him to be super-masculine, super-tough, super–self-sufficient, and super-strong. It allows him very little freedom to be that mixture of strength and weakness, independence and dependence, toughness and tenderness which a human being is."[1]

Bartolome suggested two reasons why men devote so much of their lives to their work and so little, comparatively speaking, to achieving awareness in living and experiencing their feelings. First, men are trained to become "doers," to succeed in the world of action, but they are not trained to explore the world of emotions. In the business world, men consider feelings to be a nuisance that must be coped with lest their emotions become a threat to the effective functioning of the organization. Second, men seem to enjoy their achievements; at work they can complete something, reach a goal. In their personal relationships, Bartolome's interviews showed, men often fall short of satisfying their needs.[2]

The importance of interacting with people as part of the management role was addressed in 1974 in a series of studies by Henry Mintzberg, professor of management at McGill University in Montreal. Mintzberg showed that managers spend 50 to 90 percent of their time interacting with people. Seventy percent of managers' contact time is with groups of people, and nearly half of that is with subordinates. Twenty to 40 percent of the time managers spend interacting with others involves dealing with conflict. Only 10 percent of managers' interactions are with their own bosses. In addition, Mintzberg found, managers maintain a complex network of relationships outside their own organization.[3]

In his book, *New Rules: Searching for Self-fulfillment in a World Turned Upside Down,* Daniel Yankelovich, a psychologist and analyst of social trends, sees a new ethic of commitment emerging in the 1980s. This quest for self-fulfillment was popularized by Abraham Maslow, Carl Rogers, Eric Fromm, and others who were inspired by the traditional values of self-improvement and individualism. According to Yankelovich, these psychologists influenced an entire literature of pop psychology that permeated the culture through self-help, self-assertiveness, and inspirational books and movements. Yankelovich argues that the human self cannot be wholly autonomous, solitary, contained, and "self-created," and that there is a need for a balance between concern for self and concern for others.[4]

Mintzberg and others who thought that "people skills" were important, and inevitably necessary, began to define the additional abilities required for effective management. These characteristics, called competencies, represented capabilities that managers needed to demonstrate in their jobs.[5] For example, Mintzberg identified the following competencies necessary for modern managers: ability to maintain effective peer relationships, to mediate conflict, to facilitate creative solutions, and to know oneself.[6]

Richard E. Boyatzis, author of *The Competent Manager* and president of McBer, a business consulting firm in Boston, says top managers combine the talents of empathy and self-understanding with the traditional management competencies that emphasize problem solving and productivity.[7] He sees these managers having six specific skills:

1. Knowledge: the facts, principles, theories, and frameworks needed by managers.
2. Emotional maturity: self-control, spontaneity, accurate self-understanding, adaptability, and stamina.
3. Entrepreneurial skills: concern for unique achievement, problem solving, planning, goal setting, productivity, and efficiency.
4. Intellectual abilities: logical thought, deductive thinking, memory, conceptual ability, and political judgment.
5. Interpersonal skills: social sensitivity, empathy, alliance building, nonverbal sensitivity, respect for others, counseling, and team playing.
6. Leadership skills: presence, persuasiveness, negotiation, team building, and initiative.

Lyle Spencer, a psychologist with McBer, says the firm's research into leadership competencies—those skills that enable a person to mold others to his or her own vision—recognizes "an objectivity that allows you to see clearly the other person's feelings without your own getting in the way. Another closely related ability is being able to monitor your own feelings moment to moment."[8]

Androgynous Influences on Management Styles

The new model of managerial competencies that involves both caring for people and caring for results is having an effect in newsrooms, where white males historically dominated. The presence of women and minorities is influencing the style of managing newspeople.

Alice G. Sargent, a psychologist and author of two books on changing sex roles, *The Androgynous Manager* and *Beyond Sex Roles,* says, "The workforce is no longer primarily a homogeneous, white male population. Women and minorities have brought different values and skills to management from those of white males. Women tend to be more spontaneous, emotional, expressive, and concerned with human interaction. By contrast, the prevailing management style emphasizes an analytical, rational approach that focuses on systems and tasks. Black managers show a greater concern for employees than do white managers and place a greater value on both emotions and trust. White managers tend to value change, risk, and rationality more."[9]

What happens to the diversity that women and minorities bring to management? The tendency of white males, Sargent says, is to socialize the newcomers into their own patterns of management, thereby losing the unique skills that women and minorities offer. "[Women] put on the uniform and dressed for success . . . They stopped crying and began to express anger as men do"—by pounding the desk and gritting their teeth. They were determined to prove that anything men could do, they could do better—and they honed to a fine edge their rational, analytical thinking and competitiveness.[10]

Sargent uses the term *androgyny*—which comes from the Greek *andro,* traits of males, and *gyne,* traits of females—to describe a concept that recognizes a blending of traditional "masculine" behaviors with "feminine" behaviors. As a psychological term, *androgyny* suggests that it is possible for people to exhibit both masculine and feminine qualities, and that these values, attitudes, and behaviors reside in varying degrees in each of us. In *The Androgynous Manager,* Sargent contends that modern managers must be willing to nurture and support colleagues and subordinates, to promote interactions between bosses and subordinates and between leaders and members of work teams, and to express and accept emotions. These behaviors are desirable for their own sake, she says, but they also strengthen the organization.[11]

Many androgynous behaviors are regarded as feminine and have not been thought of as appropriate for managers. White male newspaper editors, for example, have shaped their behavior on the assumption that they should be aggressive, rational, and tough-minded. Particularly difficult for male editors is how to handle a colleague who is overcome by emotion—anger, fear, or frustration. However that emotion is expressed—whether by swearing, kicking the wastebasket, or crying—the behavior is an outlet for deep feelings. Often individuals bottle up their rage or frustration until it reaches a breaking point. The lashing out or tears are really cries for help. The editor should give comfort in the immediate crisis, and in addition, he or she should seek to establish a management environment that invites individuals to air problems and frustrations before they result in behavior that makes everyone uncomfortable.

Sociologists have associated masculinity with instrumental behavior that focuses on a problem-solving approach to work and femininity with expressive behavior that involves a concern for the welfare of others and for group cohesiveness. The idea of androgyny suggests that as more women come into newsroom management, their feminine qualities will influence the behavior of male editors and the masculine qualities of the male editors will influence the behavior of the women editors. The result of this cross-influence will be a more effective management style. Male editors will be able to promote close relationships, become more intuitive, sensitive, and collaborative, realize that work provides self-fulfillment and camaraderie, and accept emotion and spontaneity as healthy expressions. Women, on the other hand, will be able to temper emotion with logic, will be more forceful in directing tasks, will state opinions clearly in the face of disagreement from others, and will be able to evaluate more objectively the performance of individuals. The androgynous influence in newsroom management holds out the probability that we might feel human and whole in both the workplace and the home—that we might express autonomy and interdependence in all our relationships and be emotionally balanced and rational people wherever we go and in whatever we do.[12]

For their book, *Black Life in Corporate America: Swimming in the Mainstream*, George Davis and Glegg Watson interviewed 160 managers, black and white, from Fortune 500 companies, seeking to gain an understanding of how blacks—who viewed themselves as more spontaneous, emotionally expressive, and human—were fitting into the white corporate mainstream. Davis and Watson said that blacks are reared with a different set of cultural values, but that a definition of those values was elusive. "The black manager might sense that the differences are affecting his or her career, but he or she doesn't know how or how much. Very often the differences affect the comfort level, but he or she will not know what to do about this because no one ever actually says he or she is different. Whites are often embarrassed to talk about racial differences, as if these discussions might reveal some embarrassing underlying assumptions of western civilization. Blacks certainly don't want to talk about them because the entire dialogue has been tainted by concepts of white racial superiority. So it is possible to walk the corridors of many major corporations and assume incorrectly that racial differences must be inconsequential or else there would be at least some talk about them."

Davis and Watson concluded that the successful black manager must be both traditional and "new breed." Blacks must "prove themselves in situations where white managers are assumed to be capable . . . They must, in short, appear to have mastered and accepted the traditional attitudes and values of business life, while at the same time keeping in mind the real deal—that corporate politics, personality, contacts, and gamesmanship are for them, as for everyone in the environment, just as important as competence and performance."[13]

OVERCOMING DISCRIMINATION

Editors who are committed to full and fair representation in their newsrooms have recognized the need to be free from stereotypes and from the rigid role definitions that have been traditional barriers to the integration of newspaper staffs. The successful newspaper editor of the next generation will know how to recruit and manage a staff that is richly diverse in its mixture of races, sexes, ages, and interests, will recognize that such diversity is an asset to the image and the quality of the newspaper, and will understand why diversity produces strength.

Women and racial minorities have had limited opportunities to demonstrate their readiness for promotion to positions of supervisory and management responsibility. Until about 1970, women typically were hired for the "soft" news departments—society, features, or food. These content areas were considered second-class journalism by the men in charge of the newspapers, so there were fewer obstacles in the way of women's attaining leadership of these departments as opposed to sports or local news. Between 1970 and 1980, however, women began to break into editing jobs in a serious way. That process was helped considerably by several well-publicized and successful discrimination suits against major news organizations. The *Washington Post, New York Times,* Associated Press, *Detroit News, Newsday,* and *Newsweek* magazine were sued by female staffers. Each organization reached an out-of-court settlement in which the discrimination charges were denied, but large sums were paid to the women who allegedly suffered from sex discrimination and programs for promoting women were established. In the case against Associated Press, racial discrimination also was charged. The AP settlement included goals for hiring racial minorities.

Dorothy Jurney, who worked as an editor for the *Philadelphia Inquirer, Detroit Free Press,* and *Miami Herald,* publishes an annual survey of women in newsroom management. Jurney compiles her report from the newspaper staff rosters published in *Editor & Publisher YearBook*. Her 1986 survey shows that men held 87.6 percent and women 12.4 percent of the directing editorships at daily and Sunday newspapers in the United States. This represented an increase over the 11.7 percent of women in directing editorships reported in 1985.[14]

There was nothing comparable to the society or food departments for racial minorities. Few newspapers had reporters who were black, Hispanic, Asian-American, or native American. The minorities who did get jobs were highly competent and, in many cases, were seen as token acknowledgments to the belief that minority groups should be represented on the news staff.

During the civil-rights movement in the 1960s, newspapers focused their powerful resources on exposing the evils of racism. There were few blacks in newsroom jobs then, and newspapers did not see it as their obligation to eliminate discrimination in their newsrooms with the same vigor and commitment they demanded of other institutions. In 1968, the President's National Advisory Commission on Civil Disorders underscored the need for the black perspective in reporting and editing. That commission, headed by Otto Kerner, then governor of Illinois, reported that the press shared with other institutions the blame for the riots in the black ghettos of U.S. cities in 1967.

"Along with the country as a whole," the commission said, "the press has too long basked in a white world, looking out of it, if at all, with white men's eyes and a white perspective. That is no longer good enough. The painful process of readjustment that is required of the American news media must begin now."[15] More to the point, the Kerner Commission said, "The journalistic profession has been shockingly backward in seeking out, hiring, and promoting Negroes . . . The scarcity of Negroes in responsible news jobs intensifies the difficulties of communicating the reality of the contemporary American city to white newspaper and television audiences."[16]

In 1968, the year of the Kerner Report, there were about 400 minority journalists in the entire U.S. newspaper population of about 40,000. By 1979, that figure had risen to 1,900 out of more than 45,000 total newsroom employees, an increase of nearly 400 percent. By 1985, the number of minorities stood at 3,402 out of a newsroom workforce of some 53,800.[17]

During the 1970s, two black journalists, Robert C. Maynard and Jay T. Harris, emerged as forceful and innovative leaders in drawing from the newspaper establishment a stronger commitment to hire minorities. Maynard was an editor for the *Washington Post* when, in 1972, he started the Institute for Journalism Education to train minorities for newspaper jobs. Harris, a journalist and an educator, founded with his wife, Christine, the Consortium for the Advancement of Minorities in Journalism Education.

Maynard and Harris had a major influence on the decision of the American Society of Newspaper Editors to make the recruitment and promotion of minorities one of the organization's principal goals. In 1978, the ASNE board established the goal that "By the year 2000, or sooner, national employment of minorities in newsrooms would be equivalent to the percentage of minority persons within the national population." Progress toward that goal has been exceedingly slow. According to an annual ASNE survey on minority hiring, approximately 6 percent of those employed as journalists on daily newspapers are minorities. Moreover, in 1985, less than 40 percent of all newspapers in the United States employed minorities. Of those minorities employed, relatively few have risen to positions of significant influence. Based on estimates of the U.S. population in the year 2000, racial parity will be achieved if blacks, Hispanics, Asian-Americans, and native Americans make up 29 percent of the total newsroom employment.

WOMEN IN THE NEWSROOM

Women journalists are not easily deterred from a profession long dominated by men. One of the obstacles facing women has been the perception of white male editors that being female would negatively affect how women do the job. Male editors have made important strides in their attitudes about women since the days when they might discourage the hiring of a female reporter because "sooner or later she's going to get pregnant" or because they thought they couldn't send her to cover a tough police story or a riot.

As a minority in the newsroom, women learned to be close observers. They discovered that success was measured as much on how closely their performance resembled what their male colleagues had accomplished as on the merits of their own work. Women learned to decode the messages of the white male world, quickly sensing put-downs and attitudes that were intended to discount or exclude.

Rosabeth Moss Kanter, psychologist and author of *The Change Masters*, pointed out that many of the characteristics frequently attributed to women supervisors—bossiness, a tendency to take things too personally, emotionalism, excessive concern with efficiency and routine details, an inability to delegate authority—are linked to women's relatively low status in the corporate managerial hierarchy. The stereotype of the "mean and bossy" woman manager "is a perfect picture of people who are powerless. Furthermore, people who feel vulnerable and unsure of themselves, who are plunged into jobs without sufficient training . . . are more likely to first adopt authoritarian controlling leadership styles. The behavior attributed to women supervisors is likely to be characteristic of new and insecure supervisors generally."[18]

In an extensive study specifically addressing management styles, Jay Hall and Susan Donnell, psychologists for a management training company, reached the conclusion that women do not manage differently from men. They matched nearly two thousand men and women managers according to age, rank in their organization, kind of organization, and the number of people they supervised. The psychologists evaluated diverse skills, from managerial philosophies to the ability to get along with people. Donnell and Hall concluded that "male and female managers do not differ in the way they manage the organization's technical and human resources."[19]

Women Editors

A three-year study of seventy-five women newspaper managers provides insight into how these women view themselves and what kinds of goals they set. The study was published in 1983 by Ardyth Sohn, associate professor of journalism at the University of Colorado. She found that the women, all of whom held midlevel management jobs, set modest goals for themselves and may have hurt their chances for promotion by thinking in terms of personal rather than institutional objectives in making five-year plans. Following are Sohn's conclusions:[20]

- The women newspaper managers in the study were willing to make a full commitment to their jobs. They recognized that to be successful on the job, they must sacrifice time they might rather spend on relationships, family, and children.
- The women set goals in a vacuum. There appeared to be little connection between their personal goals and those of the company. Few of the goals listed would earn them recognition by the newspaper company or, possibly, a promotion to the next position they desired.
- During the following five years, most of the women expected to reach no more than two levels above the position they currently held. None of the women surveyed expected to make it to the top-ranking position. The women said they did not expect to be promoted quickly, even though their careers were the focus of their lives.

The women and their newspapers could make adjustments, Sohn concluded, that would help the women meet the complex demands of their personal and professional lives. Among the adjustments mentioned were the development of flexible schedules and options, such as day-care facilities at work, plus emphasis on individual goal setting, including the freedom to reach for the top.

No individual entering the newspaper business should be surprised to be working for a woman at some time during his or her career. Today, the newspaper industry has advanced well beyond the time when the "first" women editors were made to feel as if they were part of a grand experiment.

One of the most significant trends in newspaper management during the 1980s has been the rise of women to important leadership positions. Women as publishers, editors, and advertising and marketing directors are no longer seen as rarities. While the numbers are still small, the change they represent is enormous. The barriers came down first at small and midsized newspapers. The women who became the pacesetters—with their determination and enthusiasm for risk taking and a willingness to pay a personal price for success—are making it easier for others to follow. By demonstrating strong technical skills and effective management styles, they are proving that the old stereotypes don't wash anymore.

Judith G. Clabes, recalling her work as editor of the *Sunday Courier & Press* in Evansville, Indiana, said, "It's funny how time seems to bridge so many gaps. After five years, I suppose I've settled in and the staff and community have settled in with me. I'm feeling a bit comfortable (not counting the ever-present drive to do better the next time). Everyone seems to be more comfortable, too. Either those in the community who resisted have become accustomed or resigned. Or maybe they've seen that the Sunday paper isn't going to hell in a handbasket after all. Recently, a young reporter I hired shortly after I became editor said to me: 'I can't imagine what it would be like to work for a man!' I suppose that's progress."[21]

Clabes discovered that "editors are just regular people with a job to do—and a lot more responsibility. And no one editor—male or female—does it like any other. A lot of that responsibility is to people who work for them—and who expect them to be fair, evenhanded, knowledgeable, helpful, reliable, and consistent. A great deal of the responsibility is to the community and the readers we serve—a diverse group, all around; there is surely no particular 'type' who suits them all."[22]

Fig. 17.1

CLOSE-UP

Are there qualities that distinguish women editors? Deborah Howell, executive editor of the *St. Paul Pioneer Press and Dispatch* in Minnesota, thinks there may be, and at the risk of grossly generalizing, offers this list:

- A male editor is considered exceptional if he has people skills that go beyond the ordinary requirements of the job. A woman is expected to have them.

- Having a personal talk with an employee is sometimes easier for women than for some men, especially if the employee is a woman. Men are embarrassed to cry. It doesn't bother most women if other women cry and I don't care if men do, and that's happened more than once.

- Women editors are tougher on women working for them than men are. We won't put up with it if a woman tries to lay a "helpless" number on us.

- It is easier for us to give someone a pat on the shoulder or a hug. A male editor has to watch more carefully how he uses body language lest he be suspected of being sexist.

- Women have been brought up to be more flexible, more given to looking for consensus—to keeping the family happy and together—especially when the issue is not one of principle.

- And, finally, I think our upbringing has allowed us to be more human and more humane. I'm not afraid to say I screwed up and I'm not afraid to tell people I love them.

Source: Deborah Howell, "Maybe we are different—but we still can be good editors," *The Bulletin of the American Society of Newspaper Editors,* January 1986, 6.

Stan Strick, managing editor of the *Herald* of Everett, Washington, has worked for three women editors in a newspaper career that spans more than twenty years. "Thinking back over those times, which included several stints when men were my bosses," he says, "I find it surprising to say that there seems to be little to write about 'working for a woman.' Differences of style and substance were evident, but nothing I would attribute to gender. I didn't find the men I worked for more authoritarian or the women more nurturing. If anything, the male and female newsroom managers I knew shared a common aggressiveness toward the news and a skepticism, if not outright irreverence, for things held culturally sacred. The roots of such behavior could, I suppose, be traced to *The Front Page* and is most likely to be simply an occupational trait."[23]

Still, the fact that the competitive pool is now larger and includes women and racial minorities has had an effect on white males. The most sought-after newsroom jobs—positions traditionally held by white males, as if that were the way of the world—are now being coveted by someone else.

Jayne Vogan, an associate professor of counselor education at the State University of New York at Brockport who has counseled groups of white male editors on the topic, says the discovery that the pool of competitors is larger is met, first, with "a certain amount of denial that 'this isn't going to affect me.' But when they see someone else usurping a power position that they took for granted, it makes them angry. I think that the idea of umbrage is at the root of" the white male reaction.[24]

Even if the white male gets over fear for his job, he must deal with women and minorities as professional colleagues, learning new behaviors in order to interact with them. "On the one hand," says Vogan, "the white male thinks he may have to treat these people differently, and at the same time he is being told not to treat them differently. But the people who are 'invading' his newsroom bring a whole acculturated group of interpersonal behaviors with them that the white males in power don't know anything about. So that leads to the business of what do you do with a woman who cries or a black who gets belligerent, to name two of the more obvious stereotypes. What becomes an extra burden to the white male is quite subtle. It gives rise to many white male attitudes about women and minorities getting special treatment—the whole token theory—whereas the white male thinks he is a better person but is being discriminated against in a reverse way."[25]

The tricky part is helping the white male understand why there is a need for a better mix of races and sexes in the newsroom. "The important part of it is being truthful and using that to build trust," says Vogan. "Most white male journalists will understand an explanation that we can't have everybody who is the same in the newsroom; it presents too narrow a view, it doesn't reflect the diversity of the community we serve. Assure them that, in the long run, the best performers will get ahead. Tell them they are on the right track, if they are, and what they need to do to reach their goals."[26]

SEXUAL HARASSMENT

Sexual harassment is a serious problem for the editor and the newspaper organization as well as for the individual being harassed. The number of complaints alleging sexual harassment has increased sharply as a result of guidelines issued in 1978 by the federal Equal Employment Opportunity Commission. Those guidelines confirmed that sexual harassment is a violation of Title VII of the 1964 Civil Rights Act. Although no known cash awards have been made as a result of newspaper-related sexual-harassment cases, several complaints are pending. In all industries, an estimated $180 million was paid to settle sexual-harassment claims filed between 1978 and 1980.[27]

Interpretation of Title VII by the courts is placing increased liability on employers. In a decision by the U.S. Circuit Court of Appeals for the District of Columbia, an employer can be held liable for acts of sexual harassment committed by a supervisor, regardless of whether the employer knew about the supervisor's conduct. The court said that Title VII outlaws sex discrimination by an "agent" of the employer. In this case, the supervisor was a branch manager of a bank. The court held that the manager was the bank's "agent" as far as other employees were concerned, and his unlawful practices were attributable to the bank. The court also concluded that the ruling should cover the lowest-level supervisory employees, even though they may not have the power to hire, fire, or promote personnel.[28]

Sexual harassment includes unwelcome sexual advances, requests for sexual favors, and other verbal or physical conduct of a sexual nature. Specifically, EEOC guidelines say that the basic sexual harassment categories are:

- Quid pro quo. Terms of employment reflect sexual demands, or the level of benefits—or employee punishment—depends on the granting of sexual favors.

- Environmental. An employer allows an intimidating, hostile, or offensive work environment to exist as the result of sexual advances or remarks. The courts have ruled that such an environment exists even if the employee did not lose any tangible job benefits or even if the employee submitted to the manager's advances.

- Indirect. An employee granting sexual favors receives greater benefits and/or promotions at the expense of an equally qualified employee. Sexual harassment is by no means limited to males harassing females. As more women move into supervisory positions, there may be charges from men who claim to have been harassed by their female bosses. Harassment also can occur between individuals of the same sex.

Off-color jokes and gestures, as well as more aggressive sexual advances, have been the subject of lawsuits against newspaper companies. One suit involved a good-night kiss at a Christmas party. Most of the cases have been settled. Some alleged incidents were disproved. Strong disciplinary actions were taken in other instances.[29]

Many newspapers have introduced policies on sexual harassment that spell out what behavior is not permitted and what the consequences can be for employees found guilty of sexual harassment. In addition to issuing a statement on sexual harassment, for example, the *Columbus* (Ohio) *Dispatch* requires all supervisors to take a twenty-hour course on employment laws.

Fig. 17.2

CLOSE-UP

Many newspaper companies are relaxing rules that forbid one staffer to be married to another. Their motive is to avoid losing talented employees and to forestall sex-discrimination suits by women, who typically have been the spouses who lose their jobs.

When corporations initially set the rules on office romance, their intent was to keep executives from dallying with their secretaries. In recent years, however, the presence of more women working alongside men as professionals and managers has invited office romances of a quite different order.

The *Kansas City Star* had a strict policy of forcing one member of a couple to leave if they married after meeting on the job. In April 1984, the newspaper's top features editor and the editor of its Sunday magazine became engaged and told management they wouldn't leave their jobs voluntarily, forcing the paper to change the policy or fire one of them.

That month, a notice was posted in the newsroom announcing an end to the ban on employing spouses. The new policy merely forbade one spouse to supervise the other. But the new rule wasn't liberal enough to allow both editors to continue working at the *Star*, because the features editor was the Sunday editor's supervisor.

Then a second notice appeared: The Sunday magazine was being removed from the features editor's responsibility.

A few weeks later, the marriage announcement was posted in the newsroom.

Source: Monica Langley, "Executive Sweets: Office Marriages Win More Firms' Blessings, but Problems Crop Up," *Wall Street Journal*, 16 October 1984, 1, 21.

RACIAL MINORITIES IN THE NEWSROOM

Editors and publishers are giving increasing attention to the racial and ethnic diversity in the communities their newspapers serve. Our towns and cities are populated by individuals rich in the compound influences of race, nationality, language, religion, region, and subregion. Cultural heritage remains sharply defined even as newcomers are assimilated into an "American" life-style and become U.S. citizens. The civil-rights movement aroused fresh recognition and respect for black culture and black history. The influx of Cubans, Puerto Ricans, and Mexicans to our cities has introduced Hispanic and Latino traditions. The movement of Asian-Americans to our shores, especially since the end of the Vietnam War, has increased. Even the American Indians, long ignored and discriminated against, have called attention to the values of their native American heritage by aggressively seeking redress for lands taken from them more than a century ago.

The sad paradox is that even as their struggle for equality has been chronicled in news columns and championed on the editorial pages, Hispanics, blacks, native Americans, and Asian-Americans, by and large, have been excluded from work as journalists on daily newspapers.

Seeing life on both sides is one of the fundamental tenets of journalism. Editors tried for many years to serve this master without fully understanding how the perspective of the reporter and the editor influenced the shape of the news report. The news came through filters that were white and male. The absence of women and minorities on news staffs meant that the editors and reporters, who were the custodians of fairness, balance, and completeness, were really seeing life only from one side. The belief was that objectivity knew no race or gender. If reporters and editors did their job, the other concerns would be swept away by the force of professionalism. In reality, however, the news columns were lacking cultural and ethnic diversity. Moreover, the racial minorities and the women on the staff were expected to see the world through white male eyes.

When a reporter attempts to extract meaning from an event or a file of reports and translate the information into a story, a number of individual choices are made. A black, Hispanic, or white female reporter may make a choice that a white male reporter would not make. Such culturally influenced choices underscore the ability of minorities and women to reflect the diversity of our world and our communities—clearly illustrating the value of including women and minorities on the news staff.

In her class exercises on decision making in the Kellogg Graduate School of Management at Northwestern University, Denise Rousseau puts groups of students together to resolve a crisis situation. One exercise, for example, is called "Desert Survival."[30] Groups of five or six students are told they have survived a plane crash in the desert, they have a limited amount of supplies, and they are presented with a variety of choices to make—first as individuals and then as a group—that may or may not result in their rescue. Rousseau, a psychologist, says the outcome of the exercise consistently supports the idea that heterogeneous groups—groups with mixtures of races and sexes—make higher-quality decisions than homogeneous groups. The mixed groups are more likely to survive the plane crash in the desert than are groups of white males.

One of the true challenges of integrating the newsroom is to find ways to draw on the strengths of its multicultural environment. The Asian perspective, the black perspective, the Hispanic perspective, the women's perspective—each is an important ingredient in the process of deciding how to handle the news.

Alice G. Sargent fears that companies are attempting to "mainstream" minorities rather than build multicultural organizations. "I have seen the rational decision-making management style being taught to black managers, for example, who would naturally bring a more people-oriented management style to their work; just dropping by, talking to people, doing business through people, a more human way of doing it." As a result, Sargent says, black managers end up with a "high task, low relationship" style at work, which is not their natural bent, necessarily, not the way a lot of black managers grew up. (See discussion of situational leadership in Chapter 7.)

"The whole value of cultural differences eventually has to do with the organization's ability to tap into creativity and quality. Once you shift from talking about outputs and results to talking about high performance and innovation and excellence and quality, then you know that you need to get everybody involved in what's going on."[31]

Fig. 17.3

CLOSE-UP

Ellis Cose, president of the Institute for Journalism Education, tells of being interviewed by a journalism student who was writing a paper on minorities and the press. The conversation came around to the student's own anxieties about finding a job.

"Why should a minority journalist get a job instead of me?" he asked.

"You assume," replied Cose, "that a decision on employment that takes race into consideration is unfair. Yet nearly all employment decisions are unfair. They are biased by such things as school and family ties and even by whether the interviewer likes the same music or clothes as the person applying for the job. Those biases favor white males because white males tend to do the hiring. Yet when white males get jobs, we pretend that it's only because they're competent; when minorities get jobs, we assume it's only because they're minorities. Doesn't that strike you as absurd?"

Fig. 17.3, continued

There was a long pause, which the student ended by saying, "You know, I never looked at it that way."

Later, Cose observed that "a lot of news executives, reporters, and reporters-to-be have never looked at it 'that way.' Despite their basic decency—or maybe because of it—many white editors and reporters believe that to allow ethnicity to influence hiring and promotion is to somehow taint the process. Yet they also realize that to accept the corollary is to accept the absurd: that the status quo is bias free, that we live in a world without race.

"The result is a good deal of ambivalence among those who believe in hiring and promoting minorities, but who also believe in the basic fairness of a system that routinely denies access and opportunity to minorities. Minority journalists see the ambivalence—often label it hypocrisy—and question the commitment of those editors who claim to want to help."

Source: Ellis Cose, "Keeping the Faith: Hiring and Promoting More Minority Journalists Is Not Only Right, It's Necessary," *The Quill,* October 1985, 10.

The experience of Jay Harris, a former columnist for Gannett News Service who covered the entry of Jesse Jackson into the 1984 Democratic presidential primaries, illustrates how the perspective of a minority journalist may differ from that of white male editors. Harris, who became executive editor of the *Philadelphia Daily News* in 1985, recalls that in February 1983, when he broke the story that Jackson might run for president the following year, "there were some of us who thought there was something very special going on. A movement was starting again. The story was edited with the knowledge that it was a very sensitive and nontraditional sort of conclusion that Jesse Jackson might actually run for president. My editors at GNS had enough faith in my professional ability to take it on its merits and run it. For months, others here didn't want to cover the story. They thought that, basically, I had been overcome by my blackness. And that I was doing propaganda for black people. It became apparent some time later that, in fact, we were well ahead of everybody else in reporting a change in American politics, in American life.

"The Jesse Jackson affair pointed up the absolute inability of many white editors to accept that their conventional wisdom is wrong about black voters. This whole area of black and white perspective—we have not thought about what it means. But the fact is that you and I can go to an event and we can share and honor and adhere to the same sets of journalistic standards and practices and we can write two very, very different stories. I insist that it is my right to do that as long as I honor the rules.

"Let's assume you are my editor. I think you have every right to check to make sure that I follow the rules. But if I follow the rules and you have no reason to doubt my competence, you don't get to change the conclusion. Because if you do, you are telling me a whole other thing about this craft. You are telling me that I have, ultimately, to accept your culture. Not only do I have to adhere to your standards, but I have to come to your conclusions. Then there is no role for me as an independent thinker. It is really not my judgment you want."[32]

Hiring Minorities

Nancy Hicks, former president of the Institute for Journalism Education, says that "ultimately there is not going to be a natural change or any real change [in hiring practices] until editors who are in charge believe in the competence of people of color in journalism, that they really are ready, that they really are intelligent enough to do the job. Until there is an acceptance of the intelligence and the cultural difference of minority journalists, the change in employment isn't going to be made."[33]

Despite the discouragingly slow progress, there seems to be a growing belief, nevertheless, that hiring and promoting minorities is good business. Laurence G. O'Donnell, associate editor of the *Wall Street Journal,* suggests that editors increasingly are beginning to perceive that "a newspaper is only as good as the diversity of the eyes and ears on its staff." Allen H. Neuharth, chairman of the Gannett Company, Inc., is a leader in the newspaper industry in hiring and promoting minorities and in holding his executives accountable for their performance in this area. "If your leadership does not reflect your readership," he says "you're just not going to do as well. If you have all white males putting out a newspaper, you have a minority newspaper."[34]

Although there has been an increase in the pool of minorities with demonstrated skills and talent looking for newsroom jobs, too few minorities are being attracted into college journalism programs. In a 1984 survey of 1,366 minority high school seniors for the Associated Press Managing Editors Association, Judee and Michael Burgoon of the University of Arizona and David Buller of Texas Tech University concluded that the failure of journalism programs to attract or retain minority students can be explained by the following factors:[35]

- Education and career aspirations. Business/commerce, the health professions, engineering, and computer sciences were the top preferences. Communication-related fields were listed first by less than 5 percent of the minority students.

- Academic performance and aptitude. The research indicated that, for a variety of reasons, minority students do not have the same levels of academic performance as whites. Despite the lower overall ranking, it is still evident from the data that there is a large pool of minority students with excellent academic credentials and abilities—but few of them are headed for newsrooms.

- Academic preparation. Research shows that communication-related fields may gain minority students who are avoiding math and science but may lose those whose reading and writing skills are deficient. While there is evidence that writing skills pose a problem for some minorities—as they do for deficiently prepared white students—it is clearly not the case that inability to write is a primary reason for the extremely small number of minorities now in newsrooms or working to get there.

- Interests, accomplishments, and activities. Extracurricular activities and interests are excellent predictors of educational and career choices, and many minority students are involved in activities such as the school yearbook or radio station that should whet an interest in journalism. Those who get started early with writing and reporting activities are much more likely to consider continuing with journalism as a way of life.

- Important job criteria. The ability of the workplace to satisfy the personal and psychological needs of the individual is often cited as a strong predictor of job choice. The job characteristics most often identified by minority students as being important were the opportunity for professional advancement, personal independence, responsibility, and advancement based on merit.
- Influences on choice of major subject and career. The most important influence is the personal enjoyment derived from activities involved in the job. Related to this are proficiency in writing, speaking, and language, work experience, and extracurricular activities. A second important cluster of job influences includes job prestige, job availability, and salary potential. A third factor is a student's educational preparation and aptitude for a job.
- Sources of information. Minority students do not think they are well informed about journalism as a career option. These students rely heavily on written materials about programs and colleges rather than personal contacts with college representatives or professional journalists.
- Image of journalism. Minority students who constitute the best prospects for entering journalism hold highly favorable impressions of it. They see journalistic work as challenging, important, fascinating, satisfying, and creative.

It is clear from this research that without increased recruitment efforts, it will become more difficult to attract qualified minority candidates to become journalism majors and pursue newspaper careers. The number of minorities enrolled annually in college programs is insufficient to meet the needs of the newspaper industry. The problem cannot be corrected without initiating information and recruitment programs for high school students.

Fig. 17.4

CLOSE-UP

From his own survey of fifty-two editors, David Hawpe, managing editor of the *Louisville Courier-Journal*, developed the following suggestions for minority recruitment in the newsroom:

1. A commitment from the top. The key to getting more minorities on the staff is for the person at the top—the publisher or the editor—to make a commitment and see that it gets done.

2. Everybody has to get the word. One way to do this is for the top executives to do some minority recruitment of their own. Another way is for the company to agree to hire a strong minority candidate, even if there is not an immediate and appropriate opening.

3. Those in charge have to be tough on this issue. The bosses must set specific goals, hold individuals accountable for meeting the goals, and where appropriate, use quotas. Some companies use Management by Objectives for setting minority-hiring goals. The editor's success in achieving the goals should be reflected in his or her annual bonus.

4. Find minority prospects when they are young, before they reach college. Intern programs, student newspapers, workshops, counseling, and seminars are ways of identifying promising candidates while they are in junior or senior high school.

5. Give minority students scholarships or other financial aid. Many newspapers establish scholarship programs in connection with nearby journalism schools. Others offer financial aid directly to local students who want to pursue a journalism education.

6. Work with youngsters while they are in college. Some newspapers are assisting in the creation of National Association of Black Journalists chapters on college campuses. Individual newspaper internships funded by national programs such as the Dow Jones Newspaper Fund's minority internships also are available.

7. After they graduate, give minorities training in your newsroom or introduce them to training options available elsewhere. National organizations such as the Poynter Institute, the Associated Press, the Institute for Journalism Education, the Dow Jones Newspaper

Fund, as well as individual newspapers have training programs aimed at preparing minorities for entry-level newsroom jobs.

8. Search hard for promising graduates. Editors can look for candidates at major job conferences, which are held each year, and by sending recruiters into the field.

9. Give those already on the staff, but who need more training, extra help. Involve them in seminars, institutes, and in-service programs.

10. Take special measures when necessary. This will help overcome the special financial and logistical problems that some minority candidates face—for example, co-signing for credit union loans, making adjustments in schedules, signing for deposits with utility companies. Many minorities come into the work place with a diploma and little else. The editor who is not willing to concede that and offer support is living in a dream world—or is not serious about hiring minorities.

11. Once you hire minority staffers, don't forget them. There is a need to nurture and develop minorities through routine feedback and sometimes through special training. Help them become socialized in the newsroom, be sensitive to their expectations and their needs.

12. Reach out and touch someone in the community. Meet with readers and leaders from minority communities. Listen to them. Ask them to evaluate the newspaper. And invite them to tell you of young minorities they know who might become interested in a newspaper career.

Source: David V. Hawpe, "A 12-Point Action Plan for Finding and Developing Minority Staff Members," *The Bulletin of the American Society of Newspaper Editors*, February 1985, 4–6.

In a study published in 1985 by the Institute for Journalism Education, 340 journalists—more than two hundred of them minorities—hired by newspapers in ten selected cities were interviewed about their career choices and aspirations. The report, written by Ellis Cose, president of IJE, challenges some widely held beliefs about minority journalists:[36]

- Minorities are not notorious job hoppers, despite the common perception that lack of significant upward mobility for minorities causes them to change jobs often or that demonstrated ability makes such journalists attractive candidates for larger newspapers.
- Minority journalists—women in particular—are more likely than whites to say they desire careers in newspaper management. That desire seems to be linked to the aspiration of many minorities to "effect change" both within and outside the profession.
- While minority women are particularly desirous of careers in management, they are the least likely of all groups to have been given managerial responsibilities.
- Though most minorities report they are either satisfied or highly satisfied with their jobs, some 40 percent expect to leave journalism largely because of what they report as a lack of opportunity for advancement.
- The vast majority of minority senior executives are highly satisfied with their jobs and think it extremely unlikely that they will leave journalism.
- Among all minority journalists, those who have been given managerial responsibilities are significantly less likely to think they eventually will leave the profession than their nonmanagement coworkers.

The IJE found the minority journalists it surveyed to be highly skeptical about the commitment of the newspaper industry to the goals it espouses. Cose described the situation as a "quiet crisis" in the newspaper profession because of "the belief of large numbers of minority professionals that the industry would never provide them with the opportunities they desire." The frustration of minorities is particularly acute over the lack of management opportunities. Nearly twice as many minority journalists as whites want careers in newspaper management, but few have the opportunity. Explained one black female editorial writer: "The whole reason I got into the news business was to effect change. As a reporter, I can influence one piece. As a manager, I can influence several pieces in one day."[37]

Interactions between Whites and Minorities

For the white editor who works with minorities and for the minority manager in a newsroom dominated by whites, there are patterns of behavior that will lead to successful multicultural management. Our understanding of this interaction will be helped by examining a model that represents the learning process experienced by black managers in a white organization. The model is based on research by Floyd Dickens, an engineer with Proctor & Gamble, and Jacqueline Dickens, his wife and a counselor in teambuilding, racial awareness, and career planning for black managers. A report of their research was published in 1982 as a book, *The Black Manager: Making It in the Corporate World*.[38] Although the book's focus is black managers, the phases of adjustment could apply to any minority individuals, including a white who would become an editor on a newspaper where the staff might be dominantly black, Hispanic, native American, or Asian-American.

The Dickens' model has four phases: (1) the entry phase, (2) the adjusting phase, (3) the planned-growth phase, and (4) the success phase.

1. Entry phase. The thoughts of blacks entering a white workplace are influenced by personal doubts that they can make it and by the realization that they may have been hired "because" they are black, that they may not have been the best person available for the job. The way white society perceives the competence of blacks can cause blacks to feel unsure of themselves. Although blacks may not believe these negative perceptions, they tend to internalize them to some degree.

   As blacks enter new jobs, the level of stress they experience depends on how they interpret their preparedness to work in a traditional organization. Among the concerns that produce stress are how they will fit in, both in the corporate picture and socially, whether they will get the quality of help needed to do the job, and whether their education compares favorably to that of their white peers.

Black managers typically exhibit one of two kinds of behavior during this phase: fit-in behavior or avoidance behavior. They attempt to fit in by acting "nice" around white managers so they can be seen in a favorable light. Avoidance is trying to stay away from whites as much as possible.

2. Adjusting phase. In this phase, the doubts gradually dissipate as the black managers adjust to the white organizational setting. This gain in confidence comes mostly from success on the job. Blacks who do not experience success, however, will become increasingly less confident and will continue to operate with entry-level attitudes for a long time.

One attitude that begins to change in this phase is the belief that hard work alone will bring a reward. They discover that the highly successful individuals benefit from more than just a strong work ethic. Because the number of positions at the top is limited, other considerations come into play in the competition. Blacks come to see racism as a barrier to their promotability. They recognize that many who get ahead have a senior manager to coach and guide them. A mentor-protégé relationship between whites is normal in a corporation, but the process breaks down with blacks. Blacks tend not to know how to develop a relationship with a potential white sponsor and whites don't know how to select a black protégé. A factor that inhibits blacks from getting sponsors is the black manager's need to feel emotionally attached to the sponsor. Whites tend not to have this need. Understanding the company's norms and values is an important factor for black managers in adjusting their attitudes to the corporate milieu.

When blacks detect prejudicial behavior in whites, they react by seeking closer contact with other blacks, partly for support and partly to determine whether other blacks are experiencing the same kinds of situations. Confrontive behavior is more important to the survival and success of black managers than it is to their white peers. White managers can avoid confrontation, but for blacks, confrontation is seen as necessary in many situations to avoid running the risk of having their ideas, opinions, and suggestions discounted.

3. Planned-growth phase. This is a period of consciously structured activity for black managers. If there is no change in organizational behavior toward minorities, blacks begin to accept the responsibility for changing their own styles and methods of operating. Black managers will work hard to improve their personal style of interacting with whites. They will consciously look for successes and for strokes from others to help build self-confidence. Black managers also learn how to keep others' prejudicial behavior from being obstacles to their own progress.

   In this phase, black managers will seek out mentors. They become involved in success issues rather than survival issues. They are able to separate the organization's problems from their own and focus on changing any personal behaviors that prevent them from being effective.

   In the planned-growth phase, black managers elect to keep their misgivings to themselves. They behave in a manner of trust, seeking out sponsors and using resources, racist or not. A commitment to succeed becomes the paramount goal.

   Two important skills acquired by blacks during this phase are conflict management and the management of racism. Management of racism involves behaviors developed by blacks to counteract and neutralize demeaning, prejudicial behavior directed toward them by people of another race or ethnic group.

4. Success phase. Black managers are successful when they have learned the appropriate skills that apply to their position in a white organization. One of the keys is learning that making mistakes or failing is not an option for black managers. When a white person fails, the failure is that person's. When a black person fails, the person fails for the group. Every black failure reinforces the expectations of the white system.

Successful black managers are aware of their blackness at all times and know how this affects the white corporation. They must constantly be aware of who they are and how they are perceived. To forget the impact of racism is tantamount to losing or giving up one's survival instincts. They learn to use anger and rage as part of their strategy to enhance their effectiveness on the job. They channel those behaviors into producing better results. They no longer allow emotions to be a barrier to progress.

Black managers in the success phase behave in a manner that conveys confidence, knowledge, and the appearance of being in charge. They understand how to negotiate the system. They have learned how to confront whites in a way that leaves both parties with their dignity.

INTELLECTUAL DEVELOPMENT

Intellectual development has long been recognized as a key to success. Individuals who experience the phases of adjustment identified by Floyd and Jacqueline Dickens are developing intellectually.

Jeff Howard, a Harvard-educated black social psychologist specializing in performance and motivation, says that intellectual development is one of the major benefits available to blacks as a result of the civil-rights movement and the Supreme Court decisions that guarantee access to public and private institutions in the United States.

Howard defines development as the process of building skills, competency, and self-confidence, of expanding one's capacity to contribute to the goals of the organization and to envision personal goals in an organization.

"Development is a process that some people begin engaging in very early in life and other people, for various reasons, do not engage in," Howard says. "There are problems in black culture that have generated intellectual mediocrity. There is a bias in black culture, especially black youth culture, that is really a terrible problem, and that is that kids who are academically inclined are often brutalized within their own culture. Kids who are athletically inclined, socially inclined, sexually inclined are elevated. I don't want to give the impression that this is strictly a youth problem because all those kids have parents, and problems that look like kid problems are really adult problems."[39]

Howard notes that successful groups place high value on intellectual performance. They encourage the drive to excel and use competition to sharpen skills and to stimulate development in each succeeding generation. The developed people that result from this process become the pool from which leaders are drawn. Competition is clearly not the whole story; cooperation and solitary study are valuable, too. But of the various keys to intellectual development, competition seems to fare worst in the estimation of many blacks.[40]

Howard thinks that development can be the "conceptual underpinning" for editors who want to address the question of "how do we get black newspeople who are meeting the same standards as everybody else, who are enjoying their work, and who are staying around after we recruit them. It is also a basis for reconciling the often-conflicting notions of affirmative action and merit."[41]

Expectations control performance to an important degree (see discussion of the motivational theory of expectancy in Chapter 3). By manipulating expectations, editors can influence differences in performance in two significant ways, says Howard. First, by communicating a high level of expectation, the editor can increase "the quality of performance behavior the individual is able to bring to the task." The second major effect is on the way individuals explain their successes or failures—a tendency known as *attribution*. Individuals describe successes and failures in one of two ways:[42]

1. Internal/external. "I succeeded or failed because of something about me or because of something outside of me."
2. Stable/unstable. "I succeeded or failed because of something that won't change or something that will."

Howard thinks attributions are played out in the following way among newsroom blacks: Individuals with low confidence attribute success to luck—an unstable, external factor—thereby setting themselves up for the expectation that they will not be successful the next time. Failures among individuals with low confidence are explained by lack of ability—a stable, internal factor.

Confidence is described by Howard as a "social phenomenon," which is influenced by social interaction and can be managed. "This society has managed the confidence level of black Americans around intellectual activities and has managed it way down."[43]

Following are three techniques Howard suggests to editors for managing the confidence levels and the performance development of black newspeople:[44]

1. Communicate high expectations in ways that will encourage an intensity of effort, high levels of concentration, and the willingness to take reasonable risks—all factors in the development of self-confidence and new skills.

2. Pay close attention to performance behavior and the effort being expended by minority individuals. Reinforce signs of success.

3. Take control of the process by which blacks explain what is happening to them. Emphasize that success resulted from ability (an internal/stable factor) and failure from inadequate effort (an internal/unstable factor).

THE TOTAL NEWSROOM

Management has been increasingly the focus of study and commentary. In the early 1980s, the popularity of books on management pushed many titles to the top of the best-seller lists. Tom Peters, Rosabeth Moss Kanter, Peter F. Drucker, and Kenneth H. Blanchard became oft-quoted authors, appearing on television talk shows and lecturing to audiences eager to absorb the new wisdom on management.

Going back to Henri Fayol's early writings about management (see Chapter 1) and following the recurrent themes through nearly three-quarters of a century of thought and discovery, one finds the subject of management infinitely complex, yet strikingly straightforward. The common denominator, the most effective test in recognizing why some companies succeed and others fail, is people: how they are selected, how they are treated, how they perform.

To editors and students who wonder what challenges will confront newsroom managers in the 1990s and the early years of the twenty-first century, we can suggest that the basic principles of problem solving, motivation, leadership, and reaffirming values will not change. The situations may be different, but the fundamentals of how to ensure competent handling of people and competent performance will remain.

A review of a few critical episodes during the past generation can help us understand both the influences that altered our craft and how the basic rules of management, once initiated by editors, affected the outcomes.

In the 1960s, a "new journalism" appeared, influenced by writer Tom Wolfe and his work in the Sunday magazine of the *New York Herald Tribune.* Reporters eagerly tried Wolfe's style—often with limited success—using fictional devices to tell a story and acting as advocates, interpreters, and critics rather than as the translators of events. As with most movements, the new journalism tended to get out of control. Editors were slow to recognize how reporters' experiments with a new freedom of written expression were undercutting the traditional standards of accuracy and fairness. Once they caught on, editors began to manage by enforcing traditional standards more vigorously while encouraging reporters to adopt some of the ideas of the new journalism.

The civil-rights movement, the Vietnam War, and the domestic violence they spawned influenced the emergence of reporters of social conflict who often were unable to separate their own emotions from the stories they covered. Until editors reestablished control over the reporting and editing processes, the excesses of some sociologist-journalists tarnished the thoroughly professional enterprise of many reporters covering the same stories.

And, the Watergate investigation and the reporting of Bob Woodward and Carl Bernstein of the *Washington Post,* which forced President Richard Nixon to resign, demonstrated the awesome power of the press. After Watergate began an era of exposures that saw newspapers pursue the powerful with an unchecked zeal, an era that produced a backlash against the press from readers, corporate executives, public figures, and office holders. When editors were finally convinced that a serious credibility gap existed, they began to manage the crisis by reinforcing the traditional standards of balance and fairness in the news report.

The emergence of women and racial minorities, first as the seekers of opportunity and then as competitors with white males in the fullest sense, put before editors what seemed a new kind of managerial challenge, but which, in fact, required adherence to the basic rules for sensitive, competent handling of people.

Tomorrow's challenges and tomorrow's crises will be opportunities in a variety of disguises, and editors will discover in them the strains of previous situations. We cannot predict the shape of the problems that will pass across editors' desks during the next generation; however, it is safe to suggest that editors increasingly will be faced with greater competition for hiring and keeping talented people. And the stakes for intelligent management of the staff—for training, for development, for performance evaluation, and for successfully integrating women and racial minorities at all levels of the news staff—will increase. More and more, the editor's own performance will be measured in terms of professional excellence and the quality of the newspaper he or she edits.

The editor's responsibility for participation in marketing and profit planning for the newspaper will intensify. The continuing growth of newspaper ownership groups will enlarge the opportunities for the editor to have a role in helping build the newspaper's overall strategy. The editor's ability to participate effectively in this process may be the best insurance of an autonomous news operation. In many cases, it will be the editor who fights the battle for the reader to protect staff and newshole; it will be the editor who sees the newspaper as a trust and who is compelled to invest brains and integrity in this cause. In such a future, can we have anything less than editors who are savvy, creative, caring managers who know the rules of management and who know how to use those rules to fight for their staffs and their readers?

CHAPTER SUMMARY

After years of struggle marked by lawsuits and pressure brought by leaders inside and outside the newspaper industry, the traditional white male dominance of U.S. newsrooms is slowly giving way to women and minorities.

In a workplace run by white males, as most U.S. newsrooms are, women and minorities often find that they must work harder and achieve higher performance levels to establish their competence and to demonstrate that they are the equal of their white male counterparts.

As more women rise to positions of power, the management style found in these newsrooms will become more androgynous. There will be a blending of masculine and feminine behaviors. Male editors will be more willing to accept displays of sensitivity, caring, and spontaneous emotion, while women editors will tend to be more logical and more forceful.

The newspaper industry's growing commitment to hiring and promoting women and minorities recognizes the value of bringing different cultural and ethnic perspectives to the handling of the news. This commitment has been expressed in terms of a goal set by the American Society of Newspaper Editors, which states that before the year 2000, the minority employment in U.S. newsrooms will be equivalent to the percentage of minorities within the national population.

Women have made strong inroads in U.S. newsrooms, in part by observing the performance of their white male colleagues and using the same characteristics in developing their managerial competencies. While the number of women editors is still small, the change they represent is enormous.

Employees are protected from sexual harassment by Title VII of the 1964 Civil Rights Act. The guidelines of the federal Equal Employment Opportunity Commission state that sexual harassment includes unwelcome sexual advances, requests for sexual favors, and other verbal or physical conduct of a sexual nature.

Evidence that this is a serious problem is found in the number of lawsuits filed against companies by employees who allege that they have been victims of sexual harassment.

Minorities in the newsroom add diversity to the news report, yet research shows that journalism is not among the top preferences of minority high school students for education or career choices. The evidence from the research suggests strongly that the newspaper industry and the schools of journalism must increase their recruitment among minorities at the junior and senior high school levels. Other research reports that minorities are not the job hoppers they are often characterized as, but have high aspirations for their careers and are particularly frustrated by the lack of opportunity.

The experience of black managers in a white organization emerges through a four-phase process: (1) entry, (2) adjusting, (3) planned-growth, and (4) success. By encouraging intellectual development for minorities, editors can influence their confidence levels as well as their performance.

To those who wonder what challenges and crises will face newsroom managers in the future, we can suggest that the basic principles of problem solving, motivation, leadership, and reaffirming values will not change. The situations may be different, but the fundamentals of how to ensure competent handling of people and competent performance will remain.

NOTES

1. Fernando Bartolome, "Executives as Human Beings," *Harvard Business Review*, November–December 1972, 62.
2. Ibid., 68.
3. Henry Mintzberg, *The Nature of Managerial Work* (Englewood Cliffs, N.J.: Prentice-Hall, 1980), 45.
4. Daniel Yankelovich, *New Rules: Searching for Self-fulfillment in a World Turned Upside Down* (New York: Random House, 1981), 234–35.
5. Richard E. Boyatzis, *The Competent Manager* (New York: John Wiley & Sons, 1982), 12.
6. Mintzberg, *Nature of Managerial Work*, 188–93.
7. Boyatzis, *Competent Manager*, 230.
8. Daniel Goleman, "Influencing Others: Skills Are Identified," *New York Times*, 18 February 1986.

9. Alice G. Sargent, "Competency-based Management as an Organizational Development Intervention" (Abstract, 1986).
10. Darrell Sifford, "Women in the Business World: They're Leaving All the Good Traits Behind, Consultant Says," *Philadelphia Inquirer*, 9 February 1982.
11. Alice G. Sargent, *The Androgynous Manager* (New York: AMACOM, 1985), 2.
12. Ibid., 2-3, 7.
13. George Davis and Glegg Watson, "Swimming in the Mainstream," in *Beyond Sex Roles*, 2d ed., ed. Alice G. Sargent (St. Paul: West, 1985), 317-18, 322, 325.
14. Dorothy Jurney, "Percentage of Women Editors Creeps Upward to 11.7—but Other Fields Continue to Progress Faster," *The Bulletin of the American Society of Newspaper Editors*, January 1986, 8-9.
15. "The News Media and the Disorders" (The President's National Advisory Commission on Civil Disorders, March 1968), 213.
16. Ibid., 211, 213.
17. Andrew Radlof, "Minority Hiring Up Slightly at Newspapers," *Editor & Publisher*, 19 April 1986, 126.
18. Lloyd Shearer, "Intelligence Report: 'Boss Preference,' " *Parade*, 27 April 1980, 13.
19. Ibid., 43.
20. Ardyth Sohn, "Women Newspaper Managers: Their Goals and Achievement Orientations" (Manuscript, University of Colorado, 1983).
21. Judith G. Clabes, ed., *New Guardians of the Press: Selected Profiles of America's Women Newspaper Editors* (Indianapolis: R. J. Berg, 1983), 44.
22. Judith G. Clabes, "What Is an Editor, Anyway?" *The Bulletin of the American Society of Newspaper Editors*, January 1986, 3.
23. Stan Strick, "Working for Women: They Take Their Cues from 'The Front Page,' not 'Pollyanna,' " *The Bulletin of the American Society of Newspaper Editors*, January 1986, 7.
24. Jayne Vogan, interview with author, 28 March 1986.
25. Ibid.
26. Ibid.
27. Patricia P. Renfroe, "Sexual Harassment," *presstime*, May 1985, 14.
28. "Strict Liability for Supervisors' Acts Imposed on Employers in Sexual Harassment Cases," *Employment Alert of the Research Institute of America*, 7 February 1985, 1.
29. Renfroe, "Sexual Harassment," 15.
30. J. Clayton Lafferty, Tom Webber, and Alonzo W. Pond, "Desert Survival," (Northbrook, Ill.: Human Synergistics, 1978).
31. Alice G. Sargent, interview with author, 28 March 1986.
32. Jay T. Harris, interview with author, May 1984.
33. Marcia Ruth, "Minorities: The Statistics Show Little Progress, but Momentum Is Growing for Newspaper Staffs to Reflect More Racial and Ethnic Diversity," *presstime*, August 1984, 14.

34. "Minorities in the Newsroom—1978–1985," (Reston, Va.: American Society of Newspaper Editors, 1986), 15.
35. Judee K. Burgoon, Michael Burgoon, and David B. Buller, "Why Minorities Do Not Choose Journalism: Academic and Career Orientations among Students" (Associated Press Managing Editors Association, November 1984).
36. Ellis Cose, "The Quiet Crisis: Minority Journalists and Newsroom Opportunity" (Institute for Journalism Education, July 1985), 1.
37. Ibid., 3–4.
38. Floyd Dickens, Jr., and Jacqueline B. Dickens, *The Black Manager: Making It in the Corporate World* (New York: AMACOM, 1982), 15–37.

Case Studies

CHAPTER 2

As he reflected on his first week as city editor, Peter Flynn was puzzled. The reporters had been delighted to see him get the promotion. He had been assistant editor on the city desk for six years and now, with the former city editor's retirement, he was finally in the job he had coveted.

"That's what comes of being a faithful second-in-command," he was telling his wife. "I was loyal to the boss and carried out his policies to the letter. That wasn't hard, you know, because he was in that chair for twenty-five years and the staff was familiar with his way of doing things.

"Heck, I got along pretty well with the reporters. The afternoon the promotion was announced, a group of the veterans on the staff took me out for a few beers. They told me the kind of things you hear on such occasions—you know, that I was the ideal choice to follow in the tradition of the old man.

"Of course, I didn't agree with a lot of his practices. And I didn't waste any time making a few changes.

"I switched a few beats around, got the staff in an hour earlier, and told everyone to attach receipts to their expense statements for lunch. Nothing big right now, you understand. Just a few things to let them know it's going to be different.

"There was quite a buzz in the newsroom about the beat changes. People were huddled around a couple of the desks talking about it. I noticed some of them at the bar later. I didn't pay much attention. They'll cool off after a while.

"But then a funny thing happened. Late this afternoon, two of the old-timers walked into my office and shut the door. Listen to what they said . . ."

For Discussion

1. If you were one of the senior reporters, what would you tell the new city editor?
2. How might Flynn's actions have affected the norms of the reporter group?
3. What choices does the group have if it wishes to resist Flynn's changes?
4. How might peer pressure come into play in this scenario?
5. If Flynn continues to make changes, how might the values and beliefs of the reporter group be influenced?

CHAPTER 3

In his three years on the sports desk, Tom Stevens has made his mark on the *Gazette* sports pages. He is one of four sports writers covering a community of ninety-five thousand that has an insatiable appetite for sports. Under the firm but fatherly leadership of Sam Greenwood, the sports editor, Stevens and his colleagues hustle from game to game on weekends to provide the kind of first-hand coverage readers of the *Gazette* have come to expect.

Stevens gets along well with Greenwood and likes the other men on the staff. They are all young and spend time together outside of work. During Stevens's last performance evaluation, the sports editor said he was doing a good job, working at about 90 percent of his potential. "If you'll concentrate a bit more on your locker-room interviews and speed up your writing, you'll be close to 100 percent. Let's make that your goal," Greenwood told him.

Stevens was momentarily troubled by the conversation. He had wanted to talk to Greenwood about getting some desk experience. As much as he loved sports, he knew there were other things he wanted to do at the newspaper. He recognized that there were often opportunities on other desks for which he hoped to compete.

A week later, the sports editor had a heart attack and the managing editor moved a copy editor to run the sports staff while Greenwood recovered. Stevens quickly recognized that, for him, the interim sports editor was a mismatch.

Stevens thought he could survive the harsh language and quick temper. But when the copy editor, in a fit of anger, said he could understand why Stevens was the lowest paid sports writer on the paper, things fell apart.

Stevens's interest lagged and his production fell off. The week that Sam Greenwood came back to work, Stevens was preparing to send out his résumé and clips. Greenwood called Stevens over to his desk and said, "I understand you had a difficult time while I was gone. I've got some ideas about how to fix that . . ."

For Discussion

1. Will the goals of faster writing and better interviews that the sports editor set for Tom Stevens during an evaluation interview be effective? Why?
2. What hygienes are causing Stevens to be dissatisfied with his job?
3. If Sam Greenwood can repair the damage, how might Stevens's performance change? What will his new work level be?
4. If you were Greenwood, how would you bring the concepts of expectation, equity, goal setting, and behavior modification to bear on a motivation strategy for Stevens?

CHAPTER 4

A group of reporters at the *Gazette* approached the managing editor, Christy Bolden, and said they wanted to talk about ethics.

"What do you mean?" she asked.

"Well," began Steve Caselli, the senior member of the group, "we've noticed some things that may be conflicts of interest. The newspaper would be embarrassed if they ever got out. And we'd like to talk about it."

"I think you've got your facts mixed up. Our standards are impeccable. Are you telling me that my staff is unethical?" she bristled.

"Not exactly," said Caselli.

"You better not," said Bolden.

"Can we talk about it?"

"I'll see."

A week later, Caselli poked his head in Bolden's office and asked, "Are we going to be able to talk about ethics? There really are some things you should know."

"All right," Bolden said. "I'm finishing up a project for the publisher. How about the end of next week, say Friday afternoon at four? Bring the rest of your group and we'll see what this is all about."

When the group of four reporters met with Bolden, they laid out several examples that raised questions of conflict:

- The newspaper's restaurant critic has been getting free drinks and meals from the restaurants he writes about. Shouldn't the newspaper be paying for what the critic eats and drinks?
- The city hall reporter's boyfriend is an aide to the mayor, who is facing a tough reelection fight. The boyfriend is slipping our reporter documents that are damaging to the personal life of the mayor's opponent. Isn't it a conflict for one of our staffers to be covering the mayoral race and

Case Studies

having a relationship with the mayor's aide at the same time?

- The film critic owns stock in four major film companies. He buys and sells the stock based on his inside knowledge of what's happening at these companies. Isn't this unethical?
- Last month, the desk killed a story about the sheriff's annual stag dinner at a private hunting lodge outside the city. It's an invitation-only affair, attended by top local officials and company executives, and features nude dancing and high-stakes poker. Is it true the story was killed because the publisher was there?

"Yes. I know about all of those instances and more," Bolden said. "I guess this needs to be fixed. Maybe we could work as a committee and write some guidelines."

The committee met every week for three months and wrote an ethics code.

"This is a good job," said Bolden. "Let me show it to the publisher and then we'll tell the staff about it."

Six weeks later, Caselli asked Bolden what the publisher thought of the code.

"I've been busy and haven't had a chance to talk to him about it. But I will next week."

Two months later, Caselli asked again.

"The publisher had some problems with it," said Bolden. "I had to cut a few parts out. But it's okay now and I'm going to post the code on the bulletin board this afternoon."

"But what about the committee?" Caselli interrupted.

For Discussion

1. What do you think was the reason for Bolden's defensiveness regarding the possibility of conflicts of interest?
2. Explain why the level of staff satisfaction changed as communication about the ethics problem moved from the chain of command to a committee back to the chain of command.

3. Describe the examples of poor communication and suggest ways communication could have been improved.

4. How did Bolden's verbal and nonverbal cues betray her true feelings about the problem? How might those cues influence the staff's respect for her work?

CHAPTER 5

Tina McCoy was twenty-six years old and three years out of journalism school when her city editor, Peter Flynn, called her into his office one morning to ask her to take one of the assistant city editor slots on the city desk. Henry Evans, beloved for his gentle way of working with young reporters, had announced he was retiring the next month on his sixtieth birthday.

At first, McCoy was cool to the idea. Her work as city hall reporter had just begun to show promise. Intensely critical of her own performance, she had spent the past fourteen months winning the trust of her sources and learning her way around the back rooms of city government.

The previous week, the *Gazette* had published her series on conflicts of interest between the mayor and city contractors. Her notebook was full of ideas for other hard-hitting projects and she was eager to pursue them.

McCoy was surprised that she was Flynn's choice for the job. There had been rumors about Evans's interest in taking early retirement, and in the chatter around the office and over drinks at the end of the day, the game of guessing the identity of a successor focused on several staffers—but not Tina McCoy. She paid little attention to the talk and never thought of herself as a candidate. Too little experience, she concluded, and besides, Flynn and I argue a lot over my copy.

Flynn took McCoy out to lunch the next day to talk about the new job. She pressed him for an explanation of why she was his choice. "I like the way your mind works," the city editor said.

"You're very aggressive. You've got a great news sense and a strong commitment to the newspaper. There are a lot of people who have been around here longer than you, but they are just not as professional. I'm looking ahead five years or so when I want someone to be ready to replace me. I think it's important for me to begin grooming my successor. As I look around the room, you seem to have the capacity to handle the challenge."

McCoy was elated. The conversation with Flynn had forced her thinking into a new and exciting channel. His assessment of her talent had suggested that for McCoy, the horizons were unlimited. But she also was worried. She never had managed people before. Now she was going to have to supervise a staff of fifteen reporters, a few of whom she counted among her best friends.

Always a resourceful and conscientious reporter, McCoy borrowed books on personnel management and got Flynn to give her an outline of the assistant city editor's duties. The more she read, the more she became confused. What was she supposed to do? McCoy knew she would have to establish herself fairly quickly because there were sure to be others on the staff who would be disappointed that they didn't get the job, and they would be eager to test her. A stickler for details and not one who was gifted at improvisation, she believed strongly that she had to know in advance what to do and what not to do.

A few days later, just after the last edition deadline, McCoy walked into Flynn's office and said, "I need help. My old friends on the reporting staff want to know what the inside story is and I don't know how to handle that. I've got the feeling they think I'm becoming a 'company' type. I'm not sure what my responsibilities are. I'm confused and I'm worried."

"Well," said the city editor, leaning forward at his desk and looking serious, "here is what is important about being a supervisor in this newsroom . . ."

For Discussion

1. If you were the city editor, what would you say to Tina McCoy about the supervisory responsibilities of an assistant city editor?

2. How would you counsel her on dealing with old friends on the reporting staff?
3. What special problems would be encountered by a first-line supervisor on the city desk who had been promoted from the reporting ranks?
4. How would you advise McCoy about the things she'll need to learn as a manager of people?

CHAPTER 6

Norman Gardner became editor of the *Gazette* six months ago, and this morning, the publisher sent him a note saying it is time to start planning next year's newsroom expense budget. Gardner's experience with the budget process has been limited to approving raises, buying a few features, and signing travel vouchers. On his first day as editor, he noticed a file on his desk marked "Budget." Since no one offered to explain it to him, he gave it to his secretary to file.

After reading the publisher's note, Gardner thought for a minute and then asked for the budget file. As he thumbed quickly through the pages, he noted that the current news department budget was $1 million—$800,000 in payroll costs for a staff of forty and $200,000 for expenses.

Last week the graphics director sent Gardner a note asking for an additional artist to handle the extra workload generated by a new weekly business section and an entertainment magazine. Christy Bolden, the managing editor, has been pressing Gardner for two additional reporters to handle coverage in suburban areas where zoned editions are planned. Bolden also has been lobbying to add a second wire service.

The publisher's note this morning cautioned that payroll and expenses cannot be increased by more than 5 percent in the new budget.

Gardner looked at the papers spread in front of him and sighed. "Where do I begin?" he asked himself . . .

For Discussion

1. What management roles in connection with his budget responsibility has Gardner overlooked during his first six months as editor?
2. Describe how Gardner should use each of the five basic roles of management in planning next year's newsroom spending.
3. Describe how the outcome of the budget-planning process will be different if Gardner chooses to do it all himself rather than involving others.

CHAPTER 7

Christy Bolden has been managing editor of the *Gazette* for two years. Lately she has been disturbed by the staff's performance in several areas. Principally, copy flow has been inconsistent. The paper is late most nights and both the production director and the circulation director have complained to the publisher about late press starts and the consequent problems with delivery of the paper.

Frustrated over the criticism, Bolden fires off an angry memo to the staff: No more late papers.

For two days, Bolden hears nothing. The late afternoon news conference is tense, but no one says anything about the memo. On the third day, the news editor, Doug Goodwin, knocks on Bolden's office door.

"I wonder if I could talk to you about the problem we're having with late pages," he begins. "Some of it is our fault, but not all of it is.

"As you know, we have two openings on the copy desk.

Those jobs have been vacant for four months. You've told us we can't use additional overtime to cover the vacancies. We've interviewed several candidates and made recommendations to you on whom to hire. I think those recommendations were sent to you at least six weeks ago. But, so far as we know, we don't have approval to hire the replacements.

"I know the production director has been blaming the recent run of late papers on us. And, to some degree, being short-staffed has been a factor. But you may remember the memo I sent you last month listing two problems in the composing room that contribute to the problem. The composing room lunch schedule was changed six weeks ago and several of the printers assigned to makeup are at lunch when we are ready to paste up page one and the lead sports page. Second, production has been operating with one engraving machine. The other is broken. It takes twice as long to move pages to the pressroom with only one engraving machine. I've asked the production director about it, but he says he likes working with one machine because he has been able to cut the engraving staff in half and he is saving a lot of money."

Bolden said she had both memos on her desk, but had not done anything about them because of other pressing problems.

"Can we get these new employees approved and can you tell the publisher about production's role in making the paper late?" asked Goodwin.

"Let me look into it, but I can't promise anything. Meantime, let's get the paper in on time and don't use any overtime to do it. I'm not very happy with your performance and if I don't see an improvement in our ability to get the paper out, I may have to consider a change."

For Discussion

1. Describe Christy Bolden's leadership style.
2. Using the situational leadership model, describe Bolden's approach to leading the staff and explain what maturity level she finds on the news staff.

Case Studies 633

3. What power bases does Bolden appear to be operating from in dealing with this problem? What power bases does she seem to lack?
4. Is this issue likely to become political? What elements of Bolden's leadership style would suggest that it is or is not?

CHAPTER 8

In the two years before Norman Gardner became editor, the *Gazette* news staff increased rapidly in size from twenty-eight to forty. The growth was a result of the area's booming economy, which had created new jobs, boosted population, and pushed the *Gazette*'s circulation to more than forty thousand.

When the publisher agreed to hire additional staffers, it was decided that the new slots should be reserved for reporters. They were needed to cover the issues that were emerging as the community struggled with growth. The new reporters were added to the existing city desk, reporting to the city editor and an assistant city editor.

It soon became evident that the staff had outgrown its organizational pattern. Peter Flynn, the city editor, complained that the new reporters all needed training. The new staffers complained that they were not getting any direction and were uncertain about their performance. Flynn and the other editors stretched their work days to get more done. But it was clear when Gardner became editor that the situation was a mess.

As an individual, Gardner was well liked and respected. He had been a top reporter on the paper before becoming editor. Many of the senior staff members noted with some satisfaction that when Gardner "got into management," he didn't change, he didn't abandon his old newsroom friendships. He was soft-spoken and, as was his manner, more likely to suggest than to order. He confessed to his old friends that he was unsure of himself as an executive. His friends rather admired his honesty and agreed that they liked working for Norm because he seemed democratic and attentive to them as individuals.

One day, in a meeting to plan the Sunday paper, Gardner asked why several enterprise projects were taking so long. "Because we don't have enough editors," Flynn snapped. "All these young reporters can't write. I can't get all of their stories edited without more help on the city desk. I've been telling you that for months. But you won't make a decision."

Shaken and bewildered, Gardner brought the meeting to a quick close and asked Doug Goodwin, the veteran news editor, to stay for a moment. "What was that all about?" he wondered.

Goodwin was quiet for several seconds and then said bluntly, "Norm, your people are waiting for you to clear the air. The city desk is a mess and everyone knows it. They respect you and want your leadership. They will follow any plan you give them. They'll help you come up with a plan. But you have to decide. You have to tell them what we're going to do."

For Discussion

1. Describe Gardner's management style.
2. How might Gardner go about comparing his self-perception with the staff's perception of him?
3. If Gardner decides he has been too easy and swings toward a "get-tough" style, how effective might this new management style be? Can you suggest what might happen?
4. How can Gardner develop a more decisive, "take-charge" approach to his job without abandoning his basic nature?

CHAPTER 9

The day in 1972 when Greg Fremont walked into the *Gazette* newsroom for his tryout, everyone stopped to look. Fremont was the quintessential flower child. He wore faded jeans, a colorful T-shirt, and sandals. His hair touched his shoulders and he was, in the words of one copy desk observer, "not long for this newsroom." Fremont was bright, articulate, well read, and literate. He had been a sociology major in college, and as he told the editors, he was looking for a job where he could make a difference.

John Russelow, the city editor then, took a liking to Fremont. He said he reminded him of his own son, who was with a Green Beret unit in Vietnam. Russelow persuaded the editors to take a chance on Fremont.

Fremont needed a lot of direction and coaching. Even though he picked up the news-writing style rather quickly, his work habits lacked discipline. What Russelow liked best about Fremont, however, were the crazy, offbeat story ideas he came up with. He brought to the pages of the *Gazette* a dimension the paper had lacked, stories about ordinary people and places told with sensitivity and understanding.

By the time Russelow retired and Peter Flynn became city editor, Fremont had become the *Gazette*'s projects writer. His dress was more conservative, his hair shorter, and he still had wonderful ideas. Once or twice a year, some of those ideas would turn up in a finely crafted story for the Sunday paper.

Flynn was concerned about Fremont's work habits. Creative as he was, Fremont lacked discipline and took too much time to complete a piece. Flynn asked Russelow about it once and the old city editor said, "Just leave him alone. He does things a bit differently but he turns out some great pieces."

When Flynn took over the city desk, he wrote himself a memo on what he wanted to get done right away. At the top of the list was this note: "Get more work out of Fremont."

For Discussion

1. Describe Greg Fremont's value to the *Gazette*.
2. What should be done differently in managing Fremont? Develop a list of ideas for the city editor.
3. What should Flynn do first? Describe the steps you would take in bringing a new discipline to Fremont's work.
4. How would you explain your new expectations to Fremont?

CHAPTER 10

Peter Flynn, the city editor of the *Gazette*, and two of his assistant city editors were discussing the performance of Connie Brookins, a reporter on the city desk. Brookins is scheduled for her annual evaluation interview in two weeks. She has worked for the paper for five years and, in Flynn's eyes, is one of the best reporters on the staff.

Flynn began the meeting by observing that Brookins had a knack for writing in a colorful, entertaining, informative way. Ted Valenti, one of Flynn's assistants, nodded agreement, but said there was more to the story than that. Brookins pushes her editors, he said. She has challenged Valenti's handling of her copy, a characteristic Valenti finds irritating, although the points Brookins makes are not without merit. Until recently, Valenti considered her challenging, disruptive behavior to be the price one pays for good writing.

Last week, Valenti changed the organization of one of her stories and could not reach Brookins to discuss it with her. When Brookins saw the story in the paper, she threw it on Valenti's desk and shouted at him, "You've ruined this story! You wreck every story you touch. You don't recognize good writing at all and you're a lousy editor. If I had a choice, you'd never touch a piece of my copy again!"

Liz Martin, the other assistant city editor, breaks into the conversation. Martin and Brookins came to the paper at the same time, after going to journalism school together. Their friendship has survived Martin's promotion to an editing job. They are both single parents and share concerns about child care. Martin agreed that Brookins doesn't always accept criticism gracefully. "That's because she's a perfectionist," Martin said, "but so am I. To be perfectly honest, I can understand Connie's frustration when she says that some editors are more concerned about length or graphics or rushing a story through than they are about good writing. I think her work is excellent. She delivers the kind of writing the paper needs. And if she's a little sensitive about her writing, it's worth it."

Flynn said he had heard about Brookins's blow-up with Valenti. "I don't edit Connie's copy. I usually talk to her about story ideas. I know she argues with her editors, but I just don't see her as being disruptive. More important, in my opinion, is Connie's value to the paper. The other day the publisher stopped her in the hall to praise her."

Valenti contended that Brookins's behavior was insubordinate and that she should be warned not to repeat it. "She's exploded at you more than once," Martin said. "You usually ignore it or concede she is right. Besides, what you don't know is that her child was recently diagnosed as having a serious learning disability."

For Discussion

1. How would you rate Connie Brookins on her performance appraisal? Explain your decision.
2. Did the editors make any rating errors in assessing Brookins's work? If so, explain what they were.
3. What supervisory errors did the three editors make in managing Brookins?

CHAPTER 11

One morning in midweek, editor Norman Gardner returned to his office from a meeting with the publisher and asked to see the managing editor, Christy Bolden.

"He's starting something called Management by Objectives," Gardner began. "We've got to come up with some goals for next year with specific results and a timetable."

"Goals for what?" asked Bolden.

"I'm not sure. Improvements in the newspaper, I guess. The publisher wasn't very specific. He said it had come down from corporate. We've got to have our plan ready by next week."

"What do you want me to do?" asked Bolden.

"I'll get back to you," Gardner said.

The following Monday, Gardner called Bolden into his office.

"I've got this MBO business figured out," he said, pushing two sheets of paper across the desk for her to look at. "The first page has my goals on it and the second page has yours. I tried to keep them simple."

Bolden looked puzzled and said, "After you told me about the MBO program last week, I was pretty excited. I talked to some of the other editors and we put together a few ideas. Can we talk about them?"

"That's not really necessary. Actually, I've already given our goals to the publisher. I'll let you know what he thinks."

After reading the list of goals, Bolden said, "Let me ask a question about the first goal on my list. It says, 'Raise the page-one story count.' Shouldn't we be more specific?"

For Discussion

1. How would you revise the goal for page-one story count to make it more effective?
2. What crucial steps did Gardner leave out of the preparation of the news department's MBO plan?

3. How might the publisher have improved his presentation of the MBO idea to the newspaper's executives?
4. What does Gardner's behavior in discussing the MBO planning process say about his management style and his understanding of motivation?

CHAPTER 12

As Norman Gardner listened, his stomach began to turn. The speaker was the vice-president of a firm that had completed a readership research project for the *Gazette*. The publisher had commissioned the survey in an attempt to pinpoint the causes of a slow but steady slippage in the *Gazette*'s daily circulation.

Now, Gardner, the editor, along with the publisher and the other department heads of the *Gazette* were sitting in a darkened room, fully attentive to the observations they were hearing about the loss of readers and to the numbers flashing on a screen that supported those conclusions.

"What we can draw from our research," the speaker was saying, "is that your declining circulation can be explained by three factors: (1) weak coverage of local news, including obituaries, stories about people, and an apparent lack of interest by the newspaper in helping solve community problems; (2) too much emphasis on sports and not enough on such other special reader interests as entertainment, television, religion, and fashion; and (3) the perception that the newspaper is not in touch with its readers and with the community."

After the meeting, the publisher pulled Gardner aside and said, "That was a pretty damning report, Norm. You've got a lot of work to do. Better get some things going. And let me know what you decide."

Gardner returned to his office, slammed the door, quickly rolled a blank sheet of paper into his typewriter, and began a memo to Christy Bolden, the managing editor:

"Christy: I've just seen the results of our readership research. It was highly critical of the news department. I'm not going to share the numbers with you now because I don't want them to get around the newsroom. But here are the conclusions and here are the changes I want you to make immediately . . ."

For Discussion

1. How will Christy Bolden react to Gardner's memo?
2. How will the staff react if Bolden attempts to follow the spirit of Gardner's memo?
3. Explain the causes of resistance to Gardner's changes that are likely to come from the staff.
4. If you were Bolden, how would you attempt to manage the change ordered by Gardner?
5. What responsibility for Gardner's approach to initiating change does the publisher share?

CHAPTER 13

Fifteen minutes before the first-edition deadline, Norman Gardner, editor of the *Gazette,* showed up at the news desk and peered over the assistant news editor's shoulder at the page-one dummy.

"Why are we putting a top line on the city hall story?" he demanded. "I thought that story was going in the local section."

"There was a new development," replied Sara Feldman, the assistant news editor. "The mayor . . ."

"I don't care," Gardner broke in. "The mayor's just looking for headlines and he's not going to get them from us."

"This is a pretty good story," Feldman insisted. "I hope we're not overreacting to the mayor's criticism of us on television last week."

"That has nothing to do with it," snapped Gardner, turning away and striding back to his office.

Less than an hour later, Gardner's phone rang. It was the publisher. "Norm, you've got the wrong first name in the Callaghan obit. What's going on down there?"

Gardner hung up and yelled to his secretary, "Get Flynn in here!"

A minute later, Peter Flynn, the city editor, came through the door and said, "What's up?"

"How did we screw up this obit? I want the name of the reporter who wrote it and the name of the editor who let it get in the paper. And get it fixed."

"Yes, sir," said Flynn, beating a quick retreat.

Later in the day, Flynn came back with a play-by-play of the error.

"Alright," snapped Gardner. "The reporter's new here. Give her a stiff warning and tell her one more mistake and she's out. Fire the copy editor. Sam has made too many errors. Besides, he's a union troublemaker and I can't stand his attitude. We've got to set an example for the rest of the staff. I want his desk cleaned out this afternoon."

"The union will surely file a grievance," said Flynn.

"I don't want to hear about those union guys. Who's in charge here anyway?"

Thirty minutes later, Gardner's secretary buzzed the editor and said, "The president of the union is here to see you."

"Tell him I'm busy."

For Discussion

1. What is the nature of the conflict between Norman Gardner and Sara Feldman?
2. Which of the classic approaches to resolving conflict did Gardner use?
3. Describe the defense mechanisms that Gardner used and suggest what they may say about his self-image.

4. If you were Sara Feldman or Peter Flynn, how would you attempt to cope with Gardner's difficult behavior?
5. Did Gardner take appropriate action with the reporter and copy editor who made the error in the obituary? What alternative actions would you recommend in this case?
6. What might be the union president's next step in addressing Gardner's decision to discipline the two staffers? How do you see this scenario being played out?
7. Could Gardner benefit from teambuilding training? How?

CHAPTER 14

Steve Collins, age thirty-nine, is assistant managing editor of the *Gazette*. He has been on the staff for seven years and has built a reputation as a conscientious, creative, and hard-working editor. For several years, Collins directed an investigative reporting team. Recently he was moved to nights and put in charge of the news desk. He was assured that the experience on the news desk would serve his ambition to become managing editor of the *Gazette*.

Compared to the more leisurely pace of special reporting projects, Collins found the urgency of news deadlines stimulating but exhausting. Press starts were tightly scheduled. Collins had to shift his focus from one edition to the next with no time to relax. He drank coffee and smoked more. Dinner was usually a sandwich eaten quickly at his desk in the newsroom.

He rarely got home before 2 A.M., after his wife, Sandy, and their two young children were asleep. Sandy was a social worker who rose early to get the kids off to school and leave for work by 8 A.M. As a family, their only time together was on weekends. Soon, Sandy began to complain about Collins's schedule. Her job was demanding. She had a difficult case load and found it depressing to come home and be a parent and housekeeper alone.

Collins tried to explain that his night work was an important experience in helping him fulfill his expectation of becoming managing editor. Tension and hostility increased. Sandy felt abandoned. They argued. Collins found it hard to go to sleep when he came home. Frequently, he would stop for a beer to relax so he could go to sleep.

He began to dread coming to work. He thought his life was getting out of control. He complained of frequent headaches and muscular soreness. During his annual physical examination, his doctor told him his blood pressure was in the upper range of normal.

One morning Collins woke up with a heavy cold. He stayed in bed until it was time to go to work. Just before the first-edition deadline, he told Christy Bolden, the managing editor, that he was too sick to continue and was going home.

Collins didn't shake the cold for ten days. When he returned to work, he asked Bolden if he could talk to her privately.

"I've got to get off nights," he began. "I like what I'm doing, but it's just not working out."

"Your work is good, Steve, although you seem a bit tight and weary," said Bolden. "Is there a problem?"

Collins explained the conflicting demands at home. "Sandy and I fight all the time. I don't get to see my kids. I feel rotten. I get angry so easily. I'm also worried that if I can't work nights, I'll give up any chance I have of moving up at the *Gazette*. I feel trapped and helpless."

"I'm sorry to hear about your problems, Steve. I know it is hard to separate outside problems and your responsibilities at the *Gazette*. But if you are going to become a more important part of the management team, we're going to need you at night. There are a lot of challenges and opportunities ahead. If you are going to compete for them, you are going to have get your priorities in order."

Collins left the managing editor's office with a sick feeling in his stomach.

For Discussion

1. What organizational dilemmas are raised by Steve Collins's needs?
2. What symptoms of burnout are apparent in Collins's behavior?
3. Did Christy Bolden have an obligation to ask Collins about his behavior before he brought it up?
4. What responsibilities to the *Gazette* does Bolden believe Collins would be shirking by returning to days?
5. If you were Bolden, how would you balance Collins's personal needs against the *Gazette*'s?
6. How should Collins attempt to resolve the conflict between his professional ambitions and his family role?

CHAPTER 15

One morning, Christy Bolden, the managing editor of the *Gazette*, walked into the editor's office and said, "Norm, the news is all bad this morning. And I don't mean what's on page one."

"What's up?" Norman Gardner asked, giving Bolden a hard look over his half-glasses.

"First, Jim Huffman is leaving."

"Hell, we just hired him six months ago."

"I know," said Bolden. "He says you promised to make him assistant features editor and you haven't lived up to your word. He doesn't have a job but he's got a couple of interviews at papers on the West Coast."

"I didn't promise anything. I was just trying to sell him on coming to the *Gazette*. I said that people move along pretty fast here if they do well and that an opening was coming up on the features desk."

"Well, he has done well and he thinks you made a promise," said Bolden.

"Alright, what else have you got?"

"The arbitrator ruled against us in the Simmons case. He said that we discriminated against him because of his age and that we did not document his poor performance sufficiently. He gets his job back and $7,500 back pay."

"That old geezer hasn't done a day's work in ten years. He's asleep half the time. I don't know how many corrections we've published because of his mistakes."

"We all know that," said Bolden, "but the arbitrator said that we didn't have records of his mistakes, that we didn't discuss his poor performance with him, that we didn't give him an opportunity to improve, that we didn't warn him first, and that it was wrong to just up and fire him at age sixty-three when we've tolerated his performance for nearly twenty-five years."

"Somebody better tell Jack Simmons," sputtered the editor, "that he'll regret it if he ever shows his face in this newsroom again!"

"I've got one more item, Norm," said Bolden.

"What's that?"

"Suzanne Brann turned down our job offer. Actually, none of the other editors are sorry because her tryout, as you know, wasn't very impressive. She made several factual errors on the stories she wrote here, and you'll remember, she's had three jobs in three years and not a strong recommendation from any of her former editors."

"Listen," snapped Gardner, "some of those people I hired in our newsroom didn't get rave reviews from their old papers, either. But I hired 'em and I promoted 'em. I think I've got a pretty good eye for talent. I overruled the rest of you on Miss Brann because I was impressed with her. Why did she turn us down?"

"Frankly, she was bothered by her interview with you. She objected to your questions about her divorce and about her attitudes toward women in management."

For Discussion

1. How did Jim Huffman's unrealistic expectations affect his satisfaction on the job? Why is the editor, Norman Gardner, responsible for encouraging Huffman's expectations?
2. What steps should Gardner have taken to assure that the termination of Jack Simmons would stand up?
3. What are the mistakes Gardner may have made during his interview with Suzanne Brann and in his decision to offer her a job at the *Gazette*?

CHAPTER 16

Norman Gardner, the editor of the *Gazette*, thought of his publisher as a bully. "It was awful," he said to Christy Bolden, the managing editor, after an angry encounter with the publisher one morning. "He acted as if I were a moron who'd been sitting around doing nothing before he came. He barged into my office and started shouting because he thought I should be out in the newsroom 'running the show,' as he put it. He yelled about missing deadlines and failing to cover a meeting of bankers last week. He even made a snide remark about the features editor—called her an 'old biddy.' "

"Maybe he's having an off day," suggested Bolden.

"No, this sort of thing is getting to be routine. The other day I took him our plan for reorganizing the city desk. I showed him the chart of the new lineup that the art department drew up. He pushed it aside and said, 'I don't have time for this kind of garbage.' Then he mentioned a story he had seen on television."

"What was that?"

"Some little feature about a fox hunt. We didn't have it and he chewed on me for not staying on top of the news," said Gardner. "Christy, this guy is giving me ulcers. When I try to explain things to him, he refuses to listen. He always says, 'Gardner, your job is to get results.' "

"Maybe you should just tell him what he wants to hear," said Bolden.

"Maybe I should quit," replied the editor.

For Discussion

1. How might Norman Gardner initiate a dialogue with his publisher?
2. Would it help to acknowledge to the publisher that some of his criticism is justified?
3. How might Gardner stick up for himself and his staff and, at the same time, put his relationship with the publisher on a more positive level?
4. Should Gardner quit? Why or why not?

CHAPTER 17

Four experienced reporters were huddled in animated conversation over lunch in the *Gazette* cafeteria. The four—Nancy Boyd, Fred Henry, Don Jacobs, and Cathy Barkley—were talking about the unexpected promotion to assistant city editor of a young staffer named Mitchell Stanley.

Norman Gardner, the editor, had posted the announcement just before noon. The newsroom was abuzz, not only over Gardner's selection, but also the secrecy with which he apparently had decided to make a change on the city desk.

"What bugs me about it is that no one knew the job was coming open," said Jacobs. "I would have been interested."

"Isn't there some requirement about posting jobs so that anyone who is interested gets considered?" asked Boyd.

"We should take this up at the women's network," said Barkley. "There's no way Gardner should be able to get away with giving his protégé an opportunity we'd all die for."

Henry leaned back and smiled. "That network stuff must be something. Don and I have our own black network because we're the only two around here, but it doesn't make things better for us."

"There aren't that many of *us* in the newsroom either," said Barkley. "We meet with other women in the building and give each other support and share information."

"That's some kind of pipeline! It didn't even turn up a decent rumor that Norman was going to make this move," said Jacobs.

"Mitchell has been the boss's protégé almost from the day he started here," Boyd said.

"How does that happen? How do you get to be someone's protégé?" asked Henry.

"I don't know," Boyd responded. "One day that kid's in Norman's office going over stories. Then they go out to lunch. Then Norman is stopping by Stanley's desk to pass the time of day—and he's telling the city desk every chance he gets what a great find this Mitchell Stanley is."

"Well, I hope he's keeping his hands to himself," said Barkley.

"You're not saying that Gardner is . . ." said Henry.

"No, I'm not suggesting he's gay," continued Barkley. "I've just noticed that he's got a few favorites among the women in the features department, too, and whenever he's over there I see a lot of hugging going on."

For Discussion

1. What steps should Norman Gardner, the editor, have taken to assure that everyone with an interest in the assistant city editor's job had an opportunity to be considered?

2. Explain any errors you think Gardner may have made in his mentor-protégé relationship with Mitchell Stanley.

3. In what ways might the editor's behavior make him and the *Gazette* vulnerable to legal action?

Review Questions

CHAPTER 1

1. Explain how classical management theories differ from behavioral management theories.
2. Who were the early leading theorists of classical management? Are their ideas still useful today?
3. Why is behavioral science important in the management of a newsroom?
4. Identify four early contributors to behavioral science in management and explain their ideas.
5. What are the important differences for editors between technical skills and human skills?
6. Why is newsroom management that is based on an understanding of human behavior important to reporters, copy editors, photographers, and artists?
7. Explain how an editor can link the three key elements of management expertise to be an effective manager of people.
8. Explain how the basic behavioral-science principles can be applied in the newsroom.

CHAPTER 2

1. What did Elton Mayo's findings at Western Electric suggest about why people work?

2. What was the traditional view of workers and how was that view translated into what workers felt about their jobs?

3. What kinds of groups are found in newsrooms?

4. What benefits would a peer group offer to an individual staff member?

5. How do group norms work in the newsroom?

6. Discuss how group norms might apply to various operations of the newsroom such as the copy desk, the city desk, and the sports desk. How might group norms differ for each of these desks?

7. How were the four steps in the formation of work groups acted out in the early months of *USA TODAY*?

8. How do group leaders emerge? What are characteristics of individuals who assume leadership roles in groups?

9. How can an editor discover what is on a group's agenda?

10. Describe from your own experience ways in which you have seen the principles of Solomon Asch's experiments with peer pressure acted out.

11. What are some effective ways for an editor to understand and work with peer groups?

CHAPTER 3

1. Define motivation and the way you think it works in the newsroom.

2. Describe the categories of human needs that were identified by Abraham Maslow and explain why he placed them in a hierarchy.

3. Define the human-relations approach to management and motivation and the human-resources approach. Explain how they are different.

4. Explain the purposes of hygiene factors and motivation factors in Herzberg's theories. What is their meaning for the motivation climate in the newsroom?
5. How might the expectancy theory influence the behavior of a reporter or copy editor?
6. Why do you think David McClelland's ideas about achievement are important to newspaper journalists?
7. Why are an employee's perceptions important in understanding the influence of the equity theory?
8. Describe an experience you have had where your behavior has been influenced by the consequences of the expectancy and equity theories.
9. How do the principles of B. F. Skinner's behavior-modification techniques clash with the concepts of the early motivation theories?
10. Do you think the personal characteristics of newspaper journalists fit Maslow's definition of the self-actualized person?
11. Discuss how the essential ideas of the motivation theories can help guide newspaper editors in developing strategies for motivation.
12. Describe the conditions under which a reporter and a copy editor might be motivated by money. Are there different approaches an editor might use for individuals in each job?

CHAPTER 4

1. Why is good communication important in newsroom performance?
2. What role does perception play in communication?
3. What are the responsibilities of the sender and the receiver in the communication process?

4. How does emotion influence the communication of information?

5. Identify and explain the major roles of the editor in the communication process.

6. Identify and explain the major barriers to good communication.

7. How can the editor overcome communication barriers?

8. Why is feedback important in the communication process?

9. What are the important distinctions between interpersonal and organizational communication?

10. How can an editor create a better climate for effective communication in the newsroom?

11. Under what conditions can a meeting most effectively serve the needs of the staff?

12. What kinds of support do networks offer individuals that can be important in moderating the effects of stress on the job?

CHAPTER 5

1. Explain how the role of the newsroom supervisor fits into the overall management structure of the newsroom.

2. What are some limits on the authority of the city editor?

3. Why are city editors and other first-line managers so important to the success of the newspaper?

4. In what areas should the city editor have authority?

5. How are the authority, responsibility, and accountability of the city editor related?

6. What are the characteristics of supervision that distinguish the city editor from the managing editor?

Review Questions 653

7. Describe the assistant city editor's role in the supervision of the reporting staff.

8. What problems is a new assistant city editor likely to encounter?

9. Why is it important for the assistant city editor to understand his or her role as part of the newsroom management?

CHAPTER 6

1. Explain how the five basic management roles fit into the responsibilities of the chief news executive.

2. As an editor, how would you develop a strategic plan for building suburban readership and then convert it into a tactical plan?

3. Explain the differences among programs, policies, practices, procedures, and rules.

4. Successful plans are built on four principles. What are those principles and how would you apply them in developing a plan to build suburban readership for your newspaper?

5. Identify four activities that are important in defining organizing as a management role.

6. In organizing your news staff, how would you use line authority and how would you use staff authority?

7. Describe the steps that are important to getting the right people in the right jobs in the newsroom.

8. How has Congress influenced the editor's freedom to staff his or her newsroom?

9. As editor, you have just delegated responsibility for a special section on teenage unemployment. What steps would you take to audit the progress of that news report?

10. Describe how the editor's decision-making role is carried out in the assigning, reporting, and editing of a news story?

11. How are controlling and the other management roles interrelated?

12. How does the editor use standards to establish controls in the newsroom?

13. What are the characteristics of effective controls?

CHAPTER 7

1. Compare and contrast leadership with the two other functions of management, supervising and managing.

2. Authority, leadership, and power: How are they linked, and what are their distinguishing qualities?

3. What is the relationship between leadership and such personal characteristics as physical size, intelligence, and energy?

4. Describe the five types of management behavior that can be plotted on the managerial grid.

5. Explain why the contingency theory was the forerunner of a contemporary style of leadership that stresses understanding of the individual worker.

6. What is meant by task behavior, relationship behavior, and readiness?

7. Describe the four leadership styles in situational leadership.

8. Considering the readiness or maturity of the worker, what basic leadership approaches are suggested in situational leadership?

9. Identify seven bases of power an editor can use to influence people.

10. What can cause an editor's power base to erode?

11. What are some of the influences that can cause editors to behave politically?

CHAPTER 8

1. Explain the relationship between the theories of management and individual differences among editors.
2. Describe two factors that are influential in the development of an editor's management style.
3. Why is it important for newspaper editors to have a realistic self-image?
4. What are some of the steps that take place in an introspective look at who we are?
5. What is projection and how can it affect management style?
6. Describe two kinds of inner conflict common among executives.
7. Why are the following characteristics important to editors: time frame, cognitive power, differentiation, selective decoding, and reflective articulation?
8. Describe the steps in analyzing a problem.
9. Explain the relationship between Theory Y and an editor's management style.
10. Why are followers important in any leadership situation?
11. What conditions are necessary for participatory management to be successful?
12. Why are expectations important in understanding management styles?

CHAPTER 9

1. How might Abraham Maslow's ideas about primary creativeness and secondary creativeness be carried out in the development of a news story?

2. Identify the four stages of the creative process as described by Gardner Murphy, and explain how they might work in journalism.

3. List eight steps an editor might follow in designing a strategy for managing creative people. How do these differ from the general approaches to good management?

4. What can the understanding of people's life-styles contribute to our knowledge of management?

5. In their research among journalists, Judee and Michael Burgoon identified four communication styles and three epics. What are they and what do they mean to our study of life-styles and values of journalists?

6. Identify some of the values in journalism that are important to you.

7. There are at least seven ways that the sharing of values between an individual and a company can lead to personal and organizational effectiveness. What are they and how could they be utilized at a newspaper?

8. How can newspapers encourage young, mobile journalists to share their values?

CHAPTER 10

1. Why should editors routinely appraise the work of the news staff?

2. How has the federal government influenced performance appraisals in private industry?

3. What is the role of knowledge workers in newspaper journalism?

4. Describe the characteristics of good performance-appraisal systems.

5. Define six reasons why formal feedback is important.

Review Questions 657

6. Identify each of the following: narrative appraisals, checklists, critical incidents, goal setting, and rating scales.
7. What are the advantages and disadvantages of rating scales?
8. How are standards used to rate newspeople?
9. How is the self-appraisal used in the performance-review process?
10. What two kinds of goal setting can be used in rating newspaper journalists?
11. What are some common rating errors and how can they affect the objective of a performance review?
12. How is the performance appraisal used in disciplining employees?
13. What are the reasons why editors need to be trained to conduct performance appraisals?
14. Identify three types of appraisal interviews and when they should be used.

CHAPTER 11

1. Explain why the various theories of motivation regard money as significant.
2. What are some of the activities that can be included in a wage and salary administration program?
3. Explain comp time and what the limits are on its use by editors as an option for overtime pay.
4. Why is payroll such an important part of the expense budget of a daily newspaper?
5. What are the objectives of a publisher's compensation program?
6. How does merit pay express the desire of creative workers to be paid according to performance?

7. In his view of Management by Objectives, George Odiorne suggested seven ways in which MBO could help overcome many of the chronic problems of management. List them and discuss whether they can be applied in newsroom management.

8. Discuss the ways in which the theories of goal setting and MBO are closely linked.

9. Describe two categories of creative goal setting and explain how they would work in the newsroom.

10. Explain the four common elements of Management by Objectives.

11. How should personal goals relate to the goals of the newspaper company in developing an MBO plan?

12. Why do you think editors were the last of the newspaper executives to be included in MBO programs?

13. What are some of the errors editors and publishers can make in building a plan for the year ahead?

14. Describe the three stages of an MBO plan for a newspaper editor.

CHAPTER 12

1. Discuss examples of external and internal factors that can lead to changes in a newspaper organization.

2. How do a newspaper's culture and climate of success influence staffer attitudes about change?

3. Explain how the nature of the editor's job relates to change.

4. How might the theory of force field analysis influence an editor's decision whether to proceed with change?

5. Explain three steps that usually take place in the process of creating change in an organization.

6. Why is trust an essential element in successful change?

Review Questions 659

7. Describe the six phases in Greiner's model of organizational change.

8. What problems are encountered by editors trying to change individual behavior that may not be present in attempting organizational change?

9. What are some of the reasons individuals resist change?

10. Describe the three steps in Lewin's model for individual change.

11. What roles might be appropriate for informal peer-group leaders in preparing for change in the newsroom?

12. Why is participation in a change important?

CHAPTER 13

1. Define conflict.

2. Why is conflict so common in the newsroom?

3. Explain the traditionalist, behavioral, and interactionist views of conflict.

4. Identify seven specific sources of conflict in the newsroom.

5. Describe circumstances in which conflict may be helpful to the newsroom.

6. Identify five different approaches to conflict resolution and describe the behaviors that could be expected with each approach.

7. Identify three defense mechanisms that can come into play during individual conflict.

8. What are some effective ways of dealing with difficult people?

9. Discuss problem solving, persuasion, politics, and bargaining as strategies for resolving conflict.

10. What is teambuilding and how might it be effective in resolving conflict among individual editors?

11. Why are management-union relations a source of conflict?

12. Explain management rights and discuss how an editor can use them to manage effectively in an organized newsroom.

CHAPTER 14

1. Define stress.

2. What is a nonspecific response?

3. What is the fight-or-flight response? How did it help early humans? How does it work today?

4. Describe the General Adaptation Syndrome and explain how it works.

5. What is homeostasis?

6. What are some of the stresses commonly associated with newspaper work?

7. Describe the Yerkes-Dodson Law.

8. What are the three forms of tension identified by Henry Babcock?

9. What are some of the factors that may determine whether the effect of stress is positive or negative?

10. Describe the three basic elements that determine the effect stress has on us.

11. How are personality, Type-A behavior, and heart disease linked?

12. Why are stages of life important in determining one's vulnerability to stress?

13. What are some of the conditions newspaper editors described that contribute to harmful stress?

14. When is burnout likely to occur?
15. What are some of the conflicts that arise in family life as a result of the demands of an editor's job?
16. Why is the computer a source of stress in the newsroom?
17. Identify personal characteristics that are seen as helpful in coping with stress.
18. How can the boss be effective in helping employees cope with stress?
19. What management skills are effective in reducing stress in the newsroom?
20. How is the "monkey" analogy important to editors in learning to manage time?

CHAPTER 15

1. Why may hiring new staffers be the most important function an editor performs?
2. How has recruitment of newspaper journalists changed over time? Why has it changed?
3. Describe the six qualities editors should look for in job candidates.
4. Explain how federal laws can influence how the editor carries out the hiring function.
5. What does research suggest about the effectiveness of interviewing as the basis on which to make a hiring decision?
6. What are the possible pitfalls that editors need to be aware of in the job interview and in the decision whether to hire a candidate?
7. What is the value of psychological testing in the interviewing process?
8. How are tests validated for newsroom journalists?

9. Describe the orientation of a new staffer and the steps to be taken in helping the staffer to become socialized.
10. How do training and development differ?
11. List the principles of learning that should be the basis for training in the newsroom.
12. What are some characteristics an editor should consider when evaluating a staffer who may become a protégé?
13. What are the potential problems when the mentor is the protégé's immediate supervisor?
14. What are the steps in preparing a development plan?
15. What are some of the clues to our own nonpromotability that we may recognize?
16. What are some advantages and disadvantages of turnover?
17. What is progressive discipline? Explain how it is used in terminating an employee.

CHAPTER 16

1. Three common characteristics of chief executives are their competitiveness, their ability to articulate, and their persuasiveness. Discuss why these qualities are or are not important for newspaper publishers.
2. Describe how the publisher fits into the power structure of the typical daily newspaper.
3. What sort of publisher is a Statesman, as described in research by Philip Meyer?
4. What are some of the expectations a publisher might have for his or her editor?
5. Why is communication vital to the relationship between publisher and editor?

Review Questions 663

6. What are some approaches that might be effective in dealing with a difficult publisher?
7. Define the importance of trust in the relationship between publisher and editor.
8. What are some of the questions an editor might ask in testing whether his or her publisher's behavior is supportive?

CHAPTER 17

1. What series of events raised the consciousness of editors about hiring and promoting women and minorities?
2. How does the "old-boy network" affect the roles of women and minorities in the newsroom?
3. How is androgyny influencing contemporary management styles?
4. Is it fair to say that working for a woman is different than working for a man? Why or why not?
5. What are the basic categories of sexual harassment in the EEOC guidelines?
6. Why is ethnic and cultural diversity crucial to a successful news operation?
7. What efforts can newspapers make to attract more young minorities to education and careers in journalism?
8. Why is the perspective of minorities and women important in news gathering and writing?

Glossary

Accountability (Chapter 5) Having to answer for the exercise of authority and responsibility; being responsible for results.

Achievement theory (Chapter 3) Psychologist David McClelland's theory that behavior is motivated by three needs: achievement, affiliation, and power.

Androgyny (Chapter 17) Blending the traits of males and females.

Arbitration (Chapter 13) A process in which a third party, the arbitrator, helps resolve a dispute. Arbitrators are often used to settle disputes between management and a union over the interpretation of a contract.

Authority (Chapter 5) The power to make decisions about how to commit the newspaper's resources or to instruct subordinates to do or not to do something. Authority is always governed by the organization's policies and procedures as well as the rules of society at large.

Autocratic leadership (Chapter 7) A style of leadership in which the leader acts alone, avoiding employee participation or consultation; a directive style of leadership.

Autocratic style (Chapter 8) A style of management characterized by close supervision of subordinates and lack of trust and delegation.

Bargaining (Chapter 13) Conferring with another to arrive at a resolution of a dispute or a difference of opinion; the process involves openness, objectivity, and respect.

Behavior modification (Chapter 3) A motivation technique by which work behavior is changed through learning, assessment based on observation and measurement of work behavior, and positive reinforcement.

Behavioral science (Chapter 1) A study of human behavior based on scientific research.

Behavioral theories (Chapter 1) Ideas about people's behavior at work that have been developed as a result of repeated and controlled observation.

Bilateral organization (Chapter 16) A newspaper at which two executives, a general manager and an editor, share the top responsibilities; each executive has a separate jurisdiction and they govern by consensus.

Budget (Chapter 6) A single-use plan estimating income and how it is to be used.

Building coalitions (Chapter 12) A process of obtaining support for change.

Burnout (Chapter 14) A result of working under severe stress for long periods without relief.

Career development (Chapter 10) Establishing objectives and planning activities to help a worker build skills and knowledge that will prepare him or her for new opportunities.

Central tendency (Chapter 10) In rating performance, a supervisor plays it safe by rating a worker near the average of other workers, even though the worker's performance deserves a higher or lower mark.

Chain of command (Chapter 4) Basic organizational structure in which authority flows from boss to workers.

Change (Chapter 12) A shift or alteration in the environment, practices, or policies of a company; adoption of a new and different behavior by an individual.

Change agent (Chapter 12) An individual responsible for introducing planned change in an organization; a change agent may be an insider or an outsider.

Checklists (Chapter 10) An appraisal system listing the tasks on which an employee's performance is rated.

Classical management (Chapter 1) A school of management theorists who developed ways of making production more efficient; it emphasizes the design of a preplanned structure for doing work and minimizes the importance of the social system.

Coercive power (Chapter 7) A leader's use of fear to impose his or her will.

Cognitive power (Chapter 8) Bringing an individual's perception and thinking to bear on the creative process of developing ideas or visions.

Collective bargaining (Chapter 13) Relations between employers and unions representing employees; involves the process of union organization of employees, negotiation, administration, and interpretation of agreements covering wages, hours of work, and other conditions of employment, and dispute settlement procedures.

Communication (Chapter 4) Transfer of information and meaning from one person or group to another.

Compensatory time (Chapter 11) Time off granted in lieu of overtime pay; under law, "comp" time must be taken during the same week in which it was earned.

Glossary

Competition anxiety (Chapter 8) Apprehension resulting from the fear of failure or the fear of success.

Conflict (Chapter 13) A situation in which the expectations or actual behavior of an individual or group is blocked.

Conflict maturity (Chapter 13) The ability to perceive effectively and react to a number of factors concerning self, other parties in a conflict, the work environment, and the nature of the conflict.

Connection power (Chapter 7) A leader's use of associations with influential people to achieve his or her objectives.

Contingency Model (Chapter 7) A theory in which a leader's behavior is governed by three factors: acceptance by the group, nature of the work, and the leader's power base.

Contrast effects (Chapter 10) In rating performance, a supervisor compares a worker with other workers rather than measuring the worker's performance against the requirements of the job.

Controlling (Chapter 6) One of an editor's management roles in which performance standards are used to measure progress toward goals.

Creativity (Chapter 9) The ability to innovate, to improvise, to take an inspiration and shape it into a product or a process.

Critical incidents (Chapter 10) An appraisal system based on written examples of serious problems and outstanding work.

Culture of pride (Chapter 12) The climate and traditions in a company that encourage innovation and enhance the chance of successful change.

Decision making (Chapter 6) A process of selecting a rational choice among alternatives.

Defense mechanism (Chapter 13) A reaction to conflict causing one's awareness of the threat to be reduced but which seldom affects the cause of the threat.

Delegation (Chapter 6) Assigning authority to the lowest level at which a task can be accomplished properly.

Democratic leadership (Chapter 7) A style of management in which a leader involves the staff in the decision-making process; employees have the freedom to make their own decisions; this style is supportive and oriented toward people.

Development (Chapter 15) A planned program of learning and experience designed to prepare an individual for greater responsibility.

Differentiation (Chapter 8) The ability to see distinctions between similar situations.

Directing (Chapter 6) Part of an editor's management role involving delegation and decision making.

Directive (Chapter 7) A style of leadership in which a boss tells his or her employees what to do.

Directive change (Chapter 12) New systems, practices, or policies that are imposed on individuals and the organization by the boss.

Directive interviewing style (Chapter 15) Questions asked in a way that invites specific answers.

Discrimination (Chapter 17) Treating any person differently on the basis of race, sex, age, or national origin.

Elements of stress (Chapter 14) The environment in which an individual works or lives, physical or emotional vulnerability, and stressors—the situations that are stressful.

Emotional bias (Chapter 4) Personal feelings that affect communication by distorting the message.

Emotional resistance to change (Chapter 12) Opposition that arises out of fear that the change will have a negative effect; although it appears illogical, such opposition can have strong psychological origins.

Equity theory (Chapter 3) A concept in which an employee's motivation is affected by the perception that he or she is or is not treated fairly by management in comparison to other workers.

Expectancy theory (Chapter 3) A concept in which motivation depends on an employee's perception that the behavior desired by management will result in achievement of the worker's goal.

Expert power (Chapter 7) A leader's use of expertise, skill, and knowledge to achieve his or her goals.

Extrinsic creativity (Chapter 11) Introduction of new ideas from outside of the organization.

Fair Labor Standards Act (Chapter 11) First passed by the U.S. Congress in 1938 and frequently amended, the Fair Labor Standards Act established minimum-wage, overtime-pay, child-labor, and equal-pay requirements.

Feedback (Chapter 4) The receiver's reaction to a message; feedback can be verbal or nonverbal; *(Chapter 10)* two-way communication as part of an employee's performance review.

First impression–last impression (Chapter 10) In rating performance, a supervisor makes an initial favorable or unfavorable judgment about a worker and ignores later evidence that suggests the overall performance is different from the first impression; this theory also holds when the boss gives a rating based on a strong impression drawn just before the performance review is due.

First-level management (Chapter 5) The lowest position in the organizational hierarchy at which a manager supervises other employees; these managers are called supervisors; in the newsroom, the city editor, the sports editor, and the features editor are supervisors.

Force field analysis (Chapter 12) A technique to represent the pressures to change as compared to the forces not to change.

Formal work group (Chapter 2) Part of the newsroom operation in which a group of staffers reports to an editor. Example: The city desk is a formal work group organized by the newspaper's management. Authority to run this formal work group is assigned to an editor.

General Adaptation Syndrome (Chapter 14) Hans Selye's theory that human response to stress has three stages: alarm, resistance, and exhaustion.

Goal setting (Chapter 10) A system in which a staffer and an editor agree on goals against which the staffer's performance is measured.

Goal-setting theory (Chapter 3) A concept of motivation in which goals can improve a worker's performance if the worker shares in defining the goals and if the goals are specific and challenging.

Grapevine (Chapter 4) An informal communication network, which exists in all organizations, circulating rumors and unofficial information.

Group cohesiveness (Chapter 2) How well a group sticks together by adhering to its norms and resisting outside pressure to behave differently.

Habit of creation (Chapter 9) An environment in which creative insights come more frequently to those who have them and work them through to a result.

Halo effect (Chapter 10) In appraising performance, a rating error is caused when an inaccurate generalization about one aspect of an employee's work carries over to all other factors in the employee's job performance.

Hierarchy of needs (Chapter 3) Psychologist Abraham Maslow's theory of motivation; physiological, security, social, ego, and self-fulfillment needs must be met in that order; unsatisfied needs take priority over higher needs.

Holmes-Rahe Life Event–Stress Scale (Chapter 14) A ranking of stressful events, from which it can be predicted when an individual will experience stress-related illness.

Homeostasis (Chapter 14) The body's attempt to maintain an internal balance of such bodily states as blood cirulation, breathing, digestion, and temperature that are necessary for a healthy life.

Human relations (Chapter 1) The study of how people interact and work together; *(Chapter 3)* an early school of thought about management that emphasizes the importance of employee morale.

Human resources (Chapter 3) A model of management introduced in the 1960s that concluded that such factors as incentives, social influences, the nature of the job, supervisory style, and employees' values are capable of influencing behavior.

Human skills (Chapter 1) Interaction with people; communicating, delegating, directing, controlling, and motivating are human skills which are essential to effective management.

Hygiene factors (Chapter 3) A list of work qualities, such as pay, working conditions, and management practices, identified with a worker's happiness or unhappiness on the job.

I Win–You Win (Chapter 13) A means of resolving conflict through rational problem solving and working toward mutually acceptable goals.

Incentive bonus (Chapter 11) A reward, generally cash, paid to an executive for achievement of MBO goals.

Informal work group (Chapter 2) A number of individuals in the workplace drawn together by common interests whose rules, makeup, and goals are defined by the individuals; also known as a peer group.

Information power (Chapter 7) A leader's use of information or access to information to achieve his or her goals.

Interpersonal communication (Chapter 4) Information delivered person to person.

Intrinsic creativity (Chapter 11) The discovery of new ways to perform a task.

Job description (Chapter 11) A statement of the duties, responsibilities, and conditions involved in performing a specific job.

Job evaluation (Chapter 11) A system for determining the relative money value of jobs within an organization.

Job rating (Chapter 11) A relative value given to each job following an evaluation of the job description and the job specification.

Job specification (Chapter 11) A statement of the human qualities required to fill a position.

Knowledge worker (Chapter 3) Description of an employee, such as a newspaper journalist, whose tasks require skills for research, planning, design, and innovation.

Leadership (Chapter 7) An ability to influence others to achieve willingly rather than because they are required to or because they fear the consequences of failing to achieve.

Learning curve (Chapter 15) The relationship between time and performance in the accomplishment of a task as plotted on a graph; typically, complex tasks have long learning curves and simple tasks short ones.

Legitimate power (Chapter 7) A leader's use of his or her position to achieve goals.

Glossary 671

Life-style research (Chapter 9) A way of looking at history, demographics, social movements, and trends that may suggest who we are and where we are going.

Line authority (Chapter 6) A right assigned to a manager, such as a city editor, to use reporters and other resources to accomplish an assigned task.

Mainstreaming (Chapter 17) The assimilation of women and minority managers into the patterns of management established by white males; the inclusion of minorities in a newspaper's routine news coverage.

Management by Objectives (Chapter 11) A formal management process in which workers and managers define common, specific goals to be achieved in a given period of time and against which performance will be measured.

Management rights (Chapter 13) A principle of management-union agreements in which all rights not specifically bargained away belong to management.

Management style (Chapter 8) An approach to the individual manager's work that combines theory with experience, personality, and self-perception.

Managerial Grid (Chapter 7) The plotting of five management behaviors based on the interplay of tasks and relationships; this model suggests that the best style of leadership is concerned with both production and people.

Mediation (Chapter 13) A voluntary process in which a third party assists in reaching an understanding or agreement; often used in management-union negotiations.

Mentor (Chapter 17) A manager who takes a personal interest in the individual development of a staffer and works with him or her outside the normal chain of command in the newsroom.

Merit pay (Chapter 11) A method of determining pay increases that recognizes differences in performance.

Motivation (Chapter 3) Forces influencing behavior that is undertaken because of drives, needs, or desires and is directed toward goals.

1978 Civil Service Reform Act (Chapter 10) Legislation passed in 1978 by Congress establishing guidelines for the design of performance appraisal programs for federal employees.

Narrative appraisal (Chapter 10) An open-ended essay written by a supervisor evaluating a worker's performance.

Needs motivators (Chapter 3) A list of work qualities, such as achievement, recognition, and responsibility, that were identified by psychologist Frederick Herzberg as being important factors in an employee's satisfaction on the job.

Negative and positive leniency (Chapter 10) In rating performance, a supervisor is either too hard or too easy in rating workers.

Networks (Chapter 17)   Informal communication systems through which employees can exchange support, information, and contacts.

Nondirective interviewing style (Chapter 15)   Asking questions in an employment interview that are general in nature and that give the candidate some latitude in answering.

Norms (Chapter 2)   Rules of behavior to which a group wants its members to conform; *(Chapter 15)* the typical or average performance on an aptitude or personality test.

Organizational climate (Chapter 4)   The atmosphere in a workplace that determines how receptive employees are to communication.

Organizing (Chapter 6)   A management role that involves deciding what work is to be done, who is to do the work, what authority will be delegated, and what the lines of authority are.

Participative change (Chapter 12)   A process that involves staffers in the development of plans for doing things differently.

Participative style (Chapter 8)   Management that is characterized by trust, delegation, and sharing responsibilities.

Path-Goal theory (Chapter 7)   An approach to leadership that proposes ways in which a leader can influence a subordinate's motivation, setting of goals, and efforts to achieve both personal and organizational goals.

Patterned interview (Chapter 15)   An employment interview based on a comprehensive questionnaire that asks detailed questions about the applicant's background.

Peer group (Chapter 2)   An informal organization of staffers holding similar positions. (See also *Informal work group*.)

Perception (Chapter 4)   Interpretation of a message by filtering it through personal experiences, biases, values, and attitudes.

Performance appraisal (Chapter 10)   A method of measuring an employee's performance against a standard; it most often includes a written form and an interview in which a supervisor discusses appraisal results with an employee.

Performance development (Chapter 10)   Improvements related to a worker's current job assignment.

Persuasion (Chapter 13)   A technique of conflict resolution in which one party attempts to convince the other to change its mind or agree to cooperate with a proposed solution.

Planned interview (Chapter 15)   A long, in-depth employment interview in which the applicant talks freely about his or her background, attitudes, and goals.

Planning (Chapter 6) A management role that involves setting goals and deciding on a course of action to achieve the goals.

Politics (Chapter 13) Resolving conflict by accumulating enough power to control a decision; this is often done by building coalitions.

Primary creativeness (Chapter 9) The inspirational phase in which an idea comes to mind.

Problem solving (Chapter 10) An approach to evaluation interviews in which supervisor and employee share points of view and work together to improve the employee's performance; *(Chapter 13)* resolving conflict by identifying the source of the problem, considering alternatives, and selecting the most appropriate solution to the problem.

Progressive discipline (Chapter 15) A process of punishment in which the severity increases from warning to suspension to dismissal.

Projection (Chapter 8) The tendency to look outside one's self for an explanation of a problem or a failure.

Protégé (Chapter 17) A staffer with strong potential who is selected informally by a manager for coaching and guidance. (See also *Mentor*.)

Psychological tests (Chapter 15) A series of questions or exercises that measure aptitude, achievement, and motivation.

Publisher (Chapter 16) The chief executive officer at most newspapers, responsible for managing and renewing operations.

Rational resistance to change (Chapter 12) Objections that arise because of a lack of information about what is to be done differently.

Rating scales (Chapter 10) A system built on established standards of excellence; the emphasis in rating scales is on worker behavior.

Reference check (Chapter 15) Obtaining an evaluation of a job candidate from former employers, teachers, or colleagues.

Referent power (Chapter 7) A leader's use of his or her personal traits to achieve goals.

Reflective articulation (Chapter 8) The ability to stand back from a problem, analyze the situation, and form ideas about how to resolve the problem.

Reliability (Chapter 15) The quality that enables a test to yield nearly the same score when an individual takes it more than once.

Responsibility (Chapter 5) The obligation to carry out assigned duties.

Reward power (Chapter 7) A leader's use of money, promotions, perks, or other rewards to achieve his or her goals.

Role (Chapter 6) Expected behavior associated with each position on the staff.

Salary (Chapter 11) The term commonly used to describe monetary compensation that is uniform from one pay period to the next regardless of the number of hours worked.

Secondary creativeness (Chapter 9) The phase of inspiration in which an idea is worked out as a story, a drawing, or a headline.

Selection (Chapter 15) Matching the skills and qualifications of job applicants to the requirements of a job.

Selective decoding (Chapter 8) The ability to sort out the relevant from the irrelevant.

Self-examination (Chapter 8) The willingness of an individual to seek a better understanding of his or her own strengths and weaknesses.

Sexual harassment (Chapter 17) Unwelcome sexual advances, requests for sexual favors, or verbal or physical abuse of a sexual nature.

Shared values (Chapter 9) Ideals, goals, principles, or policies that are compatible to both individual workers and the organization.

Similar-to-me (Chapter 10) In rating performance, a supervisor judges an employee more favorably because the supervisor perceives the two of them to be much alike.

Situational Leadership (Chapter 7) A model in which four styles of leadership are matched with four maturity levels of workers; a leader adapts his or her management behavior to fit the particular situation.

Staff authority (Chapter 6) The right assigned to an individual serving in an advisory capacity.

Staffing (Chapter 6) A manager's role that involves selecting and hiring the best people.

Standardized test (Chapter 15) An examination that has been pretested on a large and representative sample so that one's score can be compared with the scores of the population as a whole.

Standards (Chapter 10) Written statements of the way in which tasks are to be performed based on the work behavior of outstanding workers.

Status anxiety (Chapter 8) Tension caused by a conflict between responsibilities of the job and the need to be liked.

Strategic plan (Chapter 6) Setting long-range goals and deciding on a course of action to achieve the goals.

Stress (Chapter 14) A "nonspecific" response of the body to any demand upon it.

Supervision (Chapter 5) First-level management, which involves accountability for rank-and-file workers.

Tactical plan (Chapter 6) The basic approach used in carrying out a strategic plan.

Teambuilding (Chapter 13) A training program that attempts to build trust among employees by coaching individuals to level with each other, to face the truth about their behavior, to be nondefensive, and to drop their facades.

Technical skills (Chapter 1) The basic abilities required to perform newspaper work; examples of technical skills include reporting, writing, editing, page layout, photography, and map and chart making.

Technostress (Chapter 14) Tension that results from the frustration and anxiety of attempting to interact with computers.

Tell-and-listen (Chapter 10) A style of interviewing during a performance review in which a supervisor shares with an employee evaluation results but also listens to the employee's views about his or her performance.

Tell-and-sell (Chapter 10) A style of interviewing during a performance review in which a supervisor shares with an employee evaluation results and tries to convince the employee that a specific course of action is required to improve the employee's performance.

Test (Chapter 15) A systematic procedure for comparing the behavior of two or more persons.

Time management (Chapter 14) Analyzing what needs to be done, setting priorities, deciding the best way to do the job, focusing on what's important, and eliminating what wastes time.

Title VII of the Civil Rights Act of 1964 (Chapter 10) Federal law that approved the use of professionally developed ability tests for employment decisions, provided they did not discriminate on the basis of color, race, religion, or national origin; *(Chapter 17)* the law also created guidelines on sexual harassment and established the Equal Employment Opportunity Commission to enforce the guidelines.

Total Newspaper Concept (Chapter 11) The publisher, the editor, and the other executives of the newspaper pool their ideas and their resources to improve the newspaper.

Training (Chapter 15) A planned program of building or improving skills.

Trust (Chapter 16) An intangible quality in a relationship that is influenced by the behavior of the individuals and that relies heavily on open communication.

Type A personality (Chapter 14) Description of aggressive, hard-driving individuals who have a great sense of urgency in their lives and run higher risks of heart disease.

Type B personality (Chapter 14) Description of serious but easygoing individuals, able to enjoy leisure with no feelings of being driven by time.

Unilateral organization (Chapter 16) A newspaper with a publisher in the role of chief executive officer.

Validity (Chapter 15) The degree to which a test actually measures what it is intended to measure. To be used in hiring, a test must be job related and must predict success on the job.

Values (Chapter 9) Ideals, standards, practices, and goals that have an intrinsic worth to journalists and to newspapers.

Wages (Chapter 11) The term commonly used for the monetary compensation of employees who are paid by the hour.

Workaholic (Chapter 14) A person who has an obsession to work and who is aggressive, often hostile, achievement-oriented, and chronically rushed.

Work group (Chapter 2) Two or more people who work in close proximity to each other and who have common goals.

Yerkes-Dodson Law (Chapter 14) A theory stating that as stress increases, so do efficiency and performance.

Appendix

STANDARDS OF EXCELLENCE

The following standards for reporters, copy editors, supervising editors, photographers, artists, and librarians define the basic tasks for each of these positions. These standards of excellence were adopted by the editors and staff members of the *Times-Union* and the *Democrat and Chronicle* in Rochester, New York. Other journalists may define the standards of excellence in newspaper journalism differently. The Rochester standards are presented here as a guide for students and for editors who may wish to establish standards for the work performed in their newsrooms.

Artist

Technical Skills

Art style. The artist uses his or her primary art style and medium appropriately and effectively to complete most assignments. The artist understands the style and medium and most often exploits it to the fullest potential. He or she has the technical know-how to make the most of the technique imprint to get the best image resolution. He or she is able to troubleshoot camera or press problems. Mastery of a variety of media and the ability to work effectively in different styles allows the artist the flexibility to choose from a variety of ways to complete art assignments. Before beginning assignments, the artist always considers the creative possibilities and looks for the best solution to a visual problem, not just the solution that is easiest to implement. The artist has experience, technical know-how, and organizing ability to successfully complete assignments that require the involvement of other staffers, such as, for example, photo illustration, 3-D construction, or art that incorporates VDT tables or IBM-PC charts. The artist pays close attention to detail and strives constantly, through follow-up on reproduction and enlisting the aid of others, to make the art a technical success.

Variety of art styles. A combination of vision, creative drive, and technical know-how makes the artist a versatile problem solver. Each assignment is approached with a commitment to using the most appropriate style and medium. The artist considers the visual impact and communication power of styles and mediums available and makes choices that deliver the most effective visual communication that can be made in the time available. The artist has mastery of a variety of styles and mediums and derives satisfaction from exploring, exploiting, and learning to use new tools of the trade. The artist is comfortable in the art-director role when assignments require help from other departments to complete; for example, the artist works well with photographers on illustrative photos.

Mastery of technique. The artist can exploit a medium effectively to produce the full range of available visual effects. He or she is able to select the proper medium in all situations. The artist knows the characteristics of the medium and applies that knowledge appropriately. He or she adjusts use of the medium as necessary to compensate for conversion of continuous tone image to printable image.

Design. The artist produces graphically clean art that uses a fresh and innovative approach appropriate to story content. He or she captures the mood or story tone and visualizes critical aspects of the story. Most often, the artist strives to make art and type integrate into a "whole package." The artist thinks in terms of the overall page design rather than having a narrow focus on only a space that needs to be filled. He or she keeps the page editor or graphics editor informed of the art and its relationship to the page.

Maps. The artist develops and uses knowledge of mapmaking to capture key points, show action, and include all reference points—boundaries, streets, landmarks—to help fully identify the point of interest. The artist is alert to situations and makes sure that he or she fully understands each assignment and obtains the necessary information to complete the assignment. Maps consistently contain a text block, miles scale, and north directional indicator. Maps are consistently correct, simple, easy to read, and drawn to space allowed.

Charts. The artist produces the appropriate type of chart—fever chart, bar chart, or table—for plotting statistical information. Information in the chart clarifies facts that otherwise might be obscured or missed by the reader. The charts are a good complement to stories. Charts do not editorialize or mislead the reader. All charts contain source lines, headlines and copy blocks, and credit lines.

Diagrams. The artist creates fresh, imaginative, dramatic diagrams of news and sports events. Visual material is presented in a clear and concise way so as to help the reader understand the news event. Diagrams include text blocks to identify the situation and to permit the graphic to stand alone, if necessary. Sources are routinely credited.

Typography and style. The artist knows the newspaper's standard typographic and display style. He or she knows commands to set type for graphics and other display, and knows how to use the video display terminal to fit copy. The artist has developed a sensitivity to letter forms. He or she knows type history and has a feel for the appropriate type style to project a particular image or mood. The artist makes appropriate adjustments of letterspacing or kerning as necessary. He or she knows how to use typographic contrast to develop striking display types, logos, or sigs.

Use of color. Color use is adjusted to the subject and assignment. The artist uses color effectively for emphasis or to pull out or define key information.

Multiple-photograph layouts. The artist identifies the key elements needed to tell the story. He or she selects the primary and secondary elements—in size and in content—and links them in a series of photographs to provide a coherent story line. Photo layouts are well designed. Photos chosen show life and action and offer a variety of content, shape, and detail. Each photograph adds a different perspective to the story. The artist consults with editors on approach and keeps editors informed on progress or problems.

Care of equipment. Equipment is used and maintained with care. The artist promptly recognizes and reports the need for repairs and keeps equipment clean and secure from damage and/or theft. He or she makes sure that all equipment is put away and turned off when not in use.

Housekeeping. The artist fills out and files necessary art-request tickets at the end of his or her shift. He or she initials all work, attaches photocopies to the pink copy of the job ticket, and makes sure that the library has a copy of all maps and charts. The finished piece of artwork is delivered to the assigning editor or placed in a job-finished drawer in the department. The artist cleans the cubicle and general work area before leaving, double-checks the front, center, and back counters to make sure that all supplies are put away, and shuts down equipment according to procedure.

Journalistic Skills

Content. The artist is alert to the situation being illustrated. He or she considers visual impact, timeliness, significance, conflict, uniqueness, personality, drama, and emotion. He or she immediately recognizes the elements necessary to tell the story and eliminates irrelevant elements. Illustrations and graphics are candid when possible, capture the subject's personality, expression, or mood, and show consideration of the background and the environment. The artist's technique enhances content.

Awareness of the news. The artist shows sound knowledge of newsmakers, issues, and events in the community and beyond. He or she reads widely and thoroughly on a variety of topics not necessarily limited to his or her job. The artist makes a special effort to develop deep working knowledge on topics related to the job, keeping abreast of current issues, events, and developments and applying this knowledge to graphic arts.

Community awareness. The artist has a keen sense of the community's key figures, issues, history, present problems, and future needs. He or she draws from deep working knowledge to provide accurate references for local people, places, and things. The artist frequently brings background and recollection to art for deeper perspective on the news. He or she shares background with editors and reporters. The artist reads widely and thoroughly on local topics and brings outside knowledge to developing drawings for assignments. He or she promptly communicates information and ideas to appropriate editors.

Spelling and grammar. Graphics are free of spelling errors and typos, whether advance work or submitted on deadline. Graphics follow the stylebook.

Accuracy and attention to detail. Graphics and/or illustrations are accurate when submitted. Statistics, research, text blocks, and drawings are accurate and arranged in such a way as to convey an accurate context. Even under deadline pressure, the artist verifies facts before submitting the graphic and/or illustration or tells the editor of any information not verified to the graphic artist's satisfaction. A proof of the completed graphic is given to the editor and checked by the artist before the art piece is taken to the composing room.

Judgment. The artist senses the importance, significance, and impact of a story and completes the assignment accordingly. He or she has a sense of when additional information, detail, or clarification is needed in a job assignment and provides or asks for it. He or she promptly alerts editors to potential stories and problems. The artist knows what treatment is appropriate in handling a variety of graphics. Under deadline pressure, the artist does not unduly delay art for minor clarifications, but resists the temptation to submit art with significant problems. He or she realizes the need to keep artwork free of personal elements that would be meaningless or offensive to readers.

Research. The artist uses the newspaper library and other resources effectively to get complete and accurate information on graphics and illustrations. He or she knows where to go for background information and statistics. The artist does not wait for the editor or reporter to supply information, but seeks that information from the editor or reporter and supplements it with his or her own research. The artist anticipates the news and prepares for upcoming events, reminding the graphics editor of future news.

Use of sources. The artist uses the best possible source of information for graphics and illustrations. The best possible source is one in the position to have firsthand knowledge of a subject. In seeking help from the library, the artist uses published sources, including books and wire stories. He or she seeks counsel on sources from reporters and editors.

Attributing information to sources. The artist uses attribution properly so that readers know the sources of information in a graphic. The attribution completely identifies the source. In graphics that offer information from several sources, attribution identifies each source.

Representation of minorities. The artist keeps abreast of current issues, events, and developments relating to minority communities. He or she is alert to the impact events in the larger community may have on minorities. He or she develops a deep working knowledge of minority topics related to his or her assignment. The artist develops sources to insure swift and accurate completion of graphics and illustrations for minority representation when necessary to give full and fair views of the event. He or she is aware of minority perspective and includes that point of view in graphics and illustrations where appropriate.

Approach to routine assignments. The artist searches for and uses, if appropriate, fresh approaches to routine graphic-art assignments. He or she looks for additional information and detail that might give a routine assignment an interesting perspective. The artist treats routine assignments with care and attention.

Managing time. The artist manages time effectively. For example, he or she works on one piece of art while awaiting information for another, or draws part of a piece of art even though all the required information is not available. He or she takes advantage of quiet time to develop ideas, file, and advance projects. The artist analyzes the way time is used to be sure that the majority of time is spent on the most important aspects of the assignment. He or she eliminates activities that waste time. In conjunction with an editor, the artist effectively plans work to obtain the maximum result.

Meeting daily deadlines. The artist meets daily deadlines with complete, accurate, well-designed art requiring minimal editing. It is unnecessary for editors to supervise efforts to meet deadlines.

Meeting long-range deadlines. The artist meets deadlines for projects and long-range assignments. No major reworking of the art is necessary in the editing process. He or she consults with editors to set realistic deadlines for research, roughs, and execution of the art, and meets them with minimal supervision.

Drawing under deadline pressure. The artist draws effectively under deadline pressure. Art is well composed and is as complete as current information allows. It is accurate when submitted by deadline. When necessary, the artist identifies parts of graphics that need development for later editions. He or she prepares background for art when it is known in advance that the art will be done on deadline.

Suggesting ideas for art requests. The artist understands the value of art and graphics in conveying information, and recognizes the stories and/or situations that may lend themselves to art. He or she routinely tells editors of such situations.

Developing art idea file. The artist develops an idea file for long- and short-range assignments to insure swift and accurate completion of assignments, background information, and potential graphic ideas. Sources are those who can provide accurate information about the assignment. He or she consistently checks with those sources to make sure of information and continue to add to the personal idea file.

Use of VDTs and other computers. The artist understands the use of the video display terminals and other computer equipment that can be used on the job.

Communication

Working with editors and staff. The artist works effectively with editors, reporters, and other artists to develop graphics and illustrations. He or she seeks suggestions for concept approach and development when necessary and applies them effectively. He or she takes the initiative to clarify assignments when necessary and keeps editors apprised of the status of work in progress. The artist resolves differences of opinion with editors in a constructive, professional manner.

Keeping editors informed. The artist keeps the graphics editor and assigning editor updated on proposed graphics or illustrations and work in progress, consulting with editors to set priorities and seeking advice when uncertain of emphasis or approach or when problems arise. He or she advises the desk of his or her location when out of the office.

Using feedback for development. The artist actively seeks feedback on the quality of graphics or illustrations, technical skills, and other elements of the job. He or she uses this information effectively to make the improvements indicated. It is rarely necessary for editors to suggest the same improvement twice.

Contact with the public. The artist deals with the public in a courteous, professional manner. He or she takes the time to explain newspaper policy, answer questions, respond to phone calls, and answer letters.

Copy Editor

Accuracy

Factually accurate information. Edited copy and headlines always are factually accurate. Statistics, research, quotes, and narrative are accurate and arranged in such a way as to convey an accurate context.

Verifying identities, addresses. Names and addresses are verified, using such references as phone books and directories. The copy editor checks the spelling of names and places. When questions arise, he or she contacts the source, if possible, to verify information. The copy editor consults with an editor when verification is impossible.

Attributing information to sources. The copy editor makes sure stories carry proper attribution so readers know the sources of information. The attribution completely identifies the source. Conflicting opinions are always attributed so readers know who is offering each side. In stories that contain information from several sources, attribution identifies each source. When confidential or anonymous sources appear in copy, the copy editor verifies that appropriate steps have been taken to get sources on the record. He or she ascertains that the decision to use confidential or anonymous sources has the approval of an editor.

Using best possible sources. The copy editor makes sure that edited copy uses the best possible sources. The best possible sources are those in a position to have firsthand knowledge of a subject.

Spelling, Stylebook, Typos. The copy editor rarely submits edited copy and headlines that contain spelling errors or typos, even on deadline. Edited copy follows the stylebook.

Grammar. The copy editor uses correct grammar.

Copyediting

Identifying important story elements. The copy editor recognizes important story elements and, where necessary, rearranges them effectively. He or she makes sure that leads are based on proper criteria such as impact, local interest, timeliness, prominence, uniqueness, or conflict. The copy editor makes sure that elements such as quotations or statistics are used effectively to support the lead. He or she promptly alerts editors to potential problems and knows how to repair a story and suggest improvements.

Organizing story. The copy editor knows when story elements have been arranged in logical progression with a clearly defined beginning, middle, and end. He or she edits copy to meet these requirements, tightening copy and improving grouping of related elements for clarity and readability. The copy editor promptly alerts the appropriate editor of any need for changes. He or she always checks with the reporter on substantive changes or with an editor if the reporter is not available.

Editing copy tightly. Copy is edited so that it is succinct, but preserves the reporter's style. Leads are refined to be crisp and to the point. Duplication is kept to a minimum, but the copy editor insures that major points have adequate support. He or she tightens stories to guarantee economical word selection.

Legal awareness/sense of fairness. The copy editor has solid familiarity with libel, privacy, and youthful-offender laws. Potentially actionable or unfair material in stories is accurately identified. The copy editor immediately brings problems to the appropriate editor's attention, even on stories the copy editor hasn't handled. He or she knows and suggests the best way to correct copy while preserving the sense of a story. He or she is quick to insure that all sides of an issue are fairly represented. The copy editor is alert to sensitive material and handles it properly. He or she spots subtleties that portray subjects in an unfair light or that introduce elements of poor taste and makes appropriate recommendations to editors.

Critical judgment. The copy editor senses the impact of a story or headline on readers. He or she catches and corrects elements of bad taste and unfairness. He or she knows when fair comment is lacking and when better balance is needed. The copy editor knows how to fix these problems and promptly alerts appropriate editors when problems are found. He or she is careful to preserve the reporter's style and the story's intent. Under deadline pressure, the copy editor does not delay copy unduly for minor clarifications, but does not move copy with significant holes.

Community awareness. The copy editor has a keen sense of the community's key figures, issues, local history, present problems, and future needs. He or she draws from deep working knowledge to identify improvements needed in stories and accurate or appropriate references to local people, places, and things. The copy editor reads widely and thoroughly on local topics. He or she brings outside knowledge to improving copy, headlines, and overall coverage. The copy editor keeps track of reportage and can sort out old news from new facts. He or she communicates information and story ideas promptly to the appropriate editors and reporters.

News of minorities. The copy editor shows a sound knowledge of newsmakers, issues, and events in the local minority community and beyond. He or she recognizes when minority perspective is required to make a story complete or balanced and acts to insure that this point of view is included in the story. The copy editor spots and eliminates subtleties in copy and headlines that may cast members of minority groups in an unfair light. He or she demonstrates an awareness of minority angles in the reading and editing of wire copy and alerts editors when appropriate minority angles are missing from wire copy.

Awareness of the news. The copy editor shows sound knowledge of newsmakers, issues, and events beyond the local community. He or she reads widely and thoroughly on a variety of topics and applies this knowledge in editing and improving stories and in writing headlines. The copy editor develops expertise in special areas to enhance his or her ability to edit stories on these topics. He or she keeps track of reportage and can sort out old news from new facts.

Roundups/Packages/Series. The copy editor combines diverse elements from several stories into a cohesive and informative report. He or she is careful to keep track of overall impact, balance, and fairness of a package, especially in coverage over several days. The copy editor pays attention to detail, avoids duplication of facts, and resolves inconsistencies. He or she offers ideas for further development, sidebars, or additional stories.

Meeting deadlines. The copy editor edits copy effectively under deadline pressure. Stories are well organized, accurate, and make the deadline. The copy editor can edit "in takes" when necessary. He or she identifies areas that need development in later editions. He or she monitors stories as they develop when it is known in advance that stories will be done on deadline. The copy editor watches for specific key elements and organization. When possible, he or she gathers reference material in advance to help in meeting a deadline for a late-arriving story.

Managing time. The copy editor manages time effectively. For example, he or she edits one story while awaiting information for another or edits parts of a story even though all the information required is not available. He or she takes advantage of quiet times to improve stories between editions and to consult with staff members on their work. The copy editor analyzes the way time is used in an effort to focus on the most important parts of the job. He or she eliminates activities that waste time. In conjunction with an editor, the copy editor effectively plans work to obtain the maximum result.

Headline Writing

Identifying best headline angle. The copy editor recognizes the news peg and keys the headline to the essence of the story. Each headline idea is based on proper criteria such as impact, local interest, timeliness, prominence, uniqueness, or conflict. The copy editor assures that the headline does not ignore other sides of the issue. He or she strives for the most timely headline and knows whether a first-day or second-day treatment is required. He or she is alert to nuances or elements of bad taste and makes certain that the headline reflects the tone of the story. The copy editor alerts the appropriate editor to the need for a different headline count to accommodate the best angle.

Clarity. Headlines are clear, crisp, inviting, and easy to understand. Syntax is precise and easy to read. Words convey the exact meaning intended. Headline phrasing is direct and clear-cut. The copy editor avoids jargon and employs strong, forceful verbs and clear phrasing. Headlines are technically accurate without obscure or fuzzy words or concepts.

Flair/Creativity. The copy editor goes beyond the obvious to produce compelling, interesting headlines. Headlines may be clever, witty, or colorful while conveying the meaning of the story and preserving a sense of good taste. The copy editor uses descriptive words and details that give added dimension to the headline.

Meeting deadlines. Under deadline pressure, the copy editor writes headlines that are precise, have flair, and convey the sense of the story. He or she can write headlines on stories "in process" when necessary. The copy editor remains in control and identifies improvements for later editions. He or she monitors stories as they develop when it is known in advance that stories will be done on deadline.

Communication

Working with editors to improve stories. The copy editor works effectively with editors to improve editing and headlines. He or she seeks suggestions for approach or style and applies suggestions effectively. The copy editor resolves differences of opinion with editors on approach, style, value, and priority in a constructive, professional manner.

Using feedback for development. The copy editor actively seeks feedback on editing, headline writing, and other elements of the job. He or she uses this information effectively to make any improvements indicated. It is rarely necessary for editors to suggest the same improvement twice.

Working with other staff members. The copy editor works effectively with other staff members and is willing to share information. When working with other copy editors, he or she discusses the work in a constructive manner and shares the workload. He or she discusses copy problems and ideas with editors and reporters in a constructive, professional manner. The copy editor seeks opportunities to help reporters, particularly inexperienced or new staff members.

Keeping editor informed. The copy editor keeps the appropriate editors updated on the progress of stories as needed. He or she consults with the copydesk chief to set priorities when necessary and keeps the copydesk chief aware of stories through various stages of development, seeking advice when uncertain of the angle or approach or when problems arise. He or she never delays in alerting editors to major problems that may take time to fix.

Editor

Editing

News judgment. The editor knows which stories should be published and how they should be displayed. He or she balances significance, importance, and interest of stories in determining what coverage and display, if any, is appropriate. He or she is sensitive to taste, policy, and legal considerations. The editor identifies the important elements in stories and knows which should be followed, which need further reporting or graphics, and whether timeliness is an issue.

Headlines. The editor recognizes good and bad headlines and makes sure that bad headlines are rewritten promptly. He or she has an excellent sense of the right count and orders it, or adjusts it, if necessary, for the head to be complete. When called upon to write heads, the editor does so effectively, and does not introduce errors in writing or rewriting heads.

Production process. The editor shows a deep knowledge of each facet of the newspaper production process. He or she uses that knowledge effectively to get the freshest news into the paper without unduly delaying the production and distribution of the paper. The editor knows the best ways of resolving problems with deadlines, page flow, reproduction, and color. He or she makes editors aware of potential problems immediately. He or she knows edition and circulation structure and which stories should go in which edition. The editor notifies his or her editor of special stories or breaking stories that should be discussed with production or circulation departments for special handling or distribution.

Story ideas. The editor is aware of the community, the nation, and the world and changes that occur. He or she is aware of issues, trends, and ideas that may be newsworthy and suggests related stories. The editor draws from a deep working knowledge to identify areas for coverage and is always able to provide useful story ideas for reporters. He or she reads extensively and is well informed on most major issues, especially those within his or her area of responsibility. The editor's ideas are not limited to this area and indicate an awareness of the needs and interests of the total newspaper readership.

Story improvement. The editor recognizes strengths and weaknesses in stories. He or she knows when to leave a good story alone. The editor understands when and how to preserve a writer's style and works effectively with reporters to improve content, organization, clarity, and readability. He or she recognizes when additional factual material is needed and when standards of balance, fairness, and taste have not been met. The editor sees that changes are made before publication. In editing, he or she does not introduce errors or reach unsubstantiated conclusions. The editor knows when to coach reporters on rewriting a story and when to turn a story over to the copydesk for improvement.

Community awareness. The editor has a keen sense of the community's key figures, issues, history, present problems, and future needs. He or she draws from deep working knowledge to identify the need for covering, developing, and improving stories: whose obituary to write, which streets don't intersect, proper or inaccurate references to local people, places, and things. He or she frequently brings background and recollection to editing and to guidance of reporters for deeper perspective on the news. The editor shares background with other editors and with reporters. The editor reads widely and thoroughly on local topics and brings outside knowledge to news coverage. He or she keeps track of reportage and sorts out old news from new facts. The editor makes frequent efforts to venture out into the community to meet with newsmakers and readers and to visit organizations that are in the news.

News of minorities. The editor keeps abreast of current issues, events, and developments relating to minority communities and is alert to the impact on minorities of events in the larger community. He or she uses that knowledge to guide reporters and to direct coverage. The editor encourages the staff to develop a deep working knowledge of minority topics and to develop sources in the minority community. He or she is aware of minority perspective and acts to insure that this point of view is included in stories where appropriate. The editor spots subtleties in stories and headlines that may cast members of minority groups in an unfair light.

Layout, Design. The editor understands and executes the newspaper's graphic style to produce creative and compelling layouts that enhance the page content and invite readers into the page. He or she takes full advantage of the expertise available from graphics, photo, and other editors. He or she seeks advice on work in progress and discusses pages already published to find ways to improve future layouts.

Graphics, Photos. The editor recognizes the value of graphics and photos. He or she shows creativity in suggesting or requesting these devices. The editor knows which stories lend themselves to illustrations, photos, maps, and charts. He or she sets consistently high standards for graphics and photos and suggests revisions, if necessary, to achieve these standards. The editor works effectively with graphics, photo, and other editors to achieve the best results. He or she avoids the use of photos and graphics for decoration and searches instead for ways of using these devices to convey information that supplements and enhances stories.

Legal awareness/Sense of fairness. The editor displays a solid knowledge of libel, privacy, youthful-offender laws, and other laws related to news. He or she uses this knowledge effectively to identify and avoid actionable material. He or she is sensitive to legal concerns and consults immediately with his or her editor on stories for which legal advice is necessary. The editor knows how to counsel reporters in dealing with courtrooms, freedom of information issues, subpoenas, and other matters related to freedom of the press. The editor alerts his or her editors to these situations, in advance when possible. He or she insures that all sides of an issue are represented fairly. He or she spots subtleties that may cast subjects in an unfair light. He or she avoids elements of bad taste. The editor corrects problems immediately and notifies the appropriate editor, if necessary. He or she knows when to consult on sensitive material and does so without fail.

News policy. The editor displays complete knowledge and understanding of news policies. He or she understands when and how to apply them. The editor keeps his or her editors informed, including instances when exceptions to the policy may be appropriate or anticipated. He or she explains policies to staff to develop their understanding.

Meeting deadlines. The editor sets and meets both long-range and short-range deadlines and insures that members of his or her staff meet their deadlines as well. He or she accurately assesses the time necessary to accomplish various tasks, both those the editor must perform and those of his or her staff. The editor keeps his or her editor informed of potential problems in meeting deadlines. He or she knows when and how to stretch deadlines to get important stories into the paper without unanticipated adverse results. The editor knows when and how to release a story to meet deadlines and when to send it back for improvements, and does not delay a story unnecessarily for minor improvements.

Performance under pressure. The editor works effectively and efficiently under pressure of deadlines, breaking news, or other constraints. He or she gets the work done and does not interfere with others' attempts to do the same. He or she conveys a sense of accomplishment and challenge, not disruption. The editor knows and acts on priorities in pressure situations. The editor delays action on other matters for a more appropriate time.

Creativity. The editor looks for and uses imaginative ways of conveying the information of the day to readers. He or she encourages the staff to take a fresh approach. He or she assigns, edits, and displays stories to use available resources to the best effect. He or she uses traditional approaches when they are the most effective, but actively pursues creative treatment of stories, graphics, photos, and display, even under deadline pressure.

Managing

Selecting staff. The editor accurately determines staffing needs and identifies job requirements. He or she screens applicants to weed out unqualified candidates, conducts in-depth interviews to determine suitability, and identifies the candidate who is the best match for the job.

Assigning staff. The editor has an excellent understanding of requirements for all assignments. He or she selects the appropriate staff member for each assignment, matching requirements with staff members' strengths and weaknesses.

Evaluating staff. The editor routinely assesses the work of staff members. He or she uses specific, measurable, and observable standards as a basis for appraisal. He or she always knows how staff members are performing. The editor consistently provides feedback on both good and poor performance and offers guidance for making improvements. Staff members have no reason to be unsure how they are doing or to be surprised by results of performance reviews. Continuing attention to staff members' performance results in the collection of detailed profiles that are used as the basis for formal performance reviews. Performance reviews show an understanding of job requirements and professional standards. Conclusions about a staff member's performance are fair, reflecting a thoughtful, balanced examination of all factors involved. The editor accurately identifies problem areas and offers suggestions for improvements. He or she meets deadlines for evaluations. He or she conducts evaluation discussions in a positive, constructive manner and seeks to help each staff member understand the basis for his or her ratings and to reach an agreement on performance levels and necessary improvements.

Motivating and developing staff. The editor accurately assesses staff members' needs, interests, and values. He or she uses appropriate methods to encourage and assist them in improving performance. Staff members reporting to the editor usually work at the upper levels of their ability or show movement in that direction. The editor keeps his or her editors informed of problems and progress of staff members and seeks advice in difficult situations.

Directing work of staff. The editor determines the scope of each assignment, the approach to be used, and the deadline to be met. He or she outlines and explains this clearly and precisely and checks to be sure staff members understand what is expected. The editor monitors work in progress to be sure that assignments are being completed as outlined and that deadlines are being met. He or she moves quickly to guide an assignment back on track. He or she knows who is working on what and is aware of individual work loads. The editor encourages staff members to discuss their progress on and problems with assignments. He or she relays that information to his or her editors, as needed, and adjusts deadlines and assignments when necessary because of unexpected problems or work load.

Communicating with staff. The editor fosters a climate of openness and sharing of information. He or she encourages constructive communication and accommodates differing points of view. The editor actively solicits information, ideas, and opinions from others, and listens attentively and asks questions to be sure he or she understands what is being said. The editor gives clear instructions and direction and provides routine feedback. His or her communication with the staff shows an understanding of the supervisory role and responsibilities.

Communicating with editors. The editor keeps his or her editor informed of progress, problems, goals, and activities. He or she initiates this communication and shows no reluctance to seek advice or clarification. The editor knows when to consult and when to act. His or her editors are rarely surprised by receiving information from others that the editor should have provided. His or her editor is rarely surprised by actions taken by the editor without consultation. The editor knows what information other editors need to do their jobs. He or she shows good judgment in recognizing what information to relay.

Managing change. The editor plans and implements changes to avoid disruption, confusion, and dissatisfaction. He or she anticipates problems, discussing and counseling when necessary to accomplish smooth transitions. Staff members are not surprised by changes. The editor resolves any personal disagreements with changes before discussion with the staff.

Managing conflict. The editor knows when conflict exists and accurately identifies the origin. He or she moves to resolve conflict quickly and effectively. He or she recognizes sources of potential conflict and takes the right action to avoid problems. The editor recognizes the difference between constructive, creative disagreement and unwillingness to accept direction and responds appropriately to each.

Analyzing and solving problems. The editor quickly becomes aware of problems and can accurately assess the source. He or she seeks out the root of each problem and is not misled by the symptoms. He or she takes a constructive, logical approach and consults with others as necessary. He or she determines the proper solution and acts on it. The editor weighs the importance of finding a solution and addresses highest-priority problems first. He or she finds lasting solutions when possible, avoiding the quick or temporary fix.

Setting and meeting objectives. The editor determines what is needed to improve the newspaper, the performance of his or her staff, and his or her own performance. He or she sets clearly defined objectives to meet these needs and finds ways to accomplish the objectives, even with the pressure of daily deadlines or other constraints.

Setting priorities. The editor selects the most important objectives and focuses efforts on them. He or she weighs investment of time, people, and money against the potential return and goals. The editor knows what is important and what is not and consults with his or her editors when there is uncertainty.

Managing time. The editor analyzes what needs to be done and, after setting priorities, determines the best and most effective way to do it. He or she gets things done on time. The editor analyzes how he or she uses time in an effort to focus on the most important aspects of the job. He or she looks for things that waste time and finds ways to eliminate them. The editor delegates when appropriate.

Librarian

Library Skills

Awareness of the news. The librarian shows a sound knowledge of local newsmakers and issues and knows the community's history, present problems, and future needs. He or she draws from deep working knowledge to assist the news staff in researching stories and providing proper references to local people, places, and things. He or she reads widely and thoroughly on a variety of topics and uses this knowledge in filling the research needs of the news staff. The librarian keeps informed about the development of current events in international, national, state, business, sports, and entertainment news.

Thoroughness of research. The librarian exhausts all available sources in serving the news staff. If the information is not available in our library, he or she knows what other library or outside agency will have the information. With rare exceptions, he or she uses the best possible source material. The librarian uses a combination of the available resources—clipping file, photos, magazines, books, maps—to answer the questions of the news staff.

Accuracy. The librarian provides accurate information. He or she verifies names and addresses using such sources as directories and indexes. He or she checks spelling and titles before giving information to the news staff. When errors are discovered in news stories or in existing files, the librarian conducts a thorough search of all reference sources to assure that all corrections are immediately made. With rare exceptions, he or she provides the most recent information possible. He or she consults with the copy editor or reporter when verification is impossible.

Subject headings. The librarian uses correct subject headings when marking a news story, processing a photo, or indexing a map. He or she employs cross-references and indicates tracings. He or she creates new subject headings when necessary. The librarian updates the subject-heading list by eliminating redundant or incorrect headings, enhances cross-references, and adds tracings. He or he consults with the library manager and other library assistants to insure uniformity of headings.

Filing. The librarian demonstrates a comprehensive understanding of filing rules for all collections and follows those rules precisely. He or she subdivides overfilled envelopes. He or she is alert to misfiled envelopes and refiles them correctly.

Attention to detail. The librarian demonstrates care and attention in performing various library tasks. Clipping of news stories is done neatly, and date stamping is crisp and readable. Indexing is complete and cross-references are made as necessary. The librarian makes certain that all information necessary is provided before filing materials, and follows library style. He or she pays close attention to overdue and missing materials.

Time management. The librarian manages time effectively. For example, when finished with a specific assignment, he or she looks for ways to help other librarians with their assignments. He or she analyzes the way time is used to be sure that the majority of time is spent on the most important aspects of the job. The librarian eliminates activities that waste time. In conjunction with the library manager, he or she effectively plans work to obtain the maximum result.

Ideas for library development. The librarian suggests ways in which library procedures or resources can be improved. For example, he or she suggests the acquisition of a reference book that would improve the library's research capacity. Ideas are not limited to the librarian's assignment and indicate an awareness of the needs and interests of the total library. The librarian conveys ideas to the library manager and develops those in his or her area of responsibility.

Policy. The librarian has solid familiarity with library checkout rules, access procedures, lending policy, and copyright restrictions, and deals effectively with telephone requests.

Use of Information Sources

Clipping file. The librarian displays a broad knowledge of the clipping file and is able to locate information within it immediately. He or she knows the appropriate heading under which to find the needed information. He or she keeps abreast of how current topics are marked for filing and uses cross-references to locate all information needed.

Photo file. The librarian displays a broad knowledge of the photo file contents and locates material immediately. He or she uses the appropriate subject heading to locate photos and uses the photo card catalogue when unsure of a specific heading. The librarian understands the photo-processing procedure and follows it. He or she uses the photo master file when searching for a recent photo.

Books and periodicals. The librarian locates information immediately using the book and periodical collection. He or she is familiar with all indexes and the card catalogue and uses them to locate information. He or she knows what is contained in the book and periodical collection and what types of information can be found in each. The librarian knows of and offers additional or alternative resources to provide the fullest information possible.

Graphic sources. The librarian shows solid knowledge of graphics resources and quickly locates maps, clip art, and chart information. He or she offers editors and artists a variety of graphics material for use in developing illustrations. The librarian uses the card index when searching for locator maps. He or she displays a solid knowledge of reference material in locating graphics information.

Communication

Working with news staff. The librarian works effectively with reporters, editors, photographers, and artists on research problems. He or she welcomes suggestions and takes the initiative when necessary to clarify an assignment. He or she asks the right questions to be sure there is an understanding of exactly what information the staff member is seeking. The librarian solicits advice from the news staff when necessary in selecting a research approach and welcomes suggestions in improving research skills.

Working with library staff. The librarian works effectively with other library assistants. He or she shares knowledge with others about the location of information and reference sources. When working on a project with others, he or she discusses the problem thoroughly, then shares the work load to insure that skills are best utilized.

Keeping library manager informed. The librarian keeps the library manager updated on the status of operations, especially the filing situation, and consults to set priorities when necessary. He or she keeps the library manager aware of lengthy research projects, seeking advice when difficulties arise and pointing out potential problems.

Using feedback for development. The librarian welcomes and even seeks criticism of work methods and job performance. He or she acts immediately to make any improvements indicated. It is rarely necessary for the library manager to suggest the same improvement twice.

Contact with public. The librarian deals with the public in a courteous, professional manner. He or she takes the time to explain newspaper policy, answer questions, respond to phone calls, and answer letters.

Photographer

Technical Skills

Exposures. Film is exposed properly to yield best tonal range and for proper highlight and shadow detail. The photographer is able to select proper exposures in all situations and can create special effects as assigned. He or she knows the characteristics of film and applies that knowledge to select exposures in special situations. No adjustment is necessary during the printing process to compensate for imperfect exposures.

Composition. The photographer effectively arranges the story-telling elements in a photograph using appropriate lenses, angles, perspective, and foreground/background relationships to make interesting photographs that are well designed and direct.

Lighting. The photographer selects lighting to reflect the mood of the story. He or she uses various lighting equipment (flash, tungsten, alternative mode, etc.) to fit the situation. He or she uses natural light effectively and applies artificial light when needed to add detail, enhance content, or augment composition. The photographer uses proper lighting ratios to give depth and modeling to subjects. He or she uses highlight and shadow effectively, both in the studio and in natural light, and considers reproduction limitations.

Film processing. Film is evenly developed and fixed. Development is adjusted with the exposure and subject contrast levels to produce the best tonal ranges in high-quality prints.

Printing. Prints have a full range of tones and the proper contrast level, depth, and richness. Highlights and shadows have proper detail. Prints are free of dust and scratches. Burning and dodging are undetectable.

Housekeeping. The photographer files negatives at the end of his or her shift. Negatives marked for printing are enclosed in protective sheaths. The original copy of the assignment is enclosed with the negatives. The specifics of each assignment—name, address, story, paper, date, and photographer's name—are typed on the filing envelope. The photographer makes reprints within the three-day deadline. He or she cleans the studio, lab areas, and film room after use, wipes counters and walls in the film room, and puts away supplies. The photographer shuts down lab according to procedure. He or she scrubs sinks, cabinets, and darkroom equipment when assigned to lab cleanup.

Care of equipment. Equipment is used and maintained with care. The photographer promptly recognizes and reports the need for repairs and keeps equipment clean and secure from damage and/or theft. He or she makes sure that all lenses have protective filters at all times.

Photojournalism

Content. The photographer is alert to the situation being photographed. He or she considers visual impact, timeliness, significance, conflict, uniqueness, personality, drama, and emotion. The photographer immediately recognizes the elements necessary to tell the story and eliminates irrelevant elements. Photographs of people are candid when possible, capture the subject's personality, expression, or mood, and show consideration of the background and the environment. The photographer's technique enhances content.

Approach to routine assignments. The photographer searches for and uses, if appropriate, new and fresh approaches to routine stories. He or she looks for additional information and detail that might give a routine story an interesting perspective. He or she treats routine stories with care and attention.

Suggesting and developing story ideas. The photographer is aware of issues, ideas, and situations that may be newsworthy and suggests related stories. Ideas are not limited to the photographer's assignments and indicate awareness of the needs and interests of the total newspaper. The photographer conveys ideas to editors and follows through to develop those assigned to him or her within the agreed-upon time.

Developing news sources. The photographer develops sources for long- and short-range stories to insure swift and accurate completion of stories and access to difficult situations, background information, and potential story ideas. Sources are those who can provide accurate information about the story. The photographer consistently checks with those sources to insure photographic coverage.

Awareness of the news. The photographer shows sound knowledge of newsmakers, issues, and events in the community and beyond. He or she reads widely and thoroughly on a variety of topics. He or she makes a special effort to keep abreast of current issues, events, and developments and applies that knowledge to his or her photography. The photographer has a solid knowledge of the community's key figures, issues, history, present problems, and future needs and uses this knowledge to cover the community. He or she promptly communicates information and ideas to appropriate editors. The photographer keeps track of coverage and can sort old news from new situations.

News judgment. The photographer senses the importance, significance, and impact of news situations and photographs them accordingly. He or she promptly alerts editors to potential stories and problems. He or she knows what treatment is appropriate in handling a variety of stories. The photographer avoids elements of bad taste and unfairness. He or she does not unduly delay photographs under deadline pressure for minor improvements, but resists submitting photographs with significant problems.

News of minorities. The photographer keeps abreast of current issues, events, and developments relating to minority communities. He or she is alert to the impact events in the larger community may have on minorities. The photographer develops sources in minority communities to insure access to newsmakers and swift completion of photographic assignments. He or she is aware of minority perspective and makes sure that, when appropriate, this point of view is reflected in news and feature photographs. The photographer spots subtleties in photos that may cast members of minority groups in an unfair light.

Managing time. The photographer manages time effectively. For example, when not on specific assignment, he or she researches story ideas, develops contacts, completes routine office duties, and produces daily enterprise. He or she works on one story while awaiting information or contacts for another. The photographer analyzes the way time is used to be sure that the majority of time is spent on the most important aspects of the job. He or she eliminates activities that waste time. In conjunction with an editor, the photographer effectively plans work to obtain the maximum result.

Meeting daily deadlines. The photographer meets daily deadlines with high-quality photographs that tell the story. He or she provides complete, accurate captions. He or she keeps the editors informed of potential deadline problems.

Variety of photographs. The photographer shoots a sufficient number of photographs to allow editors a choice of composition, shape, perspective, and angle. In shooting assignments, he or she provides each with a selection of photographs that tell the story. The photographer seeks different angles, perspectives, and situations on these assignments to be sure that the paper has full coverage.

Captions. Captions are factually accurate when submitted and follow caption style. Information is arranged in such a way as to convey an accurate representation in the context of what the photograph shows. The photographer checks all names and addresses when taking the photograph, if possible. He or she also makes routine use of reference sources to check the accuracy of names and addresses. Even under deadline pressure, the photographer verifies facts or tells photo editors of any information that has not been verified to the photographer's satisfaction. He or she provides sufficient information upon which to base cutlines and seeks additional detail or background that would enhance the cutlines.

Representing situations accurately. All photographs except illustrations are accurate representations of the situations they portray. Nothing recreated, staged, or posed is represented as a candid situation. Previously shot photographs are not represented as fresh and new. The photographer is alert to situations in which straightforward photography might create an impression contrary to the facts. He or she avoids cropping a photograph in a way that would misrepresent the situation. The photographer points out questionable photographs or situations and discusses proper treatment of them with editors.

Spot news photography. The photographer recognizes and reacts to news situations as they unfold, using police and fire radios as a resource. He or she gains access to news situations, quickly assesses the important elements in the situation, and makes dramatic, clean, graphic photographs that convey the essential information quickly. The photographer produces a variety of photos, including overall shots and other secondary photos that aid in telling the story. He or she gathers as much information as deadline pressure allows from the most reliable sources on the scene. The photographer notifies editors of the situation on the scene. Photographs make the next edition whenever that is possible.

Feature photography. The photographer makes feature photographs that are well designed and graphically clean. Photographs are filled with emotion, expression, and liveliness and capture the subject's personality while relating the important elements of the story. The photographer looks for fresh and innovative treatments of feature photographs.

Sports photography. The photographer develops and uses knowledge of the sport to anticipate action, capture key plays, and show emotion and the drama of the event. He or she is alert to situations on the sidelines, in the crowd, and in the locker room that convey the mood of the game or the newsworthiness of the event. Photographs are consistently sharp, with minimal movement or blurring.

Color photography. The photographer produces color photographs that are exposed properly and that have rich, vibrant, and fully saturated tones. He or she reflects subtleties and moods by controlling lighting, exposures, film type, and filters. The photographer processes film for the correct time using uncontaminated chemicals at the correct temperature. Film is free from dirt, scratches, and stains.

Studio illustrations. The photographer creates fresh, imaginative, and dramatic studio photographs and illustrations that show understanding of graphic design and offer insight into accompanying stories. Food photos appear appetizing. Fashion photographs show good detail of clothing. Product photographs are clean and well designed. The photographer uses a variety of backgrounds, locations, props, lighting, and lenses to produce desired results. Copying is done quickly and produces a duplicate equal in quality to the original.

Multiple-photograph layouts. The photographer identifies the key elements needed to tell the story. He or she selects the primary and secondary elements and links them in a series of photographs to provide a coherent story line. Photographs are well designed, show life and action, and offer a variety of content, shape, and detail. Each photograph adds a different perspective to the story. The photographer consults with editors on approach and keeps editors informed on progress or problems.

Communication

Working with editors and staff. The photographer works effectively with editors, reporters, and other photographers to develop stories. He or she seeks suggestions for story approach and development when necessary and applies suggestions effectively. The photographer takes the initiative to clarify assignments when necessary and keeps editors apprised of the status of work in progress. He or she resolves differences of opinion with editors in a constructive, professional manner.

Using feedback for development. The photographer actively seeks feedback on the quality of photography, technical skills, and other elements of the job. He or she uses this information effectively to make the improvements indicated. It is rarely necessary for editors to suggest the same improvement twice.

Keeping editors informed. The photographer keeps editors updated on proposed stories and stories in progress, consulting with editors to set priorities and seeking advice when uncertain of the angle or approach or when problems arise. He or she advises the desk of his or her location and keeps in radio contact when out of the office.

Contact with the public. The photographer deals with the public in a courteous, professional manner. He or she takes the time to explain newspaper policy, answer questions, respond to phone calls, and answer letters.

Reporter

Accuracy

Spelling, Stylebook, Typos. Copy is free of spelling errors and typos, even when submitted on deadline. Copy follows the stylebook.

Attributing information to sources. Attribution is used properly so readers know the sources of information in a story. The attribution completely identifies sources. Conflicting opinions are attributed so that readers know who is offering each point of view. In stories that offer information from several sources, attribution identifies each source. The reporter makes every effort to get all news and quotes on the record and uses anonymous sources only as a last resort and only after consultation with an editor. The reporter protects the identity of the anonymous source. When it is necessary to go off the record, the reporter honors that commitment in writing the story.

Factually accurate information. Copy is factually accurate when submitted. Statistics, research, quotes, and narrative are accurate and arranged in such a way as to convey an accurate context. The reporter recognizes that accurate context involves representing all sides of the story fairly and completely. The reporter draws on as many sources as may be necessary to accomplish this. He or she assesses accuracy of information and credibility of sources and double-checks information routinely. Even under deadline pressure, the reporter verifies facts before submitting a story. The reporter tells editors of any information not verified to the reporter's satisfaction.

Verifying identities, addresses. The reporter verifies names and addresses using such references as phone books and directories. He or she checks the spelling of names and places. When questions arise, he or she goes directly to the source, if possible, to verify information. The reporter consults with an editor when problems arise in verification.

Using best possible sources. The reporter uses the best possible sources for information included in stories. The best possible sources are those in the position to have firsthand knowledge of a subject.

Calling errors to editor's attention. The reporter immediately calls to the attention of an editor known or suspected errors in his or her copy, regardless of their severity. The reporter alerts editors when he or she has reason to believe any story in the paper contains an error, misrepresentation, or inaccuracy.

Reporting

Gathering information. The reporter understands the process of gathering information for a story. He or she gets quickly to the heart of the story and grasps the full meaning, consequences, and implications of events. He or she determines what basic questions must be asked and makes every effort to get the answers. The reporter knows where to go for information, including the best sources and how to reach them. He or she does so quickly and requires little guidance from editors in gathering routine information. He or she does not rely on one source, but seeks out sufficient sources to provide fair, balanced, and accurate coverage. He or she draws meaningful information from reluctant sources and is able to obtain useful quotes in interviews. If there is difficulty in gathering information, the reporter quickly determines other approaches and/or sources and pursues the story. He or she consults with editors if problems persist and gathers background, if necessary, to set the story in perspective.

Approach to routine stories. The reporter searches for and uses, if appropriate, new and fresh approaches to routine stories. He or she looks for the additional information and detail that might give a routine story an interesting perspective. He or she spots unusual or offbeat ideas and elements not readily apparent that give added dimension to a story. Routine stories are treated with the same care and attention given nonroutine stories.

Suggesting and developing story ideas. The reporter is aware of issues and trends that may be newsworthy and suggests related stories. Ideas are not limited to the reporter's assignment and indicate an awareness of the needs and interests of the total newspaper. He or she conveys ideas to editors and develops those in his or her area of responsibility. The reporter sees story possibilities and angles that can be developed beyond an assigned story.

Producing enterprise stories. The reporter looks beyond routing beat/assignment coverage for stories. These stories may add depth, perspective, and analysis to the news or they may be stories that, because of their unusual natures, are not handled in the routing of the beats. These stories could also be unrelated to the beat but are of interest because of their very nature.

Developing sources. The reporter develops sources for long- and short-range stories to insure swift and accurate completion of stories, access to difficult-to-obtain material, background information, and potential story ideas. Sources are those who can provide accurate information about a subject. When feasible, the reporter deals with sources in person.

Depth, perspective, insight. The reporter looks for and uses opportunities to add depth, perspective, and insight to news coverage through development of such stories as news analyses, situation pieces, interviews with people in the news, and question-and-answer pieces.

Research. The reporter uses the newspaper library effectively to get accurate information on a story. He or she knows how to gain access to and is skillful in using public records and other background information. The reporter understands and uses statistical material, budgets, and other technical material in developing stories. He or she knows how to use results of research to properly background a story.

Awareness of the news. The reporter shows sound knowledge of newsmakers, issues, and events in the community and beyond. He or she reads widely and thoroughly on a variety of topics not necessarily limited to the beat/assignment. He or she makes a special effort to develop deep working knowledge of topics related to the beat/assignment, keeping abreast of current issues, events, and developments. The reporter applies this knowledge to reporting and writing stories, keeps track of reportage, and can sort out old news from new facts.

Community awareness. The reporter has a keen sense of the community's key figures, issues, history, present problems, and future needs. He or she draws from deep working knowledge to provide accurate references for local people, places, and things, and frequently brings background and recollection to reporting for deeper perspective on the news. The reporter shares background with editors and other reporters. He or she reads widely and thoroughly on local topics and brings outside knowledge to developing and writing stories. He or she keeps track of reportage and can sort out old news from new facts.

The reporter promptly communicates information and ideas to the appropriate editors.

Legal awareness/Sense of fairness. The reporter has solid familiarity with libel, privacy, and youthful-offender laws. He or she avoids actionable matter in stories. Potential problems are brought immediately to an editor's attention. The reporter is quick to insure that all sides of an issue are fairly represented in stories. He or she avoids subtleties that cast subjects in an unfair light and uses good taste in characterizing individuals in the news. The reporter keeps his or her own views out of stories and consults with editors on sensitive stories.

Judgment. The reporter senses the importance, significance, and impact of a story and reports accordingly. He or she has a sense for knowing when additional information, detail, or clarification is needed in a story and provides it. The reporter promptly alerts editors to potential stories and problems and knows what treatment is appropriate in handling a variety of stories.

Coverage of beat/assignment. The reporter keeps informed about the development of stories through routine channels on the beat as well as by developing special knowledge and sources. He or she knows the status of previously reported stories and reports on changes. He or she is alert to new ideas, issues, proposals, and activities that may be newsworthy. The reporter is aware of behind-the-scenes actions of newsmakers on the beat and reports not only what is happening, but why and how it is happening. The reporter never misses a significant story on the beat and usually is first with the story.

News of minorities. The reporter keeps abreast of current issues, events, and developments relating to minority communities. He or she is alert to the impact that events in the larger community may have on minorities. He or she takes the initiative to develop sources in the minority community to gain perspective in covering minorities, particularly on topics related to his or her beat or assignment, and includes this point of view in stories when appropriate. The reporter uses sources to insure swift and accurate completion of stories, access to difficult-to-obtain material, and story ideas.

Following stories. The reporter follows stories and reports new developments. He or she maintains a story idea file, knows when important developments can be expected, and pursues them. The reporter is aware of new angles and questions that should be investigated. He or she routinely looks at previous stories to determine whether an update is necessary and knows the status of important issues and proposals.

Suggesting picture and graphic ideas. The reporter understands the value of photos and graphics in conveying information. He or she recognizes the stories and/or situations that may lend themselves to illustration and routinely tells editors of such situations, whether they occur on or outside of the beat.

Meeting daily deadlines. The reporter meets daily deadlines with complete, accurate, well-written stories requiring minimal editing. It is unnecessary for editors to supervise efforts to meet deadlines.

Meeting long-range deadlines. The reporter meets deadlines for projects and long-range assignments with minimal supervision. No major reworking in the editing process is necessary for these stories. The reporter consults with editors to set realistic deadlines for research, investigation, and writing.

Managing time. The reporter manages time effectively. For example, he or she works on one story while awaiting information for another, or writes parts of a story even though all the required information is not available. The reporter takes advantage of quiet times to develop contacts or work on enterprise stories. He or she analyzes the way time is used to be sure that the majority of time is spent on the most important aspects of the assignment. He or she eliminates activities that waste time. In conjunction with an editor, the reporter effectively plans work to obtain the maximum result.

Writing

Organizing stories. The reporter digests complex material and arranges story elements in a logical progression with a clearly defined beginning, middle, and end. He or she completes one thought before beginning another so that it is not necessary for the reader to skip back and forth between points in the story. Copy does not require significant reorganization in the editing process.

Recognizing important story elements. The reporter recognizes important story elements and uses them effectively. Leads, for example, may be based on such criteria as impact, proximity, timeliness, prominence, uniqueness, and conflict. Elements such as quotations and statistics are used effectively to support the lead. All sides of the issue are represented prominently.

Copy tightly written. Copy is succinct and written to the appropriate length. Leads are crisp and to the point. Story is written tightly without the loss of interesting or essential elements. Irrelevant material is eliminated. Word selection is economical, avoiding the use of several words or a phrase when one word will do.

Word selection. The reporter uses clear, everyday language and avoids jargon and technical or governmental terminology. Words are selected that convey the precise meaning intended. For example, the reporter never uses *uninterested* for *disinterested*, *affect* for *effect*, *further* for *farther*, or *which* for *that*. The reporter is sensitive to subtleties and implications of certain words and terms, and is careful to use them judiciously.

Writing under deadline pressure. The reporter writes effectively under deadline pressure. Stories are well organized, as complete as current information allows, accurate, and submitted by deadline. The reporter can write "in takes." When necessary, he or she identifies areas that need development in later editions. He or she prepares background for stories when it is known in advance that stories will be done on deadline.

Writing style. The reporter goes beyond the basic writing elements to produce the most compelling, interesting story. He or she selects the right style for the content, mood, and tone of the story. Writing is clear and concise. The reporter provides good description, detail, anecdotes, and quotes, and blends various elements smoothly with good transitions. He or she sustains interest in long, complex stories. For example, the reporter may use pacing (varying sentence lengths to convey a mood) and transitions that lead the reader imperceptibly from one thought to the next. He or she also uses descriptive writing and details that appeal to the senses.

Grammar. The reporter uses correct grammar.

Communication

Working with editors to develop stories. The reporter works effectively with editors to develop stories. He or she seeks suggestions for story approach and development when necessary and applies suggestions effectively. He or she takes the initiative to clarify assignments when necessary. The reporter keeps editors apprised of the status of work in progress and resolves differences of opinion with editors on story approach, value, and priority in a constructive, professional manner.

Working with editors to improve stories. The reporter works effectively with editors to improve stories. He or she effectively applies suggestions for story reorganization, change in writing style, or need for additional detail. Differences of opinion with editors on these points are resolved in a constructive, professional manner.

Using feedback for development. The reporter actively seeks feedback on reporting, writing, and other elements of the job. He or she uses this information effectively to make any improvements indicated. It is rarely necessary for editors to suggest the same improvement twice.

Working with other staff members. The reporter works effectively with other staff members, sharing information gathered about another's beat and passing along tips about news stories and reporting techniques. When doing stories with other reporters, he or she discusses the story in a constructive manner. He or she cooperates in sharing the work load to make certain each reporter's skills are best utilized.

Keeping editor informed. The reporter keeps editors updated on proposed stories and stories in progress, consulting with editors to set priorities and seeking advice when uncertain of the angle or approach or when problems arise.

Contact with public. In all dealings with the public, the reporter represents the newspaper in a positive, professional manner. He or she takes the time to explain newspaper policy, answer questions, respond to phone calls, and answer letters.

Bibliography

BOOKS

Aiken, Lewis R. *Psychological Testing and Assessment.* 4th ed. Boston: Allyn and Bacon, 1982.

Anastasi, Anne. *Psychological Testing.* 5th ed. New York: Macmillan, 1982.

Argyris, Chris. *Personality and Organization.* New York: Harper & Row, 1957.

———. *Behind the Front Page.* San Francisco: Jossey-Bass, 1974.

Avery, Richard D. *Fairness in Selecting Employees.* Reading, Mass.: Addison-Wesley, 1979.

Babb, Laura Longley, ed. *The Editorial Page.* Boston: Houghton Mifflin, 1977.

Bagdikian, Ben H. *The Media Monopoly.* Boston: Beacon Press, 1983.

Baker, Bob. *Newsthinking: The Secret of Great Newswriting.* Cincinnati: Writer's Digest Books, 1981.

Bales, Robert F., and Edgar F. Borgatta. "Size of Group as a Factor in the Interaction Profile." In *Small Groups: Studies in Social Interaction,* edited by A. Paul Hare, Edgar F. Borgatta, and Robert F. Bales, 496–501. New York: Knopf, 1966.

Beach, Dale S. *Personnel: The Management of People at Work.* 3d ed. New York: Macmillan, 1975.

Beal, Edwin F., Edward D. Wickersham, and Philip K. Kienast. *The Practice of Collective Bargaining.* 5th ed. Homewood, Ill.: Richard D. Irwin, 1976.

Bem, Daryl J. "Self-Perception Theory." In *Advances in Experimental Social Psychology*, edited by Leonard Berkowitz. New York: Academic Press, 1972.

Bird, Caroline. *The Two-Paycheck Marriage: How Women at Work Are Changing Life in America*. New York: Rawson, Wade, 1979.

Bittel, Lester. *What Every Supervisor Should Know: The Basics of Supervisory Management*. 5th ed. New York: McGraw-Hill, 1985.

Blake, Robert R., and Jane S. Mouton. *The New Managerial Grid*. Houston: Gulf, 1978.

Blotnick, Srully. *The Corporate Steeplechase: Predictable Crises in a Business Career*. New York: Facts on File, 1984.

Bolton, Robert, and Dorothy Grover Bolton. *Social Style/Management Style: Developing Productive Work Relationships*. New York: AMACOM, 1984.

Boyatzis, Richard E. *The Competent Manager*. New York: John Wiley & Sons, 1982.

Bradford, Leland P., Jack R. Gibb, and Kenneth D. Benne. *T-Group Theory and Laboratory Method*. New York: John Wiley & Sons, 1964.

Bramson, Robert M. *Coping with Difficult People*. Garden City, N.Y.: Anchor Press, 1981.

Bray, Douglas W., Richard J. Campbell, and Donald L. Grant. *Formative Years in Business*. New York: John Wiley & Sons, 1974.

Bremner, John. *Words on Words*. New York: Columbia, 1980.

Broadwell, Martin M. *The New Supervisor*. 3d ed. Reading, Mass.: Addison-Wesley, 1984.

———. *The Supervisor as an Instructor: A Guide for Classroom Training*. 4th ed. Reading, Mass.: Addison-Wesley, 1984.

Brod, Craig. *Technostress: The Human Cost of the Computer Revolution*. Reading, Mass.: Addison-Wesley, 1984.

Brown, Barbara B. *Supermind: The Ultimate Energy*. New York: Bantam, 1983.

———. *Between Health and Illness: New Notions on Stress and the Nature of Well Being*. Boston: Houghton Mifflin, 1984.

Brown, Frederick G. *Principles of Educational and Psychological Testing*. Hinsdale, Ill.: Dryden Press, 1970.

Cannon, Walter B. *Bodily Changes in Pain, Hunger, Fear, and Rage.* 2d ed. New York: Appleton, 1929.

Cateledge, Turner. *My Life and the Times.* New York: Harper & Row, 1971.

Charlesworth, Edward A., and Ronald G. Nathan. *Stress Management: A Comprehensive Guide to Wellness.* New York: Atheneum, 1984.

Clabes, Judith G., ed. *New Guardians of the Press: Selected Profiles of America's Women Newspaper Editors.* Indianapolis: R. J. Berg, 1983.

Cox, Allan. *The Making of an Achiever: How to Win Distinction in Your Company.* New York: Dodd, Mead, 1985.

Cronbach, Lee J. *Essentials of Psychological Testing.* 2d ed. New York: Harper & Row, 1960.

Davis, George, and Glegg Watson. *Black Life in Corporate America.* Garden City, N.Y.: Anchor Books, 1985.

Davis, Keith. *Human Behavior at Work: Organizational Behavior.* 6th ed. New York: McGraw-Hill, 1981.

Deal, Terrence E., and Allan A. Kennedy. *Corporate Cultures.* Reading, Mass.: Addison-Wesley, 1982.

Dickens, Floyd, Jr., and Jacqueline B. Dickens. *The Black Manager: Making It in the Corporate World.* New York: AMACOM, 1982.

Drucker, Peter F. *The Changing World of the Executive.* New York: Times Books, 1982.

——. *Management.* New York: Harper & Row, 1974.

——. *Managing in Turbulent Times.* Englewood Cliffs, N.J.: Prentice-Hall, 1980.

——. *The Practice of Management.* New York: Harper & Row, 1954.

Dunlop, John T. *Industrial Relations System.* New York: McGraw-Hill, 1958.

Ebert, Ronald J., and Terence R. Mitchell. *Organizational Decision Processes: Concepts and Analysis.* New York: Crance, Russak, 1975.

Eichel, Evelyn, and Henry E. Bender. *Performance Appraisals: A Study of Current Techniques.* New York: American Management Associations, 1984.

Emery, Edwin. *The Press and America: An Interpretive History of the Mass Media.* 3d ed. Englewood Cliffs, N.J.: Prentice-Hall, 1972.

Evans, Harold. *Good Times, Bad Times.* New York: Atheneum, 1984.

Feinberg, Mortimer R., Robert Tanofsky, and John J. Tarrant. *The New Psychology for Managing People.* Englewood Cliffs, N.J.: Prentice-Hall, 1975.

Ferguson, Marilyn. *The Aquarian Conspiracy.* New York: J. P. Tarcher, 1980.

Fiedler, Fred E. *A Theory of Leadership Effectiveness.* New York: McGraw-Hill, 1967.

Fink, Stephen. *Crisis Management: Planning for the Inevitable.* New York: AMACOM, 1986.

Fitch, Stanley K. *Insights into Human Behavior.* Boston: Holbrook Press, 1970.

Friedman, Meyer, and Ray Rosenmann. *Type A Behavior and Your Heart.* New York: Knopf, 1974.

Gardner, John W. *Self-Renewal.* New York: Harper & Row, 1963.

Gherman, E. M. *Stress and the Bottom Line.* New York: AMACOM, 1981.

Ghiglione, Loren, ed. *The Buying and Selling of America's Newspapers.* Indianapolis: R. J. Berg, 1984.

Gibson, James L., John M. Ivancevich, and James H. Donnelly, Jr. *Organizations: Behavior, Structure, Processes.* 3d ed. Dallas: Business Publications, 1979.

Giles, Robert H. *Editors and Stress.* Rochester: Gannett Rochester Newspapers, 1983.

———. *Editors and Their Families.* Rochester: Gannett Rochester Newspapers, 1979.

Giles, Robert H., and Christine Landauer. *Gannett Rochester Newspapers Performance Review Program.* Rochester: Gannett Rochester Newspapers, 1984.

Gmelch, Walter H. *Beyond Stress to Effective Management.* New York: John Wiley & Sons, 1982.

Goodwin, H. Eugene. *Groping for Ethics in Journalism.* Ames, Iowa: Iowa State University Press, 1983.

Gordon, Thomas. *Parent Effectiveness Training.* New York: Peter H. Wyden, 1970.

Gray, Jerry L. *Supervision.* Boston: Kent, 1984.

Hackman, J. Richard. *Group Influences on Individuals in Organizations.* Springfield, Va.: National Technical Information Service, 1976.

Haigh, Robert W., George Gerbner, and Richard B. Byrne. *Communications in the Twenty-first Century.* New York: John Wiley & Sons, 1981.

Halberstam, David. *The Powers That Be.* New York: Alfred A. Knopf, 1979.

Hall, Edward T. *The Silent Language.* New York: Anchor Press, 1973.

Hampton, David R., Charles E. Summer, and Ross A. Webber. *Organizational Behavior and the Practice of Management.* 3d ed. Glenview, Ill.: Scott, Foresman, 1978.

Harragan, Betty Lehan. *Games Mother Never Taught You: Corporate Gamesmanship for Women.* New York: Warner Books, 1977.

Hart, Lois B., and J. David Dalke. *The Sexes at Work: Improving Work Relationships between Men & Women.* Englewood Cliffs, N.J.: Prentice-Hall, 1983.

Hegerty, Christopher, with Philip Goldberg. *How to Manage Your Boss.* New York: Rawson, Wade, 1980.

Hennig, Margaret, and Anne Jardim. *The Managerial Woman.* New York: Anchor Books, 1977.

Hersey, Paul. *The Situational Leader.* Escondido, Calif.: The Center for Leadership Studies, 1984.

Hersey, Paul, and Kenneth H. Blanchard. *Management of Organizational Behavior.* 4th ed. Englewood Cliffs, N.J.: Prentice-Hall, 1982.

Herzberg, Frederick, Bernard Mausner, and Barbara Snyderman. *The Motivation to Work.* New York: John Wiley & Sons, 1959.

Hodgetts, Richard M., and Steven Altman. *Organizational Behavior.* Philadelphia: W. B. Saunders, 1979.

Hohenberg, John. *The Professional Journalist: A Guide to the Practices and Principles of the News Media*. 3d ed. New York: Holt, Rinehart, and Winston, 1973.

Hovland, Carl I., Irving L. Janis, and Harold H. Kelley. *Communication and Persuasion*. New Haven: Yale University Press, 1953.

Isaacs, Norman. *Untended Gates: The Mismanaged Press*. New York: Columbia University Press, 1986.

Johnstone, John W. C., Edward J. Slawski, and William W. Bowman. *The News People*. Urbana, Ill.: University of Illinois Press, 1976.

Kagan, Jerome, Ernest Havemann, and Julius Segal. *Psychology: An Introduction*. 5th ed. San Diego: Harcourt Brace Jovanovich, 1984.

Kanter, Rosabeth Moss. *The Change Masters*. New York: Simon and Schuster, 1983.

———. *Men and Women of the Corporation*. New York: Basic Books, 1977.

Katz, Daniel, and Robert L. Kahn. *The Social Psychology of Organizations*. 2d ed. New York: John Wiley & Sons, 1978.

Kelly, Tom. *The Imperial Post: The Meyers, the Grahams, and the Paper that Rules Washington*. New York: William Morrow, 1983.

Kidder, Tracy. *The Soul of a New Machine*. New York: Avon, 1981.

Kiev, Ari, and Vera Kohn. *Executive Stress: An AMA Survey Report*. New York: AMACOM, 1979.

Koontz, Harold, and Cyril O'Donnell. *Principles of Management*. 2d ed. New York: McGraw-Hill, 1959.

Kotter, John P. *Power and Influence: Beyond Formal Authority*. New York: The Free Press, 1985.

LaRouche, Janice, and Regina Ryan. *Strategies for Women at Work*. New York: Avon, 1984.

Latham, Gary P., and Kenneth N. Wexley. *Increasing Productivity through Performance Appraisal*. Reading, Mass.: Addison-Wesley, 1981.

Lawler, Edward E. *Pay and Organizational Effectiveness*. New York: McGraw-Hill, 1971.

Leontiades, Milton. *Managing the Unmanageable*. Reading, Mass.: Addison-Wesley, 1986.

Levinson, Daniel J. *The Seasons of a Man's Life*. New York: Ballantine Books, 1978.

Levinson, Harry. *The Exceptional Executive*. New York: New American Library, 1968.

Liebling, A. J. *The Press*. New York: Ballantine, 1975.

Likert, Rensis. *The Human Organization*. New York: McGraw-Hill, 1967.

Locke, Edwin A. "The Supervisor as 'Motivator': His Influence on Employee Performance and Satisfaction." In *Motivation and Work Behavior*, 2d ed., 377–89. New York: McGraw-Hill, 1979.

Lyons, Louis. *Reporting the News*. Cambridge, Mass.: Belknap, 1965.

McClelland, David C. *The Achieving Society*. Princeton: Van Nostrand, 1961.

Maccoby, Michael. *The Leader: A New Face for American Management*. New York: Simon and Schuster, 1981.

McConkey, Dale S. *How to Manage by Results*. New York: AMACOM, 1983.

McGregor, Douglas. *The Human Side of Enterprise*. New York: McGraw-Hill, 1960.

———. *The Professional Manager*. New York: McGraw-Hill, 1967.

McLean, Alan A. *Work Stress*. Reading, Mass.: Addison-Wesley, 1979.

McPhaul, John J. *Deadlines & Monkeyshines: The Fabled World of Chicago Journalism*. Englewood Cliffs, N.J.: Prentice-Hall, 1962.

McQuaig, Jack H., Peter L. McQuaig, and Donald H. McQuaig. *How to Interview and Hire Productive People*. New York: Frederick Fell, 1981.

Mallette, Malcolm F. *How Newspapers Communicate Internally: Case Studies and Samplings from a Changing Workplace*. Reston, Va.: American Press Institute, 1981.

March, James G., and Herbert A. Simon. *Organizations*. New York: John Wiley & Sons, 1958.

Maslow, Abraham H. *The Farther Reaches of Human Nature*. New York: Viking Press, 1971.

———. *Motivation and Personality.* New York: Harper & Row, 1954.

Massey, Morris. *The People Puzzle: Understanding Yourself and Others.* Reston, Va.: Reston, 1979.

Mayo, Elton. *The Human Problems of an Industrial Civilization.* New York: Macmillan, 1935.

Merrill, John C., and S. Jack Odell. *Philosophy of Journalism.* New York: Longman, 1983.

Metcalf, Henry C., and L. Urwick, eds. *Dynamic Administration: The Collected Papers of Mary Parker Follett.* New York: Harper & Brothers, 1940.

Meyer, Philip. *Editors, Publishers, and Newspaper Ethics.* Washington: American Society of Newspaper Editors, 1983.

Mintzberg, Henry. *The Nature of Managerial Work.* Englewood Cliffs, N.J.: Prentice-Hall, 1980.

Mitchell, Arnold. *The Nine American Lifestyles.* New York: Macmillan, 1983.

Murphy, Gardner. *Human Potentialities.* New York: Basic Books, 1958.

Naisbitt, John. *Megatrends.* New York: Warner Books, 1984.

Neustadt, Richard E. *Presidential Power.* New York: Signet, 1964.

Odiorne, George. *Management by Objectives: A System of Managerial Leadership.* New York: Pitman, 1965.

Peters, Thomas J., and Robert H. Waterman, Jr. *In Search of Excellence.* New York: Harper & Row, 1982.

Pfeffer, Jeffrey. *Power in Organizations.* Marshfield, Mass.: Pitman, 1981.

Plunkett, Warren R., and Raymond F. Attner. *Introduction to Management.* Boston: Kent, 1983.

President's National Advisory Commission on Civil Disorders. *Report of the National Advisory Commission on Civil Disorders.* Washington: U. S. Government Printing Office, 1968.

Preston, Paul. *Employer's Guide to Hiring & Firing: Strategies, Tactics, and Legal Considerations.* Englewood Cliffs, N.J.: Prentice-Hall, 1982.

Raia, Anthony. *Managing by Objectives.* Glenview, Ill.: Scott, Foresman, 1974.

Richardson, Jerry, and Joel Margulis. *The Business of Negotiation.* New York: Avon, 1981.

Riesman, David, Nathan Glazer, and Reuel Denney. *The Lonely Crowd.* New Haven: Yale University Press, 1950.

Robbins, Stephen. *Managing Organizational Conflict.* Englewood Cliffs, N.J.: Prentice-Hall, 1974.

Robert, Marc. *Managing Conflict.* San Diego: Learning Concepts, 1982.

Roethlisberger, Fritz J., and William J. Dickson. *Management and the Worker.* 15th ed. Cambridge: Harvard University Press, 1970.

Rogers, Carl R. *Counseling and Psychotherapy.* Boston: Houghton Mifflin, 1942.

Rogers, Everett M., and Rekha Agarwala-Rogers. *Communication in Organizations.* New York: The Free Press, 1976.

Roseman, Edward. *Confronting Non-Promotability: How to Manage a Stalled Career.* New York: AMACOM, 1977.

Rucker, Frank W., and Herbert Lee Williams. *Newspaper Organization and Management.* 3d ed. Ames, Iowa: The Iowa State University Press, 1969.

Salisbury, Harrison. *Without Fear or Favor: An Uncompromising Look at the New York Times.* New York: Times Books, 1980.

Sanford, Fillmore H. *Authoritarianism and Leadership.* Philadelphia: Institute for Research on Human Relations, 1950.

Sargent, Alice G. *The Androgynous Manager.* New York: AMACOM, 1985.

Sayles, Leonard R. *Leadership: What Effective Managers Really Do . . . and How They Do It.* New York: McGraw-Hill, 1979.

Schmidt, Warren H., and Barry Z. Posner. *Managerial Values in Perspective.* New York: American Management Associations, 1983.

Scott, William G., and Terence R. Mitchell. *Organization Theory: A Structural and Behavioral Analysis.* Homewood, Ill.: Richard D. Irwin, 1976.

Selye, Hans. *The Stress of Life.* New York: McGraw-Hill, 1956.

Shapero, Albert. *Managing Professional People.* New York: The Free Press, 1985.

Shaw, David. *Press Watch: A Provocative Look at How Newspapers Report the News.* New York: Macmillan, 1984.

Sheehy, Gail. *Passages.* New York: E. P. Dutton, 1976.

Skinner, B. F. *Beyond Freedom and Dignity.* New York: Alfred A. Knopf, 1971.

Smith, Anthony. *Goodbye Gutenberg: The Newspaper Revolution of the 1980s.* Oxford, Eng.: Oxford Press, 1980.

Sohn, Ardyth, Christine Ogan, and John Polich. *Newspaper Leadership.* Englewood Cliffs, N.J.: Prentice-Hall, 1986.

Steers, Richard M. *Introduction to Organizational Behavior.* 2d ed. Glenview, Ill.: Scott, Foresman, 1984.

Szilagyi, Andrew D., Jr. *Management and Performance.* Glenview, Ill.: Scott, Foresman, 1981.

Talese, Gay. *The Kingdom and the Power.* New York: World, 1969.

Terkel, Studs. *Working: People Talk about What They Do All Day and How They Feel about What They Do.* New York: Pantheon, 1974.

Terry, George R. *Principles of Management.* 6th ed. Homewood, Ill.: Richard D. Irwin, 1972.

Travis, Carol. *Anger: The Misunderstood Emotion.* New York: Simon and Schuster, 1982.

Veninga, Robert L., and James P. Spradley. *The Work Stress Connection: How to Cope with Job Burnout.* Boston: Little, Brown, 1981.

Vroom, Victor H. *Some Personality Determinants of the Effects of Participation.* Englewood Cliffs, N.J.: Prentice-Hall, 1960.

―――. *Work and Motivation.* New York: John Wiley & Sons, 1964.

Vroom, Victor H., and Philip W. Yetton. *Leadership and Decision Making.* Pittsburgh: University of Pittsburgh Press, 1973.

Walker, James W. *Human Resource Planning.* New York: McGraw-Hill, 1980.

Walker, Stanley. *City Editor.* New York: Frederick A. Stokes, 1934.

Wanous, John P. *Organizational Entry: Recruitment, Selection, and Socialization of Newcomers.* Reading, Mass.: Addison-Wesley, 1980.

Weaver, David, and Cleveland Wilhoit. *The American Journalist.* Bloomington, Ind.: Indiana University Press, 1986.

Weiss, Donald H. *Managing Conflict.* New York: American Management Associations, 1981.

White, Theodore H. *The Making of the President 1972.* New York: Atheneum, 1973.

Whyte, William F., ed. *Money and Motivation.* New York: Harper & Row, 1955.

Whyte, William H., Jr. *The Organization Man.* Garden City, N.J.: Doubleday Anchor, 1956.

Wigdor, Alexandra K., and Wendell R. Garner, eds. *Ability Testing—Part I: Uses, Consequences, and Controversies.* Washington: National Academy Press, 1982.

Winter, Richard E. *Coping with Executive Stress.* New York: McGraw-Hill, 1983.

Yankelovich, Daniel. *New Rules: Searching for Self-fulfillment in a World Turned Upside Down.* New York: Random House, 1981.

ARTICLES

Adams, J. Stacy. "Toward an Understanding of Equity." *Journal of Abnormal and Social Psychology,* November 1963, 422–36.

Anshen, Melvin. "The Management of Ideas." *Harvard Business Review,* July–August 1969, 99–107.

Argyris, Chris. "The CEO's Behavior: Key to Organizational Development." *Harvard Business Review,* March–April 1973, 41–50.

Asch, Solomon. "Studies of Independence and Conformity: A Minority of One Against a Unanimous Majority." *Psychological Monographs* 70 (1956): 7.

Banks, Louis. "Here Come the Individualists." *Harvard Magazine*, September–October 1977, 24–28.

Barbee, Christy. "Women in the 'Bullpen.'" *Nieman Reports*, Summer 1979, 29–32.

Barnes, Louis D. "Managing the Paradox of Organizational Trust." *Harvard Business Review*, March–April 1981, 107–18.

Bartolome, Fernando. "Executives as Human Beings." *Harvard Business Review*, November–December 1972, 62–69.

Bartolome, Fernando, and Paul A. Lee Evans. "Must Success Cost So Much?" *Harvard Business Review*, March–April 1980, 137–48.

Bender, Marilyn. "When the Boss Is a Woman." *Esquire*, 28 March 1978, 37–41.

Benson, Herbert. "Your Innate Asset for Combating Stress." *Harvard Business Review*, July–August 1974, 49–60.

Benson, Herbert, and Robert L. Allen. "How Much Stress Is Too Much?" *Harvard Business Review*, September–October 1980, 86–92.

Bernikow, Louise. "The Paper Tiger: At Gannett, the Corporate Culture Must Reconcile the Small-town Newspaper Tradition with the Free-spending Ways of a Media Giant." *Savvy*, March 1983, 38–43, 84–85.

Boyd, David P., and David E. Gumpert. "Coping with Entrepreneurial Stress." *Harvard Business Review*, March–April 1983, 44–64.

Bradlee, Benjamin C. "The First Rough Draft of History." Interview by Michael Gartner. *American Heritage*, October–November 1982, 33–48.

Breed, Warren. "Social Control in the Newsroom: A Functional Analysis." *Social Forces*, May 1955, 326–35.

Brouwer, Paul J. "The Power to See Ourselves." In *Executive Success: Making It in Management*, 15–28. New York: John Wiley & Sons, 1983.

Brownell, Judi. "Listening: A Powerful Management Tool." *Supervisory Management*, October 1984, 35–39.

Burgoon, Judee K., Michael Burgoon, and David B. Buller. "Why Minorities Do Not Choose Journalism: Academic and Career Orientations among Students." Associated Press Managing Editors Association, November 1984.

Burgoon, Judee K., Michael Burgoon, David B. Buller, and Charles K. Atkin. "Communication Practices of Journalists: Insularity from the Public and Interaction with Other Journalists." Manuscript, University of Arizona, 1984.

Callarman, William G., and William W. McCartney. "Identifying and Overcoming Listening Problems." *Supervisory Management*, March 1985, 38–42.

Cameron, Daniel. "The When, Why, & How of Discipline." *Personnel Journal*, July 1984, 37–39.

Caruth, Don, and Harry N. Mills, Jr. "Working toward Better Union Relations." *Supervisory Management*, February 1985, 7–8.

Case, Robert B., Stanley S. Heller, Nan B. Case, and Arthur J. Moss. "Type A Behavior and Survival after Acute Myocardial Infarction." *New England Journal of Medicine* 312, no. 12 (21 March 1985): 737–41.

Cavanagh, Michael E. "In Search of Motivation." *Personnel Journal*, March 1984, 76–82.

Cirillo, Joan J. "Suit Suite: After Settling a Major Job-Discrimination Suit, AP Is Slowly Percolating Women and Minorities up through the Ranks." *The Quill*, December 1984, 14–18.

Collins, Eliza G. C. "Managers and Lovers." *Harvard Business Review*, September–October 1983, 142–53.

Cook, Bruce. "Reg Murphy: 'Just-Folks' Publisher of the Baltimore Sun." *Washington Journalism Review*, November 1983, 25–28, 58.

Cose, Ellis. "The Quiet Crisis: Minority Journalists and Newsroom Opportunity." *Institute for Journalism Education*, July 1985, 1–15.

———. "Keeping the Faith: Hiring and Promoting More Minority Journalists Is Not Only Right, It's Necessary." *The Quill*, October 1985, 8–13.

Costello, Timothy W., and Sheldon S. Zalkind. "Psychology in Administration: A Research Orientation." *Journal of Conflict Resolution* 3 (1959): 148–49.

Currie, Phil R. "The Journalism of Mismanagement." *The Bulletin of the American Society of Newspaper Editors,* April 1984, 26–28.

Currie, Phil R., and Mary Kay Blake. "Recruiter Tells His Story; The Students Get Some Advice." *Gannetteer,* August–September 1981, 1–12.

Day, Nancy L. "Women Journalists: Professional/Personal Conflicts." *Nieman Reports,* Summer 1979, 34–40.

Diamond, Edwin. "Tab Man: The New Editor at the News." *New York,* 28 January 1985, 28–30.

Dixon, Nancy. "Participative Management: It's Not as Simple as It Seems." *Supervisory Management,* December 1984, 2–8.

Driscoll, James W. "Trust and Participation in Organizational Decision Making as Predictors of Satisfaction." *Academy of Management Journal* 21, no. 1 (March 1978): 44–56.

Drucker, Peter F. "The Effective Decision." In *Executive Success: Making It in Management,* 464–75. New York: John Wiley & Sons, 1983.

Dyer, William. "Planned Change." In *Organization and People: Readings, Cases, and Exercises in Organizational Behavior,* 2d ed., edited by J. B. Ritchie and Paul Thompson, 384–87. St. Paul: West, 1984.

Elder, Shirley. "Journalists vs. the Unions at the Washington Post." *Columbia Journalism Review,* May–June 1976, 42–45.

Ewing, David W. "Tension Can Be an Asset." *Harvard Business Review,* September–October 1964, 71–78.

Foreman, Gene. "How Tests Can Help Evaluate Copy Editors." *The Bulletin of the American Society of Newspaper Editors,* May–June 1981, 9–11.

Fraker, Susan. "Why Women Aren't Getting to the Top." *Fortune,* 16 April 1984, 40–45.

Freudenberger, Herbert J. "Staff Burn-out." *Journal of Social Issues* 30, no. 1 (1974): 159–65.

———. "5 Ways to Short-circuit Burn-out." *Health,* April 1982, 50–51.

Friedman, Meyer. "Type A Behavior: A Progress Report." *The Sciences,* February 1980, 10–11, 28.

Glass, David C. "Stress, Competition, and Heart Attacks." *Psychology Today,* December 1976, 65–67.

Goddard, Robert W. "Negotiation: How to Win by Forgetting about Winning." *Training,* March 1984, 34, 37.

Goheen, Howard W., and James N. Mosel. "The Validity of the Employment Recommendation Questionnaire in Personnel Selection." *Personnel Psychology* 12, no. 2 (1959): 297–301.

Greiner, Larry E. "Patterns of Organizational Change." *Harvard Business Review,* May–June 1967, 121–30.

———. "Evolution and Revolution as Organizations Grow." *Harvard Business Review,* July–August 1972, 37–46.

Green, Laura. "How Much Are You Worth?" *The Quill,* February 1985, 22–26.

Grove, Andrew S. "Why Training Is the Boss's Job." *Fortune,* 23 January 1984, 93–96.

Hamburg, David A., and John E. Adams. "A Perspective on Coping Behavior." *Archives of General Psychiatry* 17 (September 1967): 277–84.

Hammer, Clay W. "How to Ruin Motivation with Pay." *Compensation Review* 7 (1975): 17–27.

Harris, Jay T., and Christine Harris. "Editors' Attitudes Reveal Wide Diversity on Employing Minorities." *The Bulletin of the American Society of Newspaper Editors,* October 1981, 10–13.

Harrison, James C., Jr. "How to Stay on Top of the Job." In *Executive Success: Making It in Management,* 436–49. New York: John Wiley & Sons, 1983.

Hawpe, David V. "A 12-Point Action Plan for Finding and Developing Minority Staff Members." *The Bulletin of the American Society of Newspaper Editors,* February 1985, 4–6.

Heide, Dorothy, and Eliott N. Kushell. "I Can Improve My Management Skills By:———." *Personnel Journal,* June 1984, 52–54.

Henneck, Matthew J. "Mentors and Protégés: How to Build Relationships that Work." *Training,* July 1983, 36–41.

Herzberg, Frederick. "One More Time: How Do You Motivate Employees?" *Harvard Business Review,* January–February 1968, 53–62.

Hobson, Charles J., Robert B. Hobson, and John J. Hobson. "Why Managers Use Criticism Instead of Praise." *Supervisory Management*, March 1985, 24–30.

Holmes, Thomas H., and Richard H. Rahe. "Social Readjustment Rating Scale." *Journal of Psychosomatic Research* 11 (1967): 213–18.

House, Robert J., and Terence R. Mitchell. "Path-Goal Theory of Leadership." *Journal of Contemporary Business* 3, no. 4 (Autumn 1974): 81–97.

Howard, Jeff, and Ray Hammond. "Rumors of Inferiority: Barriers to Black Success in America." *The New Republic*, 9 September 1985, 17–21.

Imberman, Arlyne J. "Human Element of Mergers." *Management Review*, June 1985, 35–37.

Isaacs, Norman. "'Journalism's Biggest Problem' Is Choosing Newsroom Leaders." *The Bulletin of the American Society of Newspaper Editors*, June 1985, 3–5.

Janis, Irving L. "Groupthink." *Psychology Today*, November 1971, 43–46, 74–76.

Jay, Antony. "How to Run a Meeting." *Harvard Business Review*, March–April 1976, 43–57.

Jennings, Eugene E. "The Anatomy of Leadership." *Management of Personnel Quarterly* 1 (Autumn 1961): 2–9.

Jones, Ivan. "Getting on Target with MBOs." *The Bulletin of the American Society of Newspaper Editors*, May 1981, 9–11.

Kanter, Rosabeth Moss. "Managing the Human Side of Change." *Management Review*, April 1985, 52–56.

———. "Power Failure in Management Circuits." In *Executive Success: Making It in Management*, 249–66. New York: John Wiley & Sons, 1983.

Kaufman, John A. "Effectiveness of Bilateral and Unilateral Newspaper Administrative Structure." *Newspaper Research Journal* 2 (1981–1982): 54–64.

Keefe, Reba, and Christine Russell. "Working Connections." In *Organization and People: Readings, Cases, and Exercises in Organizational*

Behavior, 2d ed., edited by J. B. Ritchie and Paul Thompson, 133–40. St. Paul: West, 1984.

Kets de Vries, Manfred F. R. "Managers Can Drive Their Subordinates Mad." *Harvard Business Review,* July–August 1979, 125–34.

Kiechel, Walter III. "How Executives Think." *Fortune,* 4 February 1985, 127–28.

Kilmann, Ralph H. "Beyond the Quick Fix: Why Managers Must Disregard the Myth of Simplicity as a Direct Route to Organizational Success." *Management Review,* November 1984, 24–28.

Kipnis, David, and Stuart Schmidt. "The Language of Persuasion." *Psychology Today,* April 1985, 42–46.

Kobasa, Suzanne C. "Stressful Life Events, Personality, and Health: An Inquiry into Hardiness." *Journal of Personality and Social Psychology* 37, no. 1 (January 1979): 1–11.

Kobasa, Suzanne C., and Mark Pucetti. "Personality and Social Resources in Stress Resistance." *Journal of Personality and Social Psychology* 45, no. 4 (1983): 839–50.

Kotter, John P. "What Effective General Managers Really Do." *Harvard Business Review,* November–December 1982, 156–67.

Kruth, Nancy. "Refining the 'Chemistry' of Good Relationships between Editors, Reporters." *The Bulletin of the American Society of Newspaper Editors,* June 1985, 6–9.

Lambert, Larry L. "Training: Nine Reasons That Most Training Programs Fail." *Personnel Journal,* January 1985, 62–67.

Lanson, Gerald, and Mitchell Stephens. "Abe Rosenthal: The Man and His Times." *Washington Journalism Review,* July–August 1983, 23–28.

Latham, Gary P., and Lise M. Saari. "Application of Social-Learning Theory to Training Supervisors through Behavior Modeling." *Journal of Applied Psychology* 64 (1979): 239–46.

Ledvinka, James, and Robert Gatewood. "EEO Issues with Preemployment Inquiries." *The Personnel Administrator* 22 (February 1977): 22–26.

Lehman, Tenney K. "A Focus on Women and Journalism." *Nieman Reports,* Summer 1979, 3.

Leonard, George. "Abraham Maslow and the New Self." *Esquire,* December 1983, 326–36.

Levinson, Harry. "The Abrasive Personality." In *Harvard Business Review on Human Relations*, 227–37. New York: Harper & Row, 1979.

———. "Management by Whose Objectives?" In *Harvard Business Review on Management*, 54–69. New York: Harper & Row, 1975.

———. "On Being a Middle-Aged Manager." *Harvard Business Review*, July–August 1969, 1–10.

———. "When Executives Burn Out." *Harvard Business Review*, May–June 1981, 73–81.

Lewin, Kurt. "Frontiers in Group Dynamics: Concept, Method, and Reality in Social Science; Social Equilibria and Social Change." *Human Relations* 1 (June 1947): 5–41.

Lewis, Neil P. "How to Motivate People." *The Bulletin of the American Society of Newspaper Editors*, March 1981, 16–18.

Likert, Rensis. "Conditions for Creativity." *Management Review* 51, no. 9 (September 1962): 70.

Livingston, J. Sterling. "Pygmalion in Management." *Harvard Business Review*, July–August 1969, 81–89.

Locke, Edwin A. "Toward a Theory of Task Performance and Incentives." *Organizational Behavior and Human Performance* 3 (1968): 157–89.

Lombardo, Michael M. "Looking at Leadership: Some Neglected Issues." In *Technical Report No. 6*. Center for Creative Leadership, January 1978, 1–41.

Lombardo, Michael M., and Morgan W. McCall, Jr. "The Intolerable Boss." *Psychology Today*, January 1984, 46–47.

Lundy, Walker. "The City Editor Then: The Toughest Guy in the Joint." *The Bulletin of the American Society of Newspaper Editors*, March 1983, 14.

McCall, Morgan W., Jr. "Leaders and Leadership: Of Substance and Shadow." In *Technical Report No. 2*. Center for Creative Leadership, January 1977, 1–22.

McCall, Morgan W., Jr., and Michael M. Lombardo. "What Makes a Top Executive?" *Psychology Today*, February 1983: 26–31.

McClelland, David C., and David Burnham. "Power Is the Great Motivator." *Harvard Business Review,* March–April 1976, 100–110.

McDonald, Alonzo. "Conflict at the Summit: A Deadly Game." *Harvard Business Review,* March–April 1972, 62–71.

McGill, Ralph. "The Values of an Editor." *Nieman Reports,* January 1961, 3–6.

McGregor, Douglas. "An Uneasy Look at Performance Appraisals." *Harvard Business Review,* May–June 1957, 89–94.

MacKinnon, Donald W. "The Nature and Nurture of Creative Talent." *American Psychologist* 17, no. 7 (July 1962): 484–95.

McMahon, J. Patrick. "The Maturity Factor: Adding Insight to Your Conflict Training." *Training,* November 1983, 57, 59–60.

Maidment, Robert. "Ten Reasons Why Managers Need to Know More about Delegation." *Supervisory Management,* August 1984, 8–11.

Marsenich, Bob. "How to Teach the Steps of Change." *Training,* March 1983, 62–63.

Martin, Desmond D., William J. Kearney, and G. D. Holdefer. "The Decision to Hire: A Comparison of Selection Tools." In *Business Perspectives,* 11–15. Southern Illinois University, Spring 1971.

Maslach, Christina. "Burn-out." *Human Behavior,* September 1976, 16.

Meyer, Philip. "News Side and Business Side: Getting Us Together." *The Bulletin of the American Society of Newspaper Editors,* July–August 1983, 26–27.

Miles, Raymond E., Lyman W. Porter, and James A. Craft. "Leadership Attitudes among Public Health Officials." *American Journal of Public Health* 56 (1966): 1990–2005.

Mintzberg, Henry. "The Manager's Job: Folklore and Fact." In *Executive Success: Making It in Management,* 414–35. New York: John Wiley & Sons, 1983.

Mobley, William H. "Intermediate Linkages in the Relationship between Job Satisfaction and Employee Turnover." *Journal of Applied Psychology* 62 (1977): 237–40.

Montgomery, Robert L. "Listening Made Easy." *Nation's Business,* October 1981, 65–68.

Morano, Richard. "Strategy for Changing Management Style." In *Human Resource Management*, 2–4. Rochester, N.Y.: Xerox Corp., 1981.

Morton, John. "Journalism Doesn't Pay." *The Quill*, July–August 1984, 15.

Natemeyer, Walter E. "Situational Leadership, Perception, and the Impact of Power." *Group and Organizational Studies* 4 (December 1979): 418–28.

Newsom, Clark. "Wages." *presstime*, August 1984, 6–9.

Odiorne, George. "MBO in the 1980s: Will It Survive?" *Management Review*, July 1977, 39–42.

Oncken, William, Jr., and Donald L. Wass. "Management Time: Who's Got the Monkey?" *Harvard Business Review*, November–December 1974, 75–80.

Oppel, Richard A. "Teambuilding: Painful, but Valuable, Lesson in Management." *The Bulletin of the American Society of Newspaper Editors*, June–July 1984, 16–17.

Opsahl, Robert L., and Marvin D. Dunnette. "The Role of Financial Compensation in Industrial Motivation." *Psychological Bulletin* 66 (1966): 94–96.

Page, Susan. " 'Til Deadline Do Us Part: Conflicts for a Couple of Reporters." *Washington Journalism Review*, March 1985, 45–48.

Payne, Richard A. "Mid-Career Block." *Personnel Journal*, April 1984, 38–48.

Pearson, Dick. "Inaccurate Perceptions about Women Managers." *Supervisory Management*, October 1984, 29–34.

Perham, John C. "How Recruiters Get the Lowdown." *Dun's Business Month*, May 1985, 60–61.

Peters, Ruanne K., and Herbert Benson. "Time Out from Tension." *Harvard Business Review*, January–February 1978, 120–24.

Peters, Thomas J., and Nancy Austin. "A Passion for Excellence." *Fortune*, 13 May 1985, 20–32.

Pettus, Allen. "Peer Review: The Tennessean's Innovative Experiment." *Newspaper Research Journal* 2 (1980): 89–92.

Pollock, Francis. "Knight-Ridder Wants to Know the Real You." *Columbia Journalism Review,* January–February 1978, 25–28.

Porter, Lyman W. "A Study of Perceived Need Satisfaction in Bottom and Middle Management Jobs." *Journal of Applied Psychology* 45 (1961): 1–10.

Porter, Lyman W., and Edwin E. Ghiselli. "The Self Perceptions of Top and Middle Management Personnel." *Personnel Psychology* 10, no. 4 (Winter 1957): 400–402.

Porter, Lyman W., and Edward E. Lawler III. "Properties of Organization Structure in Relation to Job Attitudes and Job Behavior." *Psychological Bulletin* 64 (1965): 23–51.

Price, Raymond L., Paul H. Thompson, and Gene W. Dalton. "A Longitudinal Study of Technological Obsolescence." *Research Management* 18 (November 1975): 22–28.

Quick, James C., and Jonathan D. Quick. "How Good Working Relationships Can Help Relieve Pressures on the Job." *Management Review,* May 1984, 43–45.

Raskin, A. H. "The Once and Future Newspaper Guild." *Columbia Journalism Review,* September–October 1982, 26–34.

Renfroe, Patricia P. "A Personnel Manager Tells Editors: 'We Can Help You if You'll Let Us.' " *The Bulletin of the American Society of Newspaper Editors,* October 1983, 23.

———. "Sexual Harassment." *presstime,* May 1985, 14.

———. "Succession: Grooming Replacements Should Be Company Policy." *presstime,* March 1984, 6.

"The Revival of Productivity." *Business Week,* 13 February 1984, 92.

Rice, Berkeley. "Brave New World of Intelligence Testing." *Psychology Today,* September 1979, 27–41.

Richards, Richard A. "Learning to Live with the Owl." *Training,* September 1983, 50–53.

Rousseau, Denise M., and Robert A. Cooke. "Relationship of Life Events and Personal Orientations to Symptoms of Strain." *Journal of Applied Psychology* 68 (1983): 446–58.

———. "Stress and Strain from Family Roles and Work-Role Expectations." *Journal of Applied Psychology* 69, no. 2 (1984): 252–60.

Ruth, Marcia. "Minorities: The Statistics Show Little Progress, but Momentum Is Growing for Newspaper Staffs to Reflect More Racial and Ethnic Diversity." *presstime*, August 1984, 14.

———. "Robert N. Brown: Innovator in the Heartland." *presstime*, January 1985, 42.

St. John, Walter D. "Leveling with Employees." *Personnel Journal*, August 1984, 52–57.

Salzman, Marian L. "In Search of Tomorrow's Excellent Managers." *Management Review*, April 1985, 41–47.

Sandler, Leonard. "The Successful and Supportive Subordinate." *Personnel Journal*, December 1984, 40–45.

Schuh, Allen J. "The Predictability of Employee Tenure." *Personnel Psychology* 20 (1967): 133–52.

Seliger, Susan. "Stress Can Be Good for You." *New York*, 2 August 1982, 20–24.

Shaver, Harold C. "Job Satisfaction among Journalism Graduates." *Journalism Quarterly* 55 (Spring 1978): 54–61.

Skinner, Wickham, and W. Earl Sasser. "Managers with Impact: Versatile and Inconsistent." *Harvard Business Review*, November–December 1977, 140–48.

Smith, Ron. "Employment Screening Procedures: Tests and Tryouts." *Journalism Research Journal* 5, no. 2 (1980–81): 29–30.

Smith, Ronald E. "Employee Orientation." *Personnel Journal*, December 1984, 46–48.

Sohn, Ardyth. "How Many 'Superwomen'?" *The Bulletin of the American Society of Newspaper Editors*, March 1984, 22.

———. "Women Newspaper Managers: Their Goals and Achievement Orientations." Manuscript, University of Colorado, 1983.

Speers, Richard M., and Lyman W. Porter. "The Role of Task-Goal Attributes in Employee Performance." *Psychological Bulletin* 81 (1974): 434–51.

Spencer, Daniel G., and Richard M. Speers. "The Influence of Personal Factors and Perceived Work Experiences on Employee Turnover and Absenteeism." *Academy of Management Journal* 23 (1980): 567–72.

Stogdill, Ralph. "Personal Factors Associated with Leadership: A Survey of the Literature." *Journal of Psychology* 25 (1948): 35–71.

Stoner, Charles R., and Fred L. Fry. "Developing a Corporate Policy for Managing Stress." *Personnel*, May–June 1983, 66–76.

"Strict Liability for Supervisors' Acts Imposed on Employers in Sexual Harassment Cases." *Employment Alert of the Research Institute of America*, 7 February 1985, 1–6.

Stryker, Perrin. "Can You Analyze This Problem?" *Harvard Business Review*, May–June 1965, 73–79.

Tadie, Virginia. "Management: Editors Changing Their Tune." *presstime*, February 1984, 10–11.

Tannenbaum, Robert, and Warren H. Schmidt. "How to Choose a Leadership Pattern." *Harvard Business Review*, May–June 1973, 162–71.

Taylor, Paul. "Gene Roberts: Down-Home Editor of the Philadelphia Inquirer." *Washington Journalism Review*, April 1983, 35–41.

"Teambuilding Unifies Employees by Building Trust." *Pennsylvania Newspaper Publishers Association Press*, November 1984, 8.

Thomas, Kenneth W. "Toward Multidimensional Values in Teaching: The Example of Conflict Behaviors." *Academy of Management Review* 2 (1977): 487.

Thomas, Kenneth W., and Warren H. Schmidt. "A Survey of Managerial Interests with Respect to Conflict." *Academy of Management Journal*, June 1976, 315–18.

Thomas, Kenneth W., and Louis R. Pondy. "Toward an Intent Model of Conflict Management among Principal Parties." *Human Relations* 30 (1977): 1089–1102.

Tuckman, Bruce W. "Developmental Sequence in Small Groups." *Psychological Bulletin* 64 (1965): 384–99.

Tyler, Richard F. "Motivate the Older Employee." *Personnel Journal*, February 1984, 60–61.

Unger, Craig. "Rosenthal Reported Scouting a Successor: Ferment Stirs Noted Paper." *New York,* 22 August 1983, 23–28.

VanGundy, Arthur G. "How to Establish a Creative Climate in the Work Group." *Management Review,* August 1984, 24–28, 37–38.

Watson, Gary. "The Care and Feeding of the Boss." *Gannetteer,* July 1985, 3.

Weaver, David H., Richard G. Gray, and G. Cleveland Wilhoit. "Portrait of the U.S. Journalist." Manuscript, Indiana University School of Journalism, October 1984.

Wexley, Kenneth N., and Wayne Nemeroff. "Effectiveness of Positive Reinforcement and Goal Setting as Methods of Management Development." *Journal of Applied Psychology* 60 (1975): 445–50.

Williams, Betty Anne. "Who Watches the Watchers?" *Nieman Reports,* Summer 1979, 26–28.

Wrapp, H. Edward. "Good Managers Don't Make Policy Decisions." *Harvard Business Review,* July–August 1984, 8–21.

Yerkes, Robert M., and John D. Dodson. "The Relation of Strength of Stimulus to Rapidity of Habit-Formation." *Journal of Comparative Neurology and Psychology* (1908): 459–82.

Yovovich, B. G. "A Long-Revered Paper Ponders Its Future." *Advertising Age,* 30 January 1984, M-46.

Zaleznik, Abraham. "The Human Dilemmas of Leadership." *Harvard Business Review,* July–August 1963, 14–18.

———. "Management of Disappointment." *Harvard Business Review,* November–December 1967, 59–70.

———. "Managers and Leaders: Are They Different?" In *Executive Success: Making It in Management,* 123–39. New York: John Wiley & Sons, 1983.

———. "Power and Politics in Organizational Life." In *Executive Success: Making It in Management,* 267–88. New York: John Wiley & Sons, 1983.

Index

A

Accountability, 121–22
 for delegated tasks, 157–58
 for making decisions, 233–34
 of city editor, 124
Achievement
 as focus of efforts to motivate, 72
 measurement of, 74
 need for, as motivator, 55–57
Adams, J. Stacy, 62–65
Affiliation, need for, as motivator, 57
Affirmative action, 155
Age, stress response affected by, 454–58
Age Discrimination in Employment Act of 1967, 502
Albemarle Paper Company v. Moody, 278–79
Alcoholism, 491–92
Ambiguity
 as source of conflict, 404
 as source of stress, 467
 of values, 265
American Arbitration Association, 431

Androgyny, 588–89
Anger, managing, 417
Anxiety
 competition, 221
 status, 220–21
Arbitration, 431
Argyris, Chris, 559–61
Artist, standards for, 665–70
Asch, Solomon, 32–33
Attitudes, 314–17
 appraisal of, 326
 formation of, 315–16
 influencing, as way to change behavior, 388
Attribution, 615
Authority, 121–22
 delegation of, 149
 flow of, 150, 151
 line, 151
 of city editor, 123–28
 of editors, 219
 staff, 152

B

Babbage, Charles, 3
Bales, Robert F., 20–21
Bargaining position, 431–32
Barnard, Chester, 6
Barnes, Louis D., 377
Bartolome, Fernando, 585–86

Behavior
 changing, 385–86
 masculine versus feminine, 588–90
 relationship, 191
 task, 191
Behaviorally Anchored Rating Scale (BARS), 289
Behavioral science
 application of, to management, 6–10
 principles of, 9–10
Behavior modification, 68–69
Blake, Robert R., 184
Blanchard, Kenneth H., 190
Bonuses
 distinguished from salaries, 363–64
 incentive, 362–64
Borgatta, Edgar F., 20–21
Bosses. *See* Superiors
Boyatzis, Richard E., 587
Brito v. Zia Company, 277–78
Budgets, 144, 145–46
 purposes of, 145–46
Burnout, 466, 483–86
 prevention of, 486
 situations likely to cause, 483–84

727

Burnout, *continued*
  symptoms of, 485

C

Cannon, Walter, 443–44
Career development, 313–14. *See also* Development
Central tendency, 319
Change
  agents, 384
  as opportunity, 370
  as source of political behavior, 207
  as source of stress, 466
  climate for, 370–71
  directive, 387
  editor's philosophy of, 377–80
  in behavior, 385–88
  in knowledge, 385, 388
  in skills, 388
  introduction of, 371, 380–83, 384, 388, 396–97
  management of, 141, 369–97
  newspaper as record of and object of, 369–70
  participative, 387
  planning, 394, 397
  pressure for, 382
  process of, 372–77
  reactions to traumatic, 394–95
  reasons for accepting, 393
  resistance to, 217, 370, 389–93
  responsiveness to, 374
  sources of, 370
  technological, 468
Chief executive officer. *See also* Publisher
  leadership characteristics of, 559–62
City editor, 123–28
  accountability of, 124
  assignment of resources by, 127–28
  assistant, 129–34
  rewards from, 127
  role of, 118–21
Civil Rights Act of 1964, 277, 337, 502, 522, 599
Civil Rights Act of 1968, 502
Civil Service Reform Act of 1978, 279, 319
Coalition building, 374–76
Collective bargaining, 429–30
Commitment, ethic of, 586
Communication
  as a motivator, 80
  as part of manager's job, 84
  barriers to, 86–90, 98–100
  between editor and news staff, 84–86
  breakdowns in, 79
  channels for, 102–103
  choosing style of, 197
  definition of, 79–80
  direction of, 97–98
  expectations regarding, 100–101
  facilitating, 151, 164, 428–29
  follow-up to, 103
  individual styles of, 81
  influence of organizational structure on, 81
  influence of perception on, 81–82
  informal, 238
  in implementing change, 396–97
  in meetings, 103–106
  in networks, 106–109
  interpersonal, 83–95
  listening as part of, 86, 90–95
  networks, 95–97
  nonverbal, 87, 93, 99
  of expectations, 240
  organizational, 95–106
  patterns of, 95–98
    among journalists, 268–71
  perception in, 80
  purposes of, 84
  role of, in resolving conflict, 222
  standards for, 669–70, 673, 677, 680, 684, 689
  systems for, 101–102
  through memorandums, 82–83
  to enhance creativity, 253
  upward, 102–103
Community, contact of journalists with, 268–71
Compensation. *See also* Money; Overtime
  additional time off as, 341
  adequacy of, 343–44
  based on job evaluation, 345–47
  controlling cost of, 342–43
  Equal Employment Opportunity guidelines for, 347–48
  for overtime, 336–41
  incentive bonus as part of, 362–64
  merit pay as form of, 347–50

Index

objectives of, 342–43
performance review as basis for decisions related to, 286–87
responsibility for management of, 335
roles of, 336
scheduling decisions on, 349–50
Compensatory time, 341
Competition
 among chief executive officers, 559–60
 anxiety, 221
Computers in the newsroom, 468–71
Conflict
 as source of productivity, 402
 between family and career, 474–78
 between peer groups and management, 38
 between reporter and assistant city editor, 130–31
 handling, 402
 importance of, 401–402
 inner, 220–22
 management of, 401–436
 maturity, 418
 outcomes of, 408, 409
 philosophies of, 402
 process of, 404–405
 reducing, 418–21
 resolving, 405, 406–408, 409, 417–24
 role, 403
 sources of, 403, 412–15
 union-management, 429–36
 with creativity, 250
Conformity, 32
Contingency theory of leadership, 188–89
Controlling, 172–74
 as an objective in delegation, 161
 changing approach to, 197
 importance of information in, 174
 ways of, 173
Control points, 173–74
Cooke, Robert A., 475
Copy editor, standards for, 670–73
Cost effects, 318–19
Creativity, 245–54
 as trait sought in hiring process, 507
 characteristics associated with, 246–47
 conditions inhibiting, 250
 conditions nurturing, 253–54
 definitions of, 246–48
 extrinsic, 353
 intrinsic, 353
 managing, 250–54
 needs accompanying, 248
 primary and secondary, 248
 process of, 248–50
Criticism, giving, 415–16

D

Davis, George, 590
Deadlines
 as source of stress, 463, 466
 for artists, 669
 for copy editors, 672
 for editors, 675
 for photographers, 682
 for reporters, 687, 688

setting, 160
Decision making, 167–72
 appropriate occasions for, 167–68
 emotion in, 169
 influence of thought processes on, 231–32
 judgment in, 168
 participative, 169–70, 232–33, 254
 steps in, 167, 170–72
 types of, 168–69
Decisions, culturally influenced, 602
Defense mechanisms, 408, 410–12
Defensiveness, 87, 91–92
Delegation, 157–67
 accountability remaining after, 157–58
 advantages of, 162–64
 as leadership style, 196–97
 as part of time management, 495
 choosing a style of, 160–61
 effectiveness in, 158–59
 exception principle in, 161–62
 failures in, 164–65
 guidelines for, 166–67
 objectives of, 161
 of decision making, 169–70
 process of, 159–60
 tasks suitable for, 157
Department of Labor, 430
Development
 career, 313–14
 criteria for success in, 538
 definition of, 614–15

Development, *continued*
  intellectual, 614–16
  management, 537–45
  opportunities for, outside the newspaper, 542
  performance reviews as source of, 286
  process of, 218–19, 538–40
  programs, 542
  training contrasted with, 528
Dickens, Floyd, 611
Dickens, Jacqueline, 611
Differentiation, 230
Directing, 156–72. *See also* Decision making; Delegation
  activities involved in, 156
Discipline, 319–23, 549–53
  common behavior used in, 552
  for cause, 434
  guidelines for administering, 552–53
  policy for, 550
  power to, difficult to employ in an organized newsroom, 436
  progressive, 436, 551, 551–52
  purpose of, 553
  support for decision to, 436
Discrimination, 154. *See also* Minorities; Women
  benefits of eliminating, 598, 602
  in job interviews, 512–14
  overcoming, 591–614
  sexual, 599–601
Dismissal. *See* Firing

Dodson, John D., 486–87
Donnell, Susan, 594
Driving forces, 372
Drucker, Peter F., 71–72, 81, 141–42, 170, 282, 350
Drug abuse, 491–92
Dunnette, Marvin D., 70

E

Editing, collaborative, 529
Editor
  as communicator, 84–86
  as initiator of feedback, 570–71
  as manager, 137–39
  as source of stress, 471–72
  as trainer, 531
  changing responsibilities of, 618–19
  city. *See* City editor
  executive. *See* Executive editor
  goals of, 38
  leadership style required of, 208
  management styles of, 227–31
  managing. *See* Managing editor
  middle–level, 484–85, 538
  publisher's expectations for, 568–71
  relationship of, with publisher, 564–72, 577–81
  standards for, 673–78
Employees. *See also* Subordinates
  abrasive, 412–15

  as assets or overhead, 1
  as human resources, 45, 501
  expectations of, for information, 100–101
Environment
  as factor determining effects of stress, 445–47
  of newsroom, 2
Epics of journalism, 270–71
Equal Employment Opportunity Commission, 599
  Guidelines, 502
  laws, 154–55, 156, 277–78
  standards for pay practices, 347–48
Equal Pay Act of 1963, 337, 502
Equity theory, 62–65
Ethics
  effects of values on decisions concerning, 264
  related to type of publisher, 566–67
Executive editor, 123
  responsibilities of, 138
Expectancy theory, 60–62
Expectations
  communication of, 240
  influence of, on management style, 224–28, 240–41
  influence of, on performance, 615

F

Fair Labor Standards Act of 1938, 337–41
  exemptions from, 338

Index   731

Family
  conflicts between career and, 474–78
  planning for responsibilities to, 477–78
Fayol, Henri, 4
Federal Mediation and Conciliation Service, 430
Feedback
  as part of ongoing performance reviews, 303
  as standard for supervisors, 304
  creativity encouraged by, 253–54
  high achievement linked to, 352
  initiated by editor, 570–71
  motivation linked to, 67
  performance review as, 275
  role of, 222
Ferguson, Marilyn, 106
Fiedler, Fred, 188
Fight-or-flight response, 443–44
Fillers, 82
Firing, 551–52
  grounds for, 552
  performance review as basis for decisions on, 287
  personnel department assistance with, 527
  support for, 436
Folie à deux, 575–76
Follett, Mary Parker, 7
Force field analysis, 372
Freudenberger, Herbert J., 484
Friedman, Meyer, 449–50, 452

G

Galton, Sir Francis, 246
Gantt, Henry L., 4
General Adaptation Syndrome, 444
Ghiselli, Edwin E., 217
Glass, David C., 452
Goals
  ambiguous, 206
  appropriate level for, 365
  bonus for achieving, 362–64
  confused with activities, 364–65
  contrasted with Management by Objectives, 311–12
  difficulty of, 66–67
  identified by Management by Objectives, 351
  linking organizational and individual, 335, 351–52
  Management by Objectives as forum for reviewing, 358
  measurability of, 365
  misunderstandings over, 291
  motivation to achieve, 353
  role of, in motivation, 65–68, 352
  setting, 310–14, 352–53
    as part of performance appraisal, 355
    as stress management technique, 490
    creativity enhanced by, 254
  specificity of, 66

subordinates' identification with, 227
Goal-setting theory, 65–68
Gordon, Thomas, 91–92
Grapevines, 97
Group processes, forces affecting, 37
Groups. *See also* Peer groups; Work groups
  development of, 23–24, 24–26
  informal, 17
  norms of, 29–33
  productivity and goals of, 17
  understanding behavior of, 15
Groupthink, 234–35
Growth, 218–19
Guidelines for Employee Selection Procedures, 522

H

Hall, Edward T., 87
Hall, Jay, 594
Halo effect, 317–18, 511
Harris, Jay T., 592
Hawthorne studies, 7, 16–18
Headlines, standards for, 672–73, 674
Hendrix, William, 490
Hersey, Paul, 190
Herzberg, Frederick, 50–53, 54
Hierarchy, management, 113–15, 116
Hiring, 501–527
  interviewing in process of, 509–516
  laws pertaining to, 502
  measuring qualifications in

Hiring, *continued*
  process of, 507–509
  of marginal talent, 502
  orientation as part of process of, 523–26
  process of, 503
  qualities to look for in candidates when, 505–507
  recruiting step in, 503–507
  reference check before, 508
  selection as part of process of, 523
  testing as part of process of, 517–23
  tryout as part of process of, 516
Holmes, Thomas, 447
Holmes-Rahe Life Event-Stress Scale, 448–49
Homeostasis, 443
House, James, 107
House, Robert J., 189, 190
Howard, Jeff, 614
Human relations movement, 7
Human resources, employees as, 45
Hygiene factors, 52

I

Incentive bonus, 362–64
Information channels, 29
Innovation. *See* Change
Institute for Journalism Education, 593
Integration. *See* Discrimination; Minorities; Women
Intellectual development, 614–16
Interviewing (in hiring process), 509–516
  discriminatory inquiries used in, 512–14
  low reliability in, 515
  pitfalls in, 511
  practices in, 515–16
  questions in, 510–11
  types of, 509–510
Invasion of privacy, 508

J

Jaques, Elliott, 229
Job descriptions, 345–46
Job enrichment, 42, 44–45
Job evaluation, 345–47
Job satisfaction, as source of motivation, 42
Johari Window Model, 427, 428

K

Kanter, Rosabeth Moss, 199, 370–71, 374, 594
Kaufman, John, 562
Kerner Report, 592
Knowledge workers, 72
  productivity among, 282
Kobasa, Suzanne, 479, 490

L

Lawler, Edward E., 22, 70
Leaders
  behavior of, 182–84, 190, 192, 195–98
  characteristics of, 181–82
  of peer groups, 33–35
  types of intolerable, 576–77
Leadership
  as source of stress, 464
  characteristics of chief executive officers, 559–62
  coping with poor, 573–77
  definitions of, 179–80
  environment for, 188–89
  importance of, 179
  influenced by pace of managerial work, 207–208
  inner conditions that inhibit, 220–21
  management compared to, 180, 198
  nature of, 179–84
  reflecting readership, 605–606
  situational, 190–98, 561
  styles of, 184–88, 191, 193–94, 194–95, 223
    changing, 197
    preferences for, 225
  theories of, 188–90
Learning curve, 531
Levinson, Harry, 351
Lewin, Kurt, 372–73, 388
Lewis, Neil P., 71
Libel, role of standards in suits for, 303
Librarians, standards for, 678–80
Life-styles, 254–60
  benefits of understanding, 255, 260
  categories of, 255–60
  of journalists, 266–71

Index

Likert, Rensis, 252, 563, 579
Listening
 active, 92
 improving skills in, 90–95
Livingston, J. Sterling, 240
Lombardo, Michael M., 489, 573

M

MacKinnon, Donald W., 247
Maintenance factors, 52
Management. *See also* Managerial skills
 "androgynous" styles of, 588–90
 behaviors, 184–88
 by Objectives, 350–66
  as forum for reviewing company goals, 358
  as results-oriented way to manage, 353
  as source of change, 387
  creating plan for, 356–59, 361
  elements of, 351
  employees who benefit from, 355
  goal setting contrasted with, 311–12
  goal setting in, 352–53
  goals in, 359–60, 360–61
  impact of, on management style, 360
  money in, 362

motivation with, 353
performance measurement scale used with, 363
pitfalls in use of, 354–55, 364–66
purposes of, 355–56
role of publisher or editor in, 356
sources of success of, 352
stages of, 356–58, 359
by Wandering Around, 238
development, 537–45
Fayol's principles for, 4–6
hierarchy, 113–15, 116
human interaction as part of, 586
influence of, on journalism, 617–18
of creativity, 250–54
pace of, 207–208
philosophy of, 9
results-oriented, 353
rights, 434
roles of, 2, 137
skills, 124, 587
structure, 114
 of newspapers compared with other businesses, 1–2
style, 213–41
 development of, 237–41
 editor's typical, 213–14
 impact of Management by Objectives on, 360
 influences on, 215–28, 224–28, 224–28, 237–41
 of editors, 227–31
 participative or

democratic, 232–35, 365–66, 491
theoretical versus real, 213–15
supervisory. *See* Supervising; Supervisors
theories
 behavioral, 6–10
 classical, 3–6
 scientific, 3–4
 upward, 559–81
Managerial grid, 184–88
Managerial skills
 development of, 10–12
 types of, 11–12
Managers. *See also* Executive editor; Managing editor; Leaders; Superiors
 competencies needed by, 587–90
 stereotypical role of, 585–86
 workaholics as, 473–74
Managing editor, 123
 responsibilities of, 138
Maslach, Christina, 484
Maslow, Abraham, 45–49, 54, 248, 252. *See also* Needs
Massey, Morris, 254–55, 257–60
Maynard, Robert C., 592
Mayo, Elton, 16–18
MBO. *See* Management by Objectives
McCall, Morgan W., 573
McClelland, David, 53–58, 194
McGregor, Douglas, 7, 49–50

Meetings
  communication in, 103–106
  conducting, 104–106
  functions of, 104
  scheduling, 159–60
Memorandums, as communication tools, 82–83
Menninger, Karl, 450
Menninger, Walter, 42–44
Menninger, William, 450
Mentoring, 533–36
  conditions for success in, 534
  importance of, to minorities and women, 534–35
  problems that may arise in, 534–36
Meyer, Adolph, 447
Midlife crisis, 455–56
Minorities. *See also* Discrimination; Women
  adjustment of, to white organizations, 611–14
  benefits of including, 598, 602, 604–605
  distinctive styles of, 602–603
  employment of, 154–56, 605–611
  experience of, in the newsroom, 107–109, 601–614
  fear of competition from, 598
  federal definition of, 154
  influence of, on newsroom style, 585, 587–90
  intellectual development of, 614–16
  interactions of whites and, 611–14
  journalism education for, 606–607
  limited opportunities for, 591–92
  representation of, in the newsroom, 592, 593
  support groups for, 107–109
  testing of, 522
Mintzberg, Henry, 586
Mission, editorial, 137
Mitchell, Arnold, 254–56
Mitchell, Terence R., 190
Money
  as motivator, 69–71, 335–36
  in MBO program, 362
  tied to achievement, 336
Morale
  curve, 43
  improved by effective delegation, 164
  influence of, on productivity, 41–45
Morrison, Ann, 573
Motivation, 15–18, 41. *See also* Needs
  checklist for editors, 74–76
  communication as a source of, 80
  equity theory of, 62–65
  expectancy theory of, 60–62
  goal-setting theory of, 65–68
  individualized approach to, 45
  money as source of, 69–71, 335–36
  morale as source of, 41–45
  of experienced workers, 72–73
  performance reviews as source of, 285–86
  positive and negative, 51–53
  problems in, as management problems, 71
  process of, 41, 44
  sources of, for journalists, 58–60
  theories of, 42–76
  two-factor theory of, 50–53
Mouton, Jane S., 184
Myers-Briggs Personality Type Indicator, 426

N

Naisbitt, John, 106
National Association of Black Journalists, 109
National Labor Relations Act, 337
National Labor Relations Board (NLRB), 430
Needs
  among journalists, 48–49
  Maslow's hierarchy of, 45–49
  motivators, 44–60
Negotiating, 420–24
  outcomes of, 424
Networks, 106–109
  benefits of, 107–109
Newspaper
  Guild, 433
  role of, 569
Nonpromotability, 545–47
Norms, 29–33, 517

Index

conformance to, 31–32
development of, 30
enforcement of, 30
of assistant desk editors, 31
of reporters, 30–31

O

Odiorne, George, 350–51
Opsahl, Robert L., 70
Organization
  bilateral, 562
  climate of, 102
  informal, 586
  unilateral, 562
Organizational behavior, political, 206–207. *See also* Behavior
Organizational learning, 379–80
Organizing, 148–52
  activities involved in, 148–49
  objectives of, 149
Orientation, 523–26
  goals for, 524
  personnel department assistance with, 524
  steps for, 525–26
Overhead, news staff viewed as, 1
Overload principle, 55
Overtime, 341–42
Owen, Robert, 7

P

Path-goal theory of leadership, 189–90
Pay. *See* Compensation
Peer groups, 22–39
  formation of, 23–29
  influence of, 28, 35–38
  leaders of, 33–35
  reasons for, 26–29
  standards of behavior for, 29–33
  types of, 30–31
  working with, 38–39
Peer pressure, 32–33. *See also* Norms
Perception
  as source of stress, 465
  communication influenced by, 80, 81–82
Performance. *See also* Performance review
  development, 312–13
  influence of expectations on, 615
  pay based on, 347–50
  standards. *See* Standards
Performance review, 154, 275–331
  as basis for merit-pay program, 347
  as ongoing process, 303–304
  as part of Management by Objectives, 358
  as way to manage stress, 490
  behavior, not attitudes, as standards for, 314–17, 326
  benefits of effective, 285–87
  by city editor, 126–27
  career development discussed in, 313–14
  employee responses to, 307–308
  for counseling nonpromotable staffer, 546–47
  goal setting in, 310–14, 355
  history of, 275–76
  interview, 307–310
  laws concerning, 277–80
  leniency in, 318
  limits of, 283
  listening in, 92
  of superiors, 327–31
  performance development discussed in, 312–13
  personnel department assistance with, 527
  process of, 289–310
  rating errors in, 317–19
  rating scales in, 289–302
  resistance among editors to, 276–77
  responsibility for, 305
  role of, in discipline, 319–23
  sample rating form for, 294–301
  self-appraisal and self-image as by-products of, 216
  staffer's role in, 305–307
  strategy for planning, 326–27
  successful systems for, 283–87
  techniques for, 287–89
  training to conduct, 323–27
  treated as hostile experience, 352
Personality
  as influence on management style, 238–39
  relationship of, to stress symptoms, 449–53
  tests, 519
  Type A and Type B, 450–53

Personnel department
  relations of, with news department, 526–27
  role of, during orientation, 524
Peters, Thomas J., 117, 180–81, 238
Photographer
  standards for, 680–84
  status of, under Fair Labor Standards Act, 339–40
Piecework, 4
Planning, 139–48. *See also* Goals
  family responsibilities, 477–78
  human resource, 153
  meshed with company's objectives, 140
  obstacles to, 146–48
  principles for successful, 148
  purpose of, 140–41
  questions answered by, 140
  risk evaluation as part of, 143
  strategic, 141–43
  tactical, 143–45
Policies, 144
Politics
  as vehicle for reducing conflict, 420
  related to power, 206–207
Porter, Lyman W., 22, 217
Power, 199–207
  attainment of, 205–206, 207
  definitions of, 199–200
  levels of, 204–205
  necessity for, 57–58, 200
  of editor, 219
    limitations on, 204
  of subordinates, 572–73
  of the press, 199–200
  personal, 387
  politics related to, 206–207
  sources of, 200–202
  uses of, 202–203
Practices, 145
Privacy, invasion of, 508
Problems, analysis of, 231–32
Procedures, 145
Productivity
  among knowledge workers, 282
  efforts to increase, 15, 16–18
  growth in, 280–83
  influences on, 16–18, 402
  measurement of, 1, 73–74, 280, 283
  technology and, 281
Professional employees, journalists qualifying as, 338–40
Programs, 144
Projection, 219
Promotability, 540–44
  lack of, 545–47
Promotion, 537–45
  performance review as basis for decisions related to, 286
Psychology, applied to business management, 7, 8
Publisher, 562–72
  as business person, 565
  expectations of, 568–71
  power of, 564
  relationship of, with editor, 564–72, 577–81
  types of, 566–67
Pucetti, Mark, 490

R

Racial minorities. *See* Minorities
Rahe, Richard, 447
Rating, errors in, 317–19
Readiness, 191, 194–95
Recruitment, 503–507
Reference checks, 508, 527
Relationships, as an exchange, 62
Reliability, 517
Reporters
  as source of stress, 472–73
  goals of, 38
  standards for, 684–89
Reports, as part of delegation process, 159
Resources, assignment of, 127–28
Responsibility, 121–22
  of city editor, 124
Restraining forces, 373
Rewards, from city editor, 127
Rhoads, John M., 488
Rogers, Carl R., 86
Roles, 118
  conflict in, as source of stress, 467
  conflict over, 215–16, 403
  family, 474–78
  of assistant city editors, 134
  of editors, 219
  self-image of, 215–16
Rosch, Paul, 451, 452, 480
Rosenmann, Ray, 449–50

Rousseau, Denise M., 475
Rules, 145

S

Salaries, 336–39
  distinguished from bonuses, 363–64
  rates and structures for, 337–38
Sayles, Leonard R., 238
Schuh, Allen J., 548
Selective decoding, 230
Self-appraisal, 305–307
Self-examination
  as by-product of performance review, 216
  as influence on development of managment style, 215–22
  questionnaire, 235–36
Self-fulfillment, 586
Self-image
  as by-product of performance review, 216
  at the heart of defense mechanisms, 408
  conflicts in, 216
  growth related to, 217–18
  influences on, 215
  of creative people, 247
  of journalists, 266–68
  of top and middle managers, 217
Selye, Hans, 441
Senge, Peter, 180
Sensitivity groups, 222–23
Sexual harassment, 599–601
Skinner, B. F., 68
Sohn, Ardyth, 594

Sources, importance of, to newspaper's value system, 261
Spencer, Lyle, 587
Staffing, 152–56
  laws governing, 154–56
Standards, 280, 290–92, 665–89
  for artist, 665–70
  for copy editor, 670–73
  for editor, 673–78
  for librarian, 678–80
  for photographer, 680–84
  for reporter, 684–89
  purposes of, 302–303
  role of, in defending libel suits, 303
  set by editor, 569
Status
  anxiety, 220–21
  in peer groups, 33–34
Sternberg, Robert, 230
Stress, 441–95. See also Burnout; Substance abuse; Time management
  at various life stages, 454–58
  burnout as response to unrelieved, 466, 483–86
  channeling preferred to avoiding, 445
  definition of, 441–44
  editor's view of, 465–67
  effects of, 441, 442–44, 445–59, 459–61, 478–86
  effects of shared values on, 264
  forms of, 444–45
  from difficult boss, 575
  impact of family relationships on,

474–78
  in areas of strong fears, 454
  life change as source of, 447–49
  management of, 486–91
  personality related to symptoms of, 449–53
  reducing, 492–95
  response to, 444
  sources of, 462–68, 468–73, 575
  techno-, 469
  vulnerability to, 447–58
Stressors, 458–59
  interaction of, 459–61
Streufert, Siegfried, 230
Subordinates, 118. See also Employees
  abrasive, 412–15
  anger among, 417
  encouraging frankness among, 417
  manager's confidence in, 225
  needs of, for independence, 226
  of eccentric publisher, 575
  perception by, of editor's management style, 222
  power of, 572–73
  relationship of, with boss, 564
  tolerance of, for ambiguity, 226
Substance abuse, 491–92
Succession planning, 537
Superiors, 118. See also Managers; Supervisors

Superiors, *continued*
  appraisal of, 327–31
  coping with difficult, 573–77
Supervising, 115–22
  as first experience of management, 113
  elements of, 121–22
  feedback as part of, 304
  formula for excellence in, 117
  unclear definitions of, 117–18
Supervisors, first-level, 119, 132, 138, 484
Suspension, 551–52

T

Taft–Hartley Act of 1947, 430
Taylor, Frederick Winslow, 3–4, 16
Teambuilding, 424–29
  as way to cope with stress, 491
  as way to reduce stress, 468
  truth telling required in, 429
Technical skills, 10–11
Technostress, 469
Testing
  as part of hiring process, 517–23
  guidelines for, 521–22
  laws regulating, 522–23
  psychological, 518–21
  terms used to describe, 517–18
Tests
  types of, 518–19

T groups, 222–23
Theory X–Theory Y, 7, 49–50, 182–83, 224
Time frame
  as indicator of mental capabilities, 230
  associated with job level, 229–30
Time management, 492–95
  delegation as part of, 162
  procedure for, 494–95
  training as part of, 531
To-do list, 495
Training, 528–36
  benefits of, 529, 531
  challenges in, 532
  delegation as form of, 162
  development contrasted with, 528
  errors in, 531–32
  for conducting performance reviews, 323–27
  good environment for, 528–29
  learning process in, 530–31
  mentors used in, 533–36
  transition, 395–96
Trust, 377–79
  between editor and publisher, 577–81
  building, 424–29
  necessary for negotiating, 421–22
Tuckman, Bruce W., 23
Turnover, 547–49
  minimizing, 506–507, 549
  predictors, 548
  types of, 549

U

Unions
  conflict with, 429–36
  eligibility to join, 432–34
  history of, in journalism, 433
  membership in, as condition of employment, 434
  norms of, 30
  reasons for joining, 431–32
USA TODAY, 24–26

V

Validity, 517
Values, 260–65
  ambiguous, 265
  categories of, 259–60
  effects of, on ethical decisions, 264
  formation of, 257
  influences on, 257
  of manager, 225
  of successful corporations, 262
  problems associated with, 265
  role of, in an organization, 262
  role of, in motivation, 65
  shared, 263–64
  shift in, in workplace, 585
  stress vulnerability related to, 453
  systems of, 257–60
  uniformity of, in the newsroom, 260
Vision, 230
Vroom, Victor H., 60–62, 223

W

Wade v. Mississippi Cooperative Extension Service, 278
Wage and salary administration, 336
Wages, 336–39
 for overtime, 336–41
 minimum, 337
 rates and structures for, 337
Waterman, Robert H., Jr., 180–81
Watson, Glegg, 590
Whyte, William F., 70
Women. *See also* Discrimination
 as perpetrators of sexual harassment, 600
 attitudes toward, 593
 benefits of including, 598
 editors, 594–98
 experience of, in the newsroom, 107–109, 593–98
 fear of competition from, 598
 influence of, on newsroom style, 585, 588–90
 in leadership roles, 596–98
 limited opportunities for, 591–92
 sexual harassment of, 599–601
 support groups for, 107–109
Women in Communications, 109
Workaholics, 473–74
Work groups, 18–23
 organization of, 37
 size of, 20–22
 types of, 18–20
Working, reasons for, 15–18

Y

Yankelovich, Daniel, 74, 586
Yerkes, Robert M., 486–87
Yerkes-Dodson Law, 487

Z

Zaleznik, Abraham, 198, 220–21

Index

OF JOURNALISTS AND MEDIA ORGANIZATIONS

A

Akron Beacon Journal, 163, 261, 541
American Newspaper Publishers Association, 537, 542
American Press Institute, 384, 542
American Society of Newspapeer Editors, 267, 344, 566, 592
Anderson (South Carolina) *Independent* and *Daily Mail*, 268
Anniston (Alabama) *Star*, 22
Apple, R.W., Jr., 536
Associated Press Managing Editors Association, 69, 307, 452-53, 463, 465, 467, 477, 479-80
Associated Press, 591

B

Bailey, Charles W., 578-79
Baltimore Sun, 376
Barnes, Andy, 393
Baron, Edward N., 354
Batten, James K., 358, 360, 362, 365
Beaupre, Larry, 59, 532

Bernstein, Carl, 617
Best, Eric, 59
Bingham, Barry, Sr., 261-62
Bishop, Jim, 119
Bowman, William W., 48-49, 266-67
Bulletin of the American Society of Newspaper Editors, 473, 483, 597, 609
Burgoon, Judee, 267-71
Burgoon, Michael, 267-71

C

California State University at Fullerton, 562
Capen, Richard, 565-66
Chapin, Charles E., 120-21
Charlotte News, 425, 462
Charlotte Observer, 425
Chicago Daily News, 565
Chicago Tribune, 227
Cincinnati Enquirer, 281, 571
Clabes, Judith G., 596
Clark, Roy Peter, 529-30
Cleveland *Plain Dealer*, 268

Columbia Journalism Review, 433
Concord (New Hampshire) *Monitor*, 340
Cose, Ellis, 603-04, 609
Currie, Phil, 60, 131-32, 265
Curtis, Montgomery, 384

D

Daily Camera, 100
Dallas Morning News, 344
Dallas Times Herald, 483
Dayton Daily News, 563
Democrat and Chronicle, 82, 223, 290, 349, 540
Des Moines Register, 482
Detroit Free Press, 228, 541
Detroit News, 591
Dougherty, John, 82-83, 103, 540

E

Editor & Publisher, 503, 566
Evansville *Sunday Courier & Press*, 596
Everett (Washington) *Herald*, 597

Index

F

Foley, Mike, 393
Forst, Donald H., 482

G

Gannett Center for
  Media Studies, 544
Gannett Co., Inc., 24-26,
  132, 265, 354, 453, 541,
  544, 605
Gannett News
  Service, 604
Gannett Rochester
  Newspapers, 290, 304
Gannetteer, 573
Gannon, James, P., 482
Gart, Murray J., 563-64
Giles, Robert H., 304,
  453
Graham, Katharine, 568
Grand Rapids Press, 563
Gray, Richard G., 48-49,
  266-67, 345

H

Haiman, Robert H., 59,
  122, 130, 392-93
Hampton, Jim, 565-66
Harless, Byron, 354,
  519-21, 541
Harris, Jay T., 592-93,
  604-05
Harte-Hanks
  Communications,
  100, 544
Hasert, Linda, 471-73
Hawpe, David, 608-09
Hicks, Nancy, 605
Hilliard, William, 481
Hough, Henry Beetle,
  261-62
Howell, Deborah, 596
Hoyt, George W.,
  563-64
Huffman, J. Ford, 26

I

Inland Daily Press
  Association, 344
Institute for Journalism
  Education, 609-10
Issacs, Norman, 537

J

Jarrett, Will, 483
Jennings, Max, 283
Jinks, Larry, 228, 541
John S. Knight
  Fellowships, 544
Johnstone, John W.C.,
  48-49, 266-67
Jones, Ivan, 359, 362

K

Kansas City Star, 344,
  600-01
Kansas City Times, 22,
  307, 344
Kaufman, John, 562
King, Dolly, 425-27, 429
Knight, John S., 261-62
Knight-Ridder, Inc.,
  358-59, 362, 364-65,
  384, 519-21, 541, 544

L

Lahey, Edwin A., 565
Landauer, Chris, 290,
  304
Lansing State Journal, 268
Looney, Ralph, 482
Los Angeles Times, 344
Louisville *Courier-
  Journal,* 261-62, 537,
  608
Louisville Times, 262,
  308, 537
Luedtke, Kurt, 541

M

Mallette, Malcolm F.,
  100-01
Maynard, Robert C.,
  592-93
McGrath, Kris, 69
McMillan, John, 101
Mesa (Arizona) Tribune,
  283
Meyer, Philip, 566-67
Miami Herald, 565-66,
  591
*Minneapolis Star and
  Tribune,* 578-79
Morgan, Perry, 163
Morton, John, 344
Murphy, Reg, 376
Murray, J. Edward,
  100-01
Muskogee, Oklahoma
  Daily Phoenix, 228

N

Nashville *Tennessean,*
  226
Neill, Rolfe, 384
Neuharth, Allen,
  229, 605
New London
  (Connecticut) *Day,* 268
New York Evening World,
  120-21
*New York Herald-
  Tribune,* 617
New York Times, 229,
  340, 533, 536, 579, 591
Newsday, 591
Newspaper
  Advertising Bureau,
  267
Newspaper Guild, 349,
  433
Newsweek, 281, 591
Nieman Fellowships,
  544

O

O'Donnell, Laurence G., 605

P

Pardue, Leonard, 308
Paxson, Marjorie, 228
Philadelphia Bulletin, 591
Philadelphia Daily News, 384, 604
Philadelphia Inquirer, 462, 471
Pinder, Craig, 98
Poorman, Paul, 541
Portland *Oregonian*, 481
Poynter Institute for Media Studies, 542
Poynter, Nelson, 122, 262, 519
presstime, 344
Profitt, Waldo, 483

Q

Quill, 604
Quinn, John C., 26, 541

R

Radolf, Andrew, 566
Raines, Howell, 533
Ralph Holsinger, 281
Raskin, A.H., 433
Ritter, Robert, 69
Rocky Mountain News, 482
Rosenthal, A. M., 229

S

Salem (Oregon) *Statesman-Journal*, 101
San Diego Union, 268
San Jose Mercury-News, 425, 541
Sarasota Herald-Tribune, 483
Shaffer, Ron, 564
Shaver, Harold C., 53
Shine, Neal, 228
Sifford, Darrell, 462-63
Slawski, Edward J., 48-49, 266-67
Sohn, Ardyth, 594
Southern Newspaper Publishers Association, 542
Spezzano, Vince, 26
Squires, James D., 226
St. Paul Pioneer Press and Dispatch, 596-97
St. Petersburg Times, 122, 130, 261, 392, 519, 529
Strick, Stan, 597

T

Time, 281, 579
Times-Union, 82, 103, 131, 223, 290, 349, 541
Tucker, Ken, 471-73
Tuttle, Richard, 540

U

USA TODAY, 24-26, 229
Unger, Robert, 307

V

Vancouver (British Columbia) *Sun*, 98
Vineyard Gazette, 261
Vogan, Jayne, 223, 598

W

Waddle, Chris, 22-23
Walker, Stanley, 120-21
Wall Street Journal, 601, 605
Waller, Michael, 69
Washington Post, 564, 568, 591, 593, 617
Washington Star, 563-64
Watson, Gary, 571-72
Weaver, David H., 48-49, 266-67, 345
Weiser, Ben, 564
Wenatchee (Washington) *World*, 268
Westchester Rockland Newspapers, 532
Whellan, Floyd, 100
Wichita *Eagle* and *Beacon*, 268
Wilhoit, G. Cleveland, 48-49, 266-67, 345
Wilmington (Delaware) *Morning News* and *Evening Journal*, 268
Wilson, George, 340
Wolfe, Tom, 617
Woodhull, Nancy, 26, 482
Woodward, Bob, 617